For
Gene [illegible] me
(v. [illegible] say
my enchanting young
namesake, Alexander M.,)
dear friends and
admired colleagues,
with love,
B.

9006.28

ROBERT K. MERTON

Consensus and Controversy

Consensus and Controversy

Principal Editor, Falmer Sociology Series: *Jon Clark*

1   Robert K. Merton
2   Anthony Giddens
3   John H. Goldthorpe

Editors, Falmer Psychology Series: *Sohan Modgil and Celia Modgil*

1   Lawrence Kohlberg
2   Hans Eysenck
3   Noam Chomsky
4   Arthur Jensen
5   B.F. Skinner

Falmer International Master-minds Challenged
Series Editors: Sohan Modgil and Celia Modgil.

ROBERT K. MERTON
Consensus and Controversy

EDITED BY

Jon Clark, Dr Phil

Senior Lecturer
Department of Sociology and Social Policy
University of Southampton

Celia Modgil, PhD

Lecturer in Educational Psychology
University of London

Sohan Modgil, PhD

Reader in Educational Research and Development
Brighton Polytechnic

Falmer Press
A member of the Taylor & Francis Group
London · New York · Philadelphia

UK	The Falmer Press, Rankine Road, Basingstoke, Hants RG24 0PR
USA	The Falmer Press, Taylor & Francis Inc., 1900 Frost Road, Suite 101, Bristol, PA 19007

Library of Congress Cataloging-in-Publication Data

Robert K. Merton : consensus and controversy/edited by Jon Clark, Celia Modgil, Sohan Modgil.
   p. cm.—(Consensus and controversy. Falmer sociology series)
   Includes bibliographical references
   ISBN 1-85000-550-8
1. Merton, Robert King, 1910–   . 2. Social structure.
3. Functionalism (Social sciences) 4. Science—Social aspects.
5. Anomy. I. Clark, Jon, Dr. Phil. II. Modgil, Celia. III. Modgil, Sohan. IV. Series.
HM22.U6M387   1990
301′.01—dc20   89-77736
                                                        CIP

British Library Cataloguing in Publication Data

Robert K. Merton : consensus and controversy – (Falmer international master-minds challenged).
   1. Sociology. Theories of Merton, Robert K. (Robert King)
   I. Clark, Jon *(1949–)* II. Modgil, Celia III. Modgil, Sohan
301.092

ISBN 1-85000-550-8

Jacket design by Caroline Archer

Typeset in 10/12 Times
by Mathematical Composition Setters Ltd, Salisbury, Wilts.

Printed in Great Britain by
Redwood Press Limited, Melksham, Wiltshire

Contributors

Dr Jon Clark
University of Southampton

Professor James S. Coleman
University of Chicago

Professor Stephen Jay Gould
Harvard University

Professor Piotr Sztompka
Jagiellonian University
Cracow

Professor Robert Bierstedt
University of Virginia
Charlottesville

Professor Arthur Stinchcombe
Northwestern University
Evanston, Illinois

Professor Anthony Giddens
University of Cambridge

Professor Raymond Boudon
University of Paris-Sorbonne

Professor Jon Elster
University of Chicago and Institute
for Social Research, Oslo

Professor Peter M. Blau
University of North Carolina, Chapel Hill

Professor Rose Laub Coser
Boston College
Massachusetts

Professor Richard A. Hilbert
Gustavus Adolphus College
St. Peter, Minnesota

Dr Charles Crothers
University of Auckland

Professor Marco Orrù
University of South Florida
Tampa

Professor Philippe Besnard
CNRS, University of Paris-
Sorbonne

Professor Samuel S. Wineburg
University of Washington
Seattle

and

Professor Lee S. Shulman
Stanford University
California

Professor Nico Stehr
University of Alberta, Edmonton

Professor Pierre Bourdieu
Collège de France, Paris

Professor I. Bernard Cohen
Harvard University

Professor Piyo Rattansi
University College, London

Professor A. Rupert Hall
Imperial College
University of London

Professor Hubert M. Blalock Jr
University of Washington
Seattle

Professor Mark Gould
Haverford College
Pennsylvania

Dr Simonetta Tabboni
Universities of Milan and Rome

Acknowledgments

First and foremost we would like to express our thanks to the subject of this volume, Robert K. Merton, without whose committed assistance and constant encouragement this project would simply not have been possible. Thanks, too, to all the contributors, who achieved our final deadline mostly as a result of commendable self-discipline, though bolstered in some cases by mild editorial nudges and in a few by more robust editorial arm-twisting. Thanks are due to Arthur Stinchcombe, Harcourt Brace Jovanovich and Cambridge University Press for permission to print Chapter 7 in a revised version; and to Robert K. Merton and The Free Press for permission to cite an extensive passage from *Social Theory and Social Structure* (1968) in Chapter 2.

We owe a particular debt to the academic and clerical staff of the Department of Sociology and Social Policy at the University of Southampton for their support and encouragement throughout the project. Finally, we would like to express our gratitude to Malcolm Clarkson, Managing Director, Falmer Press, for his unswerving confidence in the Sociology Series and his encouragement to give absolute priority to high standards of scholarship in the editing and production of this volume.

Jon Clark, Celia Modgil, Sohan Modgil
Hoe Gate and Old Windsor
August 1989

Contents

XIII   The Interplay of Social Theory and Empirical Research

XIV   The Sociology of Time

Part One: Introduction

I. EDITORIAL INTRODUCTION

1. Robert K. Merton: Consensus and Controversy

JON CLARK, CELIA MODGIL AND SOHAN MODGIL

THE ORIGIN AND RATIONALE OF THE SERIES

The origins of this volume on the work of Robert Merton can be traced directly, if somewhat paradoxically, to the publication in 1986–87 of a series of books on the work of leading contemporary psychologists: Lawrence Kohlberg, Hans Eysenck, Noam Chomsky, Arthur Jensen and B. F. Skinner. The success of these five volumes, edited by Sohan and Celia Modgil, persuaded the publisher, Malcolm Clarkson of Falmer Press, to initiate a parallel series of books on leading contemporary sociologists. In the autumn of 1986 Jon Clark was appointed principal editor of the new series.

The first major task was to choose the international contemporary sociologists who would be the subject of the first five volumes in the series. The choice was guided by a number of criteria. First and foremost the editors shared a fundamental belief in the distinctive intellectual interest in concentrating on the work of individuals as opposed to subject areas (education, religion, domestic life, work, mobility, health), concepts (class, power, structure, agency, gender) or 'schools' and approaches ('neo-functionalism', 'rational choice', Marxism, hermeneutics, positivism). The reader will have to judge whether this belief was justified or not. It was also agreed by the editors that the work of each scholar chosen had to be: internationally recognized in the discipline; still relevant to the core of the discipline in the 1990s; extensive in thematic coverage; and at one and the same time consensus-generating and controversial. Finally, the aim was to choose a group whose work covered a range of fields of sociological interest and countries of origin. The outcome was the choice of Robert K. Merton, Daniel Bell, Anthony Giddens, John H. Goldthorpe and Ralf Dahrendorf. For a variety of reasons the volumes on Daniel Bell and Ralf Dahrendorf did not materialize. Nevertheless, we believe that the three remaining volumes demonstrate the breadth, richness and creativity of the discipline of sociology in the post-war period.

THE FORMAT OF THE SERIES

The format of the Sociology Series is broadly similar to that of the Psychology Series. In each case the subject of the volume was invited to participate in its design so as to reflect the consensus and controversy which have surrounded their work. At the outset themes were chosen which covered the major areas of knowledge represented in their research and publications, and pairs of distinguished academics were then invited to write papers taking either a 'predominantly positive' or 'predominantly negative' view of each major area. The paired contributions were then exchanged through the editors to provide an opportunity for both parties to make a short comment on the heart of the opposing paper.

The aim of the debate format and the interchange of chapters is to highlight points of consensus and controversy. It should be emphasized, though, that the terms 'predominantly positive' and 'predominantly negative' imply no more than that the writer of the relevant contribution agrees or disagrees *in the main* with, say, Merton's approach to structural analysis—it does not imply complete agreement or disagreement, and allows contributors some degree of latitude to provide their own often more rounded view of the subject. Also, although the generic topics to be debated were determined by the editors, the contributors were given the freedom to focus on those aspects of the theme which were closest to their own research interests.

In addition to the paired contributions, this volume includes a number of introductory and 'overview' papers on themes where the 'pro' and 'con' format was felt to be less appropriate. Indeed, on one particular theme—the relation between Puritanism and science—it was decided to invite three 'overview' contributions on the simple grounds that three distinguished historians of science were willing and able to make complementary contributions to the debate.

Once completed, the manuscript was sent to Robert Merton for his consideration, and after consultation with the editors, it was agreed that he should not write a concluding comment given the exhaustive critical coverage of his work in the twenty-four contributions.

THE CONTENTS OF THE BOOK

The book is divided into two parts. Part I provides a general introduction to the work and influence of Robert Merton. It begins with a personal view of Merton the sociologist by Jon Clark. This is followed by an assessment of Merton the teacher by James S. Coleman, the internationally renowned Chicago sociologist, and an appreciation of Merton the scholar and writer of *OTSOG—On the Shoulders of Giants* (1965a)—by Stephen Jay Gould, the Harvard paleontologist, generally regarded as the finest science essayist writing today.

Part II contains twenty-one contributions covering the main themes of Merton's writings. Chapters 5 and 6 discuss whether there is a 'systematic social theory' in his work. Piotr Sztompka outlines the main components of his theory, reconstructing it out of a careful analysis of his major writings. In contrast, Robert Bierstedt argues that there is no 'general view of society' in Merton's work, and that Sztompka's open admission that Merton's social theory is 'deeply hidden' and needs to be reconstructed proves the point.

Chapters 7 and 8 examine more closely Merton's approach to structural analysis. Arthur Stinchcombe suggests that Merton's positive impact on empirical research derives from his general theory of social structure. The core process central to social structure is 'the choice between socially structured alternatives', and the core variable to be explained is 'different rates of choice by people differently located in the social order'. Anthony Giddens, on the other hand, argues that Merton's approach to structural analysis, despite subsequent modifications, perpetuates many of the well-known problems of functional analysis. In Giddens's view, the concept of function 'has no place in the social sciences and it is best to jettison it altogether'.

In Chapters 9 and 10 Raymond Boudon and Jon Elster discuss one of the most important and persistent themes in Merton's theory, the idea of the unintended consequences of social action. Raymond Boudon argues that the unintended consequences paradigm lies at the very heart of social scientific explanation, and cites in support detailed examples from the work of Max Weber and Merton himself. For Boudon, however, explaining particular social phenomena as the unintended product of other social phenomena is only plausible if the explanation is immediately understandable ('accepted by the Chinese', to use Weber's phrase) and non-tautological, i.e. if the psychological statements giving the reasons for particular behaviours are entirely independent from the phenomenon they contribute to explain. Jon Elster also regards the 'causal-cum-intentional' terminology of intended and unintended consequences (e.g. in Merton, 1936b) as the appropriate language for social scientific analysis, but is critical of those of Merton's subsequent writings which go beyond intentions and causes 'to introduce functions as a separate category' of explanation.

In Chapter 11, the first of the 'overview' papers, Peter M. Blau argues that one of Merton's most important and neglected contributions to sociological analysis, particularly in recent times, has been the elaboration of a general theory of structural constraints and opportunities. Blau also identifies an interesting parallel between Merton and Georg Simmel, suggesting that there is an analogous discrepancy between their negative reputations as general theorists and their strong actual contributions in this area.

Chapters 12 and 13 are the first in a series of papers which address more specific areas of Merton's work. Rose Laub Coser outlines his theory of role-sets, giving a number of examples—including the Western middle-class family and class differences in role-set complexity at work—of its usefulness in analyzing the dynamics of social relationships. Richard A. Hilbert, in contrast, argues that the terms 'status-set' and 'role-set' need to be located within functionalist role theory and subjected to the more general critique of functionalist explanation. Hilbert discusses examples from ethnomethodological writings—e.g. Garfinkel on rules and norms, Bittner on police peace-keeping tactics on skid row—and from Merton's own work—e.g. the status sets of Christian scientists and medical doctors—to support his case.

Chapter 14 is an overview paper on Merton's contribution to the theory of bureaucracy. Charles Crothers examines Merton's extensive writings on bureaucracy and its dysfunctions—on bureaucratic structure and personality, the roles of the intellectual and the engineer, reference groups and group behaviour, the political machine, the dynamics of leadership and voluntary organizations—and concludes that many of his insights have now been built into the conceptual foundations of organizational sociology. For Crothers, Merton's contribution to this field is a classic example of what Merton himself has termed 'obliteration by incorporation' (OBI).

Chapters 15 and 16 debate Merton's theory of anomie. Marco Orrù sees Merton, Emile Durkheim and Leo Srole as the leading figures in contemporary anomie theory and research; he argues that the appeal of Merton's approach lies in its instrumental character and its ability to identify the unintended anomic consequences of the 'American dream of success'. Philippe Besnard, on the other hand, suggests that Merton's theory of anomie is ambivalent, inconsistent and of limited use in empirical research, and that Merton's writings on anomie have established the myth rather than reality of a continuity of research since Durkheim.

Chapter 17 is devoted to a discussion by Samuel S. Wineburg and Lee S. Shulman of 'the self-fulfilling prophecy'. This is one of Robert Merton's most famous conceptual coinages, and there are now around 700 research papers which utilize the concept. Wineburg and Shulman provide an extended historical account of how it became a key concept in American education, beginning with the Supreme Court decision on school desegregation in 1956. They argue that the idea of the self-fulfilling prophecy has become so successfully diffused in the minds of American educators that—like Merton's work on organizational sociology—it has now become 'obliterated by incorporation'.

There follow five contributions which treat Merton's writings in the broad field of the sociology of science. The first two examine Merton's general approach to the sociology of science and scientific knowledge. In Chapter 18 Nico Stehr provides a descriptive analysis of Merton's sociology of science, suggesting there has been a shift in focus over the years from a socio-historical analysis of the emergence of modern science to a greater interest in the institutions and evaluation systems of the contemporary scientific community. In Chapter 19 Pierre Bourdieu pays 'critical homage' to Merton the sociologist of science, identifying his particular merit as having established the need for both an 'external' and 'internal' reading—i.e. science as both embedded in the social world and relatively autonomous from it. However, he is critical of what he believes to be Merton's 'idealistic' and 'naive' tendency to accept the norms professed by scientists at face value, although he reserves his greatest criticism for reductionist approaches 'at the opposite extreme' which relate cultural products directly to the most general economic and social conditions (Bourdieu calls this the 'short circuit effect').

The next three chapters focus more specifically on the relation between Puritanism and science, the theme of Merton's doctoral dissertation which eventually became *Science, Technology and Society in Seventeenth Century England* (Merton,1938a). In Chapter 20 I. Bernard Cohen provides a meticulous reconstruction of the circumstances surrounding the writing and critical reception of *STS*. He also demonstrates convincingly that the 'Merton thesis' is a classic example of what Merton himself later called 'a multiple and independent scientific discovery'. In Chapter 21 Piyo Rattansi provides a critical assessment of the 'Merton thesis' fifty years on, drawing on a wide range of philosophical and scientific sources—from Aristotle to Paracelsus, Bacon, Descartes and Comenius—to illuminate the continuing debate on the meaning of Puritanism. Finally, in Chapter 22 A. Rupert Hall, whose influential and highly critical assessment of the 'Merton thesis' in 1963 is discussed by both Cohen and Rattansi, provides a mature reflection on Merton the historical sociologist of science, reviewing the 'Merton thesis' in the light of the work of, among others, Thomas S. Kuhn, David Bloor and Mary Douglas.

Chapters 23 and 24 revert to the debate format, with contributions from Hubert M. Blalock Jr and Mark Gould on the interplay of social theory and empirical research. Blalock argues that Merton's case for a genuine interplay between theory and research is as valid today as it was when first presented over forty years ago. However, he suggests that sociologists have had considerable difficulty in implementing this advice, listing some of the reasons and some of the problems which are still to be resolved. Mark Gould, in contrast, argues for an 'additive' approach to sociological knowledge, suggesting that conclusions generated from within a general theoretical perspective lend credence to the empirical data and middle-range theory articulated in any one study. He illustrates his case by comparing Merton's theory of anomie and deviant behaviour with a general theory of internal disorder.

Chapter 25, the final chapter in the volume, contains an overview paper on the sociology of time by Simonetta Tabboni, who discusses Merton's early joint papers with Pitirim Sorokin as well as his current research and writings on 'socially expected durations'. Tabboni sees Merton's approach as typical of what she calls the 'Franco-American tradition', criticizing what she regards as its overemphasis on the social, normative aspects of time. She contrasts this tradition with the 'German tradition', represented by the work of Norbert Elias and Reinhart Koselleck, which emphasizes historical explanations (Elias's 'civilizing process') and also the individual experience of time. She pleads in her conclusion for future research to unite the strengths of the two traditions.

The volume concludes with biographical details about the contributors and an outline intellectual biography of Robert Merton (both compiled by Jon Clark); a full bibliography of the writings of Robert Merton from 1975 to 1989 (compiled by Mary W. Miles and Rosa Haritos); a bibliography consolidating all the references in the papers to this volume (prepared by Jon Clark); and author and subject indexes (prepared by Lyn Gorman).

II. GENERAL INTRODUCTIONS

2. Robert Merton as Sociologist

JON CLARK

Robert K. Merton has exerted a powerful influence on the development of the discipline of sociology over the past fifty years. However, as this volume testifies, the debate continues as to the relevance of his work to the theory and practice of the discipline today. The aim of this chapter is to set the general context for an evaluation of the sociology of Robert Merton, first, by outlining the main stages in his intellectual development, and second, by identifying some of his most important contributions to the discipline.

INTELLECTUAL DEVELOPMENT

Merton's sociology draws on a wide range of sources. This avowedly eclectic approach is based on the view that, in Lewis Coser's words, 'theoretical gold... [can] be found in the most unlikely ideological quarries' (cited in Coser and Nisbet, 1975: 7). There are some names, though, which recur with great regularity in Merton's writings, providing a clear indication of his own personal view of the 'founding fathers' of the discipline: Durkheim, Marx, Weber, Simmel and Cooley are perhaps the most cited, but also Comte, Spencer, Pareto, Sumner, Veblen and Mannheim—a catholic, cosmopolitan grouping, many of whom are no longer read by students of sociology today.

The prime importance of Durkheim ('pre-eminent', according to Sztompka, 1986: 24) and Marx in Merton's work will be discussed in more detail below. However, if we look at the most important living personalities who influenced his intellectual formation, six individuals stand out above all others (on this see Merton, 1968: xiii–xiv). First, there was Charles H. Hopkins, brother-in-law and dedicatee of his most celebrated publication, *Social Theory and Social Structure*: 'because this man...lived, many lives were deepened in human dignity' (*ibid.*: xiii).

Second was the man who introduced him to sociology, George E. Simpson. It was not just the first experience of conducting social research—identifying and classifying references to negroes in Philadelphia newspapers over a number of decades—as Simpson's assistant at Temple College in the late 1920s, but the 'intellectual excitement' of studying sociology that Merton later identified as Simpson's most important legacy to him. (It is worth noting that Simpson's ability to convey excitement in the subject was shared by Merton himself; see, for example, the testimony by James S. Coleman in Chapter 3 of this volume.)

Third came Pitirim Sorokin, erstwhile participant in Kerensky's cabinet in Russia in 1917, subsequently expelled by Lenin from the Soviet Union, Foundation Professor of Sociology at Harvard University in 1930 and author and teacher of a large-scale speculative historical sociology, including the mammoth *Social and Cultural Dynamics* in four volumes (1937–41). For Merton, Sorokin represented a two-fold intellectual liberation from 'provincialism', that is, the predominant focus in American sociology on US society and ideas (Merton was a voracious consumer of books from Sorokin's Europe-biased reading lists, see L. Coser, 1975b) and a restrictive concentration on 'peripheral' areas of social life (Merton, 1968: xiii).

The fourth influential figure was George Sarton (see Merton, 1985a), the Harvard historian of science who stimulated and examined Merton in his doctoral research in the substantive area which has been a focus of concern, albeit with intervals and shifts of emphasis, throughout his academic life, the sociology of science.

Fifth was Paul Lazarsfeld, with whom he worked for many years in the Bureau of Applied Social Research, 'the research arm of the Columbia Sociology Department' (Lipset, Trow and Coleman, 1956: xiii; for a biographical memoir of Lazarsfeld, see Sills, 1987). In 1941 Lazarsfeld and Merton were appointed to Columbia simultaneously on what in present-day jargon would be called a 'balanced ticket', Lazarsfeld specializing in empirical research, Merton in social theory. But the partnership which ensued, and above all Lazarsfeld's systematic approach to empirical investigation and 'sceptical curiosity' towards theory, were a continuous challenge to Merton to articulate more clearly his analytical and theoretical perspective.

Finally, there was Talcott Parsons. Parsons's influence on Merton during his period at Harvard in the 1930s was of two main kinds: the intellectual challenge resulting from the former's almost obsessive commitment to developing high-level analytical sociological theory, together with the lively and critical approach to scholarly debate fostered in the small study group which met with Parsons at this time—in the 'parsonage', of course. In later years it was debate with Parsons which helped Merton to crystallize his own particular approach to sociology, most celebratedly in his challenge to Parsons's grand theorizing at the 1947 meeting of the American Sociological Society.

In attempting to appreciate the development of Merton's distinctive approach to sociology, it is helpful to adopt Charles Crothers's schematic delineation of 'decades' in his intellectual career (Crothers, 1987a: 33–41; see also the *Intellectual Biography in Outline* in the endnotes to this volume). In the 1930s Merton laid the intellectual foundations for his future scholarly work. Apart from his doctoral thesis which eventuated in *Science, Technology and Society in Seventeenth Century England* (Merton, 1938a), he published path-breaking essays on the 'unanticipated consequences' of social action (1936b) and on social structure and anomie (1938b). In the 1940s he was involved in a number of empirical research projects linked to the work of Columbia's Bureau of Applied Social Research. In this period, too, he developed many of the theoretical and methodological ideas which culminated in the publication of the first edition of *Social Theory and Social Structure* (1949a), his 'classic' work which was substantially revised in 1957 and extended in 1968.

In the 1950s his research and increasingly influential teaching activities concentrated on key aspects of modern societies, such as the professions, bureaucracies, cities and the media. Indeed, Crothers (1987a: 38) has suggested that this work already anticipated the post-industrial imagery of Daniel Bell. In this decade he elaborated further his theoretical and methodological perspective, writing important essays on reference group behaviour (Merton and Rossi, 1950) and role-set theory (Merton, 1957c). The 1950s also saw a return to his 'first love', the sociology of science, resulting, inter alia, in the presentation of the paper, 'Priorities in Scientific Discovery: A Chapter in the Sociology of Science', as his Presidential Address to the 1957 American Sociological Society conference (Merton, 1957b). This was followed in the 1960s by a programme of research (with Harriet Zuckerman, Stephen Cole, Jonathan Cole and Thomas Gieryn) on the social and cognitive structure of science. The 1960s also saw the publication of his book *On the Shoulders of Giants* (1965a), a 'Shandean Postscript' genially celebrated by Stephen Jay Gould in Chapter 4 of this volume, and an essay on 'sociological ambivalence' (Merton and E. Barber, 1963), a concept later elevated to become the title of a collection of his writings (1976a).

Since the early 1970s, apart from reminiscences on his early work and vignettes of some of his teachers, colleagues and 'pupils', e.g. Sarton, Parsons, Lazarsfeld and Gouldner, arguably his most important publication has been the essay on 'structural analysis' (1975). This is a revised version of a thematic presentation made at a plenary session of the 1974 conference of the American Sociological Association; it will be the subject of more detailed examination below. More recently, he has published a major paper on the theme of 'socially expected durations' (1984a)—part of a wider research programme which promises to mark a new departure in the sociology of time—and issued a 'Self-Emancipation Proclamation' (in 1982) formally declaring his refusal to work to any more externally imposed deadlines!

Additional features of Merton's scholarly activities should also be noted here. First, he has exerted an enormous influence on the development of sociology by what Sztompka (1986: 18–20) has called his roles as gate-opener and gate-keeper. This refers not only to his book reviews, introductions to books, referee reports, references and recommendations, but above all to his labours as a reader and commentator on other people's manuscripts. This includes forty-five years as sociological editor for Harcourt Brace, as well as the provision of detailed comments—including the legendary rubber-stamp symbols: cautioning, questioning and occasionally, with the symbol of the noble griffin, lauding—on manuscripts sent by colleagues, former students and others for critical appraisal. Sztompka cites Merton's own calculation that, in fifty-five years of such activity between 1930 and 1985, he had commented upon around 200 book manuscripts and 2000 article-length essays (*ibid.*: 265n47).

Next, mention should be made of Merton's joy in language and his seemingly never-ending coinage of new concepts and neologisms. These include:

manifest and latent functions
social dysfunctions
self-fulfilling prophecy
self-exemplifying ideas
homophily and heterophily
pseudo-*Gemeinschaft*
goal displacement
local and cosmopolitan influentials
status-sets and role-sets
opportunity structures
anticipatory socialization
socially organized skepticism
accumulation of advantage and disadvantage
strategic research site
establishing the phenomenon
the Matthew effect
the Thomas theorem
the [Kenneth] Burke theorem
theories of the middle range
obliteration by incorporation (OBI)
OTSOG (On the Shoulders of Giants)
sociological ambivalence.

Coser has celebrated this aspect of Merton's work by dubbing him 'our foremost manufacturer of sociological thinking caps' (in Coser and Nisbet, 1975: 9).

Finally, Merton was one of the earliest users of citation data for research purposes, treating citation indices as an important quantitative indicator of the comparative amounts of attention devoted to publications by the community of scientists and scholars. This cannot be the place to discuss the strengths and weaknesses of citation indices as an accurate measure of scholarly influence, although Merton has always warned against their uncontrolled and incautious use, particularly in assessing the research performance and potential of individual scholars (see, for example, Merton, 1979a).[1] But using Eugene Garfield's benchmark of a general average of 'citation frequency' over an eight-year period (Garfield, 1980), the results are startling. Merton's 2300 citations in social science journals from 1970 to 1977 were eighty times greater than the average social scientist, and his 200 citations in natural science journals were four times the average for natural scientists! Only 40 per cent of his total citations were in sociology, with the rest spread across a range of disciplines. If one looks at particular works, *Social Theory and Social Structure* accounted for well over half the total citations (1400 out of 2500), 62 per cent in the *Social Science Citation Index* and 57 per cent in the *Science Citation Index*.[2]

Other studies of citations over different periods, mainly between 1945 and 1977, have come to very similar conclusions (see Crothers, 1987a: 46–8). Interestingly, too, they 'have shown Merton at least level-pegging with Parsons' (*ibid.*: 46) in American sociology textbooks since 1945. Mention of Parsons and Merton takes us directly to the next main section of this chapter, which assesses Merton's contribution to the discipline of sociology in the post-war period.

MERTON'S GENERAL CONTRIBUTION TO SOCIOLOGY

In this section Merton's elaboration of the principles and practice of 'middle-range theory' and 'structural analysis' will be discussed as his two most important general contributions to the discipline of sociology. The aim is not to provide an exhaustive analysis of these terms, nor to try and decipher in detail 'what Merton really meant'. Many of the chapters in this book explore these matters in detail. Instead, these terms will be interpreted as metaphors for a general approach or attitude to sociological analysis.

'Sociological Theories of the Middle Range'

Merton's distinctive approach to sociological theory can be appreciated most clearly when seen against the background of his critique of Talcott Parsons. The latter had, of course, attempted a preliminary synthesis of a number of classical social and economic theories in his mammoth book, *The Structure of Social Action* (Parsons, 1937). However, at the Annual Conference of the American Sociological Society in 1947, Parsons suggested that enough synthetical work had been completed for sociologists to embark upon a much grander project:

> ...the time is ripe for an attempt to deal with theory as a common task of the theoretically interested members of the professional group rather than with 'theories', the critical discussion of the work of a variety of different people...There is every prospect that [various current contributions] should converge in the development of a single conceptual structure. (Quoted in Merton, 1948a: 164)

Merton opposed this view, contrasting Parsons's plea for a 'single conceptual structure' with his own commitment to the development of 'special theories applicable to limited ranges of data' (*ibid*.: 165). These 'special theories' were described more accurately in a later paper as 'middle-range theories', that is,

> theories that lie between the minor but necessary working hypotheses that evolve in abundance during day-to-day research and the all-inclusive systematic efforts to develop a unified theory that will explain all the observed uniformities of social behavior, social organization and social change. (Merton, 1968: 39)

As with most 'classic' contributions to sociology, such as Weber's *Protestant Ethic* or Durkheim's *Suicide*, Merton's idea of middle-range theories can be interpreted as having both a 'strong' and a 'weak' form.[3] The strong form implies a principled rejection of the search for a 'complete sociological system' (1948a: 165). Indeed, in his paper elaborating on the idea of sociological theories of the middle range, he described the idea of a unified comprehensive theory as 'apocalyptic', having 'the same exhilarating challenge and the same small promise as those many all-encompassing philosophical systems which have fallen into deserved disuse' (1968: 45). This fundamental rejection of the holy grail of a unitary grand theory was grounded in the pluralist belief that no one theory is ever likely to have the complete purchase on knowledge or truth. In his writings Merton often refers to other 'more mature' sciences (such as physics or chemistry), which rarely deal with 'one all-embracing theory', but more often with the theory of specific types of phenomena. The young discipline of sociology ought to learn from the more mature disciplines such as physics, he suggests, which despite billions of man-hours of sustained cumulative research has only succeeded so far in generating theories of specific types of phenomena (the kinetic theory of gases or the wave theory of light) rather than one all-embracing theory or conceptual structure (*ibid.*: 47; also 1948a: 165).

The weaker thesis is less absolute. For example, in his critique of Parsons at the 1947 conference of the American Sociological Society he argued that the search for a total system of sociological theory was 'premature'—not enough preparatory work had been done on which to develop such a theory, which he suggested would be the result of a gradual consolidation of 'groups of special theories' (1948a: 165; see also 1968: 51). On this analysis the question of choosing between grand theorizing or the development of middle-range theories is a technical one of allocating sociological resources at a particular moment in time, a matter of emphasis rather than fundamentals. Both grand theory and middle-range theories are needed, but the way to grand theory is via middle-range theories rather than an intellectual leap to a master conceptual scheme.

At this point it is perhaps appropriate to give a detailed example of what Merton understands by a middle-range theory. In his various writings he quotes numerous examples—theories of social mobility, role conflict, social stratification, authority, anomie. One of the most illuminating, however, is the theory of reference groups and relative deprivation. This demonstrates, according to Merton, not only that middle-range sociological theories are able to generate hypotheses about likely patterns of behaviour, but also how they are likely to be more accurate predictors of behaviour than many less sophisticated or common-sense assumptions:

> ...the theory of reference groups and relative deprivation starts with the simple idea...that people take the standards of significant others as a basis for self-appraisal and evaluation. Some of the inferences drawn from this idea are at odds with common-sense expectations based upon an unexamined set of 'self-evident' assumptions. Common sense, for example, would suggest that the greater the actual loss experienced by a family in a mass disaster, the more acutely it will feel deprived. This belief is based on the unexamined assumption that the magnitude of objective loss is related linearly to the subjective appraisal of the loss and that this appraisal is confined to one's own experience. But the theory of relative deprivation leads to a quite different hypothesis—that self-appraisals depend upon people's comparisons of their own situation with that of other people perceived as being comparable to themselves. This theory therefore suggests that, under specifiable conditions, families suffering severe losses will feel *less* deprived than those suffering smaller losses if they are in situations leading them to compare themselves to people suffering even more severe losses. For example, it is people in the area of greatest impact of a disaster who, though substantially deprived themselves, are most apt to see others around them who are even more severely deprived....This pattern is reinforced by the tendency of public communications to focus on 'the most extreme sufferers [which] tends to fix them as a reference group against which even other sufferers can compare themselves favorably' (Barton, 1963: 62–3)....Within a particular *class* of behavior, therefore, the theory of relative deprivation directs us to a set of hypotheses that can be empirically tested. The confirmed conclusion can then be put simply enough: when few are hurt to much the same extent, the pain and loss of each seems great; where many are hurt in greatly varying degree, even fairly large losses seem small as they are compared with far larger

ones. The probability that comparisons will be made is affected by the differing visibility of losses of greater and less extent. (1968: 40–1)

Reference group theory is of course applicable to a large number of empirical phenomena apart from mass disasters. For example, workers' predominant perceptions of 'fair' wages are normally guided more by comparison with immediate 'significant others' (differentials with those immediately below and above them) than by a wider assessment of the social and economic value of their work. The important point here is that none of these examples of reference group theory has been 'logically derived' from a comprehensive sociological theory such as Marxism or Parsons's theory of action (although they could be consistent with many of them), nor are they 'mere empirical generalizations' (*ibid.*: 41) summarizing particular observed patterned relationships between variables. A middle-range theory, in short, 'comprises a set of assumptions from which empirical generalizations have themselves been derived' (*ibid.*).

The advantages and disadvantages arising from trying to put this approach into sociological practice are discussed in several contributions to this book. However, if assessed at a programmatic level, middle-range theory has multiple 'bridge-building' assets (see Sztompka, 1986: 111–12). These include linking: theory with empirical research; micro and macro focuses; scholarly cognitive (academic) and critical practical (policy) interests; and various substantive areas (reference group theory is applicable to stratification, industrial, medical, family and other specialist sociologies). Middle-range theory also provides a pluralist meeting ground for general orientations (functionalist, interactionist, Marxist, Weberian) which are often regarded as irreconcilable alternatives. In this respect, as Randall Collins has pointed out (1981: 298), middle-range theorizing, with its underlying assumption that 'theory and empirical research develop best in mutual interaction', is an 'overall strategy of analysis' independent of any particular field of sociology: 'It is the strategy that put him in the running for sociological eminence...Merton situated himself at the crossroad of a discipline of almost mutually oblivious approaches and thereby managed to come as near as anyone to directing traffic' (*ibid.*).

'Ham and Eggs': Structural Analysis as Primus inter Pares

In studies of the history of sociology and sociological theory Merton is still often seen as a 'structural-functional loyalist' (Crothers, 1987a: 18), the key figure together with Talcott Parsons in the development after 1945 of 'standard American', i.e. functionalist, sociology (see Mullins, 1973: 39). In partial defence of this view it should be remembered that Merton himself, in his influential essay (first published in 1949) on 'Manifest and Latent Functions', did pronounce functional analysis to be 'the most promising' (1968: 73) approach to sociological interpretation, although in the same paper he distanced himself from what he held to be three of its most important prevailing postulates: the functional unity of society, universal functionalism and functional indispensability (*ibid.*: 79–91).

In contrast to this emphasis on 'functional' analysis, most recent books on Merton have highlighted the 'idea of social structure' or 'structural' analysis as an equally, if not more, important paradigm of Mertonian sociology (see L. Coser, 1975a; Sztompka, 1986; Crothers, 1987a). However, while Sztompka sees no conflict between the early functional and later structural approach (1986: 143; also Chapter 5 in this volume), Crothers is rather sceptical and puzzled by Merton's adoption of the latter term (1987a: 76–81).

If we look at Merton's own writings on this matter, we find that, although he consistently acknowledges his debt to Parsons and 'structural functionalism', he does nail his colours increasingly to the mast of 'structural analysis'. Indeed, by 1975 he is describing it as the 'way of thinking about problems...more effective than any other I know' (1975: 30).

What are the distinguishing features of this approach, as outlined in Merton's article of 1975? First, it is based on a commitment to 'theoretical pluralism' in sociology. In part this is simply a reassertion of Merton's longstanding commitment to multiple theories of the middle range—such as theories of reference groups, stratification and deviance—rather than to a unified all-embracing grand sociological theory from which all lower level theories can be derived (see above). However, the 1975 version of 'theoretical pluralism' also involves a much more explicit recognition of the inherent limitations of any one approach to sociological analysis (structural analysis included) and an eclectic commitment to the complementarity of different approaches. By implication Merton is suggesting that the variety of approaches and 'isms' in the sociological firmament may simply illuminate different aspects of sociological phenomena rather than being 'better' or 'worse' in any absolute way. To illustrate what he means by this, Merton contrasts 'structural' with 'symbolic interactionist' analysis, often regarded as the two most diametrically opposed of approaches. In a rather felicitous phrase he writes: '*Many ideas in structural analysis and symbolic interactionism...are opposed to one another in about the same sense as ham is opposed to eggs: they are perceptibly different but mutually enriching*' (1975: 31; emphasis supplied).

If this commitment to theoretical pluralism marks off Mertonian 'structural analysis' explicitly from Parsonian 'structural-functionalism',[4] so does its second main feature, the stress on the structural sources and differential consequences of social conflict (*ibid.*: 37–42). Here it is perhaps possible to identify a shift of emphasis in Merton's approach. Whereas 'functional analysis' of the 1940s was heavily reliant on the Durkheimian sociological tradition, 'structural analysis' of the mid-1970s represents an explicit attempt to synthesize the best of Durkheimian and Marxian sociology. The result of the synthesis can be summarized in four main sets of propositions.

First, for Merton social structures are differentiated into interlocking and unevenly developing arrays of social statuses, strata, organizations and communities. These different social groups all have their own interests and values, some of which may be common, some actually or potentially in conflict. Social structures, then, are likely to generate social conflict as well as consensus. One of the prime concerns of sociological analysis is to examine how and how far the different social positions—based, for example, on class, occupation, race/ethnicity, gender, community, geographical location, disability, age group—of individuals shape their actions and their values.

Second, the core process central to social structure is 'the choice between socially structured alternatives', while the core variable to be explained is 'different rates of choice by people differently located in the social order'.[5] This approach incorporates concepts and emphases which are quite distinct from the 1949 definition of functional analysis. The placing of the concepts of choice and process at the centre of the analysis represents an unprecedented emphasis on human action, while underlining that (a) the choices people make in their lives are likely to be socially structured and (b) the types of choice they make (and the range of alternatives on offer) are likely to differ between different social groups.

Third, for the individuals and groups involved, the outcomes of the choices they make may be intended, anticipated and apparent (manifest), or unintended, unanticipated and not apparent (latent). The particular balance between these types of outcomes needs to be specified in each particular case.

Finally, whether intended or unintended, anticipated or unanticipated, manifest or latent, the choices people make have objective institutional consequences (functions or dysfunctions) for social structure. These consequences, in turn, affect the future structuring of alternative choices.[6] This completes the total sequence of structure—choice—outcome—institutional consequence—structure.[7]

If this set of propositions—as a 'package'—represents a shift in emphasis in Merton's approach to sociology, there is, however, at least one major continuity in his view of the tasks of the discipline. In his article of 1961 entitled 'Canons of the Anti-Sociologist', he wrote:

> Basic to sociology is the premise that, in the course of social interaction, men create new conditions that were not part of their intent. Short-run rationality often produces long-run irrationality. Public health measures may go awry; financial incentives may lead to decline rather than an increase in production; intensified punishment may aggravate rather than curb crime. Growing recognition of this has become one of the sources of an enlarged use of sociological research in such fields as medicine, public health, social work, law, education, the ministry, architecture and city planning, business, organized labor and agriculture. (Reprinted in Merton, 1976a: 184)

Merton's argument in this passage is unambiguous. A prime, perhaps the prime, focus of sociological investigation, and the area in which it brings the greatest insights, is in examining, understanding (and explaining) the relation between the conscious reasons and intentions underlying human behaviour and its outcomes and institutional consequences.

Merton's own application of this distinction to the rain dance of the Hopi tribe (1968: 110ff.) is well known, if much criticized (see, for example, Giddens, 1984: 293ff.). Merton states clearly at the outset of his discussion of the Hopi that if we wish to find out whether the manifest intention of their rain dance, to bring rain, is fulfilled or not, then we should consult the meteorologist rather than the sociologist. In contrast, the sociological approach to the same phenomenon has a different purpose and involves a number of quite different analytical stages (which are, in Merton's view, of general applicability to any kind of empirical sociological analysis).

First, the sociologist must describe the item to be interpreted. This should include not only a description of the phenomenon itself (in this case the ceremonial dance), but a systematic account of the people participating, the onlookers, the types and rates of interaction between them, and changes in the patterns of interaction in the course of the ceremonial. The description, writes Merton, must be in 'structural terms' (1968: 110), i.e. locating people and groups in the social structure.[8] Having done this it is then the task of the sociologist to examine the outcomes and objective institutional consequences of the behaviour. In the case of the Hopi tribe, what might appear on the surface to be irrational behaviour—there was no identifiable correlation between doing rain dances and the coming of rain—could have a positive (latent) meaning and outcome for the group, and as a result be socially functional for them in reinforcing group solidarity and re-kindling social energy.[9]

This general framework of analysis, first published in 1949, is of continuing relevance to present-day sociological theory and practice. Merton shows how a sociological focus on the 'manifest' side of social phenomena (structures, meanings/intentions and choice behaviour, as well as outcomes and institutional consequences/functions) simply directs our attention towards determining whether a practice instituted for a particular purpose does in fact achieve this purpose. For example, does a piece of legislation achieve a reduction in crime, does the introduction of new technology increase labour productivity (do rain dances bring rain!)? Although these are important issues, Merton argues that, if sociologists confine themselves to such questions, their enquiries are predefined and almost totally circumscribed: 'the sociologist becomes converted into an industrious and skilled recorder of the altogether familiar pattern of behavior' (1968: 119).

In contrast, the most promising areas for the development of the discipline are when the focus is extended, as in the celebrated 'Hawthorne studies', from simply examining what is manifest, intended and anticipated, to include what is latent, unintended and unanticipated. Findings arising from such a research focus are likely to deviate most from conventional understandings of social phenomena and are therefore likely to provide a greater increment in knowledge. For Merton, this more all-embracing approach should be the impulse behind empirical research rather than the requirements of social engineering. The test is no longer for the effect of a single variable (legislation on crime, technological change on labour productivity), but the description and analysis of a social situation in all its multiple facets. Such is the analytical focus which lies at the core of Merton's sociological approach and his view of the sociological enterprise.

CONCLUSION

Robert Merton's sociology has an extraordinary 'suggestiveness' (Bierstedt, 1981: 487). Whatever problems might arise with particular aspects of his approach or with the empirical application of particular concepts, they all seem to 'go to the heart of some methodological or sociological problem' (*ibid.*). It is possible to question, as does Jonathan Turner, whether Merton's classificatory theory-building adequately explains causal linkages, and it is true that the language of cause is not at the centre of Merton's sociology. But Turner also recognizes Merton's genius and the continuing appeal of his sociology, which lies 'in the substantive imagery that it depicts and the feeling...that it points to an important set of social processes' (1980: 90). It is the suggestiveness and openness of his approach and the richness of his appreciation of social life which are perhaps the most important legacies of Robert Merton the sociologist.

ACKNOWLEDGMENT

I am grateful to my Southampton colleagues Gordon Causer, Graham Crow, Neil Guppy and Alan Scott for detailed comments on a first draft of this chapter.

NOTES

1   The American discussion of citation indices is far more advanced than the British. Apart from emphasizing the need systematically to exclude self-citation, Eugene Garfield, the pioneer of citation indices in the USA, has also cautioned against the dangers of their oversimplified use. He has been particularly critical of the often held view that all citations are equal, questioning this assumption on two main grounds: the differing 'citation potential' of academic fields resulting from the different size of the literature and average number of references per article; and the different reasons or motives why authors are cited—for theory or empirical work, in affirmation, modification or rejection, ceremonial or substantive citation, one article cited again and again or a range of articles/books (see Garfield, 1980).

2   If we look at Merton's 'record' over a longer period, i.e. from 1969 to 1989, his SSCI count totals 6800 and SCI count 1350. If we deduct 50 per cent of the SCI citations as likely to be duplicated in the SSCI (a standard procedure in such cases), the total number of citations for this twenty-year period is 7500 (Eugene Garfield, Institute for Scientific Information, Philadelphia, personal communication, July 1989). This staggering figure is even more remarkable when it is remembered (a) that the citation index excludes citations in books (although it does include citations to books) and (b) it is now well established that the vast majority of citations of a paper normally appear in the first few years immediately after publication. The period under discussion (1969–89) was between twenty and forty years after the first publication of Merton's most cited work, *Social Theory and Social Structure*, and between thirty and fifty years after the publication of his celebrated papers on 'unanticipated consequences' (1936b) and 'anomie' (1938b).

3   As Merton himself has remarked (1968: 56–9, also 1957c: 108), the generic idea of the 'middle range' has well established roots, from Plato ('middle propositions') to Bacon ('middle axioms') and from J. S. Mill (*'axiomatica media'*) to Karl Mannheim (*'principia media'*), Adolph Löwe ('sociological middle principles') and Tom Marshall ('sociological stepping-stones in the middle distance').

4   In the mid-1970s Parsons gave his own view of the main differences between his own approach to sociology and that of Merton. In his comment on 'The Present Status of "Structural-Functional" Theory in Sociology' (1975: 73) Parsons identified three main differences: the centrality of the concept of 'system' (Wilbert Moore sees this as a *sine qua non* of functionalism, see Moore, 1978: 322ff.); the inevitability of abstraction; and the need to use plural system references.

5   This interpretation of Merton's approach to structural analysis has been stimulated in part by Stinchcombe's celebrated essay for the Merton Festschrift (L. Coser, 1975a: 11–33). Stinchcombe's essay has been revised for publication as Chapter 7 of this volume. The phrases cited in the text are direct quotations from the opening section of Stinchcombe's contribution.

6   My presentation and ordering of the propositions imply that objective institutional consequences (functions or dysfunctions), although exerting an influence on the future structuring of alternatives, are to be seen primarily as consequences of socially structured choices rather than the causes of them (this is a variation on Stinchcombe's famous 'loop in both directions'; see Chapter 7 in this volume). This view of Merton's general approach is accepted by Jonathan Turner at the programmatic level (1980: 77), although he argues that in practice Merton often reverses the sequencing, describing structures and behaviours in terms of the function they fulfil (*ibid.*: 77–82).

7   As an aside, it should be noted that which factor (structure/choice/outcome/institutional consequence) is seen as (1) constraining or facilitating the succeeding one or (2) constrained or facilitated by the preceding one, depends in the first instance on the point at which one enters the sequence!

8   Put another way: 'the structural description of participants in the activity under analysis provides hypotheses for subsequent functional interpretations' (Merton, 1968: 111). Note here, even in a piece originating in 1949, that the structural analysis of interaction is the generator of hypotheses for functional analysis, and not the other way around (see note 6 above).

9   This example was satirized beautifully in a cartoon in a French anthropological journal in the 1960s. The cartoon depicted members of a primitive tribe dancing around in a circle, and one is turning to another and saying: 'Do we really have to do this three times a day to maintain the social fabric?' I am grateful to my colleague Gordon Causer for this story.

3. Robert K. Merton as Teacher

JAMES S. COLEMAN

I have on occasion spoken about Robert K. Merton with sociologists who know him only through his writings. These are sociologists who have never known Merton the person, but for whom Merton the social theorist exists only through his written work. These sociologists assume *that* is Merton the sociologist; that to know his written work is to know the character and source of his impact on sociology. These sociologists are, however, incorrect, as all of us know who were graduate students at Columbia during Merton's reign. To give a sense of what 'more' there is to Merton the sociologist than can be found in his written work, I will characterize what more there is by its function, that is, by what it did for us and to us as prospective sociologists.

THE FUNCTIONAL CHARACTERIZATION OF MERTON THE CLASSROOM TEACHER

To do this involves first a reminder of what sociology is for new graduate students as they enter the field. Sociology is not like physics, well defined in the minds of those who enter it. As prospective graduate students enter a sociology department, each comes with a different conception of this new discipline about to be taken on. Early sociologists in America were often ministers' sons, and saw sociology as a means of social amelioration, a means of correcting ills and an approach to social reform. More frequent in Europe was the vision of sociology as revolutionary science, as a source of ideas that would bring down governments and radically restructure society. Some see sociology as history, only done better than historians do it; others see the discipline as a fertile field for applied mathematics. Some see sociology as a way of learning more about the social world they live in, providing guidelines for

25

living. Others see themselves as potential teachers of future youth, and sociology as the means by which they can give these youth better guidelines for living. Still others see it merely as a convenient vehicle for getting an academic job, a job with flexible hours and with summers off.

But however the new graduate students coming into a department see the discipline, the discipline is redefined for them in the first months of their careers as students. This redefinition, which creates a vision of the discipline unique to that department, may be the most important change graduate students will undergo. It shapes the way they view their work as students and as sociologists; it defines their future. There is more, however, to this change than a redefinition of what sociology is. There is a redefinition of the self, a transformation that gives one both a new direction and the force to follow that direction. A sociologist might call it a 'resocialization', but this is too weak a word to describe what happens.

What Merton did, what he did for us and to us, involves this transformation. At Columbia it was Merton, not Lazarsfeld, not Lynd, not C. Wright Mills, not Lipset, not Hyman, not Goode, not Theodore Abel, not Casey, not anyone else. It was Merton. In describing the transformation that Merton brought about in those of us who attended his lectures, I cannot be wholly general, for I know first-hand only what that experience did for me. Thus I will say a little about the before and after, the transformation which I underwent in that first year at the hand of Merton. From everything I could observe about my fellow-students, they were undergoing a similar transformation.

I came to Columbia in the summer of 1951 resolving to give educational institutions one more chance. Throughout my experiences with schools, I had looked for someone to excite my interest and capture my full attention. I had found that very seldom: once in an algebra course in grade 8, in rural Ohio, again in an advanced algebra course in grade 11, in Louisville, Kentucky, again in a political science course at Purdue University, and in a course on the plays of Henrik Ibsen and George Bernard Shaw. I was cynical about teachers in general because of their failure to generate in me this excitement with ideas. I recall once, as I was hitch-hiking to high school football practice at the end of classes for the day, saying to myself about my teachers, 'If only they would not destroy in us the interest with which we came to school, I would ask for nothing more'. I have later come to recognize that the task of capturing attention and generating excitement in students is less easy than I thought; but when I came to Columbia, my disillusion with education as I had found it was great.

I came to Columbia as a chemical engineer from a job at Eastman Kodak working as a chemist, having gradually and reluctantly concluded that chemistry did not, and likely would not, capture my energies the way it did for a few of my fellow researchers. Mixed in with all this was a strong desire to change the world for the better, in some unspecified way. Whether this was idealism or hubris or a mixture of both I cannot say. When I left Columbia four years later, the transformation was complete. I was a sociologist, having found a calling that I found worthy of lifelong dedication.

How did this come about? What was the magic potion that transformed a disillusioned 25-year-old, pessimistic about this 'last chance' for the educational system, into a dedicated sociologist, unable to conceive of himself in another calling? It was, of course, an amalgam, as all magic potions are. It is no easier to measure the separate effects of the ingredients of that amalgam than it is for an economist to measure the value of separate contributions to any joint product. But the initial, and I believe the one essential ingredient was the lectures of Merton—the only ingredient, I should add, that came in the form of classroom lectures.

I went into Fayerweather 313 on 25 September 1951 with some anticipation, anticipation that was heightened by the size and the heterogeneity of the crowd that was gathering. There were those I recognized as fellow students in sociology; there were some from preceding cohorts; there were also some who must have been from other departments; there was a contingent not quite identifiable as students nor as young toughs, with a radical-cum-intellectual air and a self-assurance bordering on belligerency. There were a few in suits from downtown who had heard about Merton's lectures. I arrived early enough to get a seat, a seat in the back where I preferred to be. The latecomers sat on the ledges of windows that hung out over Amsterdam Avenue. It was not a quiet crowd.

The course was Sociology 215, titled 'The Analysis of Social Structures'. But the title, and much about the content, were of secondary importance. The true content of the course (or as Merton might say, the latent function of the course) was to carry out the transformation that would make of this conglomerate crowd a set of would-be sociologists interested in discovering how society worked. (I must parenthetically note that this example illustrates an ambiguity in the concept of 'latent function', an ambiguity that Merton was aware of and lectured about, but unforgivably in my eyes never eliminated. A latent function is an unanticipated consequence of social action. But unanticipated by whom? Was Merton not aware that the most important consequence of this course, for many if not most students, was to induce a dedication to the sociological enterprise? Were we, the students, aware of this? And whose lack of awareness is critical for its being labelled an 'unanticipated consequence' or a 'latent function'?)

Even now I continue to pay heed to, and to argue with, those ideas and concepts that Merton laid out before us in 1951. Merton has of course discussed this objection many times; yet imagining myself back in that context, in a seat in the back of Fayerweather 313, without the courage to raise my hand in objection, I blurt out now the disagreement that I was then unable to. But I must apologize for doing so, because it gets in the way of the story.

Merton strode down the hall and entered Fayerweather 313, but the crowd did not immediately come to silence. Then he began. What ensued over the course of the next nine months was, for me, and for the other first-year students I knew in the course, an extraordinary mobilization. I left the course with no doubt that I was following the most important calling in the world. My pessimism about the educational system had evaporated. And the evaporation took place in Fayerweather 313.

It is not that all the teaching in sociology was the opposite of what had left me dispirited with high school and college. A course with Lazarsfeld was disorganized and unworthy of the subject matter; Kingsley Davis's course on the family was dry and some might say dull; Herb Hyman's methods sequence was pitched at a level far too low; Marty Lipset rambled; Robert Lynd was a mid-west preacher reminding me of the origins I had fled. I discovered later the redeeming qualities of these men. For me, Lazarsfeld's role was a special one. He gave me not only methodological problems that would occupy me for a number of years after graduate school, but also something extraordinarily important that I did not get from Merton: the confidence that I could achieve as a sociologist. The other sociologists I mentioned

played important parts in our careers as graduate students; but they were peripheral
to that early transforming experience that took place largely in Fayerweather 313. It
was also the case that the next year I found others who made sitting in a classroom
worthwhile: Daniel Bell, in a summer session course which entranced me, and Ernest
Nagel's extraordinary course in philosophy of science.

But Merton was something different. What were the components of his lectures
that made them a transforming experience? I can give only fragments of an answer
to that question, for there are ingredients that resist analysis. But some of the
components are these (and for this I draw on not only the 215–216 lectures in
1951–52, but also the 213–214 lectures in 1952–53, Merton's course in the logic of
theory construction).

1   Perhaps most important was our sense that *he* saw the process of creating
    sociological theory as all-absorbing, and was himself absorbed by it. It is, I
    think, too seldom recognized that students sense what motivates their
    teacher, and come to be similarly motivated. In the case of Merton, we saw
    his motivation as a search for the treasure, the discovery of what makes
    society work.

2   As a theorist, Merton was not content to develop his theoretical categories
    and show us their meaning. Merton went a step further than this. He asked
    how research might be used to test a proposition, and showed that it was
    possible to test 'middle-range' theories with systematic data. In this, it is
    important not to forget the time. Standardized interview techniques (includ-
    ing the 'focused interview', the interview procedures that Merton and his
    associates developed) had recently come into being, a process in which
    Merton had played an important part. Systematic sampling was a recent
    development in social research, and together with the standard interview
    schedules made possible numerical tabulations that could provide evidence
    on propositions from sociological theory.

    The times, with their methodological developments, facilitated a
    connection between social theory and quantitative research results that had
    been more difficult before; but it was Merton who, in his lectures, made the
    possibility a reality. He used, for example, the comparison of 'Hilltown' and
    'Craftown' to show in quantitative—and thus striking—fashion the effects
    of social structure on behaviour. This was before the era of national
    samples, before the period in which survey research was used to study
    characteristics of large populations or to create path diagrams for large
    populations, or to evaluate government programmes.

    There was a brief courtship, in those early days of quantitative data
    analysis, between survey data and theoretical problems in sociology. This
    courtship was apparent in Katz and Lazarsfeld's *Personal Influence*, in
    Lipset's *Union Democracy*, but most strikingly in a study that never fully
    made its way to print: Merton's 'forthcoming housing study'. It was only
    those of us in Merton's classes at that time who, in the comparison between
    Craftown and Hilltown, saw exhibited the difference that social structure
    made, saw social theory and social research come together.

    Other sociologists who were primarily theorists, like Parsons, never left
    the theoretical realm. Others who were primarily methodologists, like
    Lazarsfeld or Stouffer, were not sufficiently engrossed with the ideas central

to sociological theory that they used the methods to test the theoretical ideas. It is not even that Merton did it perfectly himself; but he strove to do it. He knew both the components; and he strove to bring them together.

3 Closely associated with Merton's linking together of classical sociological problems with the emerging quantitative methods was his background in history of science, stemming from his work with George Sarton. When Merton set us to reading some of James Conant's case studies in the history of science, and we could see other struggling young disciplines in stages similar to sociology's then current stage, this increased the sense that we were at the exciting point of the discipline. Merton constituted a bridge, not merely between the classical theoretical problems and the emerging methods in sociology, but also between sociology as it then was and other disciplines when they were searching to find their first principles. As we learned from those other disciplines, the first principles were found not by theorizing in the absence of research, nor by data collection without a set of ideas to test, but with an intimate intermixing of the two.

4 Merton, in his concern with the *process* of theory construction in sociology, gave us a set of tools with which to analyze and evaluate theoretical work. I can illustrate these tools by describing a task that Merton once set those of us in his class. Parsons's *Social System* was published in the fall of 1951, during that first semester. Merton hailed it as a great development in social theory, and eagerly set us to reading it. But he also provided some tools with which to do so. He asked us to go through the early chapters and to note each theoretical sentence, labelling it according to type: was it a *definition*, an *empirical generalization*, a *reconceptualization*, a *respecification* of a lower level empirical generalization? This led us to go through *The Social System* with a fierce intensity; and it was this task which Merton set us that, despite his accolades to the book, initiated my disillusion with Parsons—as I kept labelling statement after statement 'definition', with almost none labelled 'empirical generalization' or 'reconceptualization'.

But these tools were not only capable of exposing nakedness. They allowed Merton (and us, equipped with the tools) to discover partially hidden but brilliant insights leading to a respecification or reconceptualization. Merton's dissection of Durkheim's *Suicide* in his course on the logic of theory construction showed the inner workings of a master theorist-cum-researcher (and in the process made me into a Durkheimian for the first eight years of my career).

5 Perhaps most important of all was Merton's critical capacity in examining theoretical work in sociology. He examined theoretical work with a critical microscope from which slipshod reasoning and insufficient evidence could not escape. When he examined the work of theorists, he dissected the work in fine detail; he let the theorist get away with nothing. Merton brought from his work in history of science a set of standards, which he moulded into standards for this new discipline.

These were the Merton lectures in Sociology 215–216 in 1951–52, and Sociology 213–214 in 1952–53. It was these lectures that gave, to me and to others, the sense of mission that propelled us headlong into the discipline. But what about Merton otherwise, that is as a teacher but outside the classroom?

MERTON OUTSIDE THE CLASSROOM

The scene shifts to the staging area in Fayerweather, a bullpen surrounded on three sides by the open door of the office that contained Merton's and Lazarsfeld's secretaries, the closed door of Lazarsfeld's office, and the closed door of Merton's office. The staging area is full of people, some in an ill-formed line waiting for admittance to Lazarsfeld's office (where I more often found myself), and about the same number, probably a few more, in another ill-formed line waiting their turn with Merton. Why was I less often in the Merton line? I was 25, no longer a 9-year-old in elementary school, but when I was in the office, there was (as I see it now in memory, and no doubt as I experienced it then) a tall man behind a large desk (on a raised platform, my memory would insist, whatever the evidence) and a small boy fidgeting nervously. The tall man smiled, to be sure, and attempted casual conversation; but the small boy really had nothing to say (perhaps he forgot what he came for) and was soon out, into the open air of the bullpen.

Merton and Lazarsfeld made a study in personality contrast. The contrast at that time can perhaps be best expressed in their relation to ideas and to people. (I say 'at that time' because it is my impression that there were changes in Lazarsfeld in ways relevant to my description in his later years; and Merton is different now than he was then.) Ideas and people were important to Lazarsfeld, and were and are important to Merton. But the interaction between their pursuit of ideas and their relation to people was very different. Lazarsfeld *used* people in his pursuit of ideas. Some might say uncharitably that he used them in the way a farmer hitches up draft horses to a plough. Others, perhaps more charitable, would say that Lazarsfeld's interest in people and in ideas was so strong that he could not pursue one without making use of the other as an aid in that pursuit. Altogether, for Lazarsfeld, the pursuit of ideas and of people was inextricably intertwined.

For Merton, the pursuit of ideas was an activity to be carried out alone. If I infer correctly from the observations of thirty-five years ago, for Merton, working with ideas was an alternative to working with people. (I hesitate to say this, because I'm not by trade a social psychologist. But my own temperament is one that I see as rather similar to that of Merton's. Thus if these remarks are not correct for the Merton of thirty-five years ago—and I do not even consider whether they are correct for the Merton of today—they can serve the secondary role of self-revelation.)

It is not that Merton was not interested in people, nor that for him there was no interaction between ideas and people. The interaction was no less important than was true for Lazarsfeld. Ideas, once developed and polished through solitary work, once ready for exhibition like a fine-cut gemstone, were a vehicle for attracting people. But as in the exhibit of a gemstone, people should not be too close. Some distance was necessary, not merely for the full effect, but more important, to allow the intellectual work, a solitary pursuit, to go on.

The implications of this for Merton's actions as a teacher were several. It meant that the lecture was the centrepiece of those activities, for in the lecture ideas, developed and polished in isolation, could be exhibited. And the lecture involved people, people at the right distance, but people no less. It meant also that close working relationships were not easy, or else required a fit of personalities that was rarely found.

To illustrate from personal experience: although I regard Merton, Lazarsfeld and Lipset as my mentors at Columbia, they served very different functions for me. Lipset, closest in age and status, was my working collaborator, the research colleague with whom Martin Trow and I would thrash out problems of the ITU analysis. Lazarsfeld was my patron, setting tasks, providing funds, organizing projects and needing help in getting them done. Merton provided the inspiration for it all, pointing to a glorious future for the discipline, and providing tools for getting from the present to that glorious future. I worked *with* Lipset, worked *for* Lazarsfeld, and worked *to be like* Merton. But while there was no danger in proximity to Lipset, there was serious danger in getting too close to Lazarsfeld or to Merton. If one ventured too close to Lazarsfeld, one would be caught in an orbit, destined to circle around him forever as a minor satellite. If one ventured too close to Merton, one would be blinded by the brilliance, forced to move back in order to recover one's faculties.

The attractiveness was very great, tempting one to get as close as Merton would allow. I succumbed to this, in the hope that the magic would somehow rub off. This, alas, did not succeed. I was once, in Sociology 214 (the second half of the logic of theory course), an informal course assistant for Merton, taking notes in his lectures and writing up my comments on the lectures. I learned a great deal from this. But at one point, in a memorandum to Merton, I interrupted a restatement of the steps that Pascal took in the seventeenth century (these were steps in creating a testable hypothesis about the properties of air from an analogy between the air and a sea, steps that Merton had just lectured about). I wrote, interrupting this memorandum:

> What is my role? Am I primarily to organize, amplify, and edit the lectures, to bring them into a form for publication? Am I to do something more than this? If so, what is it? If my primary function is that of *organizer*, then I am not sure I want to embark on the program, for my primary purpose is to *learn*, and I can learn nearly as much by attending the lectures, while the amount of time spent in organization would keep me from learning in other areas. If the problem is one which primarily entails not finding out something new, but simply expositing something already known, about what authors do, then I am not very good at that. I simply have a hard time being motivated, and I don't write particularly well. My basic difficulty is this: I don't see the problem to which I am supposed to be oriented. Is it organizing what you have already analyzed and made explicit about the operations authors go through, or is it to attempt to find out more about these operations in order to somehow aid in further building of theory?

The question was never resolved. I continued as informal course assistant, and thought through the issues posed by Merton in his lectures more fully than I otherwise would have; but there was no tangible fruit to this collaboration. In the end it petered out, Merton not getting what he wanted and I never quite knowing what the problem was.

Again, an example: I came to be interested in the concept of 'social isolation', as a spinoff from Lazarsfeld's project on 'Concepts and Indices' and from my interest in Durkheim's *Suicide*. I consulted with Merton, and with his encouragement set about writing a paper on the logical character and substantive role of 'social isolation' in the work of sociologists. I wrote an early draft, received comments from Merton, then went on to extend the ideas at length. But what was its destination? Merton read it, liked it, but then it languished, till I later lost it in some reshuffling. (I thought Merton had lost it, but this was the semi-paranoia that graduate students sometimes have.) It was, in fact, the theoretical piece of which I was most proud during my days in graduate school. Yet it languished until I lost it.

It languished in part because Merton had no *need* for it. Didn't he know it was written for *him*, as a kind of intellectual offering?

With Lazarsfeld, of course, it would have been quite different. He always had too many obligations, and thus a continuing need for products to meet those obligations (though the tasks he set were sometimes ill-conceived or misguided). These needs of Lazarsfeld, and their fulfilment by graduate students, gave a closure, a product of one's activity that was often lacking after an engagement with Merton.

A large part of the uneasiness one experienced in working under Merton was due to the incisiveness of his critical ability. To paraphrase what one fellow-student who *did* attempt to do his dissertation under Merton said, 'I always feel, with every sentence I write, him perched there on my shoulder, looking at the sentence, judging what's wrong with it'. The end result was that this student didn't write many sentences. It was a catch-22: to get on with his work, one had to take Merton's detailed critique (or the detailed critique that one knew Merton *would* write) with a grain of salt. But one could not take it with a grain of salt, because the critique was *correct*: the faults as detailed were there; and now that they had been exposed, they loomed larger than any possible virtues of the piece.

CONCLUSION

What is one to make of all this? What, as a teacher, did Merton do for us and to us? To answer the first half of this is simple: Merton made sociology into a calling, a holy pilgrimage to which one, if one caught the fire that Merton held out, would devote one's life. But what of the other side of Merton the teacher: not the fire that lighted the way, but the fire that burned if one got too close? The answer, I think, is this: a student is not passive clay, nor is a teacher an omnipotent presence. A teacher is to be used: to be studied and analyzed for the sources of value, if any, that teacher contains; to be discarded if no value is found, but *if* value is found, to be used in a fashion designed to extract that particular kind of value resident in that teacher. The value that we as students found in Robert K. Merton, teacher extraordinary, was great indeed. Fortunately, Merton himself recognized where that value lay, and made it the central element of his intellectual interaction with students. The result was the kind of transformation, in us as students, that every true teacher aspires to bring about.

4. Polished Pebbles, Pretty Shells: An Appreciation of *OTSOG*

STEPHEN JAY GOULD

I do not know what I may appear to the world; but to myself I seem to have been only like a boy playing on the seashore, and diverting myself in now and then finding a smoother pebble or a prettier shell than ordinary, whilst the great ocean of truth lay all undiscovered before me. (Isaac Newton, quoted in Brewster's *Memoirs*, 1855)

I have watched the sun rise over the Taj Mahal, the Grand Canyon and the crater of Haleakala on Maui—but I have never seen anything nearly so beautiful as the south transept of Chartres in the evening light. (As an anti-romantic, I also think that sunrises are much overrated for their supposed spiritual significance. Sunsets provide an equally satisfying mirror image, and occur at much more convenient times.) My reaction to the great rose window and the five lancets below combines visceral awe with intellectual admiration—a surefire combination for academic popularity. I view the rose as a wonderful composition in reds and blues, hundreds of pieces changing in tone and intensity throughout the day as the sun moves past. I view the lancets as the finest visual image ever composed to illustrate the central tension in our quest to grasp the nature of history and knowledge—the arrow of progress versus the cycle of immanence. Four lancets surround the central figure of Mary and her child. Each shows an evangelist of the New Testament, depicted as a dwarf and seated upon the shoulders of an Old Testament prophet—Matthew on Isaiah, Luke on Jeremiah, John on Ezekiel, Mark on Daniel.

I also treasure these windows for a personal reason; in an indirect way, via R. K. Merton and *OTSOG*, they taught me the most important lesson that every decent scholar must learn sooner or later—humility. (Some who know me might deny that I have ever encountered such a notion, but external appearance and internal conviction do not always match, and only the latter is a constant companion.) I first visited Chartres at age 20, a year before my graduation from Antioch College. I saw the windows and thought that I had made a great discovery, undoubtedly never anticipated or even considered before. I recalled Newton's famous epistolary statement to Hooke: If I have seen further it is by standing on the shoulders of giants. Clearly, I had discovered hard (if fragile) evidence for Newton's lack of originality. Someday I would tell the world and make my name.

I went to graduate school at Columbia and reconnected with Stephen Cole, a boyhood friend, and then a graduate student of R. K. Merton. One day he showed me a book that his mentor had just published—*On the Shoulders of Giants*. And so I learned that pre-Newtonian usages were not only well documented, but copious enough to spawn an entire volume. Can anyone imagine a more firm or a more gentle lesson in humility? (I was even left with a solace, for Bernard of Chartres emerged as Merton's buck-stops-here starting point, and one could argue, though not with great confidence as I shall discuss below, that the famous windows are an attempt, a generation or two later, to capture Bernard's celebrated metaphor in glass.)

But if personal meaning were the criterion for a great book, I would have to rank *The Little Engine That Could* and *Lucky to Be a Yankee* among the giants of literature. The causal chain runs the other way. *OTSOG* is a great book for entirely intrinsic reasons—and great books are so generous in scope and broad in implication that they spread personal meaning in hundreds of directions. (DiMaggio's *Lucky to Be a Yankee* is anathema to Dodger fans; *OTSOG* is for the world.)

But why is *OTSOG* a great and universal book, not merely a scholarly romp or a self-indulgence, however brilliantly executed? The primal reason—joy—I postpone until the very end of this essay. The best reason lies embedded in my favourite quotation—a line sometimes attributed to the architect Mies van der Rohe, but undoubtedly older, dating perhaps to Homer or the caves of Lascaux, and worth a second volume from Merton as a little encore to be named GODDID: 'God Dwells in the Details'. (When I study Mies's buildings, I can surely accept him as a source, for, in such spare and unornamented structures, only the nuances of detail and proportion can distinguish a work of beauty from a glass box.)

The bane of scholarship is inaccessibility through failure to interest or to communicate; the opposite poles of this pervasive misfortune (surely afflicting more than 90 per cent of scholarly publication) are (1) generality so broad and so devoid of reference to tangible things that misguided attempts at comprehensiveness lapse into idiosyncracy; and (2) detail so indulged for itself alone, and so unaccompanied by any extension to broader issues of wider concern, that no one but the author gives a damn. The solution, following my geometric metaphor, is simplicity itself: go for that unexcluded middle, the *aurea mediocritas*; start with something small and fascinating (furry and friendly enough to inspire initial interest in anyone but a dolt), and then move ever outward, linking important generalities to that concrete beginning. I have tried to follow this strategy in more than 150 essays in natural history; but I am only Merton's epigone, a mere dwarf standing firmly on the ground, and looking up at *OTSOG*.

Yes, begin with details by all means, and retain them as an anchor throughout. But, as Orwell once said about animals, some details are more equal than others. *OTSOG* is a great book because it dwells in a particularly juicy, fascinating and extendable detail, not because it promotes the general and optimal methodology of working outwards from small and tangible beginnings. A true connoisseur of details could find no tidbit more enticing than Newton's comment to Hooke. It is truly top drawer, numero uno, world class, the big enchilada—and for three basic reasons.

1   The history of the statement has such an enormous range of time and personage, moving from the abbeys of medieval Europe to the computer search programs of our latter-day Bartletts, and from Bernard of Chartres through Robert Burton and Isaac Newton to Freud and Merton himself.

2   The statement itself is particularly important because it engages so many central questions in intellectual life: how does knowledge progress (or does it); what is the value of scholarship; how can novelty be balanced with fealty to the past?

3   The analysis (or just the simple story) of shifting uses and attributions beautifully illustrates most of the central questions about science as a social phenomenon—especially the three great p's of progress, priority and plagiarism. I shall devote most of this essay to expanding these three themes in order.

THE STORY LINE

An old baseball tale, perhaps apocryphal, holds that when Yogi Berra was rooming with Bobby Brown (then the Yankee third baseman, but later a famous cardiologist), Brown spent most non-playing hours poring over Gray's *Anatomy* (while Yogi preferred comic books). Yogi, puzzled by this weighty erudition, could only ask Brown how his book 'turned out in the end'.

Most fans tell the story to Yogi's disadvantage, but I would defend baseball's guru (who will contribute more sayings to the next edition of *Bartlett's* than any professor I know). Yogi was right. The story line is primary. Everything else, however elegant, is a gloss. The tracking of Newton's borrowed phrase through labyrinthine branches to unexpected roots turns out to be a great story, worthy of detective fiction at its finest, but having the extra appeal of truth. And Merton, who clearly did not miss his calling but obviously might have travelled other literary roads, is a wonderful storyteller. He knows when to rummage leisurely, when to tighten the pace, when to drop a little hint to a fulfilment fifty pages down the line, and how (above all) to spring that stock-in-trade of the mystery genre—a surprise ending. In fact, *OTSOG* is two stories, subtly intertwined: the tale of the phrase itself, and the story of Merton's hilariously wandering and non-linear mode of discovery.

Merton subtitles *OTSOG* 'A Shandean Postscript' to honour the similarity between his deliciously tangential style and our language's most celebrated opus in that genre—Laurence Stern's *Tristram Shandy*. But Merton even out-Shandys Shandy, for whereas that irreverent and tangential gentleman (who held that 'digressions, incontestably, are the sunshine...the life, the soul of reading') at least had the decency to begin at the beginning,[1] Merton starts in the middle with Newton's citation and then wanders in Brownian motion until his peregrinations reach both the beginning and the end somewhere along the way. (Jacques Barzun caught the essence of Merton's—and Sterne's—crafty craft in peering through this overt disorder into the most tough-minded generating control: 'I marveled at the maintenance of Form under the appearances of improvisation and discursiveness: *that* puts Merton in Sterne's class'.)[2]

OTSOG presents more of a story net than a story line, but one thread of Ariadne, faithful to Merton's chronology, goes something like this. Newton was no plagiarist, and laid no claim to originality. His casual use only suggests that he had cited a phrase well known to all, and therefore needing no explicit reference—as one might write to a friend from Anchorage in January about the present winter of discontent without adding an explicit note about Richard III. What, then, was the canonical source in Newton's time? George Sarton, Merton's mentor and greatest of all historians of science, had posed this question, and decided upon a citation in Robert Burton's *Anatomy of Melancholy* (1624). Now we pick up a clear hint of originality, for Burton cites his source as 'Didacus Stella in Luc. 10. tom. 2'. Leaving aside the identity of Didacus Stella (a book or a person?), Burton must be tracing the aphorism back to antiquity in the person of Lucan (39–65).

So, suspecting the eventual point of arrival, Merton is now free to peregrinate. He spends most time in his own best-known seventeenth century, primarily showing us how the aphorism became a rallying cry (for both sides) in the celebrated 'battle of the books' (so mercilessly satirized by Swift)—the conflict between ancient and modern learning, or rather the argument of the sufficiency and superiority of antiquity versus the claims of modernism under the concept of progress. Conservatives emphasize the superior height of giants versus dwarfs; modernists cite the comfortable fusion of giant with dwarf, and the elevated stature of the happily conjoined pair. (The debate could really get fierce. The archconservative Godfrey Goodman, for example, pointed out that no one had solved, or even addressed, the issue of how the dwarfs can mount so high in the first place, not to mention the vexatious problem of how they stay aloft, given the problem of vertigo. 'It is to bee feared', he writes, 'lest seeing so steepe a descent, they will rather fall to a giddines'. Now answer me that, you modernists!)

Merton wanders back, into France, Spain, through the writings of several medieval Jewish scholars, finally to the twelfth century John of Salisbury, acolyte of the celebrated Bernard of Chartres. John cited the aphorism as Bernard's invention (c. 1126), and Merton can follow it no further back. The only hint of earlier currency starts with the great cathedral windows that first inspired my interest in the aphorism. They were installed a few generations after Bernard. Could they reflect this metaphor in glass? Maybe, but Merton finds similar iconography on portals, baptismal fonts and Romanesque capitals, one example dating (perhaps) to the tenth century. Does this iconography record pre-Bernardian currency for the aphorism? Perhaps, but who knows? Recorded and preserved history seems to be silent on this question, and Bernard must tentatively prevail.

Which brings us back to the mysterious Didacus Stella and the apparent attribution to the Roman Lucan. On page 183 of *OTSOG* (I use the vicennial edition of 1985), in the middle of his discussion on Bernard and buried in a footnote, Merton gives us a sly foreshadowing of the eventual solution. He is looking at the Chartres windows and musing over the French names of the dwarf evangelists: Saint Mathieu, Jean, Marc et Luc. Could Burton's cryptic citation 'in Luc. 10. tom. 2' refer to a later commentary on the evangelist and not to a classical source? But Merton lets it pass, exclaiming: 'Enough of such stray musings, and back to our immediate search'.

And so, Merton holds his surprise for the end. Didacus Stella, he discovers, is a person, not a title, the sixteenth century Spanish scholar Diego de Estella who, among many other things, composed a commentary on—yes, you guessed it—the gospel of Luke. The assumption of scholars for centuries, the proclamation of *Bartlett's* for edition after edition, is wrong thanks to Burton's elisions, not his malfeasance. Didacus Stella is the person; Luc is the (compressed) title—not vice versa. The putative Roman source becomes a near contemporary of Burton, and the erudition of many scholars is exposed as mindless copying without checking sources.

After this *éclat* of a *dénouement*, and this affirmation of Bernard, Merton can only race forward on the other side of Newton, tracing the aphorism for three more centuries through the likes of Coleridge, Mill, Engels and Peirce to a statement of Freud so biting that the book can only end abruptly with Merton's parting shot: 'Exit Aphorism'. An undesired disciple (whom Freud disdained) made 'self-interested use' of the aphorism by claiming superior insight to Freud because, though but a dwarf on his master's shoulder, he could see farther. 'That may be true', said the master, 'but a louse on the head of an astronomer does not'. Ultimately, then, the meaning of the aphorism lies in relative sizes, and Jonathan Swift, who placed Gulliver in both categories by proper choice of contrast, spoke truly when he wrote (as cited by Merton on page 130 but not, curiously, in reference to Freud's icy retort): 'undoubtedly philosophers are in the right, when they tell us that nothing is great or little otherwise than by comparison'.

THE BIG ISSUES

Whatever our egalitarian hopes and predilections, we simply have to admit that all aphorisms are not equal. If we traced 'have a nice day', we might learn something interesting about social history, but we could never engage meaty intellectual issues because the statement is, prima facie, insipid and vacuous. But the simile of dwarfs on the shoulders of giants could not be more central to all that intellectuals hold dear in their traditions and their battles. We wonder about progress; is the concept tenable as a description of history, or does it merely capture our egotistical hopes; can fields be differentiated by the applicability of such a concept (can we accept science's conceit about the centrality of progress, and what of the talmudist's reverence for unerring text): what duty, fealty, honour, recognition do we owe the past anyway?

Can you imagine a more incisive simile for all these ambiguities than dwarfs on the shoulders of giants—for the image captures both sides of the essential tension between the relative values of past and present—our ancestors were greater for they are giants, but we know more for we build upon their greatness, however small our increment. Since the image has an inherent capacity to speak for either side, when appropriate stress or de-emphasis attends one aspect or another of the compound figure, the aphorism is not only available to anyone of any opinion, but (and here we celebrate the eternal capacity of scholars to elevate minutiae to crucial importance) the richness of detail affords endless scope for ceaseless argument.

Merton's brilliant (and hilarious) chapters on scholars, zealots and pamphleteers in the seventeenth century battle of the books show the full capacity of the aphorism. Conservatives conveniently de-emphasize the positions implied by interaction, and focus upon the two components considered separately: we are dwarfs, they were giants, and that's that. As Merton characterizes the position: 'modern discoveries are not new; if new, they are not true; if both new and true, they are not useful'. The intermediary position, the moderate stance among the modernists, takes the interaction as primary, grants the greater cognitive capacity of Plato in isolation, but argues for our superiority on the happy ground of knowledge as a cumulative process (why else be a scholar if not to preserve the past as a substrate for further advance?).

Then we have the true radicals, those who ripped the simile from its foundation and, citing a paradox formalized by Francis Bacon but with roots that (genuinely this time, not as with Lucan and Didacus Stella) go back to antiquity, cleanly invert the entire image. The ancients are not old, and we but callow youths or just born babes. They are the kiddies who inhabited the world in its innocent infancy, while we are greybeards blessed with the wisdom of all past time. As Bacon said in a famous paradox: *antiquitas saeculi, juventus mundi*—the antiquity of time is the youth of the world. Or, in the context of our simile, as George Hakewill wrote to counter Goodman's worries about vertiginous dwarfs: 'It is not so, neither are wee Dwarfes, nor they Gyants, but all of equal stature, or rather wee somewhat higher, being lifted by their meanes'.

THE SOCIAL CONTEXT

We know why Merton called *OTSOG* 'Shandean' in his subtitle, but why a 'Shandean *Postscript*'. *OTSOG* is an epistolary book, an extended response to a letter from the historian Bernard Bailyn, to whom Merton had sent a copy of his 1957 presidential address to the American Sociological Society (now, in response to the age of acronyms, the American Sociological Association) on 'Priorities in Scientific Discovery'. Bud Bailyn began his letter to Merton by thanking him for a copy of the address, and then cited dwarfs on giants as an interesting little example of uncertain intellectual property. *OTSOG* is a response to Bailyn's musings, and therefore a postscript to the more conventional scholarly address (then published as a paper, now famous, in the *American Sociological Review*) that served as its indirect source.

I am now seriously out of my depth, a paleontologist enclosed in a book of sociologists, a lamb among wolves. I must also honour an important subsidiary use of the *OTSOG* aphorism (and the one that Freud saw through so brilliantly): its value as a device for staging disingenuous allegiance to the scholarly ideal, both unattainable and undesirable in real life, of humility. I am, after all, but an ignorant dwarf....

The point is simply this: Bob Merton is the pre-eminent sociologist of science in our century. *OTSOG* is explicitly a postscript to a sociological thesis about priority disputes in science. Obviously, aside from the story line (or web) of *OTSOG*, apart from the intrinsic meaning of the aphorism itself, a third theme of light reflected from the aphorism upon sociological issues pervades this volume. But sociology is not my parish; I do not know your saints or your in-jokes (for every tidbit I get based on Latinity or the biology of size, I know that I miss ten directed to professional sociologists).

At least half a dozen themes about the social context of science intermingle explicitly (or at least overtly enough to strike a paleontologist) in this volume—and Lord knows how many others are invisible to me. The principal theme, priority, is a particularly delicious issue (and now I speak as a practicing scientist, not a scholar or analyst). The simple fact that so many major scientific discoveries are, in Merton's word (for he has brought more insight to this area than anyone else), 'multiples' of nearly simultaneous and independent origination by two or more people, rather than mysterious moments of 'eureka' vouchsafed by the Gods to unique geniuses, proves that 'hot ideas' (even those that turn out to be objectively true) must arise (or become visible even if 'eternally' valid) within a social context—for why else the rule of multiples if each item available for scientific discovery is like an independent and beautiful rose, eternally in bloom, and waiting to be plucked by the first random genius who wanders down the path. (Hey folks, I'm really sorry about that last sentence. Good Lord, a dash, three sets of parentheses and six commas. Shandyism is evidently infectious.)

In any case, the rule of multiples forms the substrate for debates about priority. But why debate at all? In the cardboard ideal preached in high school classes on 'the scientific method', scientists aren't supposed to care about priority; objective truth, not the historical contingency of who finds it, is the only thing that matters, and finders are supposed to practise the humility of not caring about personal fame (*vide* Freud on the aphorism).

Of course, one scarcely has to be a professional sociologist (or an honest natural scientist for that matter) to see through the claptrap of this nonsense; reading the local newspaper for a week or so will do (who discovered the AIDS virus; who gave the first real warning about the greenhouse effect; who worked out all that business about superconductivity; and, by the way, who won the Nobel prizes this year?). But clearly, the issue goes deeper. Anyone with a flicker of insight about human nature knows that (and a good deal of why) people vie for recognition and status, but why do scientists (and scholars in general, I suppose) pursue priority disputes in such an assiduous and unseemly way. I don't know that businessmen squabble in this manner (despite cutthroat competition in other arenas). But why should they? The currency of their status is currency—and you either have it or you don't; it is a palpable something (even if only recorded electronically in your bank). But the currency of our status is ideas—the most squishy, the most tenuous, the most slippery unit of all conceivable measurement. What are the boundaries of an idea? What is the minimal difference between two distinct ideas? What increment of mutation do we need to convert one idea into another worthy of separate recognition? It gets a hell of a lot more complicated than copyright disputes over 'Home on the Range'.

And we can't even stop here, for we must still ask why it matters so preciously much. Do scientists with the most original ideas make the most money? I don't doubt that some positive correlation exists between economic success and intellectual prowess, but this cannot be the major answer; the real money (at least in science) lies in a set of activities that preclude personal recognition for distinct ideas—commercial consultation, marketing of medical products, for example. (In my own field of paleontology, until recently, the big money lay in working for an oil company, which entailed the catch-22 of 'proprietary' information. You could do the research, usually with better funding than you could hope for elsewhere, but you couldn't publish or even tell anyone about your work, for your findings were company property. Well, the oil companies got some good people, but the best minds went to universities at one-third to half the salary—and the precious right to publish on subjects of one's own choice.) We are not martyrs, and pride goeth before a fall and all that. If our families are starving, we'll take the commercial work. But if we can make even barely adequate money with freedom to publish, we usually choose this path. Why?

This question has many answers, and 'freedom' is not an unimportant component. But a large part of the answer must be 'glory'. And now we get to the nub of the issue—and what I take to be Merton's major point. Scientists, for all their faults, actually care more about honour (and maybe even about truth) than about material reward. (As Merton says, the highest recognition of all is therefore eponymy—to become the godfather of a comet (Halley) or a theory (Darwin), or the 'father' of an entire profession, see Merton's list on page 101 of *OTSOG*.) Honour comes through priority in ideas (given the eureka myth of 'genius before its time'); ideas are slippery; most discoveries are really multiples. Mix all this together and what comes from the witches' brew? Ceaseless and acrimonious disputes about priority. Rather than purveying our holier-than-thou tsk-tsk everytime our colleagues start an unseemly wrangle about some issue in priority, we should recognize this process as not only inevitable, but as a kind of base-level indication that science is working in its canonical mode—that is, with fallible people in a social context. Better still, if a bit cynically, we should probably trumpet the 'ideal' that priority doesn't matter so long as truth prevails. The ideal can't work of course, but its public proclamation at least keeps priority disputes within bounds, as we all feign or struggle to measure up. This innocent fiction makes science a much more pleasant enterprise.

A scholar might choose many modes for illustrating these important issues (well known, no doubt to sociologists, but ever so imperfectly appreciated, if conceptualized at all, by most natural scientists): the hortatory, the elliptical, the admonitory, the minutely scholarly. But why not take a statement that everybody knows, and everybody attributes to the primary deity of all natural science, Isaac Newton himself? Why not, following the principle of God's residence in detail, write a wonderfully comic book with the entirely serious purpose of showing that the aphorism is not a unique Newtonian witticism (the analogue of eureka discovery), but part of a social tradition stretching back to the twelfth century, forward to our own day, and with Newton squarely in the middle? *OTSOG*, the documentation of a multiple among multiples, is a unique and gentle treatise on the fundamental nature of science.

As I said, Merton mixes in half a dozen or more additional principles in the sociology of science. Let me mention just one to illustrate another wonderful feature of *OTSOG*—its status as a 'participatory' document that draws all readers into the search for additional examples and principles. *OTSOG* recounts the story thus: Merton thinks he has discovered a principle in noting that scientists engaged in dispute are more intransigent and less likely to compromise or consider other views when presenting their rival opinions in public forums, but more inclined to kindness and compromise when working out their disagreements in private. But he then finds the principle beautifully enunciated by Hooke in the same correspondence that elicited Newton's *OTSOG* remark: 'I confess the collision of two hard-to-yield contenders may produce light yet if they be put together by the ears of other's hands and incentives, it will produce rather ill concomitant heat which serves for no other use but...kindle cole'. (Already I have learned something. I never knew that the old quip about heat without light went so far back.) So Merton now decides to call this concept the 'kindle cole' principle, with attribution to Hooke. But then he finds an earlier allusion in, guess where, Newton. Well, you see the point—pretty much the same theme as *OTSOG* itself, and traced a good deal back before Newton by the book's end. Now I rather suspect you could get back to the time when Chris the Cro Magnon said to Ned the Neanderthal, 'hey, let's sneak down to the stream and talk about this in private, rather than waiting for the duelling atlatl contest at tonight's campfire'. But I want to submit an entry anyway, as my contribution to the social phenomenon of *OTSOG*. Charles Darwin to Louis Agassiz, 22 October 1848 (different in its contrast of purely individual, rather than conversational, privacy with public presentation, but close enough): 'I should be glad if you would not mention my present results, partly because I should like to have the satisfaction of publishing myself what few new points I have found out and partly because one is more free to alter one's own views when they are confined to one's own breast' (he is speaking, by the way, about barnacle taxonomy, not evolution; sorry).

SUBTEXTS AND TANGENTS

If *OTSOG* only intertwined the three themes that I have already discussed—a great storyline (web), a meaty detail at the heart of intellectual life, and a set of principles about the social context of science—well, as my grandmother would have said, *dayenu*. That would have been enough. But there is more, much more, and I can only give a sampling here. We may grant an ethical primacy to means over ends, but literature also teaches us that the journey is often much more interesting than the destination (who really cares if Dorothy ever gets back to Kansas, or Alice to her garden; the adventures along the way *are* the drama). *OTSOG* is a forest of ramifying tangents and digressions. Some join and reinforce, thus fostering the central theme (as when provenance of the 'kindle cole' principle turns into a discussion of priority itself, and this apparently independent tidbit becomes one with the paternity of the *OTSOG* aphorism). But others are thrown in just for fun, as true digressions that record the scholar's most noble obligations, as sacred in wit as in any other mode, to teach, to illuminate, to connect.

Most of the digressions inform or emanate from the major subtexts—Merton's own process of discovery in rendering the patrimony of *OTSOG* (versus the main text of the patrimony itself and its meaning). As an example, consider one of my own favourite principles—the inestimable value of error. We prize truth for some undoubted moral virtues, and definite practical value (in technology at least), but for the scholarly tracing of history, truth is a dud, first class. Truth, you see, just is. It has the annoying property of universality and accessibility to anyone with the eyes to look. Truth therefore gains an infuriatingly diffuse character rendering it worthless as a guide to history—for truth is not an item, a particular something that can belong to a person or a thing, and can therefore be traced. If you want to trace lineages, you have to have error, for a mistake is a particular historical entity with a time and place of origin, and a history (all too often) of propagation.

The principle is quite general: we trace genealogies of organisms by vestigial structures (non-functional leg rudiments identify snakes as descendants of four-footed creatures), not by perfect adaptations (which erase the pathways of history); we trace medieval manuscripts by errors in dictation then propagated by lineages of copyists (if the scribe writes a phrase correctly, how can we identify a source among the proper copies?). The artist Georges Braque understood this principle when he wrote (according to the inestimable *Bartlett's*), 'Truth exists, only falsehood has to be invented'. Richard Nixon also, if sadly, came to appreciate the idea that truth just is, but lies have to be fabricated—and that when a web of falsehood becomes complicated enough, you just can't keep your story straight any more.

Merton uses this fundamental principle of historical tracing throughout *OTSOG*, but nowhere more effectively (or with better humour) than in the great Didacus Stella incident previously cited. Since the traceable buck really does stop with the twelfth century Bernard, any learned reference to a classical source in Lucan can only record the lineage of error emanating from Burton's elliptical citation 'Didacus Stella in Luc'. With this key to the tracing of a lineage, we can illustrate two foibles of scholarship. First, the enshrinement of error through its passage into canon. In science, the usual route for the elevation of particular error into general dogma is enshrinement in a textbook. Errors in textbooks last for generations, even when prominent primary literature has clearly disproved the claim—and for a particular reason: textbook writers copy from previous textbooks (without saying so). The situation might not be so serious, were it not for the second foible—scholarly pretension and one-upmanship. We all like to display our erudition by tossing off a quote from the Bard here, an epigram from Plato there. But let's face it, few of us really know the original sources as familiar friends, so we rely on a range of ponies from textbooks to *Bartlett's* (an elegant and indispensable document, but still a pony when used wrongly). This is a dangerous game, and your goose is cooked if the pony makes an identifiable mistake, and your true source lies exposed in the face of your Empyrean claims.

Textbooks are truly dangerous, for they are more often wrong than right. *Bartlett's* is usually reliable, but then even Homer nods sometimes (as Horace said, according to *Bartlett's*). In this case, however, *Bartlett's* is the chief offender. Merton found that the misattribution first occurred in the last edition (the ninth of 1891) edited by Mr Bartlett himself. Bartlett simply extended (incorrectly) Burton's citation and wrote: 'Didacus Stella in Lucan 10, tom. ii.'—thereby converting Diego de Estella into a title and shuttling the aphorism a millennium too far back. Merton then traced the citation through later editions. It did not change through the twelfth, but the Centenary edition of 1955 (the thirteenth) compounded the error a little further: 'Didacus Stella in Lucan (A.D. 39–65): De Bello Civili, 10, II'. We are now given a source in Lucan's most famous work. (It is, I confess, a bit disconcerting that no one, when finally given a traceable citation, bothered to look up the original and find the aphorism absent—if the parsing of *De Bello Civili* even has a volume 2, part 10.)

Merton stopped here (for his book appeared in 1965), but I can carry the analysis one humorous step further, for I own both the centennial *Bartlett's* and the latest edition (fifteenth) of 1980. The situation has substantially worsened, on two grounds. First, and for the very first time, the aphorism is now listed under Lucan's own entry and with the original Latin in a footnote: *Pigmei gigantum humeris impositi plusquam ipsi gigantes vident* (a taut and terse version). The aphorism is embedded in a list of statements all from 'The Civil War', with the reference '*Ib*. II, 10 (Didacus Stella)'. Now we don't know what in heaven's name Didacus Stella is supposed to be—star of...? a Roman general who says the line? a chapter title in Lucan's work? Clearly, we have a case of thoughtless copying masquerading as increasing precision and improvement through later editions. Second, and horror of horrors, the latest *Bartlett's* also makes a mistake in Newton's version (the older centennial edition omits Newton and gives the aphorism only to Burton). They cite: 'If I have seen further (than you and Descartes) it is by standing upon the shoulders of Giants'. 'Upon' should be 'on', but this is minor and we'll not quibble. But what about the added parenthetical? The reference to Hooke and Descartes may be a proper editorial explication, but these are not Newton's words—and the insertion should therefore be in brackets, not parentheses.

I chronicled this example because it tickled me, and because I could add my own little discovery to the collective work on *OTSOG*. But *OTSOG* contains literally hundreds of delicious diversions, each both funny and instructive (and showing Merton's enormous, but lightly worn, erudition—the real antidote to scholarly pretension). Each could merit several pages, but both my word limit and my readers' patience are coming to an end. Consider, then, and in no particular order, this eclectic and ever so partial list of items that caught my fancy.

No detail is too small to overlook or be made interesting by relationship to an important concept. What position, Merton asks, do dwarfs perched on giants take? Do they sit, like the evangelists of Chartres, with legs hanging down (the most stable position), or do they stand, more precariously but all the further to see? The Latin versions are not much help, for most use such non-committal language as *insidentes*, or *positi*. Merton turns to ecclesiastical art, and comes up not empty but unresolved. Most dwarfs sit, but a few stand—or as he puts it: 'modal dwarfs sit, deviant dwarfs stand'. Snatching victory from the jaws of defeat, Merton turns this ambiguity into an interesting commentary on the theory of types and the irreducible nature of variation (even with a reference to my own intellectual guru, the paleontologist G. G. Simpson).

And the play goes on, and on. Merton notes the obsession of John Aubrey (Hooke's primary champion) for describing the eyes (or 'eies' as he has it) of famous folk. Fifty pages later we learn that Ogden Nash wrote an entire poem on Aubrey's inordinate interest—another multiple. We have disquisitions on words, their etymology, their proper usage. Merton insists that 'unique' cannot be qualified by adjectival degree (and I agree); then he lists many worthy writers who have disobeyed the rule, forgiving only Arthur Miller for applying 'the most unique' to his 'singularly eumorphous bride of world-renown' (again, I agree, particularly since Joe DiMaggio was, and remains, my hero and the most damned unique ballplayer I ever saw). I did know that 'skinning the cat' referred to pre-Nautilus exercise machines (page 145), but I never realized that we owe the phrase 'sweetness and light' to Jonathan Swift, and that he was referring to the two great products of beekeeping: honey and wax (page 128). (I would read a dull book just for the privilege of learning this interesting derivation; what a pleasure to love the book, *and* learn the fact.) We travel through the byways of eponymy, even receiving a catalogue of fields with at least semi-official fathers, ranging from the ample (Boyle as the father of chemistry, but also, Merton adds, the uncle of the Earl of Cork according to his epitaph) to the suspiciously narrow (Father Johann Dzierson as the father of modern rational beekeeping, or sweetness and light).

A CLOSING COMMENT

My final thoughts, getting to the heart of my affection for *OTSOG*, are not easy to put into words. Bob Merton wrote to me on 24 February 1988: '*OTSOG* remains my favourite, prodigal brainchild'. How can a man who has done so much rank something that was such fun so high? And why not?

Haste thee, nymph, and bring with thee
Jest, and youthful jollity,
Quips and cranks and wanton wiles
Nods and becks and wreathed smiles.

(And all this from a pretty dour fellow named Milton.)

We live in an age of sharply constricting general knowledge of our long-term intellectual heritage, even among the formally well educated (though the Miniver Cheevy brigade of absolutely every generation would, no doubt, make exactly the same charge). Any scholar who loves old texts and languages must feel assaulted by a culture that knows and cares so little for this aspect of its past, and views Elvis Presley as tolerably ancient history. Whatever will happen to liberal learning if our computer banks put everything at our finger tips, and we therefore learn nothing because we can access anything when and if we really want it (but then never do because we never learned what to want)? Whatever will happen if the ideal of the scholar as polymath yields to the technocrat and the ignoramus with the right bank of buttons?

Let's face it. We don't have to be a majority. We don't even have to be popular. But we do need to persevere and, more than that, to be strong. We have much to preserve; even more to teach. How shall we show our intrinsic worth in a world pluralistic enough to leave us room (and even grant us power), but continually running away from us by any measure of mode?

I see only one general solution. It does not lie with the usual code words of 'relevance', or even 'cultural literacy'. Above all, we must show by example that scholarship is fun—yes, fun, in the best sense of a fine word. For if what we love and do is not fun, then we are lost and cannot convey our passion. Emma Goldman captured this principle elegantly in her famous statement: 'If I can't dance, I don't want to be part of your revolution'.

The danger, of course, is that fun has both cheap and sublime sources—and the former are legion. Conformity, levelling, adulteration, philistinism, revels about the golden calf, and on and on—so many that sour scholars often make the crucial mistake of equating the entire concept with its dark side. We must show the irreducible fun of scholarship without granting one iota of compromise to sources that belittle the intellect. We must dismiss the dryness of pedantry and embrace (with considerable laughter) the joy of learning. The task is not easy as a proposition in the abstract, and application is strongly hindered by a training that beats the natural inclination for fun out of most scholars.

We need some leaders of the game, scholars of impeccable erudition, and such fierce commitment that their souls could not tolerate that iota of compromise. *OTSOG* should be the manifesto of this muscular movement to depict scholarship properly as sublime fun. In composing *OTSOG*, Merton rarely ventured outside the books in his own study (sending out cries of help to larger libraries only for such truly obscure items as Diego de Estella's commentary on Luke). Yet *OTSOG* spans all the space and all the centuries of Western culture. *OTSOG* is, above all, a comedy; yet *OTSOG* engages the most important ideas of human thinking. *OTSOG* is fun, and scholarship is fun. You just don't know what you're missing if you don't read Burton, and Sterne, or study the glass of Chartres, or trace your favourite quotation through 100 years of *Bartlett's*. No apologies. *OTSOG* is a sort of holy book, and its currency is the joy of laughter.

We must give the last word to Merton's own inspiration, Laurence Sterne, who dedicated *Tristram Shandy* 'to the right honourable Mr. Pitt' in writing: 'I live in a constant endeavour to fence against the infirmities of ill health, and other evils of life, by mirth; being firmly persuaded that every time a man smiles,—much more so, when he laughs, it adds something to this Fragment of Life'.

NOTES

1 'I wish either my father or my mother, or indeed both of them, as they were in duty both equally bound to it, had minded what they were about when they begot me'.
2 For this citation, alas, I can only offer the most unscholarly: 'dust jacket of *OTSOG*'.

Part Two: Consensus and Controversy

III. SYSTEMATIC SOCIAL THEORY

5. R. K. Merton's Theoretical System: An Overview

PIOTR SZTOMPKA

IS THERE A GENERAL SYSTEMATIC THEORY AT ALL?

Daniel Bell observes: 'Writers, like runners, develop "natural" length. The man who runs the 100-yard dash will rarely be a good half-miler; wind capacity and the sense of pace are necessarily different' (1980: 13). Merton is certainly like a middle-distance runner. Most of his formidable output is in the form of extended essays, long articles, introductions, reviews, discussions—sometimes getting so long as to turn imperceptibly into a book, as that *Shandean Postscript* of 290 pages (Merton, 1965a) or that 'Episodic Memoir' of 150 pages tracing the development of the sociology of science (Merton, 1979b); but most often gathered up in numerous collections among which *Social Theory and Social Structure* (in its three major editions: 1949, 1957 and 1968), *The Sociology of Science* (1973), *Sociological Ambivalence* (1976a) and *Social Research and the Practicing Professions* (1982a) are most significant. The true 'book', in the sense so dear to the humanists and so alien to the natural scientists, he has written only once and only when he had to—his doctoral dissertation on *Science, Technology and Society in Seventeenth Century England* (1938a).

Moreover, the thematic range of his interests is very wide: from drug addicts to professionals, from anomie to social time, from friendship formation to role conflicts, from functional analysis to scientific ethos, from medical education to multiple discoveries, from bureaucratic structure to the origins of medieval aphorisms. He seems to pick up various topics at random, here and there, and study them in depth, like an artisan polishing little shining pieces for a mosaic and collecting them in a large heap.

But is there a mosaic emerging out of these pieces of coloured glass? Is there a sociological system underlying these scattered fragments of wisdom? Several commentators have answered in the negative (e.g. Bierstedt, 1981: 487–8). They are right only in the sense that Merton has never been a system-builder; he has always opposed the practice of building his own system from scratch, attempting instead to put himself firmly on the shoulders of sociological giants of the past. But the critics are grossly mistaken if implying that there are no systemic interlinks between Merton's contributions. The heuristic 'context of discovery' need not constrain the shape of a theoretical product. The seemingly unsystematic way in which he reaches his results does not preclude the systematic quality of final achievement. If I read Merton correctly, there is precisely a system of sociological thought emerging from his persistent, disciplined, even though fragmented enquiries. The building blocks of the system are given by means of disparate solutions to the many problems he finds puzzling. The unity and coherence of the whole are provided by the common frame of mind of the architect—Merton's characteristic sociological orientation.

One may ask in turn: where is this system to be found, at which level of generality? Again, several commentators are misled on this point, and the fault is partly Merton's, for two reasons. First, in his early opposition to scholastic, formalistic 'grand theory' of Parsons's brand (Merton, 1945b and 1948a), he seems to confuse the manner of theorizing with the level of theorizing. Opting for empirically grounded and empirically consequential theory, he seems to imply that it can only be attained at a middle level of generality, as a 'theory of the middle range'. But, as Stinchcombe aptly observes:

> [I]n the dialectic between Parsons and Merton, generality has been confused with woolliness. Merton, in taking up the correct position on woolliness, has tricked himself into taking up the incorrect position on general theory. The true situation is precisely the opposite. It is because Merton has a better general theory than Parsons that his work has been more empirically fruitful. (1975: 26–7)

Second, in his own theoretical research, convinced that general theory is 'premature', he has chosen to stay at the middle level, producing numerous middle-range theories—of deviance, of role conflicts, of reference groups, of sociological ambivalence, of bureaucratic structure, of scientific communities and many others—instead of the straightforward, general accounts of social structures and social processes. But there is a core theory behind or over his specific contributions. This theory, though implicit, is general. As R. Boudon observes: 'there is more systematic and general theory in Merton's work than he himself has ever confessed' (1977: 1356). Through his own life-long work Merton has contributed, even if unwittingly, to overcome the immaturity of sociology, to consolidate not only 'minor empirical hypotheses' but also numerous 'middle-range theories' into a general image of society: a specific, definite vision of social order and social change. The sketch of Merton's systematic and general theory is my goal in the remaining part of this article.[1]

THE IMAGE OF SOCIOLOGY: ITS GOALS AND SCOPE

Two of Merton's formulations come closest to his definition of what sociology is all about. The calling of a sociologist is described as 'lucidly presenting claims to logically interconnected and empirically confirmed propositions about the structure of society and its changes, the behavior of man within that structure and the consequences of that behavior' (1968: 70). And the goal of the whole discipline is characterized as follows: 'In the large, sociology is engaged in finding out how man's behavior and fate are affected, if not minutely governed, by his place within particular kinds, and changing kinds, of social structure and culture' (1976a: 184). Thus the prime subject-matter of sociology is conceived clearly as the social structure, and it is to be studied in its multiple and varied aspects; genetic (how it came to be), as well as functional (how it affects behaviour); static (how it operates), as well as dynamic (how it changes). The focus on social structure already appears as the defining trait of sociology.

This becomes even more evident when we see how Merton handles the problem of demarcation, and especially how he proposes to draw the boundary between sociology and psychology. What then is the crux of the difference dividing those two complementary and equally legitimate perspectives: the sociological and the psychological? In his view it has to do with the aspects of phenomena that are taken for granted or, conversely, treated as problematic. For the psychologist, the socio-structural aspect is given, as the context of individual behaviour, whereas the latter is problematic. For the sociologist, the opposite holds: 'the analytical focus is upon the structure of the environment, with the attributes and psychological processes of individuals being regarded as given and not within the theoretical competence of the sociologist to analyze' (1982a: 169–70). [2]

The characterization of sociology as a discipline defined by a focus on social structure allows me to hazard a conjecture concerning Merton's ontological creed, the most fundamental presuppositions of his theory. He evidently perceives society as a reality *sui generis*, possessing specific properties and displaying specific regularities, emergent with respect to the properties and regularities of individual human beings. The social reality is super-individual (as it is basically novel in relation to individuals) but it is not supra-individual (since it is not independent of individuals). The structure involves people and their actions, but it is something more than an aggregate of people and activities. It may be called the inter-individual reality, since it is produced by varied relationships among pluralities of individuals, or it may be called systemic reality, as it results in various social wholes consisting of individuals bound together by networks of interrelations. Such an ontological conception, a sort of 'structural realism', avoids the pitfall of reification, so typical of metaphysical holism. It also avoids the atomization of social reality that is found in various forms of theoretical (or 'methodological') individualism.

THEORETICAL ORIENTATION: FUNCTIONALISM AND STRUCTURALISM

Building on such an ontological foundation, Merton has devised and elaborated two specific sociological orientations: functional analysis and structural analysis. For him, 'the central orientation of functionalism' is 'the practice of interpreting data by establishing their consequences for larger structures in which they are implicated' (1968: 100–1). After the publication of his famous 'paradigm for functional analysis' in 1949, where he outlined a strikingly open, deeply revised version of functionalism, allowing for the conceptualization of social conflict and social change,[3] Merton began to be identified as a functionalist incarnate. Thus when a quarter-century later he wrote an important paper, 'Structural Analysis in Sociology' (1975), which presented a correlative sociological orientation, several commentators took it as a radical break with functional analysis, as a rejection of his own past and the formulation of a radically new approach.

Others—with whom I am in agreement—regard structural analysis as a natural outgrowth of functional analysis, complementing but not at all supplanting it. Merton's own position is explicit: 'The orientation is that variant of functional analysis in sociology which has evolved, over the years, into a distinct mode of structural analysis' (1976a: 9). Functional analysis specifies the consequences of a social phenomenon for its differentiated structural context; structural analysis searches for the determinants of the phenomenon in its structural context. Obviously, both orientations refer to the different sides of the same coin; they scrutinize two vectors of the same relationship, between a social phenomenon and its structural setting. There is no opposition between Merton the functionalist and Merton the structuralist; both theoretical orientations have been consolidated into one. This is clearly recognized by P. Blau: 'the functional paradigm is in effect a structural paradigm, which accounts for observable social patterns in terms of the structural conditions that give rise to them, except that it supplements this analysis of antecedents by stressing the importance of tracing the functional and dysfunctional consequences of these patterns' (1975b: 118).

Merton's idea of the social structure, central already for his 'functionalist' writings, includes four defining criteria. The focus on relations linking various components of society is clear already in the early characterization of social structure formulated long before the 'structuralist revolution' or 'structuralist infatuation' of modern science: 'by social structure is meant that organized set of social relationships in which members of the society or group are variously implicated' (Merton, 1968: 216). The emphasis on the patterned, regular, repetitive character of relations is one of the central themes pervading Merton's work, and the term 'patterned' is a qualifier of which he is particularly fond. As P. Lazarsfeld has noted: 'Throughout his writings, this is probably the technical term he uses most often' (1975: 57). The third constitutive criterion of social structure—the idea of a deep, hidden underlying level (corresponding to the concept of latent function in functional analysis)—is the only aspect of Merton's approach directly influenced by the 'logical-linguistic structuralism' of Jakobson, Lévi-Strauss or Chomsky. As he puts it: 'It is analytically useful to distinguish between manifest and latent levels of social structure' (1976a: 126).

But perhaps most important for Merton's notion of social structure is the fourth criterion, the idea of constraining or facilitating influences exerted by social structure on actual social phenomena (behaviours, beliefs, attitudes, motivations, etc.). The concept of 'structural context', and especially 'structural constraint', as limiting the effective field of action appears in the early 'paradigm for functional analysis': 'I assume that the structure constrains individuals variously situated within it to develop cultural emphases, social behavior patterns and psychological bents' (Merton, 1968: 177). In another connection he writes: 'Behavior is a result not merely of personal qualities, but of these in interaction with the patterned situations in which the individual behaves. It is these social contexts which greatly affect the extent to which the capacities of individuals are actually realized' (1982a: 174). But the structural context is not conceived only in negative terms, as a limiting constraint, but also as a positive influence, facilitating, encouraging, stimulating certain choices by actors or agents: 'the social structure strains the cultural values, making action in accord with them readily possible for those occupying certain statuses within the society and difficult or impossible for others.... The social structure acts as a barrier or as an open door to the acting out of cultural mandates' (1968: 216–17).[4]

ANATOMY OF SOCIAL STRUCTURE: COMPLEXITY AND CONFLICT

Within the general framework provided by his functionalist and structuralist orientation Merton develops a more specific image of the social structure. There are two traits which endow it with a distinct, unmistakably Mertonian flavour. First, social structure is seen as complex and multidimensional. It covers a plurality of components, elements, items shaped into various kinds of networks or interlinkages. There are statuses, roles, role-sets, status-sets, norms, values, institutions, collectivities, groups, organizations, interests, etc., and they are depicted as cohering on numerous levels. As Merton puts it: 'even the seemingly simple social structure is extremely complex' (1968: 370). A related, second property of Merton's idea of social structure is the emphasis on asymmetrical relationships: conflicts, contradictions, dysfunctions, strains, tensions, ambivalence. As he emphasizes: 'It is fundamental, not incidental to the paradigm of structural analysis, that social structures generate social conflict by being differentiated in historically differing extent and kind, into interlocking arrays of social statuses, strata, organizations, and communities that have their own and therefore potentially conflicting as well as common interests and values' (1976a: 124–5). Now I shall elaborate on those two characteristics of social structure.

Merton's core idea is to consider human individuals (and their actions) as structurally located, anchored in the network of social relationships. The structural location of a person is described as his or her social status; an identifiable 'position in a social system occupied by designated individuals' (1968: 368), e.g. a doctor, a student, a housewife, a father. Each social status, considered as the central building-block of a social structure, has three distinct aspects. Attached to it is a patterned set of social (shared) expectations concerning the proper behaviour of any incumbent. This is a normative aspect of a status, grasped by Merton's important concept of a 'role-set'. Similarly, each social status has an attached set of 'life chances', options, resources, facilities available to the incumbents. This is an opportunity aspect of a status. Finally, each status has an attached set of patterned beliefs, ideas, creeds typically held by any incumbent. This is an ideal aspect of a status.

Now, it is possible to change the perspective and analyze social structure in abstraction from the individuals occupying statuses and performing roles. We shall focus on the social structure per se, as a skeleton of the social world, trying to identify its dimensions and components.[5]

In one of his earliest analytic efforts Merton distinguishes the concept of cultural structure from that of social structure in the narrow sense: 'the salient environment of individuals can be usefully thought of as involving the cultural structure, on the one hand, and the social structure, on the other' (1968: 216). Both categories have been elaborated and modified in later work. Cultural structure comes to be characterized exclusively in normative terms, as a network of norms, values, roles and institutions. Similarly, the idea of social structure in the narrow sense is gradually enriched with the help of the notion of 'opportunity-structure' inspired by the idea of 'life chances' and 'vested interests'. It is understood as a hierarchically differentiated access to resources, facilities, valuables (like wealth, power, prestige, education). I think it justifiable to assume that he makes a distinction between the normative and opportunity dimensions of the social structure.

But in various places of his work a third dimension looms as well. In one place he refers to the 'state of the public mind' or 'prevalent outlook' (1968: 574); at another he speaks of perspective and outlook as 'a product of social position' (*ibid.*: 268); at still another he introduces 'the basic distinctions between attitudes and overt behavior, and between publicly affirmed and privately held attitudes' (1959a: 180). These distinctions seem to refer to the domain of social consciousness as a structural, not psychological dimension—the public, shared, patterned beliefs, creeds, appraisals, judgments, rather than the private, individual, idiosyncratic convictions. Although Merton does not introduce a separate term to refer to this domain, I shall designate it as the ideal structure.

Thus the pluralist and multidimensional anatomy of the social structure is to be represented as the combination of three levels: normative structure, opportunity-structure and ideal structure. The components of social structure at all three levels are variously interrelated, both within each level and across distinct levels. It is, in fact, only the study of those interrelations that reveals the social structure, in the proper sense of the term, as a relational network. The most important feature of Merton's analysis, which sets him apart from traditional functionalists and other proponents of social equilibrium, consensus and harmony, is his treatment of integration as problematic and contingent, not as given. The differing degrees of integration span the spectrum, from complete consensus to complete dissensus, although these extreme poles are only analytic possibilities, rarely occurring in empirical reality. It is striking that, perhaps to counterbalance the bias of 'normative functionalism', Merton focuses his analysis on situations closer to the pole of dissensus—various kinds of strains, tensions, contradictions and conflicts in the social structure. He treats them as normal, typical, permanent, and not as pathological disturbances or deviations. Against the predominant stereotype of Merton the functionalist, I believe that his is a conflictual image of society par excellence, as distant as can be from the image of a harmonious utopia. Look at some of his central theoretical categories: dysfunction, role conflict, sociological ambivalence, anomie. All of them refer to the 'ugly face' of society, as R. Dahrendorf would put it (1968: 129–50). One of the rare commentators who have recognized this is L. Coser:

> Merton's analytical strategies are characterized, *inter alia*, by his close attention to contradictions and conflicts within global structures, to ambivalence in the motivation of actors, and to ambiguities in the perceptual field to which they orient themselves. Merton's actors face role- and status-sets with often contradictory expectations and are continuously navigating between them.... The Mertonian world is a universe of warring gods. (1975b: 98)

As an illustration of Merton's concern with contradictions I choose his idea of 'sociological ambivalence', relatively less known than widely discussed notions of 'role conflict' or 'anomie'.[6] In its basic sense 'sociological ambivalence' refers to the relationship between normative standards constituting a single social role: 'The core type of sociological ambivalence stems from the socially patterned situation in which incompatible behaviors, attitudes, or values are simultaneously expected by one person in the course of one relationship' (Merton, Merton and Barber, 1983: 28). Applying the idea to the medical profession, Merton claims: 'for each norm there tends to be at least one coordinate norm which is, if not inconsistent with the other, at least sufficiently different as to make it difficult for...the physician to live up to both' (1982a: 181). One case in point is 'detached concern', a composite which combines two patently opposed norms, instrumental impersonality and compassionate concern: 'Physicians must be emotionally detached in their attitudes toward patients. But: They must avoid becoming callous through excessive detachment, and should have compassionate concern for the patient' (1976a: 68). Another patterned ambivalence is the following: 'Physicians must provide adequate and unhurried medical care for each patient. But: They should not allow any patient to use up so much of their limited time as to have this be at the expense of other patients' (*ibid*.).[7]

Normative dissensus obtains not only between the norms and values (expectations) within a single role, but also between such norms and values within a social institution. Here, as elsewhere, malintegration is the rule rather than exception: 'A major characteristic of social institutions is that they tend to be patterned in terms of potentially conflicting pairs of norms...sociological ambivalence is imbedded in social institutions generally' (1976a: 33). Once again the concept of sociological ambivalence is used, this time in its second meaning. Merton's analysis of the 'ambivalence of scientists' provides a case in point: 'In saying that the social institution of science is malintegrated, I mean that it incorporates potentially incompatible values' (*ibid*.: 36). Thus the value set upon originality, leading to a focus on establishing one's priority in scientific discoveries, is in tension with the value of humility, indicating one's indebtedness to predecessors and contemporaries; the norm of 'organized skepticism', calling for the meticulous checking and cross-checking of results, is in tension with the norm of 'communism', calling for results to be made public knowledge without delayed publication. Merton records a variety of similar ambivalence in the ethos of science.[8]

SOCIAL PROCESSES: OPERATION AND EMERGENCE OF STRUCTURES

Contrary to some simplified accounts accusing Merton the functionalist of a static bias, I am going to argue that his approach to complex and conflict-ridden social structures is clearly dynamic. By a dynamic theoretical standpoint I mean one that focuses on changes in the social structures, treating them as not only immanent 'changes in', but also as transcendental 'changes of' these structures, and recognizing both their exogenous and endogenous sources. The image of society underlying Merton's social theory is dynamic in the precise sense explicated above: incorporating structurally produced change in and of social structures. Merton does not leave any doubts about that: 'social structures generate both changes within the structure and changes of the structure and...these types of change come about through cumulatively patterned choices in behavior and the amplification of dysfunctional consequences resulting from certain kinds of strains, conflicts, and contradictions in the differentiated social structure' (1976a: 125). As the Loomises noted long ago, Merton is 'irrevocably committed to a study of the dynamics of social change no less than to stabilities of social structures' (Loomis and Loomis, 1961: 315).

There are two types of structural change which fall within the purview of Merton's dynamics. The first type involves the regular 'functioning' or everyday 'operation' of society. Such changes consist in ongoing adaptive processes which reproduce specified states of a social structure, or at least keep them within the limits which give that structure its identity. The second type of change involves the 'transformation' of society. This consists of the morphogenetic processes that disrupt the existing structure and create a basically new one in its place. The first type of change brings about the reproduction of an old social order; the second type of change brings about the production of a new social order.

The illustrations of Merton's study of adaptive processes are relatively well known. They date from the period when he was strongly committed to functionalist thinking with its characteristic idea of compensatory mechanisms, founded on the logic of negative feedback, which tend to restore the status quo once the disruptions appear. His analyses of the articulation of roles in the role-set and of the social mechanisms of adaptation in status-sets are particularly telling (1968: 425, 434). They attempt to face 'the general problem of identifying the social mechanisms which serve to articulate the expectations of those in the role-set so that the occupant of a status is confronted with less conflict than would obtain if these mechanisms were not at work' (1968: 425).[9]

But adaptive processes cover only a part of social dynamics. Changes in social structure which reduce inefficiency, conflict, strains and tensions compared with what they would otherwise be, must be distinguished from the changes of social structure which transform it significantly to produce new structural arrangements. It is rarely recognized that Merton's theory contributes also to this area of social dynamics, and he may in fact be treated as the forerunner of the 'hot' problematics of 'morphogenesis', 'structuration' or 'social construction of reality'.[10]

In Merton's theoretical orientation, the general scheme of morphogenetic process can be condensed as follows: under conditions still little understood, structural conflict brings about transformations of social structure up to a point when a new structure emerges and the structural conflict is reproduced in a new form. The basic logic underlying the process is that of amplification rather than counteraction, or, to put it differently, positive rather than negative feedback. Merton singles out two general mechanisms of morphogenesis. The first may be described as the mechanism of accumulated dysfunctions; the second, the mechanism of accumulated innovations.

There are several modalities of the dynamic mechanism based on the accumulation of dysfunctions. First is the situation when certain structural elements are dysfunctional for a social system as a whole, or some of its core segments. For example, the unrestrained pattern of egoistic hedonism, if sufficiently widespread, may lead to the disruption of the social system. The larger the number of such dysfunctional elements, and the more dysfunctional each of them, the more likely is the system to break down. Second is the case when some elements are basically functional for a social system, but have some additional dysfunctional side-effects. For example, the competitive success orientation or 'achievement syndrome' may be beneficial for the economy, but at the same time may lead to the neglect of family life and consequent breakdown of family structure. The question now becomes that of the relative weight of the accumulated dysfunctional side-effects which, passing over a hypothetical threshold, outbalance functional outcomes and lead to institutional breakdown and 'basic social change' in the form of replacement of structure. A third and, in Merton's conception, basic and empirically frequent case obtains when certain structures are functional for certain groups or strata in the society and dysfunctional for others; examples are progressive taxation, social security, apartheid, affirmative action. The net outcome—toward stability or toward change—is then determined by the comparative (relative) power of the diverse groups or strata beneficially or adversely affected by those patterned social arrangements. As groups or strata dysfunctionally affected attain sufficient power, they are likely to introduce structural changes. Finally, a fourth type occurs when some structural elements are functional for certain subsystems and dysfunctional for others. For example, traditional mores or *Gemeinschaft* forms of collectivities, certainly beneficial for the integration of society, may often stand in the way of economic modernization, thus becoming dysfunctional for the economic subsystem. The pressure for change here depends on the complex set of historical circumstances determining the relative functional significance of the subsystems dysfunctionally affected. If the dysfunctions touch the subsystems of the strategic, core significance in a given historical situation, structural change is likely. Merton sums up the mechanism of morphogenesis via dysfunctions, covering the four types of situations I have singled out, in these words: 'the accumulation of dysfunctions in a social system is often the prelude to concerted social change that may bring the system closer to the values that enjoy respect of members of the society' (1982a: 89).

The alternative mechanism of morphogenesis is the accumulation of innovations. Here Merton focuses on one selected case: the crescent change of normative structures, particularly through the 'institutionalized evasions of institutional rules'. Morphogenesis via norm evasion starts from incidents of aberrant behaviour by individuals who find the norms too demanding for them, even though generally legitimate. For example, the thief does not question the legitimacy of the fifth commandment; will be outraged if something is stolen from him; yet not particularly surprised if caught and sentenced.

Some part of evasions from norms remains fully private, invisible, undetected. But when evasions become more widespread, undertaken by a plurality of individuals, repeated on various occasions, the public awareness is apt to be awakened. When villains are identified, the examples of particularly skilful evaders may become the subject of public lore, often tainted with envy. As Merton observes: 'Those successful rogues—successful as this is measured by the criteria of their significant reference groups—become prototypes for others in their environment who, initially less vulnerable and less alienated, now no longer keep to the rules they once regarded as legitimate' (1964: 235).

The occurrence of common incentives to evasion among the large collectivities of individuals, coupled with the widespread belief that 'everybody does it' and the tendency to imitate successful evaders, account for the patterning of evasions, their regular and repeatable character. Tax evasions, cheating on exams, avoidance of customs duties and currency controls, petty theft in business firms provide familiar examples. But note that, even though rarely sanctioned, the norms here are still accorded some legitimacy.

The most crucial phase comes when, as Merton puts it, 'a mounting frequency of deviant but "successful" behavior tends to lessen and, as an extreme potentiality, to eliminate the legitimacy of the institutional norms for others in the system' (1968: 234). It is only now that his early concept of 'institutionalized evasions' fully applies. Institutionalization in this sense is more than the mere patterning, since it involves not only repetition or regularity of behaviour but the granting of a degree of legitimacy, widespread acceptance or even positive sanctioning of evasive behaviour.

This leads to the final phase of a morphogenetic process: attaining by evasions the status of sanctioned norms, fully legitimized and embedded in a new normative structure. Thus, referring to the notoriously large-scale evasions of obsolete divorce laws, Merton observes: 'should public testimony to these institutionalized evasions repeatedly occur, bringing out into the open the full extent of the gap between the principles of the law and the frequency of circumventory practices, this would also exert powerful pressure in its way for change of the law' (1963: xi). A cycle of morphogenesis ends, and of course a next one is opened, as new norms inevitably begin to be evaded, at least by some members of society, and the process of normative change starts to operate again.

TENETS OF 'REVISIONIST' INTERPRETATION

This closes my brief overview of Merton's theoretical system. I have been able to touch only some selected components of his extensive sociological writings. Starting from fundamental ontological presuppositions, I moved toward characterizing his general theoretical orientation, and concluded with the reconstruction of his substantive vision of social structure and social processes.

In the course of the analysis my main purpose was to corroborate five interpretational claims, which to some extent run counter to standard 'received' appraisals of Merton. First, I believe that in spite of the dispersed, piecemeal, fragmentary nature of his contributions, they all add up to a coherent system of thought. Of course the system is far from complete, there are many empty spots, many lacunae, many fields of 'specified ignorance'. But all the islands of enlightenment fit nicely into the overall topography; and the dark or shadowy areas provide the system with strong potentials for elaboration, suggesting further problems for fruitful enquiry.

Second, I believe that in spite of his own research focus on the middle level of generality, Merton has unwittingly produced a general theory of society. Here some of my disagreement with the critics who deny this may be due to our different conceptions of sociological theory. In my earlier work I have been able to discover and define more than twenty meanings of the term 'theory' in the current sociological literature (Sztompka, 1979: 153–6). If one takes a very rigorous stand, defining theory most restrictively as a deductive, explanatory, axiomatic system, then of course there isn't any theory of this sort in Merton's writings—nor in those of any other sociologist. The intellectual practice of our discipline, so distant from the demanding standards of the natural sciences, requires the conception of a theory in a much more liberal, loose manner. I agree with P. Blau when he warns that unrealistic, formal and logical requirements addressed to sociological theories may paralyze theoretical efforts and block any progress in our discipline (1969: 122). In my understanding any general sociological theory consists of three components: fundamental ontological presuppositions about the nature of social reality, the conceptual model providing the image of the constitution and operation of society, and empirical hypotheses allowing us to explain and (at least partly) predict actual sociological phenomena (Sztompka, 1985: 12–13). This kind of theory is certainly present in Merton's work.

Third, against the stereotypes identifying Merton as an embodiment of functionalism, I believe that his orientation is and always has been mainly structuralist. Drawing inspiration from Durkheim and Marx, he perceives all social phenomena as located in a structural context, interlinked with other phenomena within wider social wholes. Those linkages are of two sorts: causal, when a phenomenon is constrained or facilitated by structural context; and functional, when a phenomenon produces structural effects (functions). 'Functional analysis' clearly appears as a specific subtype of a more general structural approach pervading Merton's enquiry.

Fourth, contrary to a completely misguided, 'ideological' critique which castigates Merton for ignoring or neglecting social conflict, I claim that he is a conflict theorist par excellence. His image of social life is saturated with contradictions, strains, tensions, ambivalence, dysfunctions and conflicts of all sorts. There is nothing of the tranquil, harmonious, consensual, equilibrated utopia in a human drama as depicted by Merton—with its torment of uncertainty and unintended latent consequences of action; with its agony of ambivalence and cross-cutting pressures of norms, roles and statuses; with its fright of normlessness, or anomie; with its risk of defeat or self-destroying prophecies.

Fifth, against another, equally fallacious criticism, accusing Merton of a static bias, I believe that his theory is dynamic in the full sense of the term. As I attempted to illustrate in detail, he not only recognizes various modalities of change, but focuses on structural changes, i.e. those which are structurally generated and structurally consequential. He not only studies reproductive (or adaptive) processes, but devotes considerable attention to morphogenetic processes, through which new, or fundamentally modified structures are socially constructed. What more can be expected of a truly dynamic analyst?

Structural theory of society, incorporating both 'social static' and 'social dynamics', 'social anatomy' and 'social physiology', consensus and conflict, stability and change, reproduction and emergence, adaptation and morphogenesis, provides a fully fledged, multidimensional paradigm for sociology. It is deeply rooted in the classical sociological tradition of the nineteenth century, and particularly the work of Marx, Simmel and Durkheim—incidentally Merton's self-consciously selected masters. For a long time it has dictated the dominant intellectual practice of the discipline, defined a true 'mainstream' of sociology. I don't see anything wrong with 'mainstreams', and I believe the structural paradigm is far from dead. Building on the best intellectual traditions, it may still provide a viable heuristic stimulus for sociology of the future. Merton has helped to specify, clarify and codify it, erecting a bridge between the sociological masters of the past and the coming perspectives of sociological theory. Perhaps his most important service to the development of contemporary sociology is precisely the vindication of this valuable classical heritage, so needed in view of certain destructive, irrational and highly premature challenges.

NOTES

1 The search for general and systematic theory is the main directive in my 'intellectual profile' of R. K. Merton (see Sztompka, 1986). It is quite telling that an almost identical approach was taken, independently, by C. Crothers (1987a). Isn't it a self-exemplifying case of what Merton studied extensively as 'multiple discoveries'—here strikingly similar interpretational principles were reached independently by scholars from Poland and New Zealand? Needless to add, it provides some mutual corroboration to our way of reading Merton.

2 Numerous specific illustrations of this opposition may be found in Merton's writings. Thus 'anomie' is not the same as personal 'anomia', sociological ambivalence is distinct from psychological uncertainty, institutional altruism is not tantamount to altruistic attitudes, social visibility of role performance is not the same as individual perceptions, organized scepticism in science is not equivalent to personal doubts of scholars, etc.

3 I analyze this brand of 'dynamic functionalism' in considerable detail in another book (see Sztompka, 1974).

4 The most famous application of the idea is found in Merton's theory of deviance ('anomie theory') where the main explanatory condition is defined as one in which 'the social structure rigorously restricts or completely closes access to approved modes of reaching [culturally extolled] goals for a considerable part of the same population' (1968: 200). Other examples are the explanation of 'institutionalized altruism' (1982a: 110), of 'sociological ambivalence' (1976a: 4–7) and of structural limits of legal reform (*ibid.*: 209).

5 I have to warn the reader that in this part of the discussion I take considerable liberty in rephrasing, redefining and reinterpreting some of Merton's formulations. I back up my account both by Merton's explicit pronouncements and by implicit hints dispersed throughout his work. Full documentation for this kind of reinterpretation may be found in Chapter 6 of my monograph on Merton (Sztompka, 1986: 158–239).

6 For a full analysis of various meanings of these notions, and a typology of eight types of structural contradictions in Merton's work, see Sztompka, 1986: 173–82.

7 Altogether Merton lists twenty similar ambivalences inherent in the physician's social role. Other important applications of the idea are to be found in his study of the 'ambivalence of organizational leaders' (1976a: 73–89) and in the analysis of 'seeking help' (Merton, Merton and Barber, 1983). It is clearly a recurrent and pervasive theme in his writings from various periods.

8 Other institutional domains where Merton discovers numerous ambivalences are marriage and the family (1976a: 227) and bureaucratic organization (1968: 254–8).

9 He distinguishes six social arrangements which are structurally available for coping with conflict in the role-set, and a similar number of mechanisms allowing for adaptation within status-sets. I discuss them thoroughly in my book (Sztompka, 1986: 202–10).

10 These denominations are not Merton's, but those of W. Buckley, A. Giddens, P. Berger and T. Luckman respectively. [*Ed. note*: These questions are debated extensively in the companion volume in this series on the work of Anthony Giddens.]

6. Merton's Systematic Theory

ROBERT BIERSTEDT

William James tells the delightful story of returning from a solitary ramble in the woods and finding his camping companions engaged in a fierce dispute. It concerns a squirrel. Everyone knows that it is impossible to see a squirrel on a tree at close range because the bushy tailed animal always keeps the tree between itself and the man who is trying to observe it. If the man goes around the tree, no matter how fast he moves, he will fail to catch a glimpse of the squirrel because the squirrel will do likewise, always keeping the tree between itself and the man. Now there is no doubt that the man goes around the tree and no doubt that the squirrel goes around the tree. The question is: does the man go around the squirrel? On this question the campers were stridently divided, half of the company insisting that the answer was yes and the other half insisting that the answer was no. Each side implored William James to offer his opinion. He must have stunned them by saying that each side was right and each side was wrong. It all depends on what you mean by 'around'. If you mean by around that the man occupies successive positions to the north, east, south and west of the squirrel, then it is obvious that he does indeed go around the squirrel. If, on the other hand, you mean that the man occupies successive positions in front of, to the left of, behind and to the right of the squirrel, then it is equally obvious that he does not go around the squirrel. Thus an argument that was rapidly turning into a quarrel was easily solved by attending to the meaning of a word.

We may anticipate the conclusion of this paper by suggesting that something of the same kind will prove to be the case when we ask whether Robert K. Merton has produced a systematic sociological theory or whether he has neglected systematic sociological theory for stellar work instead on such subjects as the sociology of science, methodology, theories of the middle range, manifest and latent functions, anomy,[1] bureaucracy, the self-fulfilling prophecy, reference group theory and the many other phenomena that have attracted his roving mind. 'Roving', of course, is a compliment. Lewis Coser and I have independently remarked that the distinction of

Archilochus between a fox and a hedgehog has a special application to Merton. A fox knows many things but the hedgehog knows one big thing.[2] If one were forced to use only one of these words in reference to Merton, one would have to say that he is a fox rather than a hedgehog. The words are inelegant, however, and Merton himself would doubtless be happy if the name of Archilochus had never come up.

BIERSTEDT AND SZTOMPKA: THE ARGUMENTS OUTLINED

Before we get to a Jamesian solution in Merton's case, let us examine the arguments that have arisen, with Piotr Sztompka on one side and the present writer on the other. The controversy apparently has its origin in judgments I have made about Merton in my book, *American Sociological Theory*: *A Critical History*. Consider the following:

> Although he is altogether and enviably proficient in sociological theory, he has never produced a systematic theory or a system of sociology. This would seem to be a rather curious omission in one who has written so much at so high a level of competence. It is especially odd in view of the fact that both of his mentors at Harvard—Sorokin and Parsons—produced systematic sociological theory. Indeed, if I may anticipate my critical conclusion, this is the most puzzling and significant question we can ask about Merton's place in the history of sociology. There is, in short, no book about society. (Bierstedt, 1981: 445)

Consider again:

> On the critical side we have to say that Merton has the defects of his virtues. The extensive range of his interests has blurred what might otherwise have been a clear and consistent focus. As mentioned earlier in this chapter, he has given us no systematic work, no theory of the social order, no system of sociology. (*ibid*.: 487)

Finally, Merton, although he once condemned the criterion of utility in intellectual endeavour, nevertheless persistently holds the view that sociological theory is not an end in itself but an instrument to be judged by its utility in research. He does not, for example, have a high opinion of the history of philosophy, which the history of sociology tends to resemble. The systems of the great social thinkers lack all utility for research. They testify to the merits of talented men, but they cannot be used.[3] They give us no guidelines. Now of course it was not the intention of thinkers like Plato, Aristotle, Saint Augustine, Machiavelli, Hobbes, Montesquieu, Rousseau, Condorcet, Comte, Spencer and a host of others to provide guidelines for research. Their goal was to say something penetrating about the nature of human society. What is the good society and what is the source of the order it exhibits? Merton rejects this view of sociology. Sociology, on the contrary, is a science, a science that like other sciences walks on two legs, one of them called theory and the other research. Continuing from my own critical conclusion:

> Only when research accumulates can we have a body of knowledge worthy of being called sociology. The trouble with this view is that it has failed to happen. The history of sociology shows no such accumulation. If Merton had forgotten about the criterion of utility and applied his extraordinary talents to the creation of a system of sociology, his place in our pantheon would be more exalted, and more secure. (*ibid*.: 488–9)

All of these observations appear in a chapter devoted entirely to Merton, incidentally the only living sociologist treated in the book. It is a chapter replete with compliments, including a closing tribute to the sheer quality of Merton's accomplishments. Indeed, compliments are embedded even in the critical quotations that appear above.

Let us now look at the other side of the argument. Piotr Sztompka published his *Robert K. Merton: An Intellectual Profile* in 1986 and dedicated it to him in celebration of Merton's seventy-fifth birthday (which occurred in 1985). Throughout the writing he had the cooperation of his subject, whom he calls his master-at-a-distance turned friend. His admiration for Merton knows no limits and consequently he is sensitive to and even offended by any criticism of his work. He is particularly offended by critics, especially the present writer, who deny that Merton has produced a systematic sociological theory. He thus goes to the barricades to defend Merton against the charges. His master and friend has indeed produced a coherent system of sociology. More than that, 'Merton has remained for me the embodiment of *sociological wisdom*: the modern sage of social science' (Sztompka, 1986: ix).

Sztompka begins his book with a discussion of four underlying assumptions that serve as a foundation of his interpretation of Merton. The first of these is that Merton's work, in spite of its appearance as a scattered collection of miscellaneous pieces, 'constitutes a *coherent system of thought*' (*ibid.*: 1). In view of this miscellaneous character of Merton's contributions:

> It is easy to claim with Bierstedt that 'Merton alone among our American sociologists has made no effort to construct a system of sociology', and therefore, supposedly, 'he has given us no systematic work, no theory of the social order, no system of sociology'. It is true only in the sense that Merton always opposed the practice of building his own system *from scratch*, attempting instead to put himself firmly on the shoulders of sociological giants of the past. But it is grossly mistaken if intended to mean that there are no systematic interlinks between Merton's contributions. If I read Merton correctly, there is precisely a system of sociological thought emerging from his persistent and disciplined inquiry. (*ibid.*: 2)

Sztompka insists, in short, that because of the consistency of Merton's views, no matter what the subject of his attention, there is indeed a coherent sociological system.

The second assumption, perhaps an expanded corollary of the first, is that 'Merton has not stopped at the level of concrete or middle-range propositions, but has produced a *full-fledged general theory*' (*ibid.*: 3). Again one is easily misled because Merton is opposed to 'grand theory'. As a matter of fact, 'it is because Merton has a better general theory than Parsons that his work has been more empirically fruitful' (*ibid.*). Here, in parentheses, let us note that Sztompka apparently shares Merton's notion that the principal function of theory is to be useful in research. On this point Sztompka quotes Paul Lazarsfeld to the effect that 'the great variety of Merton's empirical theories is generated from a small set of common elements, organized around a core theory' (*ibid.*: 4). Beyond asserting that it exists, however, Sztompka offers no explanation of what it is or what its constituent elements are. He does say the following:

> This *core theory*, or common theme is most general; it crowns the system of Merton's more specific contributions. Since that system consists of two major parts—sociological and meta-scientific—two general theories are to be found there: *a general theory of society* and *a general theory of science*, these being interlinked and sharing a common logic. (*ibid.*)

Now we seem to have not one but two core theories, one of society and the other of science. But scepticism remains. We still wonder where in the corpus of Merton's work to look for a theory of society, an organized outline of its structural components and the logical relations they have with one another.

The third and fourth assumptions are less relevant to our current concern. The third 'holds that Merton's intellectual development over a period of some fifty years has been marked by *continuity and coherence*' (*ibid.*).[4] The fourth 'maintains that Merton's work has a set of pervasive leitmotifs—central ideas—which can be described as the classicist theme, the cognitive theme, the structuralist theme and the ironic theme' (*ibid.*). What these themes are Sztompka explains at first mention and elaborates upon in the last chapter of his book.

Sztompka also discusses Merton's essays on the relations between theory and research. There is a two-way street between them. Theory informs research and research influences theory. The following points receive emphasis. First, 'the delimitation of facts for empirical study is carried out by means of concepts, which in turn derive from a theory, an explicit conceptual outfit' (*ibid.*: 102–3). Second, 'the selection of variables is always influenced by the underlying theoretical orientation'. Third, 'the use of certain *techniques or research procedures makes sense only in view of some theoretical assumptions*'. There are five more points in this connection, but these three are the essential ones. They are all reminiscent of a proposition announced by John Dewey many years ago, and in fewer words; namely, that facts are never given, they are always taken, and taken in connection with a conceptual scheme. But all of them appear to emphasize Merton's basic view of theory, that it is a handmaiden and help to sociological research, and not a general view of society.[5]

The obverse of these propositions, and again elaborated at length, is that research is useful if not necessary in the construction of sociological theory. Merton emphasizes a number of points. 'It is my central thesis that empirical research goes far beyond the passive role of verifying and testing theory: it does more than confirm or refute hypotheses. Research plays an active roll'. 'Second, research exerts pressure for initiating theory; it fulfils an important heuristic function'. 'Third, research exerts pressure for elaborating the conceptual scheme inherent in the theory'. 'Fourth, research refocuses theoretic interest toward new phenomena, or new aspects of known phenomena'. 'Fifth, research contributes to the clarification of concepts' (*ibid.*: 103). Sztompka concludes this discussion with the following:

> The message carried by this analysis of decades ago is clear: sociological theory cannot be divorced from sociological research and *vice versa*. Attempts to conduct empirical inquiry purged of theoretical bases and components are misguided and doomed to failure. Even though this point is now taken for granted by most sociologists, it is always worth repeating. And Merton's early formulation is particularly clear and persuasive. (*ibid.*: 104)

Clear and persuasive it may be, but it is not quite correct. It is indeed possible to do research without theory and theory without research. An example of the former would be an enquiry into the number of housewives in Middletown who own microwave ovens and an example of the latter would be an analysis of social power. A final comment on this point may be in order. In discussing the masters of social thought from Plato to Spencer, I wrote the following:

If 'research' could help them, well and good—Aristotle, after all, collected the constitutions of 158 city-states—but previous theories were more relevant to their concerns. Let us in fact admire those who, because of their superior observation of the society in which they lived, their knowledge of history, and their intimate familiarity with the thought of their predecessors, could generate theory *without* doing research. (1981: 488)

THE MEANINGS OF 'SYSTEMATIC SOCIAL THEORY'

We are now ready to ask whether a Jamesian solution can be found for our fundamental question: has Merton produced a systematic sociological theory or, a question within a question, has Sztompka shown that Merton has done so? It all depends on what we mean by a systematic sociological theory. If we mean, as his disciple emphasizes throughout, that Merton's theoretical enquiries are systematic, disciplined, coherent, organized, diligent, balanced and lucid, then the answer is yes. If we mean in addition that underlying all of his major concepts there is a genuine sociological theory struggling to emerge, then the answer is again yes. If we mean, finally, that there is a conceptual scheme, whether or not fully codified (and whether or not superior to Parsons's), that can be called sociological theory, then the answer is again in the affirmative.

If, on the other hand, Sztompka cannot show us a book by Merton that gives us a general view of society, its structure and changes, together with a logical view of the elements that constitute its structure, and a weighing of the factors—geographical, biological, demographic, political, economic and ideological—that precipitate social and cultural change, then the answer has to be in the negative. There is nothing in the Merton corpus that corresponds to Robert M. MacIver's *Society* (1937), Pitirim A. Sorokin's *Society, Culture and Personality* (1947), or my own *The Social Order* (1974). It is true that Merton has discussed in detail such structural phenomena as status-sets and role-sets and has discoursed at length on the properties of reference groups, but there is no general sociological theory of the kind just mentioned.

Perhaps we should ask what Merton himself regards as theory. He examines the matter and arrives at six different meanings (1967: 140–53): (a) methodology, (b) general sociological orientations, (c) analysis of sociological concepts, (d) *post factum* sociological interpretations, (e) empirical generalizations in sociology, and (f) sociological theory. One does not quite know what to do with the last of these because here a part has the same name as the whole, and thus violates the canons of taxonomy. In spite of this list, however, Merton generally tends to conceive of theory either as a set of cumulative inductions from middle-range research, inductions that are not yet codified into a comprehensive body of knowledge, or as a conceptual scheme, an analytic tool that is useful as a guide for research.

Much of Merton's theoretical discussion falls under the rubric of methodology and is not concerned with the nature of society at all. Clearly methodological are his treatments of the history and systematics of sociological theory, theories of the middle range, manifest and latent functions, the bearing of theory on research and the bearing of research on theory. They would apply to other disciplines as well as to sociology.

Similarly, Merton has not tried to tie together the manifold concepts he has with ingenuity and style contributed to sociology. The list is long and includes, among many others, paradigms, unanticipated consequences, status-sets, role-sets, the self-fulfilling prophecy, reference group, sociological ambivalence and anticipatory socialization. But do these, taken together, constitute a theory? On this Merton himself has an apposite comment:

> It is at times held that theory is comprised of concepts, an assertion which, being incomplete, is neither true nor false but vague. To be sure conceptual analysis, which is confined to the specification and clarification of key concepts, is an indispensable phase of theoretic work. But an array of concepts—status, role, *Gemeinschaft*, social interaction, social distance, *anomie*—does not constitute theory, though it may enter into a theoretic system.... It is only when such concepts are inter-related in the form of a scheme that a theory begins to emerge. (*ibid.*: 143)

Here, of course, Merton is quite right. A 'basketful' of concepts—to use one of Sorokin's colourful words—cannot give us a general image of the contours and dimensions of society. Only propositions can do that.

Sztompka surprises us by insisting that, although it is *there*—and on this he brooks no denial—Merton's sociological theory is nevertheless hidden and has to be extricated by supposedly superior analytical talent. Consider the following:

> Throughout, I adopt a generalizing, interpretative approach, trying to reconstruct the general theory which is for the most part implicit, and sometimes deeply hidden in Merton's sociological contributions. For that reason I shall dig below the surface of particular results and literal pronouncements. (Sztompka, 1986: 6)

And even more revealing:

> Merton does not present a substantive image of society in systematic fashion. Instead of sustained, unified exposition, he chooses the method of selecting particular problems and elucidating them in a detailed and thorough manner. The result: islands of enlightenment dispersed here and there in a sea of twilight, and occasional darkness. (*ibid.*: 158)

To the observation that there is no theory of action in Merton's work, that action is not a category therein,[6] Sztompka replies once again that it is implicit and has to be reconstructed if one wants to see it. In short, if Merton has not himself given us a systematic sociological theory, Sztompka will supply one for us, even if he has to conquer a sea of twilight in order to do so.

We have said that there is nothing in Merton that corresponds to the general theories of society produced by Sorokin and MacIver, and we are tempted to believe that Merton would agree. Sorokin, for example, begins his *Society, Culture and Personality* by defining what he calls the generic social phenomenon, which is meaningful human interaction, and builds from there to a treatment of groups, norms ('law-norms' in Sorokin's terminology) and institutions. In discussing his generic phenomenon he ventures forth to consider the number of interacting individuals (two or many), their qualities (whether homogeneous or heterogeneous) and their character (whether purposive or non-purposive, whether long- or short-lived, whether conscious or unconscious). He treats meanings, values and norms in detail. The last of these especially receives extensive attention. Along the way he criticizes the definitions of predecessors, including MacIver, who wrote on these subjects. One should mention in addition that the subtitle of Sorokin's book is 'A System of General Sociology', and that is exactly what it is. The system is not hidden; on the contrary it is there for every reader to see. Sorokin goes on to treat the organized group, offers an extensive, if flawed, classification of groups, moves on to the subjects of differentiation and stratification, and uses many pages to treat the dynamics of recurrent social processes and the dynamics of cultural processes. He gives us, in short, a system of general sociology.

The same may be said of MacIver. Beginning his *Society* with a word about sociology itself, he turns his attention first to definition of primary concepts and then uses them to paint his picture of society. There is no methodological discussion here, nothing about the relation between theory and research, and few of the propositions in the book stem directly from research. Instead he writes of interests and attitudes, of the influence of environment upon society, of the social structure and its sustaining forces of code and custom, of the kinds of social codes, of social groups (including a classification); and then of specific groups including the family, the community, the city, social class and caste, ethnic groups, unorganized groups (crowds and mass communication, and the great associations, political, economic and cultural). The final section of the book is devoted to the subject of social change. Again, as in Sorokin's case, there is nothing hidden here. MacIver tells us, in graceful prose, what society is.

If I may refer to the book I know best, *The Social Order* (Bierstedt, 1974), we also find what I would call systematic sociological theory of a kind not to be found in Merton. The foundations of society rest in three factors, geographical, biological and demographic, and these are necessary but not sufficient for the explanation of society. The sufficient factor is culture and consequently culture is subjected to minute examination and analysis. The content of culture is threefold—ideas, norms and materiel—and the second of these is of particular interest to sociology because norms are of the essence of social structure. Norms are then classified as folkways, mores and laws, and consideration is given to the sanctions that support them. But norms are not 'free-floating' in society; they are attached to statuses and, as Sorokin also noted, each individual in society has as many statuses as there are groups (including statistical groups) of which he is a member. Statuses, incidentally, can be either ascribed or achieved. The subject of statuses leads to groups and their classification, which in turn leads to organized groups and the nature of organization itself, both formal and informal. Organized groups and associations are identical and it is associations, that account for orderly and recurrent procedures, which are called institutions. This proposition leads logically to an analysis of authority, which is a property of all associations, and power, which ultimately supports the social order. Thus the structure of society can be explained in terms of seven concepts—norms, statuses, groups, associations, institutions, authority, power—all interrelated and interlinked, as Merton's methodological theory requires. The remainder of the book is devoted to social differentiation and social change.

It will readily occur to the reader that the second two of these three books are textbooks.[7] MacIver's was not originally intended to be one, but it was found to be so pedagogically useful that its second edition is subtitled 'A Textbook of Sociology'. My book, somewhat to my displeasure, was openly published and distributed as a textbook. Textbooks, of course, rank low on the pecking order of intellectual accomplishments. They may run through many editions, but for the most part they do not 'last'. They receive the attention of students but not of colleagues in the profession. For many years *Sociology* by William F. Ogburn and Meyer F. Nimkoff was the leading sociology text in the United States, and a systematic work it was, but no one remembers it today. There have been great textbooks—Spencer's *Principles of Sociology* (1876), Alfred Marshall's *Principles of Economics* (1890) and William James's *Principles of Psychology* (1890)—textbooks that became classic works in their own right. But this fortunate circumstance happens only in the early history of a discipline and cannot be claimed by many. It is somewhat paradoxical, however, that in sociology the only books that give us a systematic view of society are textbooks, books whose authors often receive financial rewards but little recognition as sociological theorists.

CONCLUSION

It may be said in conclusion that Merton has no obligation to write a textbook and we should not fault him for neglect when he has done so many other things so well. But if he had done so, he would have given us the systematic sociological theory that Piotr Sztompka unsuccessfully claims can be found in his work. In any event, we return to the Jamesian solution. If we mean by systematic sociological theory that Merton's essays in theory are systematic, coherent, disciplined and balanced, then indeed he has contributed to theory, even if it must be 'extricated' by his readers. If, on the other hand, we mean by systematic sociological theory a general view of society, its structural components and their relations with one another, then there is no such book. On Sztompka's own words, that Merton's sociological theory is 'deeply hidden', I rest my case.

NOTES

1   On anomy I have to repeat what I have said in another place. Merton has persistently used the French spelling of this word rather than the English, beginning with his famous essay, 'Social Structure and Anomie' (1938b), offering as a reason that 'anomy' is a 'sixteenth century and long obsolete spelling of the word'. His contention is incorrect. 'Anomy' has consistently appeared in English dictionaries, including the *Oxford English Dictionary* and *Webster's Unabridged*, but there is no 'anomie' in recent editions of either one. It makes no more sense to use 'anomie' in an English sentence than it does to use the French 'anarchie' in preference to the English 'anarchy'.
2   Isaiah Berlin elaborates on this theme in his small book, *The Hedgehog and the Fox: An Essay on Tolstoy's View of History* (1953).
3   This does not imply that Merton demeans the endeavours of classical writers. On the contrary, 'I have long argued that the writings of classical authors in every field of learning can be read with profit time and again, additional ideas and intimations coming freshly into view with each re-reading' (Merton 1965a: 45).
4   Sztompka continues: 'To be sure, he often returns to previously stated ideas, modifying them, enriching them, following them up with new evidence. But I have not found a single instance when he would be made to reject or revoke any of them in full'.
5   The word 'theory', incidentally, comes from a Greek word meaning a beholding, a view.
6   Indeed, it should not be. I would argue that action is a category in social psychology and does not belong in sociology. My remark in context was meant to indicate that Merton is not a disciple of Parsons.
7   Sorokin's, with its 723 double-columned pages, is too large to have a classroom use.

Interchange

SZTOMPKA REPLIES TO BIERSTEDT

Professor Bierstedt is not entirely correct that our disagreement boils down to the meaning of words, and particularly to the diverse concepts of systematic theory. On the contrary, it seems to me that we have very similar, if not identical ideas of what a theory (or a good theory) is. Anyway, I am ready to accept all the characterizations of theory that he gives in passing throughout his essay. Yet I have to disagree with some crucial claims, because the true bone of contention lies elsewhere. It concerns the strategy of creating theory, and the job of a commentator or analyst who writes about theory.

Concerning theory-building Bierstedt advocates the method of writing synthetic, comprehensive, systematic treatises about society, covering all major social phenomena and their interrelations, or briefly, producing 'books about society'. He claims that Merton has no systematic theory because—quite truly—there is no such book in his bibliography.

Bierstedt's thesis about theory-building may be read in two ways. It may be treated as a normative prescription. If so, there is nothing one could say against it. It would really be great if all social theorists produced clear, orderly, unambiguous and complete 'books about society', of the rare sort that Bierstedt quotes as illustrations. Apropos of those examples, I remember myself how rewarding and pleasant it was to get my first sociological insights from MacIver and Page's *Society* (1949) and Bierstedt's *Social Order* (the first edition). Wouldn't it make the life of undergraduate students so much easier if all theorists wrote like that? Wouldn't it save thousands of tons of paper and millions of hours of interpretive, alienated labour, not to mention even more serious costs and troubles, if Marx had left a straightforward 'book about society'? Or if Weber had, or Durkheim, or Simmel?

Unfortunately, none of those great masters did, and I would claim—here taking issue with Bierstedt—that most of the modern social theorists haven't either. Let us think of the American authors he knows so well: where is the 'book about society' written by Mead or Znaniecki, or Goffman, or Blau, or Lewis Coser, or Parsons? Stay with Parsons for a minute; which of his volumes would meet Bierstedt's criterion—*The Social System* (1951), or *The Structure of Social Action* (1937), or *Societies: Evolutionary and Comparative Perspectives* (1966)? Thus, as a descriptive statement about actual theoretical practice, Bierstedt's thesis does not stand scrutiny. The strategy he advocates is in fact very rarely applied in the history of sociology, and is by no means typical of contemporary theorizing.

This opens the field for commentators, interpreters, analysts of theoretical work; for their reconstructing and systematizing efforts, 'digging below the surface of particular results and literal pronouncements'—as Bierstedt quotes me. What I was trying to do with Merton's work is the same kind of service that Bierstedt was once doing for Znaniecki, Blumer for Mead, Bendix for Weber, Cohen for Marx, Lukes for Durkheim, Coser for Simmel, Alexander for Parsons—just to mention some outstanding examples. The job comes down to unravelling the core of their theories, bringing disparate pieces of the mosaic together, giving them unified form and consistent meaning.

Of course no reconstruction of this sort is definitive or flawless. Some people do this job better than others, but the sense of the effort—whatever the result—should not be denied. The interpretation is necessary precisely because great theorists rarely write neat 'books about society'. In fact, the multiple and clashing interpretations add much flavour to contemporary theoretical debate and are certainly one of the ways in which the progress of theories comes about.

Maybe it was because they didn't want to make the life of their students easier, nor to take jobs from analysts and interpreters, nor to rob the reading public of much fun, that major theorists didn't bother about giving their theories a systematic form. Or maybe they simply had no time for writing 'books about society', so busy were they with writing about selected aspects of society; with solving concrete, scattered, miscellaneous social puzzles; with producing those 'islands of enlightenment dispersed here and there in a sea of twilight, and occasional darkness'—like Merton.

To end, like my adversary, on a conciliatory note, I am happy to acknowledge our ultimate unanimity in the overall appraisal of Merton's work. Not without a tinge of irony Bierstedt says that my 'admiration for Merton knows no limits', but then he admits that the chapter on Merton in his own *American Sociological Theory: A Critical History* (1981) is 'replete with compliments'. Maybe the man deserves them, after all.

BIERSTEDT REPLIES TO SZTOMPKA

With perseverance, industry and a commendable ardour, Piotr Sztompka continues to insist that Robert Merton has produced a systematic sociological theory. Some of his critics have taken a contrary position and this, of course, is the source of our rather mild controversy. In his chapter for this volume Sztompka again admits that Merton has devoted no book to such a systematic theory—indeed, there is no book devoted to a single subject except his doctoral dissertation on *Science, Technology and Society in Seventeenth Century England* (1938a). For the rest we have a long and impressive list of miscellaneous essays, articles and reviews. The list is impressive' enough to win for Merton a place among the most distinguished of contemporary sociologists and a reputation that will endure for an unknown number of decades to come. It is probable, however, that this reputation will rest not upon any general systematic theory but rather upon the many fertile expressions he has introduced into the literature—expressions such as theories of the middle range, paradigms, unanticipated consequences of purposive social action, sociological ambivalence, the role-set, manifest and latent functions, the self-fulfilling prophecy, anticipatory socialization, reference group and many more.

It is unnecessary in this brief response to repeat the arguments set forth in my original chapter. It is enough to say again that Sztompka concedes the principal point of my criticism, a criticism that is in fact more of an observation than an objection. Indeed, Sztompka himself, who now has perhaps a more intimate knowledge of Merton's work than anyone else, does not hesitate to declare that Merton has never been a system-builder and that he has opposed such an endeavour on the ground that it is premature. If there is a system, someone else has to find it underneath the surface in a kind of archaeological dig, and it is to this task that Sztompka has dedicated his efforts, efforts that require, in his own words, 'rephrasing, redefining and reinterpreting some of Merton's formulations'. In a sense it is good that Sztompka has done this. Without his expert sifting of the soil we would not have known about Merton's 'system'. He speaks of 'systemic interlinks between Merton's contributions', but except in a most general way does not put them on exhibition. None of this, of course, is intended to reflect upon the systematic, careful, rational and well organized character of Merton's thinking. But that is another issue.

Sztompka devotes a section of his paper to Merton's 'image of sociology', and for the most part it is a cogent and important discussion. He does not, however, enlighten us on Merton's image of society. Except for those who succumb to the temptations of methodology and meta-sociology, this is what we would ordinarily take to be the centre of sociology. Sztompka says that Merton 'evidently perceives society as a reality *sui generis*, possessing specific properties and displaying specific regularities', but the word 'evidently' gives the game away. Sztompka is apparently not sure.

Finally, in a lucid conclusion to a well written paper Sztompka candidly agrees that his interpretation runs counter to standard, received interpretations and that Merton has 'unwittingly' produced a general theory of society. It is not clear how someone can produce a solid and coherent system of sociology without knowing it. In any event Merton has so many virtues that it is unnecessary to burden him with one that he does not possess and one that, in fact, has often attracted his disapproval.

IV. STRUCTURAL ANALYSIS

7. Social Structure in the Work of Robert Merton

ARTHUR STINCHCOMBE

Of all contemporary theorists of social structure, Merton has had the greatest impact on empirical research. Investigators find it easy to understand how his general theory of social structure implies hypotheses about the pattern of behaviour and the pattern of associations between variables in the setting in which their research is conducted. The argument of this contribution is that this is due to the common logical and substantive character of all his theories of social structure. Briefly I will argue that the core process that Merton conceives as central to social structure is *the choice between socially structured alternatives*, and the core variable to be explained is *different rates of choice by people differently located in the social order*.

INDIVIDUAL CHOICE OF STRUCTURALLY PATTERNED ALTERNATIVES

If it is true that Merton has focused his theories around processes of individual choice, why do his theories look so different from those of other people who proclaim they study choice? There are many traditions in the social sciences that make that proclamation. It will be particularly useful to contrast Merton's strategy with two of these: symbolic interactionism, with choice determined by definitions of the situation (see, for example, Matza, 1969); and Parsonian theory, with choices about inherent value dilemmas determined by cultural values.[1]

Let us consider the choice between legitimate and illegitimate means in his essay 'Social Structure and Anomie' (1968: 185–214). In the first place Merton is trying to explain different rates of crime, that is, different rates of choice to do behaviour well known to land people in prison if they get caught. I presume he would agree with what I take to be the main point of the new criminology: if theft or peddling heroin were not defined as crimes, people would not go to prison for them. But that is not the situation of choice that slum dwellers are confronted with. There are connections between the choice of a career peddling heroin and the likelihood of going to prison, the likelihood of social opprobrium, the likelihood of involvement in groups with other criminal enterprises. These connections are set up by 'the society'. That is, the character of the criminal alternative to a regular career is socially structured and, by virtue of that structuring, entails multiple simultaneous consequences for the individual.

However, because the laws and sanctions of the larger society and its officials have a coercive power to define the situation, criminals cannot simply make up their minds that theft or peddling heroin are o.k., as symbolic interactionists would seem to suggest. People define situations, but do not define them as they please. In Parsonian theory I do not know which value dilemma policemen are resolving when they decide that heroin peddlars are a bunch of crooks, nor the one resolved by a person who decides then to be a crook. But it is hard to imagine that value orientations at the most general level have much to do with choosing a criminal career.

In these alternative theories of choice there is a theoretical awkwardness about the society putting together bundles of predictable social reactions to acts, so that an innovative career outside the law is either a choice of a complex of determinate definitions of the situation or a choice of the values one will live by. This theoretical attention to bundling of choices is the distinctive feature of Merton's analysis.

To take another example, the essay on the intellectual in public bureaucracy is principally organized around the choice by the intellectual between investigating all alternative policies and improving that policy that has already been decided upon. This choice comes in a socially structured form. Policy-makers tend to listen to intelligence about how to do what they want to do and tend not to listen to intelligence about why what they are doing is all wrong. The choice between having a broad and accurate assessment while being unheard in policy councils, and having the right answer to the wrong problem while being heard, is structured by the place of intellectual activity along the 'continuum of decision' (Merton, 1968: 269). Presumably, many intellectuals find both having the right problem, and having their right answer heard, rewarding or in keeping with their basic value premises. They would like to define their situation as involving both.

But they are not free to choose the combined alternative bundle of wide-ranging consideration of alternatives and of having the cabinet's ear. The eminently practical answer I once heard a college professor give to the question: 'But how can we get out of Viet Nam?' 'By getting on ships', was socially structured as woolly thinking, while the most fantastic theories of the effects of bombing or of the possibility of the South Vietnamese government becoming a revolutionary force in the countryside were socially structured as hard-headed realism. This is because the fantastic theories bore on the policy options in consideration by the cabinet, while the theory that one could come home on ships did not.

The point is that the social process presents a socially structured choice between alternative cognitive styles. People do choose among cognitive styles in order to make history, but again they do not make history as they please. This approach to society through individual choice between socially structured alternatives is the opposite of either psychological or sociological reductionism. There is, to be sure, consistent attention to the fact that people have to do all social actions. And there is close empirical analysis of norms, structures, collective representations, etc. But Merton is engaged in understanding the world, not in drawing lines between disciplines and projecting them onto the world. Externally constraining social facts have to get into people's minds in order to constrain them. But people are clever about getting what they want out of a constraining social structure. The whole question of whether social action is 'really' psychological or 'really' social appears as a fake problem.

STRUCTURAL CAUSES OF VARIATIONS IN PATTERNS OF CHOICE

The Patterning of Alternatives

The first strategic consideration in explaining patterns of choice between structured alternatives is the nature of that structuring itself. Consider the explanation for the hypothesis that ritualistic adaptations to high success goals and limited means will be more common in the lower middle class. In this class '...parents typically exert continuous pressure upon children to abide by the moral mandates of the society...' (Merton, 1968: 205). The hypothesis is then that moral constraints structure the alternatives of the lower middle class into two of the possible five adaptations: success within the norms or failure within the norms. The possible alternatives of crime ('innovation') or vagrancy ('retreatism') are excluded by the moral environment of this class (*ibid.*, 205–7). Thus the rate of ritualism as a choice should increase in this class, because the alternatives to ritualism are bundled together with dishonour, personal rejection and nagging by lower-middle-class parents. The increase of the costs of the alternatives to ritualism leaves ritualism as the only likely reaction to lack of success for that class.

The pattern of explanation is logically structured and empirically fruitful. The attachment of specific rewards or punishments (e.g. parental disapproval) by specific social structures (lower-middle-class families) to the structured bundles among which people must choose determines the motivational potential attached to the bundles. As the structurings of choice change, for example, by moving from one class to another, the rates of choice change too. They may change either by increasing the reward attached to one alternative or by increasing the punishments associated with the others.

Structurally Induced Motivation

In 'Social Structure and Anomie' Merton talks about American social structure as inducing a high motivation for success in all parts of the class system. In the sociology of science he talks about the special motivation induced by the social structure of science for prestige, especially prestige by publication. In the analysis of 'Reference Group Theory and Social Mobility' (1968: 316–25) motivation is treated in two different ways. One the one hand, attachments to non-membership groups are structurally motivated by the prospect of social mobility. On the other hand, conformity to the norms of a non-membership group is motivated by positive attachment to it.

In each of these cases we have social influences on people's goals, which in turn affect their rates of social choice. These are exogenous to the formation of the alternatives themselves, in some sense. That is, the sources of the motivation to succeed are not the same as the sources of the bundling together of innovation (crime) and prison by the criminal justice system. Promotion in university based on publication, or the public validation of arduous scientific work by publication, is not the same as the institutionalization of priority rights through publication. Nor is the induction of the goal of establishing priority among scientists directly due to the bundling of priority with publication.

Let us discuss the distinction between social structuring of alternatives and structurally induced motivation further, because the distinction is subtle. Exogenous variation in the different components of a social theory of choice is, as econometricians have often pointed out, an essential element in untangling causes that go around in circles. Since people making choices analyze the situation as a whole, the causes in theories of choice almost always go around in circles. This logical point about the structure of Merton's theories is therefore crucial, and needs further elaboration.

Consider the fact that for ordinary people to establish priority for a scientific discovery they would have to publish. Ordinary people do not publish, at least not very often, and do not worry about it. Scientists publish a great deal in journals that do not pay them—in fact, in some one may pay costs. And they worry about it a good deal. The systematic quality of the high rate of publication therefore incorporates two elements. In the first place, there is the institution of scientific journals, citation practices and so on, which ties together priority and publication. Second, there is the passion for priority among scientists, which Merton's historical studies of science evoke so well.

The institution that bundles the alternative varies over historical time. At any given time the passion for priority (the structurally induced motivation) varies over individuals, with scientists being far more passionate than ordinary people, university scientists much more than industrial scientists, scientists in fields in which one can tell whether something has been discovered or not (for example, physics) much more than scientists in fields in which one cannot (for example, sociology). The leisurely pace of publication in sociology is not to be explained entirely by different publication institutions (though the preference for books about the system of sociology as a whole over articles reminds one of ancient times in the physical sciences). Rather, it is to be explained by the different induction of the goal of establishing priority in the social structure of sociology.

Thus the distinction between the structural sources of motivation and the structuring of alternatives allows us to disentangle the motivational aspect of the structured alternatives from the goals people are trying to reach by choosing those alternatives. The two forces cause variations over different sorts of observations: historical in one case and cross-sectional in the other. That rare quality in sociology writing, of wandering easily from history to survey research without giving the feeling that one is lost, is due to Merton's pre-econometric instinct for the problem of identification in systems of interacting causal forces.

There are four main sources of variation in structurally induced motives in Merton's work: socialization into a culture, reward systems, self-affirmation in a social role, and structurally induced needs. Thus American children are taught (socialized) that people ought to succeed and that success is a measure of personal worth. There may be cultures that stress success but have alternative standards of personal worth as well. The first structural source of variable induction of motives, then, is differential socialization (Merton, 1968: 185–214). Besides being socialized to value scientific discovery, university scientists in modern societies are involved in reward systems (status systems) which make money, power, freedom at work and social honour all dependent on priority of scientific discovery. Such a status system cumulates motivations of diverse people around the same goal. Whether one wants to be rich, powerful, free or honoured, if one is a scientist in a university he or she satisfies his or her motives by establishing priority. Thus the dependence of all rewards on one performance criterion in a status system induces the cumulation of motives around that performance (Merton, 1969).

In the social psychology of reference group behaviour, the generalization from wanting to be an officer to wanting to be like an officer involves a motivational postulate of the kind now often discussed as 'ego identity.' Conforming attitudes in the military, and anticipatory socialization for becoming an officer, are partly motivated by affirming one's (potential) social role as an officer (Merton, 1968: 319–22). A fourth source of differential motivation is illustrated by the special need of immigrant ethnic groups for help, not justice, from the political machine. Many motives in people's lives (jobs, getting out of difficulties with the law, special food for ritual occasions like Christmas) require manipulation of the social structure. When people are unskilled, legally disadvantaged or poor, this manipulation poses special difficulties (*ibid.*, 73–138). A set of structurally induced special problems in satisfying the motives of everyday life creates in a person a special motive to have trusted friends in high places who can manipulate for him. That is, ordinary motives create special motives under conditions of need, under conditions in which ordinary motives can only be satisfied through a single channel. Thus there are four main structural sources of goals or motives in Merton's theories: socialization, reward systems, affirmation of identities, and needs. As structures vary in the degree to which they induce relevant motives in individuals, they will vary in the rates of choice of alternatives to which those motives are relevant.

STRUCTURAL GOVERNANCE OF INFORMATION

Information is crucial to Merton's structural analysis. There seem to be three major mechanisms by which information flows affect the pattern of structured choice behaviour. First, sanctions depend on information. One person cannot sanction another for something he or she does not know the other has done. Second, information affects people's ideas about what choices they are confronted with. People do not choose alternatives they do not know about. Third, people use information in the concrete construction of successful activities, and success in an activity makes the activity more likely to continue.

Information and Sanctions

...Social groups so differ in organisation that some promote efficient 'feed-back' of 'information' to those who primarily regulate the behaviour of members, while others provide little by way of efficient feed-back. The structural conditions which make for ready observability or visibility of role-performance will of course provide appropriate feed-back when role-performance departs from the patterned expectations of the group. (Merton, 1968: 374)

The probability of rewards and punishments is a central feature of the motivational situation in structured choices, and this probability is centrally affected by information. For example, the rate of choice to speak frankly to physicians, lawyers and priests is affected by the confidentiality of those communications. The rate of choice of a professor saying what he thinks, instead of what he thinks socially acceptable, is affected by the low observability of the college classroom (*ibid.*: 427). The troublesomeness of an intellectual in a public bureaucracy is partly that he is likely to publish the arguments for a rejected alternative (*ibid.*: 277, by implication). Although I do not find the argument explicit, it is clear that one of the reasons the functions of a political machine for the rackets are latent rather than manifest is that if they were manifest the whole group would be in jail.

Information and Alternatives

The core of the argument in 'The Self-Fulfilling Prophecy' (Merton, 1948b) is that information about what collectively is likely to happen (whether it is a priori false or true) affects the rate of choice of individuals, which affects the probability of the collective outcome. Before depositors' insurance, runs on banks destroyed many banks. The 'knowledge' that there was a run on the bank therefore caused depositors to want to get their money out. As more banks failed because of runs, it took less information on a run to start one. Thus there was a cumulation within each bank of information on a run, causing rates of choice that produced a run, and a cumulation of collective consequences producing still further information on runs in the banking system as a whole, so that there was an acceleration in the number of bank failures up to the banking reform of the New Deal (Merton, 1968: 476–7).

Information on what is going to happen puts a future-oriented animal such as man into a different choice situation. One behaves differently toward a bank that will be solvent than toward a bank that will not be. One behaves differently in providing educational opportunities for black people when he or she 'knows' black people will fail than when he or she 'knows' they will succeed. In general, what we mean by 'reality' is what will happen, and what has already happened is of very little interest unless it influences the future.

Information and Success

Merton has spent much effort on the one institution in which collective success is almost purely determined by information, namely, science. In some ways, therefore, it is no sign of extraordinary acumen that he should notice that the flow of information determines the success of activities. The communism of information in science is vitally relevant to the success of each scientist in solving his or her own puzzles. The exponential growth of knowledge in physics had a sharp downturn during World War II, a downturn not made up by a spurt of accumulated creativity after the war (Hamblin *et al.*, 1973: 143, Figure 8.6). Presumably, this is directly related to the destruction of the communism of physics by secrecy in the interests of national security (whether it is a good idea to preserve national security by maiming physics is, of course, an infinitely debatable question). No one with any experience in scientific work would be likely to doubt that upwards of nine-tenths of what he or she knows is due to the giants from whom he or she has learned. And Merton's central contributions to the sociology of science do not consist in repeating the obvious.

Though the main subject of his work in seventeenth century science was the development of science itself, he was forced to construct a theory of the information needs of practical activity. The compass was only really useful when the error of measurement of direction at different points (due to the displacement of the magnetic poles from the geographical poles) was known (Merton, 1968: 673–4). Clearly, knowing which direction is north contributes to one's success in arriving where one wants to arrive. And success in navigation was important to the social support of astronomical and magnetic investigations. The social patterning of information flows thus influences rates of socially significant choices by influencing the sanctions attached to choices, by influencing the perceived alternatives between which people choose, and by influencing the rate of success of the alternative chosen.

Structural Patterns of Sanctioning Power

Besides knowing whom to reward and punish, a person or group has to be able to reward and punish in order to control behaviour. The rate at which a person will choose to behave in a way that offends or helps another depends on whether the other can punish or reward that person. The two central mechanisms that Merton discusses are power and usefulness. These are not conceptually radically distinct, but their connotations are quite diverse. Roughly speaking 'power' connotes the capacity to get another person something (or to deny him or her something) from society at large. Thus the capacity of a bureaucratic superior to allocate blame for mistakes to his or her subordinates rests on his or her special access to organizational blame-allocating centres. This is organizationally generated power, which produces fearful ritualism in subordinates (Merton, 1968: 249–60). The cosmopolitan's 'influence' is interpreted primarily in terms of his or her 'usefulness' for, for example, managing the cultural life of Rovere (*ibid.*: 461). The distinction could be described as a strategic place in the social flow of rewards and punishments ('power') versus a strategic place in the social production of rewards and punishments ('usefulness').

Aside from information determinants of this placement in the flow of rewards and punishments, discussed above, Merton has not systematically analyzed power systems and their implications. Consequently, I will leave the topic with the note that a systematic account of the implicit theories of power in the variety of Merton's structural essays would repay the effort.

STRUCTURAL OUTPUTS OF PATTERNED CHOICE

Latent and Manifest Outputs

The output of one of these systems of patterned choice is socially organized behaviour. But Merton's crucial interest is how such patterns fold back on themselves to maintain or undermine the pattern, or otherwise to affect the structure as a whole. As a rough scheme, not to be taken too seriously, I would distinguish five types of structural implication for this causal folding back: manifest and latent functions; manifest and latent structural locations of an output; and deviant 'symptoms' of these four realities. This is all very abstract, so let me carry through an example.

When analyzing the place of publication in science, Merton talks about at least five different kinds of things. First, he speaks of the manifest function of speeding information. Since most research workers in a field read important results before they are published, and many volumes of journals are never checked out even in leading research libraries, this manifest function cannot be the whole story. Second, there are at least two latent functions of publication, namely, establishing priority for scientific discoveries and the validation to oneself that the discovery (and hence the life that went into making such a discovery) is important. This was analyzed above. Third, there is the structural place of the manifest function in the norm of the communism of science. Publication is one of many institutional devices (university education is another) that manifest the norm of communism in science, that people ought not to be excluded from ideas for one's personal benefit. The latent structural place of the output is on the curriculum vitae of the individual scientist, and consequently in the promotion system of universities and the inter-university competition for prestige and resources. That is, the latent social processing of the output is processing in scientific status systems, and it is the fact that there is a firm social structure processing the latent output (priority claims) that makes the system hang together. This is what makes the latent function of establishing priority by publication a critical one—one that makes it likely that the latent function will maintain the practice even when the manifest function is hollow. The solid social location of the latent function then produces pressures for 'deviant' behaviour according to the manifest institution of communism, namely, bitter fights over priority, over 'private property' rights in ideas. Fights over priority are not latent functions (perhaps latent dysfunctions), but rather symptoms that all is not as it seems. Sensitivity to socially patterned deviance is one of the skills Merton repeatedly uses to locate these systems of intertwined manifest and latent functions with their corresponding structural location (see Zuckerman and Merton, 1971; Merton, 1969; and Merton, 1968: 604–15).

We see the same pattern in the analysis of the political machine. The diagnostic symptom is patterned behaviour deviant from good government democratic norms (though obviously dependent on democratic norms). The latent functions include 'help, not justice', service to illegitimate business, decision-making capacity in a system of decentralized formal powers and so on. The manifest structural place of the output is the institution of democratically elected local government. The latent structural place is an organized system of ethnic groups, big businesses, illegitimate businesses and their markets and so on, which turns the latent functions into a reliable supply of social capital for the machine. Just as the tenure decision has no formal structural place in the communism of science, so the whorehouse has no formal provision in the City Charter (Merton, 1968: 73–138).

The crucial point here is that latent functions are not merely outputs of a pattern of choice that happen to come about but strategic inputs for other structures in the system as a whole. This strategic quality in turn makes them into effective causes of the maintenance of the pattern. Happenstance outputs that some people happen to like and others not to like will not effectively fold back causally to maintain the pattern.

Structural Patterns of Individual Risks

A second type of output of a patterned choice is a social distribution of life chances. The differential risk of different social classes for ending up in prison is an example. The point of the 'Social Structure and Anomie' paper is that these differential risks are built into the structure of the society and are characteristics of the structural position rather than of the individual in it. The point to note, then, is that a subtle psychological mechanism of strain in people's reactions to ends and means produces a characteristic of a social position. Such subtle transformation of levels is a speciality of Merton's. It serves the latent function for a discipline unsure of its identity of allowing us to be psychologically subtle while proclaiming our non-psychological character—nothing here but social class, the most eminently sociological of all ways to get psychology into the discipline.

WHY IT WORKS

Let me now suppose both that I have correctly identified the paradigm behind the paradigms in Merton's work on social structure and that I am right that this work has started more (and more penetrating) traditions of empirical research than that of other contemporary theorists. How might we explain this superiority?

First, I do not agree with Merton's implicit diagnosis that it is because he works on 'theories of the middle range' (1968: 39–72). It seems to me that in the dialectic between Parsons and Merton, generality has been confused with woolliness. Merton, in taking up the correct position on woolliness, has tricked himself into taking up the incorrect position on general theory. The true situation is precisely the opposite. It is because Merton has a better general theory than Parsons that his work has been more empirically fruitful. I will discuss this under the traditional general virtues of theories: elegance, power or fruitfulness, economy, precision.

Elegance

Making consensual aesthetic judgments of theories is harder than making other kinds of judgments. But I think two aspects of aesthetic experience in sociological theory would get wide assent. The most fundamental is the capacity of a theory to say with the same set of statements something complex and realistic about individual people and what they are up to and something complex and realistic about a social pattern. The impact of George Herbert Mead or Max Weber is partly explained by the fact that they both make people and structures real. Much of the sparely classical beauty of economics comes from the easy translation between market equilibria and striving individuals.

The central intractable problem for sociology has been the relation of individuals to the social order. The drive to 'bring men back in' (Homans, 1961), to develop a 'naturalistic sociology' (Matza, 1969), reflects dissatisfaction with the crude picture of individuals that structural explanations tend to give. Although the defence of professional monopoly has altogether too much to do with objections to explanations as being 'too psychological', there is also a flat obvious quality to explanations of social behaviour that come down to 'they did it because they wanted to' or 'they did it because of their thalamus'.

Merton's theoretical structure provides multiple opportunities to move back and forth from striving or thalamic men to social structural outcomes. Sometimes the psychology is obvious, as when people do not react to what they do not know about. Sometimes, as the case of audiences as central structural units in the sociology of knowledge, the connection between the behaviour of individuals and the structure is extraordinarily complex. Merton gains this aesthetic effect principally by modifying the structural concepts so that people fit as natural parts of them. A role-set is a much easier thing into which to fit one's experience of trying to figure out what a professor is supposed to do than is a Linton role. A notion of deviance that says there is something wrong with ritualistic overconformity, that the rule-bound petty officer tyrant was not what we had in mind when we passed the rules, rings truer to our experience of conformity and deviance.

If the kernel of aesthetic experience in sociological theory is the unity of social and psychological statement, the outer covering is irony. Good comes from evil, complexity from simplicity, crime from morality; saints stink while whores smell good; trade unions and strikes lead to industrial peace under a rule of law and a collective contract; law and order candidates are fond of burglary. Merton clearly loves irony. He is most pleased to find motives of advancing knowledge creating priority conflicts among scientists, and hardly interested in the fact that such motives also advance knowledge. He likes to find political bosses helping people while good government types turn a cold shoulder. He likes to range Engels and functionalists down parallel columns to show them to be really the same. The immediate subjective feeling that one has learned something from reading Merton is probably mainly due to the taste for irony.

A third aesthetic advantage is closely related to irony: the onion-like layers of the theories. That is, like Lévi-Strauss or Freud or Marx, the aesthetic effects of Merton's theory have to do with the process of moving from a more superficial view of a matter to a deeper underlying view. The onion looks brown, then light tan, then white but coarse, then white but fine-grained. Just as some of the finest effects in novels consist of shifts in point of view, so in social theory a layered structure gives an impression of movement, of learning, of an active social scientist figuring things out. There is more feeling of motion in Merton's essays than in most social theorizing.

Aesthetic qualities of a theory make it more useful in two ways. First, it makes it easier to persuade yourself to work with it, makes it fun to read and fun to play with. There is nothing duller to think about than 'Is social class really related to delinquency?' We would not have the right answer now (yes, but not strongly related) if we had not had something interesting to think about in the tedium of collecting the data.

The second is that aesthetic experience encourages a shift in perspective, breaks up and reforms the moulds in the mind. I do not know a good analysis of the relation between aesthetic experience and creativity, but I offer the empirical generalization that people who cannot experience a thrill at a beautiful idea hardly ever amount to anything in a science.

Power or Fruitfulness

In some ways the body of this essay is directed at showing, first, that there is a general theory of social action in Merton's work and, second, that it is fruitful in many different empirical problems. I have commented about how, for example, the power of the theory allows diverse evidence from history to survey research to be brought to bear on the same empirical problem. The power has its most obvious (because easiest) manifestation in the apparent effortlessness of the destructive criticism of other theorists in his essays on functionalism and on the sociology of knowledge. If it were really as easy as it looks, brilliant minds like Malinowski or Sorokin could have done it.

However, the crucial benefits in explanatory power come from two general characteristics of the theory. First, it combines attention to stability and maintenance of social patterns with attention to disruption of them. In the nature of things, if there is an equilibrium or self-maintaining state of a system, the state one is most likely to observe is that equilibrium state. If in a given setting a political machine is a self-maintaining state, then one common structure that will be found there is a machine. As in a Markov process with absorbing states, eventually everything ends up absorbed. This means that Merton's equilibrium theory has an inherent tendency to be about states of the system that are most commonly observed. But further, it focuses on the sources of variation and tension that explain deviations from these most commonly observed states. Whenever an equilibrium theory is something more than a vague notion that things will probably all work out for the best, it has an inherent advantage in explanatory power.

The second main explanatory power advantage of Merton's general theory is that it focuses attention on social magnification processes. For example, racketeers want to make money. But by being organized into a system together with legitimate business and with ethnic groups with precarious citizenship, both their capacity to make money is increased and the canalization of that impulse and the money by the machine produces a large impact on, for example, the judicial system. By canalizing the impulse to establish priority into early publication, scientific journals magnify the impulse to gain prestige from communicating results and maximize its impact on the speed of communication and on the norm of communism of knowledge. By monopolizing medical licensing and access to hospitals, and enrolling most of the profession, the American Medical Association increases the power of consensual norms in the profession about what a physician should be and becomes a stronger reference group for aspiring physicians. Magnification and canalization of causes create discriminating impacts, thus increasing the information content of a theory of causes.

The crucial feature of the theorizing that does this job of focusing on magnification is the constant attention to the structural location of a given pattern of choice. It is the structural location of corruption in the machine that makes it more than random temptation of public officials. It is the institutionalization of priority in the communication process itself that magnifies the impulse to publish. It is the location of a reference group in the power system that makes it a crucial channel for transmitting ideals.

Economy

There is one trivial kind of economy in social theorizing which many of us could learn with profit: the willingness to write about one thing at a time. The brunt of one version of 'scholarly' norms in social theorizing is that one should always introduce distinctions that might be useful in some other situation, but do not bear on the problem at hand, in order to show awareness of the tradition of the discipline. The frequent experience of not quite knowing the subject of a theoretical essay is partly due to our penchant for writing books to be entitled *The Social System* or *Economy and Society*, *The Rules of Sociological Method* and *Constructing Social Theories*, which give a cover for introducing bright ideas in the order they occur to the author. A book with a pretentious title like *Social Theory and Social Structure* is much more palatable if made up of essays making one argument at a time. It is easy in Merton to figure out which idea is being talked about at which time and what is the relevance of a conceptual distinction to that idea. Besides being an epistemological principle, Occam's razor is also a principle of rhetoric—not to clutter an argument with multiplied conceptual entities.

But I have tried to show above that the great variety of Merton's empirical theories is generated from a small set of common elements, organized around a core theory of rates of choice among socially structured alternatives. A half dozen or so major elements, in two or three major varieties each, generate structurally similar theories in a wide variety of empirical situations.

Precision

Perhaps the main epistemological mistake of sociologists is to confuse generality with lack of specificity. Newton in generalizing the theory of gravitation did not say the Earth goes sort of around the Sun, and Mars goes sort of around slower and farther out, and this is the same general kind of thing as rolling balls down an inclined plane. The theory of gravitation is simultaneously very general and very specific about exactly what will happen under various exactly described circumstances. The sociological tradition that defines a theorist by the absence of exact empirical description and prediction is completely foreign to the tradition of theorizing in the mature sciences.

Merton's theory is set up to explain variations, specifically variations in rates of choice. It is a perfectly answerable empirical question whether the establishment of scientific journals decreased the time between major discoveries and the use of those discoveries in further scientific work. The generality of the notion of socially structured alternatives is no bar to precise predictions about the rate of scientific communication. The generality of latent functions is no bar to a precise prediction about which kinds of political structures will collect higher rates of contributions from rackets. The structural distribution of delinquency and hyperconformity is precisely predictable from the argument of social structure and anomie.

There are two main elements to this precision. The first is that Merton never loses sight of the fact that the only thing that can be explained is variation. This means that no scientific theory can ever be about less than four things: two states of the effect and two states of the cause. The frequency with which this elementary matter is left implicit in sociological theorizing is little short of astounding. Whatever, for example, causes role conformity, its absence has to cause something else. That something else is a phenomenon out in the world, which has to be described before one knows what role conformity is and, consequently, what has to be explained. An entirely fictional portrayal of a Hobbesian state of nature will not do for the other end of the variable of conformity. Merton puts various phenomena at the other end, depending on his purpose—concealment or role audience segregation, having a bad attitude toward the army, hyperconformity of a ritualistic kind, solving problems by political machine methods and so on. Contextually, then, role conformity becomes a number of different things, resulting in greater conceptual precision. Further, a distance between two people or two structures along one of these conceptual scales becomes an intractable fact to be explained. Because it is conformity as opposed to ritualism, or as opposed to role segregation, or as opposed to something else, the distance between a more conforming and a less conforming person means something precise. Distances along different scales then have different explanations, but one is not reduced to 'multiple causation' or 'failure of a system to meet its functional requisites' to explain deviance.

Yet this precision is not lack of generality. Visibility occupies a stable place in the general conceptual scheme, bearing the same relation to other concepts in a wide variety of empirical circumstances. Hollow conformity likewise, at least ideally, occupies the same place when it is pretending to pursue a manifest function while really being after a latent one, as it does when it is a kind of behaviour especially characteristic of the lower middle class or of the bureaucratic personality.

Critique

This last example, however, illustrates the main difficulty of Merton's way of proceeding. Because the general theory is nowhere extracted and systematized, we are not quite sure that hollow conformity to a manifest function is exactly the same as hollow ritualism of the lower middle class, bearing the same relation to other major concepts in the system. The piecemeal presentation of the theory makes a primary virtue of its power, its extensibility into many empirical areas. Taken as a whole, the structure of the corpus of theoretical work does not forcefully communicate the elegance, economy and precision of the theory. This makes it hard to work on the lacunae.

CONCLUSION

I argued at the beginning that the core process that Merton conceives as central to social structure is the choice between socially structured alternatives. I have chosen the term 'core process' rather than independent or dependent variable for rates of choice between structured alternatives because the causal chain goes both ways. The reason it goes forward from the rates of choice is that alternatives are socially structured exactly because they are institutionally consequential. The reason the causal chain goes backward is that many aspects of structural position determine the exact nature of the structuring of alternatives for particular people.

To this basic linking process which connects structural forces to institutionally consequential choices, and thence to institutional patterns, Merton adds two kinds of causal loops. The first is the one for which he is perhaps best known, namely, the recasting of the nature of functional analysis so that institutional consequences of action act back to shape the nature of the alternatives that people are posed with. The second kind of loop is the historical development of a social character out of a systematic biographical patterning of choices. This second loop is a feedback through character formation which produces personal continuities in the kind of link a given person is between structural pressures and patterns of choice behaviour. Figure 7.1 gives a schematic outline of this structure which is common to Merton's theorizing.

I would like to conclude by making a brief comment about the relation of Merton's theoretical structure to the historical tradition of sociological theory. The striking thing about it is how many elements of different traditions there are in it, traditions that have thought themselves opposed. The core process of choice between socially structured alternatives owes a great deal (explicitly acknowledged) to the W. I. Thomas-G. H. Mead analysis of definitions of situations and self-conceptions. Where it differs from much work derived from that tradition is *not* adding to it the hopeless proposition: 'God only knows what definitions people will give to situations.'

The focus on institutional consequences of choices owes a great deal to the functionalist tradition, again thoroughly acknowledged. But Merton does not add the untrue proposition that institutions will always manage to get people to behave in the way required for their effective functioning. The analyses of character and biography clearly owe a good deal to Freud and the neo-Freudians, to Thomas's typology of character types, and many other sources. But Merton adds neither theories of the limited variety of characters that might be produced, nor theories of

Figure 7.1   Schematic Outline of the Common Theoretical Structure of Merton's Analyses

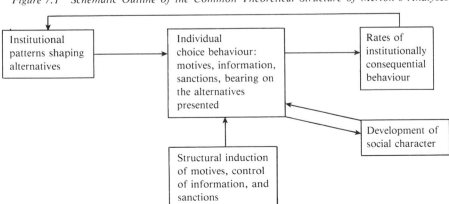

the indelibility of early experience, to the core perception of socially formed character structure.

What we find repeatedly is a free willingness to borrow and a free willingness to shear off from the borrowings the grandiosity and sectarianism of the originals, which made them fit uncomfortably with other processes in an overall theory. We will each be well served in the history of social theory if our successors constantly behave like Merton and refuse to adopt our dogmatisms while adopting our virtues.

ACKNOWLEDGMENT

This is a revised version of a paper which first appeared in L. Coser (ed), *The Idea of Social Structure*, New York, Harcourt-Brace Jovanovich, pp. 11–33. It was subsequently republished in A. Stinchcombe, *Stratification and Organization— Selected Papers*, Cambridge, Cambridge University Press, pp. 290–308.

NOTE

1   The attribution to Parsons of a social choice theory is genetic in the sense that he has never renounced the orientation of *The Structure of Social Action* (1937), especially the introductory essay. People have become much less active choosers of what to value and what to do about those values as Parsonian theory has 'matured'. It would be hard to tell from Parsons's later writings that this was a theory of socially conditioned choices of the meanings of actions.

8. R. K. Merton on Structural Analysis

ANTHONY GIDDENS

Anyone considering Merton's work must give prime place to *Social Theory and Social Structure*. This magisterial work assembles in coherent form the extraordinary diversity of Merton's contributions to sociology. The book, or some of the most important sections of it, has for decades been required reading for all sociology students. Yet if one looks at the title of the work, and compares it with the contents of the essays it contains, a noticeable imbalance is seen. The volume contains extended discussions of the nature of 'theory' in sociology and the other social sciences. Merton presents historical analyses of the development of social theory (although he often speaks of 'sociological theory' instead), sets out a 'codification' of theory in a detailed way, and provides a systematic interpretation of the proper relation between theory and empirical research. Yet no extended discussion of the concept of 'structure' is offered at all. To understand what Merton means by 'social structure', and why he regards the identification of structural forms as so significant in sociology, one has to turn to textual emendation—Merton's interpretation of the concept has to be pieced together from a diversity of contexts in which it is mentioned or alluded to.

Why is there so little discussion of 'structure' in a book which bears the term as a key part of its title? There are probably two reasons. One Merton shared with a whole generation of sociologists writing in the early post-war period. Pointing to the existence of structural characteristics of human societies, moulding and constraining human actions, became one of the main ways in which sociologists discerned a subject-matter for themselves. How many sociologists even today begin introductory courses by trying to show that the individual agent is not after all the author of his or her actions? Durkheim's *Suicide* has an enduring popularity in introductory sociology just because it apparently makes the point so well: even an individual involved in a solitary act of self-destruction bears the stamp of social influences. The point became so generally accepted that few sought to question it. Merton's work seems to bear witness to this phenomenon. The concept of social structure is presumed to be so fundamental to sociological study, and so unobjectionable, that it can be left unanalyzed.

A second reason is more to do with the specific orientation which Merton took in working out his view of the nature of sociology. Such an orientation aptly came to be called 'structural-functionalism'—structural analysis is so closely tied to a functional approach in sociology that the two are more or less inseparable. This point appears central to *Social Theory and Social Structure*, although Merton has modified it somewhat in subsequent writings.

MERTON'S CONCEPT OF STRUCTURE

Let me provide a brief exegesis of Merton's use of the notion of structure in *Social Theory and Social Structure*. There is only one point in the book, so far as I can see, where he offers something close to a definition of the concept. This occurs in the paper 'Social Structure and Anomie'. Analyzing the idea of anomie, Merton is concerned to emphasize that this does not represent a state of mind, or psychological outlook, but refers to conditions of social organization. Anomie, specifically, derives from a tension between a set of normative values in a society and the structure within which agents seek to realize those values. Merton writes as follows: '...by social structure is meant that organised set of social relationships in which members of the society or group are variously implicated.... The social structure strains the cultural values, making action in accord with them readily possible for those occupying certain statuses within the society and difficult or impossible for others.... The social structure acts as a barrier or as an open door to the acting out of cultural mandates' (1968: 216–17). The definition is a very brief one, and it is introduced almost casually. Moreover, Merton does not limit the term 'structure' to the area of social relationships. In the same passage, for example, he talks of anomie as a 'breakdown in the cultural structure'. The term 'cultural structure' is not elaborated in any way.

On virtually every occasion in *Social Theory and Social Structure* in which Merton makes reference to structure, this occurs in conjunction with an analysis of functions (or dysfunctions). Thus in his account of anomie the disjunction between social structure and cultural values produces various dysfunctions for the wider social system, coupled with various forms of functional adaptation to the strains involved. Merton makes clear the connections between structure and function in his overall presentation of the character of functional analysis in the social sciences. Functional analysis, he says, must not be focused simply upon the 'statics' of social structure. It must examine the 'dynamics' of social change, together with connecting functions and dysfunctions. Functional study, he continues, must 'explore the interdependent and often mutually supporting elements of social structure'. Social structures do not consist of a random arrangement of traits, but tend to involve mutually interconnected and sustaining attributes. Yet they also incorporate 'strains and stresses... which accumulate as dysfunctional consequences (which) will in due course lead to institutional breakdown and basic social change' (*ibid.*: 94–5).

Functional analysis, as Merton presents it, depends strongly upon the identification of structural constraint. In any given social context there is a limited range of social items which can satisfy the functional requirements of a larger system. A functionalist approach identifies what these requirements are and the range of possible variation in the items which can meet them. In close relation to this emphasis Merton introduces his celebrated distinction between manifest and latent functions. We must distinguish between the motivations for social action and the objective consequences it has. The distinction, interestingly, is taken from Freud's account of dreaming. Dreams have a 'manifest' content which conceals the 'latent' meanings that can be discerned below the surface form of the 'story line'. Latent functions are 'below the threshold' of the consciousness of lay agents in society.

Distinguishing between manifest and latent functions, according to Merton, serves to illuminate apparently irrational forms of social activity. Many social phenomena which persist, even though they do not achieve their manifest purposes, serve latent functions. The rain ceremonials among the Hopi indians do not bring rain, but have the latent function of reinforcing group identity through providing the circumstances for the collective assembly of otherwise scattered individuals. What is apparently merely a 'superstition' or 'survival' turns out to have a rational basis, although one unknown to the participants themselves.

Merton also proffers an analysis of 'machine politics' as a means of illustrating functional theory. Political machines are regarded disapprovingly by the general public, and at times contravene the law. Yet they show little sign of disappearing. Why? What accounts for their persistence? Merton answers these questions in functional terms, and along the way makes intrinsic reference to the properties of social structure. The main latent function of the political machine is to provide for the centralization of political power in a society in which it is widely dispersed and fragmentary. As Merton puts it: 'the functional deficiencies of the official structure generate an alternative (unofficial) structure to fulfil existing needs somewhat more effectively' (*ibid.*: 127). The 'structural context' renders it difficult or impossible for morally approved modes of organization to 'fulfil essential social functions', providing a situation in which the political machine steps in.

Merton's discussion of the political machine connects directly to his conception of social structure and anomie. Machine politics fulfil the function of opening out paths of social mobility for those who would otherwise be unable to live up to the success goals of the society. Those from social backgrounds which prevent them rising through 'respectable' means find in the political machine a way of achieving power and often wealth. Merton concludes with a general proposition: 'the social functions of an organisation help determine the structure (including the recruitment of personnel involved in the structure), just as the structure helps determine the effectiveness with which the functions are fulfilled.... Structure affects function and function affects structure' (*ibid.*: 136).

Among publications of Merton subsequent to *Social Theory and Social Structure* one stands out as particularly relevant to the issues under consideration here: an article entitled 'Structural Analysis in Sociology', published in 1975. In this paper Merton takes a position seemingly at odds with his earlier formulations about the character of sociology. Whereas he previously spoke of the 'codification' of social theory, in which a functional approach plays an indispensable part, he now seems to hold that sociology is irremediably pluralistic. What he has come to call 'structural analysis' is one among other theoretical orientations in sociology and 'must find its evolving place' (*ibid.*: 52). In contrast to his earlier discussion, Merton here mentions structuralism for the first time—although in order to distance himself from it and to emphasize that structural analysis emerged before, and is more deeply embedded in the social sciences as a whole, than is structuralist thought.

Structural analysis, Merton avers, is distinctively connected to functionalism. He compares the distinction between manifest and latent functions to the structuralist differentiation between 'surface' and 'deep' structures, although the point is not elaborated. Drawing upon the work of Arthur Stinchcombe, Merton argues that the central process involved in social structure is the existence of structured alternatives of action. Structure, in other words, limits the alternatives open to agents in any given context of activity. Social structure, he adds, always involves diversification, contradiction and conflict. Change is brought about as a result of structural strains and derives from an accumulation of dysfunctional consequences. Structural analysis, Merton stresses, is not intrinsically linked to any particular view of the substantive nature of social systems. It is as much a part of most versions of Marxism, for example, as it is an element of the 'normative functionalism' of Talcott Parsons.

SUBSEQUENT ELABORATIONS

It is always far easier to tear down than to construct, to find flaws in ideas rather than to produce them in the first place. The exposition of functional theory Merton offered in *Social Theory and Social Structure*, and the manner in which he connected this with 'social structure' in his more concrete analyses, were deeply impressive contributions. Yet it cannot be claimed that Merton provided a developed justification for the importance he attached to social structure, nor indeed even at any point a satisfactory exposition of the notion and its implications. The article on 'Structural Analysis in Sociology' concentrates more upon the theme of pluralism than upon elucidating the properties of structure. The fact that Merton speaks of 'structural analysis' rather than of 'functional analysis' in the paper has been taken by some to mark a distinctive break between his earlier work and his later position. If such a break does exist, it is not very dramatic and Merton has not detailed what exactly he may have abandoned in his original viewpoint. Merton says that functional analysis 'has evolved, over the years, into a distinct mode of structural analysis' (1976a: ix). But it has been left to Merton's interpreters and followers to provide a more thoroughgoing explication of structural analysis than Merton himself has given.

According to Sztompka (1986: 145–6) structural analysis *à la* Merton involves the following features:

1   a focus upon relationships between individuals or groups in society;
2   a stress upon the patterned character of such relationships;
3   an emphasis upon underlying structural characteristics of systems which it is the task of the sociologist to unearth;
4   a focus upon the ways in which social structure either constrains or facilitates forms of individual behaviour.

Sztompka refers to these four characteristics as the 'generic notion' of social structure, which he distinguishes from Merton's 'specific notion'. The more specific concept of social structure emphasizes its multidimensional character, as made up of numerous forms of groups, organizations, roles and statuses, norms and so forth.

Tensions and conflicts tend to be endemic within the diversified nature of structural relationships. In addition, this conception of social structure is 'auto-dynamic', generating transformations from within itself as a result of such tensions and conflicts. In terms of these two ideas of social structure, Sztompka argues, 'structural analysis' can mean two things: the study of social structure in a generic fashion, or analysis which situates actors and groups within structural contexts. The first of these two senses is very generalized, and covers every type of sociological analysis; only the second refers to a distinct type of orientation to social theory, which Sztompka identifies as 'sociological structuralism'. The objective of sociological structuralism is to examine a given item of behaviour or agent in terms of their positions within larger structured wholes. In Sztompka's words:

> [T]o paraphrase Merton's characterisation of functional analysis, one may say that the central orientation of structural analysis is the practice of interpreting data by establishing their determinants in the larger structures in which they are implicated.... Structural explanations are in principle valid in form, free from the risk of finalism or teleology, since they do not refer to any succeeding events or states of the social system, but rather to conditions preceding, or at most concurrent with the problematic phenomena. (*ibid*.: 4)

An example, in his view, is Merton's demonstration that social structures can exert a definite pressure upon individuals to engage in non-conforming conduct, as specified in the discussion of anomie.

Sztompka accepts that structural analysis thus defined can only be carried on in a functionalist framework. Structural and functional analysis are complementary, since the former looks for the determinants of a particular social item or phenomenon, while the latter traces its consequences. Something of a similar point of view is advanced by Stinchcombe (1975) in his attempt to systematize Merton's somewhat fragmentary thinking on these issues. In Stinchcombe's formulation the structural aspect of Merton's approach involves identifying the mechanisms which serve to define the alternative possibilities of action in any given social situation. The functional aspect concerns the ways in which alternative channels of action produce specific types of consequence for the wider social system. Drawing upon his own interpretation of functional theory, Stinchcombe proposes that structural analysis involves a causal process which goes from 'structural forces to institutionally consequential choices, and thence to institutional patterns'. According to Stinchcombe's interpretation of the logic of functional theory, functional consequences can be understood as feedback systems or causal loops. The consequences of actions which individuals or groups undertake act to reshape the alternatives with which they are faced. There is a variant of this phenomenon which Stinchcombe singles out as important. This is where the repetition of particular choices shapes 'social character', thereby conditioning choices for the future. Structural mechanisms constrain agents in an 'internal' fashion insofar as they enter into people's outlook and thereby influence what they do.

ASSESSMENT: THE PROBLEM OF FUNCTIONAL ANALYSIS

In assessing Merton's standpoint, of course, it would not be reasonable to concentrate wholly upon the formulations which others have developed on the basis of his ideas. The views set out in *Social Theory and Social Structure* remain the basic source for anyone concerned to discuss Merton's position, if only because the subsequent writings in which Merton seems to have partly modified his ideas are relatively slight in nature. We must therefore look at some of the shortcomings in Merton's early account of functional theory before moving on to consider latter-day elaborations of them. I should make my own position clear at the outset. In my view the concept of 'function' has no place in the social sciences and it is best to jettison it altogether. Moreover, I do not believe there is any such animal as 'functional explanation'. Insofar as Merton's approach to structural analysis depends upon functionalism, so much the worse for it.

It is many years since Merton's 'codification' of functionalism first appeared in print and by now numerous critical evaluations of it have been published. Thus the issues involved can be covered in fairly brief fashion. Let us first of all accept that many of Merton's own critical comments, directed at other versions of functionalism, were (and to some extent are) justified. It is a mistake to see human societies, especially the more complex types, as intrinsically consensual (the postulate of functional unity). It is an error to suppose that authors who either overtly employ the concept of 'function', or more covertly make use of 'functional explanations', are conservative in their ideological orientation. The introduction of a notion of 'dysfunction' points the way towards analyzing tensions and struggles in social systems.

Yet much of what Merton has to say in a positive way about functional analysis is either ambiguous or questionable. The distinction between manifest and latent functions, for instance, is not clearly worked out. The notion of 'manifest function' covers at least three phenomena: the intentions or purposes agents have in engaging in a given item of behaviour; the consequences they foresee in undertaking that behaviour; and the reasons actors have for doing what they do. These are not trivial differentiations. One may engage in a piece of behaviour, intending to reach a given objective, but without being able to foresee in a clear way the consequences likely to stem from it. The reasons one has for one's behaviour go beyond what one intends to do, and normally involve some assessment of the consequences of pursuing a given path of action. Consider Merton's example of the Hopi rain ceremonial. Those who attend the ceremonial presumably intend to help bring about rain to irrigate their crops. They foresee the arrival of rain as the consequence of their activity, but do not understand that one of the consequences of their regular meetings is to cohere the group. Individuals might have any number of reasons, however, for participating in the ceremonials. The wish to bring rain may be one of these reasons, but many others are likely to be involved—such as that non-attendance results in sanctions, or that it is simply recognized as 'something everyone does'. The term 'manifest function' papers over a variety of possible subjective orientations. One extremely important possibility is where at least some of the Hopi recognize that a consequence of the ceremonials is to foster group integration. It is rather difficult to believe that only sociologists would be able to see that regular assemblies tend to have the consequence of holding the group together. Insofar as some, most or all of the participants in the assembly realize what is going on in this respect, the causal elements involved in the reproduction of the ceremonial are quite distinct from where they do not.

The separation of manifest from latent functions is supposed to clarify seemingly irrational social practices. Activities which appear to be mere superstitions, or to result from human ignorance, are shown to have underlying 'structural value' where they fulfil latent functions. Calling something a 'superstition', Merton says, 'is simply a case of name calling' (1968: 118). But the same could be said of applying the label 'latent function'. If an item of behaviour has a functional consequence of which participants are unaware, this has absolutely no bearing whatsoever upon the irrationality or otherwise of their actions. What Merton is doing here, although he does not put it into so many words, is to substitute 'society's reasons' for those of the individuals engaged in the activities in question. But societies are not beings and do not have reasons for anything at all. To indicate that a social item has functional consequences for a wider social system, where those consequences are unknown to participants, shows nothing about why that item continues to exist. The same point can be made in respect of Merton's discussion of the political machine. To show that machine politics have functional outcomes which act to further the continuity of aspects of the wider social system does not explain why the political machine exists.

Use of the concept 'function' (and, for that matter, 'dysfunction') is thus unhelpful because: (1) the idea of 'manifest function' fails adequately to address basic aspects of human subjectivity relevant to the consequences of actions; and (2) explanation in terms of latent functions has no legitimate logical basis. The only instance in which we can justifiably speak of explaining an activity in terms of functions is in respect of one particular meaning of *manifest function*. This is the case mentioned above—where the functional consequence is known to participants and applied as one of the reasons for their behaviour. Functional interpretation, in my view, is only useful in the social sciences where it takes the form of counterfactual questions—which, of course, then have to be answered. In posing such questions, however, the term 'function' does not need to appear at all. We can ask: 'what would happen to item X if consequence Y were not regularly found?' This is not an explanation, but a call for one. Thus Merton's discussion of machine politics suggests interesting issues for social research and theory, although it does not offer an explanation of the phenomenon. We could ask: 'what would happen if the political machine did not exist?' on the basis of the intuition that machine politics have certain unintended consequences for the overall social system. Counterfactual thinking of such a kind plays a prime role in social analysis.

Much of this is by now generally accepted, particularly as a result of the debates involved in the 'newer controversy' over functionalism, as contrasted to that of the 1960s and early 1970s. During the former period of critique, functional theory was attacked primarily because of its presumed connection with a conservative outlook —something Merton, as has been mentioned, has consistently sought to distance himself from. The second period of controversy has concentrated more upon whether or not analysis in terms of unintended outcomes can, or should, be developed in functionalist terms. In this latter-day discussion, various somewhat novel defences of functionalist thought have been proposed. An example can be found in G. A. Cohen's attempt to reinterpret the logical nature of historical materialism (Cohen, 1978); a second appears in the work of Stinchcombe, noted above. We could readily adapt Merton's illustration of machine politics to illustrate the approach developed by Cohen and others who have been influenced by his arguments. In his defence of functional analysis Cohen brings into play the notion of 'dispositional facts' of social systems, a concept borrowed from the study of evolutionary biology. Consider the example of the long neck of the giraffe. The giraffe's long neck developed causally as a result of particular mutations altering genetic inheritance. A viable functional interpretation of the survival of long-necked giraffes is that it was a dispositional fact that long-necked giraffes have greater chances of reproductive survival than shorter-necked animals of the same species. Importing the example back into sociology, we can say that the beneficial effects for the overall system of the operation of the political machine act to ensure its survival. In the absence of these effects, machine politics would disappear much more readily than is the case. Dispositional facts of this type, it might be argued, are facts about social systems, not the states of mind of actors, and thus can figure legitimately as explanations in terms of 'structural causes'. In these terms we can account, not for the origins of the political machine, but for its entrenched character.

Can we say that anything has been explained here? The answer is that we cannot. From the dispositional fact that machine politics are beneficial to the continuity of the wider social system we cannot account for its persistence, without adding further explanatory factors into the account. We would have to show what the actual causal mechanisms are which lead influences to 'find their way' from machine politics to the wider social system and back again. In principle there are two guises in which such an account could be worked out, although in practice these mingle in a complicated way. The influences in question may be fostered through the actions of individuals who are aware of what is going on; or they may derive from a feedback cycle which no one reflexively monitors. It is only when we identify what 'happens' in such a cycle that we have an explanation of the phenomenon in question, namely the 'engrained' character of machine politics.

Stinchcombe's discussion of the logic of explanation in the social sciences, both in respect of Merton's work and in other analyses, provides an exposition of the logic of feedback mechanisms or 'causal loops'. There can be no objection to the proposal that causal relations of this type are frequently found in social systems, and are mediated through the unintended or unforeseen consequences of actions. But I think it a mistake to regard this as 'functional explanation', or to invoke the notion of function within it. Otherwise we are back in the illegitimate realm of 'society's reasons'. In Stinchcombe's discussion, and defence of, functionalist theory this kind of imagery still turns up quite often. For example, he gives the illustration that clear rules of succession tend to be more well established among upper class than lower class groups, claiming that this presumes a functional explanation of succession rules. 'Society', he continues, 'so to speak, tries hard to resolve succession conflicts when they are more severe'. He also follows Merton in suggesting that where reasons offered by actors seem to the analyst inadequate, we should start looking for latent functions. As I have mentioned previously, I do not think there is any validity in this at all. The adequacy or otherwise of the explanations agents give for their actions might direct our attention to the nature of their discursive capabilities, or perhaps to aspects of their unconscious. But it completely cross-cuts the question of whether their activities routinely produce consequences which they do not intend or of which they are unaware.

STRUCTURAL ANALYSIS: CRITICAL OBSERVATIONS

Why should those who have favoured a 'structural approach', in Anglo-Saxon social science at least, have been so attracted to functional viewpoints of one kind or another? The answer is surely to do with the point made near the beginning of this paper. Social structure is identified with conditions of social existence which act outside the scope of agents' consciousness and have a causal impact upon their behaviour. Structure, in other words, has to be seen as 'doing something'—as having properties over and above those of individual agents and constraining their activities. Those favouring a 'structural approach' have tended to see themselves as strong opponents of subjectivism in the social sciences and advocate, in some sense, a more 'tough-minded' perspective which insists that individuals are far from being the masters of their own fate.

In discussing these matters further it is helpful to follow Sztompka's distinction between the generic and specific notions of structure in Merton's writings. So far as the generic concept is concerned, we have to confront basic problems relating structure and action in social science. These are problems upon which I have myself worked extensively and it might be sensible at this point to juxtapose my position to that of Merton. It is my opinion that the social sciences have long been dogged by an unhappy dualism between structural approaches and those favouring a more 'subjectivist' outlook. It is surely right to claim, as those who have emphasized the importance of social structure have done, that social life is not plastic to the individual will and that characteristics of social organization can constrain or causally affect individual actions. It is also surely essential to acknowledge that human beings are not the playthings of social forces, pushed hither and thither by influences which they cannot resist, but are reasoning agents who always know (under some description) what they are doing as an integral part of doing it. The fundamental difficulty, which I do not think most traditions of social theory have adequately coped with until fairly recently, consists in maintaining these two emphases while relating structure and action to one another. I do not believe it is possible to accomplish this if we see social structure simply as fixed patterns of relationships which influence behaviour in a way parallel to the constraining influences of the material world. We need to give intensive thought to the notion of structure, as well as theorizing the intentionality and knowledgeability of agents in an effective and thoroughgoing fashion. The limitations of most structural approaches, including that of Merton, derive as much from the second of these points as from the first. It will not do to think of the 'subjective' side of social activity in terms of vague allusions to people's intentions, reasons or self-understandings. We must set out an analysis of agency which is every bit as systematic and sophisticated as that of structure: this is a *sociological* task, not one that the social analyst can somehow skirt or leave safely to psychology.

Theorizing agency, as I have tried to show in some detail elsewhere (Giddens, 1984), involves being sensitive to the contextualities of action across time and space. Agency is not an aggregate of intentions and reasons, but rather a continuous flow of reflexively monitored conduct. Human agents routinely 'keep in touch' with the grounds of what they do, that process in some part being constitutive of the nature of these doings. The reflexive monitoring of action, however, does not operate primarily at a conscious level, where 'consciousness' is understood as the discursive interpretation of action. No doubt there are characteristically unconscious forms of cognition which regularly influence human activities. Crucially important, however, in my view, is 'practical consciousness': non-discursive nodes of awareness built into the practicalities of day-to-day social conduct. Practical consciousness consists in all the things that agents know in knowing how to 'go on', in Wittgensteinian terms, in the context of daily activities. The failure of many of those attracted to structural approaches to take account of the richness and complexity of practical consciousness is one of the main reasons why the move from manifest to latent functions seems such an obvious and natural one. If what agents are able to say about the grounds of their activities appears slight and inadequate, it seems logical to look for some 'hidden reasons', of which individuals in question are unaware, which are the true origin of their behaviour. To see that, in virtually all circumstances, agents know a great deal about what they are doing and why—although they cannot necessarily express this in the level of discursive consciousness—is to foreclose the move from apparent irrationality to underlying social functions.

In my view social analysis does not 'begin' with the individual agent, any more than it 'begins' with society. Rather, the core subject-matter of social analysis is the study of recurrent social practices, organized across time and space. Not only an account of *praxis* but a perspective on social reproduction is a key part of this approach. The reproduction of social practices occurs through the knowledgeable use of convention, as carried primarily in practical consciousness, by means of which agents carry on their day-to-day lives. This always takes place through 'mixes' of intended and unintended consequences and against a backdrop of bounded awareness of the parameters of action. In general it seems probable that lay agents are less ignorant than at least some 'structural sociologists' suppose them to be. Most of the functional consequences identified by sociological observers are accessible to agents themselves also, and normally enter into their own reasoning. While this is the case in all societies, there is a particularly acute and complex relation between the designation of unintended consequences (functional or otherwise) and agents' own understandings and practices in conditions of modernity. Modern social systems are in substantial part constituted by the regular importation of knowledge used to alter the circumstances of system reproduction.

What of the notion of structure itself? Is there a distinctive role for something called 'structural analysis' in the social sciences? In my opinion, English-speaking sociologists should pay much more attention to insights deriving from structuralist traditions of thought than most have done hitherto. Merton is no exception in this respect, since in the article 'Structural Analysis in Sociology' he refers to structuralism only in the most cursory fashion and apparently does not see ideas from this tradition of thought as relevant to his own preoccupations. I would agree that some of the key orientations of structuralism (and post-structuralism also) have to be repudiated. But others are of essential importance. Among these I would rank in particular the idea that part-whole totalities can be understood in terms of the instanciation of 'absent' structural forms. 'Structure', in the generic sense, in my terms should be understood as the rules and resources recursively implicated in social systems. This conceptual move makes possible recognition of what I call the 'duality of structure': the fact that, in social life, structure is both the medium and outcome of human action. For 'structure' in the social sciences cannot be understood in a manner directly analogous to structures in the natural world, since it is 'carried' only in and through the activities of knowledgeable human agents. It seems to me that a range of developments in social theory converge upon the central importance of recursiveness in this sense.

Such a perspective does not in any way deny the insights of those who favour 'structural sociology'. Social systems have structural properties associated with their institutional embeddedness in time and space. These properties concern the 'fixity' of institutions, expressed in terms of stabilized social relationships. However, we have to be extremely careful in defining the nature of structural causation or constraint. Most of the advocates of 'structural sociology' have wanted to associate sociology fairly closely with the natural sciences, and have argued for models of social causation in terms similar to those associated with forces of nature. In social science, however, such a position can be at best misleading. The constraining properties of social systems only ever work in two ways: in terms of confining or shaping possibilities of action, and in terms of agents' own beliefs about such possibilities. Structural constraint, in my view, derives from the institutionalized nature of social practices in particular contexts of action. The 'givenness' of social environments can be expressed in terms of sets of feasible options open to individuals or groups. Regularities of action produced by structural constraints have the causal properties they do only in terms of decision-making in relation to such options, regardless of whether this is at the level of discursive or practical consciousness. Wherever we describe a given option as the 'only one', we presume a range of wants and a rationalization process on the part of the person or persons concerned. Where either wants or reasons become redefined, there may no longer only be one feasible option, but several potential courses of action. Many forms of contestation, opposition and active attempts at transformation derive from this circumstance.

Now this is unlikely to satisfy the 'structural sociologist', who wishes to claim that structural properties bring about other structural properties. That is to say, there is an autonomous level of structural causation somehow 'out of the reach' of individual agents. This is perfectly valid, but again we have to be careful in sorting out its logical implications. Structural properties do not change themselves. The imagery in terms of which a social system is, as it were, 'hunting around' to alter itself in relation to a functional exigency or need must simply be dropped altogether. We can trace modes of structural change, but these always presume a methodological 'bracketing out' of the circumstances of individual action. We might show, for example, how an economy 'responds' to a situation in which rates of profit drop. We could carry out the analysis in terms of alterations in the overall system, and regard the relations unearthed as causal. However, the 'moving parts' of causal relations in the social sciences are in every case (apart from some aspects of human connections with material world) individual agents. To say this is not to propose another version of methodological individualism. The structural properties of social systems cannot be reduced to the behaviour of individual actors. Structure, and the structural properties associated with institutionalized practices, are qualities possessed only by collectivities.

What in the end are we to make of the view that the main explanatory objective of sociology is to show that there are social influences affecting our behaviour beyond what we know about ourselves as individual agents? This view is unquestionably correct. As individuals, all of us follow courses of action in contexts which pre-existed our birth and which 'stretch away' in time and space from us. Our activities regularly have consequences which we neither intend nor foresee. Yet it is wrong to suppose that sociology can locate its subject-matter exclusively in terms of the study of 'forces' which mould agents' behaviour. It is just this position which alienates lay actors from the sociological enterprise, because from such a standpoint they are presented as unknowing dupes of social influences—not as human beings who knowledgeably organize what they do. Social theory has as much responsibility to provide a cogent account of human agency as to identify the structural influences with which action is intrinsically involved.

Let us now turn to the 'specific' sense in which Merton uses his concept of social structure. To my mind, this is where the Mertonian approach comes into its own—much more than in the more general formulations of structure and function for which Merton's writings are perhaps more often celebrated. Merton's work concentrates particularly upon modern societies and seeks to explore the complex yet subtle nature of the social relationships they incorporate. One of the most important features of Merton's work in this regard is that he has always sought to attack the idea that 'society' is a clearly differentiated 'super-system' which forms the prime focus of sociological analysis. Rather, Merton emphasizes that modern social life consists of many overlapping and shifting sets of systemic relationships, often having no clear 'boundaries' from one another. This seems to me very important, since sociologists have so often taken 'society' as their subject-matter, without clearly recognizing the problematic elements inherent in that notion.

Merton's interesting idea of 'sociological ambivalence' is characteristic of the mode in which he approaches the 'specific' concept of structure. His picture of characteristic forms of role relationships, and indeed other aspects of social institutions more generally, begins from the assumption that they usually embody contradictory elements. The much debated thesis relating social structure to anomie is hence part of a wide-ranging interpretation which identifies structured strains between values or norms and the actual behaviour in which individuals engage. A great deal of Merton's work concerns the tensions thus resulting.

There can be no doubt that Merton's concentration upon these issues has been enormously fruitful, stimulating important empirical work as well as renewed theoretical thinking in many areas. These matters are well explored in other papers in this volume and there is no need to analyze them here. However, Merton's work in these respects does have some fairly clear limitations and I shall address some of these in closing. Of course, no author, no matter how ambitious, can cover everything and undoubtedly Merton has sought to impose restrictions upon the scope of his work.

CONCLUSION: THE LIMITATIONS OF MERTONIAN SOCIAL THEORY

A first critical observation concerns the lack of an historical orientation in Merton's writings on 'structural sociology'. Merton is very well versed in historical study and his first major work was an historical project. But I would regard an historical perspective as much more deeply involved with the structural questions Merton addresses than he himself apparently does. Early on Merton wrote a discussion of time and social theory, and he has drawn attention to 'the perspective of historical sociology, that past and present contexts of...structures constrain or facilitate their development in certain rather than in other directions' (cited in Sztompka, 1986: 153). Yet he has made no attempt to place his discussions of the structural features of modern social institutions into an historical framework.

I do not see how we can hope more fully to understand their nature and origins in the absence of such an attempt. In criticizing earlier versions of functionalism, Merton made it clear that modern societies have characteristics which traditional ones in some substantial part lack. But he has made no move, that I know of, towards developing a typology of societies, or of the conditions which have led to transformations from one type to another. In my view, sociology cannot come to history by a roundabout route, nor can we any longer defend the view that sociology deals in abstract generalizations about social life, independent of time and space, while history concerns itself with the particularities of the past. Sociology and history share a common logical and methodological status. If it is true that all historians are now obliged to think sociologically, it is equally incumbent upon sociologists to regard an historical perspective as the natural premise of their endeavours.

Second, Merton's disinclination to treat an unexamined notion of 'society' as the starting-point for social theory is admirable in itself, but does tend rather to obscure the issue of how one should best conceptualize social totalities. In various places Merton speaks of the 'interdependent clusters' or 'institutional complexes' which compose social systems. But he gives very little attention to showing just how these clusters are organized. One can read Merton's major writings without forming any clear idea of how he conceives of the main structural features of modern societies. What makes them distinct 'societies' insofar as there are divisions between them? What role do capitalism, industrialism, the coordination of political power or ideology play in their structuring? In the absence of answers to such questions, Merton's writings often (to this reader at least) have a somewhat amorphous feel to them. They have a strong cumulative quality in respect of the stimulus provided to empirical work and logical reflection; but a good deal of effort has to be made to assemble together what Merton's account of structural forms in modern social systems actually involves.

Merton's disinclination to deal with these problems presumably derives from his desire to separate his own version of sociology in a clear-cut fashion from that of his mentor, Talcott Parsons, together with his advocacy of 'theories of the middle range'. His proposal that sociology should concentrate upon middle-range theories as the best platform for its advancement has been as widely discussed as any of his major claims or themes. So perhaps there is nothing much that is new which can be said about it. I do not myself think that it is a justifiable position. This is not because the development of sociology depends primarily upon the formulation of more comprehensive and ambitious theoretical schemes. It is rather because I would see the nature and significance of social theory in a different way from Merton. In social theory, and more generally in empirical research in the social sciences, we are not just in the business of building generalizations. The subject-matter of the social sciences—social life itself—is thoroughly permeated by generalizations, incorporated within the activities and reasoning processes of lay agents. Many of the generalizations social scientists discover are only 'news' insofar as they allow sociological observers insight into cultural settings with which they are substantially unfamiliar. Although, as sociologists, we can certainly generalize about social life, the generalizations we make are. unstable in respect of agents' knowledge of conventions and social processes.

Theory in the social sciences stands in a reflexive relation to the subject-matter for which it accounts: the activities of lay actors themselves. 'Good theory' in social science is bound up with conceptual innovation as much as with identifying and checking generalizable principles of structural causation. Merton's endorsement of middle-range theories is based upon the presumption that such theories generate propositions which are more precisely formulated, and more readily testable, than grander, speculative notions. But if the relation between social theory and social life is understood in the manner I have just mentioned, this point no longer holds—or at least its implications have to be spelt out quite differently.

Interchange

STINCHCOMBE REPLIES TO GIDDENS

I think no one nowadays would disagree with Giddens's position that humans can have socially established unconscious norms, such as the rules of English grammar; that they function much the same when they are 'practical consciousness' and not accessible to explicit discourse as when they function in a grammarian's mind; and that they are often the stuff of large social structures (e.g. the linguistic divisions in Canadian politics). That such norms or structures have the manifest function of enabling people to understand one another, and that we deliberately teach grammar to facilitate that manifest function, does not undermine the massive fact of their embedding in practical interaction without conscious 'grammatical' purposes in the actors.

Suppose we use such a structural fact to notice that many cities that had political machines in the United States had more people in them whose practical consciousness extended to Polish or Italian grammar, but not very well to English grammar. We think that perhaps the structures of the progressive movement in city government do not deliver political services and resolve political grievances as well as machines for folks who do not speak the language in which abstract public purposes are formulated for city governments in the United States. So we have a correlation between the structuring of mostly unconscious grammatical behaviour and a structure of political organization, involving intentions to win elections, favours delivered, businesses such as gambling and prostitution (which do not figure in the abstract public purposes of the progressives) protected, a structure with the welter of special purpose non-partisan administrative governmental units dear to progressives' hearts integrated into a machine system that can make decisions that serve also Italian and Polish speakers. That correlation between the demography of language use and machine politics is a structural fact to be explained, as much as the original different grammatical composition of cities is.

What Giddens demands of us, as nearly as I can see, is only that we explain the inability of progressives to talk concrete political benefits with Polish immigrants historically, instead of leaving it implicit as Merton does. And he demands that at the end of our functional explanation of the machine as an incorporator of a disadvantaged public with voting rights into effective urban politics, we add a caveat that we would like to know the detailed mechanisms that delivered to the machine-builders what they needed to make the machine go over the historical period of its growth and dominance, and the detailed mechanisms that led to its decline as Poles and Italians learned English and got law degrees and came to staff the multiple disintegrated agencies created by the progressives. I have no quarrel with that, if a scholar has time for it.

But the advice that we need to do that seems to me a counsel of perfection. Surely no one doubts that we could find those historical processes that differed between Atlanta and Los Angeles on the one side and Chicago and New York on the other, that added weight and motivation to all the various people and organizations that had to contribute to machines in Chicago and New York, and that failed to produce such contributions to cities whose population came from a depressed English speaking agricultural hinterland in Georgia or from the second and third generations of Chicago's and New York's immigration waves. To say that functionalism is shorthand for a lot of details does not make it different from any other theory.

Saying that it would be better to know the details is a strategic matter, which is sometimes good advice (if the details are problematic and would be probative of the explanation) and sometimes bad (if the details can be filled in by routine work by virtually any investigator). Whatever the epistemological virtues of filling in adequate causes for structures when we have evidence only for the strength of the functional correlation, scientists do not create new knowledge by following epistemological rules at great effort and expense, when everybody knows how the results will come out. I argue that the combination of the functional theory and the strong structural correlation seems to make filling in the historical detail bootless. However, filling in what happens when machines do *not* produce such effective cross-ethnic political contact, as in Canada, Belgium or in the Irish parts of Great Britain before independence, seems to me a promising line of work. So I believe that the functional theory, and its corresponding structural concepts, suggests a more fruitful line of research than does Giddens's alternative.

GIDDENS REPLIES TO STINCHCOMBE

I have no particular disagreement with some of the points Stinchcombe makes. It surely is, as he says, one of the most important and attractive features of Merton's theoretical work that it has stimulated so much in the way of worthwhile empirical research. I think Stinchcombe is right to say that this is not because Merton confines his attention to 'middle-range' theory. There is a difference between theoretical standpoints which are general, but relatively precise in formulation, and those which are general but vague. I am less convinced than Stinchcombe is that the empirical fruitfulness of Merton's work derives from the fact that his theoretical position is a sound and comprehensive one. The interpretation which Stinchcombe offers of the systematic components of Merton's theory has never been presented in this way by Merton himself, even though he has seemingly endorsed it. It is difficult to see that what Stinchcombe finds as the core of Merton's theoretical thinking in fact summarizes the variety of contributions to sociological research which Merton made in *Social Theory and Social Structure*.

This is a 'cleaned up' and leaner version of Merton, with much of the functionalist rhetoric removed and with the attempt at the 'codification' of social analysis which Merton originally set out now left aside. In my opinion a good deal of the impact Merton's writings have had upon empirical research comes from his talent for spotting interesting problem areas, and coining useful concepts for analyzing them, rather than from a consistently developed theoretical stance. As Stinchcombe points out at the end of his essay, apart from the programmatic efforts at 'codification', Merton's 'general theory is nowhere extracted and systematized'.

Stinchcombe chooses to find the main theoretical content of Merton's work in Merton's emphases that social structure can be understood in terms of a choice between 'socially structured alternatives' and that by this means we can explain variations in chosen patterns of behaviour by individuals in different sectors of a given social system. There are definite merits to such a conception, whether or not it is actually accurate as a representation of Merton's concerns. It avoids one of the persistent difficulties associated with many forms of 'structural sociology': the presumption that the actions of individuals can be explained as the outcome of structural forces of some kind. Stinchcombe's view preserves a fundamental role for structural factors, but at the same time focuses upon avenues of individual choice. In addition, this view does not regard motives for choices as randomly patterned in respect of structural characteristics of systems—a limited number of types of 'structurally induced motives' is recognized.

However, Stinchcombe's viewpoint has a number of limitations and I shall list them briefly here.

1 There appears to be an ambiguity in the notion of 'structurally induced motives'. The sources of motivation which Stinchcombe distinguishes seem to be cultural rather than elements of the structural features of social systems. 'Structural', when used in respect of the origins of motives, is different from the same term when applied to 'structured alternatives' which an individual in a given context faces. The ambiguity is not trivial, because it is not at all obvious that 'structure' in the second (conventional) sense has much relevance to understanding the origins of the motives which prompt individuals' actions.

2 A more sophisticated account of the relation between motives, intentions and reasons is needed than is given by Stinchcombe. His analysis centres upon the connections between motives and avenues of realizing them, the relation between these constituting choices. But as critics of the econometric literature to which Stinchcombe makes reference have pointed out, this will not suffice to provide a satisfactory account of why people act as they do. In my opinion, motives are not causal elements of action, while reasons are. The reasons people have for acting as they do form the only causal factors relevant to the explanation of human behaviour, apart from physiological and environmental influences. Any account of 'structural alternatives' has to operate from that baseline, as does any endeavour to understand the nature of 'structural causation'. Reasons, however, are not to be understood as aggregates, but as incorporated within the chronic reflexive monitoring of action which all competent human agents routinely carry on.

3 An account of the problems Stinchcombe discusses demands an interpretation of the nature of power. He recognizes this, but passes it over as though it could be tacked on afterwards without difficulty. I don't think this is acceptable. Power (generative and distributional) enters in an essential way

to the 'structuring of alternatives' which Stinchcombe discusses. Stinchcombe consistently refers to phenomena which would ordinarily be regarded as examples of the differential distribution of power, without saying how 'structure' and 'power' are to be differentiated in his analysis.

4   Under the heading of 'structural outputs of patterned choice' Stinchcombe provides an interpretation of social reproduction. I do not find this account especially persuasive, on three grounds:

   (i)   Stinchcombe persists in using the concept of function, and the distinction between manifest and latent functions, in interpreting 'structural outputs'. The passages in which he uses these notions demonstrate their characteristic difficulties. Stinchcombe argues that latent functions, in the cases taken from Merton's writings which he analyzes, are not just random outputs but 'strategic imputs' for other structured characteristics of the system in which they exist. But 'strategic' for whom? It is plainly not the fact that they are 'strategic' for the system as a whole which explains their existence or persistence. Stinchcombe recognizes this by proposing that 'happenstance outputs' are liked by some, and not by others, these preferences then 'folding back' into the reproduction of the system. But if people 'happen to like' or 'happen to dislike' the functional consequences of certain social practices, these are then manifest not latent functions (or dysfunctions).

   (ii) An account of social reproduction must recognize that in very many instances in social life the reasons agents have for what they do are not choices between 'socially structured alternatives'. On the contrary, the 'choices' which agents make in a chronic fashion in opting to follow the conventions they do in day-to-day life actually reproduce what those alternatives are. A valid analysis of social reproduction must treat this as a phenomenon of central importance.

   (iii) One of the problems in Merton's work is that he does not clearly distinguish between 'structure' and 'system'. This distinction, as a consistently observed one at any rate, also seems absent from Stinchcombe's discussion. To show where the boundaries between systems lie is fundamental to any discussion of 'structural outputs', since otherwise we do not know what defines something as an 'output', i.e. we do not know exactly what is being reproduced.

5   I would take issue with the view of causation which informs Stinchcombe's analysis. Stinchcombe appears to think that variations in social behaviour or structural characteristics can be explained in terms of universal causal conditions. I do not think such a position can be sustained in respect of the social sciences. Generalizations about social activity do not have the form of causal laws of the type Stinchcombe seems to identify as necessary. This again comes back to the role of reasons in human action, from which causal analysis in social science cannot be separated. All structural properties of social systems have to be understood in terms of mixes of intended and unintended consequences of action, where consequences only form causal conditions of system reproduction insofar as they are mediated by agents' reasons.

V. UNANTICIPATED AND UNINTENDED CONSEQUENCES: LATENT FUNCTIONS AND DYSFUNCTIONS

9. The Two Facets of the Unintended Consequences Paradigm

RAYMOND BOUDON

The paradigm according to which social phenomena should be considered as unintended consequences of individual actions has been advocated by many social scientists before and after Merton; by non-sociologists—moral philosophers such as Mandeville (1714), economists such as Adam Smith or Hayek (1952), philosophers such as Karl Popper (1967: 142–50)—and by sociologists too. Spencer's work is built on the idea that social evolution is the unintended consequence of individual actions (see Schneider, 1971). Marianne Weber (1975) has stressed the role played by the same idea in Weber's work. Merton's particular merit was to make the paradigm explicit in the field of sociology and also to illustrate it by a number of studies of his own, for example his analysis of the anti-black attitudes which developed among American industry workers around the time of World War I (see Merton, 1968: 478–9) or of the development of science in seventeenth century England (see Merton, 1970a: 112–36). In these two examples important *collective* phenomena—respectively, racism among white workers and the development of science—are made the effect of unintended *individual* actions. Merton's message has been generally well received in the sociological community. This is another way of saying that the importance of methodological individualism was recognized even though it was not always followed by this community.

However, these two examples from Merton are very different from one another in one respect. In the first one the psychological statements which are introduced to explain the behaviour of the various categories of actors are all easily acceptable. The black workers want to find a job, the union leaders are sensitive to the fact that hiring a black worker may weaken the union: coming from the rural south, he probably has no familiarity with unions and their culture. The employers' leaders use black workers to break the strikes at a time when such practices were much easier

119

than now. The union members notice that the black workers act in effect against their own interests as union members. On the whole, this example is characterized by the following features:

1 The psychological statements made about all the actors belonging in the system—union leaders, rank and file workers, black workers, etc.—are all acceptable in the sense that they are immediately *understandable* (*verständlich*). They satisfy the *empathetic* criterion: any observer can easily accept the idea that if he had been in the situation of the black worker, the union leader and all the other actors, he *could* have done what many of them actually did. One has, moreover, the impression that if an empirical study had been conducted, it would have confirmed the analysis. This does not mean that the different actors would have produced an adequate theory of their own behaviour. On the whole, the psychological statements contained in this theory raise no difficulties. They are good candidates to be accepted by the Chinese, to use Weber's phrase.

2 The collective phenomenon which Merton's analysis aims to explain is in no sense contained in the motivations or dispositions of the actors. The white workers do not develop anti-black attitudes in the particular context evoked in the analysis because they have a general diffuse anti-black attitude. To some extent they develop anti-black attitudes rather against their own will. The union leaders, as well as the rank and file unionists, are simply prudent and care about the interests of the union. In so doing, however, they increase unintentionally the difficulties of the blacks and they contribute to creating a picture of the black workers which has the effect of reinforcing their marginality.

Let us now consider briefly the other classical Mertonian analysis: science as the unintended product of the Puritan ethos and values. This second case has in common with the first one the unintended action paradigm; the macroscopic phenomenon to be explained is again explained as the unintended product of individual attitudes and actions. But it also differs from the first one in respect of exactly the same two features mentioned above. First, the psychological statement according to which the Puritan mentality should facilitate the methodical stance typical of scientific culture is not immediately understandable. This statement has not the psychological evidence of the statement relating the situation of the union leader to his behaviour. Second, one can easily have the impression that the explanation is tautological. To see the difference between the two examples on this point, one can use a mental experiment. Even if we had not known that the white workers became prejudiced against blacks, we would have easily been able to predict that, as a consequence of their role and responsibilities, the union leaders would normally prefer hiring white workers with union experience than black workers coming from the south, being without union experience and likely to threaten the union interests. In the second example, in contrast, one has the feeling that the features of the Puritan doctrine which are emphasized and retained in the analysis are selected less because they are the main or the most important ones—either in the Puritan doctrine itself or in the consciousness of the believers—than because they explain or at least can easily *be related to* the collective phenomenon to be explained, i.e. the development of science as a controlled and methodical activity. In other words, from Puritanism—like any religious movement, a complex bundle of dogmas, principles, norms, values, etc.—are retained those features which have a *substantive similarity* with the effect they are supposed to explain.

The same distinctions could be made using examples from Max Weber. In his paper on the Protestant sects in America (see Weber, 1946c: 302–22), also a classical application of the unintended consequences paradigm, Weber interprets the particular religiosity of America as the aggregate effect of easily understandable individual attitudes and actions. One of his basic assumptions is that the classical stratification symbols which—for easily understandable historical reasons—play a crucial role in social exchange in the old European societies, such as Germany or France, could not play the same role in America. In complex societies social actors need symbols through which they can quickly identify those actors whom they do not know but with whom they engage in interaction processes. Because of the historical conditions typical of America, religious symbols became to a certain extent a 'functional substitute' of the stratification symbols used in the old European societies. Moreover, the 'Protestant sects' saw very well that they could benefit from this social function of religious symbols in American society. Thus they stood in competition with one another, each trying to deliver a certificate of superior social honourableness. Weber's analysis leads him to ironical remarks where he compares American to German Lutheranism: if being a Lutheran was as expensive in Germany as in the US, there would be no Lutherans in Germany any more.

I do not want to analyze in more detail this penetrating illustration of the unintended consequences paradigm, but only to mention that the psychological statements it contains have the same features as the psychological statements contained in Merton's first example. In other words, all these statements are immediately understandable: yes, in a complex society, I need symbols through which I shall be able to identify socially the other actors who encounter me with the objective of opening and entertaining some type of social interaction; yes, it is easy to understand that the sects tried to benefit from the fact that they were in a position of distributing informal certificates of social honourableness and respectability, etc. On the other hand, these psychological statements are genuinely independent from the final collective phenomenon they explain, e.g. the particular vitality of American religious life which struck Weber at the beginning of this century when he compared it to the French or German situation. In other words, the analysis is characterized by a complete lack of circularity between the psychological statements and the sociological conclusion.

As the discussion surrounding Weber's *Protestant Ethic* has shown, the same cannot be said of his other more famous work. Unintended consequences also play a major role here. But the psychological statements which constitute the core of the theory are much less easy to accept than those in the paper on sects. One can perhaps understand that the belief in the predestination dogma had the psychological effects described by Weber. But one could as easily—perhaps more easily—understand that the same dogma would tend to generate a state of resignation on the part of the believer. Or take Weber's analysis of asceticism. Asceticism—refraining from consumption—he suggests, has the effect of facilitating the accumulation of money in the believer's bank account. This in turn can lead him to an inclination toward luxury. Thus, directly or indirectly, Puritan values can lead either to asceticism or to conspicuous consumption. In other words, when they are abstracted from their context, many psychological statements in *The Protestant Ethic* appear as ingenious, but also to some extent as arbitrary and inspired by Weber's objective to explain the congeniality between Puritanism and 'rational' capitalism. More precisely, one often has the impression that these psychological statements could easily have been different—if not contrary—if Weber had not been aware of the correlations between capitalism and Puritanism which originally inspired his work (by 'correlations' I mean here the facts that Protestants are overrepresented in economic élites in many Western countries, that capitalism was generally more successful in Protestant countries, etc.). By contrast, the psychological statements contained in the article on the Protestant sects are perfectly acceptable in themselves—they are *understandable*—and independent from the collective phenomenon constituting the *explanandum* of the analysis, i.e. the vitality of Protestantism in America at the turn of the century.

These comparisons suggest that the unintended consequences paradigm—and its companion, the methodological individualism paradigm—is of undoubted importance in sociological analysis, but also that a crucial dimension of its plausibility derives from the quality of the psychological statements that the application of this paradigm obligatorily produces. This quality in turn can be measured on two criteria: (1) the psychological statements should be acceptable, 'Chinese' should be able to understand and accept them; (2) they should in principle be entirely independent from the knowledge of the collective phenomenon they contribute to explain, in other words, they should be independent from their effects. These criteria were clearly suggested by Weber in his theoretical works. Explaining individual action means in most cases to find out the reasons which have led the actor to do what he did. When the effects are unintended, the reasons must, by definition, be independent from the effects.

I recognize the first criterion would be worth a careful discussion aimed at identifying the features which make psychological statements acceptable, debatable or even unacceptable; because of limitations of space, I cannot undertake it here. I shall assume that some sociological theories contain psychological statements easily acceptable by all, while others do not. Also, there is no general correlation between the more or less acceptable character of a psychological statement and the type of behavioural principles it introduces. Instrumental rationality, axiological rationality or the other forms of rationality which can be considered beside Weber's categories, as well as irrationality (though irrationality—see below—is of residual interest to sociology), can all provide acceptable or unacceptable principles, depending entirely on the particular aspect of behaviour under examination. For this reason, no particular behavioural model can claim general validity (see Boudon, 1988: 219–44).

As a consequence of the crucial importance of the *psychological* statements contained in a *sociological* theory following the unintended consequences paradigm, progress within this paradigm often consists in substituting a theory with non-circular psychological statements (as illustrated by Merton's or Weber's first mentioned examples) for a theory containing circular psychological statements (as illustrated by the second examples from Merton and from Weber). By circular psychological statements I mean statements where the motivations of the actors are not clearly independent from the effects they produce; and by non-circular, the opposite. Obviously, circular dispositional concepts can very well be introduced in a theory. Thus the statement 'they resisted accepting the innovation because they were traditionally minded' is neither meaningless nor empty in itself (see Runciman, 1983: 180). It supposes only that the hypothetical feature introduced in such a statement can be observed independently from its effects, more precisely, be inferred from observations independent from the observations it is supposed to explain. But very often the circularity is eliminated by modifying the psychological statements. I will illustrate this typical process—which seems to be extremely important methodologically—by some brief examples.

The first example can be drawn from discussions of Weber's *Protestant Ethic*. A number of writers raised many objections against the microscopic psychological statements included in Weber's theory: the existence of a relationship between the anxiety produced in the mind of the believer by the predestination dogma and the idea that success in this world is a sign of election can be inferred from de Bèze's sermons but seldom appears otherwise in Calvinist teaching; success in this world is seldom publicized by Calvinists; economic success is never mentioned, etc. On the whole, these objections suggest that Weber's psychological statements are empirically ill-confirmed (see Schneider, 1970: Ch. 6), besides being unconvincing from an 'empathetic' viewpoint. Trevor-Roper's work (1967) shows that the affinity between capitalism and Puritanism which intrigued Weber can be explained in another way: Erasmus had great success among the businessmen of the sixteenth century because he suggested discretely that the glory of God could be better served by conducting one's business in this world honestly, properly and efficiently rather than by practicing one's faith in a conspicuous fashion. This message was important to them since, as has been brilliantly shown by Simmel's student B. Groethuysen (1927–30), Catholicism had always had trouble finding a place in the social order for those who drew their standing in society from business: the Great and the Poor belonged to the order defined by God, but not the Rich. So the bourgeois easily became Erasmian. Later Calvinism played to a certain extent the role of a militant variant of Erasmianism, more appropriate for a time when Catholic governments tried to eradicate Protestantism by force. When the Counter-Reformation began, businessmen of Catholic countries often either emigrated toward the warmer waters of the Protestant countries or pushed their sons toward careers in the army or the church rather than toward socially disparaged business activities. This explains why seventeenth century businessmen active in Geneva or in the Netherlands never came from Geneva or the Low Countries. I do not want to go into the detail of Trevor-Roper's analysis, but it shows that the various correlations between Calvinism and capitalism, which intrigued Weber and inspired his work, can be explained in a way very different from Weber's. Most importantly, it suggests that Weber's basic psychological statements can be reversed: people, and notably the bourgeois, felt attracted by Erasmianism and then by Calvinism because they saw these world-views as more favourable to them, as giving them a dignity which Catholicism traditionally refused them. I have the impression that these new psychological statements could be more easily accepted 'by the Chinese' than Weber's original statements. They all satisfy the 'empathy' criterion ('in the same situation, I would have probably felt in the same way, done the same thing', etc.) as well as being compatible with other evidence. In other words, the psychological mechanisms described by Trevor-Roper are convincing and correlated with all kinds of empirical data (on migrations, for instance). Here the correlations between Protestantism and capitalism are again an unintended effect, while capitalism itself is no longer, as in Weber's theory, an unintended effect of Puritanism (among other causes). The change in the psychological statements affects the whole theory, although this does not mean that Weber's theory cannot also contain its part of truth.

A second classical example—Marx's theory of ideology—also suggests that progress in sociology often takes one privileged form: substituting in sociological theory for the weak ('circular') psychological statements it originally contains more acceptable 'non-circular' statements. In *The German Ideology*, notably, Marx and Engels develop the following: (1) that the dominant ideas are the ideas of the dominant class; and (2) that these dominant ideas are accepted even by those—those belonging to the dominated classes—who have an interest in not accepting them. So the theory of ideology of the 'young' Marx contains the unintended consequences dimension (unwillingly all participants in the social game contribute to the reproduction of the class structure). But it also includes 'circular' psychological assumptions: the psychological process by which members of the dominated classes accept ideas which are both false and contrary to their interests is unconscious and can only be validated in a circular fashion. Moreover, these assumptions are psychologically very cumbersome: they postulate the existence of complex and obscure psychological mechanisms for which no evidence is available. While Weber's psychological statements in his *Protestant Ethic* are controversial, Marx and Engels's psychological assumptions in the first pages of *The German Ideology* are frankly unacceptable and for this reason were—and still are—accepted exclusively by 'true believers'.

In a chapter of his *Social Theory and Social Structure* (1968: Ch. 14) Merton has drawn attention to the fact that Marx's theory of ideology is more complex than vulgar Marxists often think. Many examples can be drawn from his later works which show that he was very concerned with using 'non-circular' acceptable psychological statements in his sociological theories. Thus in *Capital* (see Elster, 1985) Marx wonders why workers accept 'exploitation' so easily. He argues that they do not tend to do so because obscure forces prevent them from seeing their 'true' interests. On the contrary, Marx sketches a theory where workers have *good reasons* for accepting exploitation: to know that they are being exploited they would need to know the difference between the value V of their work and their salary S. Now, while they know S, they do not master the theory, the methodology and the data which would give them the value V. As they still want to know whether their work is paid at a fair value, they use a cognitively functional substitute; comparing their salary with the income S' of the independent producer. If $S \geqslant S'$, they will tend to be satisfied. Even in the case where they come to understand that the division of labour generates a gain in productivity, they are not able to explain how, and see this gain as *naturally* produced at no cost by capital. On the whole, with good reason, they leave to the capitalist the benefit of the productivity gain resulting from the division of labour. Of course, the theory of surplus value which lies behind this analysis need not be considered as true. But interestingly enough, Marx shows in this analysis that, to him, an acceptable sociological theory is a theory which includes acceptable psychological statements, that is, 'non-circular' and *understandable* (in Weber's sense) statements. Another interesting point arising from this example is that it introduces a type of rationality—which can be called cognitive rationality—not explicitly taken into account in Weber's theory of action.

I have been confronted in my *Education, Opportunity and Social Inequality* (see Boudon, 1974) with the same kind of difficulties. In all countries the probability of reaching college education is much greater for a youngster from a higher class than for a youngster from a lower class. As level of education is a powerful determinant of status, this finding is puzzling since, as in the example drawn from Marx, people seem to act against their own interests. The immediate temptation is to use a 'circular' non-understandable psychological theory of the type suggested by *The German Ideology* and to suggest that people are led by forces unconsciously regulating their level of aspiration, or simply to accept the idea that the level of aspiration is mechanically produced by the social environment. I have tried to show that one achieves a more satisfactory theory by using some simple ideas derived from reference group theory. Thus it is *understandable* that, other things being equal, a youngster who has reached an educational level E will tend to see the choice between going further—to E'—or leaving the educational system in a different fashion depending on whether or not E is likely to bring him a status equal or greater to the status of his family. Such statements are not only understandable and non-circular; they also generate a theory which is confirmed by the available statistical data with much greater accuracy and completeness than competing theories.

(This point, which I cannot develop here, is both generalizable and of great importance. Very often, when non-circular psychological statements are substituted for circular statements, the resulting sociological theory generates a much richer set of consequences capable of being tested against data. In short, it is also better according to classical methodological criteria.)

Thus, as already suggested by Weber (1949)—and clearly recalled by many others such as Popper (1967)—the unintended consequences paradigm includes two organically correlated aspects: the aggregation postulate (*collective* phenomena should be analyzed as the result of *individual* actions) and the postulate that actions should be made *understandable*. In most cases, according to Weber or Popper, this means finding the *reasons* for action, and, only if this appears impossible, the *forces*—e.g. the passions—located beyond the actor's control which have pushed him to act in a particular way. I would like to emphasize this point in concluding this paper.

Without entering into a detailed discussion of the notion of rationality, I wish to argue that—unless this is shown to be impossible—the psychological statements included in a sociological theory should be in the following form: 'the members of such and such a social category had good reasons for doing X, since....' This idea was supported by Weber: the reasons can be *instrumental* or *axiological* (we saw in the example from Marx that they can also be *cognitive*), but even in this last case they are still reasons. And even in cases where sociologists have the impression that actions are *traditional*, they must in most cases—if they wish to be convincing—identify the reasons why social actors follow traditions. *Affective* actions also exist, but they have in practice only a residual importance in sociology. Popper came later to ideas very close to those of Weber in this respect. He also defended the same two crucial methodological ideas: first, that explaining social phenomena as the unintended effect of intentional actions, behaviours, etc. is one of the main tasks, if not the essential task, not only of sociology but also of the social sciences generally; second, in his notion of the *zero point* he argued that an attempt should always be made to explain social behaviour rationally. An irrational explanation is advisable only in cases where rational explanation fails.

It must be stressed, however, that the notion of rationality should be given a broad meaning, which can be described by the following definition: a piece of behaviour X is *rational* if I can explain it convincingly by a theory of the form: 'actor Y had *good reasons* for doing X, since....' As regards *irrational* actions, they will be defined as actions explained by theories of the form ' Y had no *reasons* for doing X, but... [for instance: but he was pushed by forces beyond his control, such as passion, habit, ...]' (see Boudon, 1986, 1988: 219–44).

Although neither Weber nor Popper made clear the reasons why such a postulate of rationality should be introduced in the social sciences, they can be easily understood. The main one is that irrational explanations of behaviour, while they can occasionally be valid, are often in practice ad hoc or circular. Moreover, they often result from prejudices of the observer, who projects onto the observed or analyzed behaviour data and/or frameworks of relevance to his own situation rather than to the actor's situation. Thus, when I explain that somebody has rejected an innovation because he is traditionally minded, in many cases this explanation will be accepted because it is easy rather than because it is true (it may also be true). In many cases this type of explanation will simply reflect the reaction of puzzlement which an uncommitted observer can easily have when observing that an actor acts against his interests. So the rationality postulate is the best protection sociologists can have against these *projection effects* to which they are exposed just like any observer. But again this is not the whole story: Puritans are described by Weber as having *good reasons* (reasons of the axiological type in this case) for accumulating capital, but these reasons have been considered as difficult to accept by many of Weber's readers.

Another main reason in favour of the rationality postulate is that, as the various examples which I have briefly presented show, progress in sociological explanation in effect often takes the form of substituting a rational for an irrational theory, or more generally of substituting in a sociological theory simple, understandable, easily acceptable psychological statements for less easily acceptable psychological statements. To take a further famous example, Marx and Engels's *Communist Manifesto*, in many respects and on many points a vulgar version—directed toward a particular audience and with clear propaganda purpose—of *The Poverty of Philosophy*, explains the struggle between the bourgeois and the feudal landlords by obscure historical forces which are held to have inspired the behaviour of the two classes. By contrast, in the latter work—a work evidently directed toward a universal audience—Marx develops a theory which includes simple, easily acceptable psychological statements: the sixteenth century is characterized by a lasting inflation arising from the massive importation of gold and silver from the Spanish colonies. As the landlords entertain a face-to-face relationship with their tenants, they cannot adjust the rent to the inflation rate mechanically without major risk. So they become progressively poorer and lose their influence, while the bourgeois benefit from the continuous inflation. Needless to say, the irrational explanation of the *Communist Manifesto* has convinced only believers in Marxism, while the corresponding analyses of *The Poverty of Philosophy* have been widely endorsed, by non-Marxists (like J. M. Keynes, for instance) as well as by Marxists.

So both the unintended consequences paradigm, the postulate that actions should be made understandable, and the companion rationality postulate are complementary facets of a common methodological orientation (to repeat, the rationality postulate does not say that irrational explanations should be excluded completely, only that they should in practice be considered as residual as far as sociology is concerned).

This leads to the question: why is the unintended consequences paradigm well accepted by sociologists, while the rationality postulate is given much more limited attention, if not rejected altogether? To this question a tentative list of answers can be given. First, one should mention the influence of a diffuse Durkheimian tradition in sociology, to which all sociologists are more or less exposed even when they do not feel particularly close to Durkheim. According to this tradition—which itself derives from Comtean positivism—the 'reasons' of the actor should not be considered because they cannot be observed and may be wrong; the task of the sociologist is to look for the *causes* rather than the reasons of human action. Second, one should mention the complementary influence of vulgar Marxism, notably the *psychological* principles contained in the opening pages of *The German Ideology*, according to which sociologists can legitimately assume that social actors are blinded by social forces working to the benefit of the dominant classes. Third, the influence of vulgar Freudianism also played a role, according to which sociologists are accustomed to postulate that social actors are motivated by unconscious forces. Fourth, sociologists are often very sensitive to the fact that social structures do not always leave much space to individual autonomy. This point was summarized by an economist, Duesenberry, when he said that economists explain why people do what they want to do, while sociologists are specialists in explaining why people do what they do not want to do. Moreover, sociologists often appear to be convinced that social actors never determine the rules of the social game and that the social game is deeply unsatisfactory, so that the actors have to play the game and at the same time must become convinced—by necessarily fallacious reasons—that the game is worth playing. Another reason derives from a methodological fallacy, i.e. from a misinterpretation of statistical instruments popular in sociology. The fact that a correlation can be found between two individual variables, such as social background and level of education, for instance, and that a causal interpretation can be given of the correlation, does not imply that the social background is the cause—in the sense that the spark is the cause of the fire—of the level of education and that the social actor can therefore be pictured as deprived of any autonomy, rationality and decision power. Finally, another methodological fallacy often leads to the belief that, since human beings are irrational, the *social actor* cannot be rational. The fact that anger (to take a simple example of irrationality) can be observed and play a crucial role in many novels does not mean, however, that such feelings often take the place of explanatory variables in sociology.

All the reasons militating against the rationality postulate are understandable, but it nevertheless remains true that the unintended consequences paradigm is crucial in sociology. However, its fruitfulness depends on the quality of the psychological statements which theories inspired by it necessarily include. This suggests that these psychological statements should be founded on observations strictly independent of the observations they are supposed to explain, and that the rationality principle is the best protection against poor, circular or arbitrary psychological statements. To summarize: the importance of the unintended consequences paradigm is well recognized in sociology. But it is also advisable to consider carefully the quality and validity of the psychological statements introduced into sociological theories. This is another way of saying that the *Verstehen* problem remains fundamental and worthy of closer methodological exploration. A necessarily abbreviated guideline for this methodological exploration would be the following: although statements about the psychological states of a subject cannot reflect direct observations, this does not mean that they do not have to be empirically grounded. In fact, they can be validated by procedures which are basically the same as those used in the case of statements about the 'external' world. But a number of intellectual factors—among them the lasting influence of positivism and behaviourism—have the effect that we feel entitled (wrongly) to be much more permissive and much less careful with 'psychological' statements than with statements about the external world.

10. Merton's Functionalism and the Unintended Consequences of Action

JON ELSTER

Robert Merton's article on 'Manifest and Latent Functions' (1957a : 19–84) is an acknowledged classic of modern sociology. I do not think it merits that status. It created as much confusion as it dispelled, or more. It does not seem to have generated much good empirical research, by Merton or by anyone else. In this article I do not try to document the latter claim in anything like a satisfactory fashion. For the 'anyone else' part of that claim, the reader is referred to Campbell (1982), who asserts that the concepts of manifest and latent functions, while usually referred to in sociological textbooks, are little used in actual research. For the 'Merton' part of the claim, the reader is referred to the brief discussion below of Merton's work in the sociology of science.

Merton's early article on 'The Unanticipated Consequences of Purposive Social Action' (1936b) is probably less famous than the study of manifest and latent functions, but has better claims to the status of a classic. Here Merton uses what is in my opinion the appropriate language for social scientific analysis—the causal-cum-intentional terminology of intended and unintended consequences. It is a little gem of an article, identifying several mechanisms through which the actual effects of behaviour may deviate from the intended ones. Although he does not discuss what I believe to be the most important mechanism, viz. the tendency for people to act on wrong assumptions about what other people will do (Elster, 1978: Ch. 5), the article is perfectly lucid and free of ambiguity. In this respect it contrasts favourably with the later, more famous article, which goes beyond intentions and causes to introduce *functions* as a separate category.

'Manifest and Latent Functions' does make some important contributions. It contains an impressive demolition of earlier forms of functionalism, based on the postulate of the functional unity of society, the postulate of universal functionalism and the postulate of indispensability. Also he makes it very clear that he does not rest his case for functionalism in sociology on dubious analogies from biology. Finally,

'Manifest and Latent Functions' remains worth reading for its extensive discussion of American machine politics, which almost amounts to an article within the article. Although I don't think Merton succeeds in imposing a consistent and plausible structure on this problem, the sheer richness and suggestiveness of his analysis invite further reflection.

On the critical side, the main weakness of the article is that the task of functional analysis is never made fully clear. In particular, Merton never states in so many words whether the task of functional analysis is to *explain* social phenomena or, more modestly, to identify and describe phenomena that might otherwise be overlooked. Clearly, manifest functions—intended and recognized consequences of action—have explanatory power. The question on which most of the following discussion is focused is whether latent functions—the unintended and unrecognized effects of action—can explain the actions of which they are the consequences.

Commenting on Merton's discussion of the Hawthorne experiment, G. A. Cohen writes: 'He identifies a function in the Hawthorne experiment, but fails to note it is not a function which explains why the experiment took place' (1978: 283). Cohen then adds in a footnote: 'It might be claimed in Merton's defence that he was concerned only with *identifying* functions of social patterns and institutions, not with functionally *explaining* them. This is a highly implausible reading, and if it is correct, then we may object that in an article recommending the study of functions Merton neglected their explanatory significance'.

I shall argue that the non-explanatory reading, while not 'highly' implausible, is probably less natural than the explanatory one. We may observe, nevertheless, that in a recent article devoted to Merton's distinction between manifest and latent functions, Colin Campbell (1982: 41–2) does not cite explanation among Merton's justifications for the paradigm. Instead he cites:

1 the 'desire to eliminate what [Merton] saw as a widespread confusion between the subjective categories of disposition and the objective ones of consequence';
2 the claim 'that the distinction would aid both "systematic observation and later analysis" by directing observation towards "salient elements of a situation" and preventing the "inadvertent oversight of these elements"'; and
3 the idea 'that the distinction "directs attention to theoretically fruitful fields of inquiry", by which he means that it is not enough for sociologists to "*confine* themselves to the study of manifest functions"'.

Referring to an obscure footnote in Merton (1957a: 71n90), Crothers (1987a: 71) similarly argues that functional analysis must not be confused with explanation, the latter being causal rather than functional.

In his most general statement of the 'central orientation of functionalism' Merton refers to 'the practice of interpreting data by establishing their consequences for larger structures in which they are implicated' (1957a: 46–7). It is hard to see what interpreting could mean other than explaining. Further on he argues that the latent functions of conspicuous consumption are 'gratifying and go far toward *explaining* the continuance of the pattern' (*ibid.*: 58, emphasis supplied); or, still further on, that they 'help *explain* the persistence and the social location of the pattern of conspicuous consumption' (*ibid.*: 69; emphasis supplied). He observes that labelling the Hopi rain dance a superstitious practice of primitive folk 'in no sense *accounts for* the group behavior' (*ibid.*: 64; emphasis supplied), and adds that 'given the concept of latent function, however, we are reminded that this behavior *may* perform a function for the group'. By implication this latent function does 'account for' the practice in question.

Other statements are less explicitly explanatory, but point in the same direction. Thus he refers to 'consequences [of a structure] which may provide basic social support for the structure' (*ibid.*: 72n91). With respect to the political machine he claims that 'the functional deficiencies of the official structure generate an alternative (unofficial) structure to fulfill existing needs somewhat more effectively' (*ibid.*: 73). The first statement suggests that consequences are important in maintaining (and thus explaining) institutions, the second that they are instrumental in creating (and thus explaining) them. At a more general level he makes two provisional assumptions: that 'persisting cultural forms have a *net balance of functional consequences* either for the society considered as a unit or for subgroups sufficiently powerful to retain these forms intact' (*ibid.*: 32), and that 'when the *net balance of the aggregate of consequences* of an existing social structure is clearly dysfunctional, there develops a strong and insistent pressure for change' (*ibid.*: 40). These statements amount to saying that because dysfunctional elements tend to disappear, persisting forms can be assumed to be functional and to persist because they are functional. I return to this argument. Here it is cited only as evidence for Merton's explanatory intentions.

We cannot conclude, however, that Merton intended all his analyses to have explanatory import. His comments on the Hawthorne experiment, for example, do not lend themselves to this reading; nor would it be a substantively plausible account (Cohen, 1978: 257–8). Here functional analysis—like much of what goes for 'dialectics'—seems to be little more than the discovery of surprising, paradoxical and counterintuitive consequences or, perhaps, the identification of valuable consequences (see below). His general statements about 'drawing attention to' the unintended and unrecognized effects of social phenomena also point in this direction. It *is* inherently satisfactory for the mind to discover that good sometimes leads to evil and evil to good; that less can be more and more can be less; or that individual rationality can bring about collective irrationality and vice versa. And it *is* easy to mistake the thrill of discovery for the thrill of explanation, which is what seems to have happened to Merton between the 1936 essay on unanticipated consequences and the 1949 article on manifest and latent functions. This comment, of course, is speculative and *ad hominem*. No part of my case rests on it.

Before I say more about the issue of explanation, I want to discuss some other ambiguities in Merton's paradigm of functional analysis. The classification of consequences in intended versus unintended and recognized versus unrecognized suggests four categories rather than merely two. Also, we have to ask, as Merton rarely does: intended by whom? recognized by whom? These questions, in turn, are related to another: functional for whom?

In any given item of functional analysis, there are two groups of individuals involved: those who engage in practices we want to explain and those who benefit from these practices, i.e. those for whom they are in some sense functional.[1] The question of intention arises only for the first group, the question of recognition may arise for both. The two groups may coincide, overlap or be totally disjoint. In the last case, the possibility arises that the effects are unintended by those who produce them but recognized by those who benefit from them. If, moreover, the latter have the power to sustain the activities from which they benefit, we have the ingredients of a *filter explanation* (Nozick, 1974: 21–2; Elster, 1984: 30). Although he has no place for this kind of explanation in his general dichotomous scheme, Merton tacitly admits it when he refers to activities that have a net balance of functional consequences for subgroups sufficiently powerful to retain these forms intact (*ibid.*: 32).[2] It is hard to see how power to maintain the beneficial activities would be relevant unless the benefits were also recognized by the beneficiaries.

The other category missing in Merton's paradigm is that of benefits which are intended but unrecognized. This case arises mainly when the benefits are unrecognized by the beneficiaries, as in paternalism. It is clearly of less theoretical interest than those which involve behaviour maintained by their unintended consequences. Merton would perhaps count it as a manifest function, since the effects will usually be recognized by those who intentionally produce them. This does not affect my main point, however, which is that for some explanatory purposes we need to distinguish between actors and beneficiaries. Filter explanations, in particular, rest on this distinction.

When Merton says that dysfunctions create a 'strong and insistent pressure for change', he must imply that these are somehow recognized. On the other hand, he does assert the existence of 'latent dysfunctions' (*ibid.*: 51n) which, presumably, are not recognized. I do not see how these statements can be reconciled. To bring out the point, consider two definitions of the Marxian concept of alienation (Elster, 1985: 74 ff.), as either sense of a lack of meaning or lack of a sense of meaning. One can see how the former 'dysfunction' could set up a pressure for change, provided that the victims not only perceive the problem but correctly identify its cause. The latter, however, cannot act as a causal agent in social change. For another example, consider the belief in witches. Although these tend to be dysfunctional by inducing conformity and stifling innovation (Thomas, 1973: 643–4), they provide an element of stability rather than of change. And if there can be stable bad situations, there can also be unstable good ones, like cooperation in a Prisoner's Dilemma.

Moreover, when the outcome but not the cause of a dysfunction is perceived, as is often the case if the causal chains are protracted or complex, we should not expect any pressure for change; or, if there is pressure for change, we should not in general expect it to be successful in doing away with the problem. Environmental and economic crises often defy understanding: they generate change, but no solutions. Hence we see that in addition to the distinction between recognition by actors and recognition by beneficiaries, we need to distinguish between recognition of the consequences themselves and recognition of the causal responsibility for these consequences.

Merton rightly emphasizes the need to identify the alternatives which are excluded by the activity which is subject to functional analysis or explanation (1957a: 57). But he does not draw the full implications from this insight. For one thing, he does not make it clear whether an activity, to be functional, must also be *optimal* within the set of alternative arrangements. For another, he does not explain what determines the realization of one among several equi-functional (or perhaps equi-optimal) arrangements. Merton suggests, for instance, that the rain ceremonial of the Hopi can be 'accounted for' in terms of its contribution to group unity. Now one might think, first, that an optimal common activity would be one that both contributed to group unity *and* achieved its manifest purpose, thus avoiding waste and disappointment. If he believes that the lack of success of the manifest purpose was essential to fulfilment of the latent function, he should say so and explain why; if not, he should explain the absence of another arrangement with a larger 'net balance' of benefits. Second, one might ask why the rain ceremonial, rather than any of the innumerable other joint activities one could imagine, was realized as a 'means' (*ibid.*) to group unity.

A final set of ambiguities has been so well charted by Colin Campbell that I need only cite from his discussion:

> Altogether there are at least four different meanings which Merton gives to the manifest-latent distinction. There is, first of all, that presented in the explicit formulation, i.e. the contrast between conscious intention and actual consequence. Secondly...Merton himself comes to use the dichotomy to refer to the commonsense knowledge (or sometimes the perspective of another discipline) and sociological understanding. Thirdly, there is the usage which equates manifest with the formal and official aims of organizations and latent with the purposes fulfilled by unofficial or illegal ones. Finally, there is the suggestion that manifest and latent relate to different levels of understanding, with the former equal to apparent or surface meaning while the latter concerns the deeper or underlying reality of the phenomenon in question. (1982: 33)

The first distinction is used in Merton's discussion of the Hopi; the second in his discussion of conspicuous consumption; the third in the discussion of the political machine; while the last is present throughout. Combined with the other ambiguities and inconsistencies that I have been discussing, this confusion creates something close to conceptual chaos.

Let me now confront the problem of explanation more directly. The central task for any explanation-by-consequences is to provide a *mechanism* by which the consequences uphold or maintain the behaviour one wants to explain. In the absence of some kind of feedback from effect to cause, explanation by consequence remains a totally mysterious notion.[3] It is metaphysically impossible for an event to be explained by another event that occurs at a later time. Merton's only reference to mechanisms is his suggestion that dysfunctional entities tend to disappear. Elsewhere (Elster, 1983: 61ff.) I have discussed a similar argument (proposed by Stinchcombe, 1975) at some length, concluding that it does not work. It amounts essentially to asserting that non-dysfunctional institutions, including as a special case the functional ones, maintain themselves over time, because they do not set up any pressure for change. The argument is vulnerable in at least three respects.

1 The basic premise, that non-dysfunctional institutions remain stable over time, is false. Adaptively neutral phenomena are often subject to *drift*.
2 Even if dysfunctional institutions tend to disappear, there is no presumption that they will be replaced by functional ones. Perhaps disequilibrium is a more fundamental feature of societies than equilibrium (Nelson and Winter, 1982).
3 There may be many non-dysfunctional alternatives to a given dysfunctional institution. We would like to know which of them will emerge and at what time, not simply that one of them ultimately will. Are the functional ones more likely to emerge than those which are merely neutral from the adaptive point of view? And if so, why?

Merton has nothing to say about the two most frequently cited mechanisms by which behaviours or institutions could be upheld by their consequences: natural selection and reinforcement (see van Parijs, 1981, for a thorough discussion). Evolutionary biology and animal psychology have charted these mechanisms in the utmost detail, but it remains to be shown that either can be used to support functional explanation in the social sciences. In any case, for the present exegetical purposes there is no need to discuss them at further length, since they seem very far in spirit from Merton's paradigm. In particular, both mechanisms rest on the notion that alternatives to an unsatisfactory state are generated randomly, whereas Merton argues more obscurely that they are generated by a 'pressure for change'.

I conclude by a brief comment on the language of functions in Merton's sociology of science. I shall first quote two passages at some length, and then suggest that they may give us a key to Merton's main interest in functions:

> Multiple discoveries can thus be seen to have several and varied functions for the system of science. They heighten the likelihood that the discovery will be promptly incorporated in current scientific knowledge and will so facilitate the further advancement of knowledge. They confirm the truth of the discovery (although on occasion *errors* have been independently arrived at). They help us detect a problem which I have barely and far from rigorously formulated, to say nothing of having solved it: How to calculate the functionally optimum amount of redundancy in independent efforts to solve scientific problems of designated kinds, such that the probability of the solution is approximately maximized without entailing so much replication of effort that the last increment will not appreciably increase that probability. (Merton, 1973: 80)

> [C]onsidered in its implications for the reward system, the Matthew effect [the award of disproportionate credit to senior authors for joint work or multiple discoveries] is dysfunctional for the careers of individual scientists who are penalized in the early stages of their development, but considered in its implications for the communication system, the Matthew effect, in cases of collaboration or multiple discoveries, may operate to heighten the visibility of new scientific communications. This is not the first instance of a social pattern's being functional for certain aspects of a social system and dysfunctional for certain individuals within that system. (*ibid.*: 447–8)

It is hard to believe that Merton here is using 'function' in an explanatory sense. The idea that redundancy or the disproportionate attention to seniority are *explained* by the benefits these phenomena confer on the growth of knowledge is too implausible to entertain. Merton is simply calling attention to certain consequences of behavioural patterns in science. The question is, why would he want to do this? One answer, mentioned earlier, could be that the consequences are surprising, counterintuitive or paradoxical. In the present case this does not seem to be the case. It is pretty obvious that the chances of a problem being solved increase with the number of scholars working on it, but that each new scholar creates a smaller increment of success (at least beyond a certain number). The Matthew effect owes its fame, I believe, more to the lucky choice of a phrase than to any surprising insights it has yielded.

Another, more plausible answer is that the identification of consequences can be important for policy reasons. Research councils need to know about the optimal degree of redundancy of funding. Journal editors might want to resist claims for more democracy in science, e.g. for the alphabetical listing of authors. In Merton's discussion of the political machine the policy aspects also form an important theme, and serve as basis for a warning to politicians against replacing the machine with another system that does not deliver the same goods.

What, then, are we to conclude? Does Merton simply restate Mandeville's insight, that 'those who can enlarge their view, and will give themselves the leisure of gazing at the prospect of concatenated events, may, in a hundred places, see *Good* spring up and pullulate from *Evil*, as naturally as chickens do from eggs'? Or does he claim, more ambitiously, that the evil we observe in the cause can be *explained* by the good we see in the effect? I have to report that after many readings and re-readings I still do not know. Perhaps Merton has been playing the oldest game of all, that of suggesting the strong claim without actually sticking his neck out and embracing it explicitly? More charitably and more plausibly, does his laudable love for rich empirical detail and for fine conceptual distinctions make it difficult for him to stand back from his material and perceive the larger structure of the argument? The force of the 1936 essay on unanticipated consequences, written before his mind was uncluttered with the formidable array of facts that he has since mastered and assimilated, might support this answer.

NOTES

1 I am assuming, for simplicity, that all benefits are ultimately benefits *to people*, not to some abstract entity like 'society' or 'science'. This may be a dubious assumption in some cases. In a society divided on ethnic, religious or similar grounds, an institution may benefit 'society' by ensuring a minimal level of integration even if all individuals would be better off were it to break up into two or more autonomous units. Also 'science' as a system of knowledge may well benefit from practices that provide few tangible benefits to identifiable individuals.

2 Elsewhere, however, Merton (1957a: 65) *opposes* the analysis of latent functions to analysis in terms of 'manipulation by powerful subgroups'.

3 G. A. Cohen (1978, 1982) disagrees with both statements. First, he argues, an explanation by consequences can be backed by a *consequence law* rather than by a mechanism. Second, the underlying mechanism (which must be assumed to exist but need not be exhibited for the explanation to be valid) can take the form of *causally efficacious dispositions* rather than of feedback loops. For the present purposes, these disagreements are of secondary importance.

Interchange

BOUDON REPLIES TO ELSTER

I am always surprised by the ease with which the title 'classic' is granted—or refused—to social scientists by social scientists. While it may take centuries for a musical work to become a classic, as in the case of Charpentier's *Medée*, for a sociological paper it often takes only one or two years. The two texts of Robert Merton discussed by Professor Elster are somewhat older, but I have no opinion as to whether they have 'the status of a classic'. I know only that they are important, and I have the feeling that Elster is unfair to the text on 'Manifest and Latent Functions'.

Although I cannot go into detail here, it seems to me that Merton has shown in this text—and this is not a negligible achievement—that the concept of function can have a positive and fruitful use, but also a negative and dangerous one. While he does not use these exact words, he has made clear in the paper that the concept of function is acceptable when it is used as a kind of shorthand notation summarizing social processes which can also, though more awkwardly, be described without using the concept of function. To put this idea into the form of a methodological theorem: the notion of function is useful only if it is not indispensable. Thus, when Merton showed how, at the time he conducted his analysis, the Democratic Party machine met needs among the lower classes which were not satisfied by a public social security system of the type developed, say, in Germany or France, and how this also served the interests of the Party, then he gave an illuminating example in which the word 'function' is used in a purely nominal way. This example and many others suggest that *function* is an acceptable and useful concept when it is entirely dissociated from any *functionalist* view of society. This implies a sharp distinction—again using non-Mertonian vocabulary—between what might be called methodological functionalism and substantive functionalism. As I have tried to show elsewhere (Boudon, 1980: 195–202), Merton was probably the first sociologist to suggest clearly that the notion of function was useful and perfectly acceptable in the first context, and dangerous and unacceptable in the second.

As to Merton's notion of latent function, one may not like the concept, but it points, if not to the major *function*, at least to one of the major *duties* of the social sciences. Manifest functions are visible and do not need the social sciences to be detected. Latent functions are not only invisible but sometimes half-consciously hidden. Social actors have good reasons not to recognize their existence. Thus, because producers of collective goods, such as political parties or trade unions, are exposed to the free-riding of their potential members, they have to create or take advantage of a variety of mechanisms in order to fulfil their manifest function more effectively. For example, to increase their organizational strength, trade unions may apply a range of indirect and direct pressures on non-members in order to force them to join. But these mechanisms will have to remain latent for obvious social reasons. No trade union wishes to admit or let it be widely known that it is forcing people to join its organization. A study such as Olson's *Logic of Collective Action* (1965), among others, confirms the usefulness of the notion of latent function.

ELSTER REPLIES TO BOUDON

[*Ed. note*: Elster refrained from writing a rejoinder as he felt there was nothing in Boudon's contribution with which he disagreed.]

VI. STRUCTURAL CONSTRAINTS AND OPPORTUNITIES

11. Structural Constraints and Opportunities: Merton's Contribution to General Theory

PETER M. BLAU

The specific contributions for which Robert K. Merton is probably most widely known are his paradigm of functional analysis and his conception of middle-range theories. This does not do him justice, however. It does not include any of the significant analyses from his lifelong concern with the sociology of science. What is more important, it ignores the fact that his greatest contribution, particularly in the last decades, has been to advance general theory to explain social life in terms of structural constraints.

This has been his central interest since the beginning of his scholarly career, though it has not been his sole interest throughout the half century of it. He has also advanced other theoretical approaches and schemes (as well as engaged in empirical research). Hence he is—to use his own term—a 'self-exemplifying' case of the need for pluralism in sociological theorizing. Yet there have been several trends in his work moving from earlier theoretical perspectives to a new distinct one. Three major trends are: from cultural to structural theories (as illustrated by the difference between his work on the sociology of science in the first and second parts of his life); from functional to causal-structural explanations; and from middle-range to general theorizing.

The objective of this paper is to review Merton's increasing focus on structural analysis and general theories. I am not the first to note these changes in Merton's theoretical conception. Others have called attention to them, notably Stinchcombe (1975) and Crothers (1987a), and Merton himself (for example, 1976a) has acknowledged the structural focus that has evolved in his theoretical analysis. Although my discussion will recapitulate Stinchcombe's and Crothers's reformulations of Merton's theorizing, I plan to go on to indicate that he has made even more extensive contributions to advancing a general theory of structural constraints than their analysis specifies. I shall also point out a suggestive analogy of the discrepancy between Simmel's theoretical contribution and reputation and Merton's, and note Simmel's more implicit as well as Durkheim's clearly explicit influence on Merton.

STRUCTURAL CONSTRAINTS

Durkheim is the classical theorist by whom Merton was most influenced. His first two publications (1934a, 1934b) deal with Durkheim, one of them exclusively with his *Division of Labor in Society*, and Merton frequently cites him, acknowledges his indebtedness to him, uses his analysis as a model of scientific theorizing in sociology (1945b), and employs a Durkheimian conception as starting point for his own theoretical analyses. The best example of the last is Merton's (1938b) well-known analysis of deviance, perhaps the theory of his that influenced empirical research most, in which he completely reformulates Durkheim's concept of anomie to generate an original theoretical scheme.

Durkheim's Influence

Of the great pioneers of sociology who wrote about a century ago, Durkheim is the extreme case of a pure, and essentially structural, sociologist ('social realist'). He conceptualized sociology as the study of social facts and stressed that social facts must be explained in terms of other social facts, not in terms of psychological motives or any other non-social conditions, whether geographical or biological (see Durkheim, 1895). By social fact he referred to those conditions in a population (in the social environment) that exert external constraints on its individual members. The study of social facts so conceived cannot be based on data about a sample of individuals but requires comparison of societies or other social collectivities. For social facts characterize populations, not individuals, and their relationships—like that of division of labour and solidarity or that between divorce rates and suicide rates—can only be examined by comparing social collectivities.

Durkheim also exerted another important influence on Merton, which was methodological rather than substantive. Whereas most nineteenth century forefathers of sociology did not develop theories based on quantitative research, Durkheim did—in his theory of suicide (1897). Although his statistical procedure is sometimes rudimentary, conceptually his quantitative analysis is very sophisticated. A good illustration is that he avoided the ecological fallacy—half a century before this fallacy was pointed out (Robinson, 1950)—when analyzing the influence of the prevalence of divorce on suicide rates by controlling marital status (by the simple strategy of comparing the suicide rates of only *married* men in countries that differ in the frequency of divorce). Durkheim's use of empirical data in constructing a brilliant theory undoubtedly affected Merton's burgeoning interest in systematic research as a basis for theory-building after he was appointed at Columbia University and came to respect, and later to collaborate with, Lazarsfeld.

'Structural constraints' has been a central concept in most of Merton's analysis, whether or not he explicitly used the term. It is a reconceptualization and refinement of Durkheim's social facts that exert external constraints on individuals. Merton did not dismiss motives as irrelevant, as Durkheim did. Indeed, he emphasized the significance of motivation as an intervening mechanism through which structural constraints usually become effective, but his theoretical focus is on the structural conditions as the crucial explanatory concept to account for social relations and conduct. Whereas the constraining social structure is nothing but the pattern of social relations (such as a group's social network) and positions (such as a society's class structure) of the very people who are being constrained, for each of them it constitutes external restraints on choices.

As already mentioned, Merton's first major paper is based on Durkheim's concept of anomie. He starts by reconceptualizing this concept in cultural terms, defining it by the discrepancy between cultural goals and cultural norms, specifically by the strains engendered if the cultural goals cannot be attained by following cultural norms. However, he explains the form deviance is likely to take in structural terms, that is, on the basis of the position of individuals in the class structure. The opportunity structure is closely related to the status structure. People's opportunities depend on their location in the class structure and, in turn, determine their probable adaptation to discrepancies between cultural goals and the normatively legitimate means. Thus members of the lowest classes have such poor opportunities to achieve the goal of financial success by legitimate means that they relatively often try to do so by illegitimate ones, as manifest in high rates of delinquency. On the other hand, members of the lower middle classes have been so strongly socialized to conform to cultural norms that their most likely reaction to being unable to achieve financial success is to lose their ambition and ritualistically conform to the norms of hard work and thrift without any hope of success.

From Functional to Structural Analysis

In the late 1940s Merton developed his well-known functional paradigm. Merton accepted the basic functional orientation and assumptions of his former teacher, Talcott Parsons. But he completely reconceptualized Parsons's approach to produce a methodologically rigorous and precise conceptual scheme. The importance Merton attached to the functional paradigm is indicated by his placing it first in his new major book on social theory (1949a) and by his claim that 'this framework of functional analysis...guided...all the papers in this volume' (*ibid*.: 11). Crothers (1987a: 73), quoting this statement, notes quite correctly that hardly any of them 'use functional analysis in the strict sense' and many of them do not use it at all.

As a matter of fact, a fundamental structural approach remains an element in the functional paradigm itself. Merton specifies that after tracing functional and dysfunctional consequences of an item, one must examine what alternative items could—and possibly do in other societies—serve the same function and which structural constraints have determined that the observed item rather than some possible alternative serves this function in the society studied. Note that these stipulations clearly imply that the existence of an observed social pattern (item) is not accounted for by its functions, as it is in traditional functional analysis, but by the causal influences of structural conditions. In short, the inclusion of these concepts in the functional paradigm makes it, in effect, a paradigm of structural analysis.

In the next few decades Merton moved more and more from a functional to a structural theoretical approach. The first publications that explicitly stressed

Merton's renewed focus on structuralism were an article by Barbano (1968) and a book by Wallace (1969). It was, however, Stinchcombe (1975) who explicitly formulated the structural theory implicit in Merton's writings. He suggests that Merton's emerging theory centres on 'choice between socially structured alternatives' (*ibid.*: 12). The institutional structure governs alternatives and, depending on location in the social structure, the chances of realizing various alternatives; the rates of alternative choices vary, therefore, according to people's position in the social structure. The major mechanisms that mediate the impact of the institutional structure on rates of choice, according to Stinchcombe, are motivation, information and social sanctions, all of which differ by people's location in the status structure.

Further Reconceptualization of Merton's Structuralism

Although Crothers (1987a: 85–91) praises Stinchcombe's reformulation and agrees with much of it, he takes exception to his stress on process rather than structure, and, particularly, to Stinchcombe's centering attention on individual choices rather than the structural opportunities and restraints that channel these choices by increasing the opportunities for some and limiting those for others. In other words, by concentrating on processes of individual choice, Stinchcombe minimizes the significance of structural constraints in Merton's theories. Crothers (*ibid.*: 89) also criticizes Stinchcombe for failing to give Merton credit for generally recognizing, if only implicitly, that underlying the microstructures he usually analyzes is a macrostructure (by which he often refers to the class structure) that exerts a significant influence on them.[1]

Crothers illustrates his conception of Merton's structuralism by reanalyzing his sociology of science (*ibid.*: 136–9). The starting point of his structural theory, Crothers points out, is the analysis of the institutional structure, specifically the institution's major goal, in this case the advancement of knowledge, and the related reward structure—recognition for contributions to such advancement—and opportunity structure—access to means for making contributions. This institutional structure motivates scientists to contribute to science. Thus motivation is taken into account, but only after an analysis of the institutional structure and as mechanism for implementing institutional objectives. The aggregate performance of individuals (scientists) has feedback effects which modify the institutional structural influences on individuals. Thus, Crothers concludes, Merton's theory encompasses 'both agency and structure (both free will and determinism)... [but] his focus remains unrelentingly on social structures' (*ibid.*: 152).

Whereas Stinchcombe's reconceptualization of Merton's theory (in structural rather than functional terms) centres attention on choice, Crothers endeavours to refocus it on structural constraints. But he also remains too concerned with motivated behaviour for a strictly Durkheimian interpretation of Merton's structural theory, as indicated by his positive evaluation of including 'both free will and determinism' in a sociological theory. This may be a meaningful issue in philosophy and possibly psychology, but it is a red herring in social science. It is evident that social conditions—whether economic, political, cultural or socio-structural—influence behaviour, and it is equally evident that they do not completely determine it. Whether the behaviour that cannot be explained by social influences manifests free will or psychological influences is not relevant for social scientists.[2] The distinctly sociological question is how differences in social conditions among societies or other collectivities affect the prevailing patterns of social relations or conduct, not why some individuals and not others manifest these patterns. In other words, the structural question is how variations in social structure affect the probability or rate of certain social conduct, whoever exhibits this conduct.

This can be illustrated with Merton's analysis of social deviance. Of course it is an important question what personality or background characteristics distinguish deviants from conformists, but it is primarily a question for psychologists and social psychologists, not for structural sociologists.[3] Questions for sociologists are how class and status differences influence the likelihood (rate) of deviance, or the likelihood of anomie, or the influence of location in the status structure on the probabilities of various forms of deviance.[4]

One important implication of the social structure, particularly the class or status structure, is that location in it governs access to legitimate opportunities for success, as Merton originally points out in his paper on deviance (1938b).[5] The conception of opportunity structure, which becomes increasingly important in Merton's theoretical analysis, may be broadly conceived to refer to all social conditions affecting chances, for instance, not only how the unemployment rate affects the chances of getting a job but also how a school's sex composition influences the chances of girls and boys to have dates. Opportunity structure and structural constraints are complementary concepts: restricted opportunities become constraints; fewer constraints enlarge opportunities. Another important refinement of status structure introduced by Merton are the concepts of status-set and role-set. Since these abstract terms illustrate particularly well the transition from middle-range to general theories in his work, they are discussed in the next section.

GENERAL THEORIES

Simmel did not exert as pervasive and profound an influence on Merton's thinking and writing as Durkheim, but he did influence them in various subtle ways. Merton knows Simmel's work thoroughly, used it in his courses, gave seminars on it and acknowledges its influence, particularly on his classification of group properties (see Levine, Carter and Gorman, 1976: 820).

Simmel's Significance

There is a suggestive analogy between Merton's theoretical reputation and actual contribution and Simmel's. Simmel is widely praised for his insightful substantive discussions, his specific theoretical analyses of diverse subjects, such as conflict, the quantitative dimension of social life, the stranger, and social exchange. Several authors, notably L. Coser (1965: 6–10; 1975b) and Levine (1981; Levine *et al.*, 1976), stress the theoretical contributions Simmel has made through his analysis of these and other social processes. However, the first chapter of his major book (Simmel, 1908), in which he outlined his theoretical scheme centred on the concept *Formen der Vergesellschaftung*, tends to be dismissed as formalistic, and most commentators consider him not to have made a major contribution to systematic general theory[6] (a major exception being Dahme[7]). I disagree with this prevailing negative evaluation of Simmel's contribution to social theory, for reasons I shall supply presently.

Merton is probably the most famous living sociologist, renowned for his many insightful middle-range theories. But he has also been often criticized for failing to have developed a systematic general theory. I disagree, and I am not alone, since in recent years other sociologists have called attention to the general theoretical scheme implicit in Merton's major specific theoretical analyses. I want to detour to discuss Simmel's rarely recognized contribution to general theory in order to indicate the parallel with Merton's belatedly recognized one.

Formen der Vergesellschaftung (social forms) are for Simmel not formalistic categories for a taxonomy but theoretical concepts that abstract the distinctly social aspects from diverse empirical observations of social life. He emphasized in the introductory chapter of *Soziologie* (1908) that any theory must abstract analytical elements from empirical reality, and a social form is the purely social element which diverse observable processes and structures have in common. As theoretical abstractions, pure social forms cannot be directly measured or represented by empirical variables. For they cannot be observed except as manifest in substantive contents. In real life there is no competition as such, there is only economic competition, or rivalry in courtship, or political competition, or athletic contests (indeed, only particular instances of each can be directly observed). Competition as a form of association is Simmel's theoretical term to abstract the common social element from these (and other) diverse phenomena.

An illustration of a theoretical term that abstracts a generic *structural* social form is Simmel's profound concept of cross-cutting social circles.[8] The multigroup affiliations of people, which are especially pronounced in modern society, create a social structure with many intersecting circles. The various dimensions of social differences among people are not perfectly related—particularly not in large and complex communities. This produces an intricate web of group affiliations, with every person being socially located at the intersection of a number of different groups, which often put conflicting social pressures on her or him. Cross-cutting social circles are pure forms of social structures abstracted from their empirical contents. They do not refer to the particular groups to which people belong (Catholic or Protestant) or even to the specific kinds of intersecting groups (religious and ethnic and occupational), but to the degree of intersection of group memberships whatever the nature of the groups. For instance, the question is not which ethnic groups and which religious ones are found in a community, but how weakly related ethnic and religious affiliations—indeed, any social affiliations—are.

Abstract Theoretical Terms

Simmel's theoretical term *Formen der Vergesellschaftung*, if I interpret it correctly, anticipates Braithwaite's most original contribution to the method of scientific theorizing. Philosophers of science, notably Popper (1959), Braithwaite (1953) and Hempel (1965), refined earlier advances in the method of scientific theorizing by developing critical rationalism and the hypothetico-deductive model, which they opposed to logical positivism and inductive theorizing. The gist of the model is that theories are deductive systems of general hypotheses that logically imply empirical propositions, some that are already known, which the theory explains, and others that are new predictions, with which the theory can be tested.

Conceptual analysis or refinement, however insightful, is not a scientific theory in these terms. But this does not mean that profound fruitful concepts play no role in theorizing. Indeed, Braithwaite's most distinctive contribution is to demonstrate that the higher level principles of a deductive theory must contain purely theoretical abstractions that go beyond any empirical variable or operational measure. Unless a theory includes such strictly theoretical terms, even its highest order generalizations refer merely to the relationships of empirical variables, which means that the theory can neither explain empirical observations nor be tested by making new predictions. Empirical regularities cannot be explained by simply subsuming several of them under one proposition that summarizes them, but only by discovering abstract terms that go beyond any operational variable and are used in theoretical generalizations from which the empirical regularities are deducible. Moreover, only theories that contain such terms can make new empirical predictions which make them testable.

This important conclusion of Braithwaite's about the need for abstract theoretical terms was anticipated, though only roughly and without being systematically explicated, nearly half a century earlier by Simmel's concept of *Formen der Vergesellschaftung* and his analysis of these social abstractions.[9] In other words, Simmel realized, at least dimly and implicitly, that systematic sociological theory requires, not only abstracting the distinctly social analytical elements from the diverse manifestations of social life—economic, political, educational and others—but also that explanatory principles be formulated with strictly theoretical terms. He advanced many such theoretical terms and used them in explanations. Though he never organized a systematic body of theory—as did other pioneers, notably Durkheim and Weber—by anticipating two essential but often neglected requirements of scientific theory in sociology, he made no less a contribution to the advancement of our discipline than any of its forefathers.

Status-sets and Role-sets

Merton's fruitful concepts of status-sets and role-sets were undoubtedly stimulated by Simmel's concept of cross-cutting social circles. The central idea is that people do not only occupy multiple statuses, as Linton has noted, but that each status also involves several roles and role relations with others who themselves occupy different statuses, whereas Linton attributed only a single role to each status. To illustrate in Merton's own words: 'the single status of medical student entails not only the role of a student in relation to his teachers, but also an array of other roles relating the occupant of that status to other students, physicians, social workers, medical technicians, etc.' (1968 : 423).

This conception is a substantial refinement not only of Linton's concepts of status and role, which for Linton were virtually equivalent, but also of Simmel's cross-cutting social circles. It calls attention to various implications of cross-cutting circles for the actual roles people perform in their recurrent social interaction, thereby suggesting a series of new sociological problems to Merton. Thus he analyzes how role-sets may engender cross pressures, because role partners differently located in the status structure have conflicting role expectations; the problems for ego differences in power among role partners create; and the various mechanisms that help individuals cope with these conflicts and problems. Examples of such mechanisms are: greater involvement in some role relations than in others; insulating role performance in one role from observability by other role partners; getting support from others in the same shoes (for example, other students facing the same new demands from teachers).

The concepts of status- and role-sets, and related ones like status sequence, are genuine theoretical terms abstracted from the combinations of particular social positions, particular role relations and particular status sequences, in which alone they find empirical expression and can be observed. Nevertheless, and although Merton's conceptual refinement enables him to raise various theoretical issues, he has not been able to use these fruitful concepts and suggestive issues to construct a general theory. [10] This does not mean, however, that there is no general theory underlying Merton's specific substantive or, in his terms, middle-range theories (which is not entirely explicit, although more so than Simmel's, because Merton's middle-range theories have a much more systematic and coherent structure).

From Middle-Range to General Theory

Trained in the European tradition of grand systems of social theorizing at Harvard University in the 1930s, Merton initially wrote as a broad theorist and was quite critical of quantitative survey research (see Merton, 1936b). However, he soon became disenchanted with grand speculative theories like those of Sorokin and Parsons. Shortly after accepting a junior appointment at Columbia University, where he has remained for the rest of his scholarly career, he wrote a paper (1945b) in which he emphasized the need for rigorous theory in sociology. He distinguished such theories, which consist of logically interrelated propositions that imply testable predictions, from other sociological discussions that are often claimed to be theoretical, such as theoretical orientations (like the Marxist or the psychoanalytical orientation) and ad hoc interpretations. [11] In this period he also developed a growing interest in empirical research, under the influence of his collaboration with Paul F. Lazarsfeld, another recent appointment at Columbia University.

Merton's concern with rigorous theorizing found expression in his concept of middle-range theories, which also synthesized his continuing theoretical and his emerging research interest. Middle-range theories are rooted in and testable through empirical research. As Merton puts it succinctly: 'Middle-range theory is principally used in sociology to guide empirical inquiry. It...involves abstractions, of course, but they are close enough to observed data to be incorporated in propositions that permit empirical testing' (1968: 39). [12] Promoting middle-range theories has been the most direct expression of Merton's endeavour to transform sociology from a social philosophy to a science of social life.

In rejecting general in favour of middle-range social theories as part of his criticism of speculative theorizing in sociology, Merton threw out the baby with the bathwater. Stinchcombe (1975: 26) also suggests this when he notes that 'generality has been confused with woolliness. Merton, in taking up the correct position on woolliness, has tricked himself into taking up the incorrect position on general theory'. Precise formulation, not a narrow range, is what makes a theory empirically testable and fruitful for research. Indeed, precisely formulated *general* theories are not only more fruitful but also, according to Popper (1959: 121–6), more readily testable (falsifiable) than equally precise *limited* theories, because the former have implications for a greater variety of fields and thus can make more different empirical predictions through which they can be tested.

Stinchcombe outlines the general theory of 'choice between socially structured alternatives' which he considers to be implicit in Merton's theoretical analyses. Crothers extends this line of analysis. He is critical of Stinchcombe's focus on individual choice and refocuses instead on the constraining institutional structure. Merton's general theory which Crothers infers from his various middle-range theories, particularly his theory of science, centres on the institutional status and reward structures that act as mechanisms to further institutional goals (for instance, scientific advancement) by conferring recognition and superior status on persons (scientists) in exchange for contributing to institutional goals (scientific accomplishments). Crothers's (as well as Stinchcombe's) formulation has been briefly summarized above, and so has my modification of it.

But does this general theory not reintroduce functional principles, a criticism that has been made of Merton's sociology of science, as Crothers (1987a: 135) acknowledges. The criticism is not necessarily justified. It is justified if one assumes that the status structure and reward system in science are in fact perfectly integrated with the accomplishments of scientists and thus with the advancement of knowledge, the institution's goal. (Corresponding considerations apply to other institutional systems.) One must admit that Merton's great admiration for science and scientific accomplishments sometimes makes him sound as if he made this assumption. But then one must remind oneself that Merton also introduced the analysis of such concepts as accumulation of advantage and disadvantage, priority disputes, the Matthew effect and the self-fulfilling prophecy.

The criticism is not justified if the theory is considered as a normative theory, not one that claims that scientific institutions always promote the advancement of knowledge, but one that describes how scientific institutions should be designed to serve the advancement of knowledge. And Merton's analysis of priority disputes (which encourage false claims or even falsifying evidence, and at least divert energies from scientific work) and the Matthew effect (though he himself benefits from it) indicate that he realizes that science does not function as perfectly as it ideally should, nor do other institutions.[13]

ON THE SHOULDERS...

Merton advanced concepts and paradigms suited for a general sociological theory. But he has not explicitly formulated a body of interrelated propositions that would constitute the general theory underlying his middle-range theories. Stinchcombe and Crothers outlined somewhat different versions of such a theory. I shall indicate his contribution to general structural theory another way. I shall illustrate how his concepts, notably the concepts of status structure, opportunity structure and structural constraints, have provided the building-blocks for constructing a macro-structural theory. (Although much of his own analysis has been microstructural, his conceptions apply to macrostructural as well as microstructural analysis.) For this purpose, I shall use a précis of my theory (1977) of the influence of the status structure on intergroup relations in a community as a case in point.[14]

A Macrostructural Theory

The initial problem addressed by the theory is how the structure of social positions in a society or other population influences the structure of social relations. Of special interest are intergroup relations, a term used as shorthand for relations between persons in different social positions in any respect. The population composition of a society or community governs the opportunities for establishing intergroup relations. It determines the opportunity structure for various social relations. In Spain, where most people are Catholic, and in Sweden, where most are Protestant, the chances of having a friend in a different religious group than one's own are less than in the United States, where people are distributed among many religious denominations. To be sure, the population structure is not the only factor that influences people's associates.

Cultural values and psychological dispositions naturally exert much influence on people's choices, including their choices of associates. Preferences and choices are not necessarily realized, however. The social structure imposes limits on the opportunities to realize choices. Thus the chances of upward mobility are greater in periods of economic growth than in those of decline. A man's chance to find a wife is best in cities with low sex ratios. These external constraints of the population structure on choices of associates, and other choices, are Durkheim's (1895) social facts. They influence the probabilities and rates of social relations and conduct. The central subject-matter of sociology, in my view, is the study of these structural constraints limiting the opportunities of realizing choices for many while expanding them for some, and thereby affecting the prevailing patterns (probabilities or rates) of social interaction and action.[15]

The major theoretical terms of the theory refer to the extent of social differentiation among people in a society or other collectivity. Two of them pertain to the social differences among people in a single dimension. Their empirical manifestation is the population distribution in this dimension. One of them refers to people's distribution among groups or social categories with relatively clear boundaries, such as ethnic or religious groups, the other to their distribution on an ordered status continuum, such as educational or socio-economic status. The first represents the degree of heterogeneity in a certain dimension, the second the degree of inequality in one dimension. The precise definition of heterogeneity is the probability that two randomly chosen persons belong to different groups; that of inequality is that the two members of a randomly chosen pair differ by a certain (absolute or relative) amount on the criterion of inequality (for example, by $5000 in income, or by one-half the average income), which is the same as the mean difference between all possible pairs.

Examining various differences among people one at a time does not tell us enough about the differentiation in the community (or other population), because the overall differentiation depends also on the strength to which various forms of differentiation are related. The more wealth, power, income, education and race are related, the more crystallized is the class structure. The third major concept of the theory, designed to take this important aspect of social differentiation into account, refers to the extent to which various kinds of differentiation are related or its complement—the degree to which they intersect. The intersection of social differences—which implies that social differences in one respect are not strongly related to those in other respects—represents Simmel's cross-cutting social circles. We know, of course, that variations in economic resources are not unrelated to variations in power, prestige, ethnic affiliation and place of residence. Nor are differences in occupational status unrelated to differences in education, income, sex and political affiliation. However, the extent to which one social difference is related to or (conversely) intersects with others varies among communities and among societies, which has important implications for social life.

Assumptions and Theorems

The two major primitive assumptions of the theory are: (1) social associations are more prevalent between persons in proximate than those in distant social positions;[16] and (2) the likelihood of social association depends on opportunities for contact. Most theorems are deduced (directly or indirectly) from these assumptions and the definitions of concepts. The theoretical concepts are abstractions; heterogeneity as such, for instance, does not exist; it can be empirically observed only in its specific manifestations, such as ethnic heterogeneity or occupational heterogeneity. Empirical predictions, which employ such specific operational manifestations of the theoretical terms, are deduced from the theorems, and these predictions can test the theory. Since the theoretical terms, as well as the various operational variables reflecting them, refer to structural properties of societies or other collectivities, the predictions of the theory must be tested in comparative research on many societies or other population structures; they cannot be studied in a survey of a sample of individuals.

The derivation of theorems can be illustrated with the heterogeneity theorem. It stipulates that heterogeneity promotes intergroup relations. Although this seems paradoxical, given the first assumption, it is deducible from the second assumption and the definition of heterogeneity. If the likelihood of social association depends on contact opportunities; and if heterogeneity is defined in terms of the probability that any two persons belong to different groups; it follows that heterogeneity increases fortuitous intergroup contacts, some of which are likely to develop into lasting relations, possibly friendships and even marriage. This is simply the result of mathematical probability, which is implicit in the second assumption. Nevertheless, the theorem is not trivial, as it seems to contradict the repeatedly demonstrated tendency of people to associate with people like themselves. Of course, heterogeneity does not nullify these ingroup preferences, but it does exert structural constraints for some people to set aside these preferences in one respect or other.[17]

As another illustration, the intersection theorem is derived from its definition and the first assumption. If ingroup associations occur disproportionately often, as the first assumption stipulates; and if the degree of intersection is defined by the strength of the relationships between a population's social differences in various dimensions; it follows that the ingroup tendencies of people in one dimension involve increasing numbers in intergroup relations in other dimensions the more the dimensions intersect. For much intersection implies that many people who belong to the same group (have similar ranks) in one respect belong to different groups (have dissimilar ranks) in other respects, so that their very ingroup choices along some lines involve many in intergroup relations along others.

To test the theorems, their empirical implications for the influences on intermarriage probabilities of nine forms of heterogeneity and ten manifestations of intersection were derived. These were tested with data on the population structure of the 125 American metropolitan areas with a population of more than a quarter million in 1970 (Blau and Schwartz, 1984). The research results reveal that heterogeneity is positively related to intermarriage, and so is intersection, which corroborates the theory.

Complex Social Structures

Complex social structures consist of multiple levels of structure. Societies are composed of regions, regions of counties, counties of communities and communities of neighbourhoods. The social structure of the units on any level can be analyzed. Moreover, a thorough analysis of the structure of the encompassing units should take the structure of their subunits into account. The structural properties of the larger social unit are not simply the average properties of its subunits, because there are social differences among as well as within its subunits. Thus the ethnic heterogeneity of a city may be the result of much ethnic heterogeneity within most of its neighbourhoods with little difference in ethnic composition among neighbourhoods. In contrast, another city may have the same extent of total ethnic heterogeneity although there is little heterogeneity *within* neighbourhoods because there is much *among* them (that is, different neighbourhoods are inhabited by different ethnic groups). Clearly, there is much less opportunity for interethnic contact in the second segregated city than in the first ethnically integrated one, notwithstanding the same overall ethnic heterogeneity in the two.

To detect this important difference it is necessary to decompose any form of differentiation in a complex unit into the differences within and the differences among its subunits.[18] In the study of large social units, like nations, decomposition could be repeated on several levels. Thus the economic inequality in a country (whether represented by wealth or income differences) could be decomposed into that within and among regions, that within and among counties, that within and among communities and that within and among neighbourhoods. The further down into subunits inequality penetrates, the less pronounced are class differences likely to be and the less impact they are likely to have on social life.

Intersecting social differences are the macrosociological counterpart of Merton's role-sets.[19] Since they promote intergroup associations, intersecting social circles make it likely that people have relatively large role-sets with others in diverse social positions, which promotes tolerance, engenders intellectual stimulation and fosters autonomy, as R. Coser (1975) points out in her elaboration of the implications of role-sets. But the range of people's role-sets does not necessarily imply intersecting social differences. For people in one social status can have role relations—as superiors, peers or subordinates—with others in a variety of social positions, whether or not status differences in this respect intersect with those in other dimensions. For example, a bank president is likely to supervise subordinates, negotiate with presidents of other corporations and report to the chairman of the board, regardless of the strength of the relationship of occupational status to race, education, income and wealth.

The concept of role-set is broader than that of intersection and is concerned with role relations independent of macrostructural conditions. It deals with such issues as social cross pressures, diversity of associates, variations in observability by role partners or difficulties in integrating the role-set. On the other hand, the concept of intersecting social differences centres attention on structural influences, on the probability of certain social relations independent of the particular individuals performing various roles. It focuses on such issues as the probabilities of intergroup relations or the consolidation of status differences of various sorts that are likely to crystallize the class structure. Whereas Merton centres attention on micro-sociological analysis, his fruitful concepts and theories have implications for macrosociological analysis, as I have tried to exemplify.

CONCLUSIONS

Merton has not formulated a systematic body of general theory in sociology. But he has made major contributions to such a theory by supplying many tools for it. His early distinction of propositional theories from theoretical orientations and conceptual analyses (Merton, 1945b) anticipated later formulations of methods of social theorizing. His emphasis on constructing testable theories to be substituted for the prevailing philosophical speculations and conceptual analyses has moved sociology much closer to a science of social life. Most importantly, his insightful theoretical terms do not merely summarize various empirical data or findings but are abstractions from them. Illustrations of such abstract theoretical terms are: structural constraints; status structure, notably the distribution of 'authority, power influence and prestige' (1976a: 124); opportunity structure; unanticipated consequences, analyzed in one of his first papers and influencing his work ever since; the four forms of deviance; status-sets and role-sets.

Even what others, and I too, have criticized as his limitations or errors were often—to use a phrase of his—'fruitful errors'. His advocacy of middle-range theory may well have been a needed step for moving sociology from speculative social thought to a scientific discipline. The functional paradigm, which seems now to many of us to have been a blind alley, included such concepts as dysfunction and functional alternatives which helped Merton to overcome the limits of functionalism. Although much of his analysis is on the microlevel, he refers recurrently to underlying macrostructural influences and emphasizes their importance. He idolizes the natural sciences and seems to idealize their meritocratic institutions, yet he also has analyzed priority disputes and the Matthew effect, which reflect flaws in scientific institutions. In short, Merton has provided the foundation on which future sociologists can build a science of society.

NOTES

1 But this microfocus of Stinchcombe's may have been prompted, as Crothers (1987a: 101) himself points out, by Merton's own tendency to concentrate on microstructures even though he criticizes sociologists for only rarely studying macrostructural influences.

2 From the philosophical or psychological standpoint, it may be meaningful to conjecture whether we shall ever be able to account completely for the behaviour of individuals or whether there always will remain an unaccountable residue, which may be free will.

3 Note how little space Merton devotes to the difference between conformists and deviants and that his structural analysis concentrates on variations in (the probability of) forms of deviance.

4 The recent emphasis by sociologists on the need to take into account agency as well as structure (e.g. Giddens, 1984) must not be psychologistically misinterpreted. For sociologists, its correct use refers to the need for analyzing the feedback effects of the structurally constrained patterns or rates of social relations and conduct on modifying the structure, and not to the influences of psychological dispositions and motives on individual behaviour.

5 Whereas Merton uses in this paper the concept of opportunities for access to legitimate means for success, Cloward (1959) extends it to include access to illegitimate means, e.g. opportunities for learning the role of a delinquent.

6 Even commentators as sympathetic as Levine and colleagues (1976), who do point out Simmel's theoretical contributions (823–9), state that he 'failed to articulate all his sociological principles in a systematic manner' (823). A few years later, however, Levine disagreed with this evaluation of Simmel's approach as unsystematic (without mentioning that he had shared this evaluation), stating that 'despite his reputation for being so unsystematic Simmel may well have produced the most unified conception [of sociology] of any of the classic sociologists' (1981: 65).

7 Dahme's excellent recent monograph (1981, esp. 290–319, 465–81) on Simmel concludes a careful analysis of his work and various criticisms of it by emphasizing that his main contribution was to lay the theoretical foundation for sociology as an empirical-analytical science. See also Simmel (1905), which indicates how he derived his conception of abstract social forms, and ultimately of sociology, by applying Kant's a priori presuppositions of knowledge to knowledge of historical (social) knowledge.

8 Simmel's social forms are usually exemplified by social processes, such as competition and conflict, but many of them refer to properties of social structures, such as differentiation, triad, division of labour, population diversity (of a metropolis).

9 Dahme (1981: 317–18) notes that Simmel's theoretical approach was a precursor of critical rationalism, though he does not mention that Simmel also anticipated Braithwaite's emphasis on the need for abstract theoretical terms in scientific explanations.

10 Whereas Merton's reconceptualization of Simmel's concept of cross-cutting social circles enabled him to raise a number of new theoretical issues, it also transformed the theoretical term from a macrosociological to a microsociological one.

11 As already mentioned, he illustrated such genuine theories with Durkheim's (1897) theory of suicide.

12 Although Merton discussed the concept of middle-range theory in classes in the 1940s and introduced it briefly in the first edition of his major book (1949a), he fully elaborated it only in a later enlarged edition (1968: 39–72). Interestingly, he also modified the concept there to include quite broad and general theories, such as Weber's theory of the influence of religious value orientations on economic systems (*ibid.*: 63).

13 Whereas Merton is clearly aware of these 'dysfunctions', his analysis recurrently implies an image of science as a well integrated meritocratic system.

14 In developing this theory, I have been influenced by Durkheim and, particularly, Simmel as well as Merton.

15 Since the theorems do not specify what motivates choices, but how structural conditions affect the chances of their realization, they cannot be reduced to underlying psychological principles, as Homans (1961) claims all sociological theories can be.

16 This socio-psychological proposition, for which there is much empirical support, is assumed here as given. Since this is assumed, any theorems derived about the influence of location in the social structure on social relations would be tautological. The theory is not concerned with such propositions, however, but with propositions that stipulate how conditions in the social structure (not individuals' location in it) modify these psychological tendencies and thus affect the patterns of

social relations. (The term 'proximate position' refers both to belonging to the same group (category) and to having similar rank in a status hierarchy).

17 The same data set on the 125 largest metropolitan places in the United States (see Blau and Schwartz, 1984) indicates that when individuals within each place are analyzed, disproportionate numbers marry persons like themselves, but when different metropolitan structures are compared, heterogeneity increases the likelihood of intermarriage.

18 It is apparent that structural decomposition is the theoretical (or conceptual) counterpart of analysis of variance in empirical research. The substantive focus is different, however. Analysis of variance is interested in much between-group [sic] variation, which indicates significant group differences. Decomposition is interested in much within-group variation, which indicates that the influence of a city's overall heterogeneity, for example, is not counteracted by segregation.

19 The concept of status-sets is essentially Linton's, as Merton notes, and he uses it primarily to clarify the distinct nature of role-sets.

VII. STATUS-SETS AND ROLE-SETS

12. Reflections on Merton's Role-set Theory

ROSE LAUB COSER

AN OUTLINE OF ROLE-SET THEORY

Robert Merton's theory of social roles provides an analytical tool for sociological analysis in general, but it also does something more fundamental. It goes beyond offering an understanding of some structural processes in formal organizations, as I will show later in this chapter, and does more than explain behaviour of aggregates of individuals and deviations from the norm. It is a tool for understanding individual behaviour beyond the social-psychological, because it places behaviour in a specific structural, and not merely general environmental, context. Role-set theory states the structural circumstance that a status occupant relates to several role-partners, some or all of whom may differ in their expectations owing to their own differing positions in the structure.

A role-set consists of the role relationships a person has by virtue of occupying a particular social status (Merton, 1968: 423). In each status position a person has a set of role-partners, and usually deals separately with each of the sets. For a father, the family set includes his wife, his children, their teachers, his in-laws, and siblings, his parents, as well as the pediatrician and sometimes the veterinarian. A mother has a similar, though not the same role-set; for example, it may include other children's parents with whom she shares a car pool. In the occupational set the same person deals with associates on the job, and subordinates or superordinates on different levels of the hierarchy. The several role-sets of a status-holder constitute the status-set.

A role-set or status-set is a substructure of a larger network. The concepts refer to the relationships a person has by virtue of his or her status, and to the social positions of the various role-partners. Expectations emanating from the role-set or the status-set, therefore, emanate from the partners' structural positions. These can be specified, for their incumbents are not random acquaintances. A colleague's expectations of a faculty member differ from those a student may have, not merely because of personal idiosyncracies, but because of the demands of the specific positions these role-partners occupy. It is this structural specification of role-partners that gives the particular sociological imprimatur on the analysis, for it abstracts from any personal psychological traits of the interactors. Yet, since no individual has exactly the same role-set as any other, this conceptualization makes it possible to distinguish between individuals, not merely between aggregates of individuals. If one considers that the sum total of a person's role-set is different from any role-sets of other people, even if some of their positions are similar, it becomes clear that this theory is well suited to deal with variability and individual responses.

What is so interesting about role-set theory is that it calls attention to the differences, incompatibilities and even conflicts between expectations emanating from status-holders in different positions. A status-occupant must deal with such differences and incompatibilities, so that an individual effort is required. Differences within and between role-sets provide opportunities as well as constraints for status-occupants. This conceptualization takes us beyond an analysis of constraints upon status and role behaviour, because it calls attention not merely to uniformities but to the contradictions in social life.

Perhaps the most important part of role-set theory is Merton's specification of the mechanisms that are available for dealing with the contradictions that are endemic in role relationships. I will show that, for the mechanisms to operate even with a minimum degree of efficiency, it is incumbent upon status-holders to make choices. This is how the theory points to individualistic behaviour.

As Arditi (1987) has shown, role-set theory is particularly apt to deal with modern societies, because these are highly differentiated, so that those in the role-set do not necessarily have the same values and expectations. If they did, a high degree of order would prevail (Merton, 1968: 425). As it is, variabilities in expectations within the role-set could be a source of considerable disturbance. How is it, then, that it 'seems generally the case that a substantial degree of order rather than acute disorder prevails' (*ibid.*)?

It is to be noted that Merton speaks of a *degree* of order. He does not assume social order as the main characteristic of a society; on the contrary, he assumes social *disorder*, and he searches for those mechanisms whose operation alleviates, without necessarily eliminating, the disturbances that are endemic in a role-set . 'We are concerned', he says, not with the 'generalization that social order prevails but with the analytical problem of identifying the social mechanisms that operate to produce a greater degree of social order than would obtain if these mechanisms were not called into play' (*ibid.*).

Before examining the analytical fruitfulness of these mechanisms, it is useful to summarize them.

1   The fact that role-partners are not all concerned to the same degree with a status-holder's behaviour means that the latter can, to some extent at least, ignore the expectations of those who are less involved.
2   The fact that not all role-partners have equal power over the holder of a status again makes it easier for the latter to assign priorities in orientation.
3   The circumstance that all role-partners are not present at the same time enables the status-holder to respond to those who can observe his or her

behaviour and ignore, at least for the time being, expectations of those from whom his or her behaviour is insulated.

4   The fact that the occupant of a status can act to make the contradictions within the role-set manifest for the role-partners means that the status-occupant can help the role-set overcome what Floyd H. Allport and Robert K. Merton have called *pluralistic ignorance*. 'When it is made plain that the demands of some members of the role-set are in full contradiction with the demands of other members, it becomes the task of the role-set, rather than the task of the status-occupant, to resolve these contradictions' (Merton, 1968: 430).

5   The fact that a status-holder can receive social support from others who are in a similar position vis-à-vis their role-partners can lead to collective action, in the form of coalitions or alliances, a condition that makes possible a claim for collective, rather than individual, privilege.

6   Finally, there is, in extreme situations, the fact that some relationships can be broken by bringing about a replacement of some role-partners where such choice exists, or the status-holder can simply exit. Turnover in organizations, whether high or low, testifies to the fact that this is not an infrequent solution.

It is first to be noted that for any of these mechanisms to come into play it needs both appropriate structural circumstances and individual initiative. Let's take them one by one.

1   The differential concern or interest of role-partners in a status-occupant derives only exceptionally from personal predilection; it is an exigency inherent in their structural positions. Because of differences in task involvements, a superintendent of schools is not as much interested as the principal is in the details of behaviour of individual teachers. A teacher can orient behaviour to the interest shown by the principal. Or, if these are at odds, the teacher can appeal to the more general and aloof concern of the superintendent of schools.

2   While the superintendent is more powerful than the principal, a teacher can decide to play their power against each other and thus emanate as the *tertius gaudens*, the third who rejoices within the triadic relationship (cf. Simmel, 1950).

3   Not only in modern organizations, but in modern living arrangements as well, there are different rooms for occupants of different statuses, be it in an office or in a private home. At the same time it is expected that various status-occupants can decide to close their doors and make themselves invisible, or can confer with one or the other role-partner to the exclusion of others.

4   More than the previous mechanisms, this one is dependent on the initiative of the status-holder who is called upon to use both perceptiveness and social skill in helping the role-partner overcome pluralistic ignorance. 'Confronted with contradictory demands by members of his role-set, each of whom assumes that the legitimacy of his demands is beyond dispute, the occupant of a status can act to make these contradictions manifest'. At the same time, some social structures facilitate, others hinder, such initiative. As Merton also notes, 'the possibility of redirecting the conflict so that it is one between

members of the role-set rather than, as was first the case, between them and the occupant of the status' depends 'upon the structure of power' (Merton, 1968: 431), and we may add, on their social accessibility. It is easier for a student to inform teachers of their incompatible expectations than to inform the president or the trustees of the university.

5   Again, obtaining support from others who are in the same position requires some initiative on the part of the status-occupant. First, the latter must use mechanism 4 (above), and convince those who are similarly situated of their common interests vis-à-vis their role-partners; and next, together they must devise means for making mutual support effective. But here also, perhaps more so than with the operation of the previous mechanisms, the social structure must provide the opportunity for the use of such initiative. It is easier in an employment situation, say, where a number of people can be made aware of the fact that they are all similarly discriminated against, than in the case of obtaining housing, when non-acquaintance with other victims of discrimination may prevent both awareness of this fact, and, if recognized, prevent collective action in the form of mutual support and collective demands.

6   The sixth mechanism presents similar features. It is easier to rid oneself of a role-partner if there is recognition by others that this will be useful for the smooth operation of the role-set (mechanism 4) and where there is mutual support by status-occupants of similar positions (mechanism 5), each of which depends both on individual initiative and on appropriate structural circumstance.

The list of mechanisms for role articulation is, of course, not exhaustive. Merton makes no such claim. I will show that other mechanisms can be deduced from Merton's own theory, and that there are situations in which some of the mechanisms are interrelated. The value of a theory is to be judged not only for its usefulness in systematizing and revealing new thoughts about existing phenomena, but also for its ability to generate new ideas. An important test of a theory is not only its explanatory value but the possibility of more theorizing that follows from it. For example, the concept of *sociological ambivalence*, which Merton (with Elinor Barber, 1963; see also Merton, 1976a) has developed, and which I will refer to later in this paper, can be seen as a corollary of role-set theory. What is exciting, moreover, is that with his theorizing Merton invites others to think further with him along the lines that he has sketched.

In what follows I will give two examples about the usefulness of role-set theory for understanding more fully than heretofore some dynamics of social organization. Moreover, some distinctions are in order. Merton's distinction between role-set and status-set will help clarify some aspects of the social roles of women in American society. Another distinction that I have suggested is between restricted and complex role-sets, a distinction that may reveal some social resources for generating individualism and some dynamics of gender stratification.

AN ADDITIONAL MECHANISM OF ROLE ARTICULATION[1]

At least one other mechanism, which derives from some other conceptualization by

Merton, is worth noting here. Elsewhere Merton (1959a; see also 1949d), distinguishes between different kinds of conformity: he speaks of *attitudinal conformity* when individuals grant legitimacy to designated institutional values and norms; *behavioural conformity* when, whatever their attitudes, they act in accord with values and norms; and *doctrinal conformity* when they state institutionalized beliefs to others. These different forms of adaptation are available to different persons, and to the same person on different occasions in his or her various roles. The choice in range and intensity of attitudinal commitment provides a social mechanism for the articulation of roles in addition to those that Merton has identified.

While people can often choose not to involve their internal dispositions by living up merely to behavioural or doctrinal conformity, the point here is not mainly that role-partners, especially when they are sufficiently removed spatially, can be placated through written communication in doctrinal fashion, or that a person can put on an act for the benefit of a rare visitor. Rather, selection between these types of conformity is often socially prescribed. Some status-holders may expect that a person show mainly attitudinal conformity ('it's not that I mind the way he acts, it's his attitude'); others congratulate him or her for their doctrinal conformity ('she is sure good to have around when it comes to whipping up enthusiasm'); still others demand behavioural conformity only ('why doesn't he just do his job; who cares about what he thinks?'). Such varied expectations are not just coincidences; they flow from the structural position of particular role-partners. The fact that all role-partners do not expect the same type of conformity facilitates the articulation of roles. The differences in types of expected conformity make it possible for the status-occupant to remain reasonably stable in the face of contradictory expectations.

The ability to defer expression of attitudes and to adapt behaviour is expected by some role-partners, as when they value a person for 'being able to get along with people'. Others may criticize the status-holder for being 'just an operator'. Others again may expect doctrinal conformity only, which would happen especially at ceremonial occasions. A renegade's public confession, the speech of a president at a yearly banquet of a club or a commencement address, are occasions through which beliefs are being stated to others and values are being verbally (or gesturally) emphasized.

This type of conformity is usually a means of conveying to others that their values will not be questioned. When President Reagan at a summit visit in Moscow stood up while the Soviet national anthem was being played, this was not mistaken by anyone as a manifestation of Soviet patriotism, nor as mere opportunism. The meaning of his joining with others in this concerted act was the acknowledgment of *their* values, and this is all that is required under such circumstances. The man who bends his head or salutes a flag that claims neither his allegiance nor his respect may do so because he is in the presence of others for whom it is a symbolically legitimate rite and for whom he has or is socially expected to show respect.

Doctrinal conformity is also a means of conveying to others that their values will not be questioned. Since it is required to help strengthen or at least acknowledge the value of others in well defined social situations, it is expected to occur where others can observe it. Presumably, people don't stand up in their living room when hearing the national anthem over the radio.

Doctrinal conformity takes place under conditions of observability; and so does behavioural, but not attitudinal, conformity, as I am going to show. This raises the question of the interrelation between the various mechanisms. It will turn out that the manner in which they are interrelated can also become a means for the articulation of roles.

INTERDEPENDENCE OF THE MECHANISMS FOR ROLE ARTICULATION

It is instructive to examine the relations between the type of conformity expected by some role-partners and the other mechanisms for articulating roles, i.e. the distribution of authority over the behaviour of a status-occupant, the differential observability of that status-holder's behaviour, and the socially patterned interest that these role-partners have in his or her behaviour (cf. R. Coser, 1961). Authority does not necessarily imply access to observation, nor does interest in the status-occupant necessarily imply concern with that person's attitudes. In some types of structure, certain members of the role-set are expected to have great interest in the behaviour of a particular status-occupant, and have the authority to shape this person's behaviour, but are not supposed to observe it. A case in point is the relationship between a professor of psychiatry who is a senior staff member in a mental hospital and a resident. The resident cannot be observed directly by the senior when engaged in psychotherapy with a patient. The obligation toward one role-partner, the patient, restricts the privileges of the other role-partner, the supervisor. It is assumed that the behaviour of the status-occupant will be controlled by conforming attitudes. In roles in which behaviour cannot be so easily observed, as in the case of the physician in private practice or even more so of the psychiatrist during the therapeutic hour, or the priest within the confessional, the demands on attitudinal conformity, i.e. on inner acceptance of the values and norms of the particular social system, will be greater.

The exercise of authority over a status-occupant and the observation of that person's behaviour do not always go together. Where they do, the emphasis is generally on behavioural conformity. Let me explain. The type of relationship in which an authority-holder observes the details of the subordinate's behaviour is exemplified by the foreman-operator, the teacher-pupil in grade school, the warden-prisoner or the nurse-mental patient. In these instances the person in authority is concerned primarily with the behaviour of the status-occupant, and close observation is exercised because it is assumed that behaviour is not sufficiently backed up by internalized values and cannot, therefore, be relied upon to motivate conformity. It is assumed that interests or norms are not being shared between subordinate and authority-holder. Concern here is mainly with appropriate *behaviour*. Therefore, persons in such authority positions tend to be much concerned with discipline. Moreover, they are the mediators within the hierarchy, responsible for the behaviour of the observed. They are transmitters of information to persons on a higher echelon who do not observe the behaviour in the ranks directly.

At first glance it would seem paradoxical that persons in high positions of authority do not, and do not even have the right to, observe the subordinates directly. It would seem that superior position would involve this right. Actually, the higher the person in authority, the more that person is removed from ready observation of the behaviour of those much lower in the hierarchy. If a person high in authority wants to observe behaviour in the ranks, as when a general wants to inspect the barracks, or a college president wants to visit a dormitory, or incredibly, a professor's class, this is usually patterned ceremonially. The fact that there are occasional complaints about breaches of such etiquette confirms the analytical point.

The insulation from observability of persons of high authority gives the status-occupant some leeway, for such authority-holders are initiators of important decisions that may seriously affect the status-holder's life. It is useful for a teacher that the principal should not observe the class regularly, and that the superintendent of schools be even more aloof from classroom activities.

A literary example of how functioning was felt to be impaired by violation of this informal rule comes from Tolstoy's *War and Peace*: 'While the Tsar had been at Vilna... [one party] thought and said that the whole evil was primarily due to the presence of the Tsar...; that it was for the Tsar to govern but not to lead his troops...; that the worst commander-in-chief, acting independently, would be better than the best commander-in-chief with his hands tied by the *presence* and authority of the Tsar' (emphasis supplied). I note parenthetically that this is, of course, a corollary of one of the oldest and best-known precepts in organizational functioning: the principle of chain-of-command and lines of authority (Barnard, 1938). Here this old idea is placed in a new theoretical context: observability in relation to types of conformity.

Lest it be assumed that Merton's theory is only applicable to bureaucratic organization, let me give an example from the structure of the middle-class family in Western society, which will also show how various interests of role-partners are related to differential access to observation of the status-occupant.

THE WESTERN MIDDLE-CLASS FAMILY[2]

In patriarchal pre-modern Western society, father's and mother's expectations of a child differed in some fundamental respect. There was an allocation of different types of authority between the parental figures; these tended to expect different types of conformity and to differ in their socially patterned interest in the children, as well as in the extent to which they observed the children's behaviour. The father was primarily concerned with the children's attitudes; he watched over the type of behaviour that seemed to express inner dispositions for becoming a good citizen. Mother was mainly concerned with the children's daily behaviour in terms of their immediate consequences—for their own well-being and for the smooth functioning of the household. The parent who was mostly concerned with attitudes did not observe the details of the children's daily behaviour, and the parent who had greater access to these everyday details did not focus as much on attitudes.

In this arrangement there is more than a simple distribution of authority between parental figures. There is a distribution of types of authority, of the socially patterned interest in the children, and of the extent of observability of the children's behaviour (R. Coser, 1961, 1974a).[3] Neither parent, of course, is indifferent to the primary interest of the other. A mother would have been quick to lament a child's deviation from the general, community-sanctioned value system which the father was supposed to represent. And the father, no matter how removed from practical concerns, would have been seriously annoyed at a son's or daughter's defiance of mother's exercise of authority. In the family (as in organizations) there has to be consensus between authority-holders on all levels. Yet there is leeway for a youngster in the presence of each of the parents: mother more readily than father will overlook transgressions of an attitudinal nature, and father may smile benevolently about some of the petty details of everyday behaviour about which mother is so persistent. When the child is in the presence of both, tactful parents will try not to disturb the ceremonial quality of togetherness by insisting on demands that are peculiar to each. In this ideal-type of family, leeway is afforded the child to conform in somewhat different manner to the expectations of each parent and to gain distance in order to respond to these expectations, that is, to organize his or her role.

The modern middle-class family, in contrast, puts the mother in a precarious role. The modern mother is expected to focus her attention on the children's inner dispositions for their personality development, and to make efforts to integrate the children in the community by helping them to acquire its dominant values. At the same time she must take care of the family in all practicalities, including the details of her children's behaviour. The combined interest in both behavioural and attitudinal conformity may well lead the mother to appear domineering. Her control can be pervasive because the children can hardly be insulated from her observation. Being interested in the children's attitudes as well as in their behaviour, she will be induced to weigh all behaviour not only in terms of the immediate situation, but also in terms of its symbolic meaning in regard to their future development. The mother is often called upon to make a quick choice between two conflicting modes of response. Should a child who breaks an appliance while experimenting with its mechanics be scolded for the damage, or commended for showing 'scientific interest'? A mother may alternate in her reactions and thus put the child in what Gregory Bateson *et al*. (1956) have called 'the double bind'. This is what Merton has called 'a core case of sociological ambivalence', i.e. one of 'incompatible expectations incorporated in a single role of a single social status' (1976a: 8,12).

To overcome this ambivalence, the modern mother can articulate her role through permissiveness, that is, by withholding the use of authority, and by limiting her observation, thus detaching herself in some measure from her interest in the child's behavioural conformity. This is what we would call granting the child privacy even at an early age. This will also help her overcome her own sense of ambivalence.

SOCIOLOGICAL AMBIVALENCE

This concept, which Merton (with Elinor Barber, 1963; see also Merton, 1976a) has worked out in great detail, is a corollary of role-set theory, in that 'in its core sense [it] refers to opposing normative tendencies in the social definition of a role' (1976a: 113). In my example of mother and child, the mother must make an individual decision on how to deal with the contradictory norms that are supposed to inform her motherly task. Yet the ambivalence she has to cope with has its source in the structural arrangements within the modern family, where the mother has a dual role while the father remains head of the family. She is in a position of authority, yet is not fully granted the claim. This is the second way in which sociological ambivalence is built into her role. She has to articulate her role for herself, individually, yet it is clear that the ambivalence has come to be built into the structure of her social status and role.

Merton distinguishes between different types of sociological ambivalence; he calls the above example the core-type, in which contradictory expectations emanate from the same role-partner. This is parallel to the psychological definition of ambivalence in which contradictory feelings, love and hate, are directed at the same person. Another type of ambivalence has its source in the contradictory expectations emanating from several role-partners, as in the case discussed earlier, where there are mechanisms available for dealing with the conflict of expectations. Yet a third source of ambivalence is, in contrast to the conflicts stemming from within one role-set, the conflict that stems from the fact that one person occupies different statuses, which command different interests, values and allocation of time and especially loyalty. These conflicts have their source in the status-set.

A conflict most talked about in our culture is that between the sphere of work and the sphere of the family. It is minimized in modern society by the fact that total allegiance to one or the other activity system is rarely expected. Modern life is, to a significantly greater extent than pre-industrial or medieval life, characterized by the ability of individuals to segment their roles. The modern person involves some dispositions in some roles, as my discussion about attitudinal and behavioural conformity has suggested. Nevertheless, a conflict between these two spheres is salient in regard to the role of women. In their case, sociological ambivalence does not seem to be alleviated much through role segmentation.

MEN, WOMEN AND THEIR STATUS-SETS[4]

Modern women experience sociological ambivalence because of a conflict of allegiance, not merely because of their involvement in more than one activity system. It is a conflict of normative priorities. After all, men are fully engaged in their occupations without fearing, and without being told, that they are not committed to their families. It might be said that for at least some of them precisely this commitment is the driving force for their hard work. Yet one does not think of working men as having a conflict between family and occupational obligations. It is only when there is a normative expectation that the family will be allocated resources of time, energy and affect that should not be shared with other social institutions that a conflict may arise.

Conflicts of allegiance between the family and other activity systems are not a uniquely modern phenomenon. Economic, political or religious systems often compete with the family for the allegiance of its members. There is always some tension between society's need for the family as a transmitter of status and values to the next generation, and society's claim on its members for an extra-family commitment. It would seem that such conflicts are more acute in the modern world.

Sociological ambivalence is endemic in the coexistence of family loyalties and economic or political pursuits. In some societies or organizations that have been called *greedy* (L. Coser, 1974) because they claim the total allegiance of their members, the importance of the family is played down or denied. It is in this way that we must understand the fact that the Catholic Church has prescribed celibacy for its priests, monks and nuns. And, paradoxical as this may seem, Bolsheviks tried to obtain the total allegiance of committed members through an opposite sexual pattern, that is, by extolling the virtues of free love and thereby preventing permanent unions. Similarly, in many utopian communities, prescriptions of either sexual abstinence or sexual promiscuity helped prevent permanent unions and thus served to have the energies of their members concentrated on the well-being of the community or the furthering of the cause (L. Coser, *ibid*.; Kanter, 1972).

Such restrictions on personal loyalties would seem to be less necessary in a highly differentiated society such as our own, although some vestiges remain. The rule of nepotism, which states that two members of the same family will not be permitted to work for the same employer, has its source in the functional requirement for modern organizations that they remain protected from familial concerns and allegiances during working hours. This is not only to avoid distraction; it is a response to the fact that different norms regulate behaviour in these different activity systems. If it is objected that the rule of nepotism is obsolete because of the complexity of modern organizations, where the internal separation of offices and lines of command can insulate individual members of a same family, this confirms the point that is emphasized here, that deliberate interference of familial considerations must be prevented in the sphere of work. Indeed, if the nepotism rule is obsolete, it is because normative priorities for involvement are usually assigned through separation of activities by time and place. Modern capitalism, as Max Weber has been one of the first to show, owes much of its tremendously rapid and forceful development to the fact that the place of work became separated from the home (see Parsons, 1947). This has made possible the exclusion of personal needs and desires, of affective attractions and distractions, from the rational pursuit of the efficient enterprise.

In terms of role-set theory the separation between the two activity systems makes it possible for the role-sets of family and work not to overlap; if they accidentally do, as when an associate on the job is also a neighbour, they overlap less than would be the case if the two realms were not separated. Thus, by combining Weber's notion of the importance of this separation between activity systems with Merton's concept of role articulation, it becomes clear that the mechanisms for status articulation (which are the same as those for role articulation) can operate relatively smoothly. Due to the territorial and temporal separation of activities, the mechanisms of insulation from observability, differential authority over and differential interest in the status-occupant on the part of the role-partners in each set operate more efficiently than if these activities were merged in the same place. In this arrangement the individual is not only insulated from the observability but also from the authority and the interest of the role-partners in the other set. A woman is not expected to tell her husband how to behave on the job, nor can his employer tell him how to behave at home. The fact that in both cases it can be said that 'it is none of her or his business to care' bears witness to the normative limits of interest in the status-occupant's behaviour in the other system. If it will be objected that frequently men do try to tell their wives how to behave on the job, this confirms the point: their being separated from their husbands at work makes the exercise of authority less likely, if at all possible, in the occupational realm. Thus the separation between the home and the place of work constitutes yet another mechanism for status articulation. It makes possible the operation of the other mechanisms that facilitate and, more important, routinize status articulation, that is, the decision a person must make as to which of the role-sets will be given priority. This is not to say that people will never experience contradictory demands in their different roles, but that, to paraphrase a sentence that Merton has wisely used again and again, *they will face fewer of them than if these mechanisms were not at work*.

It would seem that the mechanisms for dealing with multiple allegiances operate in the same way for men and women. Yet this is usually not the case. These mechanisms are a necessary but not a sufficient condition for routinizing status articulation. They are likely to eliminate the conflict only when they help status articulation to be routinized, and this happens only under conditions of normative consensus about priorities. It is because the expectation that during the day father will be at work and children at school is shared by all, or, to use another of Merton's concepts, it is because they have the *cultural mandate* to do so, that no decision has to be made about whether and when to take up these activities.

Where normative consensus is lacking, or where there is normative ambiguity, the routine has to be negotiated. But a routine that has to be negotiated is a contradiction in terms. This becomes especially clear if one considers emergency situations, as when a mother or father has to stay home from work to care for a sick child or has to work on a weekend instead of being available to the family. In such instances of unanticipated demands on the part of role-partners from the other role-set, that is, when the demands cannot be dealt with through ordinary normative regulation, an individual has to articulate his or her status anew by making a decision about which of the role-sets' expectations will be met.

Even today, when paternal involvement has become normatively acceptable, such a choice is not between equally weighted alternatives. In all likelihood it will be mother (and not father) who will stay home for the sick child, and it will be father (and not mother) who would give to the job the weekend time that is usually assigned to the family. The woman has the cultural mandate to give priority to the family. The fact that, even when working outside the home, she is expected to be committed to her family first, her work second, helps prevent disruptions within the family.

Non-routinized status articulation, even if it does not violate the norm, is potentially subversive. The working woman's expected commitment to her family is seen as a source of disruption of the occupational sphere because 'those involved in the role-set have their own patterned activities disturbed when [the status-occupant] does not live up to his role-obligations' (Merton, 1968: 436). This is likely to happen even if the mechanisms operate, or are being manipulated, to maximize the status-occupant's insulation from observability by the role-partners and from the exercise of their authority and interest. Incompatible expectations force the individual to articulate the status anew, to give priority to some normative demands at the expense of others. The mother who remains absent from work in order to care for a sick child creates a disruption in her place of work; the father who cannot come home for dinner because of some emergency meeting at work creates a disruption at home. *Implicit in the act of articulating one's status beyond the routine is a disruption within one role-set, whether or not the disruption is considered legitimate.*

Merton's distinction between role articulation and status articulation becomes useful for examining the significance of social disruption as a result of contradictory expectations. Status articulation involves the temporary abandonment of one role. Role articulation, in contrast, usually is aimed at better performance of the role, even if it implies some disappointment for some role-partners within one role-set.

The sanctions for such disappointments are more easily avoided than if one role has been abandoned altogether. Role articulation tends to be less disruptive than status articulation because it usually does not involve a choice between two geographically distinct places at the same time. Status articulation, in contrast, involves a whole separate role-set being abandoned if a person decides to turn to the other set.[5]

The separation between home and work does not give a wife-mother the same advantage it gives a husband-father, because if she works outside the home she is still not freed from the cultural mandate of having to be devoted to her family first. Since the separation does not make her work status immune from interference of personal concerns, it makes status articulation harder for her than for her husband. It even prevents her from combining gainful activities with her household work, and thus to alternate between the two, and neglect the one or the other in turn without this being noticed much by role-partners in either set.

Status articulation is, therefore, both easier and harder to achieve than role articulation. It is easier because the mechanisms of insulation from observability and of differential authority and interest favour the routinization of activities in the two activity systems. This happens when the cultural mandate concerning priorities is unequivocal. If, however, the cultural mandate is equivocal, that is, if a person is expected to give priority to the place of work at the same time as having to be committed to the family, routinization breaks down and the separation between the two activity systems makes status articulation most difficult. This is a core case of *sociological ambivalence.*

It follows as a consequence that the act of status articulation, when it is not routinized, produces role conflict. This is because individuals anticipate the disruption they might create in situations that would demand repeated status articulation. The conflict about priorities and about whether or how to manipulate the mechanisms for status articulation is structural not only in the sense that it stems from the structure of social relationships, but also in the sense that individuals anticipate that status articulation will create some disruption for someone in the role-set. The conflict is not only their own. While its anticipation is an individual experience, the conflict emanates from two activity systems that have legitimate demands on the actors' allegiance. Just as from the psychological vantage point anxiety helps an individual to mobilize ego defences, so *social anxiety*, which is created by the anticipation of the structural role conflict, helps activity systems to remain protected from disruptions.[6] There is a fit between the perceived need of potential recruits to occupations to minimize the conflicts that would ensue from repeated demands for status articulation and the perceived need of occupations and professions to minimize disturbances. Hence many women tend to limit their options by wanting to do what they have to do, and occupations narrow women's access to opportunities. In order to want to do what they have to do, women are aided by social arrangements that can best be understood with the help of role-set theory.

RESTRICTED AND COMPLEX ROLE-SETS

Women who do not go out to work have less differentiated role obligations than those who do. For them there is no temporal and spatial separation between their obligations to the family and their daily work, and hence there is no social separation either. Their work is family work. As a consequence, their social space is more limited than if they were to leave the home for gainful employment. Another way of saying this is that their status-set is more restricted.

Elsewhere (1975, 1986) I have distinguished between simple and complex role-sets. In the former, even if, because of authority relations for example, some role-partners are differently situated than others, they characteristically bring little difference in outlook and expectations, nor do they reveal much that is not already known. Role-partners are hardly ever changing and are thoroughly *familiar* (as in a family, as the root of the word indicates). They are fewer in number than in a complex role-set. In the latter the complexity consists of the different positions role-partners occupy, with their different expectations and, it will be remembered, their frequently incompatible expectations.

The distinction is important because a complex role-set offers, precisely because it makes incompatible demands, the structural opportunities for role articulation that are absent or inoperative in simple role-sets. In spite of the potential disturbances, their threat presents a challenge for making use of the mechanisms to cope with contradictory expectations. This enlarges the realm of choices and leads to an awareness of one's own capacities for making use of alternatives. This has already been recognized by other sociologists. Sam Sieber writes: 'Role accumulation may enrich the personality and enhance one's self-conception. Tolerance of discrepant viewpoints, exposure to many sources of information, flexibility in adjusting to the demands of diverse role-partners... all of these benefits may accrue to the person who enjoys wide and varied contacts with his fellow men [sic]....' (1974: 576).

Women have less opportunity, in general, than men do to be part of complex role-sets and status-sets (R. Coser, 1986). Not only are they less frequently employed; whether they are or not, they belong to fewer voluntary associations (Babchuck and Booth, 1969), and the associations they do belong to are much smaller in size (McPherson and Smith-Lovin, 1982). Moreover, they are more often affiliated with community organizations, while men are more often affiliated with national organizations (*ibid.*).

In contrast, when 'women are in the labour force full-time, they tend to belong to much larger organizations than housewives...' (*ibid.*: 900). But since the types of women's and men's organizations are related to their positions in the labour force (*ibid.*: and Gurin, 1987), a vicious circle is set in motion: women do not as often belong to as important and large organizations because of fewer job opportunities. Consequently, the nature of their jobs and the lack of complex role-sets further maintain women in their place.

Some evidence for this comes from an empirical study carried out by Patricia Gurin (1987) to test the role complexity hypothesis. She found that among women 30 years and older employment had an important influence on becoming more identified with other women and on questioning the legitimacy of the traditional homemaker's role. Even traditional homemakers, however, who were members of complex organizations—i.e. organizations that transcended extensions of the home-maker role such as the Parent Teachers' Association—were somewhat more critical of the legitimacy of traditional gender roles than those who did not participate in such organizations.[7]

The pattern of gender differences in participation in complex role-sets is already anticipated in childhood and adolescence, when boys are likely to play much more complex games than girls. While on the playground two girls may be sitting playing jacks, groups of boys are engaged in team games.[8] As G. H. Mead has observed, in such games they learn 'to be ready to take the attitude of everyone else involved' and to relate the players to one another; the child learns to figure out 'what everyone else is going to do in order to carry out his play', and to 'organize into a sort of unit the attitudes of the other players' (1946: 153–4). The decision as to what behaviour to select for effective action will be made in relation to the different positions of the players in relation to one another (R. Coser, 1975).

Not only in their games, but during their young lives in general, girls are more restricted than boys in the use of physical, and hence of social space. Girls do not venture far from home (Nasaw, 1985). Anthropological studies have shown that this is true in such far-away places as Kenya in two different cultures, where boys automatically played at a greater distance from home (Maccoby and Jacklin, 1974: 196). A study of chasing games of second and third graders shows that the boys' games are free-floating over a large space, while girls have safe territories to which those who are pursued can flee (Robinson, 1978). Restricted use of physical space is, of course, related to restricted social space, that is, to restriction of role-sets and status-sets.[9]

The restriction that women experience is a special case of the stratification system. In general, persons in different social positions are not equally able to make the choices that help role articulation. The mechanisms that help develop this ability are more readily available to those of relatively high than of low social status. At the upper levels in the hierarchy, whether at universities, in government or in industry, people are forced to negotiate and compromise with others of diverse interests, rank and outlook, and hence must take many factors into account, reflecting upon various alternatives of action in relation to others.

This is not to say that women have no such opportunities. Every mother knows how she has to negotiate with and compromise among the various members of her family, and between them and outsiders like neighbours or teachers—and often will do so most effectively. However, she does less of this than if she were not limited to the simple role-set of the household. The addition of a complex role-set that is situated outside the family forces women, as it does men, to articulate their roles. Middle-class women, even if they more or less limit their activities to the care of the household, have a better chance at this than lower-class women because, due to their activities in voluntary associations, they have a more complex status-set than their lower-class sisters and brothers.

CLASS DIFFERENCES IN ROLE-SET COMPLEXITY

The opportunity structure is such that there is an unequal distribution of the availability of social mechanisms that permit or challenge people to articulate their roles. For factory workers at the assembly line, there is little opportunity to make these mechanisms operate because workers are part of a narrow hierarchy, where they relate to few people in the structure who are in different positions than they are themselves. Whyte has observed that 'long, narrow hierarchies... are relatively low in economic efficiency and in employees' morale' and that in such organizations people are prevented from 'discovering what their strengths and weaknesses are' and from 'feeling that they themselves have really mastered their jobs' (1951: 306–7).

The main mechanism available to factory workers is the one, it will be remembered, that offers 'social support by others in similar social statuses with similar difficulties of coping' (Merton, 1968: 431). The very poor, who are not even on the assembly line, must rely on such support on the street corner (Liebow, 1967), that is, on those who are equally deprived of power, as well as of material and social resources.

Social structures differ in the extent to which they make demands on an individual's effort at articulation and differentiation. The mental effort needed for this is much greater under conditions of social complexity. If a role-set consists mainly of role-partners in the same status position, where only similar interests guide behaviour, one does not have to make much effort to put oneself in the position of other persons, and to negotiate and compromise. Hence, such structures leave little room for the development of what Melvin Kohn has called *intellectual flexibility*, and which he found to be associated with complexity of the job (Kohn, 1969). [10]

To operate in a complex role-set, one must gain perspective on the various attitudes of the diverse role-partners by putting oneself in the position of each of them as they relate to one another. One must keep in mind that they are different from oneself and from one another, and that this difference imposes certain adjustments in one's own stance. It is, therefore, the more individualistic rather than the less individualistic person who can adapt to the expectations of others. 'The unique selves of others enter into our own self; the grounds of our experience are made ...explicit' (Bernstein, 1971: 186).

Melvin Kohn (1963) has shown with overwhelming empirical evidence that the structure of the job situation influences people's value and cognitive orientation. It follows as a consequence that the lower class is not only deprived of material means; another important deprivation is that of structural resources in the form of complex role-sets. Some people in the social structure have more access to these resources than others. 'As the division of labour changes from simple to complex, this changes the social and knowledge characteristics of occupational roles. In this process there is an extension of access, but access is controlled by the class system' (Bernstein, 1971: 176).

Merton's theory of role-sets and status-sets gives us the opportunity to trace some sources of social inequality in addition to those with which we are familiar. However, it also makes us aware of the fact that the complexity of social relations in modern life is a source of individuation. Incompatibilities, conflicts, sociological ambivalence—these are not only burdens; the burdens are the price we pay for individuation, for the development of some measure of intellectual flexibility, and hence for creative endeavour. The theory is rich in its applications and in the corollaries that flow from it. By continuing to theorize with the help of these concepts we will add to our understanding of the modern individual, and of the dynamics of social relationships.

NOTES

1   This section, as well as the next one, are part of an earlier paper on the relation between authority and observability (R. Coser, 1961).

2   An earlier version of the following analysis is to be found in part in R. Coser (1974a).

3   See also R. Coser's (1979) analysis of a mental hospital, where a similar distribution of authority and observability prevailed.

4   This analysis of women's role conflict is part of an earlier paper by Rose Laub Coser and Gerald Rokoff (1971).

5   In regard to ego manipulation of the role structure, see Goode (1960).

6   Philip Slater (1974) has used the term 'social anxiety' to refer to the horror-stricken reaction of the public to the practice of incest.

7   Patricia Gurin (1987: 168) suggests that, as far as the fostering of women's gender consciousness and their participation in politics are concerned, unfamiliarity, diversity and instability of the role-sets associated with particular statuses are more important than their sheer number.

8   There are a number of studies on gender differences, as well as class differences, in the use and conceptualization of social space. See, among others, Lagory and Pipkin (1981), Goodchild (1974), Lynch (1977), Sutton-Smith (1979).

9   On the importance of physical space for cognitive orientation, and the relation between physical and social space, see Lagory and Pipkin (1981).

10 Although *job complexity* is not synonymous with *complexity of role-set*, there is good reason to believe that the two notions are fairly similar: see Kohn (1969).

13. Merton's Theory of Role-sets and Status-sets

RICHARD A. HILBERT

This paper offers (1) a review of Merton's theory of role-sets and status-sets; (2) a location of that theory within functionalist role theory; (3) a general critique of functionalist explanation; and (4) a return to Merton's theory to argue these critiques in the specific. No attempt is made to extend these critiques beyond Parsonian functionalism, e.g. functionalist conflict theory, substantive research that uses a functionalist vocabulary, neo-functionalism or any specific variation of role theory. Only the Parsonian explanatory system is in doubt.

REVIEW OF THE THEORY

In both his purely theoretical writings and his more concrete substantive concerns, Merton employs the terms 'role-set' and 'status-set' to describe and explain social order. Borrowing from Linton (1936) the original terms 'role' and 'status', Merton goes on to say that for any given status, i.e. for any given social position within a social system carrying its specified rights and duties, there is not, as Linton implies, but one bundle of prescribed behaviours, one role, but rather a variety of roles and their concomitant role relationships. This differs from 'multiple roles' in that the latter designates roles associated with differing statuses. A role-set, then, is a bundle of roles that goes with a single status (Merton, 1957c: 110–11). Moreover, following Linton, Merton reminds us that the same person can occupy multiple statuses, each with its respective role-set. These statuses simultaneously possessed by one individual Merton terms a 'status-set' (1968: 422–4).

A familiar example of role-set, one which Merton himself focuses on, is one that goes with the status 'scientist' (1973: 519–22). Roles attached to that social position include at least four: research, teaching, administrative, gatekeeper. Each

177

of these roles involves role relationships with a distinct set of others; together they constitute a role-set. Additionally, any given scientist may occupy other statuses, such as homemaker, each with its role-set, in this case mother, wife, PTA member, etc. Together these positions constitute a status-set.

At the analytical level there is no reason why all this complexity could not lead to multiple and simultaneous contradictory prescriptions and ultimately to chaos and disorder. Role relationships exerting pressure on a status incumbent could inhibit or stifle his or her ability to perform in other role relationships. Or the role-sets of differing statuses could come into conflict, inhibiting the incumbent from fulfilling any of them effectively. That this does not happen, or seldom does to a degree sufficient to the breakdown of social order, is Merton's observation and phenomenon to be explained.

In the case of role-sets Merton identifies 'social mechanisms' which counteract potential instability, or, in his words, 'social mechanisms which produce a greater degree of order than would obtain if these mechanisms were not called into play' (1957c: 113). The mechanisms include these observations:

1 various members of a role-set may be less concerned than others with the status associated with that role-set and will therefore exert differential pressure upon the incumbent to conform;
2 some of these members are, plainly, more powerful than others and may exert corresponding degrees of pressure upon the incumbent;
3 the incumbent may fulfil contradictory role relationships by insulating each from the visibility of the others;
4 where such contradictory pressures are fully visible to all, members of the role-set may appropriate and solve the problems as their own, thereby reducing stress upon the incumbent;
5 incumbents find solidarity among others in similar circumstances, which is itself a structural response to the troubles of role-sets; and
6 incumbents can simply terminate roles not compatible with the role-set and not resolvable in other ways (*ibid.*: 113–17; 1968: 425–33).

Similarly in the case of status-sets, potential conflicts between statuses with their respective role-sets are avoided in ways such as the following:

1 public perception of status conflict reduces the pressure brought to bear on the incumbent by role-set members within some of the statuses;
2 common value orientations regarding the relative importance of the conflicting status obligations cause certain role-set members to modify their demands;
2 structurally generated 'empathy' due to others having experienced similar status conflicts likewise reduces their pressure upon the incumbent to conform;
4 certain adaptations themselves become standardized and therefore learned and conformed to; and
5 statuses self-select, i.e. are not joined in sets at random but lead to one another through structured chains ('status-sequences')—socialization into one status inculcates values amenable to certain new statuses and not others, and so on (Merton, 1968: 434–8).

Merton is clear that these mechanisms do not reduce contradictions and conflict to nil or produce perfect social order. Quite the contrary, he suggests, social systems may operate at less than full efficiency most of the time (*ibid.*: 434; 1957c: 118). However, without these mechanisms, the present level of observed social order would not obtain.

PROBLEMS WITH THE MODEL

There is a certain tacit reasonableness to these arguments. Once provided with their terms, one would be hard pressed to claim that they are not 'true'. Indeed, Merton's analysis corresponds closely to daily life's experiences; we can intuitively pick up on what Merton is talking about in these passages and apply it to our lives. Despite the formal and categorical vocabulary, the central dynamic resonates with familiar problems and familiar solutions. We find the arguments validated through concrete cases we know of and can imagine as part of everyday routine. I personally can think of countless occasions in my own role-life that closely approximate Merton's model.

But 'closely' in the above sentence is not 'closely' in the scientific sense, and Merton's concepts are supposed to do some rather eloquent things for science. They are supposed to contribute to sociology's general explanation for social order, the explanation first put forward by Talcott Parsons (1937), who in turn said he got it by reading Durkheim and Weber (*et al.*) between the lines. The solution he settled on was socialization into a common culture which produces standard behaviour—namely the social order we observe, repetitive social events, i.e. without the chaos that Hobbes might have predicted. Culture (normative order) with its norms, roles and values was found to be exceedingly complex, corresponding to the complex factual order it produces (see Parsons, 1951; Parsons and Shils, 1951; Parsons, Bales and Shils, 1953). Merton took it upon himself to break the larger society into smaller social universes and study them as social systems in an effort to accumulate knowledge that would one day fit together toward a more systemic understanding of Parsons's general solution. These smaller social systems themselves then became complex.

There is no doubt that Merton intended his studies to contribute to the larger investigation; such was the promo behind what he called 'theories of the middle range' (Merton, 1957a: 108–10; 1968: 39–72). They were to tend more toward the local than Parsons's, the easier to manage. His concepts were nevertheless intended to be general and structural through their location in the wider normative order. They were, ultimately, to be precise, to designate formal structural causes that lie behind observed social order. I say 'ultimately' because Merton acknowledged a certain lack of precision, both due to the unfinished character of sociology's main mission and to the tendency of social systems to operate at less than full efficiency (cf. above).

Still, statuses, roles and their structured interrelatedness sustained by operating social mechanisms were to be what theoretically could produce an observed order. Their use by theorists to unravel an increasingly complex Parsonian system of norms and values indexes their place in general functionalist theory. What these moves toward simplification imply is the potential for analytic precision, that is, as we move toward progressively simple systems, unravelling, say, role-sets as we go, we eventually unravel roles as networks of prescriptions for concrete action that would, through the processes of socialization and internalization, produce the concrete action prescribed and therefore observed. Actors, at this theoretic level, need not innovate (e.g. Merton, 1968: 436).

From these considerations two objections emerge, both of which can be addressed either to Merton or to functionalism generally. The first has to do with the lack of empirical evidence supporting the existence of these normative structures *qua* structures. The second has to do with the analytic integrity of the model itself: it could not work even in the abstract. Either of these criticisms is devastating for an emerging social science. Let us take them in order.

First, the question of functionalism's empiricism. I do not wish merely to belabour the point that no one has ever witnessed a normative structure. Science in general is not limited to the five senses; subatomic physics, for example, would be sorely crippled without the scientist's ability to theorize and fill in anomalies, pointing to new ideas and new investigations. Perhaps it is within this tradition that sociologists intuit norms for concrete action and seek to validate their impressions through preferred research strategies—interviews, questionnaires, ethnography, etc. However, in the case of subatomic physics, such excursions beyond empiricism are warranted by previous empirical discovery; in sociology's case the assumption of stabilizing norms and values is simply a premise, a theoretical bedrock informing empirical work, not itself born of empirical discovery.

More to the point, if we suspend our natural common-sense belief in the constant necessity of norms and rules in order to determine if the social world will empirically yield these normative structures, we discover quite the opposite. Such was one early research policy of ethnomethodology, and it turned up findings such as the following:

1   For members of society, rules cannot unequivocally prescribe behaviour (Wieder, 1974a, 1974b; Garfinkel, 1967).
2   Members of society are quite adept at living in and participating in (producing) social order without any rules whatsoever (Bittner, 1967).
3   When people require rules, which they occasionally do, their needs are practical and in no way require precision; moreover, were they to require precision, the task would be potentially endless and impractical, thwarting the very same practical needs that generated the search for rules in the first place (Garfinkel, 1967: 36–44).
4   When people require rules, their activity includes the creation of new rules, the reinterpretation of old rules and the positing of these new understandings in the past to create the impression of having discovered the 'all along' or intended meaning of rules that had never before, as an empirical matter, been specified (Bittner, 1965; Zimmerman, 1970, 1974).
5   The future use of a rule consists not in prescription but in cautioning the membership that whatever happens may at some point have to be accountable in terms of the rule, even though exactly what that will amount to—the rule, its specific sense, or the event itself—cannot be known in advance of its construction (Wieder, 1974a, 1974b).
6   Rules are used this way by people with regard not only to action (both as prescriptive guides and retrospective judgments) but also to the mere

recognition of stable social reality or standard social structure as describable matters (Garfinkel, 1967; Wieder, 1974a, 1974b; Zimmerman and Pollner, 1970).

Thus the empirical focus on human activity reveals a world entirely different than the one assumed by advocates of the rule-governed model (cf. Cicourel, 1964, 1968; Cicourel and Kitsuse, 1963).

One study that illustrates this quite nicely is Bittner's (1967) investigation into the peace keeping tactics of police on skid row. Here actors regard their activity as regular, standardized, highly organized, indeed professional in the manner of medicine and law, yet without the faintest hint of general norms. Instead the emphasis is on the ability to improvise; to be professionally competent is to improvise well. Social constraint, as correctly postulated by Durkheim, is located not in 'abstract criteria of merit' (Bittner, 1967: 712) but in the concrete exigencies of the situation, specifically in the empirical actions and responses of other people. Thus in a sense 'normless', police nevertheless do not allow just any action to count as in conformity with what competent policemen do. They actively create, monitor and participate in social order in the course of its recognition.[1]

One might argue that while societal members may not know about the norms that guide them, these norms surely must be operative anyway; after all they are theoretically required. Without them behaviour would degenerate into instability. Such is the persistence of a commitment to the rule-governed model. We therefore must look at the model analytically, asking whether such a model could *conceivably* work, even if exerting its force within a subconscious or other empirically unavailable sphere. The source I draw upon here is Ludwig Wittgenstein, not because his linguistic philosophy is integral to sociology but because he has examined, perhaps more eloquently and exhaustively than others, the question of rule-governed procedure.

Wittgenstein does not limit his discussions to informal procedure where people do not themselves think they are following rules, as is the case in Bittner's study. He extends his analysis to the height of formality from members' viewpoint—linguistic precision, deductive logic and mathematics—the very paradigm of the rule-governed model (Wittgenstein, 1953, 1956, 1958). While the subtleties of the arguments exceed space available here, he maintains by example that none of these activities, by their inherent natures, depends upon rules for correct procedure. Yet neither are they, by their inherent natures, self-evident. Rather their self-evident or rule-dependent status turns on the practical requirements of the people engaged in them. For example, on occasion someone may want to explain a procedure to someone unfamiliar with it, or clear up a misunderstanding with somebody by referencing 'underlying rules'. This is a practical requirement in an applied setting, rather like defining a word or concept. However, we must note this about rules as they come up in such practical circumstances: their *own* meanings are neither self-evident nor in need of further clarification; they too turn on somebody's practical requirements. Moreover, there is no point in a clarification process where this would be otherwise, no point, that is, where a clarification would possess self-evident application *or* require further clarification independent of somebody's practical requirements. Thus we see Garfinkel's observations echoed here: there is no natural stopping point beyond which people cannot logically require further clarification, nor is there any analytic reason to suspect in advance that they will call for such clarification. The only thing we know in advance is that they will stop *eventually*, calling the result clear.

Another Wittgensteinian observation may help us: practical devices are in no way synonymous with that which they are used to clarify. That is, rules of procedure, used for one reason or another to clarify a procedure, are not equivalent to the procedure or related to the procedure in a precise way. Their utility resides in their ability to clear up trouble; when the trouble is cleared up, e.g. when a procedure can be successfully performed, the specific clarification device, e.g. the rules, falls away as superfluous. This can be seen in teaching someone proper use of a word like 'often'. While we might provide definitions and loose parameters, successful use of the word does not consist in 'following' these rules, nor do fluent speakers normally attend to any such recipes. They just use the word, 'point blank' as it were, finding and creating any required stability as they go.

Finally, the issue of non-reducibility to unequivocal basics needs to be addressed. Historically, philosophers have treated colour recognition as a paradigm of precision, suggesting that reality is ultimately a complex network of these basic 'simples' (Locke, 1959). Yet even this activity will not yield the sought-after precision. Wittgenstein asks rhetorically, 'could you tell me what is in common between a light red and a dark red?' (1958: 130). To those suggesting a mental image of colour, he asks:

> Which shade is the 'sample in my mind' of the color green—the sample of what is common to all shades of green? ...What *shape* must the sample of the color green be? Should it be rectangular? Or would it then be the sample of a green rectangle? So should it be 'irregular' in shape? And what is to prevent us then from regarding it—that is from using it—only as a sample of irregularity of shape? (Wittgenstein, 1953: 35)

These considerations call radically into question any model of procedure that requires a constancy of rules or norms (cf. Wilson, 1970). Not only would rules not produce the action, in sociology's case the observed order, but neither would they by necessity be operative in the first place. All cases of rules, their very presence as well as whatever degree of clarity they offer, turn on *actors'* practical requirements. That is, where actors do not require rules, rules are not required at all. Moreover, when actors require rules, such rules display whatever degree of clarity actors allow to pass as clear, or, in the other case, require whatever further clarification actors themselves require of them. It should not surprise us then that actors never require *theoretically* satisfying closure of the rule-governed model as their routine interests in rules are practical and non-theoretical. Very seldom do members of society direct themselves to a search for the precision that functionalists, in their pursuit of the Parsonian paradigm, require.

To summarize: proper procedure, or more generally the facticity of organized human behaviour, does not require rules; *people do*. And whether they do, when they do and how they do, which is now congruent with whether, when and how rules are required at all, is irremediably an empirical question. That is, norms are not required as ongoing prescriptive entities the way Parsonian functionalism supposes. In fact actors probably require rules a bare minimum of the time.

I will add to Parsonian norms their supposed organized interrelatedness, which is to say roles, and further add role-sets, status-sets and all of Merton's announced social mechanisms to this general observation, and say that all of these are practical devices for saving the appearances of an organized, factual, social universe. This can account for our intuitive sympathies with Merton's role theory indicated earlier. These are the kinds of ideas useful in structuring our everyday lives, and they are the kinds of ideas we in fact use. Once the problem of social order has been set forth, and once the problematic and its solution are presented in Merton's terms, common sense cannot argue successfully that it is not so.

Yet we are also now better prepared to argue with functionalism as it posits the *constancy* of normative structure. If functionalists insist that actors are continually following rules even when actors themselves make no such requirements, this is because *functionalists require it themselves.* Furthermore, it is easy to see why functionalists make such requirements. What for mundane actors would count as situated 'trouble', resolvable with rules, is an ongoing, chronic concern for functionalism. They have elevated the workaday problem of order to a constant theoretical concern, thereby requiring the constant use of rules in the very recognition of the phenomenon. Moreover, as the recognized phenomenon decays into its inevitable and unyielding complexity, such complexity, as recognized, will of necessity generate a corresponding network of norms and values in the very course of its recognition. The rules that *explain* order are the same rules used to *identify* that order; thus the taking for granted of a patterned factual order continues to yield to functionalism what Merton himself might call, ironically, a self-fulfilling prophecy (1968: 475–90). Functionalists are watching their own reflections.

All of this suggests that functionalism is a highly formalized example of what it claims to be studying. By sharing the common-sense assumption of order, func- tionalists generate common-sense solutions; finding objectionable looseness in these, they proceed to tighten the vision in the direction of a theoretically unrealizable deductive model. They are therefore not simply explaining organized society but are organizing society. And they are organizing society in ways that, in their terms, they cannot help but see as incomplete and in need of further work, thereby leading to more of the same activity. They are, in a word, *rationalizing* the folk-society, in Max Weber's sense. They are creating a theoretic culture of bureaucratic efficiency.

I should emphasize that the problem is not one of simply taking something for granted; all sciences so orient to their phenomena. But in this case, what is taken for granted is also what is used to explain it: a rule-governed society. As indicated, it has no empirical referent. Also as indicated, the hypothesized entity, with its designated requirements, could not conceivably function. Nevertheless, it is instructive to note that assuming its facticity enables one to 'find' intuitively convincing arguments, as well as convincing evidence, that it exists.

EXAMPLES FROM MERTON'S WORK

Readers unsympathetic with ethnomethodological commentary or who find difficulty giving up a commitment to normative structure will probably find my examples uncompelling. For those willing to entertain the line of argument, let me summarize: functionalism has no explanatory power. It generates that which it wishes to explain and it explains it in the same way. It asks us to observe the rule-governed society, which we do. Then it tells us that the reason that rule- governed society is there is that there are rules. It proceeds to prove that by showing us that for every variation in the factual structure, the behaviour, there is a corresponding variation in the normative structure, the culture. That there would *have* to be such a correspondence in order for us even to see the behavioural structure appears to escape functionalism's notice. I would like to say that the correspondence is more like a necessary congruence. Thus to explain order with norms is like explaining the shape of an inkblot by the corresponding shape of the white surrounding that comes up to its edge (cf. Wittgenstein, 1953: 85).

An easily accessible example can be found in Merton's analysis of status-sets (1968: 434–8). Why is it, he asks, that the same person occupying different social positions does not face chronic confusion or other social disorientation? Among his answers is a self-selection feature of status-sets, or in the case of his example, non-selection: committed Christian Scientists are not usually also medical doctors (*ibid.*: 436 –7). If they were, the argument suggests, there would be tension between the status commitments of the two positions. That this does not happen is due to the values associated with the statuses. Socialization into one status precludes socialization into the other. Or, more generally, people reject otherwise achievable statuses because of the value orientations internalized during socialization into other statuses. That keeps status-sets more fully integrated than they would be without this mechanism operating.

Merton's appeal to his readers to see Christian Science and medicine in potential conflict is predicated on the very same distinction in values that he then uses to explain the resulting lack of conflict. If we can see the potential conflict, we have already explained how people avoid it. There would be no perceived hypothetical conflict without the disparate values which Merton says prevent the conflict from manifesting. Rather than say, therefore, that without this mechanism there would be more status conflict, e.g. there would be more Christian Scientist physicians with all the practical trouble that carries, it might be more to the point to say that without this mechanism, Christian Scientist physicians would constitute an integrated status-set. Contrarily, what makes this possibility troublesome in Merton's hypothetical is precisely what in Merton's explanation prevents people from entering into such trouble. Why don't they face contradictions? Because that would be a contradiction.

Thus Merton is organizing the society, including its chaotic alternative, in the very process of explaining why people conform to it, including their avoidance of status conflict. He is doing what they do in the routine ordering of their lives, their decisions about consistency and non-consistency and the rest. He shares their tacit knowledge of order versus disorder and in that sense is participating in society from within rather than from a disinterested empirical standpoint. He sees the social world as they do, the difference consisting in the fact that he presses these folk explanations into the service of science. In that sense his science consists of rationalized folkways, or folk-science (cf. Zimmerman and Pollner, 1970).

The case just cited is an especially clear example of the kind of thing I am talking about in relation to functionalist theory. Indeed one would expect this transparency where Merton himself strives to clarify the underlying logic of his position. He calls the Christian Science physician example an 'extreme case' that will 'illuminate the general theoretical point', stating: 'To say that this is self-evident is of course precisely the point' (Merton, 1968: 437). However, and with due respect to Merton's overall contributions to general sociology, science rarely generates common-sense suppositions in defence of its own theoretical correctness, especially when these suppositions will not do the analytic work required by the science. Indeed, that Merton would reproduce the common sense of his society is the crux of my critique.

With varying degrees of clarity, we can see these same underlying commitments throughout Merton's discussions of status-sets and role-sets. A general observation is that wherever Merton reveals potential trouble within the functionalist idiom, that same trouble is solved within that idiom as an outcome of some presumed structural entities which societal members themselves also orient to and take for granted. Merton's solutions mirror their solutions; he solves trouble the same way; his theory is a formal version of their theory. That these solutions are specifically *structural* in Merton's theory and thereby are operative *continuously*, i.e. independently of the volition or perception of individual actors, is but an extension of the functionalist commitment to see order as continually problematic and actors thereby in constant need of solutions, rules, mechanisms, etc. My argument is that these constantly operating mechanisms are Merton's requirements, not necessarily requirements of the people observed or of their behaviour. The fact that when actors encounter routine trouble they generate precisely the solutions they require and that these solutions are a lot like Merton's solutions should not mislead us into thinking that these solutions are required by people all the time or independently of the trouble. For routine actors, social order is probably problematic less often than not.

To cite a few more examples, a Mertonian mechanism that reduces status conflict is prior agreement regarding which status obligations are more important than others (Merton, 1968: 436). Yet the world in which all conflicting statuses are considered equal, resulting either in social gridlock or chaos, is a fantasized world for which the functionalist world is supposedly the cure. Here again is the presumption of chronic trouble requiring chronic structural solutions. This is a requirement of functionalist theory. Or in the case of role-sets, conflict is supposedly reduced by the fact that relevant others exert differential pressure on the incumbent to perform, due to their differing degrees of power or practical concern (Merton, 1957c: 113–14; 1968: 425–8). The fact that people solve trouble this way when they encounter it does not mean that the solution is in effect whether or not trouble is encountered. Much less does it mean that these solutions are worked out in advance, avail themselves to actors in any precise way, or could conceivably do the analytic work that functionalists seek. Likewise, the fact that certain differing role obligations fulfilled in the open for all to see would result in some predictable conflict (Merton, 1957c: 114–16; 1968: 428–30) does not mean that their not being fulfilled that way is an ongoing solution to latent conflict. That people sometimes strategically conceal their behaviour from troublesome others does not mean that they are constantly doing it or that the terms of the strategy are structured for them prior to their attending to the trouble.

RESIDUAL DIFFICULTIES AND CONCLUDING REMARKS

American functionalist sociology shares a common-sense notion of our time, the idea that human behaviour is ideally describable as in conformity with something else, here normative structure. This is also the mentality mobilized prescriptively in bureaucratic reform (Hilbert, 1981, 1982, 1987). It is shared also by computer scientists in their efforts to write programs for cultural competence, e.g. the use of natural language (see Dreyfus, 1979). As all attempts to reduce ambiguity to literal clarification are bound to fail, indeed as all such attempts inevitably multiply aspects of human activity that still need clarification (Garfinkel, 1967: 26), so also have the goals of Artificial Intelligence been frustrated, the precision sought by bureaucrats been subject to an essential gloss for its ongoing practical utility, and the functionalist deductive model been subject to chronic repair. Merton's contribution to role theory is an example of this repair work.

A final observation concerning the rationalization of folklore concerns a new ambiguity generated by functionalist theory, an ambiguity not routinely encountered by common-sense actors: when is something a status and when is it a role? Though I can recite definitions of these two concepts, I have no idea whether, for example, 'teacher' is one or the other. It seems to be both or either, depending on how one talks about it, i.e. upon context. In 'The Role-Set', it is a status with an array of roles (Merton, 1957c: 112). In *The Sociology of Science* it is a role, part of the role-set of the status 'scientist' (Merton, 1973: 519–22). One might say that it is both, which means that functionalists are drawing distinctions that members in their ordinary lives do not have to make and therefore do not make. Contrarily, one might say that the status/role distinction is a clarification of something people do distinguish—what they are versus what they do. Either possibility illustrates my point: functionalism is a clarification of folk-theories already routinely used, clarifications beyond those that are required in everyday life, and clarifications that are ultimately less clear than that which they seek to clarify.

NOTE

1   The functionalist commitment to ongoing norms as part and parcel of Durkheimian constraint is probably what led Merton to characterize anomie as 'normlessness', though Durkheim himself never talked that way. Some interesting consequences and side issues emerge from this characterization, e.g. for Durkheim deviance functions as a hedge against anomie, while for Merton anomie causes deviance (see Hilbert, 1986).

Interchange

COSER REPLIES TO HILBERT

In my paper I have tried to show that role-set theory helps us understand some of the problems raised in specific instances of social life. Unfortunately, Mr Hilbert's criticism of Merton's role-set theory has not shown me how I could improve on my understanding.

Some of Hilbert's statements are absurd. How can he claim that Merton breaks up the larger society into smaller social universes to study them as social systems, when Merton has specifically objected to Parsons's notion of social system, preferring the concept of social structure, because he questions the notion of 'closure' that the term 'social system' implies. As to Hilbert's idea that, for Merton, actors need not innovate, I hope I have shown in my piece that implicit in Merton's theory is the capacity for individual creativity. (Hilbert might have forgotten that Merton has devoted a major part of his famous paper 'Social Structure and Anomie' precisely to the problem of the emergence of innovators.) Further, to attribute to Merton the desire to assume constancy of normative structure is not to have followed Merton's ideas, which always assume change and variability. And what are we to make of such a statement that functionalist commitment is to see order as continually problematic, when we were made to read earlier that functionalists share the common-sense assumption of order?

There seems to be little use in piling up examples of distortions and contradictions. Hilbert does not place himself on the same level of discourse as the one he criticizes. He would have preferred that Merton write his own kind of theory. I learned in graduate school (too long ago, alas!) that in order to criticize someone's ideas, one ought first to put oneself in one's own thought in the position of the author to be criticized so that one can then refine or reject the theory in question. Hilbert, however, offers us a mixture of Wittgenstein philosophy and ethnomethodology in order to criticize functionalism in general; this is interesting, but has nothing to do with role-set theory. True, at the beginning of the paper he summarizes part of role-set theory, a summary that he does not use to inform the body of his discourse. He states, however, that one would be hard-pressed to conclude that Merton's arguments in role-set theory are not true, and further that 'the central dynamic resonates with familiar problems and familiar solutions', and that 'we find the arguments validated through concrete cases'. I wish I could return the compliment that Hilbert's arguments resonate and can be validated.

HILBERT REPLIES TO COSER

In her contribution Coser (1) says Merton's theory is a 'tool for understanding individual behaviour...because it places behaviour in a specific structural, and not merely general environmental, context'; (2) summarizes the theory and expands on it from Merton's discussions elsewhere and through her own devices; and (3) applies the theory to Western middle-class families. From my arguments in the main entry, it follows: (1) the usefulness of Merton's theory is guaranteed for anyone committed to the idea of normative structure. I could not imagine that anyone beginning with Coser's premise would not find Merton's theory a useful tool. My point is that it is a tool useful for saving the appearances of non-empirical entities and for sustaining the very premise of structure in the absence of other corroborating evidence. (2) That the theory would need expanding is also guaranteed. That one can find other 'mechanisms' is not only guaranteed but required by anyone working within the theory. (3) Also guaranteed is that anyone committed to the theory will be able to apply it to just about any behaviour. That families can be conceptually organized by the theory is no surprise. It is an endlessly versatile theory.

Referring back to these three points one at a time, Coser apparently sees structure as the main alternative to social psychology and other emphases on individualistic traits. Durkheim was absolutely correct that people bump up against exterior and constraining social facts in managing their affairs. But to conclude that social facts are 'structural' in the formal Parsonian sense is empirically unwarranted and analytically indefensible. In view of Garfinkel's elegant research into the empirical (and non-individualistic) nature of exterior and constraining social facts, I fail to see why anyone would want to depend on mythological entities to transcend psychology. Still, once the commitment is made, as it is in Coser's opening remarks, Merton's theory becomes inherently useful.

I argue in my chapter that functionalists share in the ongoing project of Western culture that Max Weber called 'rationalization'. Coser's piece exemplifies the project. She embraces the project where she writes: 'What is exciting...is that with his theorizing Merton invites others to think further with him along the lines that he has sketched'. More to the point, Merton set the terms for an anomic search for logical closure that can never be fulfilled. If we take the project seriously, we are not simply 'invited' to think further with Merton; we *have* to think further with him to sustain the theory. Moreover, the project is endless. Coser situates herself within the project early on when she writes: 'It is first to be noted that for any of [Merton's] mechanisms to come into play it needs both appropriate structural circumstances and individual initiative'. That is, role theory arose to account for differentiation in conformity among the wider society; role-sets and status-sets were summoned to repair analytic anomalies in role theory; then Merton's 'mechanisms' were listed as that which allows role-sets and status-sets to work; now Coser informs us that other structural prerequisites are needed for these mechanisms to work, and she lists them. Next we will be told what the prerequisites to those prerequisites are and so on. Thus as Garfinkel demonstrates, and Weber laments, the project in the absence of inhibiting factors knows no end point. Rationalization multiplies aspects of itself that stand in need of rational repair.

As for Coser's lengthy set of examples, I find it initially interesting that she cautions us that the theory she promotes is not limited to bureaucracies and offers families to illustrate. I find this interesting in that there was little in her arguments previously to suggest such a limitation. Apparently a subliminal awareness that the model is itself bureaucratic surfaces as this warning. In any case, the question is not whether the theory applies to non-bureaucratic settings but whether a bureaucratic model, which cannot even adequately describe bureaucracy from a scientific standpoint, ought even therefore to be applied to bureaucracies, let alone anything else.

In my view the set of illustrations is a case of interesting substantive issues upstaging theoretical questions that motivated the examples. By that I mean that Coser's discussions of families are always lively, informative and insightful. Merton's vocabulary apparently serves as a useful resource for her, now and again, to make her points; I suspect that her points might just as forcefully have been made without this vocabulary. Either way, when we are recalled to the theoretical objectives of role theory vis-à-vis the problem of social order and examine Coser's illustrations *in that specific light*, we find the same *sui generis* theory maintenance occurring in these passages as those I identified relative to Merton's own illustrations.

For example, it is one thing to point out that people find solutions to problems of conflict and contradictory expectations in various situations they encounter (e.g. between work and home), quite another to say that these solutions are made possible by structured mechanisms that precede the solutions or prevent the conflict from manifesting in the first place. It is one thing to demonstrate differences between social classes concerning the complexity and variability of social relationships and the opportunity to develop social skills on the job; it is quite another to say simply that the *cause* of these differences is structural, specifically an unequal distribution of useful 'mechanisms'. In fact the latter is presupposed by the terms of Merton's theory in the very recognition of the former. Likewise, it is of little explanatory power to say that a lack of complex role-sets keeps women in their place when 'their place' has already been characterized as a lack of complex role-sets. Coser's observations on the socialization of women from an early age in terms of opportunities to develop various coping and role articulation skills are fascinating on other grounds, but the Mertonian vocabulary adds nothing but a presumptive freezing of the observations into a structural backdrop that knows no empirical referent and can do no more for the observations than to repeat them as their cause.

Indeed, this whole skill of 'role articulation' need not be made possible by structure or by 'the existence' of role-set and status-set mechanisms. That kind of analysis is roughly like saying that the reason it was possible for Mozart to compose his fortieth symphony is that the structural path, the path of composing-the-fortieth-symphony, was open and available for him to take; or reversing this it would be that Mozart did not write symphonies other than the ones that he wrote because all other paths were closed off to him. Functionalists may well argue this way, but we should keep in mind how the 'whatever' of stable behaviour will automatically congrue with the 'whatever' of normative prescription, sustaining the impression that the latter makes the former possible. This is what I mean when I say that the theory is endlessly versatile and that its usefulness within its own idiom is guaranteed for any hypothetical application.

VIII. THE DYSFUNCTIONS OF BUREAUCRACIES

14. The Dysfunctions of Bureaucracies: Merton's Work in Organizational Sociology

CHARLES CROTHERS

Although Robert K. Merton's work in organizational sociology is now seldom directly drawn on in the advancing research fronts of organizational sociology (particular exceptions are Cohen, 1970; Marcos, 1988; and Stahlberg, 1987), his early strategic input into this area is built into the conceptual foundations of the field. Indeed, this may be a meaningful silence, since, as Merton has pointed out elsewhere, obliteration by incorporation (in which a scientist's work becomes so well known that its origins are forgotten and it is no longer felt to require citation: Merton, 1968: 28) is one of the higher—if ambivalent—honours the scientific reward system can bestow!

Merton's major contribution to organizational sociology is contained in a single brief but powerful essay on 'Bureaucratic Structure and Personality' (1940). In addition, attention to the sociology of organizations is threaded through subsequent writing, in particular:

- his study of the 'role of the intellectual in public bureaucracy' (1945c);
- his critique of the social role of the engineer (1947);
- the compilation of the first reader on organizational sociology (Merton, Gray, Hockey and Selvin, 1952);

and more generally in

- his writings on reference groups and group characteristics (see Merton, 1968: 279–440);
- the use of the examples of the 'Hawthorne studies' and the 'political machine' in his essay on functional analysis (see *ibid*.: 120–2, 126–36);
- comments on the dynamics of voluntary (1958, 1966) and creative (1965b)

193

organizations, and on the orientations and dilemmas of leadership in organizations (1960, 1970b);
● discussion of the social organization of applied social research (1949f) and more briefly of 'big science' (Merton and Thackray, 1972).

Other areas of Merton's methodological, theoretical or substantive work have also been drawn on by organizational researchers, for example, in the symposium on middle-range theory in organizational studies edited by Pinder and Moore (1980); Gouldner's transferring (1957/58) into organizational studies of the notion of 'local' compared to 'cosmopolitan' attachments to community (Merton, 1949e); the employment of the concept of 'unanticipated consequences' (Merton, 1936b, in Selznick, 1948, 1949) and other studies; the widespread use of terminology from Merton's 'reference group theory' in texts on the social psychology of organizations (e.g. Katz and Kahn, 1966); Price's use of Merton's theory of 'group properties' to undergird conceptually some of the empirical measures treated in his *Handbook* (1962); or Blau and Scott's (1962), Caplow's (1964) and Evan's (1966) useful extension of the concept of 'role-set' (Merton, 1957c) at the level of individuals to the concept of 'organization-set' at the level of organizations.[1]

But much of the substantial impact of Merton's approach to the study of organizations has been absorbed and also extended by its incorporation in the work of a powerful group of Merton's students—Selznick, Gouldner, Blau and others, including Lipset—who laid down the first generation of detailed and intensive case studies of organizations. It has been further selectively passed on and partly masked by various commentaries.

This essay is mainly concerned with documenting the development of the Mertonian programme in organizational sociology. But as well as providing a descriptive account, this will be tackled in relation to a set of puzzles:

● how does Merton's work in this area fit in with other parts of his work, and how does the work of the Mertonians in this area fit in with their subsequent intellectual concerns?
● how did this programme get under way and what were the influences which drove it and shaped it?
● how does this early generation of studies relate to the present array (or disarray) of studies in organizational sociology?

The salience of these questions is given particular force in the following judicious quote—from an article by Simon Schwartzman (1984)—that points to an essential irony in the long-term trajectory of Merton's research interests: why is Merton's sociology of science so bereft of an organizational perspective, given his attention to both areas and his particularly strong interest in the sociology of science? (Note that the second book referred to in Schwartzman's statement is not Merton's PhD dissertation—Merton, 1938a—despite its very similar title.)

> The volume that brings together the classic papers by Robert K. Merton on the sociology of science contains references to universities on only seven of its 600 pages... *Science, Technology and Society* does not fare much better: it has about twenty scattered references to universities in its 600 pages. None of these references make any mention of systems of higher education in a broader sense.

The same point may be made about Merton's very limited development of an organizational perspective on the media, or on university medical schools, during his broad studies in these areas in the 1940s and 1950s.[2]

A further enigma which will be traced in this essay is the process of often unwitting displacement of the meaning of sociological concepts over time. Merton's version of Weber's sociology of bureaucracy is artfully truncated, and in turn Merton's theory of bureaucratic dysfunctions has often been reinterpreted to stress unnecessarily its attention to the social psychology of the 'bureaucratic personality', rather than its core of structural analysis.[3]

This chapter begins with a broad mapping of the history of organizational sociology, and then lays down a careful résumé of Merton's main and supplementary work in the sociology of organizations, and a briefer description of the studies in the subsequent Mertonian research programme. Then the reception accorded this work is recorded. The treatment of the early reception is focused on March and Simon's chapter (1958, Ch. 3), while later phases of influence have to be tackled more extensively. Two final sections investigate the extent to which Merton's analysis of organizations draws on and contributes to a posited general model of sociological analysis which undergirds all his sociological work, and the extent to which Mertonian organizational sociology might usefully fructify ongoing work in the sociology of organizations.

ON THE HISTORY (AND SYSTEMATICS) OF ORGANIZATIONAL SOCIOLOGY

History versus Systematics

There are two particular difficulties in tackling the historical concerns of this essay: first, general difficulties with the history of organizational sociology; and second, specific difficulties concerning Merton's organizational sociology (further specifics of the latter are laid out in more detail below).

If the current 'state of the art' of organizational sociology is chaotic, the history of organizational thought is in an even more parlous state. Although there are several studies which provide reviews of past work, most of these reviews are littered with pitfalls for the unwary historian: a superb but partial exception is Albrow's history of early 'bureaucracy theory' (1970), another is Rose's (1975) portrayal of the development of industrial sociology.[4] This lack confirms a point already made by Merton concerning sociology in general, that the careless conflation of history of sociology with the systematics of sociological theory (1968: 1–38) often produces difficulties for both.

An example of the difficulties is the laborious but useful review of organizational theory produced by Clegg and Dunkerley (1980). It covers the work of the immediate post-World War II decades in three chapters that cover typologies of organizations, the 'social system perspective' and 'the role of technology'. Although the first of these chapters covers reaction to the availability of Weber's ideal-type of bureaucracy and then discusses the typological exercises of Blau, Etzioni and then (!) Gouldner, followed by a review of Blau's double case study (which is not concerned with developing a typology), the work of Merton and Selznick is mainly discussed in the following chapter. What is even more disconcerting is that the

Merton and Selznick discussions *follow* a particularly extensive treatment of Talcott Parsons's general and organizational analyses, despite the much later date of Parsons's writing on organizations (1956, around fifteen years after Merton and Selznick). Clegg and Dunkerley do note explicitly that their presentation involves a temporal transposition in the timing of the contributors (*ibid.*: 158). But their choice in presentation does not assist understanding of the historical development of the field. It is justified by the distinctly arguable proposition that the development of organizational sociology involves, alongside the 'Weberian' approach, a 'social systems' perspective on organizations which developed out of the Henderson and Mayo interaction in spinning out the work of Pareto (*ibid.*: 171) and that Parsons led other 'structural-functionalists' in developing and applying this perspective to various social systems (*ibid.*: 185): this is surely too overdrawn a picture.[5] While some other historically oriented writers are less blatant in their Whiggish reworking of history in the service of better fitting positions into a present view of types of theoretical argument, the source material for historical work is limited, and there is very little concern for endeavouring to understand the social relationships among groups of organizational scholars as opposed to identifying common features among published work.

In this essay only a very limited attempt is made to repair these deficiencies. Attention in this section is confined to providing an overview mapping of the overall development of organizational sociology. This overview is built only on evidence contained in texts themselves and does not draw on other investigation. More pertinent detail is developed in later sections. Although organizational sociology works both as a field within sociology as well as a component in the interdisciplinary study of organizations, the review will try—somewhat artificially—only to cover the sociological themes.

A Preliminary Mapping

Despite the brute fact of the accelerating growth of organizational forms across a wide range of social areas for at least a century, at the point when Merton developed an interest in organizational studies there was very little sociological attention accorded to the structure and operations of formal organizations as a broad category of social organization, although there was some limited interest in particular forms such as firms or government apparatuses. As Albrow (1970) has documented, there had been an active 'prehistory' of writing about bureaucracy that was effectively masked by Weber's work. Other more recent writers have resurrected comments by Saint-Simon, Marx, Mosca and most importantly Michels, but these hardly constitute a developed body of writing.

For American sociology in the interwar period, Weber's ideal-type analysis of bureaucracy and of its historical role remained ignored, at least partly because it was not yet translated (it is referred to in Parsons, 1937, and made available more widely in 1946 and 1947 respectively through Gerth and Mills's and Henderson and Parsons's selections and translations). Also Weber's work in general did not have a high visibility to American sociologists. The dominant Chicago School took little interest in organizations (until its post-World War II interests in work situations and occupations: see Rose, 1975).

While relevant social research, notably the Hawthorne studies (see Roethlisberger and Dickson, 1939), was developing and there was an accelerating growth in 'management theory' (particularly in Barnard's 1938 essay on the functions of the executive), there were few attempts to conceptualize the communalities of organizations, and it was an unrecognized field. Instead, such attention as there was during this period focused on a recently constructed speciality entitled 'industrial sociology', which was coming to be regarded as an established speciality within sociology from the mid-1930s onward. One of the first signs of an active and aggressive attempt to establish 'organizational sociology' as a field in its own right came with Alvin Gouldner's brisk comments (1947) on Moore's review paper on industrial sociology. By the mid-1950s the field of organizational sociology developed out of the earlier more narrowly focused interest in 'bureaucratic theory' which Merton had ushered in with his 1940 essay. It became recognized, and was thenceforth regularly included in discipline-wide review exercises (e.g. Gouldner, 1959; Blau, 1968a). The speciality also acquired a reader (Merton *et al.*, 1952) and an introductory textbook (Blau, 1956). Whereas in 1940/41 organizational studies constituted under 1 per cent of articles published in core sociology journals, by 1965/66 they comprised about 12 per cent (Brown and Gilmartin, 1969: Table 2). It is not difficult to detect Merton's influence behind much of this (no doubt only partially considered) 'speciality-building' concern to develop organizational sociology—as Gouldner's mentor in the first set of comments, as the senior editor for the reader, and as active editor of the 1959 review exercise.[6]

The immediate impact of Merton's essay on organizations was both eclipsed, and also very considerably amplified, by the work of a group of particularly capable Columbia postgraduate students—most notably Philip Selznick, Alvin Gouldner and Peter Blau—but also a later, more diffuse group including S. M. Lipset, David Sills, the Lazarsfeld group that produced the *Academic Mind* (Lazarsfeld and Thielens, 1958), Rose Coser's study of a mental hospital (1979), and other researchers such as Michel Crozier in France. This diffuse grouping of sociologists produced a set of renowned classic organization case studies that are still highlighted, and often reworked, in current theoretical analyses of organizations.

As well as the continuing production of organizational studies, a secondary literature developed which had a major role in shaping subsequent 'reading' of the original studies (cf. Perry, 1979). Some of the features of the underlying model behind Merton's organizational sociology—and particularly the extent to which certain aspects of the model are carried into the work of Selznick and Gouldner—are pointed up by a particularly penetrating summary and critique written by March and Simon (1958). This treatment received wide attention, and material based on it is regularly included in standard organizational studies texts.

A later, and by now thinly stretched, influence lay through the polemics of Gouldner (e.g. 1955) and two summative exercises contributed by 'Columbian' sociologists—Blau (with Scott, 1962) and Etzioni (1961)—whose texts (and the latter's books of readings: 1964, 1969) provided the standard treatments of organizational sociology throughout the 1960s.[7] During this period, too, a variety of organizational studies was mounted by the Bureau of Applied Social Research at Columbia, and these were flanked by substantial attention to some of the methodological issues involved in studying organizations (for example, Barton, 1969; Coleman, 1958/59; and Lazarsfeld and Menzel, 1969).

The joint impact of the immediate 'Columbian' sequence of studies and further work was overwhelming, and it set the agenda for organizational sociology studies for at least the next decade of work during the basic formation of this field. There was little other sociological work to set alongside the early Columbian studies, with the only other notable sociologists working in this area until the late 1950s including Bendix (e.g. 1947, who continued the classical Weberian work on the historical development and political roles of bureaucracies), Dalton (e.g. 1950, who studied managers in industrial firms from a markedly conflict perspective) and Dubin (e.g. 1951, whose work was more concerned with social aspects of industrial relations systems).

However, the impact of the Columbian approach has faded over time, as this early case study approach to organizational studies gradually shifted through a concern with typologies (presaged in the early typology of Gouldner, 1954a, and by Parsons's work, 1956/57, and most notably presented in the two summaries of Etzioni, 1961, and then Blau and Scott, 1962), to quantitative structural comparative studies of organizations, which came to be the dominant approach.

Blau was one who (along with Stinchcombe, Udy and the emerging Aston group centred around Pugh) vigorously led organizational sociology towards this comparative approach. His view of the continuities that underlaid his break from the case studies tradition is captured in the following extended passage:

> Over the years, the focus of my theoretical interest shifted from seeking to gain insight into the sociopsychological processes that govern the informal relations in work groups of organizations to trying to discover the principles that can explain the structure of organizations on the basis of the relationships between organizational characteristics.... Only empirical data about many organizations make it possible to dissect the relationships between various organizational characteristics and thus to test and refine Weber's theory of these relationships. At first sight, conducting research on many organizations seems to be an impossible task, because even the study of a few work groups in one organization takes months. As I reread Weber's discussion again and again, however, I came to realise that most of the factors he analyzed do not require information obtained through painstaking observations of day-to-day operations, but merely data that can be collected on short visits to organizations, because Weber is concerned with the formal characteristics of organizations such as their size, the division of labour among official positions, the hierarchy of authority and the written rules. (Blau, 1974: 2, 3)

By the late 1970s this approach was flanked by growing critiques and alternative research programmes mounted first by microsociologists concerned with the 'negotiated social order', and then by radical organizational theorists concerned with reactivating Marxian perspectives and linking organizations back to wider social contexts (see useful collections edited by Benson, 1977, and Zey-Ferrell and Aiken, 1981, and for their contemporaries' reactions, Lammers, 1974). During this period a rather more theoretically conscious 'sociology of organizations' tended to replace the earlier 'organizational sociology'.

The present situation of organizational sociology remains confusing, with few substantial research directions gaining widespread support. Some types of study laid down earlier continue: for example, the flow of systematic and detailed quantitative structural comparative studies continues in some journals, but is not underlaid by much theoretical confidence. Another continuity that Perrow (1972, Ch. 5) has documented is the continuing concerns of what he terms, following Selznick, the 'institutional school' of organizational analysis. He sees this as a continuing tradition of close-in studies of the detailed dynamics of organizations, something of a counter to the structural-comparative approach. It may be particularly through

Table 14.1   Schematic History of Organizational Sociology

1940s		Bureaucratic Dysfunctions		
1950s		Comparative Structural		Institutional
1960s	Negotiated Order		Radical Critique	
1970s				
1980s				

this approach that the Merton/Columbian approach continues its major effect. But it seems that the core of the sociology of organizations has been occluded by the more specialist concentrations on the analysis of the 'labour process', the effects of technology and the roles of interlocking directors and similar recent focuses. Indeed, some commentators (e.g. Burawoy, 1979a: 7ff.) argue that since organizational theory ignores the historical context of the type of political economy in which organizations develop, it is appropriate for a more fine-tuned 'industrial sociology' to be restored in its place.

It might be useful to summarize this brief history using two graphic devices. Table 14.1 is a highly schematic time-plot showing some developments (for a similar periodization see Reed, 1985: 18). The second device (see Table 14.2) involves plotting the acknowledged effect of sociologists on the broad area of organizational studies by using the index to March's 1965 *Handbook of Organizations* (cf. the limited attempt to develop a history in the editor's introduction to the *Handbook*). This seems a particularly useful source for ascertaining the scholarly shaping of the field over the early era of development, although there are many dangers in inferring

Table 14.2   Sociologists Cited in March's Handbook (1965)
(only those with counts of 15 or over are included)

Blau	59
Gouldner	43
Parsons	39
Selznick	37
Whyte	37
Weber	36
Merton	35
Lipset	35
Bendix	34
Etzioni	33
Scott	33
Dalton	32
Coleman	29
Homans	24
Bales	23
Goffman	21
Warner	18
Shils	18
Janowitz	17
Dubin	16
Lazarsfeld	15

too much concerning the structure of scholarly influence from a quick and crude reference count. (For example, one major limitation is that this listing does not distinguish between influences from a scholar's general sociology as opposed to their organizational sociology.) The count has few surprises and nicely sustains the overview just developed.

Documenting Merton's Historical Role

The difficulty of inadequate general mapping and error-prone historical work in the area of organizational studies is compounded by limited secondary work on Merton's contributions in this area. Although the attention accorded organizations by Merton is moderate (perhaps something of the order of 5 per cent of his published output), it has been largely disregarded in general works on Merton. Thus the Coser (1975a) Festschrift is silent on his organizational sociology, while of the two book-length treatments, Sztompka very briefly covers his organizational concerns (1986: 194–5) and 'Bureaucratic Structure and Personality' (1940) is not even included in the bibliography, while Crothers (1987a: 37, 139) accords them the briefest mention.[8]

Moreover, within the history of organizational sociology only slight attention is paid to Merton, in some contrast to the treatment accorded the organizational writings of Parsons (Lansberger, 1961; Whyte, 1961; as well as considerable attention in Mouzelis, 1967; Clegg and Dunkerley, 1980, etc.). There is a particular difficulty with Merton's style of scholarly production which creates special chronological confusion: his 1940 essay has been reprinted in each of the three editions of his magnum opus, *Social Theory and Social Structure*, and it is usually and confusingly cited in either the 1957 or 1968 editions. (Sometimes, too, it is cited as reprinted in the 1952 bureaucracy anthology.) Finally, no personal background material on the personal circumstances surrounding this aspect of his work has been published (although some useful points might be extracted from personal correspondence, e.g. the letter to Professor C. J. Lammers, 22 September 1968). Nevertheless, textual analysis allows a relatively unproblematic reconstruction of his organizational sociology.

MERTON'S ORGANIZATIONAL SOCIOLOGY

Merton's Personal Experience with Organizations

If Weber's interest in organizations was at least partly sparked by his personal experiences in running German military hospitals, it is as well to explore the extent to which Merton's personal experiences might have shaped his own interest in organizational sociology. While Merton has a working lifetime of university service, together with participation in the Bureau of Applied Social Research and various academic bodies, several commentators have pointed out that he is not by nature an 'organization man' (Lazarsfeld, 1975; Cole and Zuckerman, 1975; Sztompka, 1986: 19–20). However, this relatively thin base of experience was extended by Merton's role for a decade and a half as consultant to the American Nurses' Association and some consulting (see Lazarsfeld, 1975) in an applied social research context that involved work with organizations (Lazarsfeld cites Zetterberg's work on a municipal museum and the material summarized in Merton and Devereux, 1964, as examples, and alludes to a considerable volume of such work).[9] However, there is evidence that, even if Merton was not interested in routine organizational maintenance, he was an effective organizational innovator, for example, intervening actively to enhance the status of nursing. Nevertheless, there seems to be only a limited link between Merton's personal experience and his organizational sociology.

The 1940 Essay 'Bureaucratic Structure and Personality'

It is important that this chapter is based on a detailed analysis of Merton's essay on 'Bureaucratic Structure and Personality' (BSP). This essay was published in *Social Forces* in 1940, and was subsequently included in *Social Theory and Social Structure* and in the Merton *et al.* anthology of 1952. By 1975 it had been anthologized in some nineteen other collections (see Miles, 1975: 501–02[10]), while another three reprints are noted in the updated bibliography by Miles and Haritos (printed as an Appendix to this volume).

No comments have apparently been published on the background circumstances which led Merton to write this essay. It was most likely (if we can extrapolate from general descriptions of his writing habits over this period) first developed during Merton's immediate-postdoctoral period at Harvard when he was part of a small circle involved in intensive theoretical work and discussion in sociology. The detailed work on the essay was probably carried out during his teaching stint at Tulane University (1939–41). It would have been presented during his course on 'social organization', presented at a conference, and then published (see Crothers, 1987a: 28; Merton's letter to Lammers, 22 September 1968, corroborates this general picture).

Where this essay generally fits into Merton's writings can be grasped from its position in the text when republished in *Social Theory and Social Structure*, where it is paired with his essay on 'The Intellectual in Bureaucracy' (1945c) as one of three pairings of essays in the main substantive section of 'Studies in Cultural and Social Structure'. Its textual position reflects its temporal location, as it is correctly aligned after Merton's work on anomie and before his late-1940s work on reference groups. In these essays Merton was developing a working perspective in sociology in which the fruits of a 'functional analysis' perspective were being realized. It fits in as one in a short series of empirically oriented theoretical essays (each of which also contains a socially critical bite) written over the late 1930s/mid–1940s period.

The essay is clearly based on the results of the intensive reading in classical European sociology carried out in Harvard over that period, especially under the auspices of Parsons. This included the attention accorded Pareto by the Henderson circle, but also a wider range including Durkheim, Simmel and Weber.[11] Although there is less visible evidence of this, there is also a definite influence from the complex network of investigations into the social organization of factories that was being carried out within the Harvard Business School during the 1930s. This work began with the Hawthorne and other related studies, but also covered the work of Warner on the social setting of the factory, Mayo's 'theological' writings on cooperation ('...offering a medieval order in the midst of a rapidly changing and expanding industrial civilization', Perrow, 1972: 75) and Barnard's insistence '...that organizations *by their very nature* are cooperative systems' (*ibid.*).[12] In many accounts of the history of industrial sociology the social context of this range of studies, and the extent to which they were centred on Harvard, is not sufficiently emphasized. However, pointing to this geographical connection should not be taken as an overestimate of their degree of integration. These studies were loosely integrated by various overlapping networks on the Harvard campus. In particular, Henderson's seminar was a focus in which several of these studies overlapped. There is no particularly direct trace of Merton's linkage to these study groups, but on the other hand it is clear that he must have been well aware of the studies being attempted, and the types of interpretations being developed. The essay also clearly reflects something of the social difficulties being experienced in North America (and worldwide) in the period of writing, where many unemployed were rescued from starvation by state charity but were subject to considerable nastiness from the bureaucracies set up to supply this relief. There must also have been an empathy with the flow of intellectuals who joined the state bureaucracies under the pulls of first the New Deal and then World War II.

At this stage in his career Merton was working through a somewhat disparate and only partially articulated theoretical programme in which he was generally attempting to apply an emerging 'functional' approach, which had largely been imported from anthropology, to the key issues of a modern society. As well as modifying the approach, Merton was concerned to focus the approach on the key social institutions of a modern society—organizations, occupations and communities—which involved something of a shift in the level of analysis from the macrosociological approach of classic functional analysis. The analysis of bureaucracies was one of a set of exercises in which this programme of attention to a middle order scale of social phenomena was set forth.

Broadly, Merton's essay can be seen as grafting onto the now classic (but then hardly visible) Weberian account of bureaucracy a wider sociology of organizations. In carrying this out, Merton's organizational sociology can be seen to parallel, at the mesosociological level, the earlier building of the analysis of the 'human relations' side to organizations at the microsociological level. Just as they added a social side to the sparse formal doctrines of the Taylor school, Mertonian organizational sociology can be seen as adding a social dimension at the mesosociological level to accounts of the formal aspects of bureaucracy.

But there is a particular theoretical approach involved in adding on this broader sociology, which is the development of functional analysis. From this perspective, Weber's analysis covers only the (*eu*)functional relationship between the social structure of a formal organization and its operation, especially its efficiency. To this Merton wished to add an analysis of *dys*functional relationships. So this essay plays a useful role in marking out the programme of theoretical work in functional analysis, even if this is not signalled in the title or directly addressed in the essay (apart from a section heading 'The Dysfunctions of Bureaucracy').[13]

The essay has three main purposes:

- to draw attention to an important piece of classical theory;
- as a set-piece illustrating the development of social theory, especially functional theory;
- to encourage empirical research into bureaucracy.

The essay itself is organized in a relatively complex way for such a short piece of work. Its basic structure is to:

- delineate the key structural features of bureaucracies which produce the vaunted machine-like efficiency of formal organizations, and then the career structure needed to staff that structure;
- *counterpose* to this 'ideal-type' image the popular image of bureaucracy as inflexibly bound by red-tape and the bureaucrat as a ritualistic pedant;
- show how these dysfunctions of bureaucracy arise because of structural difficulties built into the social organization of bureaucracies.

The opening paragraph sets up the 'efficient machine' model of a formal organization drawing on Mannheim (1935), in terms of his essentially Weberian distinction between substantive and functional rationality. The main structural features of formal organizations are quickly listed, as a social organization dedicated to producing calculable and predictable decision outcomes through a carefully designed set of formal offices. The following section builds on this through direct reference to Weber by pointing to the way in which formal organizations are 'best' set up in the form of a bureaucracy which involves a formal set of offices with an explicit division of labour, with succession to these offices being governed by a career structure of bureaucrats. This involves recruitment by formal criteria such as examinations and advancement by seniority. Bureaucracy is seen as the ideal-type of formal organization. Besides indicating the potential specifications between the terms 'formal organization' and 'bureaucracy', this analysis sets up three analytical levels for the description of a formal organization:

- the more-or-less rational predictability in the day-to-day operation of an organization;
- the structure of specified offices which are the positions involved in carrying out the day-to-day operations;
- the career structures involved in the long-term continuity of the organization.

The catalogue of the 'functional aspects' of bureaucracies continues with several further paragraphs which make interesting points, not then apparently drawn on subsequently in the essay or in any subsequent commentary apart from 'The Machine, the Worker and the Engineer' (1947). The first of these forcefully develops the Marxian point that people in many occupations are dependent on working within an organizational context because organizations have driven a wedge between a worker and his/her ownership of the tools of production. The second paragraph specifically reiterates the Weberian point that at the core of organizational structure lies the information stock that it secures, and which it holds as confidential *against* outsiders, especially in competitive contexts. This provides the basis of organizational power *against* control by either bosses or the general public. A similarly largely neglected feature of the essay is Merton's attention to the importance of terms to conceptualize bureaucracies and their operation, especially the social significance of the meaning of the term 'bureaucracy' itself.

The essay moves on to document some of the obvious dysfunctions of bureaucracy. These are seen to arise from its inability to be flexible over a range of different circumstances, and its tendency to inertia which renders it impervious to change. Merton notes that criticism of bureaucracy often becomes personalized as criticism of the individual bureaucrat. In developing an explanation of this inflexibility Merton draws on several available, more or less equivalent notions in the literature: the concept of 'trained incapacity' (Veblen); the concept of 'occupational psychosis' (Dewey); and the concept of 'professional deformation' (Warnotte). These concepts converge in the general idea that 'as a result of their day to day routines, people develop special preferences, antipathies, discriminations and emphases' (1968: 252).

After this opening ploy Merton develops a series of vignettes of organizational dynamics (including the telling pathetic case of the Norwegian aviator-explorer denied immigrant status by bureaucratic sophistry). These document the inflexibility of bureaucracies, and in particular their tendency for the 'displacement of goals', whereby 'adherence to the rules, originally conceived as a means, becomes transformed into an end-in-itself' (*ibid*.: 253). The set of theoretical explanations comprises:

- rules are followed because the organization is formally set up to do this;
- rules are followed because of primary group pressure to follow them (Merton here draws attention to the way in which social disapproval of non-rule-bound behaviour is handled by pointing to the epithets which are often used to enforce social control);
- rules are followed because the 'reward-structure' of promotion in a bureaucratic career sequence leads to compliance;
- rules are followed because they take on an emotional significance;
- rules are followed because a bureaucracy tends to recruit people of an appropriate 'personality type' that has a preference for the careful following of laid-down rules, and because such tendencies are reinforced by the experience of working in a bureaucracy.

These five approaches are used to explain conformity to bureaucratic procedure. In addition, Merton points to the difficulty of changing these procedures from outside, because of the intensity of the social forces that bind the bureaucracy internally:

- bureaucracies are often resistant to changes implemented from the top by the erstwhile controllers of the bureaucracy, and will often go to considerable lengths to subvert such external imposition of authority (especially by drawing on the complexity of information held by the organization);
- bureaucracies are often resistant to changes imposed on them by their clientele, as any such pressures tend only to be reflected back (through the mechanism of primary group pressures) into a heightened concern with enforcing the rules.

This resistance to clients among those in public bureaucracies is particularly enhanced by social class factors: although the ideology of public bureaucracies is that they are 'the servants of the people', the bureaucrats are generally lower middle class, while their clientele is mainly working class. This social class differential (and particularly because it is a relatively small social class differential) may lead to a heightening of hostility and social distance between bureaucrat and client.[14]

The essay closes with a short section on problems for research, which notes the importance of the 'social problem' which organizations constitute as a motivation for research, but then also lists a long series of theoretically relevant issues which might invite research attention.

In this short and readable essay Merton is able to take the paradox between the image of the 'efficient machine' held out by some writers (and especially the Weberian model) and the image of the 'inefficient and damaging machine' common in general public concern, and to build a sociological analysis that shows that, ironically, both models capture some of the truth: apparent rationality can have perverse and unintended outcomes. The essay makes a nice point in social commentary concerning the dysfunctions of organizations, but also develops a useful theoretical stance towards organizations. The theoretical approach has several noteworthy features:

- it draws carefully on the Continental heritage of organization sociology (through invoking Weber and Mannheim (1935); although in his comparison of several theorists, Hall (1963) identifies four points on which Merton fails to include elements in the Weberian model—differential rewards by office, administration separate from ownership, emphasis on written communication, rational discipline);
- it develops a definite set of theoretical positions; and
- it is open to ongoing empirical enquiry.

Nevertheless, the essay is also loaded with several difficulties. Some of these difficulties have hampered subsequent attention to it:

- it is not particularly explicit or systematic in its theoretical points;
- it is not based on definite empirical material (apart from what is 'generally known' about such organizations);
- in the interest of understanding the internal structure of organizations it tends to divert attention away from the relation between environment and the organization; further, it tends to replace moral concerns about the development of organizations with a 'scientific' focus;
- it never makes a very clear separation between the 'social psychological' and the 'social' levels of organizations (and indeed often seems particularly concerned with the social psychology of the bureaucratic personality, rather than the structure of organizations);
- the essay focuses on the public bureaucracy rather than the wider range of types: '...religious, educational, military, economic and political' (*ibid.*: 260), which has some longer-term limitations;
- the interesting points made in the opening substantive section about the tools of production and the politics of organizational secrecy are hardly drawn on later and in fact seem almost unconnected with the remainder of the essay.

If one tries to draw up a balance sheet ('a net balance of an aggregate of consequences', *ibid.*: 105) concerning this early essay, it seems clear that although it had a major catalyzing effect, the somewhat crowded essay format limited its impact, and left much useful analytical material buried, awaiting a later explication it never received. This essay was the earliest statement of an organizational sociology in the modern sense, and its themes were taken further in other of Merton's essays and in the subsequent development of the field of study. We now turn to these elaborations.

The 'First Wave' of Subsequent Essays

Merton's further work in the organizational area consists in two batches of scattered essays written in the mid- and late 1940s and then the late 1950s through to the late 1960s. These two 'waves' have rather different concerns and a different tone, as will become apparent.

Merton's essay on the 'Role of the Intellectual in Public Bureaucracy' (1945c) is couched as a contribution to the sociology of occupations, in this case the social science expert, and includes comments (as the title indicates) on the relation between occupations and the organizational contexts in which their members work. There is a considerable degree of personal experience and concern (albeit at least partly vicarious) which informs this essay as it traces the movement of many of Merton's contemporaries and near-contemporaries from the university settings in which they had trained into the bureaucracies of post-depression reconstruction and then the war effort. The analysis centres on the trade-off between the restrictions and time constraints imposed by working in a policy agency and the promise of a potential for helping shape policies. Merton also attempts to sketch complementary roles for 'unattached' as opposed to 'bureaucratized' intellectuals. He argues that the frustrations that often arise because of mismatching orientations and time disciplines may dissipate with time, as the intellectuals become socialized.

This work is followed by a more extensive analysis of the role of applied social research (1949f, reprinted in Merton, 1973: 70–98). Included in this essay is a briefly sketched typology (*ibid.*: 77, 79) of the relationship between types of clientele (government, foundation, business, welfare) and types of research agency (academic, commercial, in-house). This study precedes the subsequent more explicitly developed sociological interests in the relationship between staff and line and the relationship between professionals and organizations.

In 'The Machine, the Worker and the Engineer' (1947; also 1968: 616–27), Merton presents a broad perspective on the social role of technology, which, as he points out, forms the face of science to the public. His key point is that as a result of the division of labour, engineers 'come to be indoctrinated with an ethical sense of limited responsibilities' (*ibid.*: 622). Merton also generalizes this structurally induced unconcern for unintended consequences to other occupations, and pointedly indicts many applied organizational researchers for too closely adopting a management perspective.[15]

In the centre-piece essay of *Social Theory and Social Structure*, in which Merton developed his methodological restructuring of structural-functional analysis ('Manifest and Latent Functions'), the key extended example used to illustrate his approach was the 'political machine'. This belongs with his organizational sociology. Indeed, the role of the political machine forms a very nice *inverse* image to the operation of bureaucracy sketched in his 1940 essay. Whereas the official bureaucracy is honest but inflexible and paternalistic, and therefore unfriendly, the political machine is corrupt but flexible, helpful and humane. It works and because it works—at least for some groups of people—it survives and resists the efforts of civic reformers to limit its activities. The essay has no description of the political machine's internal structure, nor analysis of the limits to its operation. But the example makes clear the key importance of the relation between internal structure and environment. Although the analysis is cast in terms of a functional analysis, it can readily be shown (indeed, in Merton's own words: see 1968: 125n90) that a structural analysis can explain the situation quite satisfactorily: in a situation of competing alternative types of organization, long-term survival depends on continuing to attract or retain clients for the organization's services. The consequences of poor service may lead to difficulties for the organization, unless, of course, it has access to a captive clientele.

To these essays must be added the compilation of material in the *Reader in Bureaucracy* (Merton *et al.*, 1952), which provided the first reader in this area (although cf. Gouldner, 1950) and set the scene for organizational analysis for a period (a point made in the introduction to a later reader claiming to inherit its mantle: Grusky and Miller, 1970). The collection is dominated by the excerpts, and the editorial connecting material is thin and bland. Neither does a quick glance at the table of contents indicate much evidence of an underlying structure: the contents are bracketed by sections on theoretical approaches and on methodology and consist in a fairly standard range of material. Nor is a Mertonian stance actively pursued, with Merton's own contribution (a reprint of 'Bureaucratic Structure and Personality') being buried three-quarters of the way through in a 'Social Psychology' section. However, a closer examination shows a subtle underlying direction: the Weberian model is particularly developed and critiqued in the opening section, concern with methods (at this point covering the use of organizational documents and observations) is a continuing Mertonian interest, and the overall architecture of the book reflects a broad framework covering the environment, internal structure and career-personnel aspects of organizations.

This first group of essays by Merton share some common features:

- they have a concern for developing frameworks for organizational analysis, but also reach out to complementary frameworks;
- they have a definite socially critical tone;
- although addressing 'real world' issues, they are only loosely based on empirical studies.

Indeed, the critical tone seems later to have offended Lazarsfeld, who wrote of Merton (1975: 37):

> As late as 1945 he wrote a paper on the role of the intellectual in public bureaucracy. It is a compendium of the difficulties an academician is likely to encounter when he tries to adjust his values to agencies responsible for public service. Little sympathy is expressed for the poor bureaucrat who has to put up with the intellectual. The balanced approach of later papers is still absent.

The 'Second Wave' of Subsequent Essays

The second group of essays spans a later decade, during much of which Merton was a consultant to the American Nursing Association. The essays cover: the functions of professional organizations (1958); the role of technology and the professionalization of management (1960); the features of creative organizations (1965b); the issues of operating democratic organizations (1966); and the issues facing organizational leaders (1970b). Another essay of this period includes the only point in his writings at which Merton provides a definition of bureaucracy '...bureaucracy is a technical term designating a formal, hierarchic organization of statuses, each with its sphere of competence and responsibility' (1957e, cited from Merton, 1982a: 193).

The functional analysis of a professional voluntary association (1958) addresses manifest ('organizational aims') as well as latent functions, but does not cover dysfunctions. The functions are sorted into those for individual members, for the profession as a whole and for the community as a whole. Members (and also 'freeloading' non-members) of an association receive social and moral protective support for carrying out their professional roles, together with some opportunity and motivation to improve their standards. For the profession as a whole the association presses for '...higher standards of personnel, education, research and practise' (cited from Merton, 1982a: 204), which has the latent function of improving the social standing of the profession. The wider functions of the professional association are to provide '...one of those intermediate organizations which furnish the social bonds through which society coheres' (*ibid.*: 207) and more specifically to link the association to neighbouring professions, the government and other interests. Although this functional interpretation focuses on functions rather than structures, some organizational requirements for meeting these functions (notably the need for democratic internal structures) are specified. Merton points out that careful balancing of professional compared to societal concerns is required.

Merton's (never finalized [16]) contribution to a futurology seminar on the likely future shape of organizations (1960: 57–61, 209–12) was supposed to address the issue of the social consequences of technology (see *ibid.*: 7–9). However, he briefly dismisses this question with the surprising suggestion that there is likely to be little technology impelled change and deftly turns to his own interest in indigenous changes in the social environment, which he argues are of more importance than the effect of technology: specifically, the extent to which managers are becoming professionalized. What might have remained as a fairly standard presentation of an already fashionable unorthodoxy is instead used to stage a quickly sketched but interesting analytical framework. It is intriguing that in this essay Merton provides an analysis of the social pressures around managers that nicely complements his initial (1940) analysis of the social pressures around middle order bureaucrats. He notes that a growing social concern about the increasingly powerful role of managers is exhibited in the sharpening social images of conformist 'organizational men'. Instead, Merton counterposes his own analysis that a diversification of goals beyond sole profit maximization is occurring as standards for evaluating private and public organizations converge; the visibility of large corporations heightens; and social criticism increases as a result of more widespread formal education.

These external pressures on the value climate affecting managers are also reinforced by internal factors, such as the social pressure of esteem from fellow managers and the increasing emphasis on formal education of managers. Given this array and interplay of mechanisms, Merton argues that the trajectory of increasing 'managerialism' is secure. [17]

In commenting on the creative organization (1965b), Merton notes that supporting environments must be built at the small group as well as the organizational level, and that these may vary independently. He also points out that would-be creative organizations need to compete aggressively on the labour market to recruit highly creative people.

The essay on dilemmas in voluntary associations (1966) points out that, in order to achieve a democratic structure in which the leadership is accountable to the clientele, some trade-off between democracy and efficiency may be needed. Merton suggests that this organizational dilemma might be at least partially overcome by seeing *democratic* decision-*making* and *efficient* decision-*implementation* as alternating phases. Interestingly, he also points out that the quest for democracy can sometimes attain the extreme form of a ritualistic displacement of goals away from any concern with effective outcomes. Further, he adapts his typology of members (involved versus uninvolved and active versus inactive) to show the characteristic roles each performs in the running of a democratic and/or effective organization.

The last essay of this group (1970b) is a 'walk through' some of the dilemmas in running a business organization from the viewpoint of an organizational leader. These include the differential consequences of internal versus external promotion routes, the active versus nurturing roles in leadership, different types of leadership, dealing with internal conflicts and dealing with the wider environment. The overall thrust of the essay is an argument that, in America at least, there is an emerging strain of self-awareness and self-criticalness which constitutes a series of challenges for leadership, and that the dilemma identified must be actively tackled rather than decision-making being allowed to drift.

This group of essays shares several features. Many of the essays are particularly concerned with the interaction between organizations (more specifically voluntary associations) and professions (more specifically semi-professions). They are all aimed at lay audiences and although the theoretical literature on organizations is drawn on, the essays wear their scholarship lightly. Although the essays contain interesting observations, they do not attempt to develop insights within organizational sociology. Interestingly, as signalled by their placement when being reprinted in *Sociological Ambivalence* (1976a) and by their titles, theoretically this work is assimilated into Merton's interest in the analysis of 'sociological (more correctly 'social') ambivalence', which is a major theme in his writings of the 1960s (see Crothers, 1987a: 81–4).

At a few points the essays also draw on Merton's late 1950s work on 'group properties', in which he developed a programme of trying to elicit a consolidation of sociological material (especially from the writings of Simmel) on the characteristics and operations of groups of various sorts (including formal organizations). Some preliminary work in this area is included in the later editions of *Social Theory and Social Structure* (see 1968: 364–80), but this wider framework retains an unrealized potential for deriving particular propositions relating specifically to formal organizations.

The moral tone of these essays is much more bland and, in the absence of a critical edge, is certainly more sensitive to the concerns of organizational leaders. Various liberal suggestions about the running of organizations are recommended. In sum, this second group of essays includes a scatter of interesting sociological points, but largely constitutes gracefully written material that might be read by organizational leaders and others involved with organizations with interest and benefit.

The Mertonian Organizational Sociology of Science

Finally, there remains the nagging problem of Merton's apparent avoidance of attention to the organizational environment of scientific activity, despite the centrality of the sociology of science in both his very early and relatively recent work (see Crothers, 1987a: 33–40). It should also be noted that in general the sociology of science, despite the almost universal encapturing of scientists within organizations, seems to devote little attention to the interaction between scientific activity and organizational environments, and this topic is usually left to a residual 'applied sociology of science' approach aimed at the interests of research laboratory directors. [18]

While the role of organizational infrastructure in the development of a discipline is recognized by Merton, and the development of 'big science' noted, these are not considered to lead to major reconceptualizations of scientific activity. Indeed 'big science' is seen only to create difficulty in tracing the role performance of individual scientists, as any unique contribution becomes buried under heapings of joint writers. [19]

If Merton himself has turned only limited attention to organizational contexts, others working in a Mertonian tradition, and especially in the Columbia Programme on the Sociology of Science, have paid closer attention. Interest in organizational contexts takes three forms within the Mertonian sociology of science. One is through the description and analysis of the processes in institutions central to the processing of scientific knowledge, for example, the Royal Society (Merton, 1938a) or the operation of scientific journals (Zuckerman and Merton, 1972). A second form has been as part of the examination of stratificational systems in science (see Cole and Cole, 1973). Since these institutions are approached through fairly concrete analyses of processes, they are not particularly recognized as organizational studies. Lastly, Merton has repeated in the context of the sociology of science a point I have already reported in relation to creative organizations more generally: '...We have to conceive of the reward system as involving not only the competition *of* talent, but also the competition *for* talent' (1979b: 95).

Nevertheless, the impression that Mertonian sociology of science tends to denigrate concern with the organizational infrastructure of science is essentially correct. This relative blindness to organizational matters has at least two roots. One is perhaps a relatively trivial consequence of Merton's initial approach (1938a) to the sociology of science through study of the seventeenth century, when organizational frameworks were of less importance compared to their role in the set-up of 'big science' which now pertains. While accidental, this might have been quite diversionary. This bias has been aggravated by a focusing on the operation of the scientific élite rather than on other strata in the operation of science.

The main reason for unconcern with organizational contexts is that Merton's theory about the key processes of scientific activity is couched at an abstract underlying 'structural' level. The driving force of science is seen as the competition for the prestige which flows from making significant discoveries, but (largely) constrained within the framework of the cultural goals (and operationalized norms) laid down for proper scientific activity. Thus science needs at least two sets of institutions through which to operate: those acting as support structures to the producers of scientific work; and those acting in the overall interest of science as a social institution by permitting communication and according recognition of accepted knowledge. (In addition, teaching institutions may be required to supply the person-power.) These basic social processes of science as a social system may be able to work through any of a wide variety of actual forms of organization. The operation of science involves the generation and processing of a unique resource —the intellectual property of recognition for priority—which belongs solely to this beyond-organizational level. While organizational resources may assist very considerably in the generation of scientific knowledge, there is a crucial barrier, and organizational resources can only be converted into scientific resources across the boundary of widespread 'scientific community' recognition. Thus in the Mertonian programme interest in scientific organizations has a secondary role. In this approach scientific organizations are expected to behave in particular ways that assist the advance of scientific knowledge. Producing organizations are expected to operate to maximize their resources and prestige, while scientific organizations proper (especially journals) are expected to operate with strict fairness, solely according to the merit of the scientific ideas presented to them. For the latter class of organizations, their processes are seen potentially to threaten the fair operation of science. The risk is always hovering that the organizations supporting the neutral central functioning of science may become embroiled in, or subverted by, particular parties within the vigorous competition among the 'production organizations'. This impels empirical investigation of both types of scientific organizations: what are the factors (including organizational factors) associated with high scientific production? and what are the factors that ensure that the processing of scientific knowledge remains fair?

In the Mertonian organizational sociology of science, attention is always mainly addressed to the ways in which organizations operate in terms of the wider system of science. To a considerable extent they are seen as 'black boxes', with little attention devoted to their peculiar internal modes of operating. Thus Mertonian organizational sociology of science (at least to date) might be expected to provide only a thin offering to the advancement of organizational studies more generally. Indeed, it may be that the relative inattention to the internal structure of organizational dynamics may blind Mertonian sociology of science to key aspects of the operation of science. For example, the relations between high status and low status scientists, technicians, administrators, students and so forth become lost from view. Indeed, the extent to which the remainder of the personnel of scientific organizations, below the level of the high status scientists, are committed, either to the norms of science or to the struggle to achieve prestige, becomes highly problematic, since they are hardly likely to be able realistically to aim to secure widespread recognition. A particular lack in the theory is the failure to provide an explanation for the procuring of the resources which sustain high status organizations (and which are then able to be converted into prestige capital). While the Mertonian concept of 'cumulation of (dis)advantage' (1973: 457–8) is useful, it does not point sufficiently clearly to the sources of resources, which might flow from teaching, consultancy and other conduits. The Mertonian sociology of science needs to be able to offer a more thorough analysis at both the levels of the operation of science as an underlying structure and the operation of scientific organizations through which it must work.

Merton's Organizational Writings: Summary

It is difficult to pin down the ways in which Merton's subsequent organizational essay succeeded in extending the model developed in his first analysis. There are certainly some nice complementarities:

- while 'Bureaucratic Structure and Personality' (BSP) concentrates on the 'middle-range' bureaucrat, some subsequent essays include attention to organizational leaders and to lower order participants;

- while BSP concentrates only on line bureaucrats, a further essay examines staff positions;
- while BSP includes a critical tone, other essays are more sympathetic in tone;
- while BSP concentrates on government bureaucracies, some subsequent essays address professional voluntary associations and businesses;
- while BSP focuses on overconformity and ritualism, another essay reflects on innovative organizations;
- while BSP examines the functional requirements for efficiency, another essay examines the functional requirements for democratic accountability.

However, these ways in which BSP is extended should not be taken as the result of a systematic attempt to block out the components of a broad organizational sociology. Merton's strategy in development of theory has seldom worked in such a systematic way (cf. Crothers, 1987b). Nor was he exposed to, or created, a need for this systematic development of his organizational sociology. Such consistency as there is in his organizational analyses, I argue, derives from a constantly used underlying theoretical approach, which will be discussed in a later section. However, I also intend to argue that in the course of his unsystematic application of his more general approach to this more specific context, Merton fails to capture the essence of the functioning of organizations in the ways that his essays on anomie and on scientific priority expose some key aspects of the central workings of social structures. There is a missing centre to his analysis of organizations: he fails to capture the essence of their dynamics, and the analyses remain piecemeal. But, then, neither have subsequent analysts succeeded in capturing the unique properties of organizations, so the limitations of Merton's organizational sociology are relative only to his areas of more substantial success.

THE MERTONIAN/COLUMBIAN ORGANIZATIONAL STUDIES

The Research Literature

While Merton followed up his initial interest in the analysis of organizations in a desultory fashion, the topic attracted the attention of a particularly innovative group of Merton's students. Beyond the immediate facts that each of these had carried out graduate work in the Department of Sociology at Columbia University, and that each indicates ongoing links with Merton through acknowledgments and (less often) direct citation, it is unclear what the informal social organization of this grouping was.[20] The main writers in this group tend to cross-reference each other's work to a considerable extent, but (to my knowledge) none explicitly acknowledges any group consciousness. While Merton's influence is particularly acknowledged by Blau and Gouldner, the specifics of this influence are not given. Subsequent accounts, like that of Clegg and Dunkerley (1980) discussed above, do not always recognize the social source of possible cohesion in this group and may not even treat them as cohesive.

From Merton's own perspective the Columbian studies *did* form a programme of ongoing study. Expanding in 1957 on a comment first written in 1949 (without subsequent alteration for the 1968 edition) for the introduction to Part 2 of *Social Theory and Social Structure*, he argued:

> Sociological studies of bureaucracy are plainly needed to provide a broader and firmer base for the understanding of administration, both public and private. Thus far, sociological discussions have tended to be speculative, bare and abstract, or if informed with concrete materials, these have generally been altogether impressionistic. This conspicuous gap has belatedly attracted notice and, accordingly, a series of empirical monographs on sociological problems of bureaucracy has been initiated in the Department of Sociology of Columbia University, some of these studies with the aid of fellowships granted by the Social Science Research Council. The ... study by Selznick (1949) centers its analysis on the unanticipated consequences of organized action for bureaucratic policy; Seymour Martin Lipset's *Agrarian Socialism* (1950) examines the interplay between bureaucratic personnel and policy-makers; two monographs by Alvin W. Gouldner—*Patterns of Industrial Bureaucracy* (1954) and *Wildcat Strike* (1954) —trace out the functions and dysfunctions, both latent and manifest, of bureaucratic rules in an industrial plant; and *The Dynamics of Bureaucracy* (1955) by Peter M. Blau analyzes the conditions under which changes in the structure of two governmental bureaucracies come about. Still unpublished is Donald D. Stewart's study of local draft boards (1950) which examines the role of volunteer participation in a bureaucratic organization. Together these studies provide observational data on the workings of bureaucracy of a kind not obtainable from documentary sources alone, and begin to clarify some of the principal issues in the study of bureaucracy. (1968: 179)

A footnote draws attention to additional material in the collections by Merton *et al.* and Dubin, the introductory material of Wilensky and Blau, and also to an independent but overlapping study of bureaucracy carried out from Tulane by Francis and Stone (1956).

The foundation for the 'Mertonian/Columbian' work was laid in Merton's course 'Analysis of Social Structure' and a seminar on 'Formal Organization', which spanned several decades and covered material beyond that specifically concerned with the analysis of formal organizations in the narrowest sense. It is not entirely clear what the effects of this course were: both Gouldner and Blau report the influence on them of the general Mertonian functional analysis approach. Rather later, Hage (1980: vii) reports his introduction to March and Simon through this course. Whatever the initial effect, the direct influence of Merton was soon dissipated as the fieldwork that the key figures carried out was highly decentralized, and this was followed by their withdrawal to other institutions for writing up and subsequent teaching. Moreover, each of the key figures quickly engaged in more general contributions to the literature on the sociology of organizations.

Any further shaping by Merton was through correspondence and detailed discussion of individual reports, and no attempt was made by Merton through summative reanalysis to draw together this work into an overall programme of findings. Indeed, at the point (in the mid-1950s) when this might have become more relevant, Merton was already launched into a research programme in medical sociology that arose out of his contemporaneous work on professions and also role theory. His interest in organizations was not sustained.

The key studies in the Columbia programme were Selznick's study of the Tennessee Valley Authority (TVA), Gouldner's study of a gypsum plant and Blau's study of two government agencies (one an employment agency and the other a regulatory inspectorate). Other studies include: Lipset's study of the interaction between the Social Credit movement in Alberta and public bureaucrats (as a single chapter in a wider study of Social Credit as a social movement); his study (with Trow and Coleman) of the two-party internal democracy within the Typographical Union; and the later work of Sills on the Heart Foundation and of Lazarsfeld's group on the extent to which American universities maintained traditions of free speech during the McCarthy era. The final study from the Columbia stable was Rose Coser's investigation of the internal dynamics of a mental hospital (R. Coser, 1979).

The initial studies took a case study approach and included broad examination of each organization through extensive observation and use of organizational documents as well as some interviewing. In interpreting their data most drew on a 'Weberian' model, with some reference to Merton's essay but also to earlier authorities such as Michels and Saint-Simon. They are similar, too, in their very explicit adoption of either an 'unintended consequences' (Selznick) or a 'functional analysis' (Blau) approach. [21]

The studies were also strongly informed by ideological concerns (more accentuated than in Merton). Selznick was interested in the deflection of centrally imposed democratic concerns, the use of tight organizational structures as tools of ideologues, and in the role of leader-statesmen; Gouldner in the 'metaphysical pathos' in which 'iron laws' which battered down individuals were themselves seen as oppressive; Blau located the relationship between organization and democracy as a central issue; and Lipset was concerned with the deflection of political programmes by bureaucrats and the possibilities of internal democracy in organizations. Swedberg (1980), commenting on Selznick and Lipset who both explicitly studied communist organizations, suggests that a firm anti-communist stance has undermined the adequacy of their analyses. The extensive monographs which resulted include much structural and ethnographic description, [22] as well as analysis of the data and broad commentary on the wider theoretical issues involved in establishing a viable organizational analysis. Each made some useful contributions to the growing literature.

Selznick's writing on organizations spans two and a half decades, and includes essays on the theory of bureaucracy (1943) and a theory of organizations (1948), before he published his TVA study in 1949 (the fieldwork was carried out in 1942/43), and subsequent studies of the Communist Party as an organizational weapon (1952) and of organizational leadership (1957). Selznick's major study spans several levels of analysis including:

- a concern to develop a 'structural-functional' systems approach to organizations, which (as Wolin, 1961, has pointed out) has a strong organicist tone, especially in its treatment of leadership roles;
- a concern to critique the performance of the TVA in the light of its democratically assigned role in the area, and the extent to which it became diverted into betraying its original goals;
- a more detailed analysis of the processes through which the organizational structure became both specialized and deeply involved with local organizations and yet maintained some overall direction of purpose.

The key analyses of the TVA study were that, first, the 'grassroots' ideology developed by the TVA served as a mechanism for protecting it from extra-regional political influences (e.g. the USA government more generally), for encouraging the devolution of work to existing regional agencies and for providing for a degree of common direction and commitment to the organization; and, second, that the existing agencies co-opted and subverted the original goals set by the TVA. This empirical analysis was set alongside a theoretical schema which stressed the extent to which an organization formed a social system as a whole.

Gouldner's 1948 study of a gypsum plant in upstate New York (1954a, 1954b; see also Burawoy, 1982) involved observations of how the plant operated before and after a managerial succession. Before this crucial intervention from the higher echelons of the organization, the plant operated in a mode Gouldner describes as an 'indulgency pattern', in which implementation of rules was often loose and the men carried community life-styles into the workplace. After the managerial succession, the application of the rules was tightened up by close supervision and the rules were elaborated, with the paradoxical effect of perpetuating tensions and reinforcing low motivation. Indeed, these growing difficulties in the operation of the plant culminated in a wildcat strike.

Blau (1956) carried out a double case study of a government employment agency and a government regulatory agency during 1948/49. He found that the implementation of statistical record-keeping to monitor the performance of the staff had a series of unintended consequences which reduced overall efficiency of the operation; necessary cooperation needed to carry out effective performance tended to be overwhelmed by competition (a competition with a deviant edge). Adaptation of the official rules was often more effective than sticking to them.

Lipset (1950) found that, in Alberta, the failure of the incoming government to sweep away the existing top administrators had the effect of a very considerable undermining and modification of their radical political programme. Lipset, Trow and Coleman (1956) studied that rare exception to the iron law of oligarchy, the internal democracy within the International Typographical Union, and found that the union's internal two-party system was affected by '...the relative autonomy and decentralisation of the local subunits, the status of union leaders, the degree of participation and interest of the rank and file in union politics, the general value system of the organization and so on' (see Mouzelis, 1967: 65). Sills's work (1957) showed that when an organization's mission has been met, it may well be able to develop new goals in order to perpetuate its existence.

There are several later studies which deserve at least brief mention since they directly address the central 'Columbia School' theme of the 'theory of bureaucracy'. While Merton quotes the acknowledgment in Francis and Stone's study of an overlapping interest, it should be pointed out that their study is concerned to measure, using an impressive triangulation of research techniques, the extent to which the documents and behaviour in an organization (another employment agency!) actually do meet the characteristics laid down for a bureaucracy (rather than attempting to elicit the ways in which the organization operated, as in the Columbian studies). Crozier's (1964) double case study of two French plants also fits into the broad Columbia approach (see also Krohn, 1971; Rose, 1979). H. Cohen (1970) draws attention to the awkward discrepancy between his results, which revealed the extreme flexibility of bureaucrats, and Merton's point concerning their rigidity; he suggests that both such orientations are equivalent in effect. But besides these more direct links it becomes difficult to trace the Columbia effect through the tangled skein of organizational studies.

The final study from the Columbia stable, Rose Coser's investigation of the internal dynamics of a mental hospital, involves an intricate structural analysis of the shaping of social processes of psychiatric training and practice. As Merton points out in his Foreword (Merton, 1979d), this work is very revealing about the operation of formal organizations and he draws particular attention to this significance of her work. However, Coser's main focus lies in the development of a very careful status-and-role analysis, which is concerned with social patterns within organizations rather than linking up directly with a more global organizational analysis.

The Secondary Literature

In addition to the discrete impact of each individual study, there has been a cumulative impact of the group of studies. However, this group effect has been constructed by subsequent analysts, and different views of the cumulative effect have been developed in the literature (often without confrontation).

Ostensible members of the school had little to do with constructing the school. In his early text Blau (1956) provides no systematic framework, although various aspects of the studies are summarized at different places.[23] Nor does Gouldner's review essay (1959) provide any precise summary, and instead emphasizes the divergences between 'rational and natural' models, which tends to rend asunder the internal dynamics of the Mertonian model.

March and Simon (1958: 36–47) have provided the most important secondary analysis, made more vivid by their presentation of several graphic models. They examine Merton, Selznick and Gouldner, and conclude:

> The general structure of the theoretical systems of all three writers is remarkably similar. They use as the basic independent variable some form of organization or organizational procedure designed to control the activities of organization members. These procedures are based primarily on what we have called the 'machine' model of human behavior. They are shown to have the consequences anticipated by the organizational leaders, but also to have other, unanticipated, consequences. In turn, these consequences reinforce the tendency to use the control device. (*ibid.*: 37)

The Merton model is seen to focus on the institution of standard operating procedures or rules (with client distaste leading paradoxically to even more standardization in their implementation); while the Selznick model is seen to focus on the institution of delegated authority (which leads to subunits developing different trajectories, although this is dampened by the reassertion of overall ideologies); and the Gouldner model is seen to focus on the formalization of rules and the institution of closer supervision (which leads to lower performance and then tighter supervision).

The influence of the March and Simon construction (itself 'one of the most widely cited sections of *Organizations...*', Perrow, 1972: 152) has been immense, and has affected most subsequent treatments (Perry, 1979, cites their influence on Crozier and Pugh; the account in Mouzelis and most other texts is also based on their interpretation). But their efforts have also introduced some difficulties. To understand how these difficulties have arisen, it is necessary to understand the framework used by March and Simon into which they assimilated the Columbian work.

March and Simon attempt to build a highly sophisticated and systematic model of organizations. They interpret and construct the three studies within a framework of various 'motivational factors' which inhibit or deflect the operation of the 'machine model' of the organization. This is separate (according to Perrow, 1972) from their augmented treatment—in the second half of the book—of the way in which the 'machine model' actually works at a collective or structural level.[24]

Perrow (*ibid.*: 152) states, 'I find that these models violate the originals in several respects'. Unfortunately, he does not specify these. However, Perry identifies a specific mistake made in the rendering of Selznick's work: 'Far from summarizing the structure of the monograph, the terminology they employ and the relationships they posit are all drawn from the final four pages of a paper published some six years before the TVA study appeared and which does not even grace its bibliography' (1979: 268). However, while Perry is correct that some of the terminology is drawn from the article rather than the book, in fact, March and Simon do not develop their model from this source.[25] In any case, the effect certainly is, as Perry argues, to deflect the focus of a study which is intensely concerned with the relation between environment and organization into a focus on the internal features of that organization.

The March and Simon summary must be seen as a very useful step forward, even if it had some unfortunate effects. The models should have included Blau's work, and perhaps been more readily able to accommodate other later work, and they certainly should have been cast so as to build in external relationships; but these could be seen as challenges for later writers to correct and extend. The most important effect of their work was to stress and display the importance of feedback loops arising from organizational practices: this conveyed with great effect the essential point made by functional analysis without becoming sidetracked into some of the unfortunate explanatory difficulties which often arise with this approach.

Crozier (1964) provides the most subtle and powerful reworking of the Columbian studies. Besides reiterating the March and Simon conceptualization, while adding to it the notion that these processes involve 'vicious cycles', Crozier elicits further aspects central to these studies and also provides a penetrating critique. 'Selznick's most original thinking,...deals with the problem of the regulation of dysfunction. How does an organization limit the cumulative influence of its dysfunctions?' (*ibid.*: 181). The answer lies in the mechanisms of co-optation and of organizational ideology. However, since this analysis only '...regards the possibilities of controlling the development of dysfunctions, rather than as the source of them...Selznick still remains within the Weberian scheme'. Gouldner's contribution is seen to lie with his theory of managerial succession as a cause of the development of bureaucracy, and particularly with his analysis of the ways that rules can be used to reduce tensions within an organization, since they can be used as a bargaining tool as well as a basis for punitive purposes. Because the models do not link back to the 'rational' component of the Weberian model, the Columbian models are seen to lack a long-term dynamic of change. At best they are restricted to cyclic phases of increasing and decreasing rigidity.

To overcome some of these deficiencies Crozier attempts to build a two-layer model from his own double case study research: 'Four basic elements seem to be necessary...: the extent of development of impersonal rules; the centralization of decisions; strata isolation and concomitant group pressure on the individual; and the development of parallel power relationships around the remaining areas of uncertainty' (*ibid.*: 187). This broad framework, which can accommodate various forms of vicious cycle, explicitly enhances Merton's model: '...The vicious circle of the displacement of goals...could be explained not only by the rigidity of the human personality, which maintains itself within the mould to which it has been submitted, but the isolation of competitive strata, which use the displacement of goals to assert their influence against one another' (*ibid.*: 193). The second level of Crozier's model is to explain change and innovation, which he sees as occurring partly by change introduced by highly placed change agents or as a result of the building up of crises. Crozier also includes an interesting discussion of the application of each of Merton's modes of adaptation to the organizational situation (see *ibid.*: 190–203). While retaining a basic Columbian approach, Crozier is able to extend this to accommodate a wider range of material and to develop it from a partial analysis to a more systematic one.

Mouzelis (1967: 55–75) provides an extended account of what he terms 'The Post-Weberian Theories of Bureaucracy', covering Merton, Gouldner, Selznick, Blau and Lipset *et al*. He sees these studies as shifting the level of analysis from the political structure concerns of the classical writers to an organizational level; widening the range of empirical concern beyond 'rational elements'; and using a functional framework of analysis of the complete organization as a social system. The central feature is seen as (*contra* Crozier?) '...their dynamic and dialectical character, their emphasis on small-scale change which is due to certain inherent strains and dilemmas in bureaucratic organizations' (*ibid.*: 59). In a careful examination he points out that this grouping of studies has involved an empirical re-examination of the classical problems of bureaucracy and individual initiative and of bureaucracy and oligarchy, and in both areas they have developed rather more optimistic viewpoints than are often prevalent in that they point up '...possibilities and alternatives...' in the functioning of organizations '...which are often blurred by armchair theorizing...' (*ibid.*: 64). However, he sees this approach as limited by its methodological emphasis on single case studies and its theoretical emphasis on functional analysis.

A final and rather more elliptical account is given in Perrow's (1972) identification of a tradition of institutional studies of organizations. He sees this as a continuing tradition of close-in studies of the detailed dynamics of organizations (something of a counter to the structural-comparative approach), and as continuing to apply a 'structural-functional' approach to organizations (perhaps in the ethnographic/anthropological sense of classic community studies). This approach emphasizes:

- the whole way in which an organization is held together;
- the carrying out of case studies;
- the building up of a 'natural history' of an organization;
- attention to unplanned changes;
- exposé of the irrationalities and diversions from stated goals;
- attention to the variety among organizations;
- attention to the capacity of organizations for taking on a life of their own;
- attention to interactions with the environment.

However, he also criticizes this tradition for overattention to 'trivial organizations',[26] and for their inability to see the role of some powerful organizations to shape society (as opposed to being reactive to their environment). The institutional school is diffuse and fed by many streams of influence, not least the Chicago tradition. On the other hand, it is clearly also an extension of the main set of Columbian studies, although it lacks their analytical and theoretical concerns (i.e. their interest in cumulation of middle-range theory and their interest in tying their material back to classical writers: see also Burawoy, 1982).

It has already been mentioned that there is a major tension in several accounts (beginning with Gouldner, 1959) about the relationship between the Mertonian 'partial functional analysis' (or 'structural') and the more Parsonian 'systems functional analysis' as applied to organizations. This reflects a more general divergence in social theory between these two positions (see Crothers, 1987a: 67). Whereas the 'bureaucratic dysfunctions' approach is limited to tracing through the effects of particular practices, the 'systems' approach attempts to provide a systemic picture of the whole organization. Selznick is usually, and correctly, recognized as having a foot in both camps. Nevertheless, the difference was signalled early, and Selznick reports (1949: 252n) a caution from Merton about his tendency to attribute 'needs' to organizations.

There are other available commentaries on the 'dysfunctions of bureaucracy' approach (e.g. Albrow, 1970: 54–61; Clegg and Dunkerley, 1980: 185–90). Most add little to the above analysis. The main secondary analyses cited have been particularly important in explicating some of the fundamental theoretical and methodological issues that were largely implicit in the original studies. The models developed in this secondary literature certainly do not exhaust the material available in the original studies; they have tended to emphasize selectively some aspects (cf. Perry, 1979; Reed, 1985); they have left many loose ends not tied down into formal models; and they have had rather more effect on textbook presentations than ongoing research. But they constitute a fine example of the role of academic commentary in advancing the understanding of a phenomenon by opening up different perspectives on it.

RELATIONSHIP TO MERTON'S GENERAL SOCIOLOGY

Although some commentators on the whole corpus of Merton's work have despaired of finding any systematic underlying general model, others have argued that there are some communalities in his approach across an array of more specific analyses. These commentators differ somewhat, though, in terms of exactly what is involved with these communalities. Sztompka (1986) portrays Merton as working out of a grand systemic approach that spans several levels and is intersected by several common dimensions, whereas Stinchcombe (1975) and Crothers (1987a) develop more restrained working models from specific Mertonian analyses.

The following model is developed from a general synoptic reading of Merton's theoretical work, together with detailed exegesis of two key theoretical essays: those on anomie (Merton, 1938b) and the priority of scientific discoveries (Merton, 1957b). According to my interpretation the key components of the general Mertonian model are:

- culture
- social structure
- interaction settings
- choice situations
- social practices.

The cultural structure of a social system is seen as the set of ideas which conceptualize the world of the members of the social system and which provide goals and motivations. Any cultural structure has a complex interlocking structure in which values are consistently off-set against their counter-values. The skeleton of the social structure involves the complex set of status positions to which members are assigned (or occupy), together with the distribution of resources valued by the social system and linkages to behaviour such as reference orientations and reward systems.

At a further layer of analysis lie the social interaction settings in which networks of relationships surround a person. But perhaps the most interesting component in the Mertonian conceptual armamentum is the 'choice situation' in which individuals —albeit socially constrained by the circumstances arising from their position in the social structure—decide among various structurally offered alternatives (or possibly continue with just the one single available path of action). In analyzing choice situations, Merton develops a relatively tight logical schema at a relatively abstract level, as in the example of the paradigm of modes of adaptation in his anomie essay. Social practices are the (usually alternative) sets of institutionalized patterns of behaviour and attitudes that are constantly produced and reproduced as a result of the stream of people's choices. Finally, it is argued that different social positions are likely to attract different character types and that personality configurations are likely to be further confirmed by the day-to-day experiences of a position.

Once the components in the Mertonian model have been laid out it is possible to assemble it. Each component has a separate role. The culture provides the goal-setting that motivates the system (as in Weber's argument concerning the 'spirit of capitalism'), while different parts of the social structure work either to amplify or to dampen these culturally sourced drives by placing different emphases on them. The social structure, too, will have major effects on whether or not people are enabled to achieve the culturally set goals through differential access to resources. In particular, according to a Mertonian perspective, social structures are animated by competition or struggles between different components. For example, scientists, while denying being sullied by any personal motivation and claiming to be concerned only with the cultural goal of advancing scientific knowledge, compete (sometimes viciously) for the prestige which accrues from making scientific discoveries. It is such struggles over the allocation of important resources which provide the energy running the social machinery.

Lastly, the choices made by individuals feed back to affect the long-term future of alternative social structures. If scientists continue to emphasize publication in orthodox journals, then this form of scientific publication is likely to continue to be available. If they don't, some other form of communication may develop. Organizations have some distinctive features compared to other social groupings: the goals tend to be rather more formally and explicitly defined, and their social structure contains a much higher 'designed' component and tends to be strongly hierarchical.

The static and descriptive Mertonian framework that has so far been sketched out needs to be supplemented by consideration of a more dynamic model which underlies it. It is possible to extract a more fundamental model of how social structures work from Merton's two most analytical essays, his anomie essay and that on the ownership of intellectual property which lies at the centre of priority disputes. In both these essays he provides an analysis which shows the social system at work and which identifies the source of social energy that drives it (cf. Storer, 1973: xxiii). In the anomie analysis it is the match, or more importantly the mismatch, between the cultural drive for success and the social means for achieving it that is significant in structuring people's choice situations, and especially their ongoing decisions about orientation to (acceptance or rejection of) goals and to (legitimate or illegitimate) means. Similarly, the drive for scientific recognition that is the reward for generating scientific property provides the basic energy that drives the quests—both legitimate and not—of scientists. It is in these underlying competition/conflict models that Merton is able to grapple with the essential underlying dynamics of the social system.

The advantage of this briefly sketched two-layer model is that it not only provides a framework for description, but also helps to identify explanations of the ways in which social systems actually operate (particularly in terms of struggles over resources among various interests within a broadly agreed consensus of cultural goals). The schema provides a place for the objective levels of social reality as well as the subjective. It allows for both individual action and collective structures, and it provides some indications of the conditions under which both social change and social persistence are likely to occur. However, it has to be admitted that much theoretical work is needed to develop this model further to ensure that it meets reasonable standards of consistency and coherence.

The concern now becomes to evaluate the extent to which Mertonian organizational sociology fits, or can be made to fit, this model. Certainly, some of the main features of this general model readily apply. In particular, the essay on bureaucratic personality can be seen as a fairly straightforward extension of the earlier anomie theory essay, since it addresses the 'ritualistic' as opposed to 'innovative' orientations supposedly so characteristic of bureaucrats (see Crozier, 1964, for an extended comment on this). It also links to the earlier essay on unanticipated consequences (1936b), as this is a central imagery in the analysis. More generally, Merton's summary of Weber's description of bureaucracy could be readily reworked into the status-set/role-set/reference-group analytical apparatus for the analysis of social structure which Merton later developed more explicitly (and even partially published, mainly in 1968; see also 1973, 1976a).

However, showing the affinities with various themes does not build up a 'working model' of organizations. In the remainder of this section I attempt to reconstruct a model of the working of bureaucracy, using the raw material of observations which Merton provides, but endeavouring to construct the model in relation to his most sophisticated theoretical models. A reconstruction of a Mertonian organizational model from the perspective of the more general model easily fits the major categories (see Table 14.3).

A key, but implicit, aspect of Merton's analysis is that he sees organizations as inhabited by a set of groups: bureaucrats (those staffing the administrative

Table 14.3   Relationship of Merton's General and Organizational Sociologies

General	Organizational
Culture	Organizational objectives (and culture)
Social structure	Designed set of statuses organized around a division of labour, role-sets, etc.
	Resources allocated through hierarchy
Interaction settings	Small group milieux
Choice situations	Reliability/not in decision-making
Feedback mechanisms	Organizational control, unintended consequences

machinery), organizational leaders, clients etc. For example, his central essay (BSP) could be interpreted as an analysis of the 'middle order' of bureaucracy. These groups have their own norms, career structures and social backgrounds, which affect not only the way they operate on a day-to-day basis but also what their overall orientation to the organization might be. Perhaps a sociological analysis needs to begin by sifting through likely groupings in order to build up a profile of each together with a schema of their interrelationships. Merton offers few clues as to how this might be done, although it is possible that one could begin with the rough sorting into the three layers that seem to be implicit in his analyses: these correspond to the upper, middle and lower classes—organizational leaders, bureaucrats and lower order participants. More detailed portraits might then be added. Certainly, the sociographic tools of role-set/status-set frameworks will assist in structuring a description of positions *in relation to* other positions both inside and outside the organization. The task of establishing an appropriate set of groups is likely to be empirically problematic.

Once a portrait of the groups has been established (at least tentatively) they must then be related to the overall organization. Many organizational analyses assume that short-term 'predictability' and perhaps 'efficiency' are seen as key, if unspecified, organizational objectives. In addition (as is implied in later essays from Merton), organizations have to be concerned with their long-term 'effectiveness'. In examining the possible tensions and trade-offs between these two types of organizational goals, a wider perspective on the operation of organizations is opened up. For example, as the organization may be involved in policy development as well as programme implementation, it is clear that staff functions as well as line functionaries are needed. (The juxtaposition of these two groups will then have major implications for organizational functioning.)

The general orientation of each group to the dual goals of the organization can be described in terms of Merton's typology of modes of adaptation, as Crozier has nicely demonstrated (1964: 198–203). It is important to consider the full range of the typology rather than merely the ritualism which Merton emphasized in his main essay. Although Merton has tended to shy away from 'interest-group' theories in which action is attributed to groupings, this approach seems central to building a model. The following model draws particularly on Crozier's bargaining 'exchange' formulation (itself a development of Merton's work).

The central dynamic of organizations lies in a struggle for position and control among these groups. It is not necessarily a fully fledged struggle over the control of organizational resources (although it can be), but rather more over the trade-off between degrees of participation and commitment members of a group wish to make to an organization in return for the types of rewards (or avoidance of punishments, dirty work, etc.) they wish to receive. This is hardly a struggle which takes place on an equal footing, as the leadership strata with ownership/control over the resources and means of production play a predominant role (and, indeed, many other groups within an organization can at best resist passively). It is in the relationships between groups that rewards, control over resources, rules and even goals become weapons. This central process of organizations is not relatively neat and tidy like that pertaining in the development of scientific capital. Participants do not necessarily share the same cultural goals (or at least there is a wide range of orientations towards them) and differ markedly in their means; nor (usually) is there any endpoint to the ongoing struggle. As well as pointing up the significance of group processes in organizations, this perspective relates to the strategy and tactics of individuals, who may follow the group trajectory only to a degree.

A further point is that a Mertonian perspective might well emphasize the importance of combining organizational and occupational analyses, since the two are essentially intertwined (through the careers and trajectories of group members). Finally, the study of organizations must be seen as integrated with the wider tasks of analyzing the warp and weft of all facets of modern social life. There seems little difficulty in showing the connection between the specificities of Merton's organizational sociology and his overall approach (insofar as an overall approach can be unproblematically defined). Rather more interestingly, it can be shown that exegesis of implicit models underlying Merton's more interesting analyses can be used to build a more sophisticated Mertonian analysis of organizations.

RELATIONSHIP TO PRESENT ORGANIZATIONAL SOCIOLOGY

It is important to establish if an examination of Merton's organizational sociology is merely of historical interest or whether it also has some useful insights to offer contemporary organizational sociology. Unfortunately, this is rather too large a task to tackle without an extensive mapping and evaluation of contemporary sociology of organizations and organizational studies. Enough orientation may be provided by Perrow's challenge to allow a preliminary account to be provided: in concluding his 1972 book Perrow called for the integration of neo-Weberian structuralist views and the institutional approach. This crucial point is echoed in various ways in other commentaries which draw attention to the need to meld analysis of both the rational and irrational sides of organizations, of the formal and informal structures, of their collective level and their individual level properties.

I think that at least a modest contemporary role for Merton's organizational sociology is justified. In a complex situation marked by many divergences there may be some point to be reminded of the continuing need for a broad and balanced, theoretically organized but empirically open and systematic approach to the study of organizations. If the sociology of organizations is poised to follow up the variety of insights gained from the various lines of enquiry laid out in Table 14.1, a Mertonian framework is at least able to attempt to incorporate much material. A Mertonian framework does draw systematic attention to the various levels and areas of operation involved in an organization, including the 'bureaucratic personality', and highlights some of the ways in which these are interrelated. An organizational analyst with a background in Mertonian writings is surely alerted to complex and perhaps subtle theoretical interconnections. Perhaps such an analyst might even be able to develop further the above underlying structural model in ways which will allow the structure and dynamics of organizations to be shown to be systematically interrelated.

One theme in some current discussions is that the heritage of the first generation of organizational sociology studies should be recovered and reworked (e.g. Perry, 1979, 1981; Reed, 1985, and more implicitly, the range of historical treatments), as a foundation for a further advance. This essay has attempted to extend this process of re-examination to Merton's own contributions to this set of studies. It has shown that the original writing (now nearly a half-century old) is important for having signalled the need for sociological contributions to organizational studies, and also for the need for sociology to become more centred on the analysis of organizations. It also has attempted to show that it is rather more rich as an original contribution than is usually considered, but more importantly, that it is set within a sophisticated and useful broader framework that carries the promise of much potential for analytical development.

ACKNOWLEDGMENTS

I would like to thank Nick Perry and Georgina Murray for reading and commenting on a draft; Charles Perrow for encouragement; and Robert K. Merton for permission to cite an item from personal correspondence.

NOTES

1 The common use of the term of 'organization-set' hides some conceptual differences which require some nimble footwork to sort out: Caplow's conception differs from that of Blau and Scott, and Evan (although these two are the same). Indeed, following Blau (1975b), Caplow's emphasis on relations between the *same* type of organization might better be termed 'organizational complements' (and perhaps the collectivity involved could be termed a 'complementarity')! The Pinder and Moore volume generally exhibits a limited version of Merton's conception of 'middle-range theory', not recognizing that this approach seeks strategic formulations that cross-cut a range of concrete social areas as well as requiring theoretical work intermediate between grand theory and empirical generalization.
2 Despite Merton's own programmatic comment on the sociology of medicine, which includes attention to organizations: see Merton, 1982a: 157, 158. However, see also Merton and Christie, 1958, where Merton's interest in methodological approaches for studying organizations is displayed.
3 Such conceptual displacement is ironic since Merton's essay draws attention to processes of displacement: cf. Perry, 1979.
4 Some deficiencies in Rose's treatment of Mayo have been remedied in the second edition.
5 This approach is implied in Gouldner's theoretical typology, and is also used in Burrell and Morgan's (1979) presentation.
6 Over the last couple of decades there has been increasing sensitivity to the somewhat 'applied' or 'policy-relevant' connotations of the term 'organizational sociology', and those with more purely academic concerns indicate this by use of the title 'the sociology of organizations'.
7 Merton's influence by this time was limited, since Blau was ensconced in Chicago and was developing considerable modifications to his earlier 'functional analysis' viewpoint; the more peripatetic Gouldner was also developing a wider range of approaches; while Etzioni, although now domiciled at Columbia, was a Californian product not particularly exposed to Merton's views; nevertheless, Etzioni records the benefit of consultation with Merton in developing the contents of the first of his readers in organizational sociology.
8 Draft material incorporated in this chapter was excised from the book manuscript because of space difficulties.
9 Lazarsfeld describes the first-mentioned incident thus:

> The problem was how to increase the professional prestige of this group. Merton

> had the idea that a large conference on medical problems, called jointly by a prestigious medical association and his client's organization, would be more effective than detailed negotiations with individual hospitals, as had been originally planned. I understand that the conference was a great success and finally led to federal legislation improving the status of nurses everywhere. (1975: 60)

and the other issue;

> ... the plan which was submitted to the Columbia authorities got nowhere. The idea probably did not succeed at Columbia because Merton approved of it only in principle; he did not want to expend a second time all the effort required for a new institutional creation. (*ibid.*: 42)

10 In the bibliography published in the Coser Festschrift this essay is assigned a 1939 date, but this appears to be a mistake.

11 Of more specifically organizational writers, Michels was also apposite, but Merton admits (letter to Lammers, 22 September 1968) that, although he had earlier read Michels, he had found his causal style of presentation alienating, and thus he did not evoke Michels while developing his perspective on organizations. He only re-read Michels in the mid- or later 1940s at the instigation of some of his own students.

12 Perrow argues that Barnard's work influenced three distinct strands of organizational theory over the next three decades: the institutional, decision-making and human relations 'schools'.

13 This and other section headings were added on publication in *Social Theory and Social Structure*.

14 This point is not explicitly made by Merton: however, see his discussion of the extent to which both clerks and clientele might each feel themselves to be socially superior to the other. (*ibid.*: 258)

15 Of the limited body of social research in industry, the greater part has been orientated toward the needs of management. The problems selected as the focus of the inquiry—high labor turnover and restricted output, for example—have been largely thus defined by management, sponsorship has been typically by management, the limits and character of experimental changes in the work situation have been passed on by management, and periodic reports have been made primarily to management. No matter how good or seemingly self-evident the reason, it should be noted that this *is* the typical perspective of social research in industry and that it limits the effective prosecution of research. (*ibid.*: 625)

16 The editors include a transcription of orally delivered remarks.

17 It seems churlish in the face of the intricacy of this analysis to note, with a thirty-year span of hindsight, that Merton's precise prediction seems to be directly contradicted by the move under 'Reaganomics' and 'Thatcherism' aggressively to sweep away 'public service' concerns from both public and private sectors and to subordinate the values of the latter to the former. Nevertheless, this overwhelming disconfirmation only relates to the unduly optimistic or even naive 'content' of Merton's analytical schema: his sketching out of the mechanisms involved remains quite intact, and his essay could be readily reformulated to cover the rather different outcome.

18 A partial exception is Whitley's interest in developing complex characterizations of the organizational structures of different scientific disciplines (1984). A more important exception is the considerable analytical purchase shown by Ben-David in his sociology of the historical development of science (1971). In Ben-David's work the degree of competitiveness of the organizational environment is seen as a major impetus on the institutionalization of specialities and thus the growth pattern of scientific activity:

> Organization became a major determinant of scientific activity around 1840.... [T]he rate of scientific activity—which determined the rapidity of exploitation of the immanent potentialities of science—has been determined by a series of social innovations in the use and organization of science that occurred in different countries and have been subsequently adopted because they were

considered as the optimal available patterns by the worldwide scientific community. (*ibid.*: 170, 171)

19   ...the change toward Big Science, partly reflected in the growth of multiauthorship, makes for a change in the structure of power and authority in science where, goodwill, *noblesse oblige*, and normative constraints notwithstanding, it becomes increasingly difficult and sometimes impossible to gauge the contributions of individual scientists to the collective product of ever larger groups of investigators. (Zuckerman and Merton, 1972, in Merton, 1973: 552–3)

One consequence of this may be what Merton has termed the 'Matthew effect', the attribution of the work of junior authors solely to senior authors, leading to a strengthening of the gerontocracy and established élite of science.

20   Merton's letter to Lammers, 22 September 1968, confirms this picture of a very loose and undirected, albeit strongly supported, 'grouping'.

21   Strangely, while the former is apparently more microscale and partial and the latter more macroscale and holistic, in fact the emphases of the two writers are reversed, and in any case the two terminologies are essentially equivalent.

22   Less so with Selznick, which is surprising given his later hoisting as the model for the institutional approach to organizational study.

23   Interestingly, the later editions restore the school through a chapter on 'bureaucratic dysfunctions'; see Blau and Meyer, 1987: 139–61.

24   Indeed, there may well be a disjuncture between the two thrusts of their work that is revealed in Perrow's commentary on the March and Simon commentary:

[M]ore important, most of the factors that are supposed to be 'pathological' processes contributing to the 'dysfunctions' supposedly described by Merton, Gouldner and Selznick reappear in the second part of the book as functional. The pathologies of limited perspectives and subgroup goals and identification turn out to be necessary for the division of labour and provide means of control. Inattention to the complexities of human actors and their wants and needs proves to be necessary. The surveillance and control feature of rules and programs are no longer self-defeating, but functional and essential. (1972: 152n19)

While this might seem to argue for a conflation between the structural and individual levels, there is a crucial point concerning in whose interests particular limitations operate: those simplifications taken by management groups are one thing, similar simplifications by subordinate groups are another. This difference must not be elided.

25   In fact the terminology of the earlier article is given a twist, so that the bifurcation spoken of becomes transmuted, from the split between leaders and the led, to splits among specialist divisions. The last four pages of the 1943 article develop a theory of relationship between the leaders of a voluntary organization and it members and this does *not* inform the March and Simon model. But, then, neither does the book. March and Simon have apparently adopted a free-floating and perhaps quite apt and quite original reanalysis of Selznick's study. A similar de-emphasis occurs in their reconstruction of Gouldner in terms of the role of outside influences brought into the work situation (Perry, 1979: 9).

26   'These are the freaks, like the Townsend movement or the WCTU; the accessible welfare institutions such as general hospitals or the blind agencies; the obvious "social problem" institutions such as mental hospitals, prisons and reform schools, whose impact on a tiny majority of incarcerated individuals is frightening but trivial compared to the dominant economic institutions of our society' (1972: 197).

IX. THE THEORY OF ANOMIE

15. Merton's Instrumental Theory of Anomie

MARCO ORRÙ

There are no absolute values. There are only values which, on account of incomplete social organization, we cannot as yet estimate, and in face of these the first enterprise should be to complete the organization if only in thought so that some rough sort of estimate in terms of the other values becomes conceivable. And there is only one field within which the estimation can be made, and that is within the actual problem. (G. H. Mead, 1923: 243)

Since Robert Merton's first publication of 'Social Structure and Anomie' fifty years ago, over 250 articles and books have sought to describe, expand, test, modify, criticize or in some other way confront this sociological classic (cf. Orrù, 1987: 169–202). Any attempt to review such extensive literature in search of a final verdict on the place of Merton's theory of anomie in sociology would be a difficult and probably unrewarding task, especially within the limited space of this contribution. A more profitable use of this space would be to provide a new angle of vision on Merton's theory of anomie by identifying the elements which make such contribution a cornerstone of contemporary social theory. Accordingly, I will avoid reviewing the extensive literature on Merton's anomie theory, except to help highlight successful features of the theory; similarly, I will deal with Merton's theory in a selective fashion—the analysis will be far from exhaustive.

Merton's writings on anomie (1934b, 1938b, 1946, 1949b, 1949c, 1956, 1957a, 1957d, 1959a, 1964) are not merely one of the many contributions to the existing anomie literature. In this, as in many other sociological areas, Merton's theory towers above all others; it mapped uncharted terrains, postulated crucial requirements, identified relevant issues and set the stage for future research. One need only think of his notions of manifest and latent functions, status-sets and role-sets, self-fulfilling prophecy, sociological ambivalence and theories of the middle range to realize how much Merton's research has contributed to key theories and concepts in contemporary sociology.

Merton's anomie theory is no exception to his pattern of ground-breaking contributions. Emile Durkheim, Robert Merton and Leo Srole are readily identified as the leading figures in contemporary anomie theory and research (Garfield, 1987; Besnard, 1987; Orrù, 1987), and regardless of individual evaluations, it will be agreed that these three authors have been the standard reference for students of anomie in sociology. The relevant question, then, is: what makes Merton's theory of anomie so significant (and so appealing) in contemporary social sciences? I will attempt to answer this question by addressing the following issues: (1) Merton's new paradigm of anomie theory in relation to Durkheim's; (2) the unveiling of unintended consequences of a universalistic-achievement pattern of social action; (3) the instrumental character of Merton's anomie theory; and (4) the American nature of Merton's theory.

PARADIGMS OF ANOMIE THEORY: DURKHEIM AND MERTON

So much literature on anomie concerns itself with comparing Merton's theory with Durkheim's. The goal of such comparison is to find out whether the two theories are compatible with each other or not—whether Merton really followed in Durkheim's footsteps (cf. Orrù, 1987: 137–9). The implicit reasoning is often that straying from the Durkheimian path would automatically make Merton's theory illegitimate (Besnard, 1978; Horton, 1964; Ritsert, 1969; Chazel, 1967; Mestrovic, 1985; McCloskey, 1976). I do not subscribe to the Platonic notion that concepts, sociological or otherwise, have a timeless, fixed meaning; witness the history of the concept of anomie described in earlier writings (Orrù, 1983, 1985, 1986, 1987). For this reason, it seems fruitless to attempt to resolve issues of conceptual legitimacy in sociology—and specifically in anomie theory—by referring to the Durkheimian texts (for a theoretical defence of this position, see Skinner, 1969).

If anything, the vicissitudes of the concept of anomie in sociology show that departing from earlier definitions is not a drawback, but an asset. After all, Durkheim was acquainted with the earlier definition of anomie of the social philosopher Jean Marie Guyau, and after reviewing Guyau's work, Durkheim coined his own definition of anomie *in exact opposition* to Guyau's (cf. Orrù, 1983). Merton became similarly acquainted with the concept of anomie by reading Durkheim's *The Division of Labor*; his assessment, as shown in a 1934 review of that classic, was at least ambivalent, as he commented: 'Durkheim neglects to treat his conceptions as advisedly ideal constructions demanding appropriate alteration before they can adequately describe concrete social phenomena' (1934b: 324). Merton proposed, in antithesis to Durkheim's theory, that anomie might simply be interpreted as a reaction to the increasing division of labour, instead of an abnormal form of it. Four years later Merton proposed his own conception of anomie—no reference to Durkheim's relevant writings on anomie was to be found in that 1938 classic.

Issues of conceptual legitimacy aside, however, there is a merit in comparing Durkheim's and Merton's theories: such comparison can help us better understand each theory when set against the other's backdrop. The goal of such comparison will not be to proclaim a winner in the battle for sociological supremacy, but better to understand the location of Merton's theory vis-à-vis his sociological environment.

In the opening paragraph of 'Social Structure and Anomie' Merton wrote (1938b: 672): 'Certain phases of social structure generate the circumstances in which infringement of social codes constitutes a "normal" response'. This deceptively obvious statement made, in 1938, two sociologically revolutionary claims: that anomie *originates* in certain aspects of the social structure, and that anomic patterns are *normal* responses to socio-structural conditions.

While the two authors' theories might have much in common, Merton's notion of anomie stands opposite to Durkheim's in these two crucial respects. First, for Durkheim (1933, 1951) anomie originated in the biologically unregulated dreams and desires of individuals, and materialized on a chronic level when societal regulation weakened beyond a critical threshold. Merton, instead, locates the source of anomie squarely in specific patterns of the social structure.

Second, no matter how widespread in nineteenth century industrialized societies, Durkheim considered anomie as an abnormal social phenomenon caused by the extraordinary pace of social change. Merton, on the contrary, labels anomie a *normal response* to 'certain phases of social structure'. Underlying these differences between the two theories of anomie is a shift in the location where anomie is produced. For Durkheim, anomie originates in unregulated appetites and desires; for Merton, anomie is socially constructed—it is generated in the core cultural values of a society.

The shift in the theoretical locus of anomie is most significant for understanding the revolutionary turn produced by Merton's theory of anomie. The question is no longer: how can society provide adequate regulation to anomically inclined individuals, but rather: how can a balance be achieved between the socially constructed cultural goal which emphasizes success at all costs, and the normative rules which guarantee the fair competition of individuals in pursuit of such goal?

At the core of Durkheim's theory of anomie was his notion of *homo duplex* (McCloskey, 1976), where the unsocialized impulsive side of human nature must be restrained and controlled through socially learned morality. Merton's theory, instead, is social throughout—it does not rest on the conflict within the individual personality, but on the conflict within the social structure. Society is caught in the ambivalent position of encouraging its members to strive for success at all costs, while simultaneously regulating their pursuit of such a success goal. The anomic behaviour of individuals is, in this context, a *normal* response to the imbalance of overemphasized cultural goals and of de-emphasized institutional norms. Patterns of innovation are, to put it in Merton's own words, 'microcosmic images of the social macrocosm' (1938b: 675).

This is a key revolutionary feature of Merton's theory, for it is here that he shows how the *culturally induced pressure* to be successful generates rule-breaking behaviour as a *normal* response. Highlighting this structural link, Merton provides an instance of the unintended consequences which flow from otherwise desirable social values. This is the sociological contribution of Merton's anomie theory, and it is on its own merit that we must evaluate it—not on whether or not, or to what extent, it is a legitimate filiation of Durkheim's concept.

ANOMIE AS AN UNINTENDED CONSEQUENCE OF A UNIVERSALISTIC ACHIEVEMENT PATTERN OF SOCIAL ACTION

Merton labelled his theory of anomie as 'the doctrine of "socially derived sin"' (1938b: 672) in contrast with other sociological theories closer to the 'original sin' view of a naturally corrupted human nature. Merton's label is quite appropriate since it points to society as the source of the anomic behaviour of individuals instead of resorting to a psychological or biological explanation of deviant behaviour. But to understand the far-reaching impact of Merton's notion, we must look at the social conditions leading to the 'socially derived sin' Merton describes.

Researchers in the area of deviance have traditionally capitalized on the theory of 'Social Structure and Anomie' as it relates to the imbalance between cultural goals and social norms for individuals who are differentially located in the social structure; much less attention has been paid to Merton's analysis of the imbalance between cultural goals and institutional norms at the level of *culture patterning* (cf. Hilbert and Wright, 1979). But it is precisely here that the socially derived sin is generated.

In his description of culture patterning Merton distinguished three theoretical situations: anomie, where cultural goals overwhelm institutional norms; ritualism, where norms outstrip goals; and a 'mid-way' balanced situation, where goals and norms are well integrated (1938b: 673–4). While he presents these as equally logical possibilities, the three patterns clearly have varying relevance in Merton's scheme. Cultural ritualism is the hallmark of pre-modern societies, societies which Merton describes as 'tradition-bound' and 'characterized by neophobia' (*ibid.*). The balanced situation, instead, appears to have mostly theoretical value, since a perfectly integrated, stable society is more a hypothetical point of reference than an empirically observable phenomenon. The anomic patterning, then, is the one which best describes the situation of modern industrial societies, and of American society in particular. Merton's last type of culture patterning aptly characterized the anomic means-ends imbalance, where goals take precedence over means, as typically modern and typically American—and this must have accounted for much of the continuing appeal of Merton's theory in sociology.

The first ingredient of modern societies' anomic imbalance is the emphasis on success as a sign of social worth. This is patently a socially generated value. The measure of individuals' social esteem is not provided by their position in the social system according to inherited status, to their location in social networks or to other ascribed traits; instead, one's own talents as measured by individual achievement are the predominant (if not the only) standard of judgment.

But there is a second ingredient which, in conjunction with the success emphasis, contributes to the anomic pressure on individual behaviour. This is the universalistic thrust of the success goal as it applies most fittingly to the American case. Merton is quite direct in linking the two anomie-generating ingredients: the emphasis on success alone is not sufficient to account for patterns of anomic behaviour in individuals; beyond it, it is the applicability of the success emphasis on *the population at large* which makes for a powerful pressure toward anomie. Merton writes: 'Our egalitarian ideology denies by implication the existence of noncompeting groups and individuals in the pursuit of pecuniary success' (*ibid.*: 680); it is the strong egalitarian element in American society coupled with the emphasis on success that fosters anomic imbalance. By contrast, in a rigidly stratified society where people's expectations are differentially assigned, the anomic pressure is greatly reduced. As Merton remarks, 'poverty has varying significance in different social structures' (*ibid.*: 681); more specifically, anomie is more likely 'in a society which places a high premium on economic affluence and social ascent for *all* its members' (*ibid.*: 680).

If we paraphrased Merton's description of the conditions favouring anomie in terms of Talcott Parsons's types of social structure, we could easily identify the universalistic achievement pattern as its obvious counterpart. Parsons, as Merton had done earlier, detects in this type of social structure the tendency toward an overemphasis on the culturally approved goal of success: 'The combination [of universalism] with achievement values ... places the accent on the valuation of goal-achievement and of instrumental actions leading to such goal achievement' (Parsons, 1951: 183). Beyond identifying the tension created by a pattern of universalistic achievement, Parsons also pointed out that this type of social system rejects 'a universalistically defined *absolute* goal system' (*ibid.*); the goal of success does not specify a substantively specific type of success. Achievement cannot be restricted to a few selected instances, or it would cease to be the universally approved cultural value that it is. As Merton clarified: 'Any extreme emphasis upon achievement—whether this be scientific productivity, accumulation of personal wealth or, by a small stretch of the imagination, the conquests of a Don Juan—will attenuate conformity to the institutional norms governing behavior' (1957a: 166).

Merton illustrated the anomic dynamic by resorting to pecuniary success as a generalized cultural goal. While he cautioned that emphases on other types of success (like social recognition and esteem) are also present, he acknowledged the position held by material success in the constellation of values in American culture to be clearly pre-eminent. 'Wealth', Merton writes, 'has taken on a highly symbolic cast' (1938b: 677); and later on, 'money has been consecrated as a value in itself' (1949c: 136).

The centrality of money in the hierarchy of values in American culture did not escape Merton's attention. But while monetary success is a most popular standard of achievement, in most instances it *signifies* and reflects people's achievements in a wide variety of intellectual, physical, artistic and other endeavours. Money is literally, in this context, a *currency* for measuring achievement—but it is not necessarily an achievement in itself. This was clearly understood by Merton when he commented that 'American culture continues to be characterized by a heavy emphasis on wealth *as a basic symbol* of success' (*ibid.*: 139; emphasis supplied).

To summarize this point, a major contribution of Merton's theory, thirteen years before Parsons's *The Social System*, was not only to have described the distinguishing cultural components of modern American society, but more importantly, to have indicated how these components would create anomic strain within the social structure. Universalistic achievement is a core value of Western industrial societies, and of American society in particular—it is the source of a powerful stimulus toward instrumental efficiency and technological advancement. But Merton's theory of anomie was revolutionary in pointing out that the very features which accounted for the achievements of industrial societies were also the source of normative breakdown in these same societies. This has been Merton's favourite sociological approach, in seeking to uncover the unintended (and undesirable) consequences that flow from intended (and otherwise desirable) social action (1936b).

THE INSTRUMENTAL CHARACTER OF MERTON'S THEORY

Central to Merton's theory of anomie is the analytical distinction between means and ends of social action. As he writes: 'Among the elements of social and cultural structure, two are important for our purposes.... The first consists of culturally defined goals, purposes, and interests…. The second phase of the social structure defines, regulates, and controls the acceptable modes of achieving these goals' (1938b: 672). The distinction between ends and means is chiefly an analytical distinction—some ends are in turn means for more long-range ends, and some means can become ends in themselves. One of the key criticisms of Merton's theory (especially from a labelling perspective) was that his distinction between means and ends could not be sustained empirically (cf. Turner, 1954; Lemert, 1964). Alternatives to the means-ends scheme, however, are not easily found. For instance, while criticizing the fuzziness of Merton's means-ends scheme, Lemert chastised him for 'the failure to separate out (1) acts of individuals which embody values learned symbolically and transmitted as part of culture … and (2) acts which … are products of contingent valuation' (1964: 63). As I read it, Lemert identifies and separates ends-directed action from instrumental action; that is, he brings back, in a disguised form, the means-ends dichotomy he criticized in Merton. Lemert applies the means-ends dichotomy at the level of individual behaviour, whereas Merton had predicated such dichotomy at the socio-structural level.

Whatever the final verdict regarding its usefulness, the means-ends distinction—as an analytical device—has been part of the social science tradition at least since David Hume. Classical sociologists all dealt with the means-ends dichotomy, and had quite contrasting views regarding the priority of means or ends of action. Situating Merton's theory in the context of these views will illuminate the significance of his instrumentalist theory of anomie.

Marx's position, from a materialistic viewpoint, was that it is pointless to speak about desires or imaginary goals of action if we do not have the means to achieve such goals. In the *Philosophic and Economic Manuscripts of 1844*, speaking of the power of money in a capitalistic society, Marx points out: 'If I have the *vocation* for study but no money for it, I have *no* vocation for study—that is, no *effective*, no *true* vocation. On the other hand, if I have really *no* vocation for study but have the will *and* the money for it—I have an *effective* vocation for it' (1978: 104–5). For Marx, money transformed human potentials into chimeras, and chimeras into real powers and faculties (*ibid.*: 105). In a capitalistic society the means *create* the ends.

Durkheim stood diametrically opposite to Marx. His view, which can be labelled idealistic, was that we must first choose the ends of our action before we can evaluate the alternatives of means to achieve our ends. To quote Durkheim himself, 'If science cannot guide us in the determination of ultimate ends, it is equally powerless in the case of those secondary and subordinate ends called "means"' (1938: 48). For Durkheim, the ends are ontologically prior to the means, and only after choosing the appropriate, desirable ends of action can we get to the task of selecting the necessary means for achieving our goals.

In Max Weber we have a third, middle ground position; his view is that whereas science can help us choose among alternative means of action (e.g. in terms of efficiency or profitability), it cannot tell us which ends we should subscribe to, in the last instance. As Weber writes:

> Each new fact may necessitate the re-adjustment of the relations between end and indispensable means, between desired goals and unavoidable subsidiary consequences. But whether this readjustment *should* take place and what *should* be the practical conclusions to be drawn therefrom is not answerable by empirical science—in fact it cannot be answered by any science whatsoever. (1949: 23)

Both means and ends enter the picture simultaneously in Weber's social science, but the focus of such science is not to choose among ultimate ends, but to focus on the relational dynamic between means and ends.

Merton's theory of anomie most clearly parallels the Weberian stance on the means-ends dichotomy; it 'examines social conditions in terms of their consequences for people diversely located in the society, including the consequences that relate to values variously held in the society' (1976b: 14). Both cultural values and institutional norms are considered in Merton's theory of anomie; but the emphasis is not on whether one is ontologically prior to the other—on whether means precede ends or vice versa. Instead, Merton's emphasis is on the *relational* characteristics of a particular means-ends configuration. Ultimate values are not subjected to criticism in terms of some absolute moral standard of desirability (a standard which no social science can provide), but rather they are analyzed in their relation to institutional norms which are supposed to regulate the pursuit of socially approved goals.

The affinity of Merton's theory to Weber's was indicated in earlier research (Scott and Turner, 1965) where Merton's anomie theory was seen to parallel Weber's argument in *The Protestant Ethic and the Spirit of Capitalism*. 'Weber's Protestant ethic is a study of individuals—thrown back on themselves in pursuit of a goal whose achievement would never be known: salvation. For salvation Merton substitutes pecuniary success' (*ibid*.: 236). Scott and Turner also compare Weber's notion of instrumental rationality with Merton's category of innovation. For Weber, instrumental rationality obtains when 'the actor's choice of means is made purely in terms of efficiency' (*ibid*.: 237); for Merton, innovation characterizes the situation in which 'the range of alternative procedures is limited only by technical rather than institutional considerations' (1938b: 673). The two typologies are basically interchangeable (cf. Orrù, 1989).

But I believe the affinity between Weber and Merton to be more deep-seated at a methodological level. Both authors proceeded in their research by adopting a suspension of judgment (*epoché*) regarding the ultimate desirability of cultural values as they are found in modern societies, for the purpose of investigating the empirically observable consequences which flow from the internalization of these values and their subsequent enactment in the behaviour of individuals. This approach has been labelled as the 'value-free' approach of mainstream sociology, and it has been subjected to much criticism for its lack of a clear moral commitment. But even as vehement a critic of value-free sociology as Alvin Gouldner was willing to recognize its positive qualities. While he argued that the value-free requirement can engender 'a disorienting normlessness and moral indifference', Gouldner was quick to add that value-freedom also generated a desirable 'freedom from moral compulsiveness' (1962: 203). Value freedom, Gouldner writes, can provide 'a moral as well as an intellectual opportunity' (*ibid*.: 204).

The value-free approach opened the opportunity for the reassessment of anomie, not as a reified moral concept as it was in the Durkheimian tradition, but as an empirically observable, typical phenomenon of modern industrialized societies. This is what Merton deemed appropriate to do in his theory of anomie: to assess the adequacy of institutional means to existing cultural goals in American society.

I call this approach instrumental because it shifts the focus of analysis away from evaluating the ontological desirability of established cultural values in modern industrial societies, toward assessing the instrumental adequacy of institutional norms which aim at regulating the individual pursuit of internalized cultural values. The implicit assumption of this instrumental approach is that we cannot hope to evaluate adequately means and ends of social action independently of each other—rather, we must focus on the relational pattern between ends and means (e.g. looking at the presence or absence of appropriate emphases on both cultural values and on institutional norms). It is precisely the adoption of the instrumental posture which allowed Merton to locate anomie as a socially generated phenomenon and to describe anomie as a normal consequence of specific patterns of means-ends imbalance.

THE AMERICAN NATURE OF MERTON'S THEORY

Labelling Merton's theory of anomie as instrumentalist is not simply a way to classify his methodology; it is also a way to describe that methodology's underlying ethics. In this section I want to demonstrate the typically American character of Merton's instrumental theory, by linking his approach to the pragmatist tradition of other American social scientists and social philosophers.

The qualitative differences between European and American sociological theories and theories of anomie have been pointed out by several researchers (Horton, 1964; Ritsert, 1969; Hawthorn, 1976; Besnard, 1987; Orrù, 1987). In many instances the comparison between the two traditions has been geared more toward showing the inadequacy of American theories vis-à-vis their European antecedents than toward illustrating the American approach as an alternative to classic European sociology. The purpose of this analysis, in contrast, is not to sanction the superiority of European or American schools of social thought, but rather to identify the peculiarly American traits of Merton's anomie theory and to highlight their significance.

To speak of an instrumentalist theory of anomie is to locate such theory within the American pragmatist tradition of William James, John Dewey and G. H. Mead. The argument for an instrumental theory of anomie echoes a pragmatic moral philosophy—more specifically, it parallels John Dewey's ethical instrumentalism where means and ends are not altogether separate spheres of human action, but are parts of a totality which is in constant dialectical interaction. Cultural ends are re-fashioned by institutional means just as much as means are refashioned by ends—there is no ontological priority of one over the other. For this reason we need to look at both means and ends simultaneously, focusing on their relational aspects, rather than abstracting one from the other. Merton was aware of the crucial interconnectedness of means and ends as early as 1934: 'When instruments are fashioned for the attempted attainment of ends, by this very fact conditions are evolved which act not only in the direction of the goals, but react upon and frequently change the value-estimations' (1934b: 323).

G. H. Mead celebrated Dewey's instrumentalist position, identifying it as eminently American (1930: 231): 'John Dewey's philosophy, with its insistence upon the statement of the end in terms of the means, is the developed method of that implicit intelligence in the mind of the American community'. Mead himself took a position similar to Dewey's when he postulated an instrumental notion of cultural values:

> Society gets ahead, not by fastening its vision upon a clearly outlined distant goal, but
> by bringing about the immediate adjustment of itself to its surroundings, which the

immediate problem demands. It is the only way in which it can proceed, for with every adjustment the environment has changed, and the society and its individuals have changed in like degree. (1923: 247)

The view here, and in Dewey's instrumentalism, is that there are no fixed, unchanging goals against which social and individual perfection can be assessed; the only viable context for judging the adequacy of any social structure is to locate it within 'the actual problems' it faces. 'A scientifically trained intelligence must insistently devote itself [to define] ... our institutions, our social habits and customers, in terms of what they are to do, in terms of their functions ' (Mead, 1923: 243). This is exactly what Merton does when he comments: 'Insofar as one of the most general functions of social organization is to provide a basis for calculability and regularity of behavior, it is increasingly limited in effectiveness as these elements of the structure become dissociated' (1938b: 682). The emphasis, in Mead and in Merton, and in the American sociological tradition in general, is to do away with abstract questions concerning the ultimate validity of cultural goals and with assessing the adequacy of institutional norms in terms of some absolute moral standard; more appropriate for the American mind, instead, is to ask how we can best adjust ourselves to our surroundings.

Merton's theory of anomie, it seems to me, is precisely couched within the pragmatists' frame of thought to the extent that it rejects any a priori evaluation of cultural goals on the basis of some fixed moral standard. Merton's attention, instead, centres on the practical problems which arise in a social structure where normative institutions are de-emphasized in relation to existing cultural goals, not on whether and to what extent these cultural goals are themselves the most desirable. An achievement of Merton's theory is that it successfully takes to task psychological explanations of deviance; but a perhaps greater achievement is that it successfully highlights the deleterious effect of a certain social-structural imbalance in contemporary America, without giving in to the moralizing inclinations of classical European sociology. As R. E. Hilbert and Wright correctly pointed out 'Merton is concerned primarily with societies that emphasize cultural goals over institutional means because (1) the phenomenon of anomie (he argues) is likely to be great in these societies, and (2) he feels that American society approximates this type' (1979: 151). The problem of anomie Merton describes is not hypothetical but real; it is not a theoretical construction, but a poignantly urgent problem of contemporary America. The popularity of Merton's anomie theory results to a large extent from the immediacy of its message—it is not theory for its own sake, but theory which seeks to illuminate a particularly relevant imbalance in the social structure of a modern industrial society.

CONCLUSION

Four features of Merton's theory of anomie have been highlighted in this paper. First, Merton's theory provided a new paradigm which superseded Durkheim's; second, it demonstrated anomie to be the unintended consequence of a specific pattern of social action; third, it marked a new milestone in the anomie literature by resting on an instrumental view of the means-ends dichotomy; and fourth, it showed its American nature by adhering to the methodological and ethical canons of pragmatism. To conclude, the positive qualities of these four features will be further articulated.

First, coining a new definition of anomie is not, automatically, a sign of long-lasting sociological scholarship—witness the many attempts in this direction which have gone by the wayside (e.g. Lander, 1954; Dean, 1961; McClosky and Schaar, 1965). Merton's theory of anomie has become a classic not simply because of its originality, but also because of its ability to explain the dynamics of significant social phenomena which had previously gone unnoticed or been dismissed as irrelevant. The literature which followed on the footsteps of Merton's anomie theory earned it the high status it obtained in the sociological community.

Second, showing that anomie is the *unintended but normal* response to a specific imbalance of the social structure, Merton demonstrated a specific dysfunctional consequence of existing social patterns. More broadly, he demonstrated that malintegration and dysfunctions are not exceptions to normally functional, equilibrated social systems; rather, malintegration and dysfunctions are to be expected under *normal* circumstances. In this respect the revolutionary nature of Merton's anomie theory is further emphasized—especially when compared to its Durkheimian antecedent.

Third, the instrumental character of Merton's theory locates it squarely within the framework of a scientific sociological approach. Merton easily acknowledged that 'ends, goals, aims, are by definition not logic-experimental data but rather value judgments' (1934b: 321); at the same time he was quick to warn that an adequate understanding of social phenomena requires that we study the role played by these value judgments. Their study, however, cannot proceed by comparing the existing values in a society with the hypothetical values which guide the perfect, Utopian society. More modestly, but also more realistically, the existing values are to be analyzed in terms of their consequences in the social structure; in terms of their functional adequacy with existing social norms.

Fourth, a final asset of Merton's theory of anomie is that it is American not only in its sociological methodology, but also in its underlying moral vision. Such vision expresses a belief in the perfectibility of the social world: dysfunctions and social problems are all around us, but we can apply our scientific knowledge constantly to improve the workings of society. The method for such improvement is not to follow a Utopian blueprint of the perfect society, but constantly to re-assess the adequacy of values and norms, and their integration.

Merton's theory of anomie pointed out one significant problem which is amenable to social scientific analysis, but it did not pretend to show the way to the ultimate solution—to the mythic promised land. This pragmatic modesty is one more distinguishing quality of Merton's theory of anomie. It is the same modesty which made G. H. Mead remark: 'We, none of us, know where we are going, but we do know that we are on the way' (1923: 247).

16. Merton in Search of Anomie*

PHILIPPE BESNARD

'Social Structure and Anomie' by Robert Merton is a classic text which has given rise to an impressive number of commentaries, yet its principal difficulties and inconsistencies have not yet been sufficiently acknowledged. What has come to be called 'Merton's theory of anomie' has, though, been the object of numerous and varied criticisms: as early as 1964 Clinard (1964b) was able to identify eleven kinds of objection which had been made to it. Whatever their intrinsic relevance, none of these objections seems to go to the heart of the matter, because they all assume that there is indeed in Merton's work a theory of anomie. In contrast, the argument of this paper is that the subtle analyses of Merton (1) do not in fact constitute a theory and (2) do not actually relate to anomie. They do not constitute a theory because of the ambiguity of the concepts utilized and the absence of links between the propositions advanced; they do not constitute a theory of anomie because the status of the concept is uncertain and because it contributes nothing to Merton's overall sociological purpose.[1]

VARIATIONS ON A THEME: THE VERSIONS OF 'SOCIAL STRUCTURE AND ANOMIE' COMPARED

The opacity of the Mertonian 'theory' and its resistance to fundamental criticism result to a large extent from the fact that it has been developed in many versions stretching over twenty-six years and that commentators have rarely engaged in comparing the different texts. In addition, a degree of confusion seems to reign on the subject, for many of those who have sought to take their bearings in this difficult

---

* Translated from the French by Jon Clark.

terrain have lost themselves in it.[2] It is therefore useful, before entering on the analysis proper, to enumerate the successive variations developed by Merton around the same theme.

It was in 1938 that the first version of the Mertonian analysis was published under the title of 'Social Structure and Anomie' (Merton, 1938b). To give an idea of the breadth of the subsequent alterations, let us simply note that this review article constituted only a third of the text published later under the same title. The conciseness of this first text explains, too, why it is very often preferred to later versions in anthologies or collections on sociological theory or the sociology of deviance.

Eleven years later a new version appeared, initially published under the title 'Social Structure and Anomie: Revisions and Extensions', in a selection of texts devoted to the family (Merton, 1949c). The same text, apart from a few minor changes, was printed in the same year in the first edition of *Social Theory and Social Structure* under the title of the first version of 1938 (Merton, 1949b). We should note that this same year also saw the first reprint of the 1938 text in an anthology (Wilson and Kolb, 1949).

In 1956 the proceedings of a colloquium on juvenile delinquency held in 1955 were published. These included a communication from Merton, 'The Socio-Cultural Environment and Anomie', and his various interventions in the discussions (Merton, 1956). The following year, on the occasion of a revised edition of *Social Theory and Social Structure* (1957a), Merton reproduced the 1949 text with only one modification. However, he added a new chapter of noticeably equal length, entitled 'Continuities in the Theory of Social Structure and Anomie' (Merton, 1957d). In 1959 he replied to various criticisms advanced by Dubin and Cloward (Merton, 1959a). The last text published by Merton on this theme appeared in 1964 in a volume explicitly devoted to the discussion of his theory of anomie (Merton, 1964).

Faced with this 'sedimentation' of successive versions, the task of exegesis is not simple. To avoid slowing down the exposition considerably, it is necessary, like the mythologist faced with many versions of the same myth, to choose one basic text while taking account of the different variations. In so doing, it is not appropriate to take the original version of 1938 as the basic reference point, both because it shows very substantial differences from the subsequent versions and also because it has had virtually no resonance in the discipline of sociology. Instead, we will take as the point of departure the 1949 text (republished in 1957), which contains the essential characteristics of the theory. At the same time we will of course also note the successive variations, revisions and refocusings which have marked its development.

The aim of the analysis is to question the internal logic of the Mertonian discourse by emphasizing certain fundamental ambiguities which have escaped the vigilance of numerous commentators and users of 'Merton's theory of anomie'. We will seek in particular to answer two questions which will serve as the guiding thread of this chapter: what is the status of the concept of anomie in Merton's work; and to what extent does it contribute usefully to his overall purpose?

SOCIAL STRUCTURE AND CULTURAL STRUCTURE

Excluding a few paragraphs of secondary importance, the 1949 text is composed of two parts. It is somewhat delicate to characterize their respective subject-matters in a few words, because there is a risk, in so doing, of giving only one of the possible interpretations of this ambiguous text and of conferring on it a coherence which it does not have. However, in attempting to find a formulation which will be as neutral as possible, let us recall that the first part deals with the dissociation of two elements of the cultural structure, illustrating it by the analysis of the American dream of success, while the second sets forth a typology of individual adaptations 'to' (?) a particular cultural configuration.

The point of departure and the foundation of the whole Mertonian analysis is the distinction between two elements: culturally defined goals on the one hand, and institutionalized norms which define and regulate the modes of reaching out for these goals on the other. The first question which arises concerns the nature of the totality from which these two elements are extracted (leaving on one side for the moment the question of their precise meaning). The vocabulary used by Merton to describe this totality fluctuates considerably. He speaks, apparently without differentiating between them, of 'social and cultural structures', 'cultural structure', 'culture', 'social structure'. This lack of consistency in vocabulary has not been remarked upon by any of many commentators and users of 'Merton's theory of anomie', with the exception of Ritsert (1969: 148), who did not, though, perceive the reason for it.

It is the 'sedimentary' character of the text which explains to a large extent the inconsistency of the vocabulary. A comparison of the different versions reveals that the use of these terms has changed with time and that the passages which contain the words 'social structure' in the 1949 text are those which have been incorporated unchanged from the original version of 1938. In the Mertonian terminology of 1938, social structure comprises cultural models on the one hand and class structure on the other. In the 1949 text and more clearly still in the later texts, Merton substitutes social structure for class structure. In short, the ambiguity disappears quite quickly on a close reading of the 1949 text. Everything indicates, at least at the beginning of the text, that the two elements in question are now part of the 'cultural structure'.[3]

This is both surprising and revealing. How is it possible for Merton to publish a text in 1949 and again in 1957 where the expressions 'social structure' and 'cultural structure' are used interchangeably when it is the links between these two 'structures' which lie at the heart of his theory of anomie? In fact this terminological inexactitude is the most obvious symptom of the fundamental ambiguity of the Mertonian conception of anomie, which can be formulated thus: is anomie the result of an internal contradiction within the cultural structure or of a distortion between the cultural structure and the social structure?

FROM NORMS TO MEANS

The uncertainty about the location of the contradiction which generates anomie is intensified by a lack of precision in the definition of one of the elements of the contradiction. More exactly, the second element distinguished by Merton changes its nature during the course of the analysis. This change, which is quite marked if one looks at the whole of Merton's texts on anomie, is already detectable within the 1949 text, where the modifications of vocabulary signal and express a change in the whole scheme of analysis. This second element of the cultural structure is designated right at the beginning of the text, and even in the subheading to the paragraph, by the expression 'institutional norms'. We are concerned here with the normative definition of the means of access to (in Merton's terms 'modes of reaching out for') these goals and not the means of access themselves: norms are not means.

The expression 'means' appears quite late in the text and increasingly becomes a substitute for 'norms'. Its introduction is somewhat surreptitious, and Merton takes care to qualify these 'means' with the adjective 'institutionalized', thus conferring on them a certain dignity and making it possible to believe in the continuity of the analysis. There is of course a continuity in the analysis, which comes from the fact that it is concerned with the effects of a contradiction, or at least a tension, between two elements. But whereas one of them—culturally defined goals—remains constant, the other changes its nature progressively, becoming synonymous with the access to the means of success. This shift in usage is not without consequence for the status of the notion of anomie, which becomes increasingly elusive the more one looks at it.

The initial characterization of anomie is relatively clear. On its first appearance in the text the term refers to a particular type of internal disequilibrium within the cultural structure, namely a strong cultural definition of goals and a weak normative definition of the means which can be used to achieve these goals. But is anomie the result of this disequilibrium or is it constitutive of it, the necessary counterpart to the 'exaltation of the end' which brings about 'de-institutionalization of means'? The various formulations used by Merton are vague enough to allow both interpretations. Suffice it to say that anomie is conceived in the initial period as related to (either identifiable with or the consequence of) a particular type of disequilibrium in the cultural structure. Under this heading anomie finds its counterpart in 'ritualism', an opposite type to disequilibrium where the basic accent is placed on the institutionalized means. It is very important to note that not all disequilibrium in the cultural structure is anomic by nature, even though Merton argues that he is concerned essentially with this type of disequilibrium.

In fact, the description of the American dream of success (which was absent from the original version of 1938) is supposed to illustrate the type of anomic culture. Although it is not appropriate here to recapitulate this famous analysis, it is important to note that it illustrates well the 'exaltation of the end' but provides hardly any evidence of the weakening of the regulation of the means. This abandonment of one of the two elements of the initial contradiction is an additional index of the incompleteness of the Mertonian analysis. By only studying one form of disequilibrium in the cultural structure, by laying much more stress on the exaltation of the end than on deficiencies in the normative definition of means (which appears almost as an automatic consequence of the overstrong cultural definition of goals), Merton does not complete the analysis of the effects of various internal tensions in the cultural system, as one would have expected. He does not therefore explore to the full the analytical distinction between the two elements of culture which constitute the starting point of the text.

AN INCOHERENT AND INCOMPLETE TYPOLOGY

The success enjoyed by the 'typology of modes of individual adaptation' can be explained quite simply. There has been a wide recognition of its ability to show that what are apparently very heterogeneous forms of social conduct can be explained via the same analytical model. The typology owes a good part of its reputation to the scheme reproduced in Table 16.1 which, by its simplicity and apparent internal coherence, commands one's attention (the Table is taken from Merton, 1968: 194).

Although it is not possible to review here the many commentaries which this scheme has elicited, it is at least appropriate to recall the principal criticisms which it has encountered relating to its formal coherence and the principles by which it is constructed. At first sight it appears that type V is superfluous to a structure complete in its four parts. Indeed, Merton has recognized on many occasions that rebellion is quite a different kind of 'adaptation' from the others, since it is not situated within the existing social and cultural structure. In fact it was physically separated from the others by a line in the 1938 text.

The inclusion of rebellion allows us to draw attention to another criticism of this typology: the ambiguity in the use of the signs. As Dubin (1959) and Harary (1966) have noted, the same sign $(-)$ sometimes expresses indifference (as regards goals in ritualism) and sometimes rejection and substitution (of means in innovation). Conversely, two different signs $(-)$ and $(\pm)$ express the same notion.

However, the criticisms of Dubin and Harary remain superficial, for the ambiguity of the symbols used by Merton is but a consequence of more fundamental problems. For example, since Merton talks of individual adaptations, is it not proper to ask the question: adaptations to what? This is an apparently unnecessary question, since Merton proposes explicitly to characterize the modes of adaptation of individuals to the cultural configuration he has just described according to their position in the social structure. He indicates that he is concerned with describing the different possible adaptations or reactions to anomie. However, that was not at all obvious in the first version of the text, where Merton juxtaposed two typologies without any elaboration: having outlined 'three ideal types of social orders' (1938b: 676) defined by the relations between cultural goals and institutionalized means, he then distinguished five modes of individual adaptation without linking them in any way to one of the cultural configurations.

In fact, this apparent logic does not stand up to close examination. For example, what do 'institutionalized means' affected by the sign $(+)$ signify? We are not concerned here with a highly normative definition of the means appropriate to a given culture, since the realm of internal tensions within culture has been abandoned in order to deal with individual adaptations to a particular configuration assumed to be anomic. So, should we understand by this (1) the internalization by the individual of the duty only to use legitimate means; or rather (2) the objective opportunities for the individual to have these means at their disposal: or again (3) their effective utilization? Each of these three interpretations encounters logical

Table 16.1   A Typology of Modes of Individual Adaptation

Modes of adaptation	Culture goals	Institutionalized means
I. Conformity	+	+
II. Innovation	+	−
III. Ritualism	−	+
IV. Retreatism	−	−
V. Rebellion	±	±

difficulties; and the commentaries provided by Merton on the different modes of adaptation do not allow us to see them more clearly (for a detailed examination, see Besnard, 1987: 236–40).

The fundamental reason for the ambiguity in the Mertonian typology is the following: it tries to condense a relatively complex process, while the elements of this process and the relations between these elements are not distinguished analytically from one another. The 'Mertonian theory', insofar as it is possible to reconstruct it from the widely scattered statements by its author, needs in effect to take account of:

1   the two elements of the cultural system (goals and norms);
2   the individual internalization of the cultural system by a mode of socialization which may be related to class affiliation;
3   the position in the social structure which determines the objective chances of access to legitimate means; and
4   behaviours with regard to cultural goals and legitimate means which are adaptations to possible contradictions within 1 and 2 and between 2 and 3.

These different elements are never made completely explicit, nor fully exploited by Merton, who, in his commentary on modes of adaptation, lays stress first on one, then on another without constructing a scheme of analysis which takes them all into account. The exclusion of the cultural system from the totality of variables to be considered is understandable. The cultural configuration, characterized as anomic, may be regarded as a given, implicit in the analysis. But it is very difficult to see to what extent the behaviours described by Merton would be the consequence of an anomic cultural configuration. If the commentary sometimes seems to suggest that these adaptations assume the existence of a strongly defined cultural goal, this does not imply the absence of norms defining the legitimate means of attaining this goal. The internal contradiction in the cultural structure which Merton is concerned to describe in the first part of his text plays no further role in the analysis of 'individual adaptations'.

In contrast, the internalization of this culture by individuals appears consistently in the foreground. A complete internalization (of goals and norms) leads to conformism or retreat, while innovation, and perhaps ritualism, have their origins in an incomplete internalization of the cultural system. The mode of socialization is not sufficient to determine the mode of individual adaptation: according to the theory, as far as it can be reconstituted, it is necessary to take into account the access to legitimate means. The incompleteness of 'Mertonian theory' can be measured by the fact that, although the combination of the two independent variables is clearly specified in the cases of innovation and retreat where the mode of internalization of culture is in conflict with the lack of accessibility of legitimate means, this does not apply in the same way for ritualism and conformism. In explaining the origins of these two modes of adaptation the relation to legitimate means is not defined.

It is possible to summarize these diverse points in a scheme which shows the relationships between 'individual adaptations' and their respective origins (see Table 16.2). Out of a concern for simplicity and compatibility with Merton's typology, we will keep to the scheme of signs (+) and (−): question marks signify the lacunae in the analysis. Rebellion is excluded from the scheme, since it is heterogeneous with regard to the typology and its social origins are not made explicit at any point.

Table 16.2 Relationships between 'Individual Adaptations' and Their Origins

Internalization of		Access to	Modes of adaptation		
goals	norms defining means	legitimate means	search for goals	use of legitimate means	
+	+	?	+	+	Conformity
+	−	−	+	−	Innovation
?	+	?	−	+	Ritualism
+	+	−	−	−	Retreatism

It goes without saying that this scheme could be enriched in many ways, for example by taking account, following Cloward and Ohlin (1960), of the opportunities for access to illegitimate means and then their utilization, or again by giving up the simplistic alternative of (+) and (−), which is quite inadequate to characterize the differential opportunities of disposing over legitimate means.

Even if it is unable to resolve some ambiguities, this scheme nevertheless has one analytical virtue: it identifies individual adaptations clearly as observable behaviours in distinguishing them expressly from their antecedents. At the same time it reveals that the completeness of the final typology (that concerned with adaptations) conceals the dual incompleteness of the initial typology (that concerned with their origins). The latter is incomplete not only because of its lacunae, but also because it only considers four situations, whereas eight are theoretically possible.

Finally, it should be noted that the access to legitimate means is only specified in two cases out of four (two out of five if rebellion is included), and that in three cases out of four the theory assumes an internalization of norms which define and regulate the means which can be used to achieve the goals. In other words, this scheme expresses well the failure of Merton to realize the two main points of his programme: (1) to construct a typology of adaptations *to* an anomic culture; and (2) 'to localize sociologically', that is, by reference to its place in the social structure, the origin of the pressures leading to deviant behaviour (1956: 50).

ANOMIE: AN UNNECESSARY AND UNCERTAIN CONCEPT

This dual failure of Merton is clearly related to the uncertainty of the status of anomie in the explanatory scheme he proposes. The final remarks of the text of 1949, presented under the heading 'The Strain Toward Anomie', only serve to increase the perplexity of the commentator on this point. They begin with a phrase which, claiming to summarize the analysis as a whole, simply intensifies the ambiguities: 'The social structure we have examined produces a strain toward anomie and deviant behaviour' (1949b: 157). We should note at the outset that the notion of 'social structure' is used here in its widest sense, including the cultural structure. There is here, then, on a particularly central point, an imprecision of vocabulary the more astonishing in that the phrase was rewritten in 1949—compared with the version of 1938 'social structure' replaces 'social order' and 'anomie' is substituted for 'dissolution'—and that Merton has an increasing concern, as we will see, to link anomie to the articulation of the social structure and the cultural structure.

But what is most important to note is that this same phrase situates anomie and deviant behaviour on the same plane, even though it does not identify one with the other explicitly. It thus testifies to a reversal of the initial perspective towards the status of anomie. Anomie was conceived at the outset as a condition and constitutive element of the strain leading to deviance, now it appears as an outcome of this strain in the same fashion as deviance.

It is important to recognize that in bringing together social structure and anomie in the famous chapter heading Merton was not really concerned to confer on these terms a particularly precise meaning. Indeed it is somewhat difficult to decide which of them is more nebulous and uncertain. If one wishes, nevertheless, to try to pierce the semantic fog surrounding anomie in the text of 1949, three modes of application—one hesitates to say definition—of the term are discernible:

1   initially anomie is identified with a particular type of disequilibrium within the cultural structure, symmetrical with ritualism;
2   in the treatment of modes of individual adaptation, it appears to be linked to the internal contradiction in the mode of internalization of the cultural structure, combined with a limited access to legitimate means;
3   finally it appears as the result of the contradiction between the culturally defined goal of success and the absence of access to the means of achieving this goal.

This last 'mode of application', which identifies anomie with a particular type of deviance (innovation), is the one which has been privileged by commentators and users of the Mertonian model. There is no reason to be surprised at such a 'reduction', since it is encouraged by the general emphasis of Merton's text. It also conforms to the logic of the original version of 1938, whose final remarks represent a continuation of the exposition on 'innovation', which is given much greater emphasis than the other modes of adaptation.

The 'theory of anomie' thus conceived predicts that delinquent behaviour is most likely among the less favoured social strata who do not dispose over the means of social success. But is anomie itself not absent from this 'theory of anomie'? Indeed, it is virtually impossible to see what the term adds to such a simple hypothesis, apart from aesthetic virtue and the power to suggest some kind of 'theoretical' base. When it comes down to it, anomie proves to be as unnecessary as it is uncertain.

However, Merton is clearly attached to the term, using it with increasing frequency through the successive variations he develops on the same theme. In the 1938 version the term is used only three times in the text (of which two are on the final page) and three times in the notes (with a reference not to Durkheim but to Elton Mayo). The reference to Durkheim appears in 1949, but it is only in the subsequent texts—a colloquium held in 1955 on juvenile delinquency (Merton, 1956) and 'Continuities in the Theory of Social Structure and Anomie' (1957d)—that Merton appears concerned to justify the use of the term 'anomie'.

These later texts should have removed the ambiguities we have identified, since Merton, in attempting to define anomie, links it to the distinction (now made explicit) between cultural structure and social structure. Cultural structure is defined as 'that organized set of normative values governing behavior which is common to members of a designated society or group', while social structure is 'that organised set of social relationships in which members of the society or group are variously implicated' (1957d: 162). The insistence on such a distinction can be doubtless explained by Merton's concern to distinguish himself more clearly than in the past from the culturalist approach. The distinction between cultural and social structure thus lies at the heart of the definition of anomie which Merton proposes in the text of 1957:

> Anomie is then conceived as a breakdown in the cultural structure, occurring particularly when there is an acute disjunction between the cultural norms and goals and the socially structured capacities of members of the group to act in accord with them. (1957d: 162)

This definition is relatively clear on one point: it locates the origin of anomie in the contradiction between the cultural system and social system. But it still does not allow us to resolve definitively whether anomie is best understood as a disjunction between norms and goals (in other words the collapse of the former and the 'exaltation' of the latter) or as the collapse of the cultural structure as a whole.

Leaving on one side this continuing ambiguity, it should be noted that in the 1957 text anomie appears to have acquired definitely the status of a dependent variable in the Mertonian scheme. As for norms, they are reduced to a supporting role. In effect, far from being distinguished analytically from culturally prescribed goals, from now on they form a kind of conglomerate with them. One should not seek to locate anomie and its causes in the strain within the cultural structure but in the distortion between the totality of 'cultural norms and goals' and the social structure. It should be noted in this context that the cultural structure is defined as a totality of normative values rather than as a mode of articulation of goals and norms. Norms, having been replaced by means, thus end up by being amalgamated with goals. This strange fate illustrates the inability of the Mertonian analysis to keep to its premises and to take simultaneous account of the three elements.

This metamorphosis in the scheme of analysis is displayed in a striking manner in the programme of research which Merton considers as likely to put his theory fully to the test. He proposes that data should be gathered on (1) the exposure to goals and norms, (2) their acceptance, (3) the relative accessibility of goals, (4) the extent of discrepancy between accepted goals and their accessibility, (5) the degree of anomie, and (6) the rates of deviant behaviour of various kinds. It is clear that such a programme diverts attention away from the eventual tension between goals and norms, and places in parenthesis the legitimate character of usable means. In contrast it preserves the autonomy of anomie as a variable for which specific data must be collected. Anomie is not only the result of the disjuncture between goals and the possibility of achieving them: it is a kind of intermediary state between this structural strain and deviance, being identifiable with neither one nor the other. But the question then arises: what are to be the indicators by which the 'degree' of anomie will be measured? Merton's response is to cite the work of Srole and Lander. Srole's scale of anomie (1956) allows us to measure anomie as it is experienced subjectively; as for anomie as an objective condition, the work of Lander (1954) marks in Merton's eyes a first stage in the elaboration of appropriate indicators.

In our view this response of Merton provides additional proof of the inconsistency in his concept of anomie. These two authors are simply the only ones who have used the term 'anomie' in recent years to designate certain measuring tools or results of empirical research. But Merton does not ask at any time whether other available indicators might be more appropriate, nor does he seek to define what might be a good indicator of anomie.

The 1964 text is even more surprising on this point, as Merton goes further still in drawing up a programme of research in which the degree of anomie of a collectivity is to be measured by the percentage of individuals having a high score on the Srole scale. There is no discussion of the content of this scale and what one can measure on it. This programme of research destined to overcome the gap between theory (that of Merton) and empirical research was lacking in realism and has had no effect at all. This last effort to show the utility and autonomy of anomie—and at the same time to reappropriate the many research studies on anomie measured by attitude scales—was therefore unsuccessful.

ANOMIE: FROM DURKHEIM TO MERTON

It would be easy to provide additional evidence of the ambiguity of the Mertonian theory of anomie by comparing the various presentations which have been given of it. Alongside the already mentioned vulgar version which has predominated among 'users' (those who refer to it in a more or less ritualistic way) or in textbooks, it is possible to find very palpable differences among 'commentators'. It will be sufficient to cite one major error committed by three notable authors, Clinard (1964b), S. Cole (1975) and Dreitzel (1968). All three present Merton's theory as based on the opposition between the cultural structure, that is goals or values, and the social structure, the norms which regulate the means of access to goals. The norms are thus assimilated into the social structure, resulting in a sort of short-circuit between the beginning of the 1949 text and the beginning of the 1957 one. Coming from such shrewd commentators, this error is adequate proof that the Mertonian theory is a theory which is not 'presentable'.[4]

The Mertonian theory of anomie has given rise to a large number of commentaries relative to its intellectual antecedents and its ideological connotations. But mention has only seldom been made of the rarity of references to Durkheim in Merton's texts on anomie. At no time has Merton expounded, if only in a few words, on Durkheim's approach, not even in his text of 1964 which was supposed to review the history of the development of the theory of anomie. In fact, from Durkheim to Merton the term 'anomie' undergoes an almost complete inversion. This can probably be expressed most simply by noting that for Durkheim (above all in *Suicide*) anomie refers to the *lack of restriction on goals*, while for Merton anomie refers to the *restriction on means*. It could be argued that Merton's use of the term is too imprecise to be characterized in this way. But the shifts in usage during the course of the various texts, the demise of norms as an autonomous variable, the identification of the theory of anomie with the case of 'innovation', all come together, as we have seen, to give this final status to the notion of anomie. It is, moreover, precisely as a theory of differential access to the means of success that the Mertonian theory of anomie has been understood and utilized.

It would be easy yet tedious to give additional references on this matter. For our purpose the crucial point is that Merton regards the goals offered to individuals by culture as given, defined and uniform in the totality of the society under consideration, while for Durkheim it is the *indeterminacy of goals* which is the central characteristic of anomie. *Where Durkheim describes individuals uncertain of what they should do, so open is the horizon of possibilities, Merton presents actors certain of the goals to be attained but whose aspirations are blocked by a situation in which the possibilities of success are closed.* There is such a fundamental opposition in all aspects of the two conceptions that it is astonishing it has not been emphasized by commentators.

The situation Merton describes, in which the possibilities to realize legitimate and desired goals are blocked, is not absent in Durkheimian analysis: it is explicitly designated as the opposite situation to anomie! It exists already in Durkheim's first work, in the 'forced division of labour', where regulation resting only on force deprives the individuals of 'the means to obtain a just remuneration' and 'prevents them from occupying the place in the social framework which is related to their abilities' (Durkheim, 1893: 370, 377). Or again in *Suicide*, even if Durkheim only evokes it in its most extreme form and does everything to minimize its importance, it is the situation where desires come up against 'an intolerable obstacle', where 'the future is pitilessly closed off', that is to say, fatalism defined by Durkheim as the polar opposite of anomie (1897: 309–11). To be sure, one of the central characteristics of fatalism, an excess of normative regulation, is absent from the Mertonian analysis. It would be going too far, then, to identify Mertonian anomie totally with Durkheimian fatalism. But it is sufficient for our analysis to note that, if one looks in Durkheim for that which approximates most to Mertonian anomie, it is not anomie one finds but its opposite.

The Mertonian theory has clearly constituted an essential stage in the semantic evolution of the notion of anomie, i.e. in the movement which has led to it being identified with its opposite. Merton has not only contributed powerfully to this semantic reversal, he has helped above all to legitimate it by failing to relate his definition explicitly to that of Durkheim. One is led therefore to conclude on a paradox: Merton has succeeded in changing decisively the destiny of anomie in the sociological literature without having clearly defined the concept nor having shown what use it serves for his overall sociological purpose.

EPILOGUE

The myth of the continuity of a tradition of research on anomie, of whom Durkheim was supposed to be the precursor and Merton the prophet, has been both powerful and productive. It was one of the reasons for the fashion in the 1960s for 'scales' of anomie. These scales were extremely widespread and came to symbolize the dominant American research practice of the period. They threw up a bridge between the two pillars of this practice: reference to the classics which provided the theories; and investigation by questionnaire destined to test the hypotheses drawn from these theories.

In this period Merton's text had already acquired the status of a classic. It occupied an honoured place in the sociological canon and in the textbooks and anthologies. This success was the product of a strategy: to constitute the 'theory of anomie' as the central core of one of the major approaches of the sociology of deviance, 'strain theory' (see Besnard, 1987: 272–7). Merton took out a patent on anomie, acted as its legal trustee and treated its parallel usages like licences granted to subsidiaries of a holding theory.

This approach was, however, not successful in one important field. Merton was unable to influence empirical research on the social determinants of psychological anomie because of the water-tight barrier which existed between such studies and research on delinquency. In addition, on close investigation of the real career of the Mertonian theory of anomie in the sociology of delinquency, it is clear that this theory only had a modest and ephemeral success. It did not become diffused in empirical research until after 1959 and was only visible for a dozen years, reaching its summit in the mid-1960s. Empirical tests of the theory were rare, slow in coming and negative, thus accelerating a decline which was already in progress.

The Mertonian theory became out of phase with the evolution of empirical research. Describing the field of research on anomie and deviance in 1964, Merton took for granted that theory was at a more advanced stage than empirical investigation. It would be more exact to reverse the perspective. The theoreticians of the 1950s (Merton, but also Cohen, Miller, Cloward and Ohlin) built their theories on previously accumulated empirical generalizations and the results, essentially, of studies of delinquency based on ecological correlations.[5] Their theories became diffused in empirical research during the 1960s at a time when ecological studies were being abandoned in favour of investigation by questionnaire, which established itself as the technique par excellence of sociological research. But the results of these investigations, particularly those on the social distribution of delinquency, were contrary to what had been assumed by the theoreticians. By an irony of fate, anomie, which had initially been one arm of the fight against the sociology of the Chicago school (see Besnard, 1985), became a victim of the death of the method which this school had privileged.

NOTES

1   This text represents a highly concentrated summary of certain passages of a book dedicated to the uses of the concept of anomie in the discipline of sociology since Durkheim (Besnard, 1987). Due to lack of space, some of the detailed proofs of particular arguments have not been reproduced here.

2   Thus, in their 'Inventory of Empirical and Theoretical Studies of Anomie', Stephen Cole and Harriet Zuckerman (1964) do not distinguish between the 1938 text and that published under the same title in 1949 and 1957. Simon and Gagnon (1976) state wrongly that the 1949 text underwent a revision in 1957, including substantial additions, when in reality only one purely illustrative passage was added. Merton's research assistant, Mary Wilson Miles (1975), failed to distinguish between the different versions of the text in her bibliography of Merton's writings. Finally, Stephen Cole, specialist on the subject and a close associate of Merton, has indicated that only at a late stage, and then accidentally, did he take note of the substantial differences between the 1938 text and that of 1949 (S. Cole, 1975: 219).

3   It is worth noting that the two French translators have been somewhat led astray and translated cultural structure by 'social structure'.

4   *Translator's note*: The author is using the phrase 'non présentable' in two senses. Because it is ambiguous and inconsistent, Merton's theory is neither 'presentable' (amenable to exposition) at an analytical level, nor is it 'presentable' (in terms of 'acceptability' or 'good manners') at the sociological dinner table.

5   For a discussion of sociological studies of deviancy from an ecological perspective, see Taylor, Walton and Young, 1973: 110–24.

Interchange

ORRÙ REPLIES TO BESNARD

Scarcely a century after sociology's inception as an academic discipline sociologists tacitly agree (perhaps reluctantly) that it is very difficult, if not impossible, to analyze and to interpret sociological theories in universally accepted, univocal ways. Much of today's sociology is still preoccupied with settling conflicting claims about the legacy of the founders of our discipline, and no final verdict is in sight. The present book on Robert Merton's sociology rests on the assumption of disagreement over the legacy of his work. It should not surprise the reader, then, that Philippe Besnard and myself should have come to such contrasting evaluations of Merton's theory of anomie.

While disagreement exists, it need not be accepted as inevitable, and the present response to Besnard's 'Merton in Search of Anomie' will scrutinize some of that paper's claims and supporting arguments. Besnard's paper is very detailed in its exegesis of Merton's texts on anomie, but for economy of space I will not be able to take up the finer points of his discussion; instead, I will limit my considerations to the general assumptions on which Besnard's analysis rests, and on the consequent claims he makes regarding Merton's theory. Specifically, I will scrutinize Besnard's assertions that Merton's writings on anomie do not constitute a theory and do not actually relate to anomie. Besnard's double contention rests on four claims: that Merton's discussions on anomie (1) utilize ambiguous concepts; (2) do not link the propositions advanced; (3) provide an uncertain status of the concept [of anomie]; and (4) contribute nothing to Merton's overall sociological purpose.

As I read Besnard's paper and much of his earlier research on anomie, there are two major assumptions which underlie his work. Besnard assumes that we can distinguish unequivocally between those sociological writings which add up to a theory and those which do not; he also assumes that we can clearly separate ambiguous and unambiguous (or true and false) sociological concepts. Certainly there are cases in which a clear assessment can be made regarding the status of some theories and concepts; but these will be likely to characterize the least significant contributions to sociology. I argue, however, that the more significant a theoretical or conceptual elaboration, the more likely that it will be a target of scholarly disagreement. The true sign of theoretically and conceptually significant contributions in sociology is that these contributions influenced and still influence research in the field despite the barrage of criticism to which they have been subjected. Besnard's own work on anomie, which to a large extent evaluates the career of this sociological concept negatively, is an unwitting additional testimony to that concept's significance today.

Absolute theoretical consistency and conceptual adequacy are perhaps desirable, but who meets these criteria? Not Durkheim, not Marx, not Weber, not Merton, and alas, not Besnard. But should one throw out the baby with the bath water because theoretical and conceptual perfection has not been achieved? Besnard's verdict regarding Merton's writings on anomie is a resounding yes! Yet, even within such negative assessment, Besnard sees some redeeming qualities in Merton's theory—why would he otherwise bother to correct Merton's 'incoherent and incomplete typology' by providing his own version of a complete set of modes of adaptation? There is, then, even for Besnard, room for optimism and for improvement in Merton's theoretical elaboration.

I find still more disturbing Besnard's refusal to see Merton's as a theory *of* anomie. For Besnard, Merton's writings have nothing to do with anomie because Merton is never clear about what he means by anomie—because his use of the concept is uncertain and ambiguous. It will be of little consolation for Merton to learn that by Besnard's standards Durkheim's concept of anomie does not fare much better—it too is insufficiently elaborated, and in need of clarification. Again, Besnard sets standards for conceptual adequacy which are patently unrealistic; but more importantly, Besnard fails to acknowledge that, perhaps, the ambiguity and uncertainty he so much criticizes are constant features of sociological theorizing. He ignores the possibility that sociological ambiguity might simply reflect the ambiguity which characterizes social life. Yes, the meaning of anomie shifted from Durkheim to Merton, it shifted within Durkheim's and perhaps within Merton's own theory; but does this mean that the concept is useless? In the name of logical consistency Besnard takes leave from reality: he wants to find the 'true nature' of anomie when there is no such thing in the real world. Durkheim's and Merton's concepts of anomie are vague approximations of some social phenomenon, but just as it is impossible to grasp the true, ultimate nature of a social phenomenon, it is impossible to grasp the true, ultimate nature of the concept which attempts to describe it. In the end we can choose to make the most out of our working concepts and tentative hypotheses, or we can choose instead to recite the *requiem aeternam* of most sociological theories and concepts. Besnard seems to have made the latter choice.

BESNARD REPLIES TO ORRÙ*

Marco Orrù had an extremely difficult task: to write in praise of the Mertonian theory of anomie. He has acquitted himself as well as he can, but in doing so he is obliged to avoid the simple questions which I have asked of this 'theory', questions which Orrù knows, since he makes reference both to my book and to an earlier article of mine. These questions are, for example: what is the meaning of the word 'anomie' in Merton's writings? Why has Merton never discussed the Durkheimian concept of anomie, while letting us believe that his own analyses both continue and enlarge upon those of Durkheim? What is the meaning of the famous typology of

---

* Translated from the French by Jon Clark.

modes of individual adaptation and how coherent is it? To what do these adaptations adapt: is it to an anomic culture or not? Finally, what purpose is served by the term 'anomie' apart from that of a convenient and decorative label? Marco Orrù has taken good care not to take up the challenge that I have thrown down: to define what Merton means by the term 'anomie'. In fact no one has so far succeeded in this: an answer is still awaited.

Instead of conducting a close textual analysis Orrù prefers to adopt a global approach to Merton's writings and to defend them by arguing that it is not necessary to know which of Durkheim and Merton is the 'winner'. Contrary to what he suggests, I have never thought that 'straying from the Durkheimian path would automatically make Merton's theory illegitimate'. In fact I have written exactly the opposite. Everyone is free to define a word as they understand it, on condition that they say in which sense they are using it. Moreover, I am just as critical of the Durkheimian conceptualization as I am of Merton's. Finally, the core of my critique of Merton's essay 'Social Structure and Anomie' is not concerned with this question, even though I *do* believe it was important to have demonstrated that the Mertonian concept of anomie—to the extent that one can identify its content and such as it has been generally understood—is *opposed* to that of Durkheim on all points.

This opposition has nothing to do with the differences outlined by Orrù. Like other commentators, Orrù affirms that Merton locates the origin of human desires in society, while for Durkheim they are supposed to have a biological origin. I must admit to some difficulty in understanding how such a reading of Durkheim is possible. The whole of his discussion of anomie as developed in, for example, *Le suicide* (1897) and *Le socialisme* (1928), his whole method of argumentation and all his explanations are *based* on the idea that human desires are boundless because they are produced by society instead of being, as in the animal world, 'dependent on the body' (1897: 272).

According to Orrù, Merton has been responsible for a further 'revolutionary' innovation: the idea that anomie can be a normal phenomenon. Strange assertion: where can one find the word 'normal' applied to anomie? Not in Merton, but certainly in Durkheim (1897: 285), who devotes an extended passage to anomie institutionalized by, for example, the law on divorce. I would add that the only reference Merton makes to Durkheim in his essay of 1938 (Merton, 1938b: 673n3) is concerned precisely with the well-known theme of the normality of crime.

I am not sure I fully understand what Orrù means when he calls Merton's theory of anomie 'instrumental'. It seems to me that an instrumental theory is one which enables facts to be explained and which can be easily tested against facts. The Mertonian theory of anomie, as I have shown in detail elsewhere (Besnard, 1987: 284–97), has had hardly any resonance in empirical research, apart from ritual references and some refutations towards the end of the 1960s. This is not, in my eyes, an argument against Merton's theory. But I seek in vain for its instrumental character apart from as a pedagogic tool in textbooks.

Sociologists must accept the idea that sociological works, like all products, are subject to the effects of fashion, and that their career depends in good part on the marketing strategies of their promoters. They must also admit that the cognitive power of a theory is not to be measured by its notoriety. Like other celebrated theories, the Mertonian theory of anomie, despite the brilliant intuitions of its author, is like an overinflated balloon which bursts when one tries to seize hold of it. If one believes in sociology and its future, it is not on foundations such as these that one should build.

X. THE SELF-FULFILLING PROPHECY

17. The Self-Fulfilling Prophecy: Its Genesis and Development in American Education

SAMUEL S. WINEBURG AND LEE S. SHULMAN

In widely distributed advertisements for its long-awaited final volume, the editors of the *Oxford English Dictionary Supplement* highlighted the following new entry:

> **self-fulfilling**, ppl. a. orig. Social Sci. In phr. **self-fulfilling prophecy**: a prophecy or prediction which gives rise to actions that bring about its fulfilment (see quot. 1949).
> 1949 R.K. Merton *Soc. Theory & Soc. Structure* vii. 181. The self-fulfilling prophecy is, in the beginning, a **false** definition of the situation evoking a new behavior which makes the originally false conception come **true**.

The entry continues with examples drawn from a social psychology text, a London *Times* article on panic buying of spirits and a snatch of dialogue from a modern Russian play. Perhaps Merton's most famous single essay, certainly his most widely appropriated turn-of-phrase within the social sciences and in the world of laypersons, the self-fulfilling prophecy (SFP) remains a bit of an anomaly. Even Bierstedt, while acknowledging the essay as 'one of Merton's most seminal', relegates its discussion to the final section of his critical review of Merton's corpus of work, treating it as almost an afterthought (1981: 484).

The authors of this chapter are educational psychologists with a particular interest in teaching and learning. We are neither sociologists nor social psychologists. We will focus our discussion on the evolution and remarkable impact of the SFP from its origins in one of Merton's earliest papers (twelve years before the essay bearing its name) through its continuing impact on the field of education. The self-fulfilling prophecy has become both a concept and a phrase that occupies a central position in the thought and language of teachers, policy-makers and others who discuss the practice of education.

The centrepiece of the chapter will be an extended historical account of how the SFP became a key concept in American education, beginning with the Supreme Court decision on school desegregation in 1956, continuing through highly controversial empirical investigations of the effects of teachers' expectations on student performance in schools, and a new generation of studies both confirming the existence of the general phenomenon while adding sobering insights into its sources and mechanisms of action. Ironically, the idea's diffusion has been so successful that it has come to exemplify yet another of Merton's favourite ideas—obliteration by incorporation. As we shall see, the more firmly rooted it has become in the 'familiar furniture' of educators' minds, the less it is associated with Robert Merton.

A parallel account of the spread of this concept might surely have been written from the perspective of other fields of study, but education has been a particularly strategic site for understanding self-fulfilling prophecies, as well as for observing the ways in which social science concepts become diffused within communities of scholars and practitioners.

ORIGINS

In the fall of 1948 a seventeen-page essay appeared in *The Antioch Review* that altered how we speak about social life. It did so by inventing a concept to describe a widespread yet inadequately understood social phenomenon. The author was Robert K. Merton; the term he invented to denote the concept was also the title of his paper, 'The Self-Fulfilling Prophecy'.

Sportswriters now hurl the self-fulfilling prophecy from their columns; legislators issue it from their rostrums; and even an American President has been known to invoke it, hoping thereby to find a verbal tonic for an ailing economy (Richard Nixon, 1971, quoted in Merton, 1981b). Thousands of scholarly papers employing the term have appeared in sociology, social psychology, economics, political science, anthropology, public administration and social work. But the self-fulfilling prophecy has wielded greatest influence—and doubtless stirred the most controversy—in education.

The notion that a false but widely believed prediction could become true, simply because enough people believed in it, was certainly not shocking. Merton, in fact, related the idea to W. I. Thomas's famous dictum that 'if men define situations as real, they are real in their consequences'. But the idea, Merton avowed, predated Thomas, finding roots in Bishop Bossuet's defence of Catholic orthodoxy in the seventeenth century; in Marx's critique of the Hegelian dialectics of change; and in places too numerous to count in the work of Freud.

The self-fulfilling prophecy was a uniquely social idea with no corollary in the physical or natural sciences. While predictions of earthquakes may set Californians on edge, words do not make the ground tremble. But in the social sphere, self-fulfilling prophecies abounded. So, for example, rumours about the insolvency of banks, when widely believed and acted upon, brought doom to otherwise flourishing financial institutions. Although the term 'self-fulfilling prophecy' was new, observations of the phenomenon were commonplace. 'So common is the pattern of the self-fulfilling prophecy that each of us has his favored specimen' (Merton, 1948b: 195).

The self-fulfilling prophecy begins, according to Merton, with the false definition of a situation, which in turn engenders behaviour that brings the situation into conformity with the definition. 'The Negro is a strikebreaker and a traitor to the working class', claimed union officials in barring blacks from labour unions prior to

World War II. Hungry and out-of-work, thousands of blacks could not resist the invitation by strikebound employers to take jobs otherwise closed to them. Did blacks become scabs because of their 'inability to participate in collective bargaining', or because, excluded from union membership, they had no choice but to accept what was offered? For Merton, the final arbiter in cases of the self-fulfilling prophecy was time:

> History creates its own test of the theory of self-fulfilling prophecies. That Negroes were strikebreakers because they were excluded from unions (and from a large range of jobs) rather than excluded because they were strikebreakers can be seen from the virtual disappearance of Negroes as scabs in industries where they have gained admission to unions in the last decades. (*ibid*.: 197)

Naturally, history can play that role only if conditions permit the individuals for whom the prophecies are negative the opportunity to overcome their circumstances. Too often the prophecies constrain the options available to the actors and history can bear no witness.

Quoting Tocqueville, Merton asserted that self-fulfilling prophecies were rooted in a social structure created by humans and thus open to change by them: 'What we call necessary institutions are often no more than institutions to which we have grown accustomed' (*ibid*.: 210). Two important features of the SFP are reflected in those comments. First, the sociologically interesting genre of SFP is 'rooted in a social structure'. While most examples that are readily cited describe individuals' beliefs and their consequences for individual behaviour, Merton is particularly interested in prophecies that are collective and institutional in their origins and their means of propagation. Second, the SFP is 'created by humans and thus open to change by them'. To understand the dynamics of SFPs, therefore, is not only to grasp an essential feature of organized human behaviour; it is to discern the conditions for the amelioration and improvement of the human condition as well. Therein lay the fascination of the SFP for educators, whose social obligation is not merely to understand, but to change, to shape and to improve the human condition.

ROOTS IN MERTON'S EARLIER WORK

In the first volume of the *American Sociological Review* published in 1936, Merton published a paper that foreshadowed much of his future theoretical work. In 'The Unanticipated Consequences of Purposive Social Action' (Merton, 1936b) we observe the young sociologist beginning to shape ideas that will eventuate in his critical distinctions between manifest and latent functions. Toward the end of the essay, in the course of a discussion of the difficulties inherent in social prediction and planning, he observes:

> Public predictions of future social developments are frequently not sustained precisely because the prediction has become a new element in the concrete situation, thus tending to change the initial course of developments. This is not true of prediction in fields which do not pertain to human conduct. Thus the prediction of the return of Halley's comet does not in any way influence the orbit of that comet... (*ibid*.: 903–4)

Merton appends a footnote to this discussion, in which he cites John Venn's term 'suicidal prophecies' to refer to this process. This is the first instance in which he attaches the term 'prophecy' to such a phenomenon. He cites this earlier discussion in the classic 1948 SFP article, where he once again introduces the contrast with the return of Halley's comet (1948b: 195).

Merton himself contributes to one of the most frequent misunderstandings of the self-fulfilling prophecy when, in the first paragraph of SFP, he refers to W. I. Thomas's 'theorem basic to the social sciences: "If men define situations as real, they are real in their consequences"'. He then proceeds to discuss and give examples of the self-fulfilling prophecy. There are several misconstruals that typically derive from that juxtaposition, in particular that the self-fulfilling prophecy is nothing but a neologism introduced by Merton to refer to a restatement of the Thomas theorem, and that the subjective definition of the situation is always the most important determinant of subsequent outcomes in human affairs. As we shall see through a careful review of the history of the self-fulfilling prophecy in education, both of these misreadings contributed to an early misunderstanding of the concept in educational circles.

THE SELF-FULFILLING PROPHECY, DESEGREGATION AND TEACHERS' EXPECTATIONS

America on the eve of the twentieth century was a land that had grown accustomed to its social institutions, especially its system of separate schools for children of different colours. But by this century's midpoint much had changed, and claims that the 'necessary institutions' of separate schools were no more than 'mere customs' —and inhumane customs at that—were heard with greater frequency. Separating children on the basis of skin colour, claimed critics, flouted the ideals of a democratic society. This was not all. Segregation's effects extended beyond institutional spheres—more was at stake than inequality of social opportunity. Segregation, according to these claims, caused psychological damage to its victims, engendering maladaptive internal states that left the personality scarred. These were new and serious charges, and their documentation became a social priority. Society looked to the universities for evidence, and the universities looked to the social sciences. Psychologist Kenneth B. Clark was among those who responded to that call.

Clark's experimenters (e.g. Clark, 1955; Clark and Clark, 1939) presented black youngsters between the ages of 3 and 7 with two dolls, one black and one white, and asked them which doll they wanted to play with. At each age level the majority of children rejected the black doll. Sometimes youngsters showed extreme reactions, as did one little girl who, after choosing the white doll, called the black one 'ugly' and 'dirty'. This girl sobbed uncontrollably when the researcher asked her to identify herself with one of the two dolls. Clark, a black social psychologist then at the City College of New York, summarized the implications of such an episode:

> As minority-group children learn the inferior status to which they are assigned and observe that they are usually segregated and isolated from the more privileged members of their society, they react with deep feelings of inferiority and with a sense of personal humiliation....Like all other human beings, they require a sense of personal dignity and social support for positive self-esteem....Under these conditions, minority-group

children develop conflicts with regard to their feelings about themselves and about the values of the group with which they are identified. (1955: 63)

Not fleeting or easily healed, this feeling of inferiority was 'enduring or lasting as the situation endured, changing only in its form and in the way it manifested itself' (*Brown v. Board of Education*, 1954: 89–90). Taught by society to be inferior, black children learned to feel and act inferior. Aided by the mechanism of the self-fulfilling prophecy, the effects of racism moved from 'out there' in society to inside people's heads or, in Clark's terms, 'embedded in the personality' (1955: 50).

In his role as social science consultant to the National Association for the Advancement of Colored People in *Brown v. Board of Education* (1954), Clark was as instrumental as any other social scientist in swaying the court to dismantle this country's system of separate schools. But when many of the promised benefits of desegregation subsequently failed to materialize (cf. Cohen and Weiss, 1977; St John, 1975; Weinberg, 1975), the task of solving the problems of disadvantaged youth was seen as requiring more than mixing children of different colours in the same school. According to one explanation, it was not ghetto youth but their teachers who were the problem, and the self-fulfilling prophecy, as an explanation for differential achievement between white and black students, came to be used with ever greater frequency. Simply changing the social organization of schools would have little effect on the achievement of minority students unless a concomitant change occurred in the minds of their teachers. Therefore, because of the 'importance of the role of teachers in the developing self-image, academic aspirations and achievements of their students', Kenneth Clark (1963: 148) began a study of teacher attitudes in ten inner-city schools.

In a report describing this research (Clark, 1963), the term 'self-fulfilling prophecy' first appeared in the educational literature. Foreshadowing controversies that would rage a few years later, the term appeared in the context of a discussion of IQ tests. The argument was straightforward. Because teachers thought minority children were dumb, they didn't waste their time on them, and teachers' expectations were later borne out by students' low test scores. Clark wrote: 'If a child scores low on an intelligence test because he cannot read and then is not taught to read because he has a low score, then such a child is being imprisoned in an iron circle and becomes the victim of an educational self-fulfilling prophecy' (*ibid.*: 150).

In the late 1950s and early 1960s this view struck a responsive chord among educational researchers and practitioners. Clark's ideas about educational self-fulfilling prophecies filtered down to schoolpeople and became part of in-service training programmes. Carl Marburger, director of Detroit's Great Cities project, outlined how his city responded to the first plank of the master plan:

> One major approach is our work with teachers. Improvement of schooling depends to a great extent upon more effective teaching....At this point...we conceive the formula that teacher expectations have surprising impact on pupil achievement. Indeed we might even say that teacher expectations have a similar impact on pupil intelligence scores. (Marburger, 1963: 302–6)

Lacking empirical data to array before the participants at a conference on 'Education in Depressed Areas' at Columbia University in 1962, Marburger did the next best thing. He borrowed data and argued by analogy. Citing an unpublished manuscript (Rosenthal and Fode, cited in Marburger, 1963) by a Professor of Psychology at the University of North Dakota, Marburger described an experiment that showed that when psychology students thought their albino rats were either 'maze-bright' or 'maze-dull', the rats, after a week of maze-running, fulfilled their experimenters' expectations. The designer of this experiment was unfamiliar to most school people. But five years later there would scarcely be an educator who did not recognize the name Robert Rosenthal.

A FINDING IN SEARCH OF DATA

By the mid-1960s the notion that teachers' expectations for minority students caused them to do poorly in school was well-established in people's minds. But one problem remained. If children who did poorly in school were expected by their teachers to do poorly, it could always be argued that expectations were based, not on self-fulfilling prophecies, but on students' past performance. Thus viewed, the educational self-fulfilling prophecy became a chicken or egg problem, something to be puzzled over endlessly but never known with certainty—that is, unless this alternative hypothesis could be ruled out.

Robert Rosenthal, by the early 1960s, had moved from the University of North Dakota to Harvard. Rosenthal (1966) had earned a reputation for a series of ingenious experiments that demonstrated how researchers influenced the results of their seemingly dispassionate investigations. By 1963 Rosenthal had already begun to wonder if the expectancy effects he discovered with psychology students and albino rats (Rosenthal and Fode, 1963) might not also operate with doctors and their patients, psychotherapists and their clients, bosses and their employees, and teachers and their students. As Rosenthal, in a retrospective essay on the course of his research programme, put it, 'If rats became brighter when expected to, then it should not be farfetched to think that children could become brighter when expected to by their teachers' (1985: 44).

Rosenthal's idea to test the self-fulfilling prophecy in a school, rather than in a hospital, a factory or a mental health clinic, was apparently fortuitous. He received a request for a copy of an article on experimenter effects from Lenore Jacobson, an elementary school principal in South San Francisco. Rosenthal sent her the article along with a stack of unpublished papers and 'thought no more about it' (Rosenthal, 1985: 44). But Jacobson dashed off a second note to the Harvard psychologist and in it presented a challenge. 'If you ever "graduate" to classroom children', she wrote, 'please let me know whether I can be of assistance' (*ibid.*). From this challenge *Pygmalion in the Classroom* (Rosenthal and Jacobson, 1968a) was born.

Rosenthal and Jacobson's experiment was simple and elegant. Their research site was the 'Oak School' located in a low-income South San Francisco neighbourhood, and, in order for the experiment to work, the researchers had to violate the good faith of teachers. First, children in this elementary school were administered a little-known IQ test. Rosenthal described the procedure: 'We had special covers printed for the test; they bore the high-sounding title "Test of Inflected Acquisition". The teachers were told that the testing was part of an undertaking being carried out by investigators from Harvard University' (Rosenthal and Jacobson, 1968b: 21). An information sheet given to the teachers explained that the 'Harvard Test of Inflected Acquisition' could identify children who could be expected to 'bloom', or experience an intellectual growth spurt, during the ensuing academic year. The test was actually Flanagan's Test of General Ability (TOGA), a group administered IQ test. The bloomers had actually been chosen by means of a table of random numbers.

The subject of the 'bloomers' was brought up casually at a faculty meeting during which each teacher was given a list of about two to seven bloomers in each classroom as identified by the 'Harvard Test of Inflected Acquisition'. Four months later, and again at the end of the school year, the test was readministered. The findings of the study, as reported in the full-length book about it, were striking. 'We find increasing expectancy advantage as we go from the sixth to the first grade; the correlation between grade level and magnitude of expectancy advantage (r = − .86) was significant at the .03 level' (1968a: 74). Elsewhere, Rosenthal and Jacobson wrote, 'The results indicated strongly that children from whom teachers expected greater intellectual gains showed such gains' (1968c: 22).

The finding of 'an increasing expectancy advantage as we go from the sixth grade to the first grade' seemed to mean two things: first, that the treatment conferred an 'advantage' upon the children who received it (the bloomers); and, second, that there was some kind of progression in the data, with the magnitude of effect decreasing linearly as children became older. But did the data support this claim? Not exactly. Table 7.1 (1968a: 75) showed statistically significant results (or 'expectancy advantages') only for children in the first and second grades. In the other four grades the treatment either conferred a statistically non-significant advantage (fourth grade), no difference at all (third grade), or a statistically non-significant *disadvantage* (fifth and sixth grades). In other words, the null hypothesis could not be ruled out in 66 per cent of the grade levels.

Odd, then, were statements like 'when teachers expected that certain children would show greater intellectual development, those children did show greater intellectual development' (Rosenthal and Jacobson, 1968a: 82). The lack of qualifications in the assertions was even more striking in the light of the mixed results of a replication experiment in two mid-western schools by Evans and Rosenthal (1969). Described in a footnote on page 96 of *Pygmalion*, the results of this study showed that in these two schools, control-group girls gained about 15 points on the reasoning subscale of the IQ test, whereas the treatment-group girls gained just over 5 points, a statistically significant advantage in favour of the control-group girls.

Rosenthal and Jacobson's assertions about the effects of expectations on IQ were critically examined by the research community. Scholarly reviews of the book appeared in the American Psychological Association's review journal, *Contemporary Psychology*, and in the American Educational Research Association's major archival journal, *American Educational Research Journal*. Neither took kindly to *Pygmalion*.

Writing in *Contemporary Psychology*, Richard Snow, a differential psychologist at Stanford University, pointed out that TOGA was inadequately normed for children in the youngest grades. In one classroom a group of nineteen normal children had a mean IQ score of 31 on the reasoning subscale of the test (Rosenthal and Jacobson, 1968a: 189). Like most IQ tests, TOGA was normed to have a mean of 100. Thus the nineteen children in the 'C' track of the first grade were hardly the type of children one would expect at this run-of-the-mill school. Snow asked pointedly: 'Were these children actually functioning at imbecile and low moron levels?' 'More likely', he hypothesized, 'the test was not functioning at this grade level....To obtain IQ scores as low as these, given reasonably distributed ages, raw scores would have to represent random or systematically incorrect responding' (Snow, 1969: 198). In other words, even if some students marked their tests at random, the raw scores would have been higher than those obtained. In order to score so low, some students must have refused to put pen to paper. Snow criticized other features of the book, e.g. the fact that additional mental ability information (readily available at the school) was not used in the analysis, the reliance on simple gain scores 'even though many mean pretest differences between treatment groups equal or exceed obtained posttest differences' (*ibid.*), and the use of 'microscopic scales to overemphasize practically insignificant differences' (*ibid.*: 199). Snow concluded: '*Pygmalion*, inadequately and prematurely reported...has performed a disservice to teachers and schools, to users and developers of mental tests, and perhaps worst of all, to parents and children whose newly gained expectations may not prove quite so self-fulfilling' (*ibid.*: 198).

Robert Thorndike, an expert in educational and psychological testing at Teachers College, Columbia University, and the co-author of a widely used IQ test, was no kinder to *Pygmalion*. Like Snow's criticisms, Thorndike's had less to do with the theory behind the study or even with the design employed, than with an IQ test that produced uneven and wildly unpredictable results. Thorndike (1968) questioned the validity of a measure that would yield a mean of 150.17 among the six bloomers in class 2A, an extraordinarily high score that could only be obtained if most students received a perfect score on the subtest. But because the standard deviation for these six scores was 40 points, Thorndike wondered about the students who fell above the mean. *Pygmalion*, he wrote, 'is so defective technically that one can only regret that it ever got beyond the eyes of the original investigators!' (*ibid.*: 708).

Not only did *Pygmalion* get past the eyes of the original investigators but even before the book hit the streets, headlines about it splashed over the front page of the 14 August 1967 *New York Times* (although details of the experiment's failure to replicate received a scant column inch in the continuation of the story on page 20). Robert Rosenthal appeared on national television telling the *Today Show's* Barbara Walters that 'teachers shouldn't be allowed to teach students who they know won't learn' (NBC, 28 May 1969). Reviews of *Pygmalion* in the media hailed it as a major contribution to understanding the problems of disadvantaged students.

The reports of *Pygmalion* in the press showed how the study came to stand for whatever people wanted it to, regardless of the original research questions asked by Rosenthal and Jacobson. *Pygmalion* tested the hypothesis that teachers who believe their students are due for an intellectual growth spurt will, in fact, score higher on an IQ test than a group of comparable students for whom no expectations are held. But an article in *Time* reported that 'a new book called *Pygmalion* in the Classroom' demonstrated that 'many children *fail to learn* simply because their teachers do not expect them to' (20 September, 1968, p. 62; emphasis supplied). Not only was such an effect not documented, it was never even addressed in Rosenthal and Jacobson's study. *Time* went on to claim that the findings of *Pygmalion* 'raise some fundamental questions about teacher training' and 'cast doubt on the wisdom of assigning children to classes according to presumed ability' (*ibid.*).

One might think that only writers in the popular press would leap so quickly from the findings of a field experiment to questions of reforming teacher education and the organization of schooling. But the idea that *Pygmalion* had direct implications for teacher training, compensatory education and the ways in which the United States dealt with its poorest students was not the media's invention. Rosenthal and Jacobson themselves set the stage by forging links between *Pygmalion's* findings and questions about how to train our teachers and run our schools.

Writing in the *Scientific American* (1968c), they questioned the wisdom of federal programmes that had been trying to come up with ways to overcome the educational handicaps of disadvantaged children. They argued that the model upon which such programmes rested assumed that disadvantaged children possessed some problem, or deficit, that must be remedied. Rosenthal and Jacobson asserted that such thinking was, at best, misguided:

> Our experiment rested on the premise that at least some of the deficiencies—and therefore at least some of the remedies—might be in the schools, and particularly in the attitudes of teachers toward disadvantaged children. In our experiment nothing was done directly for the child. There was no crash program to improve his reading ability, no extra time for tutoring, no program of trips to museums and art galleries. The only people affected directly were the teachers. (*ibid.*: 23)

What conclusions were readers to draw from such statements? That compensatory education had been a waste? That changing teachers' expectancies might prove more cost-effective than programmes sponsored under the Elementary and Secondary Education Act? 'More attention in educational research should be focused on the teacher', the authors continued. Once researchers learned how the Oak School teachers were able to accomplish what they did, training packages could be designed so that 'other teachers could be taught to do the same'. This might even lead to the development of psychological instruments for earmarking teachers who could produce similar effects and weeding out those unable to do so. *Pygmalion* would thus play a role in the 'sophisticated selection of teachers' (*ibid.*). Given enough time, it seemed, *Pygmalion's* findings would revolutionize American education.

It certainly did not take long for these findings, and the underlying concept of the educational self-fulfilling prophecy, to continue their influence on the views of judges, the most influential of laypersons. In the case of *Hobson v. Hansen* (1967) in the District of Columbia, the issues were both school desegregation and the dismantling of an ability-based tracking system. Each side brought expert witnesses from the social sciences to support its claims. At one point the exasperated Judge Skelly Wright remarked, 'The unfortunate if inevitable tendency has been to lose sight of the disadvantaged young students...in an overgrown garden of numbers and charts and jargon like "standard deviation of the variable"..."statistical significance" and "Pearson product-moment correlations"' (quoted in Wolf, 1981: 265). When a decision in the case was rendered, Judge Wright wrote that the court 'has been forced back to its own common sense' (quoted in Cohen and Weiss, 1977: 96).

In spite of his avowed distrust of social science research, the judge chose to buttress his common sense with two published studies: Clark's (1963) investigation and an edited chapter on the *Pygmalion* study (Rosenthal and Jacobson, 1968b). The judge asserted:

> Studies have found that a teacher will commonly tend to underestimate the abilities of disadvantaged children and will treat them accordingly—in the daily classroom routine, in grading, and in evaluating these students' likelihood of achieving in the future. The horrible consequences of a teacher's low expectation is that it tends to be a self-fulfilling

prophecy. The unfortunate students, treated as if they were subnormal, come to accept
as a fact that they *are* subnormal. (*Hobson v. Hansen*, 1967, p. 484)

Although all of the points raised by Judge Wright may be true, the studies he
cited had failed to provide the putative evidence. Clark's research presented no data
directly bearing on the self-fulfilling prophecy. *Pygmalion* dealt with overesti-
mation, not underestimation, of children's abilities. Moreover, it presented no
observational data of teachers, so there was no information on how teachers
'treated' students. Further, no interviews were conducted with students to see
whether they accepted their 'subnormal' status. Nevertheless, so intuitively compelling was the hypothesis that studies were cited with confidence to confirm findings
that had not yet been found.

PYGMALION RECONSIDERED IN EDUCATIONAL RESEARCH

Pygmalion's influence on educational research is nothing short of remarkable. Since
the original study there have been, by one estimate (Meyer, 1985), between 300 and
400 published reports related to the educational self-fulfilling prophecy (for reviews
see Brophy, 1983; Brophy and Good, 1974; Cooper and Good, 1983; Dusek, 1975,
1985). A research tradition that began by inducing teachers to form false expectations based on experimental manipulation quickly progressed to the study of
expectations as they naturally occurred in ordinary classrooms. In the course of this
work researchers built and refined elaborate models for the communication of
expectations (Brophy and Good, 1974; Cooper, 1979; Cooper and Good, 1983;
West and Anderson, 1976) and developed finely tuned observation systems for
analyzing complex classroom interactions (Brophy and Good, 1970b). In our view
(see Wineburg, 1988) the claim that teachers' expectations could influence *measured
intelligence* has yet to be supported empirically. However, a large number of studies
have supported the hypothesis that expectations can lead to marked variations in
teachers' responses to pupils. These responses, in turn, are associated with important variations in a variety of pupil performance measures.

Brophy and Good (1970a) were among the first to study naturally occurring
expectations. They asked four first grade teachers to rank their students in order of
expected achievement and then observed high- and low-expectation students in their
respective classrooms. Interesting patterns emerged. High-expectation students
volunteered more answers, initiated more contacts with their teachers, raised their
hands more often and had fewer reading problems than their low-expectation peers,
findings which led Brophy and Good to the realization that many 'teacher
expectation effects' are best understood as student effects on teachers. But other
findings were less easy to explain this way. For instance, when low-expectation
students gave wrong answers, they were less likely to receive specific feedback, and
when they gave right answers, they were less likely to receive praise. Although all
four teachers in this study displayed relatively similar behaviour patterns, a
follow-up study (Evertson, Brophy and Good, 1972, cited in Brophy and Good,
1974) yielded less uniform results. Here only three of nine teachers resembled those
in the first study; three others displayed few differences in their interactions with
high- and low-expectation students; and the final three showed the opposite pattern
from the first, often seeking out lows for extra help and giving them more of a
chance to get the right answer. These early studies set the tone for much of the

research which followed. Expectations in the classroom were phenomena far more complex and multidimensional than most had imagined (Dusek, 1985).

As research on teacher expectancies began to accumulate, teachers looked less like the villains portrayed in the earlier studies. True, some teachers ignored information from students and held to rigid expectations, distributing turns unfairly in reading groups (Allington, 1980), criticizing some students more harshly than others (Brophy and Good, 1970b; Good, Sikes and Brophy, 1973) and smiling at some while reacting coolly towards others (Babad, Inbar and Rosenthal, 1982). Every profession includes those who do it a disservice, and teaching is no exception. But for the most part, teachers' expectations proved to be based on the best evidence in their possession (Borko, Cone, Russo and Shavelson, 1979; Shavelson, Cadwell and Izu, 1977), and most teachers were willing to abandon initial expectations when more dependable evidence became available. Indeed, a recent study suggests that those least acquainted with classroom life are often most influenced by the background information they receive about students (Carter, Sabers, Cushing, Pinnegar and Berliner, 1987). Experienced teachers tend to disregard such information, preferring to form judgments based on their own first-hand experience with students. Summarizing much research over the years on the educational self-fulfilling prophecy, Brophy concluded:

> Although there are relationships between teacher expectations, teacher-student interaction, and student achievement, most of these are more accurately construed as student effects on teachers rather than as teacher expectation effects on students. Most differential teacher expectations are accurate and reality-based, and most differential teacher interaction with students represents either appropriate, proactive response to differential student need, or at least understandable reactive response to differential student behavior...although the potential for teachers' expectations to function as self-fulfilling prophecies always exists, the extent to which they actually do so in typical classrooms is probably limited.... (1983: 634)

While it is beyond the scope of this paper to review the 300–400 studies conducted on educational self-fulfilling prophecies, it is instructive to examine one particular area of this work, an area we think provides a unique perspective on this entire body of research. Ability groupings, both within and across classes, constitute what Merton has called a 'strategic research site' for investigating the workings of the educational self-fulfilling prophecy. Because of their fixedness in the educational landscape (Austin and Morrison, 1963; Oakes, 1985), ability groups and the effects they produce are important topics of enquiry. In the following section we examine four studies of ability grouping. Three focus on the relatively narrow area of the first grade reading group, but in so doing use different methodologies that ultimately yield different conclusions. The fourth study moves from the grouping of elementary school children within classes to sorting high school students into 'ability tracks' across classes. Each of these studies tells us something different about the ways in which self-fulfilling prophecies, and expectation effects more generally, operate in educational contexts.

FIRST GRADE READING GROUPS

The first study explored the structure of reading groups once they were set into place in the first grade classroom. Weinstein's (1976) research spanned five months, from the first week of school to the middle of the school year. She was particularly interested in how reading groups were set into place and, once they were formed, the degree of mobility between them. Weinstein further studied the means by which classroom expectations were communicated: once teachers assigned students to groups, did they spend more time with the high achievers at the expense of the low achievers, as suggested by Rist (1970), or were expectations communicated in more subtle ways?

In the three first grade New Haven, Connecticut classrooms she studied, Weinstein found that initial group assignment was not nearly as binding as some had suggested. By mid-year more than half of the children had shifted from their initial placement, but it was those students placed in the middle group who moved most. Of the nineteen children initially placed in the highest group, sixteen remained; of the fifteen children in the lowest groups, ten remained. In other words, if children were initially assigned to the highest or lowest groups, there was a high probability they would remain.

In terms of achievement Weinstein found that all children gained. However, the gains of those students who remained in the highest group outpaced those of their less able peers. Thus, while a half-year grade equivalent separated students at the beginning of the year, the gap widened to a full year after five months of observation, a primary school exemplification of what Merton dubbed the 'Matthew effect' in studies of scientific communities. But how, exactly, did the 'rich get richer' in the context of the classroom? Using the Brophy-Good Dyadic Interaction System, an observation schedule for coding classroom behaviours, Weinstein looked for differences in teachers' interactions with different ability groups. But they were not to be found. Not only did she find no significant differences in the frequency of teacher interactions with three levels of reading groups, but, if anything, the lowest groups seemed to get more attention. In Weinstein's words, students in the lowest groups were 'more frequently praised after giving a correct answer and after the end of a reading turn despite their poorer performance than members of the highest reading group' (*ibid.*: 115).

Weinstein's study left open the question of mechanism. Was the dispersion among groups part of a natural process of ability differentiation or was it a function of subtle interaction processes between teachers and learners, processes so subtle they eluded the generic observation systems used to detect them? Weinstein hinted this was the case when she suggested that low achieving students may have viewed praise as indiscriminate approval, an indication that 'anything goes'. In short, praise may have been teachers' medium for conveying low expectations.

Noting the difficulties with experimenter-imposed definitions of 'good' verbal behaviours such as praise, Allington (1980) designed a coding system tailored to what goes on in first grade reading groups. Allington gathered audiotapes of twenty first grade high and low reading groups. Teachers either tape recorded themselves or were recorded by researchers; they were given no special instructions except to teach as they normally would. Believing that differences might be detected in the type of help teachers give to students, Allington analyzed teachers' interruptions during students' oral reading. First, tapes were coded for the point at which an interruption occurred: before the child made an error, after the error or whether the error was left uncorrected. Next, each interruption was coded for the type of corrective information it offered: (a) graphemic, related to the visual aspects of the word or letter identification, (b) phonemic, related to the letter-sound relationship, (c) semantic/syntactic, related to the meaning of the word or sentence, and (d) teacher intercession, those cases when teachers simply pronounced words for students.

When first grade reading groups were analyzed this way, differences were easier to detect. Poor readers were interrupted at twice the rate of good readers (74 per cent of their errors were corrected versus 31 per cent for the good readers). Moreover, if an error was semantically appropriate, good readers were allowed to continue uninterrupted 90 per cent of the time. Poor readers, on the other hand, were allowed to continue less than half (48 per cent) of the time.

Such findings lead to some interesting speculations about how teacher expectations influence student ability. Much recent research on reading points to the centrality of students' regulatory and self-monitoring processes (see Brown, 1978, for review). Believing that slower students need to be corrected frequently, some teachers may unwittingly deprive students of the very opportunities they need in order to improve. If students are always told when they make a mistake, they never get the chance to develop the independent monitoring processes that allow them to become fluid readers. Together with Weinstein's study, Allington's work exemplifies the careful specification of subtle interaction processes—processes that provide clues for how teacher expectations are transacted in the classroom. These studies also shift the emphasis from the beliefs and expectations alone to the pedagogical actions undertaken in their service.

Nevertheless, the suspicion remained that if an educational self-fulfilling prophecy effect were to account for a significant component of student performance, more must be functioning than the workings of individual teacher expectations alone. This hypothesis is beautifully explored in a series of studies by Rebecca Barr and Robert Dreeben, as they begin to identify mechanisms through which the SFP operates that transcend individual teacher-student relationships.

The study by Barr and Dreeben (1983) provides a different angle on classroom expectation effects. They too studied that most crucial of school accomplishments, learning to read at the end of first grade. They studied in longitudinal depth the educational experiences of white and black first graders of comparable ability levels across different schools. They began with the disturbing fact that even after socio-economic status and aptitude had been taken into account, the white first graders in their sample still learned about 100 words more than their black counterparts at the end of the first grade. But in accounting for these findings, Barr and Dreeben's work takes a radical turn from the other studies that have probed unequal classroom outcomes. Rather than implicating teachers, Barr and Dreeben located the causes of these differences in the structural features of schooling—features that lie outside classroom walls.

Dreeben and Barr selected nine schools in three Chicago-area districts to study. District I was a racially diverse inner-city school; District II was a largely white district in a working-class suburb; and District III was an affluent white district. Located within these districts were schools that were racially integrated and segregated, but the all-black and all-white schools were sufficiently similar in socio-economic status and exposure to different educational programmes to allow comparisons of children who differed in race alone.

Children were tested at the beginning of the year and again at the end. Two factors accounted for most of the variance in student achievement: (1) the amount of time school districts allotted to basal instruction in the first grade; and (2) the difficulty of the curricular materials provided to first grade teachers. Because most first grade teachers try to complete the curriculum in their high and middle level reading groups no matter how demanding the materials, 'the selected basal normally sets a ceiling on how much material will be covered during the school year' (Dreeben, 1987: 31). Overall they found the correlation between how many new words were covered by the assigned reading books and how much was learned by the pupils to be $r = .93$ (Barr and Dreeben, 1983: 131), an astoundingly high value. If the ceiling was high, these researchers found, teachers pushed students to work harder and achieve more; if it was low, students proceeded at a leisurely pace and learned less.

For example, the highest scoring group on the pretest was located in a poor black school. By the end of the school year, this group had learned less than white students at another school whose pretest achievement was lower. Though these black students had initially outperformed the white students by an average twelve points, their teacher spent half as much time on reading instruction as the teacher of the white students. Moreover, the number of new words introduced in basal reader for the black students was 475 words compared to 806 for the white students. At the end of the year black students learned all of the 475 words in their 475-word curriculum; white students, however, learned 768 words of their 806-word curriculum. In the two schools located in the affluent white neighbourhood 61 and 76 minutes were devoted to daily basal instruction. By contrast, in the three exclusively black schools the comparable time allotments were 49, 30 and 30 minutes. Such findings led Dreeben to this conclusion: 'Black students with higher aptitudes learned less than their white counterparts because they received poorer instruction both in terms of quantity of time and quality of materials' (1987: 33).

In examining the findings from within-class groupings in the racially integrated classes, these researchers found that within-class ability groups were formed on the basis of aptitude, not on some racially motivated factor. Regardless of race, when children of similar ability receive similar instruction, they learn about the same amount. In Dreeben's words, when ability grouping was combined with effective instruction it had 'an equalizing effect on the learning of black and white children, a result exactly contrary to the conventional wisdom that holds ability grouping to be discriminatory' (1987: 34). The problem comes, of course, when children of similar ability receive different instruction, either by way of time for instruction or quality of materials. End-of-year learning differences, at least in this study, were attributed to 'actions of district and school administrators' before classroom instruction took place. In other words, no matter what teachers did, some students who should have learned more learned less.

How, exactly, do Barr and Dreeben's findings relate to the self-fulfilling prophecy? First, the usual explanations of the working of the self-fulfilling prophecy were not supported. Systematic differences in the treatment of high and low achieving students were not found. Nor was support found for the enactment of the self-fulfilling prophecy when within-class ability groups were set into place. Instead, these researchers pointed to factors that had little to do with conventional accounts of expectation effects. If the self-fulfilling prophecy was applicable at all, it was at the level of administrative decision-making where curriculum decisions and time allocations were made.

The concept of the 'self-sustaining prophecy' (Cooper and Good, 1983) may be most applicable here. Whereas the self-fulfilling prophecy involves the false definition of a situation, the self-sustaining prophecy begins with the status quo, and assumes that because something is, it must be. While data on administrative decision-making were not part of Barr and Dreeben's study, we can speculate that decisions such as what basal reading textbook series to use are subject to the powerful forces of inertia. By infrequently evaluating curricula and decisions about time allocations, administrators may have sustained the performance levels for students who almost certainly could have achieved more. Administrative decisions (and the social forces that assign families to neighbourhoods and neighbourhoods to schools) in school systems like those of the US, in which individual districts and schools select their own curriculum and textbooks, may well provide for a far more dramatic impact of SFP on student learning than is likely to occur through individual teachers.[1]

If the assignment of children to schools and of alternative textbook materials (which thereby help drive teachers' expectations for pace and extent of achievement) are powerful influences on student learning, it is important to understand the ubiquity of the phenomenon of school tracking and the evidence that it influences what teachers do in schools even beyond first grade reading.

The final study we consider (Oakes, 1985) helps us to understand the pervasiveness of the assignment of students to tracks well beyond the first grade. It was more encompassing than the work of Dreeben and Barr, albeit less subtle in its treatment of the classroom-level interactions among teachers, students and texts. It moved from the first grade reading group to the world of the high school, and rather than looking at a limited set of classrooms, it involved twenty-five different schools, 247 classrooms and more than 13,000 students. The focus of the study was tracking, or the practice of separating students into distinctive ability groups across classes. Placements are sometimes made on the basis of teacher recommendations, student test scores or beliefs about which programme is best suited to students' career interests. But in Oakes's words, tracking is best understood as sorting—'a sorting of students that has certain predictable characteristics' (*ibid.*: 3).

The data for this study came from John Goodlad's exhaustive *A Study of Schooling* (1981), perhaps the most comprehensive and well funded project on the state of schooling in the last decade. Over 150 researchers spent six weeks in classrooms gathering documents, observing classes and administering questionnaires to teachers, students, parents and principals. In their sample of twenty-five schools, Oakes and her colleagues found tracking to be extensive: twenty-four of twenty-five schools had some kind of tracking system. Not all of the schools, however, tracked students formally. At Euclid High, a small rural high school, no official system of tracking existed and ostensibly all classes were open to all students. However, the staff in a very informal way guided student placement during registration for classes, making sure that students who were presumed to be college-bound took academic classes and those who were not did not. The result was that there were as many tracked classes at Euclid as at many of the senior highs with straightforward policies (*ibid.*: 48).

The issue of what went on in these different tracks was at the core of this study. Because tracking is justified by claims that students learn best in homogeneous groups and that slower students develop more positive attitudes when shielded from top students, Oakes wanted to see if such claims had a basis in reality. In analyzing instructional practices in 75 high, 85 average and 64 low track English-language and literature and math classes, she found a series of consistent patterns. For example, in high track English classes, 81 per cent of class time was devoted to teaching the curriculum, whereas in low track classes the corresponding figure was 75 per cent. Likewise, when teachers were asked how much time they expected students to spend on homework, they said forty-two minutes for high achievers but only thirteen minutes for low track students. Similar findings emerged from classroom observations, which showed less off-task behaviour in high track classes. When analyzing the enrolment patterns in the different tracks, Oakes found a disproportionately high number of minority students in the lowest tracks and a disproportionately low number in the highest tracks. She concluded: 'Students in some classes had markedly different access to knowledge and learning experiences from students in other classes' (*ibid.*: 74).

With the Oakes research we conclude our review of studies of the self-fulfilling prophecy in education. This gèneration-long progression of investigations was initiated by an interest in litigation regarding racial desegregation. It continued with a controversial research programme involving experimentally induced expectations that suggested a fairly straightforward effect of teachers' beliefs on the development of pupil intelligence. But this research had been consistent with several conceptual errors often made in relation to the SFP. These misunderstandings also relate to confoundings of the SFP and the Thomas theorem, to which we now turn.

SFP, THOMAS'S THEOREM AND MERTON'S LEMMA

Because of the juxtaposition of Thomas's theorem and the SFP in the *Antioch Review* article, Merton has frequently been called upon to distinguish between the two ideas. These clarifications are often made in private correspondence.

What are the essential differences between the Thomas theorem and the SFP? In a letter of 16 November 1975 to Norbert Wiley of the University of Illinois, Merton writes:

> The relation between the brilliant Thomas Theorem [and the SFP] is one between a generic idea—long before acknowledged but never as crisply formulated—that there is a subjective component in human action and that action in response to various subjective definitions will have 'real consequences' (i.e. in the observable external world), and the *sociological idea* of SFP which treats belief systems ('prophecies') as part of the external social world which constrain action so as to conform with those prophecies.
> ...The [Thomas] formulation had nothing to say about *the patterns of these consequences* (as self-fulfilling or self-defeating), the conditions under which one or the other occurs, or, socially patterned belief-systems rather than idiosyncratic ones. It is these three formal elements that are central to the notion of the SFP....W.I.'s Theorem...was only a step toward the sociological idea, which focusses on socially shared beliefs (or prophecies, as beliefs about future behavior, outcomes, etc.). This mode of analysis centers on shared beliefs as part of the socio-cultural environment which constrains action so as to have it come into accord with those beliefs.

We can thus see that Merton is particularly interested in distinguishing between the psychological SFP and its sociological analogue. The importance of the SFP for education rests precisely on Merton's critique (1976b: 22) of the subjective misinterpretation of the Thomas theorem and even of the self-fulfilling prophecy:

> Total subjectivism—'social problems are *only* what people think they are'—leads us astray by neglecting social, demographic, economic, technological, ecological, and

other objective constraints upon human beings. To ignore these constraints is to imply, mistakenly, that they do not significantly affect both the choices people make and the personal and social consequences of those choices. It is to pave the road to Utopianism with bad assumptions. In the pithy phrasing of sociologist Arthur Stinchcombe, which tempers the subjective emphasis of W. I. Thomas with the objective emphasis of Karl Marx, 'People define situations, but do not define them as they please'.

Sociological theory can take account of how people perceive and define situations without falling into the error of total subjectivism. An example is the concept of the self-fulfilling prophecy. According to this concept, *social definitions popular in groups and collectivities make up an important, dynamic part of the process through which anticipations help to create the anticipated social reality* [emphasis supplied]. Thus, when schoolteachers decide in advance that children from certain ethnic or economic origins are apt to be of substandard intelligence *and treat them accordingly*, they help bring about the retarded learning they anticipated. Subjective definitions of the situations therefore matter, and can matter greatly. But they do not alone matter.

To correct the imbalance that comes with total subjectivism and to restore the objective components of social situations to their indispensable place, we plainly need this counterpart to the Thomas Theorem:

And if people do *not* define *real* situations as real,
they are nevertheless real in their consequences.

Although expectations are enormously important, it is not the beliefs alone that influence real situations. Negative expectations must be tied to consistent negative actions and positive expectations must be accompanied by skilled, sensitive and understanding pedagogy if changing beliefs is expected to produce changed teaching and learning among disadvantaged youngsters.

AN EXAMPLE OF INTERVENTION: THE TESA PROGRAMME

The SFP's course of dissemination through the world of American education did not stop with court cases and global admonitions to teachers. The productive research programme initiated by the work of Brophy and Good led teacher educators to design programmes of in-service education to help new and veteran teachers develop habits of pedagogy that would overcome the naturally occurring tendency to treat low achieving children of poor economic or social backgrounds differently from their middle-class counterparts, thus further exacerbating the differences.

A good example of such a programme is the *Teacher Expectations and Student Achievement* (TESA) programme (Kerman, 1979). It grew out of a central finding in the Brophy and Good research: students perceived as high achievers were being given response opportunities three to four times more frequently than those perceived as low achievers. Kerman and his colleagues first surveyed more than 2000 teachers to discover why they believed that this differential opportunity to respond was commonplace. Teachers overwhelmingly asserted that it was educationally preferable to call on high achievers more frequently, because 'it might embarrass the low achievers' [to be called on], or 'the whole class benefits from a good response', or 'it is important to cover the curriculum content, which leaves little time for calling on those who are unprepared, slow, or confused'. No wonder then, observed Kerman, that low achievers eventually learn to tune out of classrooms, further reinforcing the teacher beliefs on those rare occasions when they are called upon and appear inept and out of touch.

The programme did not try to change teacher beliefs or attitudes as the primary vehicle for improving teaching and learning. Instead, it identified a number of forms of teaching interaction that were effective in promoting achievement in all children. In a series of five workshops, approximately one month apart, teachers are taught these forms of interaction. They also discuss in detail why these interactions are not as frequently practiced with low achieving children and why the ostensibly good reasons—reasonable and responsible though they may appear—are not well grounded. Indeed, these well-intentioned practices lead to the unanticipated and surely unintended consequence of producing precisely the outcome they were trying to avoid.

The teachers then observe one another at least four times using an observation form on which the observer records the frequency with which the target interactions are directed to each pupil in the class. The teachers are trying to practice those interactions with all the children. They receive feedback on their degree of success from their peer observer. The observation forms are left with the observed teacher; their purpose is to inform, not to evaluate. Evaluations of this programme have been quite positive—increased academic gains, decreased absenteeism and disciplinary referrals.[2] When beliefs are made conscious and explicit, and then tied to action, the SFP can be made to work in favour of low achieving students rather than to their disadvantage.

THE EDUCATIONAL SFP AS OBI

Our purpose in discussing the TESA programme has not been to evaluate it. Instead, we wished to portray it as part of a process in which educational SFP moved from courtroom to classroom, from flawed research to improved studies and on to teacher education and staff development. In this process, however, the connections to Merton's original paper have been obliterated. None of the later studies cited above—and they are reasonably representative of the hundreds that have been published—ever cites Merton or the SFP as a source for their work.

The more psychological studies, for example those of Weinstein (1976) and Allington (1980), are clearly within the Brophy and Good tradition, which was, in part, stimulated by Rosenthal and the *Pygmalion* study. For most of these, Rosenthal is the earliest reference, even when the phrase 'self-fulfilling prophecy' is employed.[3] These are classic examples of what Merton would call 'obliteration by incorporation' (OBI), in which a root idea—in this case invented by Merton in 1948 and introduced into the educational literature by Kenneth Clark in 1963—becomes so commonplace that it simply becomes part of common discourse, losing its original identity.

Other studies, such as those of Barr and Dreeben (1983) and Oakes (1985), were not conducted within the psychological tradition. Oakes, for example, appealed to a very different explanatory framework—the theory of social or cultural reproduction—which would cite Karl Marx, George Counts, Samuel Bowles and Herbert Gintis, Basil Bernstein, and Michael Young, and continue with a host of younger sociologists, economists and anthropologists who cast schools in the role of maintaining and reproducing the social inequities and economic injustices of the society at large. On this account students are sorted and treated, not on the basis of native ability or exhibited achievement, but on the basis of race and class alone. This is not to say that schooling has no effect; on the contrary, schools are important socializing agents. Because students must be socialized to join the unequal world of the workplace, schools prepare some students, typically the poor and minorities, to accept the menial jobs they will ultimately assume, while preparing others, typically the children of the wealthy, to assume positions of leadership. Do such studies count as OBIs, too, if they bear family resemblance to SFP-stimulated studies, but are likely to have been progeny of quite different parents?

To call something an OBI is to claim both obliteration and incorporation. In this body of educational scholarship we find a combination of what might be called 'true OBI' and 'illusory OBI'. The SFP entered the educational literature through the influence of Kenneth Clark on the Supreme Court's *Brown v. Board of Education* decision and Clark's subsequent writings. Quite independently, there appears to have been a parallel course taken by neo-Marxist social scientists who may not have been influenced by Mertonian thought at all. In this case, there was no SFP to obliterate, hence none to incorporate either. When the two traditions intersect and build upon one another, however, the influence of each is amplified, even as the likelihood increases that both families then forget their respective forebearers.

CONCLUSION

The concept of the self-fulfilling prophecy is clearly one of Merton's personal favourites. He has invoked it as an explanatory construct in both theoretical and autobiographical contexts. In a recent paper presenting new insights into the workings of the Matthew effect in science (Merton, 1988b), seen as an instance of cumulative advantage, he identifies the importance of 'an institutionalized bias in favor of precocity' in the reward system of scientific communities.

> The advantages that come with early accomplishment taken as a sign of things to come stand in Matthew-like contrast to the situation confronted by young scientists whose work is judged as ordinary. Such early prognostic judgments, I suggest, lead in some unknown fraction of cases to inadvertent suppression of talent through the process of the self-fulfilling prophecy. (*ibid.*: 613)

In a system of education in which students are regularly organized by age, precocity is always rewarded. Once these rewards begin to accumulate early in life, they tend to convince the precocious that they are indeed superior and are likely to depress the expectations of potential 'late bloomers' who become convinced that they are really dull.

In this regard, as Merton observed half a decade before Rosenthal's research,

> For most of us most of the time...tend to form our self image—our image of potentiality and of achievement—as a reflection of the images others make plain they have of us. And it is the images that institutional authorities have of us that in particular tend to become self-fulfilling images: if the teachers, inspecting our Iowa scores and our aptitude-test figures and comparing our record with [those] of our 'age-peers', conclude that we're run-of-the-mine and treat us accordingly, they lead us to become what they think we are. (Merton, 1962, as cited in Merton, 1988b: 614)

The disadvantage, needless to say, is more likely incurred by those in the less privileged social strata than by their counterparts in the middle and upper strata. At this point Merton connects this manifestation of the self-fulfilling prophecy to two other concepts with which it is associated:

> Such differential outcomes need not be intended by the people engaged in running our educational institutions and thereby affecting patterns of social selection. And it is such unanticipated and unintended consequences of purposive social action—in this case, rewarding primarily early signs of ability—that tend to persist. For they are *latent*, not manifest, social problems.... (*ibid.*: 615)[4]

Merton finds the SFP equally attractive as a way of explaining important developments in his own career, in this case in relation to his early and critical apprenticeship under historian of science George Sarton. He recollects:

> ...the few graduate students who then had any knowledge of Sarton's scholarly existence took him to be a remote, austere, and awesome presence, so thoroughly dedicated to his scholarship as to be quite unapproachable by the likes of us. Thus do plausible but ill-founded beliefs develop into social realities through the mechanism of the self-fulfilling prophecy. Since this forbidding scholar was bound to be unapproachable, there was plainly small point in trying to approach him. And his subsequently having little to do with graduate students only went to show how inaccessible he actually was. (1985a: 470)

Merton has long been fascinated by the ways in which social science ideas come to penetrate everyday discourse. In an age when social scientists and educational scholars are regularly called upon to justify the fruitfulness of their work, the frequency with which social science concepts become powerful explanatory devices for everyday life has increased dramatically. The self-fulfilling prophecy has surely followed that course. Moreover, its impact on American educational discussions has been striking.

Training programmes and courses in teacher education notwithstanding, the painful gap in school performance between children of different colours and social classes remains. This is not to dismiss the contributions made by research on the educational self-fulfilling prophecy. But writ large, the attempt to solve the ills of American schools by changing the expectations of teachers can be said to divert attention from basic social inequities by claiming, implicitly or explicitly, that the central, if not the entire, cause of school failure rests in the minds and practices of teachers.

The process by which schools inherit the responsibility for social inequity is not well understood. Yet one thing is certain—creating high expectations for school children costs less than building new housing or funding new jobs. The omnipotence of schooling is a compelling idea in a democracy, but sometimes popularity obscures falseness. Ironically, in the same article in which Robert Merton introduced the idea of the self-fulfilling prophecy, he expressed doubts about education's ability to solve the problems caused by it: 'The appeal to "education" as a cure-all for the most varied social problems is rooted deep in the mores of America. Yet it is nonetheless illusory for all that' (1948b: 197).

Merton's scepticism, however, is tempered by the great promise he found in recognizing that self-fulfilling prophecies are instances of a larger class. They are constructions of societies and institutions that then help bring about the consequences they most fear. But human constructions can work both ways. By understanding how we create the conditions for oppression and disadvantage, we can come to grasp the mechanisms for amelioration and change. While simple-minded prescriptions for social and educational revolution through changing teachers' beliefs may not work, the more general strategy of addressing problems of the human condition remains valid. Changed beliefs and perceptions must be combined with new commitments and actions. We must not stop with the modification of perceptions; we must address directly the real conditions that produce real inequities.

ACKNOWLEDGMENT

We thank Robert K. Merton, who opened his personal files and shared his reminiscences with the authors. He bears no responsibility for the argument of the chapter itself. Some sections of the essay appear in modified form in an earlier article by Wineburg (1988).

NOTES

1   The United States is most unusual in the extent to which curriculum (and even school buildings) is a responsibility of local school districts, whose administrators and faculty committees select, in the case of primary reading, among literally dozens of alternative textbook series. They may often have no idea what some of the implications of their choices may be. A growing movement within the US to institute a national curriculum (parallel in some ways to recent developments in the UK) responds in part to problems identified in research such as that of Barr and Dreeben.

2   Samuel Kerman is not a scholar on a university faculty. At the time of this work, he was a staff development administrator in the Los Angeles County Public Schools. Much important research in education is conducted outside university settings by practitioners engaged in school improvement activity.

3   A particularly striking example is an extensive piece in the prestigious *Psychological Review* by Jussim (1986) entitled 'The Self-Fulfilling Prophecy: A Theoretical and Integrative Review', which contains nary a whisper of Merton's name or work.

4   These Matthew-like confoundings of recognition for precocity and subsequent performance make empirical research on such matters devilishly difficult to perform. For example, those in higher education have been interested for years in the impact of special university scholarships or fellowships (e.g. the National Merit Scholarship for US undergraduates or National Science Foundation Fellowships at the graduate level) on the subsequent career paths of winners. Disentangling the likely career trajectories without these forms of recognition from the value added (to both self-image and the subsequent opportunities offered by others) because of the awards, has been perplexing.

XI. SOCIOLOGY OF SCIENCE

18. Robert K. Merton's Sociology of Science

NICO STEHR

For better or worse, our century belongs to science. It is therefore not surprising that science itself has become the key issue of scientific endeavours, in particular in those disciplines focusing on human culture and its varied manifestations. The theoretical and empirical work of Robert K. Merton, which spans more than fifty years of scholarly activity, quickly gained special significance and influence among socio-historical studies of the development and social organization of modern science. Merton's analyses of scientific activity and of the scientific community both exemplify his theoretical approach generally and are at the core of his sociological programme. Rather than providing an account of the varied interpretations and critiques of Merton's analysis of science, I shall first give a descriptive account of his sociology of science and then summarize and evaluate the most significant comments on Merton's sociology of science.[1]

In contrast to some of the approaches prevailing in the 1930s (e.g. Bernal, 1939; Hessen, 1931) as well as more recent efforts, Merton's analysis of science does not attempt to synthesize into a single comprehensive research programme all the specialized areas of scholarly activity whose common subject of enquiry is science, e.g. the philosophy of science, history of science and sociology of science. On the contrary, the aim of his theoretical perspective is to develop a *sociological* approach to science as an autonomous discipline, while acknowledging simultaneously the specific philosophical problematic of legitimizing claims to scientific knowledge. For Merton, the philosophy of science represents a distinct domain of enquiry and its problematic transcends direct sociological enquiry.

It is often assumed that in his study of science Merton's own foci of interest, unlike the object of his enquiry, remained basically unchanged. However, a comparison between his earlier and later works reveals distinct and interesting shifts of foci.[2] The claim that Merton's extensive enquiries into a multitude of sociology of science issues remained homogeneous, without inherent tensions, recognizable contrasts and distinct developments over half a century, quickly proves to be untenable. Nonetheless, Merton himself has frequently emphasized the importance of continuities and of their crucial role in his writings (see Merton, 1979c).

THE CHANGING FOCUS OF MERTON'S STUDIES

In the 1950s Merton's approach to science, particularly his socio-historical analysis of the emergence of modern science in seventeenth century England,[3] was regarded as too 'externalistic'[4] compared to the 'classic interpretation' of this development by the history of science of the time (Butterfield, 1949; Hall, 1954; Koyré, 1957; Gillispie, 1960). In the 1970s, however, he met with growing criticism from sociologists of science which labelled his more recent studies of the social organization of modern science as too 'internalistic', that is, as refraining from an account of the social construction of scientific knowledge and the impact of 'non-scientific' factors on this process. The radically changing evaluations of Merton's sociology of science not only reflect a shift in the theoretical emphasis of the analysis of science during the past fifty years, but also a change in Merton's own empirical interests and theoretical concerns.[5] Both Merton's writings in the sociology of science and their critical reception thus show that his enquiry into the social context and culture of science occurred in at least two distinct phases.[6]

In the 1930s and early 1940s Merton focused his attention on the social origins of modern science and its institutionalization in seventeenth century England. He later returned to sociology of science problems, but concentrated mainly on science as the specialized, more or less autonomous social system which has substantially affected the technical, economic and intellectual development of society over the past two centuries. During the second phase Merton's intellectual endeavours, not unlike those of his earlier critics, may be called in some sense ahistoric. The interdependence between science and contemporary society (e.g. scientization of everyday life, the influence of social and socio-cultural conditions—e.g. the military—on the organizational and cognitive structure of certain scientific disciplines) were rarely the explicit theme of his empirical and theoretical efforts. Instead the main focus shifted to problems connected with the highly specialized modern scientific system and the disciplinary traditions it sustains and develops. Merton has gradually moved away from a socio-historical analysis of the origins and institutionalization of modern science toward a sociological analysis of the established (academic) system of contemporary science. Most recently he has turned his attention to the social determinants of the long-term growth of scientific knowledge; but he no longer seems to be interested in the social conditions for the possibility of scientific knowledge (cf. Elias, 1971).

Not surprisingly, the occasion of the shift in theoretical interests leads Merton to a reformulation of his leading concept of science. These conceptual changes reflect also some of the basic intellectual developments in the discipline of sociology. While in the early 1930s sociology played a rather unimportant, precarious role even at American universities, later, especially in the 1960s, it grew tremendously. The growth of sociology furthered its structural change from an essentially open discipline to a much more autonomous, self-contained intellectual speciality increasingly capable of formulating and assessing problems on its own and for a professional audience mainly of fellow sociologists.

MERTON'S INITIAL CONCEPT OF SCIENCE

The essential feature of Merton's initial conception of science, as found in his publications in the 1930s, is the degree of *openness* with which he characterizes its social system (cf. Mulkay, 1975). To postulate a scientific community as open, even hospitable to influences from its surrounding social, cultural and economic context, can perhaps be expected as an almost natural outcome of a theoretical and empirical focus on the impact of external social factors on the social relations of science. But such a conception of science may have the unintended effect that one loses sight of the question of how a scientific community gradually attains and sustains a measure of independence from dominant societal institutions.

The relatively open scientific community Merton has in mind neither has to rely, as Merton (1939a: 3) himself emphasizes, on a 'vulgar' notion of materialism, which asserts an almost linear and one-sided relation between social and scientific developments,[7] nor does it require the kind of 'heroic' interpretation of crucial intellectual developments in science as frequently encountered in the 'classic' history of science. Merton examines (1937a, 1939a) possible influences of the evolving capitalist system in seventeenth century England on the selection of researchable problems by contemporary men of science, and he emphasizes that many of those scientists (Wren, Hooke, Newton, Boyle, Huyghens, Halley, Flamsteed) were influenced by society's needs for efficient means of communication and transportation. Merton (1938a, 1935) examines scientific research of the seventeenth century and concludes that the socio-economic problems and military needs of England at that time influenced to a considerable extent the range of problems selected by scientists. These studies indicate that scientific research is determined by previous findings, the logic of science and scientific rationale and also by societal, that is, extra-scientific factors. However, it was not Merton's intention to advocate the kind of interrelation between cognitive processes and existential factors Mannheim (1936: 267), for example, described as the 'existential determination of thought' (also Merton, 1937c: 493, 503).

During the 1930s Merton occasionally considered the possibility that extra-scientific factors may have a considerable impact on scientific knowledge itself and not merely on the choice of problems. He expressed this idea in an essay on the correlation between population density and rate of scientific-technological progress: 'In an admittedly round-about fashion, social and cultural factors converged to make possible Huyghens' abstract theory of the differential acceleration by gravity according to position on the earth' (Merton, 1937b: 169). The intended ambivalence of this early concept of science is apparent. For when Merton directly addresses the issue of an unmediated relation between social factors and scientific knowledge, as in his critical review of sociology of knowledge literature (Merton, 1937c), his position seems clear: he rejects the hypothesis that scientific knowledge can be influenced by social determinants.

On the other hand, in his essay on population density, social interaction and rate of scientific progress, his concept of science—even applied to the cognitive sphere of science and its dynamics—is somewhat less restrictive. There Merton advances a number of general theses about the social and intellectual organization of science which address issues currently under discussion in the philosophy of science and the sociology of science. He points out, for instance, that the degree of correlation between theorems and empirical facts is by no means the first and only consideration in adopting or rejecting scientific theories. Merton (1937b: 169) implies instead that only then is a scientific generalization considered acceptable 'when it fits into a theoretical structure the form of which is determined by preconceived ideas of what theory should be'.[8] Further, the rejection of the theory of light waves in the seventeenth century is attributable to the authoritative scientific reputation of Isaac Newton, who supported an alternative theory. Preferences based on cultural factors may also determine the fact of scientific theories. In short, there are two attributes which characterize scientific theories or laws: their congruence with observable empirical facts (i.e. their 'objective' content); and their 'meaning', which varies with prevailing cultural conceptions. The objective content of a theory is a necessary, but not a sufficient condition for its acceptance. At the same time Merton emphasizes the social basis of the justification of scientific discourse, i.e. even the objective attributes of scientific theories are not necessarily immune to the influence of social determinants.

Scientific knowledge is public knowledge, it has to be open to critical scrutiny and must be replicable (*nachvollziehbar*). Merton postulates or anticipates aspects of a critical philosophy of science: 'The work of the scientist is at every point influenced not only by the intrinsic requirements of the phenomena with which he is dealing, but more directly by his reacting to the inferred critical attitudes or actual criticism of other scientists and by adjustment of his behavior in accordance with these attitudes' (1937b: 170, cf. Gieryn, 1982). Later Merton develops this idea into the notion of a collective, e.g. socially organized and sanctioned, scepticism in science. In the same essay Merton anticipates another problematic of the sociological analysis of science currently the object of considerable discussion. Some observations, he argues, may seem 'meaningless' in one context and 'meaningful' in another; he refers to what today would perhaps be termed the 'indexicality' of scientific phenomena. Finally, he postulates that the frequency and intensity of internal and external scientific interaction may have a significant impact on the rate of scientific progress, and also on the cognitive structure and form of scientific discourse and knowledge.

Nonetheless, although Merton examines the influence of socially determined orientations on science—e.g. the hypothesis relating Puritan values with the rise of modern science in the seventeenth century (1936a, 1938a), one of the topics of his dissertation which later became known and widely discussed as the 'Merton thesis' (e.g. Kuhn, 1977: 115–22)—he restricts himself to certain 'external' demographic aspects of the scientific community, the legitimization of scientific endeavours and the personal motivation of scientists and their recruitment. In other words, Merton avoids making the direct (causal) connection between the 'internal' cognitive structure of scientific practice, in particular, the knowledge claims put forward by the scientists involved, other intellectual aspects of scientific work and the Calvinist value system.[9] Although Merton (1936a: 1) labels his research interests as concerned with the dynamic interdependence of cultural and civilizational phenomena (in the sense in which Alfred Weber used these terms), he does not deal directly with the immediate, reciprocal influence between scientific knowledge and cultural belief (cf. also Merton, 1936c). Thus it is highly improbable that the 'new' cognitive sociology of scientific knowledge could have emerged out of Merton's analysis of the genesis and institutionalization of modern science.

But curiously enough, those parts of Merton's dissertation which deal with the relation between the Puritan ethic and the emergence of modern science provided legitimacy for the post-war accusation that Merton advocated and used an externalist approach to science. During the post-war years and until the late 1960s the history of science was dominated by an idealistic pursuit of the reconstruction of heroic moments in the history of intellectual development in science. Against this background, studies undertaken in the 1930s, for example those dealing with the social origins of modern science (in particular the 'Merton thesis'), became the target of fierce criticism. A. Rupert Hall (1963: 11), a historian of science, claimed for instance that the 'intellectual change of the seventeenth century is one whose explanation must be sought in the history of the intellect; to this extent... the history of science is strictly analogous to the history of philosophy'. If this were the case, *any* analytic enquiry into the social conditions of the emergence of modern science and its subsequent development and transformation would prove to be a most dubious undertaking.

*MERTON'S LATER CONCEPT OF SCIENCE

Talcott Parsons often expressed the view that scientific (e.g. nomological) knowledge should be seen as a peculiarly *modern* phenomenon, whose advancement, codification, generalization and application require the institutionalization of specialized social roles and particular cultural conditions. The institutionalization of science can only be successful if there exists a legitimate interest in society in practical empirical knowledge. Such interest is consistent with a universalist orientation, with emotionally neutral value orientations leading to specific patterns of role expectations. Patterns of this kind are *rare* indeed and highly specialized. The differentiation of the role of scientists prompts, in turn, a gradual widening of a knowledge and communication gap between scientist and layman (cf. Parsons, 1951: 338–40). Eventually, scientific knowledge is produced almost exclusively by scientists for other scientists. Mechanisms of social control are generated within the boundaries of the scientific community and are maintained without reference to external norms. The gradual *professionalization* (cf. Parsons, 1939) of scientific conduct and scientific value orientations supports and further secures the increasing autonomy of the scientific community.

The analysis of the unique features of the social organization of the scientific system requires, according to Parsons (1951: 326), the identification of a set of norms defining and channeling scientific action because '...patterns of value-orientation are particularly central to the social system'. Both the autonomous *social system* of the scientific community and environing social systems have, however, one feature in common: certain functions supportive of the system have to be performed in each at the social level. Concretely, 'one lies in the problem of *order*, in the problem of the coordination of the activities of the various members in such a way that they are prevented from mutually blocking each other's actions... the second focus is on the adequacy of *motivation*. The system can only function if a sufficient proportion of its members perform the essential social roles with an adequate degree of effectiveness' (Parsons, 1948: 159; emphasis supplied; cf. also Parsons, 1970: 849).

Merton, no doubt, valued and accepted programmatic statements of this kind, yet approached other functionalist theorems and strategies of theory construction with considerable reservation, even objecting to some with vigour. He thinks highly of Parsons as one of the eminent social theorists who, in his analytic enquiries into the social organization of societal institutions, into the system of social norms and values, the role of collective factors, and the problem of primary functions of social systems (which Merton, contrary to Parsons, sees as dynamic functions; cf. also Gouldner, 1967; Isajiw, 1968; Savage, 1981: 138–45), alerted sociologists to central sociological issues. But he rejects those Parsonian theorems which proclaim the necessity of constructing general, abstract sociological theories for complex social systems, since we cannot expect 'any individual to create an architectonic system of theory which provides a complete *vade mecum* to the solution of sociological problems' (Merton, 1948a: 165). [10]

Merton's most important contribution to the debate about the role of functionalist theorizing in sociology is his essay 'Manifest and Latent Functions', an attempt to clarify, codify and 'pragmatize' a number of contentious methodological and theoretical issues, including the term 'functionalism' itself.

One of his most significant modifications to the objectives of functionalist analysis is expressed in his statements about 'structural constraints' and 'structural context'. These concepts are intended to capture the idea that the conditions for the possibilities of human behaviour are delimited and therefore constrained by specific interrelated elements of the social structure. They imply at the same time that the relevant social structure is the source of conflict, contradictions and discrepancies in social action as well the motor of social change (Merton, 1957a: 121–30; also 1975, 35–9). [11]

This shift in emphasis in Merton's concept of science is evident in a paper co-authored with Bernard Barber and published in 1963; it represents a critical discussion of their teacher Sorokin's *idealistic* sociology and macrosociological theory of science. Sorokin's (1937, Vol. 2: 455) core thesis is that a society's dominant scientific development is the direct outcome of relatively ambivalent but general 'cultural mentalities'. In their critique, Merton and Barber (1963: 343–9) point out that Sorokin's thesis is in danger of becoming merely tautological and that, given its high degree of abstraction and generality, it is incapable of explaining contradictory intellectual developments within the scientific community. Their main complaint, however, is aimed at Sorokin's failure to develop a *theory* concerned with the changing (cognitive and social) autonomy of different *societal subsystems*, which might have led him to analyze the varying dependency or historically specific autonomy of science in society.

Merton's more recent concept of science emphasizes the social autonomy of the scientific community, the degree to which the growth of scientific knowledge is self-sustained and the functional operation of the social structure of science. During the post-war years his empirical and theoretical focus is almost exclusively concerned with the *modern* differentiated social system of science, which relates to society in an entirely different manner from the emerging scientific community of seventeenth century England.

Merton's analysis of modern science, centred mainly at universities and non-academic research institutions, concentrates on an exemplary theoretical and empirical enquiry into the social organization of the scientific community, a fact which even many of his recent critics freely acknowledge (e.g. Barnes and Edge, 1982: 15–20). Merton enquires into the institutionalized processes of the scientific community which warrant or further the realization of its goals of producing and validating expanding knowledge claims, examining the nature, unique features and contribution of its system of communication, motivation, competition and rewards toward the goals of science. It is thus the *sociological analysis of the public and structured evaluation of claims to have generated valid scientific knowledge* which is at the core of Merton's most recent research efforts in the sociology of science. He has discerned and analyzed a range of relevant, interdependent collective processes and has described in detail how they operate within this system designed to assess knowledge claims. The allocation of scientific reputation, insiders and outsiders, social stratification and social control within science, multiple discoveries, priority disputes, deviant behaviour and the system-induced ambivalence of the scientist are some of these socially patterned phenomena. To put it briefly, the question central to Merton's recent approach to science is also the key question of his sociological theory generally: how can specific aspects of the social structure induce and limit patterns of social action? Stating the central issue in this manner implies, of course, that in his recent approach to the sociological analysis of science Merton is not striving for any immediate sociological analysis of the genesis, construction and legitimation of the substance of scientific knowledge claims. On the other hand, he does not disregard the sociological analysis of cognitive aspects of science altogether, but it is not his focus of theoretical and empirical attention.

The fact that Merton's recent observations on intellectual problems of scientific development have mainly focused on the social sciences and are primarily centred on the context of discovery (see Merton, 1959c, 1959b) forces the conclusion that these empirical observations and theoretical efforts are not designed to advance arguments favouring a sociological analysis of the validity of scientific knowledge claims. [12]

The critical challenges from different disciplines to Merton's recent concept of science and his analysis of the social organization of the scientific community are based on a variety of assumptions and issues (cf. Mulkay, 1969; Barnes and Dolby, 1970; Whitley, 1972; Martins, 1972; Sklair, 1972; Mitroff, 1974; Weingart, 1974). [13] The core of the critique may be reduced to a more or less common objection. It identifies and objects to the affinity between Merton's rationalist sociology of science and the explicit support for a history of science which describes it also as the accumulation of knowledge. This critique of Merton's concept of science, aspects of which appear in the meantime to have become rigid and orthodox themselves, emphasizes in contrast the historically contingent features of the development of scientific knowledge and the possibility—as well as the need—for a sociological perspective on the construction and collective assessment of scientific knowledge claims. While a sociological approach to the question of the validation of scientific knowledge claims may well be compatible with Merton's sociological analysis of the *social structure* of scientific evaluation systems, his theoretical framework for his programme, generally speaking, may also prevent the sociological analysis of scientific culture from degenerating into a programme of mere *idealistic conceptions* which deals exclusively with cognitive processes. In fact, the importance of society for science and science for society, Merton's early theme, is now a widely neglected topic, at least within science studies.

The sociological critique of Merton's recent analysis of science is not so much the independent outcome of intellectual developments within sociology as an example of the success which Thomas Kuhn's *Structure of Scientific Revolutions* (1962) and related theories of science (Toulmin, Lakatos, Feyerabend) have enjoyed in the sociological community. Merton's critics interpret Kuhn's historiography of science as signalling a distinct deficit in Merton's analysis of science, namely Merton's lack of interest in a sociology of scientific knowledge and his denial of the need to analyze either the cognitive processes in science or the interdependence of cognitive and socio-structural processes. Yet in Kuhn's critique of the dominant internalist approach in the history of science, he referred mainly to the neglect of *external* factors. Kuhn's and Merton's conceptions, which emphasize the role of the social structure of science, have been seen by some at least as compatible notions (cf. Cole and Cole, 1973: 3; Kuhn, 1974: 460–1; Merton and Gaston, 1977: 107; Kuhn, 1977: xxi; Pinch, 1982). It would seem that the intellectual distances between Kuhn's historiographic approach and Merton's sociological analysis are not insurmountable, and this despite efforts to construe them as contradictory projects (e.g. Barnes, 1972, 1974, 1981; Bloor, 1976, 1981; Collins and Cox, 1976; Barnes and Edge, 1982).

CONCLUSION

It is one of the peculiarities of social science debates that they rarely produce a clear 'winner'. Social science controversies are per se unresolvable, although a theory is allowed to dominate for a time—a commonplace situation in science. The likely result will be that different generations of social scientists and historians of ideas and science will encounter Merton's different emphases and conceptions of science and its social and intellectual organization retroactively and will variously interpret or deny their relevance as forerunners and exemplars of their own work.

NOTES

1   I have made use of observations on Robert K. Merton's sociology of science found in Stehr (1985). The essay has benefitted from a critical reading by Volker Meja and Thomas F. Gieryn.
2   My discussion makes use of those publications whose contents, as far as I have been able to determine, were clearly Merton's primary responsibility; excluded are publications in the 1930s written at Harvard in close cooperation with Pitirim A. Sorokin (see in particular Sorokin and Merton, 1935, 1937b).
3   [*Ed. note*: for an account of the relevant history of Merton's Harvard doctoral dissertation see Chapter 20 by I. B. Cohen in this volume.]
4   Regarding this claim, the British medical historian Roy Porter (1982: 13) points to the intellectual kinship between Merton's works of the 1930s and the works by Boris Hessen and J. D. Bernal, two Marxist historians and sociologists of science, on the origin of scientific work and thought patterns and the development of certain outstanding scientific findings. On the other hand, Porter also refers to the classic interpretation of the scientific revolution where the formulation of hypotheses and goals is much more restrictive and emphasis is on the autonomy and special status of science. For an account of the internalist/externalist controversy cf. Barnes, 1974; Johnston, 1976; and Macleod, 1977.
5   In contrast, Norman W. Storer (1973) describes Merton's enquiry into science as a series of studies which complement each other, evolving in a continuous natural sequence spanning a period of nearly fifty years. Storer (1973: xvi) claims that Merton's analysis of Calvinism already anticipates the theses of his later work on the ethos and social organization of science (see also Storer, 1968: 203). Although in a general sense both of these studies deal with the question of values in and of

science, the common denominator is more a formal rather than substantive similarity over time. But some of Merton's critics seem to share Storer's view; his war-time essay on the ethos of science (Merton, 1942), for instance, is seen as a programmatic for the foundation of a functionalist sociology of science (e.g. Weingart, 1972: 29). This implies that there has been virtually no further development in Merton's research, that it is cast in one mould, showing a high degree of continuity.

6 The intellectual differentiation noted in Merton's work should not be misunderstood, however. It is by no means implied that Merton focused exclusively on early modern, seventeenth century science at one time and on sociological problems of modern, large-scale science at another. This is not the case. Merton (1957b, 1969) comments, for instance, on historical materials in his analysis of priority disputes in science, and deals with aspects of contemporary science in his essay on the ethos of science (1942). In fact, one might want to argue that Merton's work on the social norms of the scientific community constitutes a linkage between his early and later work in the sociology of science. The discussion of the ethos of science is, on the one hand, concerned with the social prerequisites for the possibility of (cognitive) scientific work, while the same essay deals, on the other hand, with issues which foretell Merton's later work on the social organization of the scientific community.

7 In this context Merton (1939a: 6) emphasized at the time that he would not classify the work of Marx/Engels or the investigations of the Russian physicist Boris Hessen (1931) as examples of the vulgar materialism he rejects. For a more detailed evaluation of Hessen's work by Merton in the 1930s, see Merton, 1938a: 501–2, 544–6; Merton's own early studies of science are, as he remarks, 'heavily indebted to Hessen's work' (*ibid.*: 565).

8 Merton refers to Erwin Schrödinger (1935) for elucidation and confirmation of his thesis, and in particular to his reflections on the symmetry between culture and science first published in 1932 in an essay entitled 'Ist die Naturwissenschaft milieubedingt?' Schrödinger examines whether there are certain socio-cultural structures without which even science cannot function properly, and which are then reflected in the structure of scientific discourse and scientific knowledge. Schrödinger refers, for instance, to objectivity, relativity and similar principles.

9 In his first enquiry into these issues Merton (1936a: 1) carefully and cautiously states the problem in the following manner: 'It is the thesis of this study that the Puritan ethic, as an ideal-typical expression of the value-attitudes basic to ascetic Protestantism generally, so canalized the interests of seventeenth-century Englishmen as to constitute one important *element* in the enhanced cultivation of science'. In a response to a critique of his work on the Protestant ethic by Becker (1984) Merton described the working hypothesis of his dissertation (or of the 'Merton thesis', as it became known), given the Weberian mandate (Merton, 1973: 181), as holding that: 'at a time in Western society when science had not become elaborately institutionalized, it obtained substantial legitimacy as an unintended consequence of the religious ethic and praxis of ascetic Protestantism' (1984b: 1093).

10 Later Merton (e.g. 1975) supported a pluralistic theoretical programme for sociology even more explicitly. While Parsons (1948: 157) stated categorically, 'the time when the most important fact about theory in our field was its division into warring schools or the personal systems of individuals is, if not already completely passed, in my opinion passing', Merton's (1948a: 165–6) disagreement is already evident. Thus, his consent for a time in the immediate post-war era is not without implicit and explicit criticism of Parsons's theoretical and methodological programme. In particular, it is the high degree of abstraction and generality of sociological theories which Merton holds responsible for sociology's persistent theoretical controversies and frequent apparently unresolvable disputes, since general theories rarely allow for cognitive consensus; as a matter of fact, they make such agreement practically impossible.

11 As far as the intellectual ancestry of these ideas is concerned, Merton (1957a: 53) points to Goldenweiser's (1918) 'principle of limited possibilities' for a blueprint of these notions; Merton refers to the Goldenweiser principle for the first time in an essay dealing with Durkheim's theory of the division of labour (Merton, 1934b).

12 Merton's distinction between plausible truths and plausible untruths—a dilemma faced not only by social scientists—may serve as an example of his concern with cognitive issues. Although he readily admits that the distinction between the two notions is difficult, he suggests that the differentiation can be sustained and that it is constitutive of scientific discourse. Social scientists are faced with the problem of either having to affirm plausible truths, i.e. statements which are already considered true in everyday life, or of identifying plausible untruths, i.e. beliefs accepted as truths in everyday life. In the first case the social scientist is merely confirming what is well-known and consequently is

in danger of undermining his own reputation; in the second case he is in danger of losing this legitimacy entirely.

13   The literature cited, which initiated and largely dominated the critical discussion of Merton's programme within science studies, deals to a large measure with Merton's theory and his elaboration of the norms of scientific conduct, namely universalism, communism, altruism and organized scepticism (Merton, 1942; also Stehr, 1978).

19. Animadversiones in Mertonem*

PIERRE BOURDIEU

This somewhat pompous title is meant to denote, *cum grano salis*, that I wish to take advantage of the famous example of Leibniz's *Animadversiones* on the work of Descartes in order to give to the critical homage I want to pay to one of the greatest contemporary sociologists and historians of science the form—at first sight loose and informal—of a series of fragmentary notes on 'Three Fragments from a Sociologist's Notebooks' (Merton, 1987).

> In the cognitive domain as in others, there is competition among groups or collectivities to capture what Heidegger called the 'public interpretation of reality'. With varying degrees of intent, groups in conflict want to make their interpretation the prevailing one of how things were and are and will be. (Merton, 1973: 110–11)

I would readily adopt this proposition, which Robert Merton put forward for the first time in *The Sociology of Science* (1973), as my own. I have often stated that if there is a truth, it is that truth is the stake of struggles (*enjeu de luttes*). This proposition is particularly valid in the case of those relatively autonomous social universes which I call cultural 'fields', in which professionals of symbolic production engage in struggles where what is at stake is the imposition of legitimate principles of vision and division of the natural world and the social world. It follows that one of the central tasks of a science of science consists in establishing what the scientific field has in common with other fields—the religious field, the philosophical field, the artistic field, etc.—and in what ways it is different, even unique.

One of the great merits of Robert Merton is to have established that the world of science must be analyzed sociologically, and this through and through. Which is to say that the proponents of the so-called 'strong programme' in the sociology of science were 'crashing through an open door', as we say in French, when they

---

* Translated from the French by Jon Clark.

declared amid great hullabaloo that 'all knowledge, whether it be in the empirical sciences or even in mathematics, should be treated through and through as material for investigation' (Bloor, 1976: 1). Did not Merton say as early as 1945 that the Copernican revolution consists in the hypothesis that not only errors, illusions and unfounded beliefs, but also the very discovery of truth, are conditioned by society and by history (Merton, 1945a)?

In contrast to his 'radical' critics, Merton has established furthermore that science must be examined in its two-fold relation, on the one hand to the social cosmos in which it is embedded—the *external reading*—and on the other to the social microcosm constituted by the scientific universe, a relatively autonomous world endowed with its own rules of functioning which must be described and analyzed in themselves—the *internal reading*. On this point the proponents of the 'strong programme' represent in reality a regression. In accordance with a logic which can be observed in all sciences of cultural works, i.e. in matters of history, of law, of art, of literature and of philosophy, they break with the internal (or 'tautegorical', as Cassirer called it) reading which all these learned universes claim to impose only to fall headlong into the most brutally reductionist pitfalls of the external (or allegorical) reading by *directly* relating cultural products to the most general economic and social conditions (this is what I call the 'short-circuit effect') and by overlooking the specific—and truly social—logic of the world of professional symbolic production and of professional producers, artists, writers, philosophers and scholars.

But if Merton takes note of the existence of the world of scientific production, he continues to apply to it analytical categories which are imposed on him by this very world itself, so that what he presents as a description of its positive laws of functioning is often little more than a record of the normative rules which are officially professed by its members. He therefore departs only in appearance from the 'internal' reading which, in the history of art and the history of philosophy as in the history of science, goes hand in hand with a hagiographic vision of those who produce art, philosophy or science. More precisely he omits to raise the question of the relation between, on the one hand, the ideal values proclaimed by the 'scientific community' (another indigenous mythology), such as objectivity, originality and utility, and the norms which it professes, universalism, intellectual communism, disinterestedness and scepticism, and, on the other hand, the social structure of the scientific universe, the mechanisms which tend to ensure 'control' and communication, evaluation and reward, recruitment and training. Yet it is in this very relation that the foundation of the specificity of the scientific field resides. It is in this relation that we find the basis of the dual truth which defines its specificity and equally eludes both the idealized and naively irenic vision of the 'Mertonian programme' and the reductionist and naively cynical vision of the proponents of the 'strong programme'. We are confronted here with one among many cases of the 'forced choice between alternatives' (*alternative obligée*) which can be observed in the most diverse areas of analysis of the social world. The naivety of the first order, which consists in accepting at face value the representation which symbolic powers (the State, Law, Art, Science, etc.) give of themselves, in a way calls forth a naivety of the second order, that of the 'half-wise', as Pascal called them, who are not prepared to believe what they are told. The pleasure in feeling clever, demystified and demystifier, in playing the disenchanted disenchanter, lies at the root of many scientific errors: if only because, among other reasons, it inclines us to forget that the illusion denounced is part and parcel of reality and that it must be included in the model which is designed to explain it, although initially the model can only be constructed against it.

If, obeying the principle of reflexivity that they themselves invoke (Bloor, 1976: 8), the proponents of the 'strong programme' took the trouble to turn the gaze of the sociology of science upon their own practice, they would immediately recognize in the falsely revolutionary 'breaks' that they effect the most common form of strategy of subversion through which new entrants seek to assert themselves against their predecessors and which, because they are well suited to seduce the lovers of novelty, constitute a good means of realizing at little cost an initial accumulation of symbolic capital. The grandiose and arrogant tone of self-validating declarations, which are more suggestive of the literary manifesto or political programme than of the scientific project, is typical of strategies through which in certain fields the most ambitious—or pretentious—pretenders assert their will to 'break', a will which, by casting discredit on established authorities, aims to bring about a transfer of their symbolic capital to the benefit of the prophets of radical renewal. The ultra-radicalism of a sacrilegious denunciation of the sacred character of science, which tends to cast discredit on all attempts to establish—even sociologically—the universal validity of scientific reason, naturally leads to a sort of nihilistic subjectivism. Thus the cause of radicalization which inspires Steve Woolgar and Bruno Latour drives them to push to the limit or, better, to extremes, the kinds of analysis, such as the ones I proposed more than ten years ago, which endeavour to transcend the (false) antinomy of relativism and absolutism (see Woolgar and Latour, 1977; Latour, 1987; Bourdieu, 1975). To call attention to the social dimension of scientific strategies is not to reduce scientific demonstrations to mere rhetorical exhibitions; to highlight the role of symbolic capital both as weapon and stake of scientific struggles is not to make the pursuit of symbolic profit into the exclusive goal or *raison d'être* of scientific conduct; to uncover the agonistic logic of the functioning of the scientific field is not to ignore the fact that competition does not exclude complementarity and that from competition itself can arise, under certain conditions, the 'controls' and 'cognitive interests' which the naive vision records without posing the question of the social conditions of their possibility and genesis.

If the scientific analysis of the functioning of the scientific field is so difficult to elaborate or so easy to caricature by means of a reduction to one or other of the opposing stances which it must transcend (irenicism and cynicism, absolutism and relativism, internalism and reductionism, etc.), it is because it presupposes a *double break* with social representations which, after all, are almost equally expected and thus equally rewarded socially: a break with the ideal representation which scientists and scholars have and give of themselves; and a break with the naively critical representation which, reducing professional ethics to a 'professional ideology' by a simple inversion of the enchanted vision, forgets that the *libido sciendi* is also a *libido scientifica*, i.e. a libido produced by the scientific field and regulated by immanent laws which rule its functioning and which have little in common with the ideal norms advanced by scientists and scholars and recorded by hagiographic sociology, without being for all that reducible to the laws which regulate practices in other fields (such as the political field or the economic field, for example).[1]

The idea that scientific activity is a social activity and that the construction of science is also a social construction of reality is not much of a stupendous discovery and it only has meaning to the extent that it is *specified*. Indeed, it is necessary to remember that the scientific field is both a social universe *like the others*, in which, as elsewhere, questions of power, of capital, of balance of forces, of struggles to maintain or transform the balance of forces, of strategies of preservation or subversion, of interests, etc., are at issue, and a *world apart*, endowed with its own laws of functioning which mean that every single one of the characteristics designated by the concepts used to describe it takes on a specific form which is irreducible to any other.

Scientific activity emerges out of the relation between the regulated dispositions of a scientific *habitus* (which is the product of the incorporation of the immanent structural logic of the scientific field) and the structural constraints exercised by this field at a given moment in time. This means that epistemological constraints, those which are uncovered *ex post* by methodological treatises, operate through social constraints. The *libido sciendi*, like any passion, can be at the basis of all kinds of actions that violate the ideal norms uncovered by Merton, whether in the case of the most ruthless struggles for the ownership of discoveries (so judiciously analyzed by Merton himself[2]), or in practices of plagiarism, more or less well concealed, or in strategies of bluff and of symbolic imposition of which we have met some examples above. But the same *libido sciendi* can also be at the basis of all the scientific virtues when, in accordance with the Machiavellian model, the positive laws of the Scientific City are such that the citizens of science have an interest in virtue; or better still, when the 'reward system distinctive of the social institution of science' (Merton, 1973: 371–82) or the laws that determine the material and symbolic prizes attached to scientific activities and scientific works are such that they impose in practice—beyond any normative injunction and, more often than not, through the dispositions of the scientific *habitus* which are progressively adjusted to the requirements of these laws—the cognitive norms to which researchers must willy-nilly submit in establishing the validity of their statements. In a scientific field which has attained a high degree of autonomy (which is not the case today of the field of sociology), the drives of the scientific *libido dominandi* can only be satisfied on condition that they submit themselves to the specific censorship of the field which requires them to take the paths of scientific reason and of argumentative dialogue such as the field defines them, that is to say, that they sublimate themselves in a *libido sciendi* which can triumph over its adversaries only by conforming to the rules of the game, opposing theorem to theorem, refutation to demonstration, scientific fact to another scientific fact. Such is the principle of the alchemy which transmutes the appetite for recognition (*appétit de reconnaissance*) into an interest in knowledge (*intérêt de connaissance*).

TRANSLATOR'S NOTE

I would like to thank Pierre Bourdieu, Loïc J. D. Wacquant (Chicago) and Bill Brooks (Southampton) for helpful comments and suggestions on earlier drafts of the translation.

NOTES

1   The 'radical' vision and the 'ideal' vision form an 'epistemological couple' (Bachelard) whose elements are opposed to each other in the reality of social existence in the form of the social division between an optimistic vision and a pessimistic vision (symbolized by the name of La Rochefoucault). It follows that the advocates of the first position tend, often without even realizing it, to reduce the scientific vision to a 'radical' vision and that 'radicalization' in the manner of Woolgar and Latour, which conceals, behind the appearance of a radical advance, a regression to one of the common-sense positions with which science must break, provides ammunition to strategies of amalgamation and contamination (on this see, for example, Isambert, 1985).

2   I had elected to focus on a recurrent phenomenon in science over the centuries, though one which had been ignored for systematic study: priority-conflicts among scientists, including the greatest among them, who wanted to reap the glory of having been first to make a particular scientific discovery or scholarly contribution. This was paradoxically coupled with strong denials, by themselves and by disciples, of their ever having had such an 'unworthy and puerile' motive for doing science. (Merton, 1987: 21)

This summary of Merton's famous article on multiple discoveries (cf. Merton, 1973: 371–82) expresses the whole *paradox* of the scientific field as a field which simultaneously produces the struggle of interests and the norm which imposes the denial of interests.

Interchange

STEHR REPLIES TO BOURDIEU

[*Ed. note*: Stehr felt there was no need to write a 'reply' to Bourdieu's self-contained contribution.]

BOURDIEU REPLIES TO STEHR

I have read the article by Nico Stehr with great interest. I have little or nothing to add to it by way of commentary. I find it both clear and informative. It reinforces my own conviction that the 'paradigm' opposed to that of Merton is present in his work, but in the background, and in a comparatively unsystematic form. This is something which often happens in the history of thought.

XII. THE 'MERTON THESIS': PURITANISM AND SCIENCE

20. Some Documentary Reflections on the Dissemination and Reception of the 'Merton Thesis'

I. BERNARD COHEN

THE 'MERTON THESIS': PURITANISM AND SCIENCE IN SEVENTEENTH CENTURY ENGLAND [1]

In a celebrated essay of 1961 Robert K. Merton discussed the question of 'Singletons and Multiples in Scientific Discovery' (1961b). I had the good fortune to be present when Merton first presented this paper in 1961 during a celebration of the quatercentenary of the birth of Francis Bacon. As I listened to Merton's impressive array of multiple discoveries in science and his analysis of their significance, my mind leapt backward to a major event in my life—to a time a fourth of a century earlier, in 1936, rather than the four centuries of our Baconian celebration—to the time of my first encounter with the history of science as an academic subject. [2] In the spring of 1936, while a junior in Harvard College, I enrolled in George Sarton's course on the development of the sciences from Newton to the near-present. In the next academic year, 1936–37, my final year as an undergraduate, I became one of three registered (or 'credit') students in Sarton's graduate seminar in the history of science, then being taught for the second time. In the autumn of that same year (1936) I decided to shift my academic allegiance from mathematics to the history of science and to pursue a programme of graduate study leading to the newly established degree of PhD in the History of Science and Learning. [3] So it may be understood why in 1936—twenty-five years before the Bacon celebrations in Philadelphia—Merton was an impressive figure on my intellectual horizon; he was the only person within my ken who had completed a PhD with a thesis in or relating to the history of science. I was introduced to him when he came to Sarton's office one day, presumably to discuss some aspect of the publication of *Science,*

307

Technology and Society in Seventeenth Century England (Merton, 1938a). As was his custom, Sarton had very generously assigned me a desk in his outer office,[4] to facilitate my research in preparation for the term paper for his seminar. It was the very same desk to which Merton had been assigned while he was undertaking the study and research for his doctoral dissertation.

As I listened to Merton's paper in 1961, there were many reasons why my mind leapt back through twenty-five years to the time of my formal introduction to the history of science. First and foremost among these, I believe, was the occasion—the first time that I ever heard Merton lecture on his own research.[5] There flashed into my mind the circumstances of that first meeting with Merton, soon after I had decided to become a historian of science. The subject of his lecture, furthermore, triggered a series of free associations, and I quickly recalled the circumstances of that year 1936, when I had first encountered Merton. I have mentioned that I was then working on my first research paper in the history of science, the assignment for Sarton's seminar. As I relived those bygone days in my imagination, I was suddenly startled by the recollection that the subject I had chosen for my seminar paper twenty-five years earlier had been multiple independent scientific discoveries, the very same subject that Merton was exploring for us in celebration of Francis Bacon.[6] That the two of us should have independently explored this same topic is yet another instance of the 'self-exemplifying multiple' that Merton has discussed.

Merton's presentation was of interest to me for yet another personal reason. When I taught my own graduate seminars, I always introduced the historical insight concerning the special role of Puritanism in the rise of science in England as an illustration of independent multiple discovery by three different scholars: Dorothy Stimson, Robert Merton and Richard F. Jones. This gave me the opportunity to show that independent discovery occurs in the history of science as well as in science itself. In the 1930s these three investigators were in geographically separate parts of the country, working in widely different academic specialities, coming to more or less the same conclusion by wholly different routes.

Merton has recorded that he began research for his dissertation in Harvard's Department of Sociology in 1933 (1970a: vii). He completed a first long statement on Puritanism and science in the early part of 1934; in revised form this became his article on 'Puritanism, Pietism and Science' (Merton, 1936a). He fulfilled all the requirements for the doctoral degree (including the dissertation and examinations) two years later, to be awarded the PhD at the mid-year commencement in early 1936. A revised and rewritten version of the dissertation, with a new title, was published in *Osiris* in 1938.[7] In 1934, a year after Merton had begun his research, Dorothy Stimson (a historian and a long-time Dean of Goucher College in Baltimore, Maryland[8]) read a paper at the December meeting of the History of Science Society in Washington, DC, on 'Puritanism and the New Philosophy in 17th Century England'. A revised version was published in May 1935, at a time when Merton's thesis had already been all but completed, one year after Merton's own essay on this subject had been subjected to a scorching criticism by his major professor, Pitirim Sorokin (see below). In her published article, Stimson proposed 'the theory that Puritanism was an important factor, hitherto little regarded, in making conditions in England favorable to the new philosophy heralded by Bacon and in promoting the type of thinking that helped to arouse interest in science and to create a ready reception for the work of the geniuses produced in that century' (Stimson, 1935b: 321–2). In Chapter 4 of *STS*,[9] Merton mentioned that 'since the completion of this study' the Stimson article (and books by Olive Griffiths and R. F. Jones) 'have appeared' and 'will be considered in a later chapter'. He does so, as we shall see below, near the beginning of Chapter 6, on 'Puritanism, Pietism and Science', in a discussion of 'Puritan Elements in the Royal Society'.

In *STS* Merton buttressed his own independent conclusion 'that the originative spirits of the Society were markedly influenced by Puritan conceptions' by referring to the work of 'Dean Dorothy Stimson'. 'In a recently published paper', he wrote, Dean Stimson 'has independently arrived at the same conclusion' (Merton, 1970a: 114). Dean Stimson did more than hazard an opinion upon her subjective historical intuition. She actually made a start at counting heads to provide numerical evidence for her assertion. Even though she gave no tables of data, the very fact that she did give some numerical information is remarkable. She records that there were 119 Fellows of the Royal Society on the original list. Of these she writes:

> With the facilities at my disposal I can find no information whatever about thirty-two of these 119. Of nineteen more I cannot tell where their political sympathies lay before 1660 nor what their training was, though several of these men were in 1645 but boys of eight and ten, too young for the important decisions of those days. Forty-two of the remainder are Puritan in their training or parliamentary in their affiliation or both, even though they later accepted the Book of Common Prayer along with the Restoration and were conforming to the Church of England. Only twenty-six were definitely royalist before 1660. If the thirty-two unknown names are subtracted from the total of 119, then almost half, or forty-two, of the remaining eighty-seven had had Puritan experience in greater or less degree. Surely this is evidence showing at least a strong Puritan tinge in the Society which led the scientific work of that age. (1935b: 329–30)

By comparison with Merton's later heroic quantitative assault this may seem to be a very modest effort. Yet in those days very few historians of science introduced numerical considerations of any sort.

At this same time Richard F. Jones, a professor of English literature at Washington University in St Louis, came to a somewhat similar point of view during his investigations of the influence of Francis Bacon, notably on education in seventeenth century England. In his dissertation Merton had made use of two of Jones's earlier papers: on 'Science and Prose Style in the Third Quarter of the Seventeenth Century' and on 'Science and Language in England of the Mid-Seventeenth Century' (see Merton, 1970a: 19n30, 20n34). But Jones's great work, *Ancients and Moderns*, in which he argued explicitly for a confluence of Puritanism and Baconian useful science,[10] did not appear in print until 1936. Published too late to be used by Merton in his dissertation, *Ancients and Moderns* appeared early enough to become embalmed in a long Mertonian footnote in *STS*. In that note Merton recorded Jones's suggestion that 'after the restoration, ardent royalists impugned science, and particularly the Royal Society, because of the close connection between these, Baconianism and Puritanism'. Merton shrewdly observed that this very fact 'suggests that contemporaries recognized the strong Puritan espousal of the new experimental science, as indeed they did' (1970a: 85n5). Merton also summarized Jones's work in general as supporting his own conclusions. Professor Richard Foster Jones, he wrote, 'adds further evidence':

> His extensive survey of seventeenth century writings on the contemporary natural philosophy reveals clearly the affinity between Puritanism, Baconianism and the new science. Moreover, as Professor Jones demonstrates, this relationship was widely recognized at the time. Many worthies of that day took the occasion to comment upon

the close connection between the reformers of religion and of science. In fact, one of Stubbe's devices for discrediting the Royal Society was to point out its strongly Puritan cast! As Professor Jones has suggested: 'The part which the Puritans played in furthering the values of science has so faded from view that it is hard to realize how conscious of the fact the Restoration was'. (*ibid.*: 114)

A little chronology will be helpful at this point. Dean Stimson read her paper in December 1934 and published it in May 1935. We shall see below that she and Merton were engaged in epistolary exchanges of information by 1934, and that she told him she had written paragraphs in 1933 (as a conclusion to an article on Comenius) suggesting a link between Puritanism and the new science. Jones's book appeared in January 1936. Hence, Merton does not refer to it in the dissertation. Merton's first essay on 'Puritanism, Pietism and Science' was written in the first months of 1934 and was published in the *Sociological Review* in January 1936 (1936a). He submitted his dissertation in December 1935. Merton's first publication of his findings, 'Puritanism, Pietism and Science', thus postdates the publication of the article by Stimson and appeared in the same month as the book by R. F. Jones.

This congruence of ideas of three independent scholars would have had a special appeal to the mature Merton in 1961, when he was devoting a major research paper to multiple discoveries as a feature of science. But in 1938 Merton merely stated the fact without any illuminating comment—and in the driest academese. 'Since the completion of this study', Merton wrote, there 'have appeared several papers and books ... which trace, with varying degrees of detail, a positive connection between Puritanism and science'.

When, during a recent rereading of Merton's *STS*, I came upon this statement, appropriately relegated to a footnote, I was at once struck by the fact that Merton cited three other authors, not merely the familiar two: Dean Dorothy Stimson and R. F. Jones. Since, like other members of the profession, I had often referred to Merton, Stimson and Jones as an example of multiple independent discovery—along with such famous examples from the sciences as the doctrine of conservation of energy and the principle of natural selection—it may be imagined how astonished I was to find Merton, in the footnote quoted above, referring not merely to Stimson and Jones, but to Stimson, Jones and Olive Griffiths. I freely confess to my ignorance. Who was Olive Griffiths? A later footnote of Merton's (1970a: 99n49) identified her as the author of an 'excellent monograph' on Presbyterian thought prior to the 'foundation of the Unitarian movement', a work related to Merton's study of the religious background of the seventeenth century in England, but not really a primary work for me or for most historians of science.

R. F. Jones became a celebrated figure in the scholarly world—in English literature, not the history of science. His *Ancients and Moderns* was considerably revised and reprinted and has enjoyed a considerable life in print as a paperback. His career as a scholar was celebrated by a remarkable Festschrift (Jones, 1951), containing a very moving evocation of his life and accomplishments written by Marjorie Hope Nicolson. But Jones did not go on to produce any further major works relating directly to the development of the sciences. Dorothy Stimson achieved some prominence as a president of the History of Science Society and author of a history of the Royal Society. In scholarly gatherings and in private discussions she would almost at once tell young scholars how she had been one of three independent researchers who had simultaneously produced the theme of

Puritanism in relation to the rise of science. From her tone it would be at once evident that she wanted to be assured of her priority and given credit for what had become known as the 'Merton thesis'. This was, furthermore, not the only occasion on which she had had to assert her claim to share in a historical discovery. She would tell us also how she had found, studied and edited the full text of 'The Ballad of Gresham College' and had proved it to be a major part of the early history of the Royal Society. She was proud to have been the first person to publish the complete text (see Stimson, 1948: 56–63).[11] From her remarks and her tone of voice it was obvious that she continued to be disturbed and quite justifiably offended after F. Sherwood Taylor later published the text of this ballad (based on quite different manuscripts) as an independent discovery (Sherwood Taylor, 1947) without any reference to her prior publication, which had appeared in *Isis*, the foremost journal of the history of science.

A curious aspect of this multiple discovery of the role of Puritanism in the development of modern science appears in Merton's 'Preface' written in 1970 for the reprint of *STS* (Merton, 1970a). Here he introduced the issue of the multiple independent discovery in what must seem to be an odd fashion. Writing almost a decade after his celebrated Philadelphia paper on singletons and multiples, Merton now mentioned this episode without any discussion of (or even reference to) his own very significant work on the general aspects of multiple independent discoveries and priorities. Furthermore, he declared: 'some time ago, Dorothy Stimson, Raymond Stearns, and the author of this monograph arrived at much the same results ... in finding a distinct Puritan cast among English scientists in the latter part of the seventeenth century'. The old quattuorvirate of Stimson, Jones, Griffiths and Merton of the original text of *STS* has given way to a new triumvirate of Stimson, Stearns and Merton. Merton's only comment in 1970 on this multiplicity in discovery (several authors arriving at 'much the same results' in 'social arithmetic') was that 'one might hope [this] would be the case with independent computations of substantially the same data'. A careful reading of Merton's brief statement in 1970 indicates that he was here referring solely to 'independent computations' with 'substantially the same data'. He was not at all introducing the name of Stearns as a possible co-discoverer (along with Merton, Stimson and Jones) of the Puritanism-science thesis, but rather as one who had confirmed Merton's numerical results by a wholly independent analysis.

Ray Stearns was a first-rate scholar and a personal friend of long standing.[12] I had thought I was familiar with his whole *oeuvre*, but I never encountered any publication of his in which he displayed such a quantitative Mertonian study. Merton's text did not give a direct reference to Stearns's study in question, but Merton's 'Selected Bibliography 1970' (written for the new printing of *STS*) lists two of Stearns's publications. In one of these, published in 1960, I found the statement:

> A large problem is the relation between English Puritanism and the new science. Robert K. Merton, Dorothy Stimson, and others have pointed out that there was something about Puritanism that was remarkably receptive to natural philosophy. Fulmer Mood and I some years ago made a survey of the 115 original Fellows of the Royal Society of London and found that nearly 80 per cent of them were of Puritan origins. (Stearns, 1960: 70)

Stearns does not indicate what year he had in mind in the phrase 'some years ago'. Perhaps in the course of his research into the early years of the Royal Society he had decided to make an independent test of the Merton thesis.[13] A careful reading of his publications yielded no clue that he might possibly have done so in the pre-Merton era.[14] Merton himself does not remember ever having had any direct contact with Stearns.

It will certainly seem odd that Merton's essay (1961b) on 'singletons' and 'multiples' does not include Puritanism and science in England among the examples listed or analyzed, even though Merton's presentation was not strictly limited to mathematics and the natural sciences, but contained a few examples from the social sciences as well.[15] Nor is this topic explored in his partly autobiographical book on the sociology of science, although he does there discuss a quite different episode of simultaneity related to the history of science (Merton, 1979b).[16] There is yet another odd feature of this episode. It is that Merton's seminal paper on singletons and multiples (1961b) is not listed in the extensive 'official' or authorized bibliography of his writings (Miles, 1975). Such omissions occur in even the most carefully prepared bibliographies and autobibliographies.[17]

Merton's dissertation contains seeds of important concepts which he (and others) were to develop later. An example is the significance of multiple discoveries. We shall see below Merton calling attention to this feature of thought in his first reply to Dorothy Stimson in 1935. An examination of *STS* shows how much he focused on multiples in his graduate student days. Thus he discussed the 'largely independent discoveries of Torricelli and Guericke, of Boyle and Mariotte, and possibly also of Hooke and Papin', which—he observed—'derived from the intense concentration of contemporary scientists on a relatively limited sector of mechanics' (1970a: 154). It is of more than passing interest that graduate student Merton should already have accepted such independent multiples as a norm in scientific advance rather than as an anomaly, and should even have put forth an explanation. A little later on, Merton referred to the rival claims to priority in watch design—Hooke versus Huygens—leading to the following observation:

> These simultaneous inventions are a resultant of two fundamental forces: the intrinsically scientific which provided the theoretical materials employed in solving the problem in hand and the non-scientific, largely economic, factor which served to direct interest toward this general subject.

This provoked a further reflection:

> The frequency of disputes concerning priority which, to my knowledge, first becomes marked in the sixteenth century, constitutes an interesting problem for further research. It implies a lofty estimation of 'originality' and of competition; values which were largely foreign to the medieval mind which commonly sought to cloak the truly original under the tradition of earlier periods. The entire question is bound up with the rise of the concepts of plagiarism, patents, copy-rights and other institutional modes of regulating 'intellectual property'. (*ibid.*: 168–9)

This subject had to wait about a quarter of a century before a sociologist—Merton himself—took up this 'interesting problem for further research' (see Merton, 1957b).

Independent invention and discovery appear elsewhere in *STS*, e.g. the examples of Newton and Hadley on the sextant (1970a: 173), Boyle and Mariotte (*ibid.*: 187–8), Wren and Huygens (*ibid.*: 218), and Richer and Halley (*ibid.*). Merton asked (*ibid.*) 'how it happened that the original observation [of the need to alter the length of a pendulum in an accurate clock, as an observer changes his latitude] could have been made by Richer, and independently by Halley?' The graduate student answered this question in a way suggestive of the later mature scholar by reference to 'the complex interlocking of the social factors which affect science'. He called attention to the intervention of 'social elements' that made possible the multiple discovery, among them the problem of the longitude and the financing by governments of expeditions to determine the longitude of important places throughout the world. He concluded by indicating the 'admittedly roundabout and complex fashion' in which 'social and economic factors converged' in making possible an abstract theory of how gravity varies with terrestrial latitude.

Merton's *STS* is a veritable treasure-house of ideas and information. For example, as several reviewers noted in the late 1930s, Merton (Ch. 11) formulated a new and challenging interpretation of the seventeenth century idea of progress. Others had related the idea of progress to the genuine and rather striking achievements in the sciences, but Merton called attention to two 'important elements in the culture which account for the acceptance of progressivism': 'changes in the social organization and the application of canons of imperialism'. Another topic introduced by Merton, and one not as yet fully exploited, was the way in which an 'increasing population density' acted to facilitate 'the advance of science and technology'.

SOME CONSEQUENCES OF THE FORM OF PUBLICATION OF MERTON'S MONOGRAPH

Merton has described his good fortune in having his doctoral dissertation converted into a published monograph at a time when most scholars were able to get their dissertations into print only if they could personally subsidize the publication, which Merton 'manifestly' could not afford to do (see Merton, 1985a).[18] The serial *Osiris*, edited by George Sarton, in which Merton's work appeared was, however, a very obscure medium of publication.

In those days, it must be remembered, the history of science was not yet a fully recognized and established academic subject. Even George Sarton, an acknowledged founder, was not then a tenured faculty member with the proper rank of professor.[19] The journal *Isis*, of which Sarton was founder and editor, had—in the 1930s—barely 500 subscribers the world over. Sarton founded *Osiris* as a companion volume for longer monographs and for dry-as-dust but useful bibliographical tools. For instance, practically the whole of Volume 6 was devoted to a dreary catalogue of alchemical manuscripts. Volume 4 was divided almost equally into Merton's monograph and a bare-bones short-title checklist or catalogue of 'Incunabula Scientifica et Medica' by Arnold C. Klebs, a retired physician, book collector and medical historian living in Lausanne; his personal library, together with those of Harvey Cushing and John F. Fulton, formed the nucleus of the Historical Library at the Yale Medical School. Because most volumes of *Osiris* were of little interest to historians or subscribers to *Isis*, very few copies of *Osiris* were distributed. Sarton reported that in the years before 1942 fewer than 100 copies of each of the volumes of *Osiris* were sold to purchasers or subscribers (see I. B. Cohen, 1988). To make matters worse, *Osiris* was printed in Bruges in Belgium, where almost all of the unsold copies were stored. Within a year of the publication of *STS*, the great conflagration had broken out in Europe. After Belgium was overrun by the Nazis, there were no more copies of *Osiris* available for purchase. The only source was Merton's private stock of offprints.[20]

In assessing the reception of Merton's *STS*, furthermore, we must keep in mind that Merton was pioneering a new domain of learning. Today there are many academic programmes devoted to aspects of 'Science, Technology and Society', but in 1938 this was an unusual combination of words—perhaps the first such usage. If there were few historians of science at that time, there were even fewer sociologists of science. So the potential audience for Merton's monograph was predictably small. There were additional problems preventing an easy and widespread dissemination of *STS*. First there was the primary question of whether *STS* was a historically oriented work in sociology or a sociologically oriented work in history of science. I well recall my own puzzlement over this dichotomy. The question of definition continues to vex scholars today, just as it did a half-century ago. I am here mostly concerned with the fate of *STS* in the history of science community. We shall see below that historians found a real barrier in the language and intellectual framework of sociology. Furthermore, Merton put off all but the hardiest of his readers by the *chevaux de frise* of numbers—displayed in quantitative tables and bar graphs, which were not then part of the usual armoury of historians. There were also such vexing questions as whether Merton's conclusions could be applied more generally: to other cultures? to other time periods? to science other than in an emergent state? Furthermore, Merton was not always using the terms 'Puritan' and 'Puritanism' in the generally accepted fashion of historians to designate specific religious belief and affiliation, but seemed rather to be encompassing by these terms a set of general values known as the 'Puritan ethic' (or 'ethos').[21]

An examination of the initial response to *STS* (see below) shows no consensus on the part of reviewers concerning the main or defining feature or features of Merton's monograph. Thus Marjorie Nicolson, a historian of English literature concerned with science and the literary imagination in the seventeenth century, particularly lauded Merton's study of the decennial shifts in intellectual interest and was notably impressed by his discovery of a shift from poetry to prose, a feature of *STS* that is often not even mentioned in discussions of Merton's monograph. We shall see that the 'Merton thesis' was not at all the primary focus of all reviewers.

If Merton's monograph was available only in a relatively small number of libraries until the reprint of 1970, how could it have produced its influence? The answer is two-fold. First, Merton had a number—fifty, perhaps 100—of reprints which he distributed, some going to journals for review. Second, and even more important, Merton published five articles, based on his dissertation, which tended to disseminate his findings and his point of view:

'Science and Military Technique' (1935);
'Puritanism, Pietism and Science' (1936a);
'Some Economic Factors in Seventeenth Century English Science' (1937a);
'Science, Population and Society' (1937b);
'Science and the Economy of 17th Century England' (1939a).

Of these, the one that attracted most attention was the study of 'Puritanism, Pietism and Science' setting forth the 'Merton thesis'. It was published as a separate pamphlet that was widely used in courses as part of the Bobbs-Merrill Reprint Series in the Social Sciences; and it was included in all three editions of Merton's widely read collection of essays, *Social Theory and Social Structure* (1949a, 1957a, 1968), which, according to the official bibliography of Merton's writings, has been reprinted in translation in a number of different languages.[22] Second in popularity, but without quite the 'box office' appeal of the essay on Puritanism, was the enquiry into science and the economy (1939a), which was also reprinted in *Social Theory and Social Structure*. The official bibliography (Miles, 1975) lists no reprintings of the essay on population (1937b) or on science and warfare (1935).[23]

The article on 'Puritanism, Pietism, and Science' generated an enormous literature of discussion, comment and criticism, which the other articles (and subjects) did not.[24] The result has been the almost ubiquitous eponymy of *the* 'Merton thesis'—the relation between Puritanism (or radical Protestantism) and science. In assessing the impact of this thesis, in relation to others contained in *STS*—for example, on the influence of the economy or of warfare on problem-choice—we must try to recapture the 'climate of opinion' of the 1930s.

Today, after some fifty years of extensive discussion of the Merton thesis, we are apt to take for granted that, in the founding centuries of modern science, religion (or at least the religious background or religious values) exerted a positive force on the development of science. Influenced by many studies linking science and scientists with religious beliefs and values—by Alexandre Koyré, Walter Pagel, Joseph Needham, R. S. Westfall, Paul H. Kocher, John Dillenberger, Charles Raven, Karl Heim, and others[25]—scholars no longer hold to the view expressed simply and dramatically in the titles of such books as John W. Draper's *History of the Conflict between Religion and Science* (1874) or Andrew D. White's *A History of the Warfare of Science with Theology* (1896). For historians, the juxtaposition of these two domains no longer produces the simplistic dichotomy of science as rationality and truth based on experiment versus religion as superstition and belief based on blind faith. Historians are now generally aware of the important religious component in the thought of such figures as Kepler, Newton and van Helmont. The issue of science and religion is no longer confined to such events as the condemnation of Galileo by the Inquisition and the burning to death of Michael Servetus. But, of course, there is an awareness of the active opposition of fundamentalists to the teaching of Darwinian biology.

In the 1930s this dramatic change had not yet occurred. The Merton thesis was thus a challenging idea, one that went against the grain of many scholars. Two primary examples will show this to have been the case. When Merton presented his ideas on Puritanism (and radical Protestantism in general) to his thesis adviser, Pitirim Sorokin, he was told in blatant terms that he had been a gullible victim of Ernst Troeltsch and Max Weber. Sorokin pooh-poohed both Merton's subject-matter and his conclusions, with a side-swipe at his methodology.[26] When George Sarton, a die-hard Comtean rationalist, agreed to publish Merton's dissertation in *Osiris*, he strongly urged that Merton greatly cut down the discussions of religion, which Sarton obviously considered irrelevant to science.

In the late 1930s there was, among historians and scientists (but not socio-logists), a general appreciation that modern science had had many close links with the needs of warfare. A number of historians of science, furthermore, were beginning to be aware of the economic factors in scientific activity—chiefly, I believe, as a result of the more radical position taken by their Marxist brethren. Boris Hessen's 'The Social and Economic Roots of Newton's *Principia*' and its companion piece by N. Bukharin (see Bukharin *et al.*, 1931) had produced an awareness that the 'history of science is not a mere succession of inexplicable geniuses' and that scientists 'do not live in a vacuum', because 'the directions of their interest are ever conditioned by the structure of the world in which they live' (quoted from Needham, 1934: xvi).[27]

Hence Merton's studies on the economic motivation for scientific research (mining and transportation) or the relations of science to warfare could be seen as amplifications or documentations of positions already accepted—in varying degrees—by historians and by sociologists. But the religious component was of a different sort, producing a direct confrontation with long established primary beliefs. Merton was saying, in effect, that the traditional view of religion as the direct enemy of science should be abandoned, or at least seriously modified. He was arguing that religious values and beliefs could provide an ethos that justified the emerging new professional commitment of being a scientist, and that particular religious values could lead to and validate the performance of experiments and the establishment of knowledge based upon an experimental and generally empirical foundation.

There is yet a further difference between Merton's article on Puritanism and the one on the economy. The former comes to us in a vigorous style, admirably suited to its topic, with its overtones of resounding Puritan sermons. It opens with a challenging thesis, 'that the Puritan ethic, as an ideal-typical expression of the value-attitudes basic to ascetic Protestantism generally, so canalized the interests of seventeenth-century Englishmen as to constitute one important *element* in the enhanced cultivation of science'. Merton concludes his presentation in an interesting and arresting paragraph, suggesting (especially in the final five words) that his results were of far more general applicability than might otherwise have been expected:

> The association [of Protestantism with scientific and technological interests and achievements] is largely understandable in terms of the norms embodied in both systems. The positive estimation by Protestants of a hardly disguised utilitarianism, of intramundane interests, of a thorough-going empiricism, of the right and even the duty of *libre examen*, and of the explicit individual questioning of authority were congenial to the same values found in modern science. And perhaps above all is the significance of the active ascetic drive which necessitated the study of Nature that it might be controlled. Hence, these two fields were well integrated and, in essentials, mutually supporting not only in seventeenth-century England but in other times and places. (Merton, 1957a: 595)[28]

By contrast, the study of science and the economy begins on a minatory tone, decrying the simplistic approaches to the problem: 'misguided efforts' such as 'a vulgar materialism which seeks to find simple parallels between social and scientific development'. This leads Merton to an exploration of 'three common but unsound postulates', followed by several pages of negative exposition, before he is able to deal with the subject proper. The conclusion lacks the bell-ringing positive clarity of the article on Puritanism. It consists of a paragraph containing the following single sentence: 'On the grounds afforded by this study it seems justifiable to assert that the range of problems investigated by seventeenth century English scientists was appreciably influenced by the socio-economic structure of the period'. This reads as if it were a parody of the concluding sentence of *STS*: 'On the basis of the foregoing study, it may not be too much to conclude that the cultural soil of seventeenth century England was peculiarly fertile for the growth and spread of science'.

Two further observations may be made. The volume of scholarly criticism and discussion aroused by the article on Puritanism was of so great a magnitude, and of a quality so intensive, that Merton was impelled to write a twelve-page summary (with a reply and defence) under the title of 'Bibliographical Postscript'. This was included in the 1957 edition of *Social Theory and Social Structure* (1957a: 595–606).[29] No such addendum was ever needed for the paper on science and the economy (1939a; 1968: 661–81). Second, it has been only after the re-publication of *STS* in book form that the monograph as a whole, rather than the part dealing with the Merton thesis, has come under general scrutiny and has at last aroused the serious and full discussion it had merited for so many decades of relative silence. Notable among such studies are those of Gary Abraham in 1983 and the late Joseph Ben-David in 1987.[30]

MERTON'S DISSERTATION IN RELATION TO THE MONOGRAPH KNOWN AS *SCIENCE, TECHNOLOGY AND SOCIETY IN SEVENTEENTH CENTURY ENGLAND*

There is a common misapprehension concerning the publication of Merton's *STS*. Most writers and commentators refer to the 1938 publication in Volume 4 of *Osiris* as if it were a printing of Merton's 'thesis' or dissertation. Thus the editor's introduction to the 1973 collection of Merton's writings on the sociology of science refers to Merton's 'dissertation', *Science, Technology, and Society in Seventeenth-Century England*.[31] The fact of the matter is that the above title, known widely throughout the scholarly world, was *not* the title of Merton's dissertation. Merton's dissertation, still available to readers in the Harvard University Archives, bore a quite different title from that of the printed work. The official title was 'Sociological Aspects of Scientific Development in Seventeenth Century England'.[32] Merton told me that he had originally conceived the dissertation under a title much like that of the final published version. His thesis committee, however, considered that to be too grandiose for a mere graduate student and suggested a more limited subject, expressed in the title of the dissertation.

Merton completed his dissertation by the autumn of 1935 and officially submitted it in December 1935 'in partial fulfillment of the requirements for the degree of Doctor of Philosophy in the Division of Sociology'. The examining committee consisted of Pitirim A. Sorokin, George Sarton, Carle C. Zimmerman and Talcott Parsons, whose names appear on the certificate of acceptance in that order. The preface, dated 14 December 1935, expressed the customary acknowledgment of indebtedness to each of the four committee members. We may note that Sarton was thanked 'for his kindly encouragement, thoughtful suggestions and constant guidance in a field where my knowledge is but that of the neophyte'.[33] By completing his degree work early, Merton (as indicated in the commencement programme, June 1936) was listed under the heading 'Iam Medio Anno Declarati', indicating that the degree had been awarded earlier in the academic year.

To today's reader the most striking physical feature of Merton's dissertation is the high quality of the typing. Merton—like other graduate students of those days—did his own typing. He was evidently a skilled typist and the neatly typed tables, of great complexity, would be the envy of many a professional of our own day. But, of course, in those days of mechanical typewriters the impression of the type from different keys was far from uniform and the end-product did not have that elegant finished appearance so easily obtainable with today's electric and electronic typewriters and word processors.

When George Sarton agreed to publish a version of Merton's dissertation, he proposed certain revisions. I have already mentioned that Sarton urged Merton to 'condense' the whole work, 'notably the religious part'. Merton, fortunately, did not follow this suggestion. But he did take seriously Sarton's advice that the final chapter of the dissertation be broken up into separate chapters. This final chapter of the dissertation (Chapter 9) bore the title 'Military Technology and Science'. It consisted of two parts (of which the first was unnumbered, while the second bore the heading of 'II'). The first part was indeed concerned with 'military technology'. But the second part was more general, beginning with a presentation of the means of determining 'the relative amount of scientific research which was influenced, directly or indirectly, by socio-economic needs'. Since this bore little or no relation to the first part (on 'military technology'), it made sense to split it off to become a separate entity.

In the printed version, however, this more general second part was expanded to become two separate chapters. In the first of these, Chapter 10, entitled 'Extrinsic Influences on Scientific Research', there is an opening general discussion of 'the relative importance of intrinsic and external factors in the determination of the foci of scientific interest'. Chapter 11 of the printed work is entitled 'Some Social and Cultural Factors in Scientific Advance', and is of the general character befitting of the conclusion of an investigation on the scale that Merton had presented. Today's reader of the dissertation will no doubt be puzzled why the general material to be found in the final two chapters of the printed work had been compressed into the second part of the final chapter of the dissertation, allegedly devoted to the more limited subject of 'Military Technology and Science'. By what strange quirk, one must wonder, did these two subjects become so intimately tied together? One can guess that Merton was so pressed to complete his dissertation in time for a degree at the February commencement that he hastily threw all his conclusions into a Part II of the last chapter, rather than expanding this material into one or two autonomous chapters.[34]

Merton produced his dissertation in a day when there were no xeroxes and no inexpensive copy or reproduction processes. Fortunately for Merton, there were then no grants available for typing and retyping. Hence, to produce a ribbon copy for the printer Merton could not merely reproduce the completed dissertation, with minor stylistic emendations. Rather, he had to retype the complete text himself and in the process—as was then the custom—he considerably rewrote the work, section by section, paragraph by paragraph, sentence by sentence. The result is a much improved book, with many alterations.

The difference between the dissertation and the printed version may readily be seen by a comparison of two extracts:

Dissertation (1935)	**Osiris** (1938)
Opening of Chapter 9	*Opening of Chapter 9*
The seventeenth century in England was one in which war and revolution were rife. Not only were there fifty-five years of actual warfare during this period, but also the two greatest revolutions in English history. A number of changes in military technique occurred coincident	It was not until the seventeenth century that England attained its position of military and commercial leadership. Frequent recourse to force of arms attended this rise to power. Not only were there fifty-five years of actual warfare during this century, but also the

with this prolonged warfare. The dominance of firearms—both muskets and artillery—over side-arms first became marked at this time. The period represents a turning-point in the history of armanents: swords and pikes disappear almost completely as significant weapons (save as they are incorporated in the removable bayonet about 1680) and firearms are used almst exclusively....

greatest revolution in English history. Coincident with this prolonged warfare occurred a number of changes in military technique. The dominance of firearms—both muskets and artillery—over side-arms first became marked at this time. The period represents a turning-point in the history of armaments: swords and pikes disappeared almost completely as weapons of importance (save as they are incorporated in the removable bayonet about 1680) and firearms were used almost exclusively....

Opening of Chapter 9
(Part II)

In order to determine the relative amount of scientific research which was influenced, directly of [*sic*] indirectly, by socio-economic needs, recourse was had to the minutes of the Royal Society as transcribed in Birch's *History of the Royal Society*. The only feasible, though in many ways inadequate, procedure seemed to be a classification and tabulation of the researches discussed at the meetings of the Society.

Opening of Chapter 10
(second section)
A Statement of Procedure
The minutes of the Society as transcribed in Birch's *History of the Royal Society* provide one basis for such a study. A feasible, though in many ways inadequate, procedure consists of a classification and tabulation of the researches discussed at these meetings, together with an examination of the context in which the various problems came to light. This should afford some grounds for deciding roughly the extent to which extrinsic factors operated directly or indirectly.

In the printed version Merton introduced some notes about recent additions to the scholarly literature. At the end of Chapter 10 in the printed version there is an 'Addendum', not of course present in the dissertation, in which Merton takes up G. N. Clark's criticism in 1937 of the essay of Boris Hessen (see endnote 86). There is also a paragraph about R. F. Jones's *Ancients and Modern* (see endnote 10).

Many of the revisions made by Merton in preparing the text for printing consist of improvements in style and expression. Each chapter was now broken up into subdivisions with headings. Hence, introductory passages were required. The final paragraph of the whole work was shortened and made to refer to 'the foregoing study', whereas in the dissertation Merton wrote only of 'the last three chapters'. Finally, the conclusion was made more general in its assertion that the 'cultural soil' of seventeenth century England was 'peculiarly fertile for the growth and spread of science'. In the dissertation Merton—in good 'thesis-ese'—only 'tentatively maintained' that the 'selection of subjects of investigation' had been 'influenced considerably' by 'socio-economic needs'. The texts of the two final paragraphs are as follows:

Dissertation (1935)	STS (1938)
On the basis of the data presented in the last three chapters it may be tentatively maintained that socio-economic needs influenced considerably the selection of subjects of investigation by scientists in seventeenth century England. Speaking roughly, about thirty to sixty percent of the contemporary researches seem, directly or indirectly, to have been so influenced.	On the basis of the foregoing study, it may not be too much to conclude that the cultural soil of seventeenth century England was peculiarly fertile for the growth and spread of science.

The change speaks for itself!

PURITANISM AND THE NEW SCIENCE AS SEEN IN THE CORRESPONDENCE BETWEEN DOROTHY STIMSON AND R. K. MERTON

Dorothy Stimson's first essay in the area of science in seventeenth century England was an article on John Wilkins (Stimson, 1931). In her presentation there is no statement of any aspect of the general theme of Protestantism or Puritanism and science. This theme would, in fact, have been a novelty in the 1930s, even though it had been the subject of a short chapter in Alphonse de Candolle's book of 1873.[35] By 1933, however, Miss Stimson had reached the conclusion that Puritanism was related to 'the new philosophy' in seventeenth century England.[36]

In December 1934, when she presented her findings in Washington at a joint meeting of the History of Science Society and the American Historical Association, Miss Stimson had announced that she had made a count of the number of Puritans among the founding Fellows of the Royal Society and had come to the conclusion that forty-two out of sixty-eight were Puritans.[37] In her brief account of her findings, published in May 1935 (Stimson, 1935b), she did not define what criteria she had used to establish the Puritanism of the Fellows in question.[38] She probably did not grasp that at least half a year before the Washington meetings Merton had already written a full-length study (early in 1934) of the whole issue of 'Puritanism, Pietism and Science'.

At that time scholarly attention had been called to the 'Protestant ethic' in general by the book of Max Weber on *The Protestant Ethic and the Spirit of Capitalism*, issued in an English translation (by Talcott Parsons) in 1930.[39] Weber did not introduce any quantitative data nor—so far as I know—did he ever even hint that his ideas might be susceptible of a numerical test. It is also of significance that Weber's book did not include the natural sciences in its subject-matter, although Merton was later at pains to show that Weber had not been wholly unaware of the issue of Protestantism and science.[40]

In the 1930s, even though Candolle and others had intimated that there might be a link between Protestantism and science, the thesis about radical Protestantism or Puritanism was not at all obvious. Nor did the theme of religion and science then have the centrality that it later attained. Some examples will show this to have been the case. When Sarton agreed to publish Merton's dissertation in *Osiris*, he suggested to Merton (as we have seen above) that he reduce the discussion of religion, which may seem odd to today's readers since *STS* has become generally best known for the 'Merton thesis', which specifically relates science to Puritanism. Furthermore, as we shall see below, this theme in *STS* was not stressed by any of those who wrote book reviews. Additionally, this feature was absent from the title of both the dissertation and the published monograph; neither one included the term 'Protestantism' or 'Puritanism' or 'Religion', although Merton could have argued that religion (especially a 'Puritan ethos' or a 'Protestant ethic') was subsumed under the general rubric of 'society'. Yet this theme was stated plainly in the title of his article, based on his spring 1934 paper on 'Puritanism, Pietism and Science'. We have also seen above that Pitirim Sorokin, the founder of Harvard's Sociology Department, rejected the whole concept of there having been a possible connection between Puritanism and science in seventeenth century England.[41]

Some time after Merton began his dissertation in 1933, George Sarton informed him about Dorothy Stimson's studies and suggested that he make contact with her.[42] Accordingly, in February 1934, when Merton had already done research for his paper completed in the spring of that year, Merton dutifully wrote to her about his plans.[43] To judge from her reply, his initial letter would have indicated (or perhaps have stressed) that he was producing a doctoral dissertation in sociology and not in the history of science.[44]

She replied on 3 February 1934, declaring that 'to the best of my belief there is no overlapping in your work & mine that need bother you'. She stressed that her work 'is historical, with the emphasis on the earlier part of the century up to 1662 rather than after it'. Then, after referring to three of her articles (which 'would show you the lines of my work to some degree'),[45] she called his attention to 'Thorstein Veblen's essay "The Evolution of the Scientific Point of View" in his book, *The Place of Science*' and 'Ogburn and Thomas's discussion on "Is Invention Inevitable?" in the *Political Science Quarterly* for March 1922 (vol. 37)'. She then summarized their views:

> They contend that great minds are present in all centuries, but the cultural environment must be suitable—'the time be ripe'—to make possible great discoveries. Pasteur could not have done his work in 1600, had he been alive then, for the compound microscope with achromatic lenses had not been developed. Also measurement is at the basis of scientific work: the early 17th century saw the development of many instruments of measurement and precision from the telescope and logarithms to the pendulum clock and the thermometer.

Finally, after delivering herself of this schoolmarmish mini-lecture (as if Merton had been an undergraduate neophyte in her introductory course at Goucher), Miss Stimson concluded, 'But you probably are fully aware of all this'. She ended the letter cordially, 'I shall be interested in seeing the results of your researches'.

A year later, almost to the day, on 9 February 1935, Miss Stimson wrote to Merton about her paper, which—she said—was scheduled to appear in the June issue of the *New England Quarterly*. From the context this may have been the paper based on her talk in Washington a few months earlier; it did not appear in the *New England Quarterly* but in the *Bulletin of the Institute of the History of Medicine* (Stimson, 1935b).[46] Describing it as, 'of course, in one sense a progress report and not a complete study', she hastened to assure Merton that 'it will not infringe upon your work'. She doubted 'if it contains anything that is not already well known to you'. Merton had evidently asked to see a copy of the paper, since she concluded by asking, 'will it be time enough for you to see it when it is printed?' The previous letter had been written in long-hand, but this one had evidently been dictated and typed by a secretary; the stationery bore the heading 'Office of the Dean'. Whereas in long-hand she had ended the first letter 'Yours sincerely', she now subscribed herself 'Very sincerely yours'.

In May 1935 her paper on 'Puritanism and the New Philosophy' was published and on 14 May Merton wrote to say that 'I have just read' it. 'I was both gratified and astonished', he declared, 'at the complete identity of both the thesis and the proof thereof which you develop and my own treatment of the subject'. He then told her:

> The section of my dissertation dealing with 'Puritanism and Science' which Dr. Sarton read last year and which led him to suggest my writing you presents almost precisely the same analysis as yours, save that it is done, of course, in somewhat greater detail. Truly a case of 'independent duplicate discovery'!

The final sentence indicates how early in his career Merton became aware of the phenomenon of 'independent duplicate discovery', which became so important in his later development of the sociology of science.

Two days later, on 16 May 1935, Miss Stimson (or: Dean Stimson) wrote to Merton in a somewhat agitated state. She began by a frank confession that Merton's recent letter had 'quite startled' her and had sent her 'in haste to my files to re-read your letter of February 1934'. She thus found that Merton had written that his 'approach to the problems of science in the 17th century is sociological', whereas her own 'approach is historical'. She had 'felt sure then', she wrote 'as I do now', that Merton's work 'would not interfere' with hers nor hers with his. Then she observed:

> It is indeed interesting that we should have had the same theory about Puritanism. The theory has long been germinating in my mind, and in the last paragraphs of a paper Dr. Sarton has yet to print, written in 1933, I sketched this theory. Being asked to speak in Washington last Christmas compelled me to work up what evidence I had in its support as a kind of progress report.[47]

She asked Merton whether she might 'borrow' a copy of his dissertation. She would, she said, 'be much interested in seeing your presentation of the matter and your evidence'. It is clear from this letter that she was quite taken aback on discovering that the sociologist Merton was not proceeding in the manner that she had imagined a sociologist would, but had been engaged in deep and broad historical research of a quality that could put many professional historians of science to shame. (Parenthetically I may observe that this has been a marked feature of many of Merton's papers. Their content is on the highest level of historical research, displaying acquaintance with a vast range of the primary and secondary literature.)

Dean Stimson concluded her letter by remarking how 'others are working along the same line'. She had in mind two papers 'using New England evidence', one by Theodore Hornberger, the other by Clifford Shipton.[48] 'Obviously', she observed, 'a number of us are approaching this idea from various angles'; and then she ended on a rueful note, 'I imagine there is room for us all!'[49]

In response to Dean Stimson's letter, on 23 May 1935, Merton dutifully sent her 'a rough draft of the section of my dissertation which deals with' the relation of 'Puritanism and scientific development'. He informed her that he had 'not as yet fully developed the implications of the theory since for some time I have been collecting data concerning the "shifts of vocational interest" in seventeenth century England'.[50] He then announced his intention 'further to investigate the relationships between Pietism and science in Germany, and Puritanism and science in New England'. Commenting on her references to the papers by Hornberger and Shipton, he told her that he was 'glad to hear' that the 'latter connexion is being studied'. He concluded by gracefully asking Miss Stimson for 'any critical marginalia' she might 'care to inscribe'.

Dean Stimson replied on 29 May 1935, 'enclosing a page of specific comment on details that impressed me'. In a puzzling statement she averred that 'I am inclined to agree more with the pencilled comments along the margins than I am with some of your own arguments'. I do not know whose 'pencilled comments' appeared on the pages of the text that Merton had sent her. Possibly these were part of Sorokin's scorching commentary.[51] Nor is there today any trace of her page of comments.[52] But she did take specific issue with Merton for not having 'done full justice in your argument to scholasticism and, indeed, to the Christian religion, particularly in the early part of the chapter'. The exact sense of this criticism is far from obvious. But then she stated strongly her own difficulty with the Mertonian presentation. Merton had not written history in the ordinary manner and style of historians and, as she admitted, 'the field of sociology is quite foreign to me'. Even 'its vocabulary', she declared, 'at times becomes rather difficult, particularly in your first section'. I have mentioned my own puzzlement on first reading *STS* and my difficulty in deciding whether this was a historically based study of primarily sociological interest or a sociologically oriented historical monograph. Today this distinction would not appear so great as it did then. The reason is that historians have become familiar with and now use fruitfully the concepts and the language introduced into historical discourse by Merton, which then seemed so alien to Dorothy Stimson.

In his letters to Dean Stimson, Merton had remarked on the fact that she and he had 'reached the same conclusion although by different paths'. She echoed this sentiment in her letter of 29 May 1935. She reiterated her position 'that there is ample room for many workers in this particular field in which we are both interested'.

In the event Merton had already written up his findings in the article on 'Puritanism, Pietism, and Science', which was published in *The Sociological Review* for January 1936, more than half a year after Dorothy Stimson's 'Puritanism and the New Philosophy' (1935b) had appeared in the *Bulletin of the History of Medicine*. It was the draft of this paper which Sorokin had criticized in the spring of 1934 and which Merton had sent to Dorothy Stimson in May 1935. Merton was not the first to put into print a complete statement about Puritanism and science in seventeenth century England. In his article he very gracefully acknowledged Dorothy Stimson's independent quantitative research toward the same end:

Dean Dorothy Stimson, in a recently published paper, has independently arrived at this same conclusion. She points out that of the ten men who constituted the 'invisible college', in 1645, only one, Scarborough, was clearly non-Puritan. About two of the others there is some uncertainty, though Merret had a Puritan training. The others were all definitely Puritan. Moreover, among the original list of members of the [Royal] Society of 1663, forty-two of the sixty-eight concerning whom the information is available were clearly Puritan. Considering that the Puritans constituted a relatively small minority in the English population, the fact that they constituted sixty-two per cent of the initial membership of the Society becomes even more striking. Dean Stimson concludes: 'that experimental science spread as rapidly as it did in seventeenth-century England seems to me to be in part at least because the moderate Puritans encouraged it'.

As soon as the article appeared in print, Merton sent Dean Stimson a reprint, which she acknowledged in a letter to him dated 25 March 1936 as having come 'early this month'. She thanked him 'heartily' for 'your generous use of my article' and expressed her pleasure 'that it furnished you with further ammunition for your thesis'. She declared that 'you have proved the point clearly and forcefully' and she found that 'your German evidence is particularly interesting'. She was sending him a reprint of her article on Comenius 'because of your references to him and to Hartlib'.[53]

In the version of *STS* corresponding to this article, Merton reproduced the paragraph about Dean Stimson's findings, more or less as it appeared in his article. But he now added a lengthy quotation to the mere footnote reference that had appeared in the article:

> Dean Stimson's brief, but meticulous and convincing, study proposes 'the theory that Puritanism was an important factor, hitherto little regarded, in making conditions favorable to the new philosophy heralded by Bacon and in promoting the type of thinking that helped to arouse interest in science and to create a ready reception for the work of the geniuses produced in that century'.

This quotation was followed by a bibliographical reference to Dean Stimson's article on Comenius, of which she had sent him a reprint. It is apparent that Merton was not unhappy to find in her writings some strong support for, and validation of, his own point of view. On rereading Merton's footnote, however, in the light of the magnitude of his own quantitative research, one cannot escape the feeling that he quite intentionally added the qualifying words 'brief, but' to his phrase about a 'meticulous and convincing study'.

The final letter in the series was written by Dorothy Stimson to Merton on 21 August 1938, acknowledging the receipt of a copy of *STS*.[54] She said that she 'had intended saying Thank you for both [your letter and your study] *after* I had finished reading the study'. She found, however, that she was 'being so interrupted' that she didn't know when that would be. She had read only 'some 30 pages' and found herself 'very much interested in your work'. Then she gave Merton her preliminary judgment. 'It is decidedly valuable for me, I am certain', she wrote, adding at once that 'I am glad I wrote my lectures before I started reading it'. I assume she is referring here to her forthcoming lecture at Radcliffe College (given in October 1938) on 'Amateurs of Science in Seventeenth Century England'. Perhaps she was implying that she might have become engrossed in *STS* to a degree that might have prevented her from giving full time and attention to the impending presentation in Cambridge; or, she may have been expressing the fear that she might have been too influenced by Merton and would not therefore have expressed her own conclusions in full independence.

Merton must have winced a little on reading Dean Stimson's earlier comments about his use of sociological jargon and, in his letter accompanying the gift of *STS*, he evidently said something about its prose style. She responded, 'And since you referred to your English may I comment that I find your style intelligible and readable even tho' I am not a sociologist'. She then remarked, 'Isn't Mr. Needham's note interesting? If I can get the study "noticed" for you I shall be happy to do so'.

She concluded by thanking Merton for allowing her to 'have one of your few copies' and expressed her appreciation of his 'kind use of my articles'. This final comment was accompanied by a parenthetical remark, 'You see your index works!'

I attended Dean Stimson's lecture at Radcliffe College on 26 October 1938. Merton was still in Cambridge; his appointment at Tulane University did not begin until September of 1939. Merton recalls that he also attended her lecture and that they met on this occasion. But he has no memory of the subject of their conversations. Nor have I been able to find any record of Dean Stimson's further reactions to *STS* after reading more than the first thirty pages. I assume that she would have read more than these initial pages. Yet I have no way of determining what she thought of Merton's findings concerning shifts in intellectual interest or vocation, of his explorations of military, mining and transportation technology as determinants of fields of scientific research, or the other topics in which *STS* so richly abounds.[55]

SOME FIRST ENCOUNTERS: THE INITIAL CRITICAL RECEPTION (AND APPRECIATION) OF MERTON'S MONOGRAPH

Although Merton's *STS* was published in a journal of limited circulation, it did attract a certain amount of attention through reviews. I shall present the views of the chief reviewers and also the reactions of James B. Conant and A. Rupert Hall. Dorothy Stimson did not write a review as did Richard F. Jones, the other independent claimant to the Puritanism thesis. J. B. Conant, President of Harvard, had a genuine interest in this topic that later matured into an independent point of view expressed in a learned journal.

Each of the reviewers tended to stress his or her own focus of interest: the Puritanism theme, the shift of intellectual concerns during the century, the economic factors; and there is some disagreement among them, for example, on how convincing they found Merton's quantitative investigations. All in all, the roster of reviewers is most impressive—a real tribute to a young scholar's first major work.

These reviews were occasioned in part by Merton's having sent to various journals a reprint of *STS*, from the stock furnished to him by the editor, George Sarton (see endnote 20). In some cases Merton sent a reprint to a scholar (e.g. Walter Pagel) with an expression of hope that his work be reviewed in some journal. There was no review by a sociologist in a major sociological journal.[56] The review in the *American Sociological Review* was written by Marjorie Nicolson, a historian of English literature, who devoted only two paragraphs to the contents of *STS* and did not discuss any of the aspects of Merton's work that might be of interest to sociologists.

There was one review of *STS* by a 'mainline' sociologist, Howard Becker, a theorist at the University of Wisconsin (not to be confused with Howard S. Becker of Northwestern). This review was published in 1942 in *Rural Sociology* (Vol. 7, p. 110), a journal whose very title reminds us of a topic which—in the years before World War II—was of central importance in sociology. We have mentioned that one of the members of Merton's doctoral committee was Carle Zimmerman, a specialist in rural sociology. Becker introduced a note of apology for the four-year time lapse since the publication of *STS*: 'The book was placed in my hands in 1938'. This review appears in retrospect as odd in the extreme. Although short (occupying less than a page), almost half is devoted to a discussion of the politics of 'our commercialized university presses' with respect to scholarly works, notably dissertations. It was 'with intent', Becker declared, that he had said 'little' (in fact, he said nothing at all) about Merton's 'striking erudition, wide range of research, methodological stringency, and analytic grasp'. The intent was apparently merely 'to spread the news that the much-demanded "substantive sociology of knowledge" is fittingly exemplified in Merton's work'. Citing the titles of a few early chapters, Becker announced that Merton had brought us 'beyond the mere juggling of "ideology and utopia" and the futile weighing of plausibilities'. But there was not a word on Merton's bold quantifying innovation, nor even on the sociologically interesting theme of Puritanism in validation of the new profession of scientist. There was no reference to Merton's original and striking presentation of mining, shipping and warfare, but Becker did say that Merton had 'driven to the head and clinched' Weber's contention that 'non-material factors' are 'quite as necessary' as 'material factors' in the development of technology. Merton was praised for having provided a refutation of Ogburn's 'crude epiphenomenalism *re* the role of ideas in social change'.

There was no review in the *American Journal of Sociology*. In the summer of 1940 Merton wrote a letter to Everett G. Hughes, a member of the board of advisory editors, about the failure to publish a review. On 3 July 1940 Robert F. Winch, editorial assistant, wrote Merton a letter of apology, explaining that 'the book was received' in 1939 and that 'before the book could be sent out for review, it disappeared from our book room'. The editors agreed to attempt 'to make tardy rectification of our error'. Since the publisher was in occupied Belgium, however, there was no way to order a replacement review copy. Merton was asked how the journal might 'procure another copy'. The letter ended with a promise that if another copy could be obtained, they would 'endeavor to get a prompt review and early publication for it'.

Merton replied on 31 July, announcing that he was sending another copy. He expressed his thanks for the 'promise of a prompt review'. In August, Merton received a letter from Louis Wirth, the sociologist at the University of Chicago (who, with Edward Shils, had published a translation of Karl Mannheim's *Ideology and Utopia* in 1936), informing him that he had been asked to review *STS* for the *American Journal of Sociology*. By this time the affair had become a comedy of errors. Wirth told Merton that the journal didn't have 'a copy of the book' and that 'the copy which I bought has disappeared'. He therefore put 'the case before' Merton for providing a replacement. Merton replied that he had just sent a copy to Hughes, adding that if 'this copy has been misplaced, please let me know and I shall immediately send another to take its place'. In the end, thirty-two years were to pass before a review essay finally appeared. It was written by Benjamin Nelson on the occasion of the 1970 reprint (Nelson, 1972).

One sociologist who did write a contemporaneous review of *STS* was Bernard J. Stern. He, however, wrote only a very brief notice, a single column (half of a single page) in length. Perhaps the reason why Stern did not offer a useful sociological commentary was that his own speciality as a sociologist was medicine and society, a topic not really treated by Merton. Stern wrote that Merton's 'most significant contribution' was to have provided 'excellent documentation' of the 'interrelation between economic developments and the growth of science and technology'. Stern held that Merton had proved 'conclusively that the pure scientists of the seventeenth century defined their problems and focused their research in terms of the practical interests and needs of the new industries and commerce stimulated by capitalism'. Stern also praised Merton for his 'discussion of the role of Puritanism in scientific progress of the period', which likewise goes beyond previous studies in this field. What such 'previous studies' might have been is left to the imagination of the reader.

Stern, however, did not believe Merton had been fully 'successful in his attempt to apply a statistical method to an analysis of the shifts in vocational, scientific, and technological interests'. Nor did he find Merton's book to 'attain the integrated maturity' (whatever that might mean) of Martha Ornstein's study of scientific societies (Ornstein, 1938). He also criticized Merton for 'an unnecessary, unanalytical citation of authority'. But he did appreciate (as no other contemporaneous reviewer apparently did) that Merton had suggested 'future lines of research in fields hitherto neglected by American sociologists' (Stern, 1939).

A one-paragraph review, written by one C.A.M.E. (= Ewing), criticized Merton for his procedure in 'thumbing carefully' through the pages of the *DNB* to select figures of prominence 'in the various fields of science and technology'. Despite his objections to Merton's 'methodology' (and the examination of data which are not 'so satisfactory as those in the truly scientific fields'), Ewing concluded that Merton had 'formulated some worthy generalizations'. Among the latter he cited Merton's 'comments on the utilitarian causation for most of the advance in science' and his conclusions concerning 'the conspicuous place which Protestants occupied in innovating discoveries' (Ewing, 1939).[57]

A review by the physical anthropologist M. F. Ashley-Montagu, in the *University Review*, stressed Merton's 'clarification of the role which protestantism, and its peculiar form in particular—Puritanism—played in the "sacerdotalizing" of scientific pursuits'.[58] He referred briefly to the second half of *STS*, 'the part played by other ideologic values, such as the concept of utilitarianism, and the important influences of economic and military activities upon scientific and technologic development'. Ashley-Montagu concluded on a note of the highest praise, which must have been a source of delight and satisfaction to the young author. Merton, he said, 'has written a monograph distinguished by its breadth of view, urbanity, and scholarship'. This work was 'a model of its kind', one 'to which all students of science and technology in the seventeenth century must hereafter remain indebted' (Ashley-Montagu, 1939).

More significant, if only because it reached a wider audience, was a general article in *Nature* on *Osiris*, featuring Merton's *STS*.[59] Here an account was given of Volume 4, Part 2 of *Osiris* (containing *STS*) and the whole of Volume 5 (a general miscellany). In rather sterile language this anonymous presentation states that the *DNB* 'has been selected [by Merton] as the source of information of an occupational census and the data subjected to a tabulation process'. It is said that, as well as these data, 'a further survey of discoveries based on Darmstädter's *Handbuch...*' was compiled, which 'indicated the particular interests which arose in different times in the period studied'. What those 'interests' were, how they shifted and what significance these shifts might imply were not even suggested to the reader. It is the same for the ambiguous reference to the 'influence of religious movements such as Puritanism', concerning which we are told only that it 'is considered'. In the same manner, a statement is made that the 'influence of external factors is carefully examined'. This leads to the pathetic conclusion that the 'whole study is very interesting and suggestive in many fields'.

These book reviews called the attention of scholars to the existence of Merton's *STS*. But the real influence of *STS* on the scholarly community did not begin until after World War II. The impression given by the reviews in the late 1930s may be contrasted with the experience of encountering *STS* in the 1940s by examining Rupert Hall's discovery of *STS* during the course of a systematic reading of the literature in the set of *Osiris* in the University Library in Cambridge (see below). This episode is of more than ordinary interest, since Hall's 'Merton Revisited' (A. R. Hall, 1963) has long been considered the classic response of a main-stream historian of science to *STS*.

Richard F. Jones

We have seen that R. F. Jones was one of the three writers who independently came upon the Puritanism-and-science thesis in the 1930s. Merton sent him a reprint of his article 'Puritanism, Pietism and Science' soon after it was published in January 1936. Jones was then in the Department of English at Washington University, St Louis. On 19 March 1936 Jones wrote to Merton, expressing his gratification that Merton, 'approaching the problem of Puritanism and science from a different direction and with an eye on the continent, [should] reach results which bolster up my own opinion'. Jones was particularly impressed by Merton's 'statistical logic', which he found to be 'inescapable'. He himself had been 'aware of the emphasis upon scientific subjects in the Dissenters' academies', but he felt bound to admit that Merton's 'continental researches opened my eyes'. He concluded by expressing the hope that Merton's article would achieve 'the recognition it deserves for its material, the skilful and logical manner with which you handle the material, and above everything else, the importance of your findings'. He added a sentence in which he stressed the particular significance of Merton's findings in combination with his own research on the influence of Francis Bacon. Merton had made him 'more convinced than I was that the essential characteristics of our modern civilization are to be discovered in the union of Protestantism (especially Puritanism) and Baconian science'.[60]

In 1938, when *STS* was published, there were two obvious candidates for the book review in *Isis*: R. F. Jones and Dorothy Stimson.[61] Each of them had written about the central theme and each could be considered independent progenitor or developer of it. I do not know why Sarton chose Jones, but perhaps he wanted to enlist Jones—who had not as yet contributed anything to *Isis*—as a potential author. He needed articles badly and Dorothy Stimson had already published in *Isis*.[62]

In due course Jones's review appeared in *Isis* (Jones, 1940). It ran to about two pages and a half. Jones began with a quotation from the concluding paragraph of *STS*, that Merton's purpose was 'to prove' that 'the cultural soil of the seventeenth century England was peculiarly fertile for the growth and spread of science'.[63] Jones wrote:

> The method employed consists of an analysis of various factors and values of the times, which are shown to have been unusually conducive to the development of science, and of economic activities which did much to determine the specific direction pursued by scientific investigators.

There follows a succinct account of Merton's quantitative studies on interest in science, but without reference to Merton's analysis of the shifts in interest in England in the seventeenth century and without even a mention of Merton's use of Darmstädter's *Handbuch*. Curiously enough, Jones deflates Merton's study of the *DNB* from the approximately 6000 entries used for *STS* to 'nearly a thousand'.

Jones appreciated that the 'social and cultural values' to which Merton had ascribed 'the greatest importance are those contained in the religious movements of Protestantism, Pietism, and Puritanism, with especial emphasis upon the last'. The 'close connection between science and the Puritans', according to Jones, has 'in no small degree' been clarified and established by Merton and 'should in a short time become almost a truism in the history of science'.

Jones's review was not a simple laudation. He was concerned by Merton's assertion that 'Puritan theology found a sanction for science' in 'the glorification of God through works, which he [Merton] thinks were interpreted in terms of experiments' and in 'the manifestation of God's attributes in nature'. Jones felt that 'greater detail' of evidence and analysis was needed to support the view 'that "works" came to be equated with experiments'. He also offered two 'tentative objections to the idea that the Puritans integrated their science and theology'. [64]

Jones's review concentrated heavily on the issue of Puritanism, the subject of Jones's own investigations, giving only the briefest hint concerning the rest of the book. Curiously enough, Jones did not even refer to Merton's discussion of Continental activities or the relation between Merton's findings and his own about Bacon—both of which had been the occasion for his warm praise of Merton in his letter two years earlier.

Jones barely mentioned Chapters 8–10, comprising at least a third of the monograph, dealing with 'Science, Technology and Economic Development', 'Science and Military Technique' and 'Extrinsic Influences on Scientific Research'. He describes these in a single sentence in a curious way, saying that 'Merton, by a comprehensive and critical use of modern economic treatises on the period' has demonstrated 'that the development of economic activities such as mining and transportation, and uneconomic activities such as military science, inspired the scientists to solve the problems presented by them'. I am not at all certain what Jones meant by the phrase 'modern economic treatises on the period', since the adjective 'modern' would suggest 'treatises' of the present or of the recent past. Merton, it is true, does cite many economists and economic historians of the late nineteenth and the twentieth century, but he also—and rather obviously—draws here (as elsewhere) heavily on primary sources.

Jones summarized the final chapter of *STS* by noting merely that it 'comprehends discussions of various social and cultural factors which assisted in the advancement of science'. This chapter, he commented, 'would have found a more natural place earlier in the volume'.

Jones concluded his commentary by expressing his own view, contrary to Merton's, that 'belief in progress' seems 'rather a result than a cause' of scientific progress. He did admit, however, that 'when once inspired, it [i.e. belief in progress] furnished a strong motive for the support of science'. A final paragraph praised the author for his display of 'the true spirit and method of conscientious scholarship', for having gathered his evidence 'from wide sources' and for having produced an 'important treatise'.

Marjorie Hope Nicolson

In the 1930s a number of scholars who concerned themselves with the history of science came from the profession of literary history.[65] Chief among them was Marjorie Hope Nicolson, then Dean of Smith College in Northampton, Massachusetts, later professor of English (the first woman to receive such an appointment) and chairman of that department at Columbia University. In 1938 she was at the height of her creative powers, author of a series of stunning path-breaking studies on the telescope and the microscope and English literary imagination.[66] They were soon to be followed by her extraordinary monograph on the influence of Newton's optics (Nicolson, 1946) and many others. (Parenthetically I may add that she spoke in public (on the several occasions on which I heard her) in perfect prose—by which I mean completed sentences, framed in carefully ordered paragraphs. When a typed transcription was made from one of her talks, it could be sent directly to the printer with hardly an editorial emendation being required.)

As a specialist in seventeenth century English thought in relation to science, Majorie Nicolson was an obvious choice as reviewer of *STS*—there were not many other available candidates with her credentials. But what will surely come as a surprise to many readers today is that she should have been chosen to write the review for the *American Sociological Review*. This fact may possibly be taken as an index of the lack of available sociologists concerned with science.[67] But it was also the case that the few such scholars were primarily interested in current problems of science and society and knew precious little about seventeenth century science. They could not have approached a historically based work such as *STS* with any real critical competence. Another possible factor may have been the desire of the editors to combine a review of *STS* with accounts of some other historical works dealing with more or less the same historical period.[68] In any event the choice of Marjorie Nicolson and the joint review of three books was an inevitable guarantee that whatever sociological message Merton's *STS* may have had—in its content, its methodology or its conclusions—would not be dramatically brought to the sociological community comprising the readership of the *American Sociological Review*, the official journal of the American Sociological Society.

On 13 October 1938 Marjorie Nicolson wrote a very cordial letter to Merton, inviting him to participate in a session she was organizing, for the coming December meetings of the Modern Language Association (MLA), on 'the influence of science upon literature'.[69] In the early part of the letter she mentioned that she had 'just been reading with much interest your publication on science and society in *Osiris*'. She then announced that, 'As a matter of fact, I am supposed to review it for two different periodicals in two different fields'. As far as I can tell, however, she did not write more than the one review.

Of particular interest in the present context is Marjorie Nicolson's expression in her letter of her great interest 'in the charts you incorporated in your volume, and in the study of the shifts of interest in various fields'. She observed that these charts 'are particularly interesting to students of literature' to the degree that 'they show the rapid decline of poetry and the rise of prose'. So far as I know, she was the only scholar ever to seize upon this finding.

Marjorie Nicolson devoted only a single paragraph in print to *STS* as such. Almost a third of her review dealt with Merton's analyses of 'shifts in cultural interest during the seventeenth century'. She was impressed by Merton's 'charts and tables', his demonstration of 'the decline of the clergy, the rise of certain forms of the plastic arts, the fallow periods in drama, the gradual decline of poetry and the corresponding rise in prose'. Literary historians have long generalized about such matters, she wrote, but never before has there been a real documentation of their opinions. Then, in a sudden transition, she tacked on a single sentence about Puritanism. Merton's 'conclusions in regard to the relation between Puritanism and the scientific spirit', she said, were 'opposed to many of the older generalizations'. His conclusions, however, were 'entirely in line' with those 'drawn during the last few years by literary historians'. Presumably she had primarily in mind the writings of Richard F. Jones. In retrospect it will seem odd that Marjorie Nicolson did not so much as give a hint concerning what conclusions Merton had drawn about Puritanism and science. Nor did she mention the fact that Merton had devoted considerable thought and study to economic and military incentives. Perhaps, as a student of literary and intellectual history, she could find no grounds for even a sympathetic reading of chapters written in a sociological (or externalist) framework. Be that as it may, her review showed that parts of *STS* could have a wide appeal beyond a narrow circle of historians of science or sociologists concerned with science.

Joseph Needham

Joseph Needham was always a man of great style—a feature displayed in his scientific work and historical writing and in personal contacts. I shall never forget the verve and the richness of example in a lecture he gave at Harvard just before the outbreak of Wold War II, when I was a beginning graduate student in the history of science, more or less at the time of publication of Merton's *STS*. Even so, I was astonished when Merton sent me a xerox of Needham's request for a reprint of *STS*. Unlike the crude and cold postcards we receive today, Needham's card was handsomely printed in elegant Latin. At the top was a salutation in English '*from* JOSEPH NEEDHAM, *Caius College, Cambridge, England*', but the rest was in the best style of any author of university citations, beginning with a classical form of greeting: 'Josephus Needham apud Anglos in Universitate Cantabrigiensi scientiae naturalis doctor, Collegae clarissimo *Roberto K. Morton* salutem'. The '*Roberto K. Morton*' (*sic*) was, of course, written in long-hand. The rest of the message continued in Latin with a reference to the title of *STS* and the journal *Osiris* in which it appeared, and a request that a copy be sent. The conclusion, of course, was 'Vale', followed by 'Cantabrigiae ex Aula Annuntiationis vulg. dict. Gonv. & Caij *die 18/5/38*'.[70] Needham appended a note in English: 'Of course I am willing to pay any necessary charges'.

In the event Needham wrote a long review (five and a half pages) in the American Marxist quarterly, *Science and Society* (Needham, 1938). At this time he was by profession a biochemist, Sir William Dunn Reader in Biochemistry in the University of Cambridge. He had already published a learned and well written *History of Embryology* (Needham, 1934) and was known for his religious writings and his general Marxist point of view. A passionate devotee of the history of science, Needham had combined forces with Walter Pagel to arouse a serious interest in this subject in Cambridge University. They organized a series of lectures later published under the title, *Background to Modern Science* (Needham and Pagel, 1940), of which the centrepiece was a brilliant autobiographical account of nuclear physics by

Lord Rutherford.[71] Of course it was an honour that a doctoral dissertation by a beginner in the history of science should be reviewed by such an established scientist and scholar.

Needham's review, however, is in retrospect a very curious production. Like many of the contributions in today's *New York Review of Books*, it is more an essay on seventeenth century England in general, and on certain aspects of science at that time, than a review of *STS sensu stricto*. Following about two pages of generalities, Needham refers briefly to the writings of Clark and Tawney and concludes: 'Since capitalism, therefore, went hand-in-hand with Puritanism on the one side and with science on the other, we should expect to find a correlation between the scientists and the Puritans'.[72] This leads directly to the first mention of *STS*: 'Mr. Merton's book demonstrates that we do find exactly this'. But Needham does not then, as we might have been led to expect, describe or analyze or even criticize how Merton has made such a demonstration. Rather, he discusses the attitude toward science of such Puritans as John Wilkins, William Derham and Noah Biggs, with extensive quotations from their writings but with no additional mention of either Merton or of *STS*. A page later Needham introduces a comparison of the two universities, Cambridge and Oxford, to conclude that after the Civil War, Cambridge ('the traditional home of the East Anglican puritans') was the place to which 'the science movement repaired'.

We thus approach the end of Needham's essay with as yet no real sense of the subject-matter, the aims or the methods of *STS*. Then, in an aside, there occurs the second reference to Merton, in the statement that in 'Mr. Merton's book there is only one serious omission—he does not once mention the Levellers'. This group, says Needham, were 'in many cases peculiarly well aware of the impact of the coming scientific movement upon social relations'. Rather than develop this theme, however, or even explain the sense he intended of the phrase 'social relations', Needham gives a quotation of about a page and a quarter in length from a 1652 pamphlet by Gerrard Winstanley. This is followed by a comment that Winstanley exhibited 'a vivid appreciation of the importance of science for human welfare ... with a truly revolutionary political belief and activity'. Needham strongly advised Merton to 'include in another edition of his admirable work a chapter on the Levellers'. Merton's personal copy of a cutting of this review contains an arrow pointing to Needham's advice, but I do not find that Merton discusses the Levellers in either his 1970 'Preface' to the reprint of *STS* or the several revisions of his essay on 'Puritanism, Pietism, and Science'.

In the final page of the review Needham at last turns to the book itself. 'The association between puritanism and the early scientific movement is not', he writes, 'the only subject taken up by Mr. Merton'. He points out that Merton has 'a quantitative sense unusual in a historian', and proceeds to summarize Merton's methods and findings in relation to shifts of interest and work (based on the *DNB*) and his quantitative study of important discoveries (based on Darmstädter's *Handbuch*). He also gives a brief mention of the very valuable quantitative analysis of the proportion of papers in the early volumes of *Philosophical Transactions* devoted to pure as opposed to applied science. He informs his readers that 'like all students of the period', Merton 'has to admit the powerful influence on science of armaments, navigation and mining'. Needham concludes with a brief discussion of Merton's insight that 'the origin of the conception of progress' was 'associated with a favorable attitude toward change in all compartments of culture' and not only 'from the writers who were primarily concerned with the advancement of science'.

All in all, Needham's essay remains, after half a century, a stunning example of his splendid prose style. The quotations are relevant in content and they enrich a general essay on seventeenth century English culture. If the space devoted to Merton and to *STS* as such is small, nevertheless most of the main features of the book are mentioned. The only significant omission may be a lack of stress on Merton's thesis about the ethos of Puritanism serving to justify or to validate a new intellectual enterprise.

Walter Pagel

On receipt of a copy of *STS* from Merton, Walter Pagel wrote a cordial letter of acknowledgment. Today, in retrospect, we tend to think of Pagel as primarily a historian, author of seminal works on Harvey, Paracelsus and van Helmont. But in those days his historical research, however important, was a side-line, to be pursued in evenings and moments he could snatch away from his main occupation, which—as he explained in a letter to Merton (Cambridge, England, 25 May 1938)—was pathology.[73] In this letter Pagel admitted to Merton that he was 'of course not competent to say how much this work means for the progress of history and sociology', but he hoped Merton would 'allow me to tell you that I have never read a book which convinced me so much as yours'. We can easily imagine the feelings that such a statement would have aroused in a young scholar.

At this time Pagel's own research and writing had become directed toward the religious and philosophical matrix of scientific and medical thought. I remind the reader that he and Alexandre Koyré were to become the two major scholars who opened the eyes of historians of science to the riches of this form of 'externalism' and impelled them to depart from pure chronology or even the simple filiation of scientific ideas removed from any intellectual, philosophic or religious context.[74] At this time Pagel had just published the first of his explorations of the religious component of the thought and thought-process of life scientists and medical figures, his classic study of 'Religious Motives in the Medical Biology of the XVIIth Century' (Pagel, 1935).[75] Accordingly, he would have been predisposed in favour of a general discussion of any aspect of science and religion and would have been especially receptive to Merton's study of Puritanism or radical Protestantism in relation to the rise of science. In the letter he indicated 'how much I enjoyed the broad discussion on the significance of religion for the development of Science Technology and Sociology'. For 'the first time', he said, we now have 'the scientific basis for statements which were always made in a vague manner and were rather felt then scientifically proved'.

In his reply (14 August 1938) Merton expressed his gratification that Pagel had so warmly approved his work in this epistolary ceremony of laying-on-of-hands. He freely admitted that producing *STS* had been 'a labour of love' and that 'in such instances one can no more avoid emotional identification with intellectual, than with flesh-and-blood, offspring'. After mentioning some scholars—'enthusiasts from virtually every academic field'—who 'offer their research allegiance to the century of genius', he concluded with a request that Pagel might find it possible to review *STS* 'for some journal with which you are connected'. He had 'but a limited number of copies for review', he wrote, and he wished ('understandably enough perhaps') to 'have as extended a range of editorial notice as possible'.

Pagel complied. Unfortunately, his review did not appear in an influential journal such as the *Bulletin of the History of Medicine*,[76] but rather in a local publication, *The Cambridge Review* (Pagel, 1938). As might be expected, Pagel produced an intelligent and sympathetic account, introduced by reference to Merton's having adduced 'evidence in a most original way'. Merton's 'facts and theories', he declared, 'convince the reader in all essential points'.

For Pagel, as for Marjorie Nicolson, 'the main subject of this learned monograph' was 'the shift of emphasis and interest from theological to scientific studies'. Pagel then devoted the major part of his review to examining Merton's analysis of the 'social processes [that] were involved in shifts of interest from one division of human activity to another'.

After a discussion of Merton's statistical investigations, Pagel introduced the factor of 'short-time fluctuations in scientific interests' which 'depend upon the internal history of the science in question'. As an example, he cited the influence of Harvey's great discovery of the circulation of the blood. He contrasted this kind of effect with 'the appearance of the general types of problems, which are bound up with the dominant "values" and interests of the day'. Noting that religion is a 'factor of general importance', Pagel then proceeded to summarize Merton's general conclusions (in his own paraphrasing) in relation to the 'Protestant and Puritan ethic' and 'religious pragmatism' as 'a powerful incentive for research into Nature'.

At this point Pagel interjected his own 'opinion' that 'the motives are of a complicated character'. The reason is that 'there is as much praise as deprecation of human reason and its power'. That is, 'empiricism and experimental work are' in his view 'by no means invariably bound up with reasoning'. He then interjected a very personal note in observing (on the basis of his own work) that 'religious mysticism as opposed to the juridical reasoning of scholasticism has indeed played its part in the rise of modern science'.

Pagel concluded with a somewhat briefer presentation of Merton's studies of the influence of economic and military factors on the choice of research topics, and applauded Merton for his conclusion that there was 'no divorce of technology and science in the XVIIth century'. Pagel saluted Merton for a 'brilliant representation of his subject' and a 'meticulous collection of an overwhelming material'. Merton, he said, had established 'fundamental facts in a field which is often inadequately and unscientifically treated'.

By far the most cogent of all the reviews I have read, this one suffered only from the limited readership of a local university publication.

J. B. Conant

Presumably at George Sarton's suggestion, Merton sent a copy of *STS* to Harvard's president, James Bryant Conant. In acknowledging receipt of a copy of *STS*, in a letter dated 21 October 1938, Conant said that he had 'taken time off to read it because I am interested in that subject' and he wanted Merton to know 'how much I enjoyed your work': 'Having read somewhat extensively in this period on a strictly amateur basis, I was delighted to find that my tentative conclusions were exactly those which your exhaustive work had determined'. He concluded with a suggestion that Merton might have lunch with him 'so that we might on a strictly non-academic and unofficial basis talk about the history of science'.

It was a rare honour for a young scholar to be invited to lunch with the president of the university, but it must be remembered that Conant was far from being the ordinary president. Throughout his career as university administrator, and later as ambassador, he was always keenly interested in intellectual topics. Furthermore, as I and many others can testify, he loved intellectual exchanges, a feature of which was to put younger scholars at ease so that information, criticism and even complete dissent were possible—without any special deference to his rank (see I. B. Cohen, 1978). Furthermore, it was not often that Conant encountered so original and so important a study in an area in which he was personally interested. The lunch, arranged soon after in the President's home, was a meeting of two rather extraordinary scholars.

It should also be noted that Conant, a chemist by profession, had a longstanding sincere interest in the history of science, going back to the days when he had been a teaching assistant in T. W. Richards's Harvard course in the history of chemistry (see Conant, 1960). Under Conant's administration as President of Harvard, Sarton's academic position was at long last regularized with a promotion from Lecturer to Professor; the degree of PhD in History of Science was established in 1936 and was a featured topic in the annual report of the President of the University for 1937; and Sarton was awarded an honorary degree. A close adviser of Conant's was L. J. Henderson, famous for his research in biochemistry, who was an avid amateur of the history of science. In the 1930s Henderson had been initially responsible for Sarton's coming to Harvard and he had generously abandoned his own study in Widener Library so that Sarton might have it. I have referred above to Henderson's course for undergraduates at Harvard. Henderson had been a President of the History of Science Society; he became inaugural chairman of the new Harvard Committee on Higher Degrees in the History of Science and Learning (of which Merton was a member and Sarton the Secretary).

Conant's interest in the history of science became of real importance in the educational system when the Harvard report on *General Education in a Free Society* (1945) recommended that introductory courses have a strong historical component, if not be fully based on historical case histories. He expounded his own thoughts on such courses in his Terry Lectures at Yale, published under the title *On Understanding Science* (1947), expanded as *Science and Common Sense* (1951). He himself later participated in such a course (together with his protégés T. S. Kuhn and L. K. Nash) and edited a series of 'case histories', of which his own contribution dealt with the work of Boyle and his contemporaries, that is, science in seventeenth century England, the time and place of Merton's *STS*.[77]

In later years Conant wrote a historical study on 'The Advancement of Learning during the Puritan Commonwealth' (Conant, 1942).[78] Here, among other topics, he scrutinized the relations of 'Puritanism and Science'. He began by calling attention to the work of Dorothy Stimson, Robert K. Merton and Richard F. Jones. He pointed to the numerical studies which had shown that almost two-thirds 'of the charter members of the Royal Society came from a Puritan background'. He quoted Jones's thesis 'that our modern scientific utilitarianism is the offspring of Bacon begot upon Puritanism'. Merton was said to be 'particularly interested in Puritanism as an aspect of the relation of Protestantism to both science and technology'. Merton in this regard 'carries forward and illustrates with much new material the point of view first put forward by Max Weber'.

Following this review of the work of Stimson, Merton and Jones, Conant admitted that he found himself 'vacillating between a tendency to pursue this [Stimson-Jones-Merton] road even further than those who opened it and the contrary tendency to question some of the implications of this hypothesis'. He illustrated his problems in accepting the hypothesis in all its aspects by referring to the situation at Oxford in the 1650s. While all but two of those then in residence who later became Fellows of the Royal Society were Puritan and Parliamentary rather than Anglican or Royalist in their affiliations, Conant noted, they were 'none of them strongly Puritan in the sense that they espoused the strict Calvinist point of view, nor were they members of the Presbyterian party'. Indeed Conant finds them to have been only moderate Puritans, whose stance was 'in opposition to the strict Puritans, who were actively concerned with theological matters'. Conant found it notable that, at the Restoration, 'the future members of the Royal Society [were] readily conforming'. Conant thus stressed their character as 'lukewarm Puritans at best' and he observed how different they were from those 'who felt deeply the theological cleavages of that revolutionary period' and who 'seemed to have been little concerned with the new science'.

Conant concluded his examination of the Stimson-Jones-Merton thesis by calling attention to 'a group of *young men*' who 'preferred the Parliamentary cause to that of the King' and who 'were the progenitors of the establishment of experimental science on a firm foundation'. Admitting that 'the predominant influence of Cromwell and his followers' was 'demonstrably' responsible for the flourishing of these young men 'in Oxford during the Commonwealth', Conant agreed that to this extent, at least, 'the Puritan may be counted a friend of the new learning'.

We may note that Conant did not address the intellectual problem raised by Merton and by Jones of Puritanism in relation to utility. Nor did Conant even mention the Mertonian issue of the Puritan ethic as a factor in the legitimation of a new enterprise or profession—experimental science—although he did mention that 'Dr. Merton discusses the relation between the Protestant ethics [*sic*] and the new experimental science'. Conant was more interested in the general point of view, which he called the 'conclusions of all three scholars' (which 'are, roughly speaking, the same'), 'that Puritanism was helpful rather than harmful to the furtherance of the new experimental philosophy'.

Conant was not writing a review of the Merton monograph, nor was he attempting to give a critical analysis of that work or of the Stimson and Jones publications. Indeed Conant's discussion of 'Puritanism and Science' was only one of six sections of his article, and a rather short one (four out of twenty-nine pages) at that. His main purpose was to examine the legacy to learning of the Puritan decades, and he found that, paraphrasing Clarendon's 'famous left-handed tribute to General Monck', the Puritans of the 1640s 'were instrumental in bringing mighty things to pass, which they had neither the wisdom to foresee, nor courage to attempt, nor understanding to continue'. Among these mighty things 'which slowly came to pass', Conant listed 'religious toleration, representative government, modern science, and universities as we now know them'.

In 1971 Conant acknowledged the receipt of a copy of the reprint of *STS*. He was 'particularly glad' to have 'this copy with its new preface', he said, because he had lost the original. He reminded Merton that he had 'had an interest in this field for a long time'. He was, he concluded, 'enjoying rereading your contribution'.

A. Rupert Hall[79]

Rupert Hall's encounter with *STS* illustrates the way in which a serious scholar of the 1940s, eager to learn what had been written in the history of science, first came in contact with Merton's work. Hall later wrote one of the most important of the critiques of *STS*, 'Merton Revisited' (A. R. Hall, 1963). In that study Hall did not describe his 'first visit'.

Like many others, I had long assumed that Hall might have turned to *STS* in the course of preparing his own doctoral dissertation, which was on a subject directly related to a Mertonian theme—the possible relationship between theoretical studies of kinematics and dynamics and the practical art of gunnery.[80] When I recently re-examined Hall's book on this topic, however, I found to my great amazement that Merton's name does not appear in the index, although *STS* is listed in the 'Bibliography', along with Alexandre Koyré's *Etudes Galiléennes*. Furthermore, there is no mention of either Merton or Koyré in the 'Preface'.[81]

This aspect of Hall's book seemed all the more striking in the light of a recent bold assertion:

> Merton had great impact, but of a negative kind. Following Koyré, the emerging professional history of science tended to shun his viewpoint. The English historian A. R. Hall used Merton's citation of ordnance as the jumping-off point for a brilliant monograph showing that history did not follow Merton's sociological formulation, specifically that Merton simply did not know the facts. He followed that up with an influential critical essay, 'Merton Revisited'. (Reingold, 1986: 253)

It was with this statement in my mind—and with an awareness of the lack of direct reference to, or rebuttal of, Merton's work in Hall's book—that I conducted an interview with Rupert Hall in his home in Tackley, outside Oxford, on Easter Day 1988.

When I opened the conversation by asking about the origins of the dissertation, I was astonished to learn that Hall's choice of topic bore no direct relation whatsoever to Merton's *STS* and was in no way conceived as a test of whether or not history might 'follow Merton's sociological formulation'. Rather, Hall told me that he had undertaken a dissertation on this topic at the specific suggestion of G. N. Clark, then the Regius Professor of History at Cambridge University. At that time Clark was one of the leading figures in modern history in England, with a wide range of interest in every aspect of the seventeenth century: political and military history, cultural and scientific developments, technological and economic issues. He was the author of a major work focused on the problems of science and society ('social welfare') in seventeenth century England, a lengthy rebuttal to Boris Hessen's famous monograph.[82]

Hall had returned to Cambridge in 1945 after military service and had won a college scholarship at Christ's, where he was 'encouraged' to enter the new field[83] just being opened of history (and philosophy) of science.[84] At that time Hall had thought of pursuing economic history, but the new subject appealed to him because he had been an avid reader of the books by Eddington and Jeans and had found 'the historical notes in E. J. Holmyard's textbook of inorganic chemistry to be even more fascinating than the scientific text'. The new field combined his interest in history with a 'long-standing concern with science'.

Hall informed me that G. N. Clark served as his thesis advisor for about a year, during which time Hall saw him 'only three times—twice officially and once in a barber's shop'. So, although Clark had suggested that Hall undertake a study of the history of ballistics,[85] he did not direct Hall's work; in fact, he left Cambridge for Oxford to become Provost of Oriel College within a year. Hall, of course, read Clark's *Science and Social Welfare in the Age of Newton*, which—he recalled —'naturally led him to the work of Hessen', and he was fortunate in finding a copy of the original KNIGA printing in the University Library.[86] But Clark's book did not mention Merton or *STS*, even in the revised second edition.[87]

When Clark left for Oxford, the History Faculty assigned Hall to F. P. White, a mathematician and Fellow of St John's, where he was librarian. White was a good choice because he was an amateur historian, had an extensive personal library of older mathematical books (which he made available to Hall) and could help Hall with various technical questions.

Hall recalled that he had supposed, at the start of his research, that the scientists who developed the mathematical theory of trajectories in the sixteenth and seventeenth centuries would have exerted an important influence on the practice of gunnery. But he found that artillery men of that era used very crude empirical methods and that the work of the mathematicians did not affect the day-to-day practice of gunners until well after the seventeenth century.

It is to be noted that Merton was concerned with a quite different question than Hall's. Hall's study was directed toward a possible influence of theoretical or mathematical science on the practice of gunners. But Merton had rather explored the needs of gunnery as a stimulus for scientists and mathematicians to undertake the study of projectile motion and the computation of trajectories.

My final question to Hall was an obvious one: how had he encountered Merton's *STS*? It is an index of how little *STS* was read that none of Hall's teachers or advisers had directed him to Merton's work. I have mentioned the fact that Clark did not refer to Merton's work in the revised edition of his book. F. P. White was a professional mathematician and an amateur historian of his subject; it is not likely that he would have kept up with *Osiris* or even that he would have been interested in Merton's monograph if he had actually encountered it.

Hall recalled that soon after he became convinced that he would pursue the history of science as his academic speciality, he 'quite naturally turned to the journals in that field', of which there were then not many (a situation very different from today). Fortunately, the University Library owned these journals 'in complete runs', and he began to read through them all, beginning with Volume 1. 'I even read Boncompagni's old journal', he told me, and 'the *Archeion* or *Archivio*', but 'primarily *Isis* and *Osiris*', which naturally brought him into contact with Merton's monograph.

The way in which Hall encountered Merton's *STS* and the fact that no one in Cambridge had directed him to it may seem, in retrospect, a little odd—especially considering Hall's field of interest. This fact underlines the remark that I made earlier, that the influence of Merton on historians was not produced (before 1970) by the full-length study in *Osiris*, which was not generally read, save by scholars with a special interest.[88]

CONCLUSION: THE CONTINUING DEBATE AND THE LASTING SIGNIFICANCE OF MERTON'S *SCIENCE, TECHNOLOGY AND SOCIETY*

Since the publication of *STS* in 1938 the central Mertonian thesis about Protestantism has been discussed, debated, rejected, revived and reworked. Although on at least two occasions scholars have said that this was a dead issue, the stream of commentary continues without apparent abatement. Of how many doctoral dissertations (including those published with revisions) could it be said that they provoked or stimulated a half-century of such active research?[89] The only one that comes to mind is Emile Durkheim's *The Division of Labor in Society* (1893).

Many writers assume that the 'Merton thesis' is a single entity concerning the role of Puritanism in validating and legitimizing the new science. But some scholars have indicated that the 'Merton thesis' has two parts, just as there are two major topics in Merton's monograph on *Science, Technology and Society*. The latter part of *STS* is largely concerned with the influence of economic demands (primarily mining and shipping) and military needs on the foci of scientific interest. This latter topic was studied by Merton in two ways. First, a series of three chapters (7, 8, 9) explores in detail the extensive economic and military problems studied by, or related to, the researches of English scientists of the late seventeenth century. Second, a numerical analysis is made (in Chapter 10) of the topics introduced at meetings of the Royal Society, as transcribed in Birch's *History*, in categories of pure science, research for direct application to practical problems, and research that is only indirectly related to practice.

This pioneering aspect of Merton's monograph has not proved to be as challenging to scholars as the issue of Puritanism.[90] The reason may be that historians, notably Marxist historians, had already made forays in this direction. At a time when many scholars held that the significant new feature of the 'new science' was its reliance on experiments, it made sense that this science would have contacts with the experiential practice of artisans. Criticisms of this aspect of Merton's work have taken the form of an exploration of ideological incommensurability between this traditional and experiential view of science and a quite different one, adopted by many historians of science (see notably A. R. Hall, 1963). Influenced primarily by Alexandre Koyré, they have stressed the role in the scientific revolution of a new way of thinking, including the significance of Renaissance Platonism (or neo-Platonism), the rediscovery of Archimedes, the destruction of the Aristotelian cosmos and the geometrization of space.[91] Following Koyré there has not only been a denial of the importance of practical experiments, but also a stress on thought experiments as part of the new 'thinking cap' that produced modern science.[92]

Merton's work has been criticized because he did not explore what practical effects, if any, resulted from the efforts of scientists.[93] Even his numerical data have been challenged. A different mode of classification of the entries in Birch's *History* yielded a computerized analysis that indicated a much smaller proportion of topics related to such practical concerns as commerce, agriculture, mining, shipping and manufacturing (see Frank, 1975).[94]

For many scholars, however, the 'Merton thesis' does not include the two parts but simply refers to the theme of Puritanism and science. Here a continuous issue of criticism has been the definition of Puritan and Puritanism. As sociologist Merton used the term 'Puritan' (and 'ascetic Protestant') to denote a set of shared values and a point of view found among Puritans, in the sense that Max Weber had written of a Protestant ethic (or ethos) in his classic *The Protestant Ethic and the Spirit of Capitalism*. But many historians have not been willing to accept such a definition. For them a Puritan is defined by such factors as doctrinal allegiance, ritual and religious practice, membership in an organized church and anti-royalist politics. The resulting intellectual confrontation has even affected the Mertonian statistical analysis, since that depends on who is and who is not counted as a Puritan.[95]

An example in point is John Wilkins. He was reared in a Puritan environment, married Cromwell's sister and—during the Interregnum—was appointed Master of Wadham College. But after the Restoration he was ordained in the established church and rose to be Bishop of Exeter. In considering his post-Restoration career as a scientist and scientific amateur, are we nevertheless to consider him a Puritan? Merton would answer in the affirmative, others in the negative. [96] In recent years such issues have given rise to studies of the role in the science of the seventeenth century of such non-Puritans as Latitudinarians, Anglicans, Catholics and royalists. [97] In the 1960s Christopher Hill widened the terms of the debate by linking the Mertonian themes of Puritanism and science with a Marxist theme of Puritanism and capitalism. The ensuing debate heightened interest in the original Merton thesis. It is now generally agreed that Merton's findings about the value system and the institutionalization of science are valid, but that a serious modification is required of the element of 'Puritanism'.

In retrospect, however, I believe that Merton's major influence on the history of science was a primary demonstration that the development of science could be more than the narrowly conceived filiation of great discoveries that constituted this subject in the 1930s. For me, as for many others, Merton's *Science, Technology and Society* showed that the history of science had many dimensions and might be enriched by considerations external to science proper, that is, by introducing circumstances other than experiments, concepts and theories. [98] It was not clear that Merton's formal analysis could be simply transferred to other situations. I, for one, did not ever envisage that I would produce research in the style of *Science, Technology and Society*. But Merton did make me aware of the need to consider science in its total environment. As historian, and under the influence of Alexandre Koyré, I—like others in the history of science—primarily explored the intellectual environment rather than the social environment of science. [99] But it was Merton who brought a real awareness that the environment was worthy of exploration and that a study of external aspects of science could enrich the understanding of the historical development of the sciences and bring our historical presentations and interpretations into greater congruence with the events of the past. [100]

ACKNOWLEDGMENT

The research on which this study is based was supported by a grant from the Richard Lounsbery Foundation, New York City.

NOTES

1   The present study is based on a longer and more detailed presentation scheduled to appear as an introduction to a work I have edited, entitled *Puritanism and the Rise of Modern Science: The Merton Thesis*, to be published by Rutgers University Press (henceforth cited as I. B. Cohen (forthcoming)). This work contains selections from the major criticisms, discussions and amplifications of Merton's monograph of 1938, *Science, Technology and Society in Seventeenth Century England* (Merton, 1938a). The present version draws heavily on printed and manuscript materials and correspondence from the personal archive of Robert K. Merton in New York City, which were made freely available to me. I have also profited from many conversations with Merton. I have, additionally, made use of manuscript documents and records in the Harvard University Archives.

2   In those days at Harvard the general presentation of the history of science was given in two parts. In the autumn semester the physiologist and sociologist L. J. Henderson lectured on science from Hipparchus through Harvey and Galileo; in the spring semester George Sarton dealt with science from Newton to the very recent past. It was a curious fact that Henderson, a practicing scientist, should give the course on early science, while Sarton, whose major publications were on ancient and medieval science, presented the modern era.

3   The graduate degree programme at Harvard was established in 1936. Two degrees were offered: an MA and a PhD in the History of Science and Learning, administered by an interdisciplinary committee. I later learned that the 'and Learning' had been added to 'History of Science' in order to include the work of Professor Robert Ulich (of the Graduate School of Education) on the history of universities. Sarton's graduate seminar had been given for the first time during the academic year 1935–36. When I enrolled in the seminar during the academic year 1936–37, there were some regular auditors or non-credit students. The credit students, in addition to myself, were Aydin M. Sayili, the first student to complete his doctorate under the programme, and A. R. Goldsmith.

4   Sarton then occupied a set of rooms in Widener Library, of which the smaller one (Widener 185) was his private office, with a connecting door to the outer office (Widener 189), which housed continuous runs of almost all journals relating to the history of science, a good working research library, and Sarton's vast collection of reprints—sent to him so that their titles could be included in the critical bibliographies which he regularly prepared for *Isis*. In this outer office there were five or six desks, one for his secretary, one for his assistant (at one time Mary Catherine Wellborn, later Alexander Pogo), and others for visiting scholars and students. I was assigned to one of these desks to facilitate my writing my seminar paper, while Sayili also had a desk. At this remove in time I can no longer remember exactly when I was first introduced to Merton, but I believe the meeting occurred during 1936–37, while I was still an undergraduate taking Sarton's seminar. Although Merton had conducted one of the meetings of Sarton's seminar in its inaugural year, 1935–36, he did not do so during the second year, when I was a student.

5   The only time I had heard Merton speak, prior to his presentation of 'Singletons and Multiples', was when he gave a rather informal commentary on Rupert Hall's paper on 'The Scholar and the Craftsman in the Scientific Revolution' (Merton, 1959b) during the Institute of the History of Science Conference held at the University of Wisconsin, 1–11 September 1957.

6   Whereas in Merton's paper many examples were adduced in order to lead him to some general conclusions about the nature of the scientific enterprise, mine was more narrowly focused on three examples: the independent invention of the calculus by Newton and Leibniz, the discovery of the principle or law of conservation of energy (by Helmholtz, Joule and Mayer) and the conception of natural selection (by Darwin and Wallace). I did a quite extensive search through the literature of the subject, however, and came upon an early discussion of this topic by M. F. Mentré which has not entered the general literature, and, so far as I know, has only once been cited by a recent author, Merton, who lists his name (without a bibliographical reference and without any discussion) as one of those who has been aware of the existence of simultaneous discoveries. I was astonished to find that this work had not been analyzed by Merton, because he usually provides an extensive review of the literature and a complete pre-history (or history) of the subject. Mentré's article was based on a paper given at the *Congrès International de Philosophie* conference at Geneva in 1904. The 'cinquième section' of the conference was devoted to 'Histoire des Sciences' and constituted the 'IIIme Congrès international d'Histoire des Sciences'. There were papers by Paul Tannery, Pierre Duhem, H. G. Zeuthen, Karl Sudhoff and others. Mentré presented simultaneous discoveries grouped in categories of mathematics, astronomy, mechanics, physics, chemistry, biology and sociology. Rejecting the possibility that such simultaneous discoveries could result from pure chance or be the product of collusion, Mentré argued that the only remaining possibility was an external 'cause objective', that is, a 'déterminisme social'. In developing the dichotomy between a 'déterminisme externe' and a 'logique interne', Mentré may have been the first scholar to put forth the distinction between 'externalist' and 'internalist' history of science.

Chapter 10 of Merton's 1938 monograph *Science, Technology and Society* is entitled 'Extrinsic Influences on Scientific Research'. The opening sentence raises the 'question of the relative importance of intrinsic and external factors in the determination of the foci of scientific interest'. Note that although the title of the chapter contains the phrase 'extrinsic influences', the text does not pose a dichotomy of 'extrinsic' and 'intrinsic' but rather 'external' and 'intrinsic' (not 'internal'). In the third paragraph of Chapter 1, however, Merton referred to 'the internal history of each of the fields of culture'. On Merton's position in the history of the debate over externalist history, see further I. B. Cohen, 'The First Discussion of "Internalist" and "Externalist" History of Science', to appear in *Isis*.

7   For information concerning the publication in *Osiris* see I. B. Cohen (1988).

8   Dorothy Stimson had received her doctorate from Columbia University for a thesis entitled *The Gradual Acceptance of the Copernican Theory* (privately printed in New York in 1917). Her later historical work dealt with seventeenth century England, notably figures associated with the Royal Society. Her major work was *Scientists and Amateurs: A History of the Royal Society* (1948).

9   I join the company of Mertonians who refer to Merton's work as *STS*.

10 Jones's book has undergone a number of significant changes. Originally entitled *Ancients and Moderns: Study of the Background of the Battle of the Books*, it was published in 1936 as a volume in the Washington University Studies. A revised edition, published in 1961 by the Washington University Press, was considerably rewritten and had a new subtitle so as to become *Ancients and Moderns: A Study of the Rise of the Scientific Movement in Seventeenth-Century England*. Since then there have been paperback reprints, two by Dover Publications, New York, including one in 1982.

11 In her article on 'The Ballad of Gresham College' (Stimson, 1932), she pointed out that she had been put on the track of this ballad by the Yale historian Wallace Notestein. She also indicated that extracts of the ballad had been previously published in Weld, 1848: 79–80; and Masson, 1925: 48–9.

12 Stearns obtained his PhD at Harvard, working primarily with Samuel Eliot Morison. Although he produced some studies of seventeenth and eighteenth century England, his primary area of research was the development of scientific activity in the New World. His magnum opus is *Science in the British Colonies of America* (1970).

13 Stearns's celebrated work on this subject was 'Colonial Fellows of the Royal Society of London, 1661–1788' (Stearns, 1946).

14 Since both Stearns and Mood are dead, this curious mystery does not have an easy solution.

15 For example, Merton referred to the fact that 'recently, the sociologist Talcott Parsons is recorded as having described the threefold, or possibly fivefold 'discovery of "the internalization of values and culture as part of the personality" as "a very remarkable phenomenon because all of these people were independent of each other and their discovery is ... fundamental"'. Quoted from the reprint in Merton, 1973: 356.

16 The index includes a single reference under 'multiple discoveries'—'multiple discoveries: in sociology of science'.

17 [Ed. note: This omission has been made good in the Supplement to Miles, 1975, printed as an *Appendix* to this volume.]

18 On page 476 Merton quotes a letter from Sarton to him agreeing to publish his dissertation 'if H.U. [Harvard University] or another agency is ready to share the financial and burden of risk with me'. Merton comments: 'In the event, neither Harvard nor any other agency shared the burden and the risk; my mentor himself provided the functional equivalent of a publishing grant from the nonexistent National Science Foundation'. Merton, however, was in error. A grant was made by Harvard's Committee on Research in the Social Sciences, a subvention of $375. For further details see I. B. Cohen (forthcoming).

19 For further details on Sarton's career see Merton and Thackray (1972).

20 Sarton apparently made a gift to Merton of twenty-five or fifty free reprints. Merton apparently ordered (and paid for) an additional number.

21 Merton was using the term in the accepted sociologists' meaning, as featured in Max Weber's writings on the *Protestant Ethic* (1930). Historians, however, were aware of the English Civil War and made a sharp distinction between Puritans and other Protestants. This contrast between historians and sociologists has plagued much of the commentary on (and criticism of) Merton's *STS*.

22 *Social Theory and Social Structure* has been translated into French, Italian, Japanese, Spanish, Hebrew, Portuguese, Hungarian and Polish (and in *Samizdat* editions, Russian and Czech) and the article itself had been reprinted twice (see Miles, 1975).

23 The article on science and the military (1935) was apparently never reprinted until Merton's *The Sociology of Science: Theoretical and Empirical Investigations* (1973).

24 This article was also printed separately as a pamphlet in the Bobbs-Merrill Reprint Series in the History of Science.

25 E. A. Burtt's seminal study, *The Metaphysical Foundations of Modern Physical Science* (1932), did not have much influence on historians of science until after 1945.

26 Sorokin's commentary and Merton's reply (of mid-1934) have been published in the May 1989 issue of *Science in Context*. See also note 51 below.

27 On the history of Hessen's essay, see the 1971 reprint of Bukharin *et al.*, *Science at the Cross Roads*, with an introduction by Gary Werskey and a foreword by Joseph Needham.

28 This paragraph appears on page 649 of the 1968 edition of *Social Theory and Social Structure*, and corresponds more or less to the penultimate paragraph on page 136 of the 1970 edition of *Science, Technology and Society*.

29 The 'Postscript' was not upgraded anew for the enlarged edition of 1968, where it appeared on pages 649–60 (Merton, 1968).

30 Both are reprinted in I. B. Cohen (forthcoming).

31 Those interested in bibliographical curiosities may take note that in the original publication in *Osiris*, the title is given in the form, 'Science, Technology and Society in Seventeenth Century England', without a comma after 'Technology' and without a hyphen in the compound adjective 'Seventeenth Century'. On the title page of the paperback reprint (New Jersey: Humanities Press, 1978), an ampersand has been substituted for the word 'and' and there is no hyphen; yet on the front cover the original 'and' is maintained but a hyphen is introduced into 'Seventeenth-Century'. The hyphen is used, but not the comma, in the list of Merton's writings given in Merton (1973); Norman Storer's introduction (p. xv) introduces both the comma following 'Technology' and the hyphen in 'Seventeenth-Century'.

32 This title may be compared with the opening sentence of the 'Preface' to the version published in *Osiris*, where Merton says that his 'study might be more exactly entitled "some sociologically relevant aspects of certain phases of the development of science in seventeenth century England"'. On the title page of Merton's dissertation, as submitted for the degree, the hyphen was not used in 'Seventeenth Century', but there is a hyphen in the title of the dissertation typed at the head of the signed certificate of acceptance.

33 Further information on Sarton and Merton is presented in my 'Introduction' to I. B. Cohen (forthcoming) and in Merton (1979b).

34 This would account for a Part II tacked on to the end of the final chapter, originally conceived without a separately headed Part I.

35 A selection from de Candolle's discussion on Protestantism and science is included in I. B. Cohen (forthcoming).

36 Theodore Rabb has said that 'the first hint' of the thesis that Puritanism was 'of considerable importance' in the 'rise of science in XVIIth century England' was given by Dorothy Stimson in her 1931 article 'Dr. Wilkins and the Royal Society' (Rabb, 1962: 47n2). This statement has been repeated by Charles Webster.

A careful reading of the Stimson article on Wilkins, however, has failed to reveal even the slightest 'hint' that Puritanism might have provided a favourable impetus to science. On the contrary, the article contains such statements as that in a 'time of political and theological faction continuing through the civil war and the Commonwealth into the Restoration period, men of varied interests' found 'relief and recreation in the new science'.

Although she mentions that Wilkins had 'Puritan antecedents and training', she stresses that he and Seth Ward 'were pre-eminent among the Anglican divines who gave reason, according to Sprat, for the Church of England to be entitled "Mother of this sort of knowledge"'. She notes that 'these divines ... found in the ... Anglican Church of those days ... a comfortable indifference to their scientific concerns'. The Anglican Church was not 'likely to be perturbed ... about the scientific pursuits' of its ministers. This situation is contrasted with 'the lack of such comfortable security ... especially after 1662' of non-conformist ministers, a situation which (she says) may help to 'explain why nonconformist ministers were not equally conspicuous with Anglican divines in the ranks of the Royal Society'.

In a quite different article, on Comenius, which was submitted to Sarton for publication in 1933 (Stimson, 1935a), there is a hint of the possible significance of Puritanism for science.

37 In our circle of historians of science Dorothy Stimson was almost always addressed as 'Miss Stimson', 'Professor Stimson'. I never heard her referred to (or addressed) as 'Dean' Stimson, although this mode of address was perhaps used at Goucher College. Merton, and others (perhaps following his example), referred to her in print as 'Dean' Stimson. Her first letter to Merton was

written in long-hand on personal stationery, bearing the letterhead, 'Miss Dorothy Stimson' (not 'Prof. Dorothy Stimson' or just plain 'Dorothy Stimson')—a permanent visible token of her times, her upbringing and her adopted persona.

    I vividly recall a conversation in the late 1940s, at the home of John F. Fulton, on Deepwood Drive, in Hamden, on the outskirts of New Haven. The occasion was a reception and dinner for the members of a committee appointed by Fulton (then President of the History of Science Society) to explore the role of history of science in the science courses then being established at many American colleges and universities as part of the General Education programmes. During a pre-dinner conversation Miss Stimson turned to my wife, after staring (perhaps glaring) at Henry Guerlac and me. In her typical strident voice she compared her situation as a scholar to ours, expressing her envy—not because Henry and I were on the faculty of major universities gifted with great research libraries, but rather because (as she put the matter simply and directly) 'I [!] have no wife to help me!'

38   So far as I know, Miss Stimson never stressed this subject in later publications. In particular the Puritan thesis is mentioned only briefly in her history of the Royal Society (Stimson, 1948).

39   First published in London in 1930 by George Allen and Unwin. Parsons is identified on the title page as 'Tutor in Economics, Harvard University'. In the main body of the text (p. 50; uncorrected in the second printing, 1948) Benjamin Franklin appears as 'Benjamin Ferdinand' and there is a reference to the 'state of Philadelphia'.

40   In 'Puritanism, Pietism and Science' (Merton, 1968: 634n18), Merton discusses the statement imputed to Weber that 'the opposition of the Reformers is sufficient reason for not coupling Protestantism with scientific interests'. See further, *ibid*.: 649, 656–7; also *STS* (*passim*). See too Weber's *Protestant Ethic* (1930: 168, 249n145).

41   The positions taken by Sarton and Sorokin are especially relevant since Sorokin was the nominal director of Merton's dissertation and Sarton was the faculty member under whom Merton had prepared himself to deal with the subject-matter of the history of science. Both men signed the dissertation and—despite their reservations—were active in assuring its publication. Sarton offered to include *STS* in a forthcoming issue of *Osiris* if a partial subvention could be obtained; Sorokin obtained a grant of $375 to help defray the costs of publication.

42   There is no way of now ascertaining the exact date.

43   The following presentation is based on R. K. Merton's personal archive, which he very kindly made available to me. The first letter available is from Dorothy Stimson to RKM on 3 February 1934, in reply to a letter of his which has not been found.

44   One can only guess at the contents of RKM's letter from her replies.

45   At that time, 3 February 1934, Dorothy Stimson had not as yet made a public announcement of the Puritan thesis; that occurred some months later (in December 1934) at the Washington meeting of the American Historical Association.

46   A careful search of the *New England Quarterly* has revealed no trace of an article or of any communication by Dorothy Stimson.

47   The paper in question was 'Comenius and the Invisible College' (Stimson, 1935a). On page 374 she stated that: 'In addition to probable European influences, the movement resulting in the formation of the Royal Society seems also more closely related to Puritanism than has hitherto been made clear; for that attack upon authority in the church and in the state had its effect upon authority in science also'.

48   Evidently a reference to Theodore Hornberger's 'Puritanism and Science: The Relationship Revealed in the Writings of John Cotton' (1937). There are two relevant works by Shipton published at the time: 'Secondary Education in the Puritan Colonies' (1934); and 'A Plea for Puritanism' (1935). The last-mentioned paper had been read at the American Historical Association on 29 December 1934, during the same meetings at which Dorothy Stimson read her paper on Puritanism and the 'new philosophy'.

49   The total lack of mention of Jones in the Merton-Stimson correspondence indicates that his views about Puritanism and science in relation to Bacon were not evident to other scholars prior to the publication in 1936 of *Ancients and Moderns*.

50   The results of this research were presented in Chapter 2 of *STS*.

51   I wonder whether these marginalia may have been pencilled in by Merton's fellow graduate student, Theodore Silverstein, a brilliant scholar and acute critic. Silverstein is thanked by Merton in the original preface to *STS* (dated 4 April 1937).

    On further reflection, and after a discussion of the matter with Merton, I have come to believe that most likely the comments in question were those written by Sorokin on the draft of 'Puritanism, Pietism and Science' that Merton had submitted to him in the spring of 1934. Sorokin objected (see text to note 26 above) to what seemed to him to have been oversimplification in 'Weber's-Troeltsch's-Merton's specifications of so called leading socio-moral-principles of Protestantism'. 'On margins here and there', he wrote, 'I note that these supposedly specific principles of the Protestant *Geist* can be found in the pre-reformation Christ[iani]ty, in other Oriental religions etc. Why so violently twist the real situation and make such a blunder?' Such marginal comments, in Sorokin's characteristic and inimitable style, would obviously have attracted Miss Stimson's interest.

It should be noted, furthermore, that Sorokin said that Merton's 'attempt to give the statistical corroboration (*contra* to Weber who did not give anything except one miserable—second-hand—table) is also very dubious'. He concluded by a reference to his own ideas which 'much better fit to the "facts" than half-fantastic "derivations" of Weberian "Protestantism-Capitalism" and Mertonian "Protestantism-Scientism"....' He advised his graduate student that the one-time fashionable theory of Weber, Tawney and others is now 'punctured'—so 'entirely' that 'hardly any serious historian or scholar...subscribes for it'. He concluded that 'It is definitely "over". Why to follow "back-numbers"?'

52   These may eventually turn up among the papers in the Merton archive.

53   The reference here is to Stimson's 'Comenius and the Invisible College' (1935a). In this same letter of 25 March 1936 Dorothy Stimson wrote to Merton that she had written it in 1933 but it was not published 'till last Sept'.

54   Perhaps further information may be available in Dorothy Stimson's papers. She evidently did not choose (or was not asked) to write a review of *STS*.

55   Merton had no further epistolary contact with Dorothy Stimson. He recalls that in the early autumn of 1938 (a date engraved in the memory because of the destructive forces of the great hurricane of September) he visited her in her home in Stonington, Conn. At this remove, however, he is unable to recall any of the discussions that took place during that social visit.

56   B. J. Stern and C. A. M. Ewing each wrote a review (see below), but not for a major sociological journal.

57   Ewing began his comments by observing that Pitirim Sorokin's 'impetus' had 'substantially increased' the 'professional study of the rise of science' in recent years.

58   Merton and Ashley-Montagu later collaborated in writing about criminals and the work of E. A. Hooton.

59   *Nature*, Vol. 143, 22 April 1939, pp. 674–5. The only other view of *STS* in a scientific journal was by Grant McColley (1939). This was a highly laudatory summary of Merton's main points, chapter by chapter.

60   A major focus of Jones's research was the influence of Francis Bacon and of Baconian science. See note 64 below.

61   Jones's magnum opus, *Ancients and Moderns*, was published in 1936, too late to be used (or mentioned) in the dissertation, but it was discussed in the revised version printed two years later in *Osiris*. Merton reviewed *Ancient and Moderns* in *Isis*, 1936, Vol. 26, pp. 171–2.

62   Jones published an article on 'Puritanism, Science and Christ Church' in *Isis* in 1939 (Jones, 1939); in it he developed a point mentioned in his review, about a proposal 'to turn Christ Church into an experimental science institution'.

63   The Germanic-sounding misquotation (or misprint) of 'cultural soil of the seventeenth century England' was not corrected on the galley proofs sent to Merton.

64   Jones suggested two possible objections to 'the idea that the Puritans integrated their science and theology'. The first is that 'Bacon, whose influence at this time was exceedingly great, clearly separated the two [i.e. science and theology], and there is evidence that the Puritans followed him in this attitude'. The second, that Sprat (in his *History of the Royal Society*) makes 'no mention ... of the glorification of God through works, i.e. experiments'.

65   In her joint review of *STS* and the books by Martha Ornstein (1938) and G.N. Clark (1938), Marjorie Nicolson devoted almost the whole of her final paragraph (almost as much space as she had used to discuss *STS* itself) to the activity of literary historians in studying the development of science. This she described as a new field of research which had been steadily growing in importance in the last decade:

The fact that these two volumes [Merton's and Martha Ornstein's] appear at a time when groups of the Modern Language Association are devoting themselves to a study of the interrelationship between science and literature, when various journals in the field of history are publishing articles on scientific subjects, when sociologists discuss the pros and cons of 'the social determination of ideas', indicates that a new and important field of investigation has been opened for scholars in many fields. Only by a succession of such volumes, dealing with the interrelationship of science, literature, economics, politics can the true history of science be written.

The development of historical studies of science and literature (and Richard F. Jones's role in such studies) was a feature of Marjorie Nicolson's introductory essay to the R. F. Jones Festschrift, *The Seventeenth Century: Studies in the History of English Thought and Literature from Bacon to Pope* (1951).

66   These have been assembled in a volume entitled *Science and the Imagination* (1956).

67   Merton has addressed this subject in his autobiographical retrospect on the sociology of science (Merton, 1979b).

68   The other two works were G. N. Clark's *Science and Social Welfare in the Age of Newton* (1938) and Martha Ornstein's *The Role of Scientific Societies in the Seventeenth Century* (1938).

69   In the event, a previous commitment prevented Merton from participating in the MLA session.

70   A reference to Gonville and Caius College, Cambridge, of which he was a Fellow. Later he became President and Master.

71   The volume contained 'Ten Lectures at Cambridge arranged by the History of Science Committee, 1936'. The 'Introduction' described the activities of this committee in attempting to establish the subject of history of science at Cambridge; Needham was the chairman, Pagel the secretary.

72   This curious example of intellectual *legerdemain* is as stunning as it is unsound. In essence, it says that since *C* was associated with *P* and *C* with *S*, it follows that *P* and *S* must be equally associated—which is perhaps a not immediately obvious paralogism, masked by an optimistic belief in the conclusion.

73   Pagel did say (in this letter) that 'I have some plans for future work in history and if providence allows me to publish something again I shall certainly care [take care?] to send you the first reprint'.

74   Pagel and Koyré were the primary scholars who introduced my generation (and succeeding ones) to intellectual externalism in the history of science, just as Merton and Hessen, but primarily Merton, introduced us to social externalism. On this score, see my 'Introduction' to I. B. Cohen (forthcoming) and Chs 9 and 10. Gary Abraham (1983) has analyzed some of the major differences between the historical sociology of Merton's *STS* and the externalism practised by many of today's historians of science.

75   This was Pagel's first full-dress study in history. See the bibliography of his publications in the two-volume Festschrift, Allen G. Debus (ed), *Science, Medicine and Society: Essays to Honor Walter Pagel* (1972).

76   It is rather curious that Merton's *STS* was not reviewed in the *Bulletin*, since the editor (Henry E. Sigerist) was notably interested in all aspects of science and society. The *Bulletin*, furthermore, had published Dorothy Stimson's paper on Puritanism and science.

Of course, Merton did not discuss medicine and could be faulted for having stressed the physical sciences (in relation to mining, transportation and military arts) rather than the life sciences (in relation to agriculture and health).

77   See J. B. Conant (ed), *Harvard Case Histories in Experimental Science*, 2 vols (1957). Conant personally contributed two 'case histories': one on Boyle and pneumatics, the other on the chemical revolution.

78   Less than three full pages of this study are actually devoted to science.

79   See further Hall's chapter in this volume (Chapter 22).

80   Hall's doctoral dissertation was published in 'a slightly different form' under the title, *Ballistics in the Seventeenth Century* (1952).

81   Since Hall's book draws heavily (almost entirely) on primary sources, there are not many references in the text or notes to the monographs or books by recent historians. Thus there is no mention of (or reference to) Merton, although a note on page 91 mentions Koyré's *Études Galiléennes* and another on page 79 refers to Jones's *Ancients and Moderns*.

82   G. N. Clark, *Science and Social Welfare in the Age of Newton* (1937). His best-known work was *The Seventeenth Century* (1935); a second edition appeared in 1947. He had also written a review of

English economic history, *The Wealth of England, 1496–1760* (1946), in the Home University Library series.

83　Hall told me that, of course, college authorities cannot force scholarship students to change or to choose fields, but they do exert a tremendous intellectual pressure on junior scholars. Evidently, the college authorities thought 'it would be interesting to have someone in the college pursue this new field'.

84　The most active promoter of this new subject at Cambridge had been Joseph Needham. Just before the outbreak of World War II Needham and Walter Pagel had organized a series of lectures intended to arouse an academic interest in the history of science (see note 71 above). After the war the history of science entered the Cambridge curriculum, even achieving status as a tripos subject. Herbert Butterfield's popular book, *The Origins of Modern Science 1300–1800* (1949), later revised and often reprinted, originated in a set of lectures planned to advance this subject. See Hall's reminiscences in Chapter 22 of this volume.

85　In his book on *Science and Social Welfare in the Age of Newton* Clark did not mention the problems of pure and applied ballistics. Nor did he address himself to the questions of science and warfare, although he did discuss 'the direct effect of military needs on technology' (1937: 51ff.). His chief motivation was to dispute Hessen's thesis, to show that 'an economic impulsion' (*ibid.*: 73) was but one of four, the others deriving from the arts, healing and warfare. He even stressed that 'the stimulus to science from the desire to succeed in war is not identical with that from the desire to enjoy and create' and gave examples to prove his point.

86　Clark's book was first published in 1937, based on a pair of articles in the *Economic Journal* and the *Economic History Review*. In a second edition of 1949, Clark introduced 'some further references added at the ends of the chapters', but these did not include Merton's monograph, nor any of his articles, even though these were of evident importance for Clark's general theme.

87　Merton reviewed Clark's book in *Isis* in 1938 (Merton, 1938c).

88　In J. G. Crowther's *Fifty Years with Science* (1970: 178) there is a paragraph containing his impressions of Robert K. Merton, whom he met at Harvard in 1937. Although Crowther lavishes praise on Merton for his contribution to our understanding of science and society, he cites only the article on 'Science, Puritanism and Pietism', without even a reference to *Science, Technology and Society in Seventeenth Century England*.

89　A convenient review of some of the early literature concerning the 'Merton thesis' is given in Kemsley (1968). Merton himself has given a set of summaries and replies to some early criticisms and comments in a 'Bibliographical Postscript' to the republication of his 'Puritanism, Pietism and Science' (Merton, 1968: 649–60). A review of the literature, plus a bibliographical listing of relevant writings, is also given in the 1970 reprint of Merton's *Science, Technology and Society* (Merton, 1970a). These two discussions by Merton are reprinted in I. B. Cohen (forthcoming), where section 10 of my 'Introduction' contains a summary of some of the major issues raised by the 'Merton thesis', and section 11 contains an annotated checklist of the major writings discussing the 'Merton thesis' over some fifty years.

90　For example, in the 1970 reprint of *Science, Technology and Society* Merton responded to criticisms and discussions of the Puritan-Protestant-science thesis, and listed in the bibliographical appendix a number of authors who had written on this subject; but there was no similar response needed for the economic-military chapters in the 1970 reprint, nor in the reprint of his essay, 'Science and Economy of 17th Century England', in his volume *Social Theory and Social Structure*.

91　On the essential problem raised by these two different approaches to the scientific revolution, see T. S. Kuhn (1968).

92　This new viewpoint has been conveniently summarized and presented by Herbert Butterfield, *The Origins of Modern Science, 1300–1800* (1949).

93　We have seen above that Rupert Hall's study of ballistics in the seventeenth century indicated that the theoretical studies of dynamics did not have much influence on practical gunnery. It would be interesting to know what effects, if any, the practically oriented studies of scientists in the Royal Society had on the day-to-day practices of artisans in different areas. On this topic, see Michael Hunter, *Science and Society in Restoration England* (1981, Ch. 4).

94　One reason for the difference in the numerical results obtained by Merton and by Frank is that they used quite different and wholly incompatible statistical categories. Merton's presentation indicated that this was a first essay. Clearly, this is a subject that still calls for more research.

95　Among the writers who have discussed this question are T. K. Rabb, Barbara J. Shapiro, Lewis Feuer, J. M. Cooper, James W. Carroll and Bernard Barber. This question has been summed up neatly by John Dillenberger, *Protestant Thought and Natural Science* (1960). On John Wilkins, see Barbara J. Shapiro, *John Wilkins, 1614–1672: An Intellectual Biography* (1969).

96   A convenient collection of writings dealing with this subject, excerpted from the British Journal *Past and Present*, has been made by Charles Webster, *The Intellectual Revolution of the Seventeenth Century* (1974).

97   Hill's presentations and the reactions to them are available in Charles Webster's anthology, cited in note 96 above.

98   A similar influence is discerned in retrospect by many observers of the British scene, where the famous paper by Boris Hessen, 'The Social and Economic Roots of Newton's *Principia*', presented in 1931 at the London International Congress of the History of Science and Technology, is held to have produced a profound effect on many British historians of science and scientists interested in the history of their subject. A comparison and contrast of the influence of Hessen and Merton in this regard is given in section 9 of my 'Introduction' to I. B. Cohen, *Puritanism and the Rise of Modern Science* (forthcoming). Some information on both the positive and negative impact of Hessen's paper may be found in P. G. Werskey's new 'Introduction' to the 1971 reprint of Bukharin *et al.*, *Science at the Cross Roads* (1931).

99   Often the writings of Alexandre Koyré are held up as models of 'internalism' in history of science because he eschewed all aspects of possible economic and social influences. Thus in Rupert Hall's 'Merton Revisited', the work of Koyré is presented as a direct antithesis to Merton's *Science, Technology and Society*. Nevertheless, from the very narrow point of view of history of science as it existed in the 1930s, Koyré's work partook of 'externalism' to the degree that it introduced non-scientific considerations such as philosophical currents, religious or theological beliefs and so on.

100 For many of my generation it was Merton rather than Hessen who opened our eyes to the richness of history of science, to the possibilities that this subject has more dimensions than narrow internal scientific considerations. The fact is that Hessen's work was crude, often erroneous and written from a simplistic Marxian point of view of dialectical materialism. As such, it could not be fully convincing to non-Marxist scholars. Merton's monograph, on the other hand, was written in impeccable historical style, although using extensively the language and concepts of sociology. In fact, Merton's work was so fully documented and so well historically researched that it could easily have been submitted as a successful doctoral dissertation in a department of history or of history of science.

21. Puritanism and Science: The 'Merton Thesis' after Fifty Years

PIYO RATTANSI

MERTON AND THE WEBERIAN CHALLENGE

Max Weber's name does not make its appearance among the footnotes to Robert K. Merton's *Science, Technology and Society in Seventeenth Century England* (1938a) until the fifty-ninth page, and then only in the company of Sombart, Troeltsch and their contemporaries. Yet Weber obviously provided the model for that part of Merton's investigation which has dominated scholarly interest during the succeeding half-century. Merton's work would be said today to fall squarely within the Weberian 'research tradition'.

Weber's *The Protestant Ethic and the Spirit of Capitalism* was itself part of a much grander comparative-historical enterprise, which traced the historical origins of the animating 'spirit' of Western culture and institutions, setting it apart from all other civilizations of past or present. It was essentially the 'spirit' of rationalism, a proportioning of means to ends unfettered by all those influences that could restrict its fullest application. It rested on a 'disenchantment of the world', that is, the assumption that rational calculation was, in principle, capable of unlimited application, denying the existence of any mysterious entities beyond its reach. Existing in a highly developed form in the legal and juridical systems and in the patterns of economic organization, government and administration, its influence was equally evident in music and architecture. It perhaps found its supreme embodiment in the science and technology of the modern West.

By what historical route had that 'spirit' come to pervade and shape Western culture? In the *Protestant Ethic* Weber selected a key area for study: the emergence of mercantile capitalism in early-modern Europe. Weber worked backwards from a remarkable sociological feature of the Germany of his day. When the religious composition of its élite, made up of the captains of industry and commerce and

351

of the higher technical personnel, was analyzed, the Protestants were found to be greatly overrepresented in proportion to their share of the population. The preference for the modern was equally evident in the educational choices of Protestant parents for their children, when compared to Catholic parents. How far back could it be traced? In the sixteenth century it was the economically more highly developed cities which had gone over to the Reformation. Was that because they sought greater freedom for economic activities, untrammeled by religious restraints? However, the reality had been quite different. Far from loosening religious control, Protestantism had reinforced it over all aspects of life. Calvinistic Geneva had carried that tendency to its extreme. Indeed, historical investigation revealed a seemingly paradoxical coexistence of business acumen and expertise with a deep and genuine piety among certain Protestant groups. Why had so many of those who had proved so adept at operating its key institutions belonged to groups that had shown such hostility to certain distinctive characteristics of emerging modern society?

At the end of his far-ranging investigation Weber reached the provisional conclusion that Calvinist Protestantism had moulded a character-type ideally suited to manage successfully the new form of mercantile capitalism. It was the unintended consequence of an 'elective affinity' between the ethos of Calvinist Puritanism and the 'spirit' of capitalism. The mediating mechanism was the Calvinist theology of predestination. Some individuals had been elected for salvation and others for damnation by God even before He embarked on creation. The intolerable psychological burden the dogma imposed on the believer was partially mitigated by Theodore Beza's rider that diligence in a 'calling' was a sign of election. Weber regarded the concept of a 'calling' as a quite novel Reformation innovation. Each individual was to perservere in his calling through systematic and methodical labour, in the spirit of an innerworldly asceticism. Commerce, in contradistinction to classical and medieval attitudes, occupied an assured place among approved callings. It was an attitude which proved well adapted to guarantee success to those engaged in a quite novel form of capitalism, sanctioning the quest for profit not through piracy, plunder or adventurism, but from 'rationally and systematically' pursued and formally peaceful exchange, with the accumulated gain being ploughed back into business rather than squandered in riotous living or conspicuous consumption (Weber, 1930: 56).

Weber was at pains to emphasize that he had not merely substituted a 'spiritual' interpretation for an equally one-sided 'materialistic' or Marxist one. He had not tracked down the historical cause of capitalism, nor located it in the Reformation. A full explanation would be a synthesis of these divergent approaches. He was convinced, nevertheless, that he had succeeded in providing strong proof that the Puritan ethos was linked with Western capitalism. The failure of such an ethos to occupy an equally significant place in China and India would throw light on why a Western-style capitalism had never emerged in those civilizations. Weber was hopeful that his analysis of the influence of Calvinism would yield rich gains in historical understanding when extended to other areas of Western culture, in particular to science, art, politics and the legal systems.

The challenge, as far as science was concerned, was taken up by Robert K. Merton in 1938, focusing on seventeenth century England. By the mid-seventeenth century England had assumed a scientific lead among European nations. Merton argued that progress in science depended on two sets of conditions, one of them being internal to science, the other being cultural or sociological. The internal one comprised the accumulation of a sufficient stock of knowledge and the development of effective methods which could be applied to it. The external or sociological one was the esteem enjoyed by scientific pursuits in a particular society. The latter was of crucial importance, as it influenced the flow of talent into science (Merton, 1970a: 56). The medieval period had proved unfavourable on both counts. The sixteenth and seventeenth centuries provided a much more fruitful environment. There was a steady accumulation of data, and the experimental method attained full maturity. What of the flow of talent into science? By an ingenious use of the *Dictionary of National Biography* Merton confirmed to his own satisfaction a marked shift of interest on the part of the English élite towards science, reaching a climax by the mid-seventeenth century (*ibid.*: 26). What accounted for the shift? It reflected a significant change in the prevailing system of values. Since religion was the dominant expression of values in that period, any enquiry must focus on changes in the religious ethos (*ibid.*: 56).

Emulating Weber, Merton studied the way in which 'Puritanism' had moulded contemporary attitudes to the pursuit of science. By 'Puritanism' Merton understood not the belief that the English church was to be reformed in accordance with a Presbyterian pattern, but rather 'a common attitude of mind and mode of life' which he believed was common to all the major English denominations and sects. Its expression, as an ethos, was to be culled not from arid theological treatises, but from the sermons and works of advice which directly influenced the daily life and conduct of believers. Like Weber, Merton found it particularly well expressed in Richard Baxter's *Christian Directory* (1664–65), 'a typical presentation of the leading elements in the Puritan ethos..,' (*ibid.*: 60).

Puritanism could have led men towards science, away from it, or perhaps had not influenced such preferences at all. Merton detected in its ethos elements which could have promoted a favourable attitude to the new empirical and experimental science. Puritanism made the chief end of life the glorification of God. It regarded the study of God's work as the best way of accomplishing that end. It dedicated the fruits of such study to the public weal. The medievals, too, had believed in glorifying God through studying his works. The decisive difference was in the spirit in which these duties were now undertaken: through an 'innerworldly' activity, employing a combination of empiricism and rationalism. 'Puritanism altered social orientations. It led to the setting up of a new vocational hierarchy, based on criteria which inevitably bestowed prestige upon the natural philosopher' (*ibid.*: 94). Merton, like Weber, invoked the Puritan's psychological need for the conviction of being among the elect, and the relief offered by a novel idea of 'calling' (*ibid.*: 57). The active scientific study of nature was useful to establish proof of being in a state of grace, since it led to the glorification of God through the study of His works and dedicated the fruits to the enlargement of man's empire over nature for the common good.

It still remained to show that there was a consonance between the values of Puritanism and the 'spirit', or, in Merton's words, 'the motive force of the new science' (*ibid.*: 80). Merton combed the works of men like Boyle, Barrow, Grew, Newton, Ray, Wallis, Wilkins and Willoughby to establish the motives which had inspired those engaged in science, and the method by which they thought nature was to be studied. He found a 'point to point correlation' between the Puritan ethos and the 'avowed attributes, goals and results of scientific investigation' (*ibid.*: 89). The new science had 'patterns of behavior which are congenial to Puritan tastes. Above all, it embraces two highly prized values: utilitarianism and empiricism' (*ibid.*: 90).

After all, 'the combination of rationalism and empiricism which is so pronounced in the Puritan ethic forms the essence of the spirit of modern science' (*ibid*.: 92).

An 'elective affinity' still demanded the proof of a 'crucial experiment'. Whether the thesis was true or not could only be demonstrated by examining the actual composition of groups who helped to found the Royal Society at the Restoration, and were prominent in its activities. Merton believed the facts totally vindicated his thesis. Dorothy Stimson had already shown a decisive predominance of Puritans in the London group of 1645 and among the original members of the Royal Society. Moreover, the fact that the Society's origins lay in a period of Puritan dominance was further confirmation of the thesis, for many Puritan natural philosophers had urged such a cooperative grouping.

The link between Puritanism, empiricism and utilitarianism remained strong even after the political defeat of the Puritans, through the new ideal of education following the Restoration. During the revolutionary period the Bohemian educator Comenius was invited to England to establish the visionary scientific institution sketched in Francis Bacon's *New Atlantis*. The Dissenters, excluded from the universities, now gave scientific studies prominence in the academies they founded. Locke had formed his influential educational ideas in a Puritanical milieu. The association of Puritanism and science was to be found in other Protestant lands. Governor Winthrop had probably invited Comenius to establish a scientific college in New England, and its Puritan clergy promoted the study of the new astronomy. Comenian ideas were put into practice in Germany by the Pietists. The new university of Halle gave science and technology prominence. The link between Protestantism and science had remained unbroken until the present day, as many recent studies had amply confirmed.

Like Weber, Merton disavowed any intention of offering a 'complete explanation' through a linkage between Puritanism and science. The two were components of a 'complex system of dependent factors'. It would be quite wrong to regard religion as the independent, and science as the dependent variable (*ibid*.: 104–5). If his conclusions seemed, like Weber's, to challenge 'materialistic' interpretations of the growth and development of modern science, Merton displayed much greater sympathy to an economic explanation for the other major problem he analyzed in the rest of his study: why the greatly enhanced interest in science had come to focus predominantly on the *physical* sciences.

THE CRITIQUE OF THE MERTON THESIS: RUPERT HALL

In the half-century since its publication Merton's characterization of the new science and of the Puritan ethos has attracted a great deal of criticism and debate. By 1963 A. Rupert Hall, undertaking a reassessment of the thesis, saw it as the product of a bygone age. How could historians of science find convincing a thesis which characterized modern science in terms which must appear deeply mistaken in the light of the work of Alexandre Koyré and others? The change from medieval to modern could not adequately be conveyed as one from rationalism to empiricism, or from passive contemplation to active observation and contemplation, as sociologizing historians had done. Rather, it was conceptual and in the last resort metaphysical. It could best be described as beginning with a 'mathematization' of the world-picture and culminating in its 'mechanization'. As Koyré, turning the tables on a conventional view, had strikingly expressed it, the rise and growth of experimental science was not 'the source but, on the contrary, the result of the new *theoretical*, that is, the new *metaphysical* approach to nature that forms the content of the scientific revolution, a content which we have to understand before we can attempt an explanation (whatever that may be) of its historical occurrence' (Koyré, 1965: 6). If the scientific revolution was an intellectual transformation, then according to Hall, its origins must be sought in intellectual history, for 'to this extent...the history of science is strictly analogous to the history of philosophy' (A. R. Hall, 1963: 11). It was indeed 'fundamental and absolute', not a mere by-product of the Reformation or the rise of capitalism.

Hall was pointing to a singular weakness in Merton's work. While Merton had cited E. A. Burtt and A. N. Whitehead, his conception of the new science made little use of the insights they had to offer. Burtt had attacked the assumption that science underwent a revolution due to more careful and precise observations or the steady application of a more 'mature' experimental method to accumulated data. He showed that it was the fruit of a metaphysical change, transforming the terms in which nature was conceived. Merton's 'rational-empirical' method was anchored in a metaphysical shift which had replaced one ontology with a different one. It provided the new framework in which the leading men of the Royal Society undertook their scientific work. Merton had absolved the sociologist from the duty of concerning himself with the fine detail of scientific ideas. The sociologist would thereby be confined to the study of the public face of science. He could analyze the public image fashioned by scientific publicists or men of science when they sought to attract lay interest and patronage. He certainly would not be able to reveal, for example, why scientific interest had come to focus on particular sorts of enquiry. By analyzing the activities of the Royal Society in the light of the economic and technological needs of English society, Merton had turned science into little more than an instruction book for a bag of tricks, which enabled men to master nature or each other.

Hall went too far, however, in his claim that by making the history of science a branch of intellectual history, it could effectively be insulated from any influences originating in the social or economic spheres. Those influences would make themselves felt as *ideas* (as Mary Hesse has pointed out), and it remains the task of historical study in each case to determine the extent to which such influences impinged on particular scientific developments. Nevertheless, an adequate analysis demanded a far more persuasive definition of the 'new science' if its consonance with a 'Puritan ethos' were to be established. The same care that Weber had shown in analyzing the characteristics of the new capitalism as a distinct entity had to be deployed in analyzing the nature of the new science. The sociologist would presumably have to determine the extent to which Puritanism or Protestantism had proved congenial to the mathematization and, later, the mechanization to whose initial accomplishment Catholic men of science, from Copernicus to Galileo and Descartes, seemed to have initially made the most important contributions.

Recent historical work has also raised problems concerning the 'disenchantment of the world' which Weber had regarded as promoted, however unintentionally, by Puritanism. 'Disenchantment' was for Weber indispensable for the full emergence of that rationalism which was a distinguishing characteristic of modern Western culture. By divesting the world of its traditional and magical attributes, it had made it possible to apply systematic rational thought to an ever-widening range of human endeavours. However, historical research now makes a 're-enchantment' a more prominent feature of the early-modern period rather than a Weberian 'disenchantment'. Already in fifth century Athens Aristotle had disenchanted mathematics by attacking Pythagorean numerology and insisting that abstract numbers and shapes could not act as causes. When Aristotle's influence became dominant in the medieval West, St Thomas Aquinas was faithful to Aristotle's rejection of action at a distance to erect in his *Summa contra Gentiles* (written around 1258–64) an intellectual structure which enabled scholastic thought to restrain magical currents by a classical distinction between the natural, the miraculous and the demonic. The rising tide of opposition to scholasticism prepared the way for a break with Aristotle and a rehabilitation of Platonism during the Renaissance.

'In a sense, Plato and Pythagoras stand nearer to modern physical science than does Aristotle', Whitehead had written, adding: 'The two former were mathematicians, whereas Aristotle was the son of a doctor...' (1926: 36). Burtt, too, gave Platonism an important role in motivating Copernicus's great innovation, giving him the courage to persist in holding fast to the heliostatic cosmology when it was vulnerable to so many powerful objections (1932: 1–60). The appeal of Copernicanism as a cosmology, moreover, remained confined within the rest of the sixteenth century to those who, like Kepler and Galileo, shared that philosophical orientation. Ultimately, the Copernican innovation was to pave the way for a quasi-Weberian disenchantment, described by Koyré as 'the violent expulsion from scientific thought of all considerations based on value, perfection, harmony, meaning and aim...' (Koyré, 1965: 7). But it began quite differently. Copernicus had condemned the Ptolemaic cosmology because it failed to meet a 'Platonic' aesthetic requirement, and his strongest argument for his new cosmology was the pleasing orderliness which he claimed it had restored to the universe. Similar motives and reasonings had guided Kepler's initial acceptance of, and his subsequent momentous break with, Copernicus. Numbers and figures had thus been re-endowed with an ontological significance which Aristotle and his medieval scholastic successors had resolutely attempted to deny them.

Moreover, Platonic influences were not confined to developments in which, retrospectively, we can catch glimpses of the beginnings of modern science. Re-enchantment was taken much farther by numerous thinkers who were attracted by the magical side of the neo-Platonic tradition. They wished to use its metaphysical scaffolding to remove the taint of demonic aid from any attempt to enlarge human powers over the world. Neo-Platonism could legitimate the idea of a 'natural' or non-demonic magic, since it claimed that it depended entirely on the manipulation of the forces of sympathy and antipathy pervading nature, and on tapping the stellar powers which conveyed virtues from the celestial to the sublunary realm (Walker, 1958). The Florentine Academy of Ficino and Pico, which Burtt had accepted as a powerful centre of the Platonic revival, had given fresh impetus to these magical currents, if in a scholarly and genteel manner. A much more populist and anti-authoritarian version of them was propagated beyond the Alps during the course of the sixteenth century, and coalesced with the social and spiritual tendencies of the Reformation era. It found an original and strident expression in the work of Paracelsus (1493–1541), who wished to substitute an authentically Christian philosophy of nature for the 'heathen' doctrines adopted by the Church from Greek philosophy (Pagel, 1982). Although retaining his Catholic allegiance, Paracelsus bequeathed his ideas to a succession of Protestant thinkers who viewed the Reformation as the beginning of a great transformation of religion, society and learning, constituting a preparation for the last age and the second coming of Christ. The outbreak of the Thirty Years War (1618–48) and the devastation it caused seemed to some of them a fulfilment of scriptural prophecies of the battle with the Anti-Christ and led some of them, including J. A. Comenius, to turn to England as the focus of their hopes for a Christian resurgence.

Re-enchantment, rather than disenchantment, seems thus to mark the beginnings of the transformation of the sciences in the sixteenth century, although it took different forms, as seen in the history of astronomy and cosmology, and in the natural-magical and Paracelsian movements. A genuine attempt at a comprehensive disenchantment is more characteristic of some of the Aristotelian thinkers of Padua, who attempted to purify Aristotle's teachings from later Islamic and medieval-Christian accretions (Rattansi, 1988: 8–10).

Only with 'mechanization' in the first half of the seventeenth century was there a development which could be described as a comprehensive disenchantment in Weber's sense. The lead was taken by French thinkers. The development of a corpuscular and mechanistic scheme of scientific explanation was regarded by Mersenne (Lenoble, 1971), Gassendi and Descartes as essential to safeguard Christianity when it was threatened from two directions, as the hold of scholastic Aristotelianism had slackened. It came, on the one hand, from a renovated Aristotelian 'naturalism' and, on the other, from a revived natural-magic. Mathematics, too, secured disenchantment with the development of a new symbolic conception of number and a new algebra. Galileo proclaimed that the Book of Nature was written in the language of mathematics, but mocked attempts at a ranking of shapes in terms of baseness or nobility (Galileo, 1957: 263).

Historical work has thus revealed the existence not of a single 'new science', but of a variety of competing approaches, methods and goals for scientific enquiry in place of the discredited scholastic natural philosophy. It has brought fresh challenges for any future attempt to revive the Merton thesis.

THE RESURGENCE OF THE PURITANISM-SCIENCE THESIS: CHRISTOPHER HILL AND CHARLES WEBSTER

Writing in 1963, Hall had seen a marked diminution of interest in the social and economic relations of science as the attention of historians of science had been diverted to the conceptual structure of the new science, following the pioneer explorations of the philosophical historians Burtt, Koyré and Cassirer. However, a resurgence of interest in the Puritanism-science thesis became evident only a few years later in the publication of Christopher Hill's *Intellectual Origins of the English Revolution* (Hill, 1965). Hill saw the new science as one of the forces that had prepared men's minds for revolution during the earlier part of the seventeenth century. While Merton had dismissed the disturbed period between 1640 and 1660 as scientifically unproductive (1970a: 41), Hill regarded it as the culminating achievement of an alliance of merchants, artisans and the new science. Hill declared that the civil war had also been a fight between Parliamentary heliocentrics and Royalist

Ptolemaics, and that the mechanical philosophy had been the philosophy of the 'rude mechanicals'. Merchants and artisans, disgusted by the moribund state of the universities, had turned to Gresham College in London, providing new and useful scientific knowledge in the vernacular to artisans and sailors. Francis Bacon had articulated the new ideal of science in a form which attracted enthusiastic Puritan support.

Hill's work sparked off a new debate over Puritanism, capitalism and science. Other historians found Hill's major theses, linking Puritans, artisans and merchants with new science, gravely defective. Hugh Kearney pointed out that Gresham College was never cut off from the universities, and its curriculum included not only mathematics and navigation, but the traditional disciplines. Patronage for applied mathematics was hardly confined to merchants, and came equally from landowners, courtiers, the Crown and the gentry. If Puritanism meant an emphasis on inward religious experience and a hatred of universities and theological learning, than few men of science had been Puritans. They were far more likely to lean towards 'Latitudinarianism' or moderation in religion, being, indeed, the greatest enemies of the sort of Puritanism described by Hill. Moreover, Hill had concentrated on only one element in Baconianism in postulating an affinity between it and Puritanism. Men like Hartlib, Petty and Webster, and the Parliamentarians who invited Comenius to England, were drawn mainly to Bacon's 'experiments of use'. The utilitarian element was to be incorporated in the programme of the future Royal Society. But Hill had neglected the other indispensable element, expressed during the revolutionary period in the Oxford group, which drew more from Descartes and Galileo than from Bacon, looked to mathematics rather than to Baconian induction, placed greater value on experiments of 'light' than on immediate use, and sympathized with a religious outlook that was profoundly non-Puritanical. Kearney found Hill's association of science and Puritanism unconvincing, neither entity having been correctly or persuasively defined (1964: 81–101).

A much more formidable reinforcement of the 'Merton thesis' appeared in 1975, in Charles Webster's *The Great Instauration*. In a work of nearly 600 pages, based largely on unexplored manuscript sources including the Hartlib Papers at Sheffield University, Webster provided a rich and detailed picture of scientific activities during the first half of the century. He clarified a number of contentious issues through a balanced and judicious examination and evaluation of the evidence from source materials. Among them were the controversies regarding the role of Gresham College, the nature of Boyle's 'Invisible College', the part played by the London and Oxford group in developments that led to the foundation of the Royal Society, and the activities of the College of Physicians during the revolutionary period.

Webster reaffirmed the central importance of Puritanism for scientific activities in seventeenth century England. Its values were in consonance with those of experimental science. In addition, it had provided a positive motive for engaging in science. The leading role in science of those who were Puritan and Parliamentary by background, outlook and association amply confirmed that. Webster was not merely restating the Stimson-Merton as well as the Hill theses. He emphasized a different element in the religious motivation to which he, too, attached overwhelming importance. Following Weber and Troeltsch, Merton had attached great significance to *soteriological* considerations. Webster, by contrast, stressed *eschatological* ones (1975: 1–31, 505–6). Belief in the imminence of the millennium influenced many Protestants and Calvinists on the Continent, and exercised great influence on English Puritans by the seventeenth century. The key scriptural text to which they turned was Daniel 12:4. It was interpreted as promising in the last times not a general decline, but rather, the'attainment of the greatest perfection of knowledge. The confusion of tongues would be reversed. The decay of human senses and reason would be repaired by the provision of new aids. Man would recover the Adamic powers he had possessed over creatures in his unfallen state in Eden. That inspiring vision made the Puritans engage in scientific enterprise, and to strive to reform education at all levels. It promised them full success in their endeavours. The soteriological motive accounted for the fact that the 'rise of the English scientific movement correlates extremely closely with the growth in the strength of the puritan party' and that the 'entire puritan movement was conspicuous in its cultivation of the sciences...' (*ibid.*: 503).

Experimental science, particularly as described in the work of Francis Bacon, appealed to the Puritan reformers because it harmonized with their own values. It relied on proof by experiment, not on authority. That was analogous to their resort to personal revelation in religion. Theirs was a spiritual religion. It lacked 'rigid' links with metaphysics or divinity. In its place was a natural theology, to which experimental science, as a study of God's works, could greatly contribute. Moreover, experimental science lent itself to the practical application of its results, which accorded with the Puritan social ethic (*ibid.*: 189).

Webster acknowledged that, while sympathetic to experimental science, the Puritans differed widely in their adherence to particular scientific doctrines and approaches. In the concluding part of his work he traced the roots of those differences, declaring: '...it can be shown that their scientific beliefs were framed with a conscious reference to their religious views, each section within the puritan sphere of influence developing a scientific outlook consistent with its doctrinal position' (*ibid.*: 503). The situation remained fluid and an individual could make a transition from one position and group to another, although it was possible at any time 'to discern a mosaic of competing groups wedded to different value systems'.

The bulk of the work was a detailed examination of the period and in particular of the activities of a 'puritan' intellectual group linked to the Palatinate refugee Samuel Hartlib, an indefatigable 'universal intelligencer'. Puritanism had suffered a reverse with the rise, with royal support, of the Arminian party in the church and the universities during the early part of the reign of Charles I. However, members of the group continued to enjoy the patronage of a puritanically inclined section of the gentry and nobility. Confident of a proliferation of inventions and discoveries that would bring man ever closer to the state of prelapsarian Adam, the Puritans gave great attention to education at all levels, to medicine and to the improvement of arts, crafts and agriculture.

An interpretive framework, placing the activities of the Hartlib group in the historical context of the period, had already been sketched in a brilliant essay by H. R. Trevor-Roper (1960: 3–20; 1967: 237–93). He had traced an alliance between the ideas and ideals of Hartlib's group and those of the disaffected 'country gentry'. That party's preference for laicization and decentralization made them sympathetic to the apocalypticism of Comenius, who had fashioned a vulgar Baconianism: 'serious, Puritan, dull, only with its dullness lit up here and there by lunatic flashes' (1967: 248). Bacon's experiments of light turned into millennial speculations, his experiments of fruit into 'the uncontrolled elaboration of gadgets' (*ibid.*: 258). Serious hopes of implementing their larger designs waxed or waned with the fortunes of Parliamentary ascendancy. In the end, they succeeded in influencing the programme of the early Royal Society, but only when John Wilkins took their vulgarized version and allowed it to be 'quietly transformed, elevated again into the pure Baconianism of Bacon' (*ibid*.: 289).

Webster dissented from the tendency to regard chiliasm as the last desperate resort of economically declining groups in their most pessimistic moments, and pointed out that Bacon's own *instauratio* was conceived in a millenarian context. It had provided a positive motivation, and scientific work inspired by it had been far more productive and significant than generally acknowledged. That was due to the fact that the attention of historians of science had been almost wholly transfixed by the revolution which the physical sciences were supposed to have undergone during that period. The influence on the Royal Society, too, had been consistently underestimated.

When the Hartlib group turned its attention to education, they did not concern themselves with the reform of the schoolmaster alone, like earlier educationists, but with the widest range of pedagogical problems. They wished to reform the universities too. Webster summed up the evidence relating to scientific studies at Oxford and Cambridge as proof that they had failed to keep up with the latest developments, and provided little encouragement for those wishing to explore areas ignored by the curriculum (Webster, 1975: 119–22). Mathematics was neglected, and experimental science denied official countenance. Medical teaching lagged far behind the best Continental teaching. Innovative approaches were more likely to be pioneered in Puritan academies.

With the Parliamentary victory in the civil war, a great change came over the universities. While the scholastic bias persisted on the arts side, many tutors and students felt free to explore novel paths in scientific studies. 'For the first time since the middle ages the English universities appeared to have become the focal point for developments in medicine, science, mathematics and philosophy' (*ibid*.: 178). Critics outside the universities were hardly satisfied and their campaign of sweeping reforms reached a climax during the Saint's Parliament of 1653. John Webster composed 'the most extensive critique of scholasticism produced by the reformers'. His opponents retorted that a learned ministry demanded a scholastic curriculum, and one of them pointed out that 'a school for Tongues and Arts cannot be a shop for Trades' (*ibid*.: 203).

Battle was joined, too, in medicine. Paracelsians and, by the 1640s the Helmontians, had placed orthodox physicians on the defensive, and their ideas were eagerly expounded and adopted. Far more medical works, many in the vernacular, were printed than ever before. Medicine was accused of being a monopoly and came under attack with other monopolies. Numerous far-reaching plans for reform of medicine and improving public health were advanced. To deflect criticism the College of Physicians was compelled to publicize its interest in chemical medicines. Webster brought new evidence to show that the College was by no means backward or inactive at this time, and was engaged in anatomical and physiological researches under Harveian aegis. To the contemporary Puritan that would have seemed like a dereliction of duty in the face of pressing problems of medical care, although in the backward glance of the historian of science it would appear to have promoted experimental science while remaining a faithful guardian to a system of classical medicine (*ibid*.: 323).

The radical improvement of technology through the conscious application of scientific principles had been a cardinal theme of Bacon's work. Truth and utility were for him the very same thing, for to possess genuine scientific knowledge was also to know how to work changes in nature. In his own lifetime Bacon's interest had shifted from inductive logic to natural history and finally to the compilation of a history of arts and crafts. The study of patents showed that many ingenious men worked on innovations in mining, navigation and surveying. In the absence of state support they depended on such patronage as was provided by the great merchant companies. With Parliamentary victory the Hartlib group was hopeful of state involvement. Among the numerous projects for advancing arts and ingenuity were *Macaria* (shown by Webster to have been written by an associate of Hartlib) and William Petty's *Advice*, addressed to Hartlib. Boyle's 'invisible college' involved itself in a saltpetre project, and saw no conflict between performing experiments of light or of use, as Bacon had termed them (*ibid.*: 382–3).

Webster anticipated the objection that he was merely describing activities which, guided by utilitarian zeal, diverted scientific endeavour into channels where the inadequacy of scientific knowledge and the backwardness of techniques condemned them to failure. He selected five areas where he claimed that significant advances had been undeniably achieved. In the chemical field useful techniques were disseminated and improvements effected. The interest of chemists in the technology of coining had led to improvements in the Cromwellian reign. The attempts to inculcate a scientific attitude to husbandry, forestry and horticulture laid the foundations of future developments and led to a marked quickening of pace in the latter part of the century. Boyle and others took up the Baconian ideal of natural history as an analysis of agriculture, industry, trade and society. It inspired the *History of Ireland* of the Boate brothers, Petty's famous Down survey and John Graunt's population studies. The analysis was extended to social and economic problems, and influenced the setting up of the Council of Trade and the enactment of the Navigation Acts. In sum, only when historians of science shifted attention from the physical sciences would they come to appreciate the achievements of the Bacon-inspired science of the Puritans.

The major conclusions of Webster's *Great Instauration* have been summarized here at some length, since they show how a work drawing in part on Merton's thesis has greatly enlarged our knowledge of a very significant area of scientific endeavour during the seventeenth century.

THE MERTON THESIS: AN ASSESSMENT

To assess Webster's contribution to the Puritanism-science debate, it is necessary to recall the criticisms to which it has been subjected. Merton had proposed a division of labour between the historian of science, concerned with the detail of short-term fluctuations, and the historical sociologists, uncovering long-term fluctuations, such as the shift of interest from *belle-lettrist* pursuits to science, or, within the sciences, from the bio-medical to the physical sciences.

The justification Merton offered was that at any given time a social scheme of values assigned differential esteem to various disciplines. A marked shift in preferences, like the one detected by his *DNB*-based survey, signalled a change within that scheme. Religion exercised an influence on that scheme at the time, and offered a suitable object for sociological enquiry. Similarly, a shift towards the physical sciences was revealed by a content analysis of the topics discussed in the pages of the *Philosophical Transactions* and at the meetings of the early Royal Society. It was appropriate to relate them to the economic needs of England at that time. Interest had, indeed, been channelled into scientific problems which had led to 'those inventive achievements which aided England in the quest for economic dominance; in the fields of textile manufacture, agriculture, mining and shipping' (Merton, 1970a: 146).

To Hall such an approach revealed a grave misunderstanding of the very nature of the scientific enterprise. If scientific interests came to focus on the physical sciences, that was, according to Hall, the outcome of processes internal to science and, in the last resort, philosophical in nature, leading to the mathematization and subsequently to the mechanization of the world-picture. Others would have criticized Merton for having held an 'inductivist' conception of science, regarding it primarily as a method applicable to any chosen field. It was easy for him to think then of the choice of its application as being subject to sociological influences. While Hall's 'internalist' stance may have been too restrictive, it had the merit at least of drawing attention to the fact that the sociologist could not shirk the duty of defining the nature of science more precisely and considering the history of science in much finer detail than Merton had considered necessary. Moreover, in the period which Merton had chosen to investigate there were several rival claimants for the place formerly occupied by scholastic-Aristotelian natural philosophy. Perhaps there were different sorts of linkages between various religious tendencies and the various styles of scientific approaches, beliefs and their characteristic domains of interest. Among them were currents of 'nature-mysticism', as had been pointed out in the work of Walter Pagel, cited by Merton a number of times but exerting little influence on his argument (Pagel, 1935; Merton, 1970a: 71, 102, 110.)

Part of the originality of Webster's contribution lay in his accepting the existence of links between Puritan values and specific kinds of phenomena and domains of interest. Experimental physiology, following up the research of William Harvey, was according to him the preserve of Anglican men of science, while the study of agriculture chiefly attracted Puritan-Parliamentarians. Puritans gravitated to those subjects which were of particular concern to a still largely agrarian nation, with an embryonic industry. These were chemistry, as applied to medicine, technology, natural history, mining and metallurgy. The appeal of Hermeticism and the ideas of Paracelsus, Comenius and Boehme was largely confined to Puritans and sectarians.

THE CONCEPT OF PURITANISM: THE CONTINUING DEBATE

Have those sceptical of the 'Merton thesis' been converted by Webster's powerful reinforcement? The major difficulty remains the definition of 'Puritanism', a protean term which has come under even greater onslaught from revisionist historians in recent decades. It has been condemned as vague and ambiguous, misleading when used as Weberian 'ideal-type' (George and George, 1961: 117–23; for a different view, see New, 1964.) It has been castigated as expressing a favourable or unfavourable view of certain historical developments, rather than as making any genuine contribution to historical understanding. By making Puritanism the seedbed of many modern ideas, including those of individualism, democracy, religious liberty and toleration (e.g. Woodhouse, 1974: 37), historians are said to have supported a Whig-Protestant version of English history, in which progressive forces came into an inevitable collision with the old order during the English civil war. Yet, according to the critics, it has proved impossible to define in a convincing way any common core of doctrinal beliefs uniting those loosely described as Puritans (e.g. Finley, 1983).

Such a critic would presumably object that Webster's *Great Instauration* has not demonstrated through case studies, nor illustrated in any detail, the influence exercised by allegedly Puritan values in motivating intellectuals or their upper-class patrons to engage in science, or guiding their preference towards particular scientific outlooks and domains. If the eschatological motive had such deep roots in contemporary English culture and was of overwhelming importance in inspiring men to choose science in preference to *belle-lettrist* pursuits, then the rapidity with which it generally faded after the attainment of the immediate political and military objectives needs more explanation than we are offered.

There are difficulties, moreover, about the suggestion that a number of core Puritan values were in harmony with the approach and methods of the new science. Thus Puritan anti-authoritarianism is said to have been at odds with the hearkening to the authority of Aristotle, which was a pronounced feature of scholastic natural philosophy, and more compatible with the belief that all truth about nature was to be derived through the immediate testimony of direct observation and experiment. However, the varieties of the 'new science' were based on differing metaphysical standpoints, and in that sense acceptance of the authority of a particular conceptual framework was inescapable.

Moreover, Protestant anti-authoritarianism was primarily religious and expressed in the assertion that no human authority could take the place of the revealed word of God in scripture. Human traditions were consequently devalued as a source of knowledge, while scripture, reason and experience gained in importance. The balance between reason and experience, too, tended to shift in favour of experience. Reason had been corrupted by the Fall, and the Greeks were often accused by Reformers of having sinned by their exclusive reliance on it, demonstrated by the central place granted to logic in Peripatetic philosophy.

The resulting implications for natural philosophy were not, however, unambiguous and proved controversial. Did scripture provide the rule in religious matters only, or were all problems, including the settling of the basic principles of natural philosophy, to be resolved by recourse to it? Those who looked for all truths in revelation sometimes combined it with the belief that the divine revelation was not confined to the Bible, but was supplemented by other bodies of esoteric knowledge. They included a secret cabbalistic teaching, received by Moses on Mount Sinai, and transmitted through a rabbinic succession: or that taught by a chain of elect sages, illuminated to the fullest extent by the *lumen naturale* and encapsulating their knowledge in such themes as the 'music of the spheres'; or by the succession of true alchemical adepts, providing commentaries on the alchemical creation account in the *Tabula Smaragdina*. Since the two books of scripture and nature were assumed to be perfectly harmonious, such beliefs could lead to the view that, although knowledge of nature was to be sought primarily through experience, it would be confirmed and deepened when examined in the light of those authoritative if enigmatic sources. Paracelsus, for example, conceived divine creation as a chemical distillation through his interpretation of the text of Genesis (Pagel, 1982: 89–95). Oswald Croll, who adapted Paracelsian teaching to a Calvinistic framework, believed in a chain of sages who, over the centuries, responded to a constantly renewed message from the Book of Nature (Hannaway, 1975: 50–51, 114). The Cambridge Platonist thinker Henry More was for a time the most fervent exponent of Cartesian ideas in England, presenting Descartes as a rediscoverer of a lost Mosaic philosophy which had combined atomism and mechanism with doctrines which were much later absorbed into Plato's philosophy (More, 1662: Vol. 2, 104).

In a traditional society change tended to be presented not as absolute novelty but as a return to older and more authentic traditions. The Italian Renaissance claimed to be a reversion to classical culture from the corruptions supposedly introduced during the intervening, or 'middle', period. Northern humanism, more pietistic, represented itself as a return to the oldest traditions of Judeo-Christian culture, while the Reformation took the form of a return to the original revelation from God to man in the Bible, in place of the Roman Church as an authoritative intermediary. The rejection of scholastic natural philosophy and the substitution of supposedly 'older' and hence more authentic views was a tactic that cut across the Catholic-Protestant divide. Even those advocating a mechanistic and corpuscular approach could, like Gassendi (Bloch, 1971: 39–43), claim to be renovating a *philosophia perrenis* whose elements were to be gathered from sound and ancient philosophical doctrines.

Those continuing to adhere to the Peripatetic tradition, which was now under sustained attack, could assert that their preference for it was based not on deference to authority but the test of experience and reason. William Harvey, who had imbibed the purer Aristotelianism which at Padua had spurred new physiological and biological research, dedicated his *De Motu Cordis* (1628) to the true men of science who 'suffer not themselves to become enslaved and lose their freedom in bondage to the traditions and precepts of any, except their own eyes convince them' (Harvey, 1628: 6). A general adherence to Aristotelian concepts and guiding principles was not for Harvey incompatible with a firm commitment to empiricism. Newton's early scientific notebook at Cambridge was to bear the proud motto: *Amicus Plato, amicus Aristoteles, magis amica veritas* (McGuire and Tamny, 1983: 336). It was a declaration to which men of very different religious and scientific allegiances could vow adherence.

Bacon and Descartes were exceptional in rejecting a recourse to revelation, as well as ancient opinions in natural philosophy, and calling for a wholly new science of nature. Bacon retained more of traditionalism in the millennarian vision which inspired his *Great Instauration*, and believed that the task was to help man reacquire the power over creatures he had originally possessed in Paradise. However, the true knowledge of nature which would enable him to do so was not to be regained from the traditions of the past, but to be reassembled by using a new and refined inductive procedure. Bacon was particularly wary of those who sought it in the Bible, being well acquainted with the dangerous consequences which ensued when it was drawn into other secular controversies, such as the ideal form of ecclesiastical organization or the relation between state and church. He condemned the Paracelsians and others 'that have pretended to find the truth of all natural philosophy in the scriptures, scandalizing and traducing all other philosophy as heathenish and profane' (Bacon, 1966: 248).

Descartes scarcely acknowledged any historical debts, and doubted that men in earlier ages could have gained access to the knowledge he himself had established since they had at best caught only a glimpse of the new method for acquiring truth which he was the first to discover (Descartes, 1955: Vol. 2, 6 and 18). The edifice of knowledge had to be reconstructed, on the foundations of the first principles found imprinted as clear and distinct ideas on the human mind, leading to an essentially deductive mechanical-mathematical account of the operations of nature. Although at one in their repudiation of the authority of the past, Bacon and Descartes differed in important ways in their ideals of science and scientific method.

An anti-authoritarian stance is therefore of doubtful value by itself in enabling us to distinguish Puritans or the scientific approach favoured by them. It could lead to sympathy with either the Baconian or Cartesian approach. Modified by other Reformation currents, stressing divine revelation as the source of all true knowledge, and sometimes supplementing the divine revelation in scripture with other bodies of esoteric knowledge, it was compatible with a preference for a variant of an original 'Mosaic philosophy' (Brucker, 1790: 652–60) or with Paracelsian doctrines. That was strikingly evident in the work of Comenius himself. While praising Bacon, he criticized him for having only given a method whose laborious application would postpone complete knowledge of nature for a long time. Since the millennium was imminent, and sense and reason were slow or even powerless to resolve a great many problems, God must have intended man to resort to scripture for the truth. Comenius believed that his own interpretation of Genesis yielded the basic principles by which all the operations of nature were to be explained (Comenius, 1651: Preface, Chs 1 and 2; 1642: 2, 16, 18, 30, 76).

Similar queries could be raised about the alleged Puritan disposition to find proof by experiment more congenial since it was analogous to the demand for personal revelation in religion. Experiment and experience carried a very different significance in the various scientific approaches which competed for dominance during this period. Even for Aristotle, as champions like Harvey never tired of pointing out, experience was the source of all valid knowledge. He had believed, however, that the mind abstracted the 'natures' of objects from experience, and these were best disclosed when they were observed in their 'natural' state and least interfered with. Bacon objected that it was nature 'vexed' or 'brought to the rack' that was more likely to yield knowledge of the simple natures on which, like an alphabet, all qualities ultimately depended (Bacon, 1960: 25). Knowledge would then truly be power, for knowledge of natures would at the same time make it possible to 'superinduce' them in suitable matter (*ibid.*: 121). There were unanswered difficulties, though, about a programme, supposedly free from all preconceptions, to provide guidance about the sorts of observations which were likely to prove most fruitful, or to generate the theories which would bind those observations. Experiments were much more profitably employed in a 'hypothetico-deductive' manner by William Gilbert, in spite of earning the condemnation of Bacon for succumbing to the 'premature hurry of the understanding' (*ibid.*: 61–2), and by Galileo, for whom experiments were primarily aids to that conceptualization of the quantitative aspects of phenomena which contributed to the establishment of a mathematical science of nature.

Paracelsus, too, sought knowledge of the powers and virtue of things. It would partly be derived from experience, when it taught, for example, how a herb exercised a healing power in the human body. It became 'science', however, only when the investigator identified with the herb and 'overheard' the secret of the power which enabled it to produce a particular effect (Pagel, 1982: 59–61, 336). 'Experimental' knowledge had already been distinguished from ordinary perceptual experience in medieval times by Roger Bacon and by the alchemists who claimed to prove their principles through a direct testimony, giving it the status of a suprarational and incommunicable knowledge, resembling the mystic's insight into divine matters. The directness and immediacy of such knowledge, eliminating the need to resort to a 'pagan' intermediary like Aristotle, seemed to be in harmony with the initial teachings of the Protestant Reformers, who stressed the authority of the inner testimony of the spirit when compared to the patristic traditions and scholastic theology on which the Roman church relied. However, the Protestants, too, were soon confronted by the problem of authority facing any sect as it became a church. They had increasingly to curb individual liberty to interpret scripture in the light of inner illumination, and to reinstate the authority of 'reason', as they created new ecclesiastical institutions and struck bargains with earthly powers. While Melanchthon and Erastus (Pagel, 1982: 311–33) believed that Protestant education must rest on the authority of Aristotle, others, notably Bacon, strove to deprive the word 'experiment' of the affinity to mystical experience it had acquired and to confine it to a process yielding freely communicable 'facts' in a mind purged of all preconceptions.

Protestant attitudes to the various new approaches substituting experiment for authority were, therefore, complex and varied from one period or cultural region to another. Merton, ironically, cited Richard Baxter's condemnation of those who pretended to have received knowledge through immediate illumination and his praise of reason as an 'essential' Puritan trait, although Merton was well acquainted with that work of Troeltsch, in which the religious dilemmas of sects which were tending to develop into *ecclesia* were discussed at great length (Hughes, 1961: 235–6). Baxter's attacks on 'deluded men' who set reason and faith against each other were, in fact, the product of his experience of sectaries during the revolutionary period, being part of a more widespread reaction against enthusiasm (Merton, 1970a: 104; cf. Baxter, 1931: 110; Williamson, 1960: 202–39; Knappen, 1965: 354–66).

Another reason for Puritans to take a favourable view of the new science is said to be its independence from scholastic metaphysics and divinity, and the contribution it made to the Puritan emphasis on a natural theology, ancillary to a spiritual religion. Scholasticism, following Aristotle, had made metaphysics a fundamental 'first philosophy', and the metaphysician into the 'kind of thinker who is above even the natural philosopher...' (Aristotle, 1941: 736). However, the relation between metaphysics and natural philosophy was conceived in a number of different ways in the seventeenth century. Bacon had stood the Peripatetic conception on its head, and in the *Advancement of Learning* made metaphysics itself, as traditionally conceived, into 'a branch or descendent of natural science' (Bacon, 1966: 102). Perfect clarity about 'the natures and principles of things' was not to be expected at the beginning of enquiry, but would emerge only at the conclusion (1960: 106). Although final causes were excluded from physics, which was to be concerned only with physical causes, Bacon gave an important place to natural theology, which was that knowledge of the power, providence and goodness of God conferred by 'the contemplation of His creatures' (1966: 105). While it sufficed to conquer atheism, it could not 'inform religion'. Bacon could not be said to be articulating a characteristically 'Protestant' doctrine, since the Catholic Gassendi was led to embrace a position similar to Bacon's and contrary to the standpoint of Descartes. Descartes rejected scholastic metaphysics but remained nevertheless convinced that a new one must take its place, for only on that basis would it be possible to erect a new scientific edifice in place of the old one, now irreparably ruined. All the major errors he detected in Galileo seemed to him to flow from the absence of such a foundation (Gilson, 1930: 176–7). In a famous comparison, Descartes saw Physics as a tree whose roots were in Metaphysics, with Mechanics and Morals as its branches (Descartes, 1955: Vol. 1, 211). His ideal of a unified science, rooted in metaphysics, was not favourable to natural theology, and he acknowledged that it seemed rash to him 'to investigate the ends of God' (*ibid*.: 173). Gassendi protested that by doing so '...you have rejected the principal argument whereby the divine wisdom, foreknowledge, power and existence as well, may be established by our natural light...' (*ibid*.: Vol. 2, 175–6).

Gassendi's nominalistic approach, resembling that of Bacon, had great appeal for a number of the Oxford group of natural philosophers during the 1640–60 period. On the other hand, it was Descartes's grounding the new science in a new metaphysics, the whole comprising for them a lost 'Mosaic' doctrine, that first drew the Cambridge Platonists to Descartes's teachings (Webster, 1975: 148–150; McGuire and Rattansi, 1966: 131–3). Mechanistic accounts would otherwise have the perilous consequence of leading to a deterministic and materialistic picture of the world, as the system of Hobbes amply demonstrated.

Comenius himself lamented the fact that the once proud claim of metaphysics to be a *regina scientiarum* had been discredited so far that the Ramists had excluded it from the scope of philosophy and Gustavus Adolphus had banned his subjects from reading books on it and booksellers from importing them on pain of confiscation (Comenius, 1642: 10). Yet a man not versed in metaphysics could scarcely be a good natural philosopher. Astronomers could not have raised such contradictory hypotheses, nor Copernicus a 'new and plausible Astronomy out of his Optick grounds, but such as will in no way be admitted by the unanswerable principles of naturall Truth' (*ibid*.: 16; similarly Bacon, 1966: 123). By a combination of sense, reason and scripture it would be possible to consolidate knowledge in such a way that all controversies would come to an end. Baconian induction was insufficient, requiring the industry of many men and many ages, and its success was uncertain. It needed a more universal rule, which Comenius believed could be supplied by the principle that God had framed all things according to an idea, and these were to be searched for in nature, with the help of His word in scripture. For Comenius nature was a 'lively image of God' and his method was based on tracing analogies between God, the universe and man—whereas Bacon had warned against the use of the macrocosm-microcosm analogy since man alone was made in the divine image (Bacon, 1966: 104). Comenius was convinced that it would provide a surer insight into 'common natures' than Bacon's slow and laborious method. Eventually, the general precepts of Pansophy would emerge, being 'real and practical axioms' providing the key to knowledge and a guide to practical operations (Comenius, 1642: 43).

Another claim is that the promise of applicability to the solution of practical problems offered by the new science accorded well with the social ethic of Puritanism. Once more, we find that many varieties of the new science offered to solve pressing technical problems and contribute to the comforts of everyday life.

Peripatetic philosophy had a contemplative orientation and, while giving some attention to the extension of the power of human limbs through the use of mechanical devices, assumed that such powers would remain severely limited since nature could not be 'cheated'. In its scholastic version it led to the assertion (in a classic discussion by St Thomas Aquinas) that only through confederacy with the devil could the bounds of human power be significantly enlarged (Aquinas, 1928: Vol. 3, 60). A radical change in that attitude was evident during the Renaissance. By the late fifteenth century the Florentine neo-Platonists envisaged a 'natural' or non-demonic magic, legitimated by a neo-Platonic world-picture. Similar doctrines were asserted by others in northern Europe during the sixteenth century. Hopes of constructing marvellous mechanical devices were entertained, at the same time, by practical mathematicians, whose numbers multiplied in response to the needs of navigation, trade, war and the burgeoning cities. They took as their ideal Archimedes—the defender of Syracuse against the Romans, with his war-engines, rather than the thinker who had disdained the application of mathematics to vulgar use. They followed the pattern set by painters, sculptors and architects and demanded recognition as 'artists' rather than craftsmen because their practice had its basis in the liberal art of mathematics (Kristeller, 1965: 163–227; Rossi, 1970: 1–62; Rattansi, 1976: 63–77).

It would be misleading to attribute the changing attitude to man's power over nature almost entirely to 'Hermeticism' (cf. Yates, 1972; and Heilbron, 1978). Bacon, nevertheless, accepted their ends while condemning the means they employed, being as at best inefficacious and at worst 'unchaste'. His own inductive method would lay bare the 'forms' which gave rise to the various qualities or powers possessed by bodies, and simultaneously teach men how they could be 'superinduced' in bodies, thus dissolving the ancient split between contemplative and operative knowledge. Even those, including Descartes, who doubted whether Bacon's method would lead on to true knowledge, accepted his assumption that scientific knowledge would make men 'masters and possessors of nature' (Descartes, 1955: Vol. 1, 119). Galileo continually sought useful applications which would draw patronage and enable him to pursue his more theoretical enquiries, and chose to explore the 'misbehaviour of machines in the concrete as compared with their ideal counterparts' in a dialogue set in the shipbuilding yard at the Venetian Arsenal (1974: 49–116). While the Paracelsians and others may be said, by the volume of their translated publications in England, to have reached the height of their influence between 1640 and 1660, the battlelines were being drawn more clearly between them and others, as is indicated by the care taken by John Wilkins in his *Mathematical Magick* of 1648 to distance himself from authors of a Hermetic or Paracelsian tendency, citing rather the mechanical marvels discussed by authors like Ramelli, Besson and Mersenne (Wilkins, 1970: 150, 180, 182, 226, 231). The applicability of a new science to practice, resulting in achievements far surpassing the results of the available technology, was promised by proponents of many different approaches to the study of nature.

CONCLUSION

Despite recent attempts to buttress it, Merton's basic thesis, linking Puritanism and the rise of English science, remains controversial. Defining 'Puritanism' by isolating a common core of values has drawn even greater critical fire in recent years. The values selected as specific to Puritans turn out to have been much more widely shared and were compatible with a great variety of scientific approaches which raised their claims as a replacement for the discredited 'Aristotle of the schools'.

One important reason for granting religious motives a particularly important role in explaining the scientific lead taken by England by the Restoration was the assumption that the universities had provided little encouragement and were out of touch with the great advances on the Continent. Webster summarized the existing evidence and was disinclined to challenge the conventional view (1975: 117–41). Tyacke, however, has shown that the Laudian ascendancy at Oxford and the rise of Arminianism led to no discouragement of scientific activities, but, rather, a great deal of patronage of mathematical studies from that scourge of the Puritans (Tyacke, 1978: 73–93). A longer study by Feingold, concentrating on mathematical studies during the period from 1560 to 1640, concluded that an able corps of mathematicians introduced undergraduates at both universities to new scientific ideas, providing opportunities for further study to those with scientific inclinations, and has traced the emergence of a scientific community which embraced the universities and Gresham College in London (Feingold, 1984).

It would be impossible to study the history of science in the early-modern period without taking full account of religious issues and allegiances. The most promising way ahead seems, however, to lie through detailed case studies. Hannaway's exploration (1975) of the ways in which the Calvinism of Oswald Croll and the Lutheranism of Andreas Libavius mediated their responses to Paracelsian teachings provides one model of the kind of historical study which may enhance our understanding of the interaction between Protestant religious currents and science during the period.

Bacon once remarked that truth was more likely to emerge from error than from confusion. Merton's famous study restated the earlier and much vaguer suggestions of a connection between Puritanism and science in seventeenth century England as a clearly formulated thesis, applying new sociological methods to historical enquiry. The resulting debate has greatly enhanced our knowledge of the interrelationship between science, society and religion in that period. It is a signal tribute to its novelty and originality that it should continue to arouse such interest and passion half a century after its publication.

22. Infant Giants Are Not Pygmies: The 'Merton Thesis' and the Sociology of Science

A. RUPERT HALL

...il y a parmi eux [les sociologues] ... des esprits rigoureux qui cherchent avec raison à préciser la part de l'élément social dans l'histoire, mais qui ont une tendance à tout expliquer par ce seul élément... (Henri Berr, 1903)

HISTORICAL SOCIOLOGY

Generally speaking, historians do not probe far into personal motivations. They claim no expertise in psychological investigation and often argue that the surviving evidence is not sufficiently abundant to render psychological reconstruction a profitable and safe exercise. If the biographer is cautious about the precise cause of Henry VIII's ulcers, or indeed the demise of Napoleon, he may show still greater prudence in delineating sketchily the character, temperament and mentality of either man. Moreover, historians tend to suspect explanations of events in terms of the personal intellects and foibles of the principal characters involved in them: there was more to the English reformation than Henry's desire for Anne Boleyn, more to the Austrian marriage than Napoleon's boredom with Josephine. Of course I do not mean that a historian would fail to provide reasons for Mr Neville Chamberlain's three visits to Hitler in September 1938, or that he seek to do so without some personal references to the Prime Minister; but his tendency would be to explain Chamberlain's frequent recourse to the aeroplane in terms of a *policy*—a set of ideas, estimations, objectives shared with others and evolving over a period of time—rather than in terms of Chamberlain's timidity, need of a father-figure or even his dislike of communism. Historians tend, rightly or wrongly, to prefer the examination of policies to the analysis of persons, and to treat persons as those who implement or develop or modify policies almost as though these had an existence independent of the minds that conceive them.

The historical sociologist, on the other hand, starts from the consideration of people in all their interrelationships which constitute society. He is as aware as the historian of the impossibility of obtaining a complete individual portrait of Tom, or

371

General Dick, or Prince Hal, nevertheless he is confident of his ability to create pictures of the various societies of which in their respective times these persons were members—a picture complete enough to enable the characteristics of that society to occupy a central role in historical explanation. What these characteristics are and what causal roles they play in the run of events may be established from sociological investigations of men and women in general, from historical sources, from philosophical argument or from social anthropologists' studies of primitive communities. For the present purpose—to reflect upon the historical sociology of science—it may be sufficient to start from the principle stated by Robert K. Merton in 1970:

> the socially patterned interests, motivations and behaviour established in one institutional sphere—say, that of religion or economy—are interdependent with the socially patterned interests, motivations and behaviour obtaining in other institutional spheres—say, that of science ... [T]he social, intellectual and value consequences of what is done in one institutional domain ramify into other institutions, eventually making for anticipatory and subsequent concern with the interconnections of institutions. Separate institutional spheres are only partially autonomous, not completely so. (Merton, 1970a: ix–x)

Applied to intellectual history, as it is by Merton, this means that one cannot write the history of one field (say, science) without consideration of others (such as, say, religion). Few would dispute this proposition with respect to large issues (Copernicanism, Darwinism) which were universally considered during the relevant historical periods to possess transcendental significance, or with respect to institutional matters because of the large role of churchmen of all denominations in education, and of religion in every kind of intellectual activity, before the present century. It is perhaps less clear that confessional allegiances have any relation to technical matters such as Hevelius's lesser success in selenography as compared with Riccioli or the dispute between Lavoisier and Priestley. At a certain level of technical intensity the internal logic and structure of a subject predominate over matters of wealth, religion or nation. One feels almost like saying that Riccioli is a more significant astronomer than Hevelius *in spite of* his Catholicism, which of course impelled him to embrace the geostatic picture of the universe.

SCIENCE INTERNATIONAL

In the same sort of way most historians of science have argued for the (European) internationalism of science throughout medieval and modern times; in their view it has never been fitting to speak of 'German science' or 'Italian physiology'. So Aldo Mieli (1919):

> I have many times had reason to observe that one may speak of Greek science, Indian science or Chinese science, but that on the other hand there is no such thing as a German science or an Italian or French science. There exist only the contributions made by German, Italian or French scientists to the general development of modern science. (cited in di Meo, 1986: 350; transl. A.R.H.)

There are obvious, partial limitations to be imposed upon this view, besides those arising from modern wars between nations. For institutions, journals, educational and research provisions are by no means identical in each state. Laws governing animal research show wide variation: immobilization by curare may be allowed in one country when total anaesthetization is required in another. Laws control the kind of experiment that can be performed. Then it is well known that institutions, informal research groups and 'schools' (the Cavendish Laboratory, the Société d'Arcueil), which may or may not possess a national character, have enjoyed at different times a singular importance in defining lines of thought and experiment. We hear indeed of the 'Copenhagen interpretation'. In this case, oddly enough, it almost seems that the closer one gets to the cutting edge of research, the more significant (temporarily) these national differences become. In a by now classical study Paul Forman explained the 'movement to dispense with causality in physics' within Weimar Germany as primarily an effort by German physicists to adapt the content of their science to the values of their intellectual environment. In this case a school of theoreticians (not all German by nationality) imposed on physicists world-wide a concept of nature which—according to Forman—was generated in response to particular national conditions (Forman, 1971: 3).

Presumably Forman would argue for the stronger line here: had Weimar Germany's 'environment' been identical with that of France or the USA, the rejection of causality would not have occurred there—which is not to affirm that the same rejection would not have occurred elsewhere in different circumstances at some other time. In *his* work, however, Merton has rejected the firm step from correlation to causality. If I may reverse the order of two of his sentences:

> [I]t is certainly not the case that Puritanism was indispensable [to the rise of English science] in the sense that if it had not found historical expression at that time, modern science would not then have emerged. Such an imputation betrays a basic failure to understand the logic of analysis and interpretation in historical sociology. In such analysis, a particular *concrete* historical development cannot be properly taken as indispensable to other concurrent or subsequent developments. (Merton, 1970a: xviii)

If I understand correctly, Merton makes no more than the prudent claim that Protestantism was a sufficient but not a necessary condition for the emergence of science in England, whereas Forman seems to be asserting that the peculiar environment of the Weimar Republic was necessary for so strange a step as the abandonment of causality in physics.

MERTON AND HISTORY

This is one example (among many) of the common-sense and prudence of Merton's *Jugendwerk*, indicating his scholarly attachment to the discipline of the historian, as well as that of the sociologist. As he remarks, 'The statistical evidence is laboriously assembled and sometimes laboured' (*ibid.*: xv). One may wish to dispute his arguments in detail, but his is an evidential methodology applied to materials of unquestionable relevance to his subject—materials which themselves were extremely copious (2000 communications to the *Philosophical Transactions*, 6000 lives in the *Dictionary of National Biography*). The monograph certainly owes some debt to the theoretical principles of certain historians and sociologists, but nothing to philosophical contentions about the nature of science nor to the theoretical speculations of anthropologists.

For some six years Merton was closely associated at Harvard with George

Sarton, and if his apprenticeship to the history of science was 'short, incompleat, and sometimes unruly', it was one that gained him 'a flow of gifts, freely bestowed [by Sarton] which in their cumulative outcome may have affected my life and work in ways that have little or nothing to do with substantive doctrine or method of inquiry but much to do with discovering the pleasures and joys, as well as the nuisances and pains, of life as a scholar' (Merton, 1985a: 472, 474). More specifically in terms of historical interpretation, Merton was thoroughly exposed to Sartonian progressivism. To repeat a sentence from a letter quoted by Merton: 'The scientific activity is particularly interesting from the historical point of view because it is not simply creative but *cumulative*' (*ibid*.: 486). I am far from suggesting that Merton shared this faith of Sarton's; on the contrary, he makes it clear that Sartonian progressivism 'was far removed from the sort of sociological framework adopted in my dissertation' (*ibid*.: 484)—that is, the celebrated monograph. But Merton has never lost his esteem for scholarship, even of the more arid kind, when it is sincere and deep, nor failed to consider whatever merits historical analysis may possess.

The questions to which he addressed himself were modestly and practically framed. He did not ask: what were the social roots of the mechanical philosophy of nature? Rather, he tried to discover (1) what kind of people interested themselves in natural philosophy and mathematics? and (2) what kinds of topics of investigation did they pursue? His conclusions (as we all know) were that Protestants were more likely to study nature than Catholics, and that 'socio-economic needs influenced considerably the selection of subjects of investigations by scientists in seventeenth century England' (Merton, 1970a: 206).

According to my sense of words, Merton was certainly concerned in the monograph with the sociology of knowledge. But it was not his aim to determine, from the characteristics of English society, the way in which the content of English science actually evolved. It did not concern him to know whether the solar parallax was then taken to be fifty or fifteen seconds of arc, whether the whale was thought to be a mammal or a fish, whether the decrease of gravity was taken to be as the second or third power of the distance. Merton to a large extent (about half the pages in his book) explored the sociology of scientists rather than the sociology of science abstractly; to a less extent (just over one-third) he examined problem-selection (*ibid*.: xii).[1] The latter investigation is directly related to the crucial questions: why does old knowledge die? where does new knowledge come from? For if the answer to these questions is: knowledge dies when a changing society no longer needs it, new knowledge springs from the changes in that society, then in a sense the individual characteristics of the executioners and midwives of knowledge become of minor importance.

Abbreviating slightly Merton's own summary in the 'Preface' to the 1970 reprint of his monograph, we read:

> What are the modes of interplay between society, culture and science?... What makes for those sizable shifts in recruitment to the intellectual disciplines—the various sciences and humanities—that lead to great variations in their development?... Under which conditions are changes in the foci of attention the planned results of deliberate policy, and under which the largely unanticipated consequences of value commitments among scientists and those controlling the support of science? How did these matters stand while science was being institutionalized and how do they stand since its thoroughgoing institutionalization? And once science has evolved forms of internal organization, how do patterns and rates of social interaction among scientists affect the development of scientific ideas?... (Merton, 1970a: ix)

Now it seems to me that some of these are straightforward historical questions. Some were considered by G. N. Clark in *Science and Social Welfare in the Age of Newton* (1937), published in the year before Merton's monograph. Other scholars have greatly developed during the last half-century the history of scientific institutions—let us admit, under some spur from sociologists. The question of the education of scientists has also begun to receive deeper attention from historians. On the subject of science and government much has been published by historians of science. I mention here only *Science and the Federal Government* (1957) by Hunter Dupree, because of its pioneer importance, and the more recent volumes on *Atomic Energy in Britain* by my colleague, Margaret Gowing. The discipline of history of science has changed, broadened, one might say become richer, in a variety of ways since Merton first bearded Sarton in Widener 185, not least through the influence of Merton's own publications. Obviously historians and sociologists do not write the same books. But in the sociology of science as Merton presented it there was convergence and alliance with historians.

The sociological question, 'Who were the men who...?' is also a familiar one to historians. Charles Beard in 1913 asked, 'Who were the men who introduced the constitution of the United States?' Lewis Namier in 1929 posed the question, 'Who were the eighteenth century Whigs?' Beard's book was concerned with a very small group; at the other extreme Merton analyzed a large community of 'scientists', many of whom will forever remain obscure. The principle is the same. The methodology of Merton's two statistical investigations seems to me profoundly historical and his conclusions too seem to owe as much to the historical as to the sociological tradition of scholarship. It is perhaps significant that Merton's supervisor, Pitirim Sorokin, rejected them because they departed from Sorokin's own conception of sociological theory (Merton, 1985a: 484–5).

If there were notable developments in the historical sociology of knowledge during the quarter-century after the publication of Merton's monograph, they made little contact with the history of science. The war changed much, and after it for a time everything savouring of economic determinism fell out of academic favour. When I made a review of the state of the historical sociology of science in 1963, it appeared to be a neglected subject, for there was little to record save a notable monograph by Sam Lilley (1949). A change of mood and—in Britain at least—a return to something more like the spirit of the 1930s occurred only in the 1960s. Now, as then, some historians of science, like Robert M. Young, affirmed their intellectual commitment to Marxism and their acceptance of its principles as guides to historical understanding (see on this Corsi, 1986). Christopher Hill (1965) lent his powerful support to the 'Merton thesis'—at least so far as it concerned the Puritan influence upon English science in the seventeenth century—not without protest from other quarters (see Lilley, 1949; also Kearney, 1973). [2] The same decade also saw systematized interest in 'social studies' of science and in 'science policy'. A journal of *Science Studies*, later *Social Studies in Science*, began in 1971.

COGNITIVE RELATIVISM

An event modifying future discussions of the relations between the history, philosophy and sociology of science was the publication of Thomas S. Kuhn's *Structure of Scientific Revolutions* in 1962, mainly because this book brought these three fields of analysis into close juxtaposition. Kuhn was certainly conscious of writing about the 'community of scientists' and he had reflected upon the difference in intellectual tone between the social sciences and the natural sciences, but it is fairly clear that it was not his main intention to direct a particular message to sociologists of knowledge. Not until 1970 did he publish material with 'explicitly sociological' content. He has, moreover, disavowed those 'Kuhnian' sociologists who 'think it absurd to conceive the analysis of values as a significant means of illuminating scientific behaviour' and who have accordingly devalued certain of Merton's researches (Kuhn, 1977: 291–2, 320–39).

Kuhn's primary interest was in the dynamics of theoretical change in science, drawing as much upon philosophical presentations of scientific thinking as upon the analysis of historical examples. It was in a sense *malgré lui* that Kuhn furnished sociologists with powerful batteries to breach the citadel of scientific theory. Particularly, they have turned to Kuhn for reasons for doubting the supposed objectivity of natural science and its claim to progress asymptotically towards an account of the real structure of nature. They realized also that Karl Popper's philosophy of scientific discovery, though wholly counter to Kuhn's system, could be used in flank support of Kuhnian relativism (see Bloor, 1974). Though Popper affirmed his commitment to the objectivity of the scientific process, his philosophy rejected simple cumulation and progression.

If a well grounded and widely accepted proposition in science is to be denied objective truth, that is, if one may not suppose it to be verifiable by all competent observers at all times, then it must be held to be only relatively true, that is, true for certain observers at certain times. We cannot press inductive consistency so far as to claim that a contingent proposition can never be falsified. Not least, in real human terms, the capacity of observers may be variable. So the relativism of the truth of propositions is obvious enough in a historical context: a proposition universally accepted as true at one stage in intellectual history ('All men and women are descendants of Adam and Eve') becomes false at a later, more 'advanced' stage. The ordinary common-sensical historian is satisfied that primitive notions are replaced by more sophisticated ones (such as the concept of biological evolution) because the latter possess in greater richness such merits as placing much information into a consistent pattern, avoiding reliance upon arbitrary authority (the Hebrew Bible) and giving greater power of prediction of future events. That is, the new proposition marks a degree of progress over the old. The true relativist, however, is not content with such historical relativism and its associated idea of progress. He will deny that there are absolute standards by which the merit of different scientific prepositions can be tested. If the point is made to him that the Copernican system is superior to the Ptolemaic, he will ask, 'In whose opinion?' Priestley will not agree that the oxygen-theory is superior to the phlogiston theory; in general (the relativist argues) we always find the victorious system superior only because we ourselves are of the party of the victors. (It should be said, though, that there are examples counting the other way.) The relativist argues that, at every point in the history of science, alternative pathways were possible, each of which could have seemed 'true'. The reason for the choice of one rather than another is not its greater truth-value but its usefulness, its conformity with the thoughts and needs of the people anxious to follow it.

To what, then, is each *Weltbild* related? Why do not all men, at least at similar stages in their technical exploration of nature, form similar images of the composition and pattern of nature? (We know that in fact they do not.) The answer, given by the modern sociologists of science rather than by Thomas S. Kuhn, is that such images of nature are the reflections of the particular societies in which they are formed; they differ because societies differ. So early in the post-Kuhnian age as 1971, a writer in *Science Studies* declared:

> If we accept that theories and hypotheses, the most uncertain elements in scientific inquiry, can come to prominence partly through the stimulation of institutional and general cultural factors, then these arguments lead us to recognize a sociological and cultural relativity in *all* scientific knowledge-claims. (Dolby, 1971: 10)[3]

The thrust of this assertion is that sociology is not limited to the kinds of questions we have seen defined by Merton, or to making the simple point that only industrially sophisticated societies can perfect the elaborate technical method of research upon which some knowledge-claims depend (for instance, those of radio-astronomy). Rather, the sociologist is to seek within the characteristics of a society for the origins of the most deep and subtle ideas in the theoretical fabric of its science. (An example of this in Paul Forman's study of science in Weimar Germany has already been noted.) Again, a more recent author, looking back with a special glance at Kuhn, writes:

> One upshot of post-Kuhnian social study of science is the increased self-assurance with which sociologists and others confront their phenomenon. Whereas the inner workings of science were previously treated as a black box, the very content of scientific knowledge is now said to be amenable to sociological investigation. (Woolgar, 1986: 310)

Once a reading of Kuhn has destroyed the image of natural science as mysterious and majestic, because approximating to reality, the sociologist believes that it can be subjected to his kind of analysis, though (it goes without saying) Kuhn's book does not make the technical content of any science one whit more or less intelligible per se then it was before Kuhn put pen to paper.

There are curious paradoxes to be discerned in this argument. Firstly, it was not Thomas Kuhn but David Hume (1711–76) who stated that because scientific propositions are contingent they can never be made infallible. The formalism of a theory tells nothing about nature; and for however long the contingent propositions of the theory remain unfalsified, the impossibility of their falsification cannot be asserted. Nevertheless, for 200 years or more—since not long after the death of Newton—mathematicians, chemists, astronomers, physicists and biologists have continued to experiment and theorize as though Hume had never written. Whether or not they were, each and every one, aware of Hume's correct claim about the limitation upon scientific knowledge, they worked as though content to strive towards an unattainable goal. The most interesting feature of scientific knowledge is that Hume's valid contention has discouraged no one from trying to attain to it. How odd, therefore, to discover the essential key to the understanding of science in a philosophical contention which the whole progress of modern science has set aside!

The right of the sociologist of knowledge to dominate intellectual history has been forthrightly expressed by David Bloor, in outlining what he has called the 'strong programme in the sociology of knowledge':

> All knowledge, whether it be in the empirical sciences or even in mathematics, should be treated, through and through, as material for investigation [by the sociologist]. Such

limitations as do exist for the sociologist consist in handing over material to allied sciences like psychology or in depending upon the researches of specialists in other disciplines. There are no limitations which lie in the absolute or transcendent character of scientific knowledge itself, or in the special nature of rationality, validity, truth or objectivity. (Bloor, 1976: 1–2)

For these are illusions. The reluctance of sociologists to enter the technically rebarbative, but really vulnerable, provinces of science and mathematics, even after mankind had entered the post-Kuhnian era, Bloor attributes to 'lack of nerve and will', a cowardly belief that defeat would be inevitable. David Bloor's aim in a powerful (if mixed) metaphor 'is to put weapons in the hands of those engaged in constructive work to help them attack critics, doubters and sceptics' (*ibid.*: 12–13).

He recognizes that natural science is largely theoretical, and that its abstract and sometimes highly formalized theories might be thought to be isolated from social pressures, but the true case is far otherwise: 'The theoretical component of knowledge is a social component, and it is a necessary part of truth, not a sign of mere error' (*ibid.*: 29). That is, the *élément social* in science, to repeat Henri Berr's phrase, is no mere contaminant introduced into the abstract objectivity of science because men are men, not pure intellects, but actually shapes and directs theorization. But theory cannot be treated as an arbitrary fabrication, a fantasy, because its ramifications are restrained by experience: the transmission and acquisition of experience are social processes. Our view of nature in the light of this experience is a 'convention', since we have no means of measuring our experience against reality. 'The indicator of truth that we actually use is that the theory works' (*ibid.*: 33). That is, it enables men to rationalize and control their environment. It may be useful, Bloor concedes, to employ such words as 'true' and 'truth', but these have no absolute validity since their application to propositions varies from one society to another, and also in time: 'It should be possible to see theories entirely as conventional instruments for coping with and adapting to our environment' (*ibid.*: 35). Again, he insists that the notion of conventionality does not imply arbitrariness, for there are constraints upon the theories that scientists can formulate. However, these are not constraints derived from the characteristics of nature—such quantities, for example, as the mass of the electron or the velocity of light—but from elsewhere: 'There is indeed truth in the conviction that knowledge and science depends [*sic*] on something outside of mere belief.... What is "outside" knowledge; what is greater than it; what sustains it, is of course society itself' (*ibid.*: 72).

Since (on this view) it is a mistake to view natural science as in any way providing an image of reality, an image that might become capable through the increasing enlargement and improved reflectivity of the theoretical mirror of giving an ever sharper image, because science is instead a conventional artefact serving the needs and interests of society, there can be no continuity, no progress, no cumulation. Here of course the Kuhnian doctrine of the life of science alternating between 'scientific revolutions' and periods of 'normal science' comes into play. (It is easy to overlook the fact that Kuhn's examples of such 'revolutions' do involve the transmission, the continuous validity, of an enormous mass of knowledge.) In Bloor's view the cumulative view of intellectual history can only be justified by a biased selection of evidence: 'If an historian should desire to show the cumulative character of mathematics then his interpretive apparatus will enable him to do so' (*ibid.*: 115).

Now Bloor does not mean that such a scholar compiles an account that is inaccurate or unprofessional; it may contain all the scholarly virtues, but 'it should be said that these virtues are all employed in the interests of an overall progessivist vision, and it is this which must be challenged' (*ibid.*: 143). Again the combative metaphor! David Bloor invites Humpty Dumpty to enter the Empire of New Clothes: here every proposition is valid so long as no one denies its validity, and *true* is a nice word for everything that meets with society's approval, whether in morality or mathematics. 'There need be no such thing as Truth, other than conjectural, relative truth, any more than there need be absolute moral standards rather than locally accepted ones. If we can live with moral relativism we can with cognitive relativism' (*ibid.*). To which the answer may be: do we have to?

GROUP/GRID ANALYSIS

The name of David Bloor has also been prominent in another development of the 'strong programme' in historical sociology, that is, the application to historical materials of an analytical tool devised by the anthropologist, Professor Mary Douglas. In this individuals are located (according to the judgment of the analyst) in a space defined by two rectangular coordinates, representing two variable parameters.

> One, *group*, refers to the extent to which an individual's conduct is limited by obligations to others and by experience of the exercise of authority—that is, roughly, by the strength of group membership and loyalty. The other, *grid*, is concerned with the extent to which an individual's conduct is guided by more abstract notions of role, by codes and rules.... The essential claim of this approach is that the cosmology of an individual is closely correlated with the 'quarter' of the grid/group diagram in which that individual falls, where 'cosmology' is taken 'to include the ultimate justifying ideas which tend to be invoked if part of the natural order'. (Edge, 1983: 255)

David Edge's description makes it clear that (apart from the rather unusual meaning attributed to the word 'cosmology') the assessment of an historical individual in terms of grid and group must be highly subjective, and that it disregards intellectual qualities altogether. No clear reasons seem to have been offered for supposing that this tool, however illuminating in its original function, should also throw light on the activities and careers of mathematicians, chemists and astronomers. However, a few scholars—David Edge, David Bloor and Martin Rudwick—have adopted it with enthusiasm. Bloor especially has claimed good results for it *a posteriori*:

> I hope that enough has been said to show the utility of taking Mary Douglas's grid, group theory out of its anthropological context and extending it into scientific knowledge. Clearly the approach is not confined to mathematical examples but should illuminate the workings of the natural sciences too. For instance, it should help to show when and why an anomaly is turned into a crisis-provoking anomaly in Kuhn's sense, or why in Lakatos's terms a research programme can be said to be degenerating. (Bloor, 1978: 266: see also Worral, 1979)

Since Merton has not applied anthropology to the study of scientific knowledge, it is pointless to pursue the matter further than is necessary to indicate, by contrast, the historical character of his style of writing.

THE MERTONIAN PARADIGM

It would be a mistake to suppose that all writers on the historical sociology of science are deeply committed to cognitive relativism. For those who have been concerned with the other side of the coin—not the influence of society upon science, but the influence of science as it has actually developed upon society—the question of the ultimate fallibility of scientific propositions has no significance. A *locus classicus* is J. D. Bernal's *The Social Function of Science* (1939), but much more has been written in the last fifty years (for a recent examination see McGucken, 1984). Among others, J. R. Ravetz, while asserting that T. S. Kuhn has 'created the new paradigm which we all follow' (Ravetz, 1971: 73n), in fact makes little conceptual use of Kuhn's ideas. Rejecting that impossible ideal of scientific knowledge that demands of it reality, distinctness and eternal validity (for all the works of men are imperfect), Ravetz nevertheless finds room for empiricism and cumulative progress:

> That which we can recognize as scientific knowledge has achieved its state only by surviving a long series of ruthless selections, and of drastic changes in the meaning of its objects. It thus contains within itself a segment of human history; its roots in experience of nature are tough and necessarily manifold; and it still grows through involvement with new scientific problems, new results, and new functions. (*ibid.*: 235)

Ravetz's thought seems to be that because the process of creating scientific knowledge is contingent upon experience, it is fallible; yet (within the universal liability to imperfection) we need to distinguish—and do distinguish—those elements in scientific knowledge that are ephemeral from those that are permanent, enduring 'as long as does the framework of reality in whose terms they are cast' (*ibid.*: 236). He is very far from claiming that such knowledge is an unstable offshoot of the society with which it is associated.

Like Ravetz, Joseph Ben-David and many others, Merton has been concerned as much with the behaviour of scientists as a professional group as with their cognitive processes. What Norman W. Storer calls 'the social structure of science' formed the core of his work during the 1940s and 1950s. He defined the norms of scientific conduct; he examined the effect of institutions both within and without science itself. '[N]ot until the late 1960's', writes Storer, were 'the tactical advantages to be gained from drawing a sharp distinction between the social structure of science and its specific substantive output... realized... and the time was ripe [for Merton] to pay attention once more to the reciprocal relations between the social structure of science and scientific knowledge' (Storer, 1973: xix–xx).[4] His earlier work had, indeed, been criticized on the ground that it took little account of the substantive content of science (*ibid.*: xxviii). Then in the late 1950s emerged what Storer has called the 'Mertonian paradigm': the peculiarly effective cognitive processes of science arise not, of course, from the mere cumulation of evidence but from the combination of its reward system with its institutionalized normative system:

> Like other social institutions, the institution of science has its characteristic values, norms, and organization. Among these, the emphasis on the value of originality has a self-evident rationale, for it is originality that does much to advance science. Like other institutions also, science has its system of allocating rewards for performance of roles. These rewards are largely honorific, [and] are to be meted out in accord with the measure of accomplishment. When the institution operates effectively, the augmenting of knowledge and the augmenting of personal fame go hand in hand....

> In providing apt recognition for accomplishment, the institution of science serves several functions, both for scientists and the maintenance of the institution itself.... The community of science thus provides for the social validation of scientific work.... The organization of science operates as a system of institutionalized vigilance, involving competitive cooperation.... Only after the originality and consequence of his work have been attested by significant others can the scientist feel reasonably confident about it. (*ibid.*: 323, 339)

Merton demonstrates that the desire for recognition by one's scientific peers is no mere consequence of egotism, and he is so far from needing to prove that scientists should not regard themselves as infallible that he stresses the humility and diffidence of those who actually make discoveries: 'Few scientists have great certainty about the worth of their work'.

Although Merton's writings on the sociology of science between 1962 and 1973 include a number of allusions to Kuhn's *Structure of Scientific Revolutions*, they all are incidental to his own lines of argument.[5] None indicates that Merton himself underwent a 'paradigm shift' as a result of reading this book, unlike the younger sociologists whom I quoted earlier. Nor does Merton make any appeal to the historical examples studied by Kuhn in his book, as they do. Historical examples—which continue to be very important in Merton's later papers—are very much his own, even recalling his association with Sarton twenty years before (see, for example, 'Priorities in Scientific Discovery', Merton, 1957b). There seems to be an obvious reason for this relative imperturbability in the face of Kuhn's thesis, which is Merton's merely passive interest in the philosophy of science. He has read the philosophers extensively—in *The Sociology of Science* (Merton, 1973) I find allusions to May Brodbeck, Carnap, Lakatos, Medawar, Popper and Russell (probably without exhausting the list) though not to Max Black nor to Paul Feyerabend—without discovering anything in their writings to serve him as a major *point d'appui*. All the references to philosophers turn on points that are fairly trivial. Particular views about the essence of science—whether its method is deductive, inductive or hypothetico-deductive, proceeds by falsification or by research programmes—all these burning issues hardly influence his writing one way or the other. His aim has been, not to construct a sociology of science from a theory of scientific knowledge, but to found sociology on examinations of the behaviour of scientists individually and collectively in institutions. (A classic of the latter sort is his article with Harriet Zuckerman on institutionalized patterns of evaluation in science: Zuckerman and Merton, 1971). Merton draws the material that he submits to sociological analysis directly from the life of science.

SCIENCE IS NOT AN IDIOT'S TALE

The philosopher John Watkins wrote recently: '... even if we set aside its industrial, medical and military applications, and consider science as a purely theoretical system, a systematic attempt to describe and explain the workings of the world we live in, it is still extraordinarily impressive' (Watkins, 1987: 455).

He was no less correct, obviously, when he added that if we ask philosophical questions about the cognitive status of a scientific proposition, 'we get no clear, cogent, positive, and generally agreed answers'. Now a historian must be conscious that while confidence in the truth of a scientific proposition is no argument for its permanent status as a truth, there are among all these propositions of admittedly dubious cognitive status some that seem now so secure, so firmly established, that in practice we cannot conceive of their falsification (as Ravetz pointed out). It may be in the future that no reasoning man or woman on earth will suppose it to be a planet circling the sun; but this would seem to imply a disaster to learning, not its advance. While the historian, like the philosopher, recognizes that many scientific propositions once taken to be indubitably true are now with equal or greater confidence taken to be false, and vice versa, and from this may infer that some propositions now held to be true will in the future be falsified, this recognition and inference do not disturb him, any more than the historian is disturbed by the seeming eternal vicissitudes of economic and political life through which mankind survives in spite of the constant threat of disaster. One can study comparatively the collapse of empires or the downfall of theories of nature without falling into the despairing belief that efforts to attain stable theories or stable societies are futile and pointless.

When a historian investigates the downfall of a theory, such as the theory of the spontaneous generation of living organisms, he is concerned with the arguments pro and con, with the formation of a rival view of the phenomena to that taken by the believers in spontaneous generation, and its successful elaboration to the point where no defenders of the old view are left. The historian is not concerned with our contemporary opinion of the rightness (or perhaps the wrongness) of the process of refutation that he is studying. Still less, if he reviews the establishment and triumph (in its own day) of a refuted theory, will he wish to judge it from our contemporary point of view. In these respects sociology is surely at one with history. To set a scientific theory or institution in its social context we do not need to know whether the theory, or the experiments made in the institution, have been falsified or not. To say this is not to deny that there can be historical, psychological and sociological interest in enquiring why erroneous opinions or estimations were in the past held to be true. We should absurdly cripple our understanding of ourselves and our past if we failed, for some purposes, to exploit the historical hindsight that we possess. The crucial commitment in an historian or a sociologist is that he should respect early achievements in the study of nature, especially those which (as so often in Aristotle) are highly rational and fundamentally mistaken.

In the minds of some scholars, the realization that scientific truth is less than absolute has created a disrespect for contemporary science. In the words of John Watkins: 'There is at present time a vociferous group who hate and despise modern science; and to them these negative results are most welcome; for they seem to imply that science is just another irrational ideology, on a par, say, with Zande magic' (*ibid.*: 456).[6]

If magic may be held to satisfy the needs of a community recorded by an anthropologist as well as our complex science satisfies our own society (an assumption that can be neither proved nor disproved, by the way), and if it is philosophically impossible to affirm that either magic or science is absolutely true (though, by the way, it is perhaps less impossible to prove that one system is more false than the other), the cognitive relativist may ask: what is there to choose between them in intellectual status? To answer this question one must consider the whole intellectual history of mankind, and one who does so can hardly conclude that it is an idiot's tale, without meaning. Certainly Robert K. Merton has always been aware of the increasing richness, complexity, depth and precision acquired by the scientific idea of nature through modern times. This truth is no less patent to him than is the historical growth of science as a profession and a social force. The essence of his sociology of science from the famous monograph of 1938 onwards is an enquiry into the social reasons for the peculiar, progressive ascendancy of science since the seventeenth century.

It is time to complete Merton's quotation of a Sartonian letter of 1935, from which I took one sentence above. The letter ran straight on:

> Our artists are not greater than artists of the past, our saints are not better than those of the past, but our scientists are undoubtedly more knowing. Michel Angelo stands upon the shoulders of Phidias, but that does not make him any taller. On the other hand Newton stands upon the shoulders of Galileo and because of that he can see further....
> (Merton, 1985a: 486)

Many years later Merton was to publish a Shandean history of the trope that Newton had made famous by using it in a letter to Robert Hooke—admittedly with a certain false modesty: pygmies can see further than giants when they are raised upon the giants' shoulders. Only such a scholar as Merton who accepts the real possibility of there being intellectual pygmies and giants, and who understands the intellectual debt of each generation to its ancestors, would have undertaken to follow the tortuous path of Laurence Sterne.

NOTES

1   The analogous distinction between sociology of mathematicians and sociology of mathematics is made by David Bloor (1976: 74).
2   Kearney wrote, rather inaccurately: 'Merton himself abandoned the bleak fields of the history of science for the lush pastures of sociology some little time ago and much of the credit, or blame, for the continuing vivacity of the Merton thesis must be laid at the door of that vigorous historian of Puritanism, Christopher Hill'. The title chosen by Kearney for this article, 'Merton Revisited', was first used by myself in 1963 (see A. R. Hall, 1963). There is a bibliography (1923–49) of publications on 'Science and Society' in Sarton (1952: 94–7), of which little or nothing is relevant to the present discussion.
3   Having quoted this sentence, I must admit to being puzzled by it. Would it not be more to the point if the most *certain* 'elements in science' could be traced to 'institutional and general cultural factors'—I mean such things as the values of constants, determinations of magnitude and velocity?
4   It seems clear that the date '1960s' is a misprint for '1950s'.
5   The longest of these is on pages 554–5. The discussion serves only to introduce the point that Kuhn is 'ambivalent' about a possible correlation between youth and scientific originality.
6   The beliefs of the Azande people are discussed by David Bloor (1976: 123–9). His conclusion to this section begins: 'This all suggests that the Azande think very much as we do. Their reluctance to draw the "logical" conclusion from their beliefs is very similar to our reluctance to abandon our common sense beliefs and our fruitful scientific theories....'

XIII. THE INTERPLAY OF SOCIAL THEORY AND EMPIRICAL RESEARCH

23. The Interplay of Social Theory and Empirical Research

HUBERT M. BLALOCK JR

Nearly forty years have elapsed since the publication of Merton's classic work, *Social Theory and Social Structure* (1949a), in which he argued forcefully for theories of the 'middle range' and devoted separate chapters to the bearing of sociological theory on empirical research, and the bearing of research on theory. Merton was concerned that the sociology of that time seemed to be evolving along two contrasting lines. On the one hand were the grandiose and highly general theoretical schemes epitomized by the identifying motto: 'We do not know whether what we say is true, but it is at least significant'. On the other hand were the radical empiricists for whom the motto was essentially: 'This is demonstrably so, but we cannot indicate its significance' (*ibid.*: 83).

Merton urged patience, in the form of fewer ambitious attempts to develop highly general societal laws prior to the cumulative development and testing of much more specialized ones and the need to recognize the very long historical development of presently mature sciences such as physics and astronomy. The trick, in this process, is to move from well established 'empirical generalizations' to corresponding 'social laws' that are derivable from specialized theories, which do not stand alone but afford the opportunity to tie together apparently diverse empirical findings.

How seriously has his advice been taken? And was it basically sound in the first place? I believe the answer to the second question is a resounding 'yes', though I cannot give an unequivocal answer to the first. As I reread these essays four decades after they were written, I find very little with which to quarrel, and my sense is that the overwhelming majority of at least American sociologists subscribe, in principle, to the major messages Merton was attempting to convey. But we have had considerable difficulty implementing them, partly because the methodological roadblocks are much more complicated than anyone of that period could have anticipated. Nor have we been organized and properly motivated to coordinate our theoretical and empirical activities sufficiently to move efficiently toward the kind of cumulative process that Merton envisioned.

Merton did emphasize, however, that cumulation in science occurs only very gradually and that one must examine the matter from a much longer time perspective than most of us are willing to employ. The implication may be that if we are in too much of a hurry, the kind of bifurcation between grand theorists and extreme empiricists may persist even if there were a general consensus that a more balanced development is desirable.

Thus is it essential that we re-examine Merton's general thesis with an eye to elaborating on it, noting why his advice is sometimes difficult to follow and listing some of the problems we must resolve if we are to move toward a more genuine interplay between theory and research, rather than a mere token endorsement of the general thesis that such an interplay ought to take place. Let us turn, first, to a brief listing of some of Merton's principal arguments.

SOME MAJOR THEMES

In his chapter on the bearing of theory on research Merton suggested that the notion of 'theory' has a number of connotations or meanings. One connotation is that theory basically consists of very general theoretical orientations involving 'broad postulates which indicate *types* of variables which are somehow to be taken into account rather than specifying determinate relationships between particular variables' (1949a: 85). Another very common type of theory consists of post factum interpretations of major historic phenomena, such as the rise of capitalism, peasant revolutions or political and economic development. Such post factum interpretations may, indeed, be highly plausible, but since there will almost inevitably be a wide variety of alternative ex post facto explanations for nearly every social phenomenon, such a type of explanation 'does not lend itself to nullifiability, if only because it is so completely flexible' (*ibid.*: 90–1).

The sociological literature, according to Merton, also contains a number of discrete empirical generalizations that summarize observed uniformities between two or more variables. Research becomes directed, however, only when 'empirical inquiry is so organized that if and when empirical uniformities are discovered, they have direct consequences for a theoretic system' (*ibid.*: 92). Although Merton is not entirely clear about what he does and does not include under his notion of 'theory of the middle range', he definitely implies that it must contain sets of *interrelated* empirical generalizations that are 'derivable' from an explicit theory.

As an illustration he uses the finding that Protestants have higher suicide rates than Catholics, which can be derived from Durkheim's more inclusive theory that posits a positive relationship between social cohesion and psychic supports provided to group members, with such supports in turn being inversely related to suicide rates. Adding to this middle-range theory a series of specific assertions, such as 'Catholics have greater social cohesion than Protestants', then makes it possible to place the empirical generalization in a broader theoretical context, which may also be used to explain other particular phenomena as well.

Thus the scope of the original empirical finding is extended, and this also helps provide for the cumulation of both theory and research findings (*ibid.*: 93). Critical in this process is the raising of the level of abstraction in the proposition, by substituting more abstract constructs (e.g. social cohesion) for those that are bound by time and place. Presumably, it is in this sense that scientific laws are derivable from theory, although the word 'derivable' perhaps suggests a far more logically tight, deductive theoretical formulation than Merton had in mind.

Merton also indicates that a substantial activity of social theorists consists of the analysis of basic concepts, including their clarification and definition. He points out that it is only when such concepts are *interrelated* in terms of a theoretical scheme, and are transformed into the variables between which empirical relationships are to be sought, that genuine theory is being produced. A disjointed set of concepts, alone, cannot constitute a theory.

One very important function of conceptual clarification, however, is to 'make explicit the character of data subsumed under a given concept' (*ibid*.: 88). As a case in point, he cites Sutherland's (1940) re-examination of the concept of 'crime' and his extension of the concept to include white-collar crime. Such clarifications may provide for the reconstruction of data by indicating more precisely what phenomena should be included and excluded under the concept, thereby reducing ambiguities encountered in linking theoretical constructs with measured indicators. Conceptual analysis may also help to resolve certain apparent inconsistencies or anomalies, showing that they may be more apparent than real. The essential point, I believe, is that Merton considers careful conceptual analyses to be necessary but not sufficient activities leading to the development of fruitful middle-range theories.

Merton also stresses the importance of precision in our theories, though he also cautions us against becoming prematurely obsessed with the need for both precision and logical coherence, lest this lead to an inadvertent blotting out of significant problems (*ibid*.: 95). The reason we will ultimately require greater precision, however, is that highly precise predictions are easily falsified, thereby considerably reducing the number of plausible rival alternatives that will also yield (nearly) identical precise predictions. Although Merton does not say so directly, the implication is that sociology contains far too many alternative explanations, most of which are ex post facto, with the result being that the theoretical scene remains far too cluttered. I might add, rather cynically, that it is often to the advantage of any given theorist to provide imprecise, unclear and highly flexible interpretations that can then withstand elimination via standard scientific criteria.

Finally, in a separate chapter Merton stresses that empirical research may contribute to theoretical understanding in a number of important ways. There will almost inevitably be serendipitous, or unexpected anomalous empirical findings that pique the curiosity or that suggest needed theoretical reformulations. The critical factor in this connection, however, is that such unexpected results must be 'strategic', in the sense that they 'permit of implications which bear upon generalized theory' (*ibid*.: 99). It is the observer or theorist, of course, who must be alert enough to perceive this strategic character of a finding, since there may be any number of miscellaneous peculiar findings that have little or no bearing on the theory in question. The implication, clearly, is that empirical research that is not guided by theory is relatively unlikely to produce such strategic findings. Elaborations or refinements of the original theory may then be required to account for these findings.

Empirical research may also force a clarification of concepts, for example, when several supposedly equivalent indicators of the same construct yield very different empirical results. An excellent example of such a clarification process, which took place slightly after Merton's chapter was written, involved a widely divergent set of empirical results produced by several different indicators of residential segregation (see Jahn *et al.*, 1947; Williams, 1948). This led to an important clarifying paper by Duncan and Duncan (1955), who pointed out that several of these measures involved undesirable mathematical properties that confounded degree of segregation with the minority percentage, whereas two others (the Gini Index and Index of Dissimilarity) were defined in such a way as to almost guarantee an extremely high correlation between them.

In some instances new methods of data collection, or new kinds of empirical information, may also lead to new foci of theoretical interest. Floyd Hunter's (1953) pioneering study of the Atlanta power structure, for example, led to a series of studies of community power, which in turn helped to generate theoretical discussions of pluralist versus élite orientations to power in Western societies, as well as a somewhat later development of network approaches to the study of power.

COMPLICATIONS IN IMPLEMENTING MERTON'S SUGGESTIONS

We now know a good deal more about the methodological complications one may expect to encounter in attempting to construct theories of the middle range in such a fashion that genuine 'scientific laws', capable of falsification, can be established and a cumulative knowledge base established. Our difficulties stem from a combination of sources that are not individually peculiar to the social sciences, but which, taken together, have produced a number of formidable obstacles. At base, a combination of multiple causation, the necessity of indirect measurement, a lack of 'universal constants' or highly repetitive events and a bewildering array of social phenomena to be explained have made it difficult for us to achieve a sufficient degree of consensus on the definitions and measurements of basic concepts, or ways of constructing reasonably closed theoretical systems that are at the same time reasonably good models of real-world processes. In short, the nature of the reality we are attempting to study has made the task far more difficult than many early discussions, including that of Merton, seemed to imply.

Multiple causation means that our theoretical systems cannot be 'cut off' by confining ourselves to a relatively small number of variables, as, for example, the Durkheim illustration implies. If one must include thirty or forty interrelated variables in an explanatory causal model of, say, deviance or discrimination, then in any given piece of research there will necessarily be many omitted variables the net impact of which will have to be summarized in a disturbance term. But when we come to making assumptions about the behaviours of such disturbance terms, we will need the more inclusive theories to justify them. Simple bivariate propositions of the form, 'the greater the X, the greater the Y', even if strung out, cannot form the basis of a 'deductive' or axiomatic theory of the sort that Zetterberg (1965) proposed or that Gibbs and Martin (1964) utilized to account for suicide rates. As noted by Costner and Leik (1963), among others, the existence of disturbance or stochastic terms means that causal linkages between remotely connected variables in a simple causal chain can become extremely weak, so that predictions become virtually indeterminate and imprecise.

As we have become increasingly aware of the econometric literature on simultaneous equation systems involving reciprocal causation, where there is no single dependent variable but instead an entire set of mutually interdependent endogenous variables, we now recognize that many theoretical systems will be under-identified, even under ideal circumstances where all variables can be perfectly measured. This means that there will be indefinitely many structurally equivalent models, involving very different sets of parameter values, that cannot be distinguished empirically without making some rather strong additional assumptions about lag periods or causal connections with exogenous variables. Thus even very carefully constructed theories involving clearly defined and perfectly measured variables can prove to be intractable.

Indeed, the more complicated our models become, in the sense of their including additional causal paths between pairs of variables, the less easy it becomes to test them. If Gouldner and Peterson (1962) are correct that the fundamental postulate of functionalism is that 'everything causes everything else', then to the functionalist the situation is indeed hopeless. To begin somewhere, one must assume a 'block recursive' real world, in which at least some *sets* of variables are not caused by other sets. For those of us who would like to begin with simple explanatory models and add complexities a few at a time, the message is disconcerting. It means that as more and more complexities are added, we shall need to compensate, somewhere, by being much more specific about the assumptions we are willing to make so as to keep the number of empirical unknowns below the pieces of empirical information needed to estimate causal parameters. It also means that our data collection efforts will need to become increasingly ambitious and well coordinated.

We also now understand considerably more about fundamental measurement (Krantz *et al.*, 1971; Blalock, 1982), what it takes to approximate legitimate interval and ratio scales and the dependence of measurement in the physical sciences on the existence of natural constants or relatively simple regularities that permit indirect measurement. Where postulated constructs (such as elementary particles) are concerned, precise measures of mass depend on the validity of theoretical laws linking such postulated properties to behaviours that can be inferred, in the aggregate, by indirect means. If we were to contrast such theories and empirical regularities in physics—even in the presence of micro-level stochastic processes—with those we encounter in attempting to infer abilities, motivations or subjective utilities, we begin to see that the limits that 'nature' may place on measurement precision in the social sciences are likely to be very considerable. Our multiple-indicator approaches to measurement errors, even with the assistance of sophisticated computer programs such as LISREL (Jöreskog and Sörbom, 1981), have helped to make it abundantly clear that our problems of indirect measurement are formidable and can only gradually be reduced to acceptable levels.

There are other kinds of measurement conceptualization problems that are likely to place severe restrictions on the precision of our empirical estimates, and thus our ability to evaluate precisely formulated theories. Many group norms and social boundaries are fuzzy. How does one obtain a precise measure of 'deviance' about imprecise norms? Can one simply take suicide rates (which have a precisely defined zero point) and equate these with 'deviance'? Not unless all forms of suicide are defined as deviant in all societies, and certainly this is not the case. If a friendship clique or urban area has fuzzy boundaries, one can obtain a precise measure of its size by creating arbitrary boundaries. For example, one may construct precise measures of residential segregation by using politically defined city boundaries and subunits defined as either census tracts or 'blocks', but there will then be comparability problems if in other cities the boundaries are defined somewhat differently, or if the blocks are larger or do not correspond with 'natural boundaries'.

This fuzziness of social reality thus creates a dilemma. We can obtain precise measures based on arbitrary decisions, or we can reduce the precision or allow for variations that depend on our selecting alternative boundaries or zero points (in the case of normative deviation). There is thus a kind of sociological 'uncertainty principle' that muddies the water. It means, at the very least, that we must place a heavy reliance on a combination of multiple indicators and sensitivity analyses in assessing the predictions of our theories. But if we attempt to carry out these empirically based strategies without an accompanying 'auxiliary' measurement theory that states explicitly what we are assuming, we shall merely add to the confusion by implying that almost anything goes.

When we attempt to address the problem of raising levels of abstraction to develop more inclusive scientific laws, which subsume empirical generalizations as special cases, we run into further methodological complications. If we begin, for example, with a simple empirical generalization involving a linear equation with constant coefficients (e.g. $Y = a + bX$), and if we wish to extend the generalization to other populations or time periods, the so-called 'constants' a and b are likely to have to be altered. This means that they are not constants at all, but variables that also need to be explained by introducing an additional set of variables into the theoretical system.

Thus the push toward extending the scope of the generalization usually results in further complexities. Furthermore, as one adds realism to the picture in the form of feedback loops and temporal delays, still more factors will need to be considered. If the level of abstraction of the concepts themselves is to be raised, for example, from that of suicide to that of lethal aggression or intrapunitive responses, one must also anticipate that additional variables will have to be invoked to differentiate among these responses and to explain the conditions under which one, rather than another, can be expected. In short, complexities in one's theories are to be anticipated as one attempts to extend their scope.

The additional variables needed to handle these complexities will also be imperfectly measured, may have peculiar non-additive joint effects, and may themselves be partly explainable in terms of other variables in the theoretical system. So generalizability is often purchased at the expense of parsimony. Auxiliary measurement theories needed to link constructs and indicators will also vary across settings, which creates additional measurement comparability problems. There is thus a host of tough methodological problems that arise, over and above those of 'raising the level of abstraction' to formulate more inclusive scientific laws. Where these complications are not anticipated in advance, and where measurement assumptions are not made explicit, there are likely to be ambiguities in interpreting empirical results, with lots of room for slippage and post factum interpretations.

In principle, many such complications can be handled, but they require a combination of technical sophistication and a willingness and ability to undertake large-scale research projects that are capable of collecting the necessary data to include measures of the complicating factors. This, too, means that a considerable price must be paid if we are to take Merton's advice seriously. I believe we should do so, but thus far we have not. Nor do we seem well enough organized to do so.

Careful conceptual analyses of the sort that Merton (and I) believe are desirable also sometimes involve methodological complications that may lead to temporary dead ends or intriguing intellectual traps. Lenski's early dissatisfaction with simplistic unidimensional categorizations of 'social class' gave rise to his and others' discussions of a number of distinct status dimensions and to 'status inconsistency' models that had features in common with earlier discussions of mobility effects (see Lenski, 1954; Jackson, 1962; Blalock, 1967b; and Hope, 1975). The problem then arose of distinguishing effects of single status dimensions from those of inconsistencies among them, for example, high ethnic but low income status. But the fact that status inconsistency was taken as a derived construct, and measured as an exact difference between two (or more) statuses, created an extreme collinearity problem that is unresolvable unless non-linearities or other restrictions can be introduced in the *theory*, rather than merely inserted in an ad hoc manner in order to arrive at an empirical estimate of the separate effects. A similar problem has arisen in the case of age-period-cohort models, with the tendency remaining that of bypassing the theoretical problem by making use of ad hoc empirical devices (Glenn, 1976).

Problems of this sort illustrate the general point that conceptual clarifications very often introduce methodological difficulties, which cannot be resolved unless the original theory is clarified. This also illustrates a cumulative process involving the interplay between theory and research, an interplay which brings methodological considerations to the forefront. Indeed, if one takes Merton's definition of methodology as involving the study of the logic of the scientific method, rather than the development and mastery of specific techniques, we reach the conclusion that the study of methodology, in this broad sense, is essential in facilitating and explicating the interplay between theory and research.

Another critical topic, which Merton did not discuss explicitly in the essays under consideration but which his own theoretical work influenced considerably, is that of the linkage between micro and macro levels of analysis. Two related bodies of methodological research have emerged: the one concerns so-called 'contextual effects' and the other deals with problems of aggregation and disaggregation. The problem encountered in contextual effects models is that of separating out the effects of individual level variables, say those pertaining to the characteristics of a student, from those of the social context. If the latter is measured in terms of group means, then for the ith individual in the jth group, the independent variables may consist of a series of X_{ij} representing individual characteristics plus another set of variables represented by group means $\bar{X}_j$ on these same or other independent variables.

Not only are there likely to be extreme multicollinearity problems in such models, but contexts may be nested within one another (classrooms within schools within districts), group means on the *dependent* variables may also affect individual level dependent variables (Erbring and Young, 1979), there may be self-selection into some but not other contexts, and the boundaries of contexts may be blurred or overlapping. As might be anticipated, as soon as one begins to open up the obvious possibility of contextual impacts, a host of sticky methodological problems arises, most of which require additional data for adequate resolution.

W. S. Robinson (1950) pointed out long ago that data and theory may be at different levels, and that a so-called 'ecological fallacy' may result if one uses aggregated data to infer individual level effects. A considerable body of literature has developed since that time, the impact of which has been to emphasize that careful conceptualization and an explicit statement of one's assumptions are absolutely critical if we ever hope to make headway on problems of this nature (see Hannan, 1971; Firebaugh, 1978; and Langbein and Lichtman, 1978). Nowhere have the debates been as sharp and enlightening as in the school effects literature that developed as an offshoot of the work of Merton's student, James S. Coleman (Coleman *et al.*, 1966). How does one separate the effects of school climates, school systems or other system variables from those of the students themselves and their parents? Should one use data aggregated at the classroom level, the school or district level, or not aggregated at all? These are not questions that can be resolved by an examination of the data alone or by resort to theory alone. They can only be answered by making a series of critical assumptions, whether stated explicitly or not; and they require careful attention to the technical methodological literature. I cannot think of a better example to illustrate some of the critical points Merton makes in the chapters under consideration.

CULTURAL AND ORGANIZATIONAL ROADBLOCKS

Are sociologists behaving in such a way as to implement the implied Mertonian programme? Do we accept the objective of reducing the gap between theory and research and of working toward a scientific model of knowledge accumulation? There are some social scientists who reject the notion that sociological knowledge should be supported by empirical evidence and that a 'value free' orientation is either approachable as an ideal objective or even desirable. Those who take such a position, with which I cannot quarrel on 'scientific' grounds, are perfectly free to do so, and there is little more that can be said about the matter. But even were we to assume a consensus on the ultimate objective, there still remain a number of difficulties that, strictly speaking, go beyond issues that were considered in Merton's work. I will mention only a few.

First, we are for the most part organized in such a way as to preclude close and continuing working relationships among sociologists with highly similar 'middle-range' interests. Most of us are members of academic departments that are organized to maximize diversity and to assure adequate instructional coverage of nearly the entire discipline. Therefore, there are usually at most two or three persons in each department with similar interests. Those whose intellectual orientations are closest to our own are usually widely scattered. We may exchange working papers with them and attend occasional conferences, but the continued intensive collaboration of, say, ten to fifteen race relations or deviance specialists is virtually precluded organizationally.

Nor is long-term, programmatic research encouraged, either by funding agencies or hiring and promotion policies. We are rewarded to get research out quickly, to apply for short-term grants and to work on several projects simultaneously. Careful conceptual work, exploratory research, replication studies and the planning of entire research programmes are neither strongly encouraged by one's senior colleagues nor institutionalized in the normative climate of the discipline. Publication outlets for work of this nature are inadequate, as are research funds. Sociologists who find themselves in non-academic settings, or even in university research institutes, are often faced with the necessity of 'moving on' to another project before they have had time to digest the findings of the prior one.

Pressures and incentives to study 'new' social issues and to move into fashionable subfields of the discipline also tend to support the proliferation of subspecialties that are defined in an ad hoc and atheoretical way. This makes it very difficult for anyone to 'add up' or integrate the highly diverse findings reported in the growing number of highly specialized journals that are now available in our libraries. This, in turn, means that none of us can ever hope to keep abreast of the empirical literature in more than a tiny fraction of the discipline. And, for most of us, this means that we have virtually no interest in a very substantial proportion of the journals and books that other sociologists produce. If anything, the field has become more fragmented than during the period to which Merton was referring. Perhaps 'middle range' now means something closer to 'lowest quartile range' or 'bottom decile range'. If so, the task of the theorist has become all the more formidable.

I am not so sure, either, that our instructional programmes have reinforced the flavour of Merton's recommendations. The cutting edge in quantitative methodology has certainly moved to the point that one or two semesters of required statistics leave students woefully behind the times. There is very little time left, then, for students to take advanced courses in measurement, even in the few departments where these are available. Theory training often remains confined to a study of dead sociologists, as one of my former colleagues used to put it. Nor are there any signs that the intellectual credentials of our undergraduate pool of sociology majors are any better than they were forty years ago. Indeed, they may have deteriorated.

CONCLUDING REMARKS

Yet there are some positive signs. Since there are many more of us, there are also more good pieces of research and carefully formulated theory than existed at the time when the Merton thesis was developed. There is also more bad research and bad theory. The trick is to assure us that the former will drive out the latter, rather than the opposite. This presupposes that we can distinguish the former from the latter and that neither ideological nor personal factors will influence this selection process.

As a cumulative development that originated rather more from the empirical than the theoretical side, let me cite the status attainment literature that was stimulated by the Blau and Duncan (1967) study of American occupational structure, which was quickly followed by a very substantial number of monographs and journal articles that elaborated on the basic causal models that were used in these earlier studies. As a somewhat later development, a series of more critical, theoretical and conceptual articles has more recently led to an extension of the earlier models, which essentially focused on individuals and their career patterns, to add structural or contextual level factors relating more to the 'demand' side of the occupational attainment process. Theories accompanying this growing body of empirical literature have, for the most part, not been couched in highly abstract language, but the level of abstraction involved seems to be very close to what Merton had in mind by theories of the middle range. Post factum interpretations have suggested falsifiable predictions that have subsequently been tested.

Coming more from the theoretical side, there is now a growing body of literature, mostly but not exclusively social psychological, dealing with power, dependence and positions in exchange networks. Stimulated by the theoretical work of Blau (1964), Emerson (1962, 1972) and Homans (1974), a series of social psychological experiments has now been conducted to assess theoretical predictions and refine earlier notions about bargaining, equity, coalition formation and network structures. This literature is also gradually becoming linked with that developed out of the primarily methodological literature on social networks in a manner that illustrates Merton's point that new data collection approaches may help to reorient developments in theory.

Finally, Merton alluded very briefly in his work to what he referred to as 'codification', which I interpret to mean efforts to examine the literature with a view to organizing it more systematically, to 'purifying' its terminology by weeding out redundant concepts, and explicitly presenting interrelated propositions to provide readers with a reasonably simplified but organized view of some substantial body of literature. At the time of Merton's essays I came upon two such efforts that impressed me: Homans's *The Human Group* (1950) and Williams's *The Reduction of Intergroup Tensions* (1947). Now there are many more works that attempt to cover reasonably delimited but general topics by explicitly listing interrelated, say, 100 or more, propositions and using reasonably consistent terminology (see, for example, Bacharach and Lawler, 1980; Blalock, 1967a; Blau, 1977; Collins, 1975; and Goode *et al.*, 1971). Most of these works also contain discussions of the supporting literature, or at least indicate which propositions seem relatively well established and which are being put forward much more tentatively as hypotheses to be investigated in subsequent research. In the spirit of Merton's recommendations, I hope that we will see many more such efforts in the near future.

24. The Interplay of General Sociological Theory and Empirical Research: 'In Order Thereby to Arrive at a Causal Explanation of its Course and Effects'

MARK GOULD

Robert Merton's understanding of the relationship between social theory and empirical research is derivative from his understanding of the codification and development of knowledge in the natural sciences. According to Merton, both progress incrementally through the articulation of falsifiable theories of the middle range.[1] The pattern of incremental development which has led to so much success in the natural sciences will lead to a parallel success in the social sciences when a commensurate number of personhours have been devoted to the task (Merton, 1968: 47). The attempt to find a general theoretical framework from which middle-range theories might be derived or within which they might be codified is a phantasm. In this essay I question the viability of Merton's programme for the development and codification of social theory. I do this from within his orientation towards sociology as a science, as I agree, unlike many of his critics, with the view that sociology should aspire to be a science formulating empirically grounded propositions (*ibid.*: 141–3), albeit a science of social action with its own distinctive theories and methods.[2]

The essay has five sections. First, I comment briefly on a central difficulty we face in doing scientific sociology. Second, given the conditions under which we do sociology, I argue that the articulation of a general theory is vital for at least a tentative codification of social research into grounded theory. Third, I discuss the differences between Merton's theory of anomie and deviant behaviour and some subsequent work on theoretically analogous topics, emphasizing, in section four, the conceptualization of scientific revolutions. I show the advantages of working from within a general theory, in contradistinction to the attempt to formulate discrete, even if generalizable, theories of the middle range. Finally, I argue that viable social research requires a theoretically comprehensive picture of the social system under examination. We will find that scientific sociology, when articulated in institutional conditions not allowing for the full development of sociology as a science, looks very much like a hermeneutics, where our theory provides a point of entrance into the otherwise unbroken circle.

AN OVERABUNDANCE OF THEORIES

Merton's discussion of secondary analysis is, in my opinion, an accurate characterization of all social research conducted in the absence of the institutional conditions required for doing science.[3] Merton criticizes secondary analysis as post factum; the reseacher provides plausible interpretations of extant data, explanations dependent on the validity of the theory which generates the interpretations. Yet, Merton argues, there is not a single instance of a sociological law which satisfies its 'logical criteria' (*ibid.*: 150). Thus, at best, secondary analyses are plausible speculations with low evidential value.

The problem with secondary analysis is not merely its post factum form. If new data contradicting early results are discovered, Merton correctly suggests that the researcher will once again find an intepretation to fit the facts. The problem here is not timing, rather it is the capricious nature of the theory (*ibid.*: 147). One can do a post factum analysis of an historical situation and then articulate propositions intended to be applicable to another set of events about which one is ignorant. One can even do further primary historical research to uncover 'new' facts. This looks very much like 'directed research' (*ibid.*: 149–50), where hypotheses are predictive rather than postdictive. The problem is that if one discovers, in either pre or post factum analyses, that one's arguments are false, one will merely reformulate one's theory in the light of the data, or argue that the data are not adequately representative of one's theory. This process goes on ad infinitum.

Sztompka contends that Merton does not provide us with adequate guidelines for distinguishing between good and bad theory. Merton's 'explicit methodological analysis of the research process remains open-ended and incomplete, leaving the sociologist somewhat at sea, faced with an overabundance of competing and seemingly incommensurable theories' (1986: 118). This theoretical indeterminacy stems from the absence of 'compelling evidence' (Merton, 1968: 147), and the absence of compelling evidence is a consequence of the institutional conditions under which we do sociology. There is no experimental unification of theory and practice in sociology, nor is there controlled observation as in astronomy. Consequently, the determinate conclusions one finds in the natural and biological sciences are absent.

DO WE NEED A GENERAL THEORY?

The next two sections are devoted to a brief discussion of certain strategies which may be useful in allowing us to begin 'squaring the circle', doing viable social science where the institutional conditions to do social science are not in place. In this section I outline why I believe that a cogent general theory, including a coherent conceptual schema, is essential if we are to accomplish this task. In the next section I depict the different outcomes which result from an attempt to formulate a middle-range theory of deviance and a general theory of internal disorders.

Merton's viewpoint on the development and codification of theory is summarized as follows: 'Sociological theory, if it is to advance significantly, must proceed on these interconnected planes: (1) by developing special theories from which to derive hypotheses that can be empirically investigated and (2) by evolving, not suddenly revealing, a progressively more general conceptual scheme that is adequate to consolidate groups of special theories' (1968: 51).[4] Middle-range investigation is concerned with 'theory, a set of logically interrelated assumptions from which empirically testable hypotheses are derived', and not with 'empirical generalizations', 'isolated propositions [s] summarizing observed uniformities of relationships between two or more variables' (*ibid.*: 66, see also 61, 68, 149ff.). While theories of the middle range 'have great generality, extending beyond a particular historical epoch or culture...these theories are *not* derived from a unique and total system of theory' (*ibid.*: 64).

At first glance it is hard to find fault with such statements. Here and elsewhere Merton presents a clear image of the dialectical relationship between the articulation of theory and empirical research. He recognizes that empirical research plays a crucial role in the *development* of theory: '[I]t does more than confirm or refute hypotheses. [Empirical] research plays an active role: it performs at least four major functions which help shape the development of theory. It *initiates*, it *reformulates*, it *deflects* and it *clarifies* theory' (*ibid.*: 157; Ch. 5, *passim*).

On the other side of the fence, Merton has always understood that 'in the design and in the reporting of empirical research, it might be made a definite convention that hypotheses and, whenever possible, the theoretic grounds (assumptions and postulates) of these hypotheses be explicitly set forth' (*ibid.*: 154). He understands that continuity in empirical research is possible only when such research is theory driven (*ibid.*: 153–4). He recognizes that concepts are the variables between which empirical relationships are sought and in consequence understands that the choice of concepts is crucial and that one of the major tasks of empirical research is the clarification of concepts (*ibid.*: 143ff.).

The simplest way to recognize the fundamental problem with Merton's point of view is by focusing on one of the issues he appears to understand:

> The choice of concepts guiding the collection and analysis of data is, of course, crucial to empirical inquiry. For, to state an important truism, if concepts are selected such that no relationships between them obtain, the research will be sterile, no matter how meticulous the subsequent observations and inferences. The importance of this truism lies in its implication that truly trial-and-error procedures in empirical inquiry are likely to be unfruitful, since the number of variables which are not significantly connected is indefinitely large. (*ibid.*: 144)

Merton appears to be referring to the relationship between middle-range theory and empirical generalizations. He never adequately discusses a crucial question: from where do we derive the concepts within which middle-range theory is articulated? Or put a little bit differently, does there not need to be a dialectical relationship between middle-range and general theory as a vehicle both to codify and to generate the propositions which constitute a middle-range theory?

Merton's own discussions are ambiguous on this point, perhaps because his conceptualization of middle-range theory is ambiguous. If they are '...empirically grounded theories—involving sets of confirmed hypotheses...' which are logically integrated and connected (*ibid.*: 61), what is the nature of this integration? He tells us that middle-range theories 'consist of limited sets of assumptions from which specific hypotheses are logically derived and confirmed by empirical investigation' and that they 'are consolidated into wider networks of theory' (*ibid.*: 68). Either this process of consolidation occurs only inductively (cf. the quotation from Bacon cited in note 4), or there must be a body of general theory dialectically interacting with middle-range theory and in consequence assuming an active role regulating its formulation.

For Merton there appear to be three levels of theoretical articulation: empirical generalizations, middle-range propositions explaining these generalizations, and the logical integration of middle-range propositions (cf. Sztompka, 1986: 106; Merton, 1984b: 1095–7). He recognizes that the generation and codification of empirical generalizations are fruitfully organized by middle-range theory; he recognizes that the integration of empirical propositions is aided by the autonomous and creative role of middle-range theory in guiding empirical research. Yet he fails to grasp that the generation and codification of middle-range propositions are fruitfully organized by an autonomous general theory. This does not, needless to say, imply that at either level the movement is a one-way street. Just as corrections and developments in middle-range theory are often initiated by empirical research, corrections and developments in general theory are often initiated by theoretical work at the middle-range and by empirical research.

In his early discussion of 'paradigms' Merton does give some indication of his sensitivity to the problem of codifying middle-range theory (1968: 69ff., and the essays he cites in 1976a: Ch. 7, note 52). In this discussion he emphasizes the need to specify the assumptions which guide sociological analysis. 'If true art consists in concealing all signs of art, true science consists in revealing its scaffolding as well as its finished structure'. The paradigm reveals the scaffolding within which a sociological analysis is constructed.[5] Paradigms provide 'a compact arrangement of the central concepts and their interrelations that are utilized for description and analysis' (1968: 70). They 'lessen the likelihood of inadvertently introducing hidden assumptions and concepts, for each new assumption and each concept must be either logically derived from previous components of the paradigm or explicitly introduced into it'. They advance the cumulation of theoretical interpretation and 'suggest the systematic cross-tabulation of significant concepts and can thus sensitize the analyst to empirical and theoretical problems which he might otherwise overlook' (*ibid.*: 71).

While this image of a paradigm looks very much like the notion of general theory Merton often criticizes,[6] when one looks at the paradigms Merton has constructed, the differences become very clear. While his paradigms often provide little more than 'orienting propositions', with the exception of the paradigm for functional analysis (*ibid.*: 104ff.), they all refer to specific middle-range theories. They focus on deviance (Ch. 6), on the sociology of knowledge (Ch. 14), on racial intermarriage (1976a, Ch. 12) and racial discrimination (*ibid.*: Ch. 11). Thus the codification that Merton seeks is within the various middle-range theories he articulates; it is not a codification which seeks to regulate and interrelate these theories. The latter task looks too much like the attempt to articulate a *theory* of social action, 'a unified theory that will explain all the observed uniformities of social behavior, social organization and social change' (1968: 39, 45), instead of *theories* of social action, for it to be acceptable to Merton (1976a: 129ff.).

In the next section I present a brief explication of a more useful and realistic image of general theory by way of an example. I infer that the failure to develop general theory as a logically integrated set of concepts resulting in deductively generated propositions condemns sociology to searching for relationships between unrelated variables.

ANOMIE AND DEVIANCE VERSUS THE THEORY OF INTERNAL DISORDER

In this context it would be fruitless to provide a laundry list of the functions fulfilled by a viable general sociological theory. Instead, in this section I provide an indication of some of these functions by drawing a comparison between Merton's theory of anomie and deviant behaviour and a theory of internal disorder articulated from within a general theory of social systems. I hope that the superiority of the latter will be manifest even though, in this context, I cannot hope to present an adequate picture of the general theory from which it originates. In the following section I suggest how the theory of internal disorder helps us not only to make sense of scientific revolutions, but also suggests a multi-level image of sociological endeavour which includes a crucial place for general theory.

In his commentary on Dubin's 1959 paper on deviance, Merton writes that 'After all the purpose of the classification is not merely to *identify* forms of socially deviant behavior [as is the case in Dubin's essay]...the purpose is to derive these forms by combining a limited number of defined elements, and so to discover the relations of each form to all the rest' (1959a: 184–5). He contrasts Dubin's goal of classification with his own and Cloward's (1959) goal, 'to identify social and cultural conditions that combine to make for differing rates of various types of deviant behavior among people occupying differing positions in a social structure, with the typology only instrumental in that purpose' (Merton 1959a: 186). Inauspiciously, Merton's own schema for doing this is marred by many conceptual confusions, some of which might have been eliminated if his arguments were referred upward to a more general theoretical framework as well as downward to empirical materials. The test of whether a general theory 'works' is whether its use generates more powerful explanations for the activities under examination.[7]

Merton's primary insight in his work on anomie lies in a criticism of the utilitarian assumption that ends may be treated as given, or somewhat differently, the position that some might derive from Freud or Durkheim, that ends are biologically determined impulses exogenous to the structure of social relationships. In contrast, he argues that ends are culturally regulated and that pressures for deviance are manifest when legitimately available, socially structured means to attain culturally mandated goals are not adequate (1968: 188, 199, 228). In Stinchcombe's felicitous terms, 'the core process that Merton conceives as central to social structure is *the choice between socially structured alternatives*...[F]or Merton the utility or reinforcement of a particular alternative choice is thought of as socially established, as part of an institutional order' (1975: 12; Merton, 1976a: 124).[8]

This image of anomie is, unfortunately, conflated with a second conception.

Here Merton sees anomie as manifest where there is an exceptionally strong emphasis on the attainment of cultural goals without a corresponding emphasis on adherence to institutionally appropriate procedures leading to these goals. In this case agents are seen as acting in an instrumentally rational fashion, selecting those means most efficient in the attainment of their ends, whether or not these means are culturally legitimate. This is a situation of normlessness, what Merton specifically labels anomie (1968: 188–9).[9]

Merton's various discussions should be praised for their insight in recognizing that both aspirations and the opportunities to attain one's aspirations are socially structured (albeit, as he would surely acknowledge, this insight is earlier found in Marx, Durkheim, Weber, Parsons and many others). As a theory leading to the explanation of various forms of deviant action, however, they are significantly marred by their conceptual confusions. These confusions preclude an adequate analysis of the variables which lead to deviance, prevent an adequate categorization of the various types of deviance and finally inhibit the articulation of the relations between these independent and dependent variables. In his discussion Merton confounds values and goals, and facilities and norms.

Merton refers to 'culturally defined goals, purposes and interests, held out as legitimate objectives for all or for diversely located members of the society' (*ibid.*: 186). Elsewhere he refers to 'culturally accepted values and the socially structured difficulties in living up to these values...' (*ibid.*: 245). Goals are situational and while their selection may be regulated by social values, values are much more abstract. Values define an image of desirable and binding social interactions and are ideally institutionalized by all actors in a social system. As such they may involve the subsumption of private utility to what is believed to be 'right and good' (Merton, 1973: 270). They may not only regulate private interests, they may interpenetrate them, constituting what individual actors desire. These socially regulated desires, which may or may not be consistent with social values, are goals.[10]

What has come to be known as anomie generally refers to the disjunction between socially defined goals and the legitimate opportunities to attain these goals. In Merton's discussion the (legitimate) opportunity structure, the availability of (lawful) facilities to attain social goals, is conflated with institutionally prescribed conduct (1968: 189), with the normative expectations that regulate the selection of means. Facilities are the elements in a social situation that actors manipulate to attain their goals. Norms define expectations for differentiated actors within a social order. Social norms constitute the limits of acceptable conduct for actors subject to their jurisdiction. Norms may, for example, define the use of certain means as illegal, and a violation of a norm may entail a sufficient negative situational sanction to result in the avoidance of those means of attaining one's goal. This indicates that there are legal and illegal means, or somewhat differently, legal and illegal opportunity structures, but access to (il)legal facilities and their (il)legality should not be conflated.

These distinctions constitute a reconstruction of one version of the components of social action identified by Parsons.[11] Their importance for both the categorization and explanation of various types of deviance will be clearer if we briefly examine the brilliant work undertaken in Cloward and Ohlin's (1960) *Delinquency and Opportunity*.

Prior to Cloward and Ohlin's work, Merton had written about four types of deviant adaptations, the outcome depending on actors' orientations to cultural goals and institutionalized means: where the goals are accepted and the means rejected (or unavailable) deviant innovation is manifest. While Merton sometimes had a tendency to equate its definition with the independent variables leading to its occurrence—innovation 'refers to the rejection of institutional practices but the retention of cultural goals' (1968: 230)—deviant innovation is more profitably thought of as a rational utilitarian violation of institutionalized norms.

Ritualism is both the consequence of, and is defined by, the rejection of cultural goals and the ritualistic adherence to institutional means (i.e. for Merton, norms) (*ibid*.: 194, 203–4, 237). Retreatism is the product of, and is defined by, the rejection of both cultural goals and institutionalized means (*ibid*.: 194, 207, 241). Lastly, rebellion entails a rejection of both cultural goals and institutionalized means and a substitution of new goals and means for those rejected (*ibid*.: 194, 209, 244). [12]

Cloward and Ohlin focused on one of the generating conditions Merton examined, the discrepancy 'between culturally induced aspirations among lower-class youth and the possibilities of achieving them by legitimate means' (1960: 78), but sought to discuss three possible outcomes of that condition. [13] Focusing on juvenile delinquency, they suggested that depending on the illegitimate opportunity structure available to them, lower-class youths oriented towards economic improvement, but without the opportunities needed to succeed in legitimate activities, might respond in one of three ways. If they lived in an area with an open illegitimate opportunity structure facilitating their socialization into a criminal world of deviant innovation, they might enter into a criminal subculture. If they lived in a disorganized community without connections to an illegitimate opportunity structure, their response might be to enter a conflict gang. Finally, those who failed in both legitimate and illegitimate organizations were seen to be candidates for various forms of retreatism.

While a considerable improvement over Merton's original model, Cloward and Ohlin's discussion is also marred by conceptual confusions. We can use the concepts we have extracted from our discussion of Merton to clarify a few of them. Cloward and Ohlin confuse two distinct types of variables: three varieties of strain, 'an impairment of the relations among and consequently inadequate functioning of the components of social action' (Smelser, 1962: 47), and three types of opportunity structure. [14] They have in reality outlined three types of strain and within the situations characterized by these impairments have discussed the learning mechanisms, opportunity structures, leading to particular forms of deviance. The response to the first type of strain, strain at the level of facilities, a 'condition of *ambiguity* as to the adequacy of means for a given goal' (*ibid*.: 51), involves instrumentally rational activities within the context of a criminal subculture.

When they discuss a conflict subculture, however, their analysis undergoes a subtle change. They ignore that a disorganized community is poorly integrated in terms of its normative structure and fail to note that this normative disorganization constitutes a different variety of strain. Normative strain entails situations where actors are confronted with either equally legitimate conflicting expectations or an ambiguity with regard to expectations. Cloward and Ohlin's conflict gangs are one variety of deviant conflict, the response to strain at the level of norms.

In their discussion of retreatist subcultures they make a similar error. They ignore their implicit suggestion that these deviants are withdrawing from society owing to their rejection of societal values. This strain at the level of values, an ideological ambivalence towards or rejection of the dominant values of the society, generates various forms of withdrawal (cf. Merton, 1968: 244–5). As in the case of strain at the level of facilities and strain at the level of norms, withdrawal is guided by the illegitimate opportunity structures available to actors.

There is, however, one additional type of deviant response to one further type of strain. Merton mentions Cohen's criticism that the theory of anomie and deviant behaviour does not account for non-utilitarian crime (*ibid.*: 231–2). We might hypothesize that this type of criminal activity results from a situation where, for example, 'lower-class' adolescents are oriented towards the middle class and feel relatively deprived compared to its members (Cloward and Ohlin, 1960: 90–7; Merton 1968, Chs. 10, 11; cf. 1988a). Relative deprivation is a variety of strain at the level of goals.

It should be clear that this reconstruction of one aspect of Cloward and Ohlin's argument has reintroduced the four components of social action (values, norms, goals [motivational mechanisms, collectivities], facilities [roles]) we discovered in reconceptualizing Merton's argument. I have used these notions to conceptualize various forms of deviance (utilitarian crime [deviant innovation], non-utilitarian crime [deviant aggression], deviant conflict and deviant retreatism), but I have also used them to conceptualize crucial variables leading to these responses, respectively, strain at the level of facilities, goals, norms and values. In Cloward and Ohlin's work there is no relationship between the nature of strain and the deviant response. In contrast, I suggest that the occurrence of strain limits the possible type of response, while the nature of the illegitimate opportunity structure confronted by actors in situations of strain narrows their possible response *within* each of the four types of deviance I have outlined. They are mobilized for a particular type of deviance from within the illegitimate opportunity structure.

One final clarification will further illuminate the power of the general theoretical framework I am utilizing. The reader will remember that in Merton's discussion of anomie there was a confusion between (1) the disjunction between goals and means and (2) where owing to the depth of the actor's desire he or she acts in an instrumentally rational fashion in selecting means to his or her goal, regardless of the legitimacy of those means. The former is clearly a form of strain at the level of facilities. The latter, however, is something completely different. It involves the genesis of an expedient attitude toward some set of 'law-like' expectations. If confronted with a situation of strain, many actors will not engage in deviant activities. They are precluded from doing so because they feel that such activities are morally wrong. In order for them to do so, they must have rejected this moral commitment in favour of a calculating attitude toward the norms in question, where a violation will occur if the actors feel that they will profit from the deviance under examination. This sense of benefit may be no more than a belief that they will get away with the crime. The point is that the calculating attitude is both analytically and empirically separable from each of the four varieties of strain and must be present in conjunction with strain if deviance is to occur.

If we recognize, once again drawing on the conceptualizations available in our general theory, that there is a classifiable variety of institutional structures within a society, we can further chart the direction of what I have elsewhere called internal disorder, motivated violations of the normative component of any institutional structure. These violations may either attempt the reconstruction of the structure attacked (as in the four types of political revolutions, restructuring the set of role relationships, collectivities, norms or values of the polity) or merely attack that structure, perhaps legitimizing the attack within a disorderly subculture, but making

Figure 24.1   Hypotheses Concerning Motivated Violations of Institutional Structure

Type of strain present within the system	Component at which disorder is directed	Is the component redefined?	Media deflated			
			Money	Power	Influence	Value commitments
At the level of values	values	yes		Total revolution		
		no			Deviant retreatism	
At the level of norms	norms	yes		Normative revolution		
		no			Deviant conflict	
At the level of goals	collectivities	yes		Rebellion		
		no			Deviant aggression	
At the level of facilities	facility roles	yes		'Facilitory rebellion'		
		no			Deviant innovation	

Source: This is a simplified version of the figure in Gould, 1987: 67.

no attempt to restructure the component attacked (as in the four types of deviance). These hypotheses are outlined in Figure 24.1.

In fact, my arguments can be made much more powerful. It is possible to show that they may be inferred from the functionally defined systems-analytic framework that Parsons and his students have developed (Parsons and Smelser, 1956; Gould, 1976; 1987: Ch. 2). Theory crafted using functionally defined concepts formulates societal (social) universals, propositions intended to be valid for all societies. Premised on the understanding that any system requires specifiable resources to function adequately, it asks about the consequences of an imbalance between these resources. No claims are made that the resources are actually present; instead, the theory poses causal hypotheses about the consequences of the relative dearth or plethora of one or another of them.

Calculating attitudes to the various normative orders are a consequence of deflations in what Parsons has labelled the generalized media of action (money, power, influence and value commitments). Thus a situation where the real resources controlled by the polity exceed the legitimate symbolic scope of its power is a situation of power deflation, and this deflation entails a calculating attitude towards the norms of political authority. In this situation actors will adopt an expedient orientation to political decisions, no longer accepting them as binding. Power deflation is a consequence of imbalances in the inputs to the political subsystem in a society.

Further, the four types of strain that I have enunciated may be conceptualized within the interchange system. Each of the four functionally defined subsystems provides factors of production to the other three subsystems (facilities from the economy, motivational mechanisms from the polity, normative justifications from the societal community and evaluations from the pattern maintenance subsystem). An impairment stemming from any of these inputs will generate social strain. As I have noted, depending on the location of strain, disorders will be directed at one or another component of social action. Depending on the location of the medium imbalance, the disorder will be directed towards the affected subsystem. For example, strain at the level of norms coupled with a deflation of power will generate a political disorder (a revolution or a riot) directed to the normative structure of the polity.[15]

One problem with working from within a general theoretical framework in a discipline where that framework is not readily accepted nor understood is the necessity of presenting the crux of the model in every essay. I am aware that my discussion in this paper is at best schematic. I hope, nonetheless, that it has made clear that I agree with Merton that useful conceptual schemes must result in the formulation of explanatory propositions. The general theory that I have utilized enunciates 'concepts...[that constitute] the definitions (or prescriptions) of what is to be observed; they are the variables between which empirical relationships are to be sought. When propositions are logically interrelated, a theory has been instituted' (Merton, 1968: 143).

Merton recognizes that data can exert pressure 'upon the research worker for successively so modifying his concepts that, with the recasting of the data in terms of the new concepts, there emerged a set of suggestive uniformities in place of the previously untidy aggregation of facts' (*ibid.*: 444). My discussion in this section has had the goal of demonstrating that a general theory may have similar results, leading to a formulation of empirically verifiable hypotheses. In consequence, I hope that my discussion lays to rest the myth that general theory is unconcerned with the formulation of explanatory propositions. While empirical research is not presented in this essay, I further hope that it is clear that these propositions both require and are suited for empirical evaluation. These claims may become clearer with the specification of the theory of internal disorder to a discussion of scientific revolutions.

THE STRUCTURE OF SCIENTIFIC REVOLUTIONS

'Paradigm' is a term with little theoretical content. In a discussion of scientific change Merton uses it to refer to the actually operating theoretical structures in sociology. 'As mini-structures of basic ideas, concepts, problematics, and findings, paradigms were held to represent unpretentious but organized claims to a limited kind of scientific knowledge' (1976a: 132). As is well known, Masterman (1970) has shown twenty-one different uses of the term 'paradigm' in Kuhn's *The Structure of Scientific Revolutions* (cf. Merton, 1976a: 133–4). It should be clear that 'the first step in the search for sociological order amid apparent disorder is to re-examine, in theoretical terms, the *concepts* in terms of which the data are reported. More often than not [and surely in this case], it will be found that these concepts may profit by clarification and reformulation' (Merton, 1968: 307). With any luck, reconceptualization will suggest 'the relevance of a previously developed body of theoretic propositions, thus reducing the *ad hoc* nature of current interpretations and making for *continuity* of present findings and theories of the past' (*ibid.*: 313, 144, 363).

Scientific revolutions consist of actions in violation of institutionalized norms within a scientific community;[16] they may include actions that are conforming within some other collectivity, including what may be termed a 'revolutionary subculture'. If we reconstruct Kuhn's notion of a paradigm, we will find that there are a variety of different types of scientific revolution, each of which is suggestive of a different type of scientific activity. Institutional structures are one form of social structure. They are moulded out of the four components of social action that we have already discussed: values, norms, goals [motivational mechanisms, collectivities] and facilities [roles]. As an institutional structure, a scientific discipline is constituted by relations between these four components. It will help in understanding the analysis which follows if I sketch out, in less abstract terms, how these components of social action are present in scientific organizations.

Facilities-roles are manifest in the directions guiding scientists' interaction among themselves and with the objects they study. The latter, as social structurally defined, involves the utilization of scientific theory as a guide in establishing interrelationships between scientific objects. This theory defines the nature of those objects and points towards types of instruments capable of relating to them (see Koyré, 1968; Merton, 1968: 141n2, 166n3). This aspect of the science does not involve the specification of problems, but rather the application of methods in the resolution of those problems, whether this involves conceptual operationalization, observation or instrumental application. These are instrumentalities in the specification and representation of theory, here utilized as an instrument in scientific practice.

Within this context it is justifiable to relate motivational mechanisms-collectivities to the structured goals which we may take as definitive of a scientific collectivity (cf. Parsons, 1960: Chs 1, 2). It is important to recognize that any such collectivity or discipline will be focused on a series of goals, and that, strictly speaking, goals are situationally defined. Thus a transformation of the collectivity structure within a scientific community need not transform the identity of that community itself. Motivational mechanisms-collectivities refer, within the context of science, to the theoretical and other definitions of problems and to the collective pursuit of the resolution of those problems. The nature of problem definitions is not uniform throughout science, but within 'normal science' these problems are usually specifications of the theories which might be taken as constitutive of the discipline. In Kuhn's terms this is the component of a paradigm which allows for the identification of puzzles, supplies clues to their solutions and in some sense guarantees success in finding a solution. Within scientific disciplines social norms may be most readily conceptualized as the standards controlling admissible problems and acceptable solutions. In the context of a smoothly functioning normal science, these standards are, at least in part, constituted by general theories, which define the concepts used and allow for the derivation of relationships in concrete research applications.

Finally, values define the nature of the desirable scientific community. They are embodied in the commitments of what it means to be a member of a discipline, how one is morally obligated to act, and they come to define a standard of scientific imagination within that discipline. This includes the social (as against the cultural) aspects of what Polanyi calls 'tacit knowledge'. As Kuhn points out, in his somewhat different use of the term, values may be shared by those who differ in their interpretation, application and implementation (1970b: 185–6; cf. Parsons, 1969: Ch. 16). Drawing on the theory of internal disorder already articulated, it should be clear that we may formulate a set of hypotheses capable, we have some reason to hope, of explaining various types of scientific revolution. The combination of one of the four varieties of strain and a calculating attitude towards the institutionalized normative structure attacked, a deflation of reputation (the form of influence operative within scientific communities [17]), determine the outcome. [18]

Much of what Kuhn discusses under the rubric of an anomaly is a form of strain at the level of facilities, an ambiguity with regard to the required facilities to attain some socially defined goal. Anomalies may be viewed from two perspectives. In the first they simply define puzzles to be resolved within normal science; in the second they are perceived as counterinstances and may give rise to the crisis which Kuhn usually views as a precondition for scientific revolutions. In the latter case, the puzzle is seen as a recognition that nature has violated paradigm induced expectations: a piece of equipment has failed to perform as it should, a problem presumed capable of resolution by known procedures resists solution, a new phenomenon capable of explanation within the theory appears within science's scope of perception, repeated specifications of theory fail to yield adequate results. In each instance facilities have proven inadequate to attain a socially defined goal.

Anomalies are present throughout normal science and channel much normal research. They are one aspect of the open nature of a scientific activity. Anomalies, strains at the level of facilities, become relevant to scientific revolutions only when coupled with other variables, most importantly, with a deflation of reputation. The latter generates a calculating attitude towards the regulating principles in the scientific system under examination; within this context conduct generated in response to an anomaly may involve a violation of normative codes.

The revolutionary response associated with facility strain within scientific communities involves a redefinition of scientific instrumentalities, when that redefinition violates the institutionalized norms which regulate scientific activity. This 'facilitory scientific revolution' will usually involve the introduction of previously banned or not previously conceived methods as instruments of research or modes of doing research. It will thus involve a redefinition of role performances within the context of extant collectivity structures, performances justifiable in terms of existing expectations. Thus it involves the redefinition of scientific roles as instrumentalities in pursuit of solutions to current problems.

Strain at the level of goals is also discussed by Kuhn under the rubric of an anomaly. It entails what he refers to as the 'breakdown' of the old theory. This occurs within the context of the theory's inability to guide normal problem-solving activity. It is not a question of inadequate facilities to resolve some problem, but of the nature of the theoretically derived problems themselves. Strain at the level of goals occurs when theoretically guided actions fail to yield results in a regularized fashion. In acute form this involves what Popper refers to as the falsification of a theory. A brief discussion of falsification will help us to see the difference between strain at the level of facilities and goals, as falsification can generally occur only when facility strain is not present.

Strictly speaking there is no such thing as falsification, as there is no clear-cut way to differentiate between two separate occurrences: if empirical procedures, experimental or of another sort, result in data contrary to the theory, there are two possible interpretations: the first is that the theory is false; the second is that the theory has not been properly operationalized, that the empirical materials are not valid representations of the theoretical concepts, and therefore the theory is not invalid, instead the operations are not adequate (cf. Merton, 1984b). The former circumstance is a variety of goal strain and must be based on a stronger belief in the efficacy of the method than of the theory; the latter is a manifestation of facility strain. Falsification, interpreted as one form of goal strain, is possible only when the methods are accepted within the community as adequate to the theoretical task. While it is essential to distinguish analytically between strain at the level of facilities and strain at the level of goals, it is also essential to recognize that the two may be conflated in concrete historical situations. When this entanglement occurs, and it is especially likely to occur in major scientific revolutions, any successful response will be to both types of strain.

Falsification is not a scientific revolution. The latter occurs only when an attempt is made to restructure the theory in question and when that attempt is in violation of the institutionalized norms of the scientific system under examination. The most important of this type of scientific revolution occurs when the reconstructed theory is partially definitive of the identity of the discipline or speciality under examination. In this case the collectivity of workers will itself be redefined and the positions of political control, the ability to set and implement goals within the community, will be reallocated to those who have constructed the new exemplar for the doing of the science. Often this process of redefinition results in the genesis of competing images of the new science and this can result in normative strain. This process is comparable to the situation of dual or multiple power during political revolutions and may involve the establishment and utilization of provisional theories recognized as unacceptable, but nonetheless necessary 'for the time being'.

Strain at the level of norms involves situations of role ambiguity, where an actor is either confronted with incompatible expectations or where the norms to which she is expected to conform are not specific or detailed enough to guide her actions (cf. Merton, 1976a: Part 1). Normative strain involves, therefore, a confusion with regard to expectations, because of either their surplus or dearth vis-à-vis specific situations. Kuhn refers to this variable often, usually when discussing a scientific crisis. The implication, since he usually assumes that crises precede scientific revolutions, is that all revolutions are in response to strain at the level of norms. This, in part, explains Kuhn's concentration on revolutions of wide scope, those which attack the rules, spoken or unspoken, which define admissible problems and solutions within a discipline. This transformation entails a redefinition in the standards which control normal science, a shift in the general theory which regulates a discipline's normal scientific research and thus a shift in the disposition of the discipline. The expectations which define interrelations among community units are altered. This is comparable, within political revolutions, to shifts in regime from, for example, a monarchy to a republic. We must not, however, assume that all scientific revolutions are of such scope, nor that all are in response to normative strain.

The last type of strain focuses at the level of values. It involves an ideological alienation from or ambivalence to the values institutionalized within a given system. Its roots are many, but one common source of this strain is the conjunction between two diverse communities which have institutionalized substantially different values.

Thus the confrontation between them yields, for the one subsumed within the other, value strain. This strain can be mitigated through the maintenance of autonomous structures, but when this autonomy is absent or when it is loosened, value strain may be manifest. The response to strain at the level of values leads to a transformation of the commitments which exemplify the discipline. This entails, as Kuhn puts it, a transformation of the world-view within which science is done. [19] These are the types of transformation emphasized in the work of Bachelard for the natural sciences and Althusser, for the social sciences; they involve 'epistemological breaks'. These involve the redefinition of what it means to do 'sociology' and in terms of what values the doing of 'sociology' is legitimized.

We have a categorical schema which allows us to organize systematically the components of social action within a scientific community in such a way that we are able to make considerable progress towards the explanation of the revolutionary transformations of these components. An obvious conclusion from this perspective is that scientific revolutions are not either-or affairs. Even if one focuses only on disorderly movements, there are several different varieties of scientific transformation. Not all scientific development is incremental, derivative from the resolution of puzzles within or outside normal science. Some transformations occur at other levels of scientific activity, for example, in shifts in the principles which regulate admissible problems and justifiable solutions. Work at these other levels of scientific practice, whether revolutionary or 'normal', must be grounded in empirical findings, but it may be autonomous from empirical research (cf. Alexander, 1982).

Any concrete scientific activity is always a combination of all four components (see the quotation from Parsons in note 11). For example, there is no problem-solving activity which is not, at least implicitly, regulated by normative expectations. 'Nevertheless, the four categories or components are, in the nature of the case, independently variable. Knowing the value pattern of a collectivity does not, for example, make it possible to deduce its role-composition. Cases in which the contents of two or more types of components vary together so that the content of one can be deduced from another are special and limiting, not general, cases' (Parsons, 1966: 19).

These independent, if interdependent (Parsons, 1937: 25n2) variables in our theory represent independent, yet interdependent, performances on the part of scientists. Each contributes to the success of scientific endeavours. If it is true that the higher ordered components cybernetically control the lower ordered activities, it is just as true that successful scientific activity is limited by the empirically grounded practices at the lowest level of the series, practices themselves limited by the nature of the external world.

CONCLUSION

I want to conclude by suggesting a few strategies which emerge from the analysis in this essay. These are second-best alternatives given the reality we face as social scientists. For the most part they are in accord with things Merton has long since argued. It goes without saying that, as Durkheim put it, our research must be undertaken with method, as systematically as is possible. It is a major contention of this essay that our theory must be articulated just as systematically. Not every sociologist need be proficient as a theorist, but if sociology is to advance, there must be systematic theory behind the work of virtually every sociologist. Merton has pointed out that verified predictions do not prove a theory. Alternative hypotheses, drawn from other theories, might just as well explain the data under examination. The task then becomes to find situations where the two theories generate different predictions. This is possible, needless to say, only when the theories generate sufficiently precise hypotheses to allow for a crucial experiment or observation (1968: 152–3).

If this process is not to remain totally ad hoc in form, we must recognize that 'the internal coherence of a theory has much the same function [of helping us to decide between competing hypotheses], for if a variety of empirically confirmed consequences are drawn from one theoretic system, this reduces the likelihood that competing theories can adequately account for the same data. The integrated theory sustains a larger measure of confirmation than is the case with distinct and unrelated hypotheses, thus accumulating a greater weight of evidence' (*ibid*.: 153). In my opinion, this insight forces us to recognize the role of general theory. If we are able to formulate a logically coherent set of interrelated concepts which allow us to develop and ultimately to deduce a wide range of hypotheses, the aggregation of plausible conclusions in terms of this one systematic framework will add weight to our confidence in both the whole and the parts.

The trick here is to straddle the line between concepts and propositions too flexible to evaluate and the 'premature insistence on precision at all costs [which] may sterilize imaginative hypotheses' (*ibid*.: 153). The key is to recognize that the concepts we articulate cannot become adequately precise until they are utilized in a variety of research settings. One task of research must be the clarification of concepts (cf. *ibid*.: 168–71) and some research may lead to the modification of concepts, rather than to the 'falsification' of propositions. The constraint on this type of activity, which I have labelled 'cheating', is found in the aggregate nature of research. One's conceptual redefinitions must be consistent across research projects (Gould, 1987: 64–5; cf. Merton, 1968: 143ff.).

Another way of stating the same point is that in the absence of experimental conditions and/or controlled observations, our task is to generate logically coherent images of bodies of empirical materials, where the empirical materials are almost as suspect as the theories we utilize to explain them. This hermeneutic representation applies not only to our empirical research endeavours, but also (contrary to most hermeneutic arguments) to our articulation of theory. Unlike traditional historians who try to tell a meaningful story based on their singular interpretations of the particular data at hand, we have a way of breaking into the hermeneutic circle. The coherence of our story must be consistent with and thus certified by the theory we utilize, just as the validity of that theory must be confirmed by the adequacy of our explanations. If our theory is general, it must also affirm the coherence of other empirical stories and in consequence it provides a considerable warrant for believing each individual explanation, just as each coherent explanation provides a bond for the theory's veracity.

Merton has long argued for a theoretical pluralism'—distinct paradigms and theories of the middle range—rather than a single actual or soon-to-be attained comprehensive theory' (1976a: 129; 1981a). At the same time he has suggested that 'the *ideal* of a unified comprehensive theory is not here in question. Like other ideals of the Pareto type T, this one may be functional, even when not attained, for advancing the state of sociological knowledge' (*ibid.*: 117–18). While I can make no claims that the ideal general theory exists, I have argued that just as the dialectic between hypothesis and empirical research is crucial for the development of sociology, the dialectic between hypothesis and coherent, logically integrated theoretical system is crucial for the development of our discipline.

NOTES

1   While Merton recognizes the importance of discontinuities in scientific development (1968: 9, 13, 23n47; 1984b: 1107–8), his clear emphasis is on the process of incremental growth and the continuities of development. Needless to say, Merton does not suggest that scientific development is simple and direct. He is a master at demonstrating that science is a form of social activity and like every other social activity moves with 'intuitive leaps, false starts, mistakes, loose ends, and happy accidents...' (1968: 4; 1973; 1970a).

2   In this essay I have focused only on social action and have refrained from considering either subinstitutional, culturally mediated interaction or autonomous personality systems.

3   Merton suggests that secondary analysis has the logical status of clinical enquiry. This may be the case when the clinician gathers a case history and interprets it prior to a therapeutic intervention, but clinical work also allows for the theoretical guidance of interventions and when this occurs the clinician is in an excellent situation to articulate and evaluate predictive theory. There is no a priori reason why this dialect between theory and intervention cannot constitute the clinical relationship, though its prospect is greatly enhanced as our theoretical knowledge increases (cf. Freud, 1963: 120–1).

4   An even clearer statement of this position is found in a long quotation from Bacon, who, according to Merton, 'more than anyone else before him...emphasized the prime importance of "middle axioms" in science' (1968: 56):,

> ...But then, and then only, may we hope well of the sciences, when in a just scale of ascent, and by successive steps not interrupted or broken, we rise from particulars to lesser axioms; and then to middle axioms, one above the other; and last of all to the most general. For the lower axioms differ but slightly from bare experience, while the highest and most general (which we now have) are notional and abstract without solidity. But the middle are the true and solid and living axioms, on which depend the affairs and fortunes of men.... (*ibid.*: quoting Bacon, *Novum Organum*, Book I, Aphorism CIV)

Merton views codification as equivalent to induction and formal derivation as equivalent to deduction (*ibid.*: 154n28). When one reads his texts carefully, the latter appears to include the derivation of empirical hypotheses from middle-range theory, but not the derivation of middle-range from general theory.

5   In his most famous discussion of paradigms as aids in the codification of sociological theory (1968: 69ff.), Merton appears to limit their functions to assisting qualitative (rather than quantitative) analysis. He implies that paradigms allow for the approximation of the logical, if not the empirical, rigour of quantitative analysis. 'The procedures for computing statistical measures and their mathematical bases are codified as a matter of course; their assumptions and procedures are open to critical scrutiny by all' (*ibid.*: 71). In this discussion he appears to confuse the narrowly statistical validity of an empirical study with the interpretation of empirical results. The latter is always a theoretical task; it is irrelevant whether the empirical study is quantitative or qualitative.

6   Merton writes that

> [A] large part of what is now described as sociological theory consists of *general orientations toward data, suggesting types of variables which theories must somehow take into account, rather than clearly formulated, verifiable statements of relationships between specified variables*. We have many concepts but fewer confirmed theories; many points of view, but few theorems; many 'approaches' but few arrivals. (1968: 52)

On the same page, in a footnote, he quotes Parsons's characterization of general theory, which looks very much like his own characterization of a paradigm. He suggests that this depiction, which he sees as downplaying the importance of general theory, does 'not differ significantly in principle from those who see the best promise of sociology today in developing theories of the middle range and consolidating them periodically' (*ibid.*: 52n17; cf. 39–53).

7 There is, needless to say, a problem in arguing by example. It may well be that the general theory I utilize is not efficacious, while some other theoretical formulation might be more convincing. It is also true that a convincing argument in this one case may reflect more about the inadequacies of one particular middle-range theory than the virtue of general theory in assisting in the formulation of explanatory propositions, or that the relationship between the explanatory propositions and the general theory is merely coincidental. I nonetheless proceed by example as I agree with Merton that it is time to demonstrate what can be done, rather than to continue to talk about what might be done if....

8 Sztompka, following Stinchcombe's lead, argues that Merton has articulated a '*full-fledged general theory*' and he sets out to 'dig into the matter, searching the structure of Merton's thought' in order to reconstruct it (1986: 3–4). He does not ask how the necessity for this reconstruction jives with Merton's own charge to reveal not only the finished structure of one's research, but also its scaffolding (Merton, 1968: 70, as quoted in the text above and as quoted in Sztompka, 1986: 1).

9 There is a third image of anomie in addition to those discussed in the text. Here 'it is the conflict between cultural goals and the availability of using institutional means—whatever the character of the goals—which produces a strain toward anomie' (Merton, 1968: 220, 216). Once again anomie is equated with a breakdown in norms, normlessness (*ibid.*: 217), but here anomie is a dependent variable along with deviant behaviour (*ibid.*: 230).

10 There is an important difference between *desired* and *desirable*. The former refers to what is wanted, to the actor's goal; the latter to the moral value which regulates the selection of norms, goals and facilities. Thus I use the term 'value' to refer to the desirable, and the term 'goal' to refer to what is desired. While what is desired and desirable may overlap, they need not be the same and they are often contradictory. The reader should not be confused by other conceptual frameworks which refer to 'values' as what is desired.

11 Parsons's warning concerning the proper use of these components is worth quoting in some detail:

> *any* concrete structural unit of a social system is always a combination of all four components—the present classification involves *components, not types*. We often speak of a role or collectivity as if it were a concrete entity, but this is, strictly speaking, elliptical. There is no collectivity without member roles and, vice versa, no role which is not part of a collectivity. Nor is there a role or collectivity which is not 'regulated' by norms and characterized by a commitment to value patterns. (Parsons, 1966: 19)

12 As deviance, all of these presumably entail the violation of some institutionalized norm, and Merton was aware from the very beginning about the ambivalent position of ritualism as a form of deviance (1968: 204).

13 Cloward and Ohlin define the pressure leading to deviance as is indicated in the text. Like Merton, however, they then go on to discuss anomie as 'a state in which social norms no longer control men's actions' (1960: 78).

14 The four types of strain I treat were first systematically articulated in Smelser's (1962) *Theory of Collective Behavior*, an essay generated from within the general theoretical framework I am discussing.

15 The theory of internal disorder is discussed in much greater detail in Gould, 1987, where I explicate additional independent variables not mentioned here, the logic of the model, and attempt to evaluate it in the light of an examination of the English revolutions of the seventeenth century.

16 It should be clear that many major developments in science were not revolutionary in form.

17 Reputation is a form of influence, 'a way of having an effect on the attitudes and opinions of others through intentional (though not necessarily rational) action...' (Parsons, 1969: 406). An actor attempting to influence another must justify her assertions 'with reference to items of information...The function of justification is not actually to verify the items, but to provide the basis for the communicator's *right* to state them without alter's needing to verify them' (*ibid.*: 417–18). In Luhmann's terms, alter accepts ego's experiences as his or her own (1976); the acceptability of ego's experiences is legitimized in terms of his or her prestige within the system under examination (cf. Merton, 1973: Ch. 20).

18 In this context I do not attempt a discussion of the deflation of reputation and will merely outline one possible manifestation of each of the four types of strain. In my paper 'A Theory of "Scientific

Revolutions"' I enunciate the theory in much greater detail, including a number of other independent variables (Gould, 1989). I have drawn freely from this essay.

19 When the transformation involves a progression from one stage of scientific development into another, it may entail a reformulation of the notion of 'truth' within the discipline (see Gould, 1977).

Interchange

BLALOCK REPLIES TO GOULD

In all honesty I do not understand what the differences are between Gould and either Merton or myself, but in this regard much may depend upon how one conceives of 'general theory' and 'theory of the middle range'. Gould, for example, asks 'from where do we derive the concepts within which a middle-range theory is articulated?' But the same could be asked about the concepts of a general theory. He also speaks about institutional conditions that inhibit the development and testing of middle-range theories, but I assume that many of these same conditions also inhibit the development of general theory as well. As I have tried to indicate, many of the problems we face, at any level, are fundamental and methodological in nature.

I read Merton as conceiving of 'general theory' as basically an orienting framework, devoid of either empirical generalizations or specific theoretical propositions linked by explicitly formulated assumptions. To me such general theory is typified by a work such as Talcott Parsons's *The Social System* (1951) or many of the highly abstract discussions of general theoretical orientations that regularly find their way into the sociological literature. But Gould may have something far more specific in mind by the notion of 'general theory', as indeed I infer to be the case from his discussion of a theory of internal disorder. To me such a theory of internal disorder, if clearly formulated into a series of explicit propositions, would be another example of a theory of the middle range. It *may* be more general than Merton's own discussions of anomie and deviance, but the notion of 'middle range' certainly does not preclude the possibility that successive theories may subsume earlier ones as important special cases. Nor does Kuhn's (1962) notion of 'paradigm revolution' help very much. Perhaps the issue is primarily semantic.

What I believe to be the essential points are the following. Whatever we call our theories, and whatever level of abstraction is involved, it is crucial that:

1 propositions be explicitly stated;
2 assumptions needed to justify and link these propositions also be made as explicit as possible;
3 there be clear statements about the conditions under which the theory does and does not hold;
4 considerable attention be given to the conceptualization of important variables in such a way that the move to measurement or operationalization is also based on explicitly formulated measurement assumptions; and

    5   social scientists make concerted efforts to agree on definitions of these basic
        concepts and how they are to be measured in specific contexts.

If all of these conditions are met, I would consider the theory to be 'middle range'.

    I thoroughly agree that it is important to place all such middle-range theories into reasonably general frameworks and to make every effort to link as many such middle-range theories to one another as is feasible in the light of currently available empirical evidence. What I infer bothered Merton, and what certainly bothers me, is that efforts to formulate highly general theories are often premature and overly ambitious and that such efforts practically always result in highly diffuse and confusing formulations, vaguely defined concepts, inattentiveness to measurement and discussions that are far too abstract to suggest specific, researchable propositions capable of falsification. If all of these defects can be corrected in any given 'general theory', then I, for one, would welcome the product. In my judgment, however, too many such efforts to develop highly general theories have been distracting at best, and productive of meaningless theoretical disputes at worst.

    As middle-range theories become increasingly inclusive, or as several such theories are joined into a more inclusive theory, we must be prepared to find that they also become increasingly complex. As I have tried to indicate in my earlier remarks, the search for parsimony does not seem compatible with the desire for increasing inclusiveness *if* we also wish to explain a considerable proportion of the variance in a wide variety of specific studies. Thus I see the move from highly delimited middle-range theories to more abstract ones as also requiring us to admit of more, rather than fewer, complexities. But if this must be accomplished by obscuring logically and empirically interconnected theoretical propositions by means of 'big words' and obtuse arguments, as well as vague references to the philosophical literature, then much will have been lost. My own reading of the general theory literature that has been produced over the past forty years is that it has been far too removed from empirical research. Lenski (1988) has made much the same point in connection with the macrosociological literature.

    I see much of this as a matter of the tactics we prefer in theory construction, as well as that of optimal timing in our efforts to produce a cumulative set of findings and theoretical interpretations, rather than a series of endless disputes among scholars favouring one or another 'school' of sociological theory. Merton is obviously calling for patience in our efforts to construct such theories by building upwards from discrete empirical generalizations to more abstract theoretical generalizations linked by a set of explicit assumptions and careful conceptualizations. It is in this sense that I fully endorse the strategy of the approach that he appears to be endorsing. One does not get to fully general theories 'full blown'. Ultimately, perhaps, we may move increasingly toward such an objective, but along the way we need to be far more careful about the methodological and empirical underpinnings than many so-called 'theorists' in our discipline seem to be.

GOULD REPLIES TO BLALOCK

Blalock voices agreement with Merton's call 'to move from well established "empirical generalizations" to corresponding "social laws" that are derivable from specialized theories'. He does this while acknowledging the ambiguity of Merton's image of middle-range theory, even though he devotes most of his essay to explaining the methodological problems 'in attempting to construct theories of the middle range in such a fashion that genuine "scientific laws", capable of falsification, can be established and a cumulative knowledge base established'. This emphasis on the methodological obstacles to carrying out Merton's project complements the theoretical arguments I have made in my essay, even though Blalock's comments are made in an apparently inductive argument.[1] My essay argued for the importance of general theory in empirical research. I will not repeat that argument here. In these comments I briefly focus on two of the issues Blalock raises: (1) why is it so difficult to formulate viable sociological theory; and (2) what is the nature of the basic concepts we must utilize in constructing our theoretical models?

(1) Blalock focuses on a set of methodological complications we confront in our attempt to develop explanatory theory—including multiple causation, the necessity of indirect measurement and the absence of universal constants. While I do not dispute these problems, it seems to me that they reduce to the claim that the social world is harder to explain than the natural world. Either these methodological problems are tractable or they are intractable. If the latter, Merton's, Blalock's and my own faith in the possibility of social *science* is misplaced. If the former (as Blalock seems to suggest), we need an explanation for why they have proved more unyielding in the social sciences than comparable problems in the natural sciences, an explanation more subtle than the claim that inadequate manhours have been devoted to their resolution.[2]

In *Reading Capital* Althusser makes an astonishing claim: 'It has been possible to apply Marx's theory with success because it is "true"; it is not true because it has been applied with success' (Althusser and Balibar, 1970: 50). This claim seems absurd to us as we are very likely to be sceptical of the truth claims Althusser makes for Marx's theory. On what grounds could such claims be based? What, however, of the following contention? 'It has been possible to apply Newton's theory with success because it is "true"; it is not true because it has been applied with success'. This claim makes sense to us if we argue that 'true knowledge' is produced within a realm of scientific practice, where scientific activity consists in the articulation *and* evaluation (via, for example, controlled observations and experimentation) of scientific theory. Here a determinate and autonomous product, knowledge, emerges from the realm of scientific activity. This knowledge might then be applied in, for example, engineering projects. The question we must ask is whether this image of scientific practice and its application is a legitimate one for both the natural and the social sciences.

In physics it is clear that a relatively autonomous institutional framework of scientific practice may exist within a capitalist social system and that from activities *within* this framework knowledge might be produced. It is then reasonable to speak of the application of this knowledge. If I put forward Gould's theory of mechanics and suggested testing it by building a bridge across the Delaware River, most of my readers would be reticent to be the first to drive across the bridge. You would, no doubt, suggest that this new theory would be better tested in the laboratory, where it might be determined to be valid under specifiable conditions, and then used in the construction of a bridge. In other words, true knowledge emerges from within the realm of physics, only to be applied in the construction of a bridge. It is possible successfully to apply Newton's theory because it is true and we know of its truth from the activities of physicists, not those of engineers.

In the social sciences, however, even if theory is articulated within a scientific problematic, there is virtually no autonomous realm of evaluation. The various techniques that social scientists have developed to adjudicate between theories are indeterminate. They allow neither for experimental tests nor for controlled observation (as in astronomy). While the amount of knowledge gained in social scientific research should not be minimized, and while the errors eliminated by good research have been considerable, it is nonetheless the case that virtually all of the theories and models we have developed remain subject to contention among those qualified to judge among them.[3]

It is impossible to imagine the emergence of an autonomous institutional realm where social scientists might practice. Here, unlike in physics, the production of scientific knowledge is possible only within the realm of 'political action' and thus only within the realm of the production of a 'political product'. In other words, the evaluation of scientific theory within the social sciences, including the evaluation of Marxist theory, is inextricably bound up with the application of that theory. The autonomous production of such knowledge without impinging on the lives of those studied is very unusual. Each instance where this impingement ensues will necessitate the evaluation of the consequences of scientific-political action by the people on whom these actions impinge. Their systematic evaluations are analogous to the empirical consequences of an experiment. In a capitalist social formation such evaluations are generally precluded, as structural constraints mandate action not in search of truth, but in search of profits and guided by various socially sanctioned prejudices. Distortions in the system impede the enactment of quasi-experiments. For the social sciences to be successfully undertaken, the structure of society will have to be transformed into a scientific community. In other words, unlike in physics, the institutional conditions required for the successful doing of social science must constitute the institutional structure of the society in which we lead our everyday lives. Then the unity of theory and action might be meaningfully implemented. Within the realm of social theory, evaluation will always imply both the production of knowledge and the implementation of goals.

(2) In my essay I argued that a general theory of action provides crucial guidance in the construction of powerful explanatory propositions. It articulates a set of interrelated concepts from which we may develop and in some instances derive such propositions. Even at our current level of knowledge theories must do more than simply orient us towards interesting questions, yet our conceptualizations cannot pretend to a precision which will emerge only after their continued use in examining wide varieties of empirical materials.

Both Merton and Blalock recognize that one task of empirical research is the clarification of concepts. Both appear to see this task largely in terms of the construction of indices operationalizing these concepts, 'in linking theoretical constructs with measured indicators' (Blalock), in 'developing *standardized measures* of each of the properties under review' (Merton, 1968: 379). For Merton, 'The index, or sign of the conceptualized item, stands ideally in a one-to-one correlation with what it signifies (and the difficulty of establishing this relation is of course one of the critical problems of research)' (*ibid*.: 169).

This empiricist view permeates much of Merton's writing.[4] While recognizing difficulties in establishing this one-to-one correlation, Merton seems to feel that such indices are achievable (cf. Sztompka, 1986: 100–1). Yet such an image runs directly counter to many of the most valuable theoretical insights we may derive from his work. For example, in his discussion of deviance and anomie Merton recognizes that poverty need not be correlated with crime (deviant innovation). The variable which generates crime is the disjunction between social goals and available legitimate means. Poverty is only related to crime when coupled with unattainable aspirations (Merton, 1968: 201, 201n22), and a wide variety of social goals may lead to deviance if the legitimate resources required to attain them are not available (1973: Ch. 14).

Likewise his analysis of Durkheim's discussion of suicide is premised on the recognition that social cohesion cannot be linked with any substantive attributes. Catholics may commit suicide less frequently than Protestants, but the theoretical explanation for this has nothing to do per se with Catholicism. The argument is that suicide is inversely related to social cohesion (although this is much too simple a summary of Durkheim). The derivation of a substantive hypothesis from this argument is dependent on the specification of this theory within a concrete social situation, and this specification is variable across situations (Merton, 1968: 151–2; also Blalock).

Further, as Durkheim well understood, in empirical analyses concepts may be overdetermined. Even in one situation the presence of a variable may be manifest in a variety of forms, any one of which would lead to activation of the variable in our proposition. It isn't that these forms are not subject to systematic empirical identification, it is that their identification will require the use of judgment on the part of the researcher, a judgment guided by a coherent theoretical perspective. No one operation can identify the variable forms a concept may take, both within and across social situations. Additionally, any particular operation may identify two or more disparate concepts in different situations.

All of these problems are accentuated by two issues implicit in their articulation. The first is the fact that sociologists study action and not behaviour. Social action is mediated by structures of meaning; two phenomenologically identical performances may have completely different meanings and, in consequence, may represent very different concepts. If our theories and the research we conduct to evaluate them do not recognize that 'interpretive understanding' is necessary in order to generate causal explanations, we will not be successful in articulating relationships (Weber, 1947: 88; the translation in Weber, 1978, reduces causal explanations to interpretive understanding). Second, invariant relationships across social systems must utilize functionally defined concepts. Here units are identified in terms of their consequences for the system as a whole.[5] Concepts must be defined in abstract functional terms to encompass the seemingly infinite variety of particular cases and to take note of the fact that the 'same' substantive phenomena may have various functions and in consequence various roles in scientific propositions. The enunciation of arguments in substantive, instead of in functional terms, leads to absurd conclusions. For example, in his essay on 'Manifest and Latent Functions' Merton examines the functional role of religion. He faults earlier theorists for postulating only an integrating role for religion and for failing to recognize the disintegrating consequences of religious conflict. He then comments that 'such functional analyses may, of course, mean that religion provided integration of those who believe the *same* religious values, but it is unlikely that this is meant, since it would merely assert that integration is provided by any consensus on any set of values' (1968: 84). Without judging the authors Merton discusses, surely what they *should* have examined is the consequences of value homogeneity and value heterogeneity on the stability of social systems.

A general theory cannot be formulated using concepts which are institutionally specific and which presume a determinate function for any concrete variety of institutional complex. To do so would be to assume that Protestantism instead of egoism is correlated with suicide. As Merton himself recognizes, the existence of functional substitutes requires that concepts be defined in a way which is not substantive (1968: 88, 106). This leads to the conclusion that there is no one-to-one correlation between substantive attributes and sociological variables. It should also lead to the conclusion that general theory is essential in guiding the formulation of middle-range theory, if only because the facts under examination are conceptual statements about phenomena, and the systematic articulation of a conceptual framework is one province of general theory.

NOTES

1   Theorists who argue for the significance of general theory usually recognize the importance of inductively derived contributions. Unfortunately, 'middle-range theorists' and 'methodologists' often fail to reciprocate the compliment. Given the dominance of 'methodology' in sociology departments, this dismissive attitude has as a possible consequence the bifurcation of sociology to the point where theory occupies a position not dissimilar to its role in political science, where too often it is reduced either to political philosophy or to intellectual history.

2   Blalock does mention a number of cultural and organizational roadblocks inhibiting knowledge accumulation in the social sciences, including the isolation we face in our academic departments and the fact that grant and promotion policies favour short-term research projects. While these are important barriers—especially to those of us who are (1) theorists, whose work tends to be long-term in nature, and (2) members of small departments—they are not, in my opinion, adequate explanations for the retarded development of the social sciences.

3   This discussion is not meant to be comprehensive. I want merely to state the obvious: social scientists have no autonomous realm of activity in which to conduct experiments. Further, unlike astronomers, we do not have any agreed upon methods allowing for the systematic observation of the objects of our research. The capacity of astronomers in this respect is itself dependent on theory evaluated within laboratories. We do not have comparable theoretical resources. Social scientists are thus in the paradoxical position of having to find ways of doing social science while the institutional conditions for successfully doing social science are absent.

4   In this context Merton sees an empiricist position as one which fails to pay due regard to the variables involved in research (1968: 168). For me an empiricist position is one which accepts as valid concepts only those directly generalizable from observations. Empiricists reject theoretical constructs like the 'unconscious', which are required to explain observations, but are not directly reducible to observations, and in consequence they favour an invariant relationship between index and concept.

5   Elsewhere I have argued, specifically with regard to a theory of societal crisis, that viable explanations require a three-dimensional conceptual framework, including structural and developmental perspectives as well as the functional dimension. Structural models are only valid for one stage in the development of societies and include constructs which, unlike some functionally defined concepts, are not abstractions from 'simple descriptions' (Gould, 1985; see also 1987).

XIV. THE SOCIOLOGY OF TIME

25. Robert K. Merton's Contribution to Sociological Studies of Time

SIMONETTA TABBONI

The study of time has not been an issue that has absorbed Merton to any great extent, although he has returned to it from time to time over the years. It is sufficient to say that there are almost fifty years between his first and his most recent essay on the subject. Nevertheless, Merton's contribution to this field has made a considerable impact and pointed the way for future studies in this area. Merton is significantly well equipped to give a detailed account of the American approach to the analysis of temporality, as it was he and Pitirim Sorokin who laid the basis for a theoretical study of time in 1937. This paper, 'Social Time: A Methodological and Functional Analysis' (Sorokin and Merton, 1937a), broke new ground in the United States, marking the beginning of a completely new line of research. In 1982 he developed these ideas further in a lecture (Merton, 1982b), and then went on to write an essay on the social aspects of duration, which was published in 1984 (Merton, 1984a).

Merton's work was in the great European tradition, building on the pioneering studies of Emile Durkheim, Henri Hubert and Marcel Mauss, whose studies on the theme of time provided many profound insights. However, the intellectual climate of the late 1930s did not seem particularly favourable to a renewal of interest in the study of time, and American sociologists showed no particular interest in Merton's attempts to develop it further.[1] The themes put forward in Merton and Sorokin's essay were not taken up by anyone else, although Sorokin, who had been the moving force behind these studies, remained interested in these issues and went on to develop them in *Social and Cultural Dynamics* (1937/41) and *Sociocultural Causality, Space, Time* (1943).

In retrospect these initial studies can be seen as premature and isolated attempts to transplant European and Durkheimian ideas into a somewhat unfertile and non-receptive American soil. They met with little success. Still, when American social scientists become interested in the subject of time again, they will no doubt

427

take up from where Merton and Sorokin left off, continuing the Durkheimian emphasis on the normative and collective aspects of time and the way in which time is seen as a unifying force.

The works of Moore (1963), Coser and Coser (1963) and especially Zerubavel (1981) are direct developments of the themes of the 1937 essay, firmly rooted in the Durkheimian tradition.

In this sense Merton's second essay on time of 1984, which focuses on the concept of socially expected durations (SEDs), marks the logical conclusion of a particular line of research which had been started in the United States by Merton and Sorokin, following on directly from Durkheim. Perhaps this explains Merton's comment on the relation between his essay on SEDs and the large body of work produced on the subject of time from the 1960s: 'However, these and kindred materials, both early and contemporary, provide part of the substantive basis for a methodical analysis of the concept of socially expected durations in connection with the sociological problems and understanding it helps to generate' (Merton, 1982b).

This amounts to saying that the diverse approaches to the theme of time adopted by American sociologists need to be supported by an adequate theoretical framework if they are to stand up to close scrutiny. Merton put considerable emphasis on the fact that social time and SEDs formed part of the same continuum, both in the paper he presented at San Francisco in 1982 (1982b) and in the interview with Anna di Lellio in 1985, in which he said:

> In highly industrialised societies, certain types of social expectations of time are highly complex and have a considerable impact. This can be more clearly understood if we bear in mind the concept of social time as explained by Sorokin and I in an article we wrote in 1937. Even although at that time we had no idea of what social expectations of time were, in that article we maintained, in the best Durkheimian tradition, that the more there is a generally perceived social need to co-ordinate and link aspects of time, the greater the development of models of social time which are distinct from calendar time and time as measured against the movements of the stars. (Merton, 1985b: 8)

After having made clear the basic premises of Merton's approach, a number of questions remain to be answered. The first concerns the exact nature of Merton's project and the theoretical directions he is following within the American tradition of studies on the 'sociology of time'. We must attempt to identify the strengths and weaknesses of his contribution to the study of social time and to ascertain what are likely to prove the most promising developments of his line of thought.

In his essay on SEDs, as on many other occasions, Merton goes back to Burke's theorem to explain his intellectual development, the reasons for his particular approach, why it proved to be particularly fruitful and why he left other directions relatively unexplored. Burke's theorem must have fascinated Merton and provided the answer to a question which, although apparently banal, often arises when assessing the evolution of a theory, namely why certain issues are explored in great depth while other related fields of enquiry are left unexplained, neglected or considered not to be relevant. According to Burke: 'A way of seeing is also a way of not seeing. If we focus on object A, object B gets left in the shadows' (Burke, 1935: 70).

I would like to apply Burke's theorem to Merton's work. Thus I will not only elucidate fully those aspects of his work which he himself has highlighted and which lend themselves, as in fact happened, to being taken up and developed further; I will also attempt to give an account of those elements which have hitherto been neglected. It is particularly interesting that the aspects which Merton failed to develop in depth take on a particular importance if they are viewed in the context of his exhaustive treatment of other aspects of temporality and the fascination which certain themes and theoretical orientations exercised on him throughout his intellectually productive years.

I would like to show how Merton's focus on the normative and integrative aspect of time, his emphasis on collective representation and the supreme importance of the social, prevented him from recognizing that the study of time was of greater sociological interest than he had first realized. Another consequence of Merton's approach was that the world of the social and the world of the individual were seen as potentially opposed rather than interwoven. This opposition between the social and the individual provides the basis for his relatively static vision of the social aspects of temporality and his neglect of historical tools of analysis.

THE OPPOSITION BETWEEN SOCIAL AND INDIVIDUAL TIME

In his essay of 1937 with Sorokin, Merton made it quite clear that he accepted and wished to develop his own version of the Durkheimian tendency to regard collective representations as sacred, to ascribe a positive value to the social and to see it as an extremely powerful, almost omnipotent force. Merton makes no mention at all of the issue of individual time and the way it is closely connected with changes in social time, actually helping to bring them about. The very fact that Merton is able to describe in such detail the essential harmoniousness of temporal norms, the basic patterns which carry a determined set of collective meanings, seems to indicate that social time is implicitly set against individual time, although this is never stated directly. Like all other norms, collective temporal norms are imposed on the individual consciousness with an almost divine authority. In short, individual time is not considered as a problem.

However, this means that we have no way of understanding how and why individual time contributes to forming the structures of social time, which are the main focus of Merton's attention. As he puts it apropos of SEDs, they 'constitute a fundamental class of patterned expectations linking social structures and individual action' (Merton, 1982b). Individual time tends to be seen as existing between certain patterns of opposition or adaptation. It is never perceived as a creative force. In fact Durkheim was even less convinced than Merton that these two aspects of time could have a reciprocal influence upon each other. He expressed grave doubts about the possibility of bringing these two levels of human experience together and breaking down the barriers between them. For Durkheim, the gulf between social time and individual time could not be bridged.

The individual and society could only be brought together if society were very much the dominant force. When, in the concluding pages of *The Elementary Forms of the Religious Life*, Durkheim asks how it comes about that '...the individual is capable of raising himself above his own peculiar point of view and of living an impersonal life' (Durkheim, 1964: 445), when, in other words, he raises the issue of the relationship between individual and society, he expresses the solution in the following way:

Perhaps some will be surprised to see us connect the most elevated forms of thought with society: the cause appears quite humble, in consideration of the value which we attribute to the effect. Between the world of the senses and appetites on the one hand, and that of reason and morals on the other, the distance is so considerable that the second would seem to have been able to add itself to the first only by a creative act. But attributing to society this preponderating rôle in the genesis of our nature is not denying this creation; for society has a creative power which no other observable being can equal. (*ibid.*: 446)

Merton's analysis of social time bears some of the traces of the Durkheimian emphasis on a sociological definition of time, which stresses time's social and integrative quality. For Merton, time extends beyond the domain of measured time, beyond the abstract chronology of the days and hours measured on the clock face to which modern societies turn because they need a common language and which allows them to understand each other and to coordinate their common activities. Time for Merton is the sum of change experienced and observed: the essence of social time lies in the experience of the collectivity. Thus Merton not only paid scant attention to the notion of individual time, he also largely ignored the aspects of time which were linked to the theory of action (on this see Sztompka, 1986: 27).

Merton's theories about the social origin of time, its qualitative nature and the ways in which it differs from measured and quantitative definitions of time do not bring out the uniqueness of individual time and the choices it involves, neither do they clarify how social and individual time are connected. There is a considerable imbalance between the subtlety of Merton's analysis of the social aspects of temporality and the fact that he largely ignores the individual's experience of time and how individual time contributes to modifying the rules we call social time.

If we return to Burke's theorem, it appears that the fact that Merton lays particular emphasis on the normative aspect of time makes it difficult for him to become aware that it is the very adoption of a temporal perspective that makes it possible to approach a solution to one of the most difficult dilemmas of sociological theory, namely the search for ways of connecting theories of action and theories of structure. In fact Merton continued to devote his attention to this difficult issue, but he tried to find a solution to it by pursuing other avenues of enquiry.

If we consider that people really use the notion of time to describe experiences of change[2]—and a norm which connects directly the social and the natural at the level of the individual—then this makes it easier to establish a link between these different planes of human experience. As Norbert Elias has maintained, to understand what time is we have to abandon the dichotomies which have tradition- ally been used in the West to separate the individual from the social and the natural. Elias's definition of time can help forge a link between the different zones of human experience: 'In its present state of development time... is a symbolic synthesis on a very high plane, a synthesis which enables us to relate natural, social and individual processes of change' (Elias, 1986: 23).

Elias's analysis of time complements the Durkheimian approach to the ques- tion. His approach progresses along the same lines, but enriches it with new insights. Elias is not content merely to demonstrate the social nature of time: he also offers an explanation of why time has become what it is today. Elias attributes the develop- ment of a series of changes wrought over the centuries of human society, which he refers to as 'the civilizing process'. Time is no longer merely the collective rhythm of different activities, but a social construction which varies in the course of the process of civilization, becoming today one of the most constraining social habituses, an extremely abstract symbol, a cognitive instrument borrowed from the natural sciences.[3]

This work of historical reconstruction is not accomplished by reference only to the normative definition of time. In addition to the social norm, Elias takes into account the active intervention of individuals and their different experiences of time in explaining the historical change that this concept has undergone throughout the centuries and its concomitant changing social practices and representations.[4] These reflections on the theme of time enable us to reach some understanding of how the social, the individual and the natural levels of human existence are linked. Elias's work gives us an insight into how normative bonds and subjective intentions, constraints and choices contribute to the solution of what constitutes individual time. Individuals construct a wide range of different time schemes, they each have their own particular way of going about things and coming into contact with the collective temporal norm. People are continually adjusting and readjusting the facts to suit their own particular needs and skills and continually reassessing the relationships constituted by different social times.

The study of time helps us understand the interplay of structural constraints and individual intention in social action. It is likely that one of the reasons why the various elements of time have exerted such a fascination for sociologists is that the study of time offers a good opportunity to explore the nature of individual choice. Time implies order, constraint, but also meaning and a degree of free choice. The study of individual and collective temporality seems to offer sociologists a way out of a deadlock and opens up an interesting perspective on an extremely complex theoretical issue: how and to what extent do social structures determine individual behaviour, and how in turn do individuals modify social structures to suit their own purposes?

THE CONCEPT OF SOCIALLY EXPECTED DURATIONS

In Merton's second essay on time from 1984 (Merton, 1984a) the focus alters slightly; he refines and improves his method of approach, leaving aside previous lines of enquiry. The concept of SEDs evolved over a long period. It gradually took shape during various collaborative empirical research projects that he undertook. The idea began to take shape on the basis of the findings of a study of the behavioural patterns of the inhabitants of Craftown—a new community of about 750 working-class families which had been set up in 1911 in an industrial area near New York. Merton found that the inhabitants' relationships with others and their readiness to make friends and to participate in leisure activities were directly dependent on how long they expected to stay in Craftown. As he put it: '... it was found that the *expected* duration of residence worked independently of the actual duration to affect these behaviors' (1984a: 275). When Merton temporarily gave up empirical research at the end of the 1950s to return to more theoretical study, his intention was 'to identify the major properties of social structure' (*ibid.*: 278). He now felt ready to attempt a definition of the broad concept of the social expectations of duration.

Merton distinguishes three types of SEDs. The first are socially prescribed durations supported by institutions. Second, there are what he describes as collectively expected durations (these include, for example, predictions about how long an economic crisis or a government coalition will last). This type of socially expected duration is difficult to define precisely. Finally, there are the temporal expectations which are to be found in interpersonal relations of various types, ranging from formal contractual relations to more intimate and community-oriented relations. Although these types of relations are generally more stable, they too are expected to last for a particular length of time.

Merton's notion of socially expected durations introduced the theme of time into social theory. It must be said, however, that although Merton was fully aware that time was part of the social structure, the impact of his approach was blunted by his failure to take account of the origin and evolution of the concept. Merton has always been primarily interested in social structures, in the elements of collective life which exert a powerful constraining influence on human behaviour. By focusing on the social expectations of duration, which is how Merton sees human behaviour in relation to time, he largely ignores the sphere of individual experience and the fact that an individual's experience of time is historically conditioned.

In addition, although the concept of the social expectations of duration enabled Merton to develop a structural analysis of the social world, he often failed to take into consideration the historical dimension. Although the historian Reinhart Koselleck uses the concept of time in a completely different way from Merton, it is nevertheless instructive to compare his approach with Merton's, as it provides an interesting counter to an approach which focuses too narrowly on normative expectations. The starting point for Koselleck's study of temporal structures (Koselleck, 1979) is an analysis of the reasons why certain linguistic usages occur, take root and spread and the circumstances in which this comes about. The basis of Koselleck's approach is a detailed analysis of the links between social history and the history of concepts. Koselleck's exploration of the development of meaning is certainly far removed from the empirical social scientific approach adopted by Merton from which the concept of socially expected duration gradually arose.

Koselleck also highlights the importance assumed by what he defines as 'the horizons of expectations' in collective life and in the way people choose to behave. However, unlike Merton, Koselleck considers that if this concept is to be used to explain the past and possibly to predict the future, then it must be seen in relation to what he describes as 'the regions of experience'. Koselleck discusses expectations and experiences in general, and his perspective remains a historical one. Nevertheless, it is still possible to compare his approach with Merton's, given that both are primarily concerned with the temporal factors which influence collective behaviour and that expectations and experiences of time form part of the wider sphere of expectations and experience. All this brings home the fact that Koselleck and Merton use the term 'expectations' to suit their own particular purposes; neither makes any reference to general definitions of the concept.[5]

For Koselleck, then, 'horizons of expectations' are inextricably linked with 'regions of experience'. Experience and expectations are antithetical temporal concepts which can only be understood if they are seen as interrelated. All human action springs from the reciprocal tension that is generated between these two related concepts. If expectations are a structural element of every society and if society exists in a diachronic dimension, what defines history is the ever-present and necessary difference between expectations and experiences. This process works in both directions: expectations never confirm experiences, something new is always happening, which in turn modifies previous expectations, thus altering the overall picture. Experiences do not confirm expectations, but are modified retrospectively by the appearance of new experiences, so that the past is never a closed book, it keeps evolving and changing and is continually being modified by successive events. The past is continually being brought to life and remodelled as events progress.

The difference between expectations and experiences, which according to Koselleck is a basic anthropological fact, is all the more significant—and its effects more widely felt—in the modern era, in which time takes on a new meaning, the future is seen as unpredictable and unsettled, and people are generally convinced that things will happen in the future that would have been inconceivable in the past. It is indeed the case that Merton developed the concept of SEDs on the basis of empirical research findings which showed that there was a precise correlation between SEDs and the ways in which the working-class inhabitants of Craftown behaved.

However, this does not necessarily imply that these findings would have been borne out by other research conducted in different socio-historical contexts. Indeed it is possible to envisage cases in which such a correlation could be explained by other factors. It could be linked, for example, to certain forseeable aspects of economic and collective life, to a general sense of stability and security which gives people confidence in the norms or conventions on which their social expectations of duration are based. Alternatively, if similar research were carried out against a background of socio-economic crisis and fluctuating rates of employment, for example at the end of a war or in a climate of general uncertainty where the overwhelming experience was of a general lack of stability, it is unlikely that this correlation would be found to exist. If the socio-historical circumstances of the workers studied by Merton had been different, if, for example, they had experienced periods of unemployment or underemployment or participated in political or union struggles, their experience would have had to be considered a significant variable forming an interactive nexus with expectations of various types. Experience and expectations have a reciprocal effect on each other, just as the expectations which influence human behaviour, like any other structural variable, develop on the basis of past experience as well as on the basis of a more or less binding normative system.

Individual experience is also part of what we call SEDs, and SEDs themselves are the result of the interaction which takes place between experiences and expectations. In fact, expectations arise out of existing norms, convictions and customs. How does it come about that SEDs play such an important role in social life? How is it that individuals behave predictably as regards the expectations which they hold on the basis of certain rules—some of which have a formal-legal character and some of which are rooted in custom or derive from generally held beliefs?

Rules alone cannot explain certain forms of behaviour unless they are viewed within the historical framework in which they occur, develop and are used. If we do not take into consideration the experiences which constitute the background and support of a normative system, either ensuring that the rules are enforced and guaranteeing their legitimacy or alternatively providing evidence of fragility and precariousness, then we cannot be fully aware of the true nature of socially expected durations. SEDs evolve out of a historical process; they are the product of the interaction between expectations and experiences which develops over a period of time.

The concept of SEDs is an extremely useful research tool if it is conceived as the product of a historical process in the course of which individuals compare their expectations and experiences. It is a useful concept for describing how the various social actors view the reliability of the norms and customs in force on the basis of their own experiences.

THE SOCIOLOGY OF TIME TODAY

Reviewing sociological studies of time today, we can single out two approaches which have been extremely influential in determining the course of research. First, there is the French tradition, dominated by Durkheim and developed by Merton and Sorokin, which provided the real inspiration for American research on the issue. Second, there is the German tradition, largely based on historical tools of analysis, including scholars such as Elias and Koselleck, Luhmann and Rammstaedt. These two traditions have tended to develop along separate lines and have had little or nothing to do with each other. It seems likely that the proponents of these different approaches would come up with more interesting findings if they were prepared to learn from one another and adopt elements of each other's approaches. Fresh impetus has recently come from the Franco-American tradition, led by Merton, with the formulation of the concept of socially expected durations. This has had the effect of focusing attention on the social origins of time and on its innate capacity to order human life.

Current developments have meant that the focus of research has become increasingly sociological in the strict sense of the word. There has been a tendency to focus on the integrating function of temporal norms and to uncover the vast range of conventions and temporal norms upon which social life rests (the work of Eviater Zerubavel is a case in point). Present research aims to make increased use of theoretical concepts—such as Mertonian SEDs—in an attempt to impose some order on the mass of empirical observations and findings and to make them part of a coherent system. It is primarily the normative aspects of time which are being studied at the moment; the study of temporality is being brought back to the study of social structures.

In the German tradition, on the contrary, the concept of time is first and foremost defined from a wider historical point of view.[6] Experience is also a subject of investigation,[7] and attention is focused not only on the temporal norm, but also on the historical development of the notion of time and the factors which appear to have influenced it most in the course of its history.[8] In this tradition the main interest lies in the changing form which time has assumed while common experiences and prevailing values were also changing, and how time has fulfilled a variety of different functions throughout history. Attempts have been made to identify the variables which may have influenced the change, and the emphasis has been on a historical approach rather than a sociological one (if it can be assumed that this distinction is meaningful).[9] Both these traditions, the Franco-American and the German, are rich in relevant concepts and characterized by acute insight, although both have their own particular 'blind spots' *à la* Burke. For this reason it would be useful to bring the two approaches together, starting with the work of scholars such as Merton.

To return to the question asked at the beginning of this paper, it now appears that Merton's contribution to the sociology of time could be developed further in two directions. First, it could follow the lead of other studies which have demonstrated an increasing awareness of the fact that temporal norms are closely interwoven with the fabric of social life. Second, advances can only be made if the range of analysis is broadened to include new approaches. Merton has already shown that he is aware of this and is continually extending his interpretive scheme.

In his paper of 1982 Merton outlined some possible future developments of the concept of SED:

> The further analytical and interpretative questions are legion: what are the attributes and parameters of SEDs? How do SEDs vary in structure, operation, and consequence? What, in particular, are the anticipatory behavioral adaptations of individuals, groups, organizations, and collectivities to social expected duration of the several kinds? In short, how do SEDs come to take certain forms rather than others; what are the parameters of the various forms; and finally how do they operate as temporal components of social structure to affect patterns of organizational and individual behavior?

However, it is not possible for Merton to pursue his interest in the normative aspects of time much further as long as they continue to be analyzed independently from changing social experiences. Although he has to some extent investigated how the concept of time has evolved throughout history (Sorokin and Merton, 1937a), he does not seem interested in studying why and how the concept changes or in identifying which kind of long-term processes influence it. Above all he does not tackle the problem of how the mutual interaction between social and individual time develops, how individual initiative modifies existing temporal constraints while partially accepting them. Interactions can only be analyzed historically. In short, what is missing in Merton's entire approach is an attempt to find points of contact between the two poles of the 'paradox of human action' (Abrams, 1982)—freedom and constraint.

NOTES

1   This is confirmed by Merton in his ASA paper of 1982 in which he describes his own work and the intellectual climate in American sociological circles during that time. He also mentions the intellectual isolation of his mentor, Pitirim Sorokin (see Merton, 1982b).
2   There are many classical psychological studies on time which link thinking on time to broader perceptions of change (see, for example, James, 1909; Fraisse, 1967; Piaget, 1971). This issue is dealt with convincingly by a number of sociological studies (see, for example, Rammstaedt, 1975; an unpublished paper by Cavalli, 1986; and some passages in Norbert Elias's *Saggio sul tempo*, 1986).
3   Norbert Elias deals with these themes at some length in his *Saggio sul tempo*.
4   This does not mean that the concept of time should be 'historicized', nor indeed was this what Elias was saying. On the contrary, although its historical evolution should also be taken into account, it remains the main task of the sociologist to arrive at a definition of the concept per se. If the notion of time as it stands takes into account the relation between the subject and a particular experience, the analysis of its genesis enables us to arrive at a better understanding of the context and the social circumstances in which the concept takes on meaning.
5   An exploration of the concept of 'expectation' would have been useful before formulating the concept of SEDs. As C. Mongardini has pointed out:

> The expectations of role, or, more generally, structural expectations in the broader sense as used by Merton, are only the same facade covering microprocesses which go against the current of the production or reproduction of collective life. These microprocesses help the social actor adjust to his environment. This adjustment process in turn produces expectations and consequently action. These microprocesses comprise the following elements: a) the gathering

of information on and perceptions of the environment which are the preconditions of action; b) the awareness of the fact that the social actor is able to alter the situation to his advantage, and indeed is likely to do so. This has some effect on the way he sees what he is going to do; c) the setting up of a plan for interaction which is composed of partial expectations and expectations of expectations (which are attributed to the other). (Mongardini, 1985: 104–5)

6   As far as I am aware, Norbert Elias is the only sociologist to tackle head on the problem of the sociological definition of time. His lucid definition forms an invaluable base for future developments in the study of time: 'The concept of time is dependent upon... man's capacity to link two or more sequences of continuous changes. One of these sequences acts as a yardstick for the other or for others' (Elias, 1986: 89). Elias expresses this idea more clearly still: 'the word "time" is... a symbol of a link which a group of people, that is a group of living beings with the biological capacity to remember and to make sense of their experiences, establishes between two or more series of events. One of these is then used as a frame of reference or yardstick for the other or others' (*ibid*.: 59).

7   I am referring to the previously quoted studies by Rammstaedt (1975) and Koselleck (1979).

8   Both Elias (1982, 1986) and Koselleck (1979) have made important contributions to this particular area of study.

9   On this point see Philip Abrams's brilliant polemic, *Historical Sociology* (1982). I am in broad agreement with the views expressed in Abrams's book.

Notes on Contributors

Philippe Besnard is Director of Research at the Centre National de la Recherche Scientifique and also teaches at the Institute of Political Studies in Paris. He has been an active member of the Groupe d'Études Durkheimiennes for many years, and is joint editor of the *Revue française de sociologie*. Among his current research interests are social aspects of consumption, and social rhythms and seasonal variations. His recent publications include (as editor) *The Sociological Domain—The Durkheimians and the Founding of French Sociology* (1983), *L'anomie: ses usages et ses fonctions dans la discipline sociologique depuis Durkheim* (1987) and *Moeurs et humeurs des Français au fil des saisons* (1989).

Robert Bierstedt is Commonwealth Professor Emeritus at the University of Virginia. He has taught and lectured at a number of universities, including Munich, Edinburgh, Glasgow, Oxford, Cambridge and the London School of Economics. His publications include *The Social Order* (4th ed, 1974) and *American Sociological Theory: A Critical History* (1981). A collection of his essays has been published under the title *Power and Progress* (1974).

Hubert M. Blalock Jr is Professor of Sociology at the University of Washington in Seattle. His research interests are in applied statistics, causal modelling, theory construction, conceptualization and measurement, and race relations. His recent publications include *Conceptualisation and Measurement in the Social Sciences* (1982) and *Basic Dilemmas in the Social Sciences* (1984). He is currently working on a book dealing with power and conflict processes.

Peter M. Blau was educated at Elmhurst College, Elmhurst, Illinois, and Columbia University, New York, where he was awarded his PhD in 1952. He is at present Robert Broughton Distinguished Professor of Sociology, University of North Carolina, Chapel Hill, and Professor Emeritus of Columbia University, where he was Quetelet Professor of Sociology from 1970 to 1988. He has been editor of the *American Journal of Sociology* (1961–66), Pitt Professor at the University of Cambridge (1966–67) and President of the American Sociological Association (1973–74). He is also a Fellow of the American Academy of Arts and Sciences and of the National Academy of Sciences (USA). His major books include *The*

Dynamics of Bureaucracy (1955), *Exchange and Power in Social Life* (1964), *The American Occupational Structure* (with O. D. Duncan, 1967), *Inequality and Heterogeneity* (1977) and *Crosscutting Social Circles* (with J. E. Schwartz, 1984).

Raymond Boudon was born in 1934 and educated at the École Normale Supérieure de la rue d'Ulm. He is a doctor of letters and human sciences and Professor of Sociology at the University of Paris-Sorbonne. He has been Visiting Professor at a number of universities, including Harvard, Chicago, New York, Columbia, Geneva and Stockholm. He is a member of the American Academy of Arts and Sciences and of the Academia Europea, and president of the editorial board of the *Année Sociologique*. His major publications include *À quoi sert la notion de structure?* (1968), *La logique du social* (1983), *L'inégalité des chances* (1985) and *L'idéologie* (1986).

Pierre Bourdieu was born in 1930 at Denguin in Béarn. He is now Professor of Sociology at the Collège de France, Director of Studies at the École des Hautes Études en Sciences Sociales, and Director of the Centre of European Sociology at the Collège de France and the École des Hautes Études. He also directs the review *Actes de la recherche en sciences sociales*, which he founded in 1975. Among his principal publications are *Sociologie de l'Algérie* (1958), *Le métier de sociologue* (1968), *Esquisse d'une théorie de la pratique* (1972), *Questions de sociologie* (1980), *Homo Academicus* (1984) and *La noblesse d'état* (1989).

Jon Clark was born in 1949, studied at the Universities of Birmingham (England), West Berlin and Bremen (West Germany), and was awarded a doctorate of the University of Bremen *summa cum laude* in 1979. He has held research posts at the London School of Economics and the Groupe de Sociologie du Travail, University of Paris, and was appointed in 1978 to the Department of Sociology and Social Policy at the University of Southampton, first as Lecturer, then in 1985 as Senior Lecturer. He has authored and co-authored a number of books, including *Trade Unions, National Politics and Economic Management* (1980), *Bruno Schönlank und die Arbeitersprechchorbewegung* (1984) and *The Process of Technological Change —New Technology and Social Choice in the Workplace* (1988). He has also co-edited *Culture and Crisis in Britain in the 30s* (1979), *Labour Law and Politics in the Weimar Republic* (1981) and *Labour Law and Industrial Relations* (1983). He is Principal Editor of the Falmer Sociology Series.

I. Bernard Cohen received an SB Degree *cum laude* from Harvard College in 1937 and his PhD in the History of Science from the same University in 1947. His whole teaching career has been spent at Harvard University, where he is currently Victor S. Thomas Professor (Emeritus) of the History of Science. His major publications have dealt with scientific instruments, the scientific thought of Benjamin Franklin and Isaac Newton, and the history of computing and computers. His most recent books are *Revolution in Science* (published by Harvard University Press) and *Puritanism and the Rise of Modern Science: The Merton Thesis* (published by Rutgers University Press).

James S. Coleman was born in Bedford, Indiana in 1926. He received his bachelor's degree from Purdue University in 1949 and was awarded a PhD from Columbia

University in 1955. From 1959 to 1973 he was Associate Professor and Professor in the Department of Social Relations at Johns Hopkins University. Since 1973 he has been a Professor of Sociology and Education at the University of Chicago. He is a member of the National Academy of Sciences, the American Philosophical Society, the American Academy of Arts and Sciences, the National Academy of Education and the Royal Swedish Academy of Sciences. His recent publications include *The Asymmetric Society* (1982), *Individual Interests and Collective Action* (1986), *Public and Private High Schools: The Impact of Communities* (1987) and *Foundations of Social Theory* (1990).

Rose Laub Coser received her PhD in sociology from Columbia University. She is past President of the Society for the Study of Social Problems and of the Eastern Sociological Society, and past Vice-President of the American Sociological Association. At present she is Adjunct Professor of Sociology at Boston College and Professor Emerita at the State University of New York at Stony Brook. In the past she has held posts at Wellesley College, Harvard Medical School, Northeastern University and Radcliffe College. She is the author of several books, including *Training in Ambiguity: Learning through Doing in a Mental Hospital* (1979) and *In Defense of Modernity: Complexity of Social Roles and Individual Autonomy* (1989).

Charles Crothers was awarded a BA in Geography in 1968 from the University of Waikato, New Zealand, and a BA (1970) and PhD (1978) in sociology, both from the Victoria University of Wellington. He has been Lecturer (1983–85) and is now Senior Lecturer in the Department of Sociology, University of Auckland, New Zealand. He was previously Senior Research Officer at the Town and Country Planning Division, Ministry of Works and Development, Wellington (1978–82), and Junior Lecturer in the Department of Sociology, Victoria University of Wellington (1975–78). In 1987 he published a monograph on *Robert K. Merton* in the Ellis Horwood/Tavistock Key Sociologists series. His research interests are in social theory, the sociology of social science, methodology, urban and occupational sociology, and the analysis of New Zealand society.

Jon Elster was born in 1940 and is Professor of Political Science and Philosophy at the University of Chicago and Research Director at the Institute for Social Research, Oslo. His publications include *Logic and Society* (1978), *Ulysses and the Sirens* (1979), *Sour Grapes* (1983), *Explaining Technical Change* (1983), *Making Sense of Marx* (1985), *The Cement of Society* (1989), *Solomonic Judgements* (1989) and *Nuts and Bolts for the Social Sciences* (1989). He is currently engaged in an empirical study of distributive justice.

Anthony Giddens was born in 1938 and studied at the Universities of Hull, London and Cambridge. He was Lecturer in Sociology at the University of Leicester (1961–69), Fellow of King's College and University Lecturer in Sociology, University of Cambridge (1969–85), and was appointed Professor of Sociology at the University of Cambridge in 1985. His major publications include *Capitalism and Modern Social Theory* (1971), *The Class Structure of the Advanced Societies* (1973), *New Rules of Sociological Method* (1976), *Central Problems in Social Theory* (1979), *The Constitution of Society—An Outline of a Theory of Structuration*

(1984) and an 800-page introductory text, *Sociology* (1989). He is the subject of a further volume in the Falmer Sociology Series.

Mark Gould is Professor of Sociology and Chair of the Department of Sociology and Anthropology at Haverford College, Pennsylvania. He received his PhD in sociology at Harvard University, where he studied with Talcott Parsons, Barrington Moore Jr and Kenneth Arrow. He is the author of *Revolution in the Development of Capitalism: The Coming of the English Revolution* (1987). His current work involves an attempt to reconstruct microeconomic theory sociologically.

Stephen Jay Gould was born in 1941 in New York City. He studied geology at Antioch College, where he gained an AB in 1963, and was awarded a PhD of Columbia University in 1967. In the same year he became Assistant Professor of Geology at Harvard University. In 1973 he was appointed Professor of Geology and Curator of Invertebrate Paleontology at the Museum of Comparative Zoology, Harvard University, and in 1982 Alexander Agassiz Professor of Zoology at the same institution. He has honorary doctorates from over twenty American colleges and universities, is a member and fellow of a number of learned societies in the USA and Europe, and a distinguished writer of essays and reviews for leading scientific and literary magazines. He has also received a number of awards for his research and publications. His major books include *Ever Since Darwin* (1973), *The Panda's Thumb* (1980), *The Mismeasure of Man* (1981), *Hen's Teeth and Horse's Toes* (1983), *An Urchin in the Storm* (1987) and *Wonderful Life* (1989).

A. Rupert Hall was born in 1920. He was Professor and Head of the Department of the History of Science and Technology at Imperial College, University of London, from 1963 to 1980. He is the author of *Ballistics in the Seventeenth Century* (1952), *The Scientific Revolution, 1500–1800* (1954), *Philosophers at War* (1981) and a number of other works. His critical article 'Merton Revisited', published in 1963, contributed to a reawakening of interest among historians and sociologists in Merton's work on the emergence of science in seventeenth century England. He was elected a Fellow of the British Academy in 1978, and has been Emeritus Professor of the History of Science and Technology at the University of London since 1980.

Richard A. Hilbert received his PhD at the University of California at Santa Barbara and is at present Associate Professor of Sociology at Gustavus Adolphus College, Saint Peter, Minnesota. His past work addresses such diverse topics as teacher education and chronic physical pain. He is the author of a forthcoming book about classical sociological theory and ethnomethodology.

Marco Orrù is Assistant Professor of Sociology at the University of South Florida, Tampa. He was awarded his PhD from the University of California at Davis in 1984. His research has appeared in the *British Journal of Sociology, Rassegna italiana di sociologia, Archives européenes de sociologie, Journal of the History of Ideas* and Japan's *Financial Economic Review*. His book, *Anomie—History and Meanings*, was published in 1987.

Piyo Rattansi was born in 1930 at Nyeri, Kenya, and studied at the London School of Economics, where he was awarded his BSc in 1956 and PhD in 1961. After appointments at the Universities of Leeds, Chicago, Cambridge and Princeton, he was appointed in 1971 to his present post of Professor and Head of the Department of the History and Philosophy of Science, University College, University of London. He has published widely on sixteenth and seventeenth century science, religion, philosophy and politics, and is author of the much reprinted *Isaac Newton and Gravity* (1974).

Lee S. Shulman is the Charles E. Ducommun Professor of Education and Professor (by courtesy) of Psychology at Stanford University, California, where he has taught since 1982. From 1963 to 1982 he was Professor of Educational Psychology and Medical Education at Michigan State University, where he was also founding co-director of the nationally supported Institute for Research on Teaching. His research is on teaching and teacher education, with special emphasis on the relationships between teachers' knowledge and their teaching performance. In 1984–85 he was President of the American Educational Research Association and in 1989 was elected President of the (US) National Academy of Education.

Nico Stehr was born in 1942 and studied at the Universities of Cologne and Oregon (where he received his PhD). He is currently Professor of Sociology at the University of Alberta, and a Fellow of the Royal Society (Canada). He is a founding editor of the *Canadian Journal of Sociology* and has held a number of visiting appointments in Europe and the United States. He is co-author (with David Kettler and Volker Meja) of *Karl Mannheim* (1984) and *Politisches Wissen* (1989), and has co-edited a number of books, including (with Rene König) *Wissenschaftssoziologie: Studien und Materialien* (1975) and (with Volker Meja) *Society and Knowledge: Contemporary Perspectives on the Sociology of Knowledge* (1984) and *Knowledge and Politics* (1990). His research interests centre on the sociology and philosophy of the social sciences, the history of sociological thought, the use of social science knowledge, and the 'knowledge society'.

Arthur Stinchcombe was born in 1933, was awarded his AB in Mathematics from Central Michigan College in 1953, and his PhD in Sociology from the University of California at Berkeley in 1960. He has held academic posts at a number of universities, including the Johns Hopkins University and the Universities of California at Berkeley, Chicago and Arizona, and visiting professorships and fellowships in England, Holland, Norway and Australia. Since 1983 he has been Professor of Sociology, Political Science and Organizational Behavior at Northwestern University, Evanston/Illinois. In 1968 he published *Constructing Social Theories*, which was awarded the Sorokin prize, and his recent books include *Economic Sociology* (1983), *Organization Theory and Project Management* (with Carol A. Heimer, 1985) and *Stratification and Organization* (1986). His current research interests are in economic sociology, organization theory, social change, and methods.

Piotr Sztompka was born in 1944 and is a Professor of Sociology at the Jagiellonian University in Krakow, Poland. He has held teaching posts and research fellowships at a number of institutions, including Columbia University, the University of California at Los Angeles, Johns Hopkins University, the Universidad Nacional de Mexico and St Catherine's College, Oxford. His principal publications are *System* *and Function* (1974), *Sociological Dilemmas* (1979), *Masters of Polish Sociology* (1984) and *Robert K. Merton: An Intellectual Profile* (1986).

Simonetta Tabboni was born in Bologna, Italy, in 1937. She works and teaches in the general area of the sociology of culture, and has conducted research and published recently in the fields of education and the sociology of youth. She has also participated in a major research project on 'The Uses and Perception of Time among Young People', and is coauthor, with A. Cavalli and others, of the volume *The Time of Young People*. She teaches a course in general sociology in the University of Rome and holds seminars in the University of Milan on the politics of time. Her recent publications include *Vicinanza e lontananza. Modelli e figure dello straniero come categoria sociologica (Nearness and Remoteness. Models and Images of the Foreigner as a Sociological Category)* (1986), and *La rappresentazione sociale del tempo (The Social Representation of Time)* (2nd revised edition, 1988).

Samuel S. Wineburg is Assistant Professor of Educational Psychology at the University of Washington in Seattle (USA). He holds a BA in Religion from the University of California at Berkeley and a PhD in Educational Psychology from Stanford University. He is a cognitive psychologist who studies the teaching and learning of history as well as the intellectual work of mature historians. His publications have appeared in a number of journals, including *Educational Researcher* and the *Educational Psychologist*.

Robert K. Merton: Intellectual Biography in Outline

1910	Born 5 July in Philadelphia, USA: younger of two children of working-class immigrant parents from Eastern Europe
1915–27	Educated in the elementary and secondary public schools of Philadelphia
1927	Wins scholarship to Temple University, Philadelphia. Majors in philosophy, then sociology under George E. Simpson
1931	Graduates with BA degree from Temple University, awarded graduate fellowship at Harvard University
1932	Gains Harvard MA
1933–35	Writes doctoral thesis on the emergence of modern science in seventeenth-century England
1936	Awarded PhD of Harvard University. Examining Committee: Pitirim Sorokin, Carle Zimmerman, Talcott Parsons (all of Department of Sociology) and George Sarton (historian of science)
1936	Appointed instructor and tutor in sociology at Harvard: publishes article on 'The Unanticipated Consequences of Purposive Social Action'
1937	Publishes article 'Social Time: A Functional and Methodological Analysis' (with Pitirim A. Sorokin)
1938	Publishes book *Science, Technology and Society in Seventeenth Century England*; also first version of 'Social Structure and Anomie', the most cited article in American sociology
1939–41	Associate Professor, then Professor of Sociology at Tulane University, New Orleans
1940	Publishes article 'Bureaucratic Structure and Personality'
1941–	Member of Department of Sociology, Columbia University: Assistant Professor (1941); Associate Professor (1944); Professor (1947); Head of Department (1961); Franklin Henry Giddings Professor of Sociology (1963); University Professor (1974), a title shared by only three other professors at Columbia; Special Service Professor and University Professor Emeritus (1979–85); University Professor Emeritus (1979–)
1942	Publishes article 'A Note on Science and Democracy'

1942–71   Associate Director, Bureau of Applied Social Research, Columbia University
1946   Publishes *Mass Persuasion*
1947   Engages in celebrated debate on sociological theory with Talcott Parsons at the annual meeting of the American Sociological Society (published 1948)
1948   Publishes article on 'The Self-Fulfilling Prophecy'
1949   First edition of *Social Theory and Social Structure*, including the monographic 'Manifest and Latent Functions' (2nd revised edition 1957; 3rd enlarged edition 1968); also publishes article 'Patterns of Influence: A Study of Interpersonal Influence and Communication Behavior in a Local Community' introducing the concepts of 'local and cosmopolitan influentials'
1950   Publishes article 'Contributions to the Theory of Reference Group Behavior' (with Alice S. Rossi)
1956   Publishes *The Focused Interview* (with M. Fiske and P. Kendall)
1957   Elected President of the American Sociological Society and publishes, as the presidential address, 'Priorities in Scientific Discovery: A Chapter in the Sociology of Science'; also publishes article 'The Role-Set: Problems in Sociological Theory' and *The Student-Physician* (with G. G. Reader and P. L. Kendall)
1961   Publishes article 'Singletons and Multiples in Scientific Discovery: A Chapter in the Sociology of Science'
1963   Publishes article 'Sociological Ambivalence' (with Elinor Barber)
1964   Publishes article 'Anomie, Anomia and Social Interaction: Contexts of Deviant Behavior'
1965   Publishes *On the Shoulders of Giants: A Shandean Postscript (OTSOG)*. The enlarged vicennial edition appears in 1985
1967   Establishes the Columbia University Program in the Sociology of Science (with Harriet Zuckerman, Stephen Cole and Jonathan R. Cole); also publishes articles 'On Sociological Theories of the Middle Range' and 'On the History and Systematics of Sociological Theory'
1968   Publishes article 'The Matthew-Effect in Science: The Reward and Communication Systems of Science'
1972   Publishes article 'Insiders and Outsiders: A Chapter in the Sociology of Knowledge'
1973   Publishes *The Sociology of Science* (edited by Norman W. Storer)
1973–74   Introduces project on the 'Historical Sociology of Scientific Knowledge' (with Harriet Zuckerman, Arnold Thackray, Joshua Lederberg and Yehuda Elkana) as part of the Program on Science, Technology and Society of the Center for Advanced Study in the Behavioral Sciences, Stanford, California
1974   Makes thematic presentation on 'Structural Analysis' at annual conference of the American Sociological Association (published in revised form in 1975)
1975   Lewis Coser edits Festschrift, *The Idea of Social Structure*, on the occasion of Merton's sixty-fifth birthday
1976   Publishes collection of essays under the title of *Sociological Ambivalence*

1977   Publishes *The Sociology of Science: An Episodic Memoir* (republished in 1979)

1979   Appointed Adjunct Professor, The Rockefeller University; appointed Resident Scholar, Russell Sage Foundation, New York

1980   The New York Academy of Sciences initiates a Festschrift for Merton, *Science and Social Structure*, edited by Thomas F. Gieryn, on the occasion of his seventieth birthday

1982   Publishes *Social Research and the Practicing Professions*

1983–88   MacArthur Prize Fellow

1984   Publishes article on 'Socially Expected Durations: A Case Study of Concept Formation in Sociology', part of a wider research program on the sociology of time

1987   Publishes article 'Three Fragments from a Sociologist's Notebooks: Establishing the Phenomenon, Specified Ignorance, and Strategic Research Materials'

1988   The semi-centenary of *Science, Technology and Society in Seventeenth Century England* is commemorated by international conferences and publications, including a symposium in the journal *Isis* and a volume edited by I. B. Cohen. Also publishes article on 'The Matthew Effect in Science II: Cumulative Advantage and the Symbolism of Intellectual Property'

1990   In his eightieth birthday year, publication of *Robert K. Merton: Consensus and Controversy* in the Falmer Sociology Series

Appendix: The Writings of Robert K. Merton, 1975–1989

compiled by MARY W. MILES and ROSA HARITOS

Editor's Introduction: This bibliography of Merton's writings from 1975 to 1989 is a supplement to 'The Writings of Robert K. Merton, 1934–75', compiled by Mary Wilson Miles and published in Lewis A. Coser (ed), *The Idea of Social Structure —Papers in Honor of Robert K. Merton*, New York, Harcourt Brace Jovanovich, 1975, pp. 497–522. It retains the same basic format as the earlier bibliography, comprising chronologically listed references to all Merton's published writings from 1975 to 1989—books, translations and compilations, articles, unpublished lectures, introductions and forewords, miscellaneous writings, review essays and reprints —plus all known further reprints and translations of pre-1975 books and articles. It also contains an updated bibliography of books and articles on Merton's work listed alphabetically according to first named author. In general these commentaries are confined to discussions of Merton's sociological ideas rather than, for example, their application and utilization by others.

Some dimensions of the range and variety of these commentaries are worthy of brief note. First, they transcend not only national, linguistic and geographical boundaries (covering North and South America, Europe and Australasia), but also conventional boundaries between different types of social system—for example, there are commentaries not only from the 'capitalist' West, but also from the 'socialist' East, including Russia, Poland, Rumania and Yugoslavia.

Second, the commentaries cover virtually all the principal themes in Merton's writings: structural analysis; middle-range theory; the unintended consequences of action; manifest and latent functions; functional analysis; role-sets and status-sets; anomie and deviance; the sociology of bureaucracy, organizations and the professions; the sociology of science and knowledge; Puritanism and science; the relation between theory and research; and the sociology of time.

Third, while virtually all the commentaries cited have been published in the last fifteen years, they refer to the whole gamut of Merton's writings, from the two famous papers of the 1930s, 'The Unanticipated Consequences of Purposive Social Action' (1936b) and 'Social Structure and Anomie' (1938b), to the 'Three Fragments from a Sociologist's Notebooks' of 1987.

Finally, the commentaries also transcend conventional 'academic' boundaries, covering journals and subject areas from a range of disciplines including sociology, politics, psychology, philosophy, history, medicine and health, and engineering.

Jon Clark

BOOKS

1976   *Sociological Ambivalence and Other Essays*. New York: The Free Press.

        1979 *A Ambivalência Sociológica e Outros Ensaios*. Rio de Janeiro: Zahar Editores.

        1980 *Ambivalencia Sociológica y Otros Ensayos*. Madrid: Espasa-Calpe, S.A.

1977   *The Sociology of Science in Europe*. (edited with Jerry Gaston). Carbondale: University of Southern Illinois Press.

        1980 *La Sociologia della Scienza in Europa*. Milano: Franco Angeli Editore.

1978   *Toward a Metric of Science: The Advent of Science Indicators*. (edited with Yehuda Elkana, Joshua Lederberg, Arnold Thackray and Harriet Zuckerman). New York: John Wiley.

1979   *Qualitative and Quantitative Social Research: Papers in Honor of Paul F. Lazarsfeld*. (edited with James S. Coleman and Peter H. Rossi). New York: The Free Press.

1979   *The Sociology of Science: An Episodic Memoir*. Carbondale: University of Southern Illinois Press.

        1983 Japanese translation. Tokyo: Saiensu-sha Co. Ltd.

1980   *Sociological Traditions from Generation to Generation: Glimpses of the American Experience*. (edited with Matilda White Riley). Norwood, NJ: Ablex Publishing.

1981   *Continuities in Structural Inquiry*. (edited with Peter M. Blau). London: Sage Publications.

1982   *Social Research and the Practicing Professions*. (edited by Aaron Rosenblatt and Thomas Gieryn). Cambridge, MA: Abt Books.

1985   *On the Shoulders of Giants: A Shandean Postscript*. The Vicennial Edition with a new Preface by the author and an Afterword by Denis Donoghue. San Diego: Harcourt Brace Jovanovich.

TRANSLATIONS & COMPILATIONS

1979   Ludwick Fleck, *Genesis and Development of a Scientific Fact* (from the German). Edited with Thaddeus J. Trenn. Chicago: University of Chicago Press.

1980   *Dissertations in Sociology* (compiled with Harriet A. Zuckerman). New York: Arno Press, 61 volumes.

ARTICLES

1975   George Sarton (with Arnold Thackray) In Charles Coulston Gillispie, ed. *Dictionary of Scientific Biography*. New York: Charles Scribner's Sons, 12, 107–114.

1976   Social Problems and Sociological Theory. In *Contemporary Social Problems* (edited with Robert Nisbet). New York: Harcourt Brace Jovanovich, 4th ed., 1–43.

1976   The Ambivalence of Scientists: A Postscript. In R. K. Merton, *Sociological Ambivalence*. New York: Free Press, 56–94.

1976   The Uses of Institutionalized Altruism. *Seminar Reports* (Columbia University), 3, 105–117.

1978   Institutionalized Altruism: The Case of the Professions (with Thomas F. Gieryn) In Man Singh Das, ed. *Sociocultural Change since 1950: Essays in Honor of Carle C. Zimmerman*. Bombay: Vikas Publishing Co., 309–344.

1979   Remembering Paul Lazarsfeld. In *Qualitative and Quantitative Research: Papers in Honor of Paul F. Lazarsfeld* (edited with James S. Coleman and Peter H. Rossi) New York: Free Press, 19–22.

1980   On the Oral Transmission of Knowledge. In *Sociological Traditions from Generation to Generation: Glimpses of the American Experience* (edited with Matilda Riley) Norwood, NJ: Ablex Publishing Corp., 1–35.

1980   Remembering the Young Talcott Parsons. *The American Sociologist*, 15 (May), 68–71.

1980   The Shoulders of Giants. *Columbia*, Fall, 27–28.

1981   Remarks on Theoretical Pluralism. In *Continuities in Structural Inquiry* (edited with Peter M. Blau) London: Sage Publications, i–vii.

1981   Our Sociological Vernacular. *Columbia*, November, 42–44.

1981   On the Fleckian Sociological Epistemology and Structural Analysis in Sociology. Introduction to the Polish translation of *Social Theory and Social Structure*, 1–19.

1982   Alvin W. Gouldner: Genesis and Growth of a Friendship. *Theory and Society*, 11, 915–938.

1983   Florian Znaniecki: A Short Reminiscence. *Journal of the History of the Behavioral Sciences*, 10, 123–126.

1983   Client Ambivalence on Professional Relationships: The Problem of Seeking Help from Strangers (with Vanessa Merton and Elinor Barber) In B. M. DePaulo *et al.*, eds., *New Directions in Helping*, Vol. 2: *Help-Seeking*. New York: Academic Press, 13–44.

1983   Sociology of Science in Poland. *Science of Science* (Poland), 3, 179–191.

1984   Socially Expected Durations: A Case Study of Concept Formation in Sociology. In W. W. Powell and Richard Robbins, eds., *Conflict and Consenus: In Honor of Lewis A. Coser*. New York: Free Press, 262–283.
        1985 Le aspettative sociali di durata. *Rassegna Italiana di Sociologia*, XXVI.

1984   The Fallacy of the Latest Word: The Case of Pietism and Science. *American Journal of Sociology*, 89, 1091–1121.

1984   Texts, Contexts and Subtexts: An Epistolary Foreword. In Louis Schneider, *The Grammar of Social Relations*. Jay Weinstein, ed. New Brunswick, NJ: Transaction Books, ix–xlv.

1984   The Kelvin Dictum and Social Science: An Excursion into the History of an Idea (with David L. Sills and Stephen M. Stigler) *Journal of the History of the Behavioral Sciences*, 20, October, 319–331.
        1986 In Brenda Spatt, *Writing from Sources* 2nd ed. New York: St. Martin's Press 27–31.

1985   George Sarton: Episodic Recollections by an Unruly Apprentice. *Isis*, 76, 477–486.

1985   Basic Research and Its Potentials of Relevance. (revised) *The Mount Sinai Journal of Medicine*, 52, 679–684.

1985   The Historicist-Presentist Dilemma. *History of Sociology*, 6, 137–151.

1987   The Focussed Interview & Focus Groups: Continuities and Discontinuities. *Public Opinion Quarterly*, 51, 550–566.

1987   Three Fragments from a Sociologist's Notebooks: Establishing the Phenomenon, Specified Ignorance and Strategic Research Materials. *Annual Review of Sociology*, 13, 1–28.
         1987 Italian translation, *Studi di Sociologia*, 25, 387–415.

1988   Reference Groups, Invisible Colleges and Deviant Behavior in Science. In H. J. O'Gorman ed., *Surveying Social Life: Papers in Honor of Herbert H. Hyman*. Middletown, CT: Wesleyan University Press, 174–189.

1988   Sociological Resonances: The Early Franco Ferrarotti and a Transatlantic Colleague. R. Cipriani and M. I. Macioti, eds., *Omaggio a Franco Ferrarotti*. Rome: Siares, 83–91.

1988   Some Thoughts on the Concept of Sociological Autobiography. In Matilda White Riley, ed., *Sociological Lives*. Newbury Park, CA: Sage Publications, 17–21.

1988   The Matthew Effect in Science, II: Cumulative Advantage and the Symbolism of Intellectual Property, *Isis*, 79, 606–623.
         1988 Flemish Translation (with a prologue and epilogue as the Inaugural Sarton Lecture) *Tijdschrift voor Sociale Wetenschappen*, 33, 325–355.
         1988 Sartoniana. Volume I, pp. 23–51.

1989   Le molteplici origini e il carattere epiceno del termine inglese per 'scienziato'. *Scientia* (in press).

1989   Unanticipated consequences and kindred sociological ideas: A personal gloss. In Carlo Mongardini and Simonetta Tabboni, eds. *L'Opera di Robert K. Merton e la sociologia contemporanea*.

1990   *STS: Foreshadowings of an Evolving Research Program in the Sociology of Science*. In I. Bernard Cohen, ed. *Puritanism and the Rise of Modern Science: The Merton Thesis*. New Brunswick: Rutgers University Press (in press).

1990   Epistolary Notes on the Making of a Sociological Dissertation Classic: *The Dynamics of Bureaucracy*. In Craig Calhoun, Marshall W. Meyer and W. Richard Scott, eds. *Structures of Power and Constraint: Papers in Honor of Peter M. Blau*. Cambridge and New York: Cambridge University Press (in press).

UNPUBLISHED LECTURES

1977   A Memory of George Sarton. Presidential Remarks, Society for Social Studies of Science. Cambridge, October 14.

1981   On Sociological Ways of Thinking. Cambridge: American Academy of Arts and Sciences (bicentennial meeting).

1981   Some Reflections on Progress in Science. Philadelphia: Temple University.

1988   An Epistolary Gloss on the Origin of the Thomas Theorem: A Spurious Case of Institutionalized Sexism. New York.

INTRODUCTIONS AND FOREWORDS

1975   Introducción a un libro de Marías. *Revista de Occidente*, 148 (July), 99–111.

   1986 Introduction. Julian Marías. *The Structure of Society*. University of Alabama Press.

1979   Introduction. Rose Coser, *Training in Ambiguity: Learning Through Doing in a Mental Hospital*. New York: Free Press, xi–xiii.

1979   Foreword. The Evolving Grammar of Citation Analysis. Eugene Garfield, *Citation Indexing: Its Theory and Application in Science, Technology and Humanities*, New York: John Wiley & Sons, vii–xi.

1983   Foreword. Eugene Garfield, *Essays of an Information Scientist*. Vol. 5: 1981–1983. Philadelphia: ISI Press, xv–xix.

1986   Foreword. André Cournand. *From Roots...to Late Budding: The Intellectual Adventures of a Medical Scientist*. N.Y.: Gardner Press, vii–xiii.

1986   Foreword (with Eugene Garfield). Derek J. de Solla Price, *Little Science, Big Science...And Beyond*. New York; Columbia University Press, vii–xii.

1987   Foreword. *Contemporary Classics in the Social and Behavioral Sciences*. Philadelphia: ISI Press, vii–ix.

1988   Foreword. Helen Rose Ebaugh, *Becoming an Ex: The Process of Role Exit*. Chicago: University of Chicago Press, ix–xi.

MISCELLANEOUS WRITINGS

1975   On the Origin of the Term: Pseudo-Gemeinschaft. *Western Sociological Review*, 6, 83.

1980   Citation Classic: Social Theory and Social Structure. *Current Contents*, 21, May 26, 12.

1980   On New York Scientists. *The Sciences*, December 20, 9–10.

1988   André Cournand, 1895–1988. Memorial Service, Columbia University, March 17. Meriden-Stinehour Press, 21–26.

1988   Tribute to a Distinguished Career: Notes on the Retirement of David L. Sills. *Items*, Social Science Research Council, December 1988, 97–98.

1990   Social Time and Socio-Cognitive Networks: Remarks on Becoming an Honorand of Jagiellonian University. *International Sociology* (in press).

REVIEW ESSAYS

1968   Making It Scientifically. Review of *The Double Helix*, by James D. Watson. *New York Times Book Review*, February 25, 41–45.

   1980 Gunther S. Stent (ed.) *The Double Helix: A Personal Account of the Discovery of the Structure of DNA* (Text, Commentary, Reviews, Original Papers). New York/London: W.W. Norton & Co., 213–218.

1978   The Sociological Study of Scientific Specialties (with Thomas F. Gieryn). *Social Studies of Science*, 1978, 257–261.

PRE-1975 BOOKS: REPRINTS AND TRANSLATIONS

1938   *Science, Technology and Society in Seventeenth-Century England*.

   1970 New York: Howard Fertig, Inc.

   1975 *Scienza, technologia e societa nell'Inghilterra del XVII secolo*. Milano: Franco Angeli Editore.

   1978 Atlantic Highlands, New Jersey: Humanities Press.

1983 Japanese translation. Tokyo: Ochanomizu Shobo.

1984 *Ciencia, technología y sociedad en la Inglaterra del siglo XVII.* Madrid: Alianza Editorial, S.A.

1988 New York: Howard Fertig, Inc.

1951   *Social Policy and Social Research in Housing* (edited with Patricia S. West, Marie Jahoda and Hanan C. Selvin).

1963 *Sociología de la vivienda.* Buenos Aires: Colección hombre y sociedad, serie sociología urbana.

1965   *On the Shoulders of Giants: A Shandean Postscript.*

1980 *Auf den Schultern von Riesen: Ein Leitfaden durch das Labyrinth der Gelehrsamkeit.* (translated by Reinhard Kaiser) Frankfurt am Main: Syndikat.

1983 *Auf den Schultern von Riesen: Ein Leitfaden durch das Labyrinth der Gelehrsamkeit.* Suhrkamp Taschenbuch edition. Frankfurt am Main: Suhrkamp.

1967   *On Theoretical Sociology.*

1979 *O Teorijskoj Sociologiji.* Zagreb: Biblioteka Pitanja.

1968   *Social Theory and Social Structure*
[1949,
1957]   1953 *Éléments de méthode sociologique.* Paris: Librairie Plon.

1959 *Teoria e struttura sociale.* Bologna: Il Mulino. 2nd edition, 1986.

1960 *Teoría social y estructura social.* Santiago, Chile: Andres Bello.

1962 Japanese Translation. Tokyo: Misuzu Shobo Publishing Company.

1964 *Teoría y estructura sociales.* Mexico: Fondo de Cultura Economica.

1965 *Éléments de théorie et de méthode sociologique.* enlarged edition. Paris: Librairie Plon.

1970 *Sociologia, teoria e estruttura.* Sao Paulo: Editoria Mestre Jou.

1971 *Teoria e struttura sociale.* Bologna: Il Mulino. 3rd edition, Three volumes.

1971 Hebrew translation. Tel Aviv. Yachdav United Publishers Co.

1972 *Social Theory and Social Structure.* Indian edition. New Delhi: Amerind Publishing Company.

1980 *Társadalomelmélet és Társadalmi Struktúra.* Budapest: Gondolat.

1982 *Teoria Socjologiczna i Struktura Spoleczna.* Warsaw: Panstwowe Wydawnictwo Naukowe.

1973   *The Sociology of Science: Theoretical and Empirical Investigations.*

1977 *La sociologia de la ciencia.* Madrid: Alianza Editorial. 2 volumes.

1979 Chicago: University Press, Phoenix edition.

1981 *La Sociologia della scienza.* Milano: Franco Angeli Editore.

1982 Chinese Translation. Beijing: Commercial Press.

1985 *Entwicklung und Wandel von Forschungsinteressen: Aufsätze zur Wissenschaftssoziologie.* Frankfurt A.M.: Suhrkamp.

ARTICLES: FURTHER REPRINTINGS
First Published:
1936   Puritanism, Pietism and Science.

1973 C. A. Russell, ed., *Science and Religious Belief: A Selection of Recent Historical Studies.* London: University of London Press Ltd., 20–54.

1937   The Sociology of Knowledge
        1976 Kewal Motwani, ed. *Sociology of Knowledge*. Bombay: Somaiya Publications Pvt., 83–125.
1938   Social Structure and Anomie
        1970 Sozialstruktur und Anomie, in A. Fischer, ed., *Die Entfremdung des Menschen in einer heilen Gesellschaft*. München: Juventa, 123–136.
        1976 Rose Giallomobardo, ed. *Juvenile Delinquency*. New York: John Wiley, 95–103.
        1977 Stephen Schafer and Richard D. Knutden, eds., *Criminological Theory*, Lexington, MA: D.C. Heath, 195–201.
        1978 Barry Krisberg and James Austin, eds., *The Children of Ishmael*. Palo Alto, CA: Mayfield Publishing Co., 155–166.
        1978 Delos H. Kelly, ed., *Delinquent Behavior: Interactional and Motivational Aspects*. Belmont, CA: Wadsworth Publishing Co., 47–56.
        1978 Leonard D. Savitz and Norman Johnson, eds., *Crime and Society*. New York: John Wiley, 115–123.
        1978 Sir Leon Radzinowicz and Marvin E. Wolfgang, eds., *Crime and Justice* (Vol. I: *The Criminal in Society*). New York: Basic Books, 565–596.
        1978 Ronald A. Farrell and Victoria L. Swigert, eds., *Social Deviance*. Philadelphia: J. B. Lippincott Co., 2nd ed., 167–179.
        1978 Peter Worsley, ed., *Modern Sociology*. London: Penguin Books, 2nd ed., 615–622.
        1980 Stuart H. Traub and Craig B. Little, eds., *Theories of Deviance*. Ithaca: E. Peacock Publishers.
        1981 William E. Thornton, et al., eds., *Delinquency and Justice*. Glenview, IL: Scott Foresman, 672–676.
        1982 Lewis A. Coser and Bernard Rosenberg, eds. *Sociological Theory*. New York: Macmillan, 397–406.
        1982 Leonard D. Savitz and Norman Johnson, eds. *Contemporary Sociology*. New York: John Wiley & Sons, 45–53.
        1983 James D. Orcutt, *Analyzing Deviance*. Homewood, IL: The Dorsey Press.
        1987 R. A. Farrell & V. L. Sweigert, eds. *Social Deviance*. Wadsworth Publishing Co., 3rd ed.
1940   Crime and the Anthropologist (with M. Ashley-Montagu)
        1980 Carroll Klein, ed. *Readings in the Sociology of Deviance*. Richmond, Canada: Open Learning Institute.
        1984 Robert W. Rieber, ed. *Advances in Forensic Psychology*, Vol. I. Norwood, NJ: Ablex Publishing Corporation, 147–170.
1940   Bureaucratic Structure and Personality.
        1979 George H. Rice, Jr., ed. *Industrial Organizations*. Austin, TX: Lone Star Publishers.
        1979 George Ritzer, ed. *Issues, Debates and Controversies*. Boston: Allyn & Bacon.
        1981 Joseph A. Litterer, ed. *Organizations: Structure and Behavior*. New York: John Wiley & Sons.
1942   A Note on Science and Democracy

1972 Wissenschaft und demokratische Sozialstruktur. In Peter Weingart, ed. *Wissenschaftssoziologie*. Frankfurt A.M.: Athenäum Verlag.

1945   Sociological Theory
1986 O znaczeniu teoril socjologicznej dla badan empirycznych. In Antoni Sulek, ed. *Metody Analizy Socjologiecznej*. Warsaw: Wydawnictwa Uniwersysteu Warsawskiego, 11–25.

1946   The Focused Interview (with Patricia L. Kendall)
1979 Das focussierte Interview. In Christel Hopf and E. Weingarten, eds. *Qualitative Sozialforschung*. Stuttgart, West Germany: Klett, 171–204.

1948   Mass Communication, Popular Taste, and Organized Social Action (with Paul F. Lazarsfeld)
1983 Zhang Li, ed. and Huang Lin, translator. *Mass Communication*. Beijing, China: People's Daily Publishing House, 157–183.

1948   Discrimination and the American Creed.
1977 John Stone, ed. *Race, Ethnicity and Social Change*. Belmont, CA: Wadsworth Publishing Co., 26–44.

1948   The Self-Fulfilling Prophecy
1958 Arabic translation In *Readings in the Social Sciences*. Dar Al-Ma'aref Printing House (Auspices UNESCO). 49–76.
1964 La profecia que se auto-realiza. In *Colección Derechos Humanos*. Buenos Aires: Ediciones D.A.I.
1965 Ernst Topitsch, ed. Die Eigendynamik gesellschaftlicher Vorsaussagen. In *Logik der Sozialwissenschaften*. Köln: Kiepenheuer & Witsch.
1978 Ronald A. Farrell & V. L. Swigert, eds. *Social Deviance*. Philadelphia: J. B. Lippincott Co., 2nd ed., 65–69.
1980 Lewis Coser, ed. *The Pleasures of Sociology*. New York: New Atheneum Library, 29–47.

1949   Patterns of Influence: A Study of Interpersonal Influence and Communications Behavior in a Local Community.
1972 Roland L. Warren, ed. *Perspectives on the American Community*. Chicago: Rand McNally and Co., 3rd ed., 277–290.

1950   Contributions to the Theory of Reference Group Behavior (with Alice S. Rossi).
1981 Lewis A. Coser & Bernard Rosenberg, eds., *Sociological Theory*. New York: Macmillan Co., 232–240.

1954   Friendship as a Social Process: A Substantive and Methodological Analysis (with Paul F. Lazarsfeld).
1982 Patricia L. Kendall, ed. *The Varied Sociology of Paul F. Lazarsfeld*. New York: Columbia University Press, 298–348.

1957   The Role-Set: Problems in Sociological Theory.
1971 Kenneth Thompson and Jeremy Tunstall, eds., *Sociological Perspectives*. London: Penguin Books.
1977 Stephen C. Brown and John N.T. Martin eds., *Human Aspects of Man-Made Stress*. Great Britain: Open University Press, 200–209.
1978 Peter Worsley, ed. *Modern Sociology*. London: Penguin Books, 2nd ed., 341–351.
1981 Lewis A. Coser & Bernard Rosenberg, eds., *Sociological Theory*. New York: Macmillan, 282–291.

1957 Priorities in Scientific Discovery
   1958 *Shakaigaku Ronsoh*, 11, 3–45.
   1973 In Peter Weingart, ed. *Wissenschaftssoziologie: Wissenschaftliche Entwicklung als sozialer Prozess*. Frankfurt A.M.: Suhrkamp, I: 124–164.

1957 Bibliographical Postscript to 'Puritanism, Pietism and Science'.
   1962 Bernard Barber and Walter Hirsch, eds., *The Sociology of Science*. New York: The Free Press of Glencoe, 55–66.

1960 The Mosaic of the Behavioral Sciences.
   1968 El mosaico de la ciencias del comportamiento. B. Berelson, ed. *El Hombre: Su Comportamiento*. Mexico: Pax-Mexico.

1961 Singletons and Multiples in Scientific Discovery: A Chapter in the Sociology of Science. *Proceedings*, American Philosophical Society, 105, 470–486.
   1961 *New Scientist*, 12, 306–308.

1962 The Ambivalence of Scientists.
   1976 R. S. Cohen, P. K. Feyerabend and W. M. Wartofsky, eds. *Essays in Memory of Imre Lakatos*. Dordrecht: D. Reidel Publishing, 433–455.

1963 Sociological Ambivalence (with Elinor Barber).
   1981 Lewis A. Coser & Bernard Rosenberg, eds., *Sociological Theory*. New York: Macmillan, 493–507.

1964 Anomie, Anomia and Social Interaction.
   1967 Anomie, anomia e interacción social: contextos de conducta desviada. In M. B. Clinard, comp. *Anomie y Conducta Desviada*. Buenos Aires: Paidos, 201–336.
   1970 Anomie, Anomia und soziale Interaktion: Beziehungen zu abweichendem Verhalten. In A. Fischer, ed. *Die Entfremdung des Menschen in einer heilen Gesellschaft*. Munich: Juventa, 137–143, 156–161.

1967 On the History and Systematics of Sociological Theory.
   1981 Wolf Lepenies, ed. Zur Geschichte und Systematik der soziologischen Theorie. In *Geschichte der Soziologie: Studien zur kognitiven, sozialen, und historischen Identität einer Disziplin*. Frankfurt A.M.: Suhrkamp Verlag, 4 Vols., Vol. I, 15–74.

1968 The Matthew Effect in Science.
   1977 Walter P. Metzger, ed. *Reader in the Sociology of the Academic Professions*. New York: Arno Press.

1969 Behavior Patterns of Scientists
   1975 Paul Weiss, ed. *Knowledge in Search of Understanding: The Frensham Papers*. Mt. Kisco, NY: Futura Publishing Co., 148–170.
   1978 Martin Goldstein and Inge F. Goldstein, eds., *How We Know: An Explanation of the Scientific Process*. New York: Plenum Publishing, 255–278.
   1983 In Robert S. Albert, ed. *Genius and Eminence: The Social Psychology of Creativity and Exceptional Achievement*. Oxford/New York: Pergamon Press.

1969 The Social Nature of Leadership.
   1976 Sandra Stone et al., eds. *Management for Nurses*. St. Louis: C. V. Mosby Co., 97–106.

1970   The Ambivalence of Organizational Leaders.
        1979 Marjorie Beyers, ed. *Leadership in Nursing*. Wakefield, MA: Nursing Resources, Inc., 145–153.
1971   Social Problems and Sociological Theory.
        1975 Soziologische Diagnose sozialer Probleme. In Karl Otto Homdrich, ed. *Menschliche Bedürfnisse und soziale Steuerung*. Hamburg: Rowohlt, 113–129.
1971   Patterns of Evaluation in Science: Institutionalization, Structure and Functions of the Referee System (with Harriet Zuckerman).
        1979 A.J. Meadows, ed. *The Scientific Journal*. Dorchester, England: Henry Ling Ltd., 112–146.
1971   Insiders and Outsiders: An Essay in the Sociology of Knowledge.
        1979 Edward A. Maziarz, ed. *Value and Values in Evolution*. New York: Gordon and Breach, 47–69.
        1979 James C. Hackler, ed. *The Prevention of Youthful Crime*. London: Methuen Publications, Ltd.
        1986 Simonetta Tabboni, ed. *Vicinanza e lontananza: Modelli e figure dello straniero come categoria sociologica* (Elias, Merton, Park, Schutz, Simmel, Sombart). Milano: Franco Angeli, 211–266.
1975   Thematic Analysis in Science: Notes on Holton's Concept.
        1976 Analiza tematycnza w nauce: uago o koncepcji Holtona. In *Zagnadnienia Naukoznawstwa*, 12, 3–4. Warsaw: Polska Academia Nauk.

COMMENTARIES ON MERTON'S WORK
Books:

Clark, Jon, ed.	*Robert K. Merton: Consensus and Controversy*. London and Philadelphia: The Falmer Press, Taylor and Francis, 1990.
Cohen, I. Bernard, ed.	*Puritanism and the Rise of Modern Science: The Merton Thesis*. New Brunswick: Rutgers University Press (in press).
Coser, Lewis, A., ed.	*The Idea of Social Structure: Papers in Honor of Robert K. Merton*. New York: Harcourt Brace Jovanovich, 1975.
Crothers, Charles	*Robert K. Merton: A Key Sociologist*. London & New York: Tavistock Publications, 1987.
Feldhay, Rivka and Yehuda Elkana, eds.	*"After Merton": Protestant and Catholic Science in Seventeenth-Century Europe. Science in Context*, entire issue 1989, 3.
Garcia, Jesus L.	*Merton: La estructura precaria orden y conflicto en la sociedad moderna*. Mexico: Editorial Edicol, 1979.
Gieryn, Thomas F., ed.	*Science and Social Structure: A Festschrift for Robert K. Merton*. New York: The New York Academy of Sciences, 1980.
Herpin, Nicolas	*Théorie et expérience chez Robert K. Merton*. Paris: Sorbonne, 1967, unpublished dissertation.
Hill, Robert B.	*Merton's Role Types and Paradigm of Deviance*. New York: Arno Press, 1969.

Mongardini, Carlo and Simonetta Tabboni, eds.	*L'Opera di Robert K. Merton e la sociologia contemporanea.* 1989.
Passas, Nikos	*Merton's Theory of Anomie and Deviance: An Elaboration.* Edinburgh University, Ph.D. dissertation, 1988.
Patel, Praven J.	*Sociology of Robert K. Merton.* Ahmedebad: Gujarat University Press, 1976.
Restrepo, Gabriel	*Las teories intermedias de Merton y la sociologia Norteamericana.* Universidad Nacional de Colombia, Faculdad de Ciencias Humanas, 1971.
Stzompka, Piotr	*Robert K. Merton: An Intellectual Profile.* London: Macmillan/New York: St. Martin's Press, 1986.

Articles & Chapters:

Abraham, Gary A.	"Misunderstanding the Merton Thesis: A boundary dispute between history and sociology." *ISIS*, 1983, 74: 368–387.
Auping, John	"Een Kritiek op Robert Merton's 'Science, Technology and Society in 17th Century England'." *Sociologische Gids.* 1973, 20: 98–112.
Barbano, Filippo	"Sociologia e sviluppo della scienza nel pensiero di R. K. Merton." In Merton, *Scienza, technologia, e societa nell'Inghilterra del XVII secolo.* Milano: Franco Angeli Editore, 1975, 11–32.
	"Introduzione" to Merton and Jerry Gaston, eds. *La Sociologia della Scienza in Europa.* Milano: Franco Angeli Editore, 1980, 10–32.
	"Introduzione" to Merton, *La Sociologia della Scienza.* Milano: Franco Angeli Editore, 1981, i–xxvii.
	"La recezione dell'opera di Robert K. Merton." In Filippo Barbano, *Sociologia, Ermeneutica, Storia.* Torino: Editrice Tirrenia Stampatori, 1988, 207–220.
Beauchamp, Murray, A.	*Elements of Mathematical Sociology.* New York: Random House, 1970, 8–16.
Becker, George	"Pietism and Science: A critique of Robert K. Merton's hypothesis." *American Journal of Sociology*, 1984, 89: 1065–1090.
	"The Fallacy of the Received Word: A reexamination of Merton's Pietism-Science Thesis." *American Journal of Sociology*, 1986, 91: 1203–1218.
Behling, Orlando	"Functionalism as a base for midrange theory in organizational behavior." In Craig C. Pinder and Larry F. Moore, *Middle Range Theory and the Study of Organizations.* Boston/The Hague/London: Martinus Nijhoff, 1980, 212–224.
Bell, Wendell	"Anomie, social isolation and the class structure." *Sociometry*, June 1967, 20: 105–116.
Ben-David, Joseph	"Emergence of national traditions in the sociology of science." *The Sociology of Science* (Jerry Gaston, ed.) San Francisco: Jossey-Bass, 1978.

Beres, Mary Elizabeth and Karl Price — "Middle-range organization theorizing: Role theory as an example". In Craig C. Pinder and Larry F. Moore, *Middle Range Theory and the Study of Organizations*. Boston/The Hague/London: Martinus Nijhoff, 1980, 257–272.

Besnard, Philippe — "Merton in search of anomie." *Revue française de sociologie*, 1978, 19: 3–38.
L'Anomie. Paris: PUF, 1987, *passim*.

Besozzi, Elena — "La circolarità teoria e ricerca empirica: il contributo di R.K. Merton." *Studi di Sociologia*, 1986, 24:442–464.

Bierstedt, Robert — "Robert K. Merton." In *American Sociological Theory – A Critical History*. New York: Academic Press, 1981, 443–489.

Blissett, Marlan — *Politics in Science*. Boston: Little, Brown & Co., 1972, 65–89.

Booth, Allan and Nicholas Babchuk — "Personal influence, networks and voluntary association affiliation." *Sociological Inquiry*, (Spring 1969), 39: 179–188.

Boskoff, Alvin — "R. Merton." *Encyclopaedia of Biography*, 1987, Volume 14, 491–493.

Boudon, Raymond — *Effets pervers et ordre social*. Paris: Presses Universitaires de France, 1977, Chapters 1 and 7.

Brannigan, Augustine — *The Social Basis of Scientific Discoveries*. Cambridge: Cambridge University Press, 1981, 52–64.

Burns, Kenneth — "Recent periodical literature on a crucial issue in the sociology of sociology." *Newsletter*, International Society for the Sociology of Knowledge (January 1976), 2: 15–18.

Burrell, Gibson and Gareth Morgan — *Sociological Paradigms and Organisational Analysis*. London: Heinemann, 1979, 87–108.

Busch, Charlotte — "Les consequences inattendues de l'action humaine, ses rapports avec la liberté individuelle et l'organisation sociale." *Revue Internationale de Sociologie*, 1982, 18: 79–88.

Cahnman, Werner, J. — "Robert K. Merton." *Encyclopaedia Judaica*, Jerusalem, 1972, 1394–1395.

Campbell, Colin — "A dubious distinction? An inquiry into the value and use of Merton's concept of manifest and latent functions." *American Sociological Review* (February 1982), 47: 29–44.

Caplovitz, David — "Robert K. Merton as editor: Review essay." *Contemporary Sociology*, 1977, 6: 142–150.
"Principles of sociological writing." In David Caplovitz, *The Stages of Social Research*. New York: Wiley, 1983, Chapter 16.

Carroll, Leo and Pamela I. Jackson — "Inequality, opportunity, and crime rates in central cities." *Criminology*, May 1983, 21: 178–194.

Cataño, Gonzalo — "Bibliografia sobre teoria sociologica: Robert K.

	Merton." *Sociologos y Sociologia* (Boletin de la Asociación Colombiana de Sociologia), 10, April 1984.
Celinshi, Andrzej	"Critical analysis of Merton's theory of deviational behavior." *Studia Socjologiczne*, 1974, 3: 117–140.
Chapman, Ivan	"A critique of Merton's typology." *Quarterly Journal of Ideology*, Winter 1977, 1: 13–18.
Chazel, François	"Considerations on the nature of anomie." *Revue française de sociologie*, 1967, 8: 151–168.
Cohen, I. Bernard	"The publication of *Science, Technology and Society: Circumstances and consequences.*" *ISIS*, December 1988, 79: 571–582.
	"Robert K. Merton and the 'Merton Thesis'." Part One of I. B. Cohen, *Puritanism and the Rise of Modern Science: The Merton Thesis*. New Brunswick, NJ: Rutgers University Press, (in press).
	"Some documentary reflections on the dissemination and reception of the 'Merton Thesis'." In Jon Clark, ed. *Robert K. Merton: Consensus and Controversy*. London & Philadelphia: Falmer Press, Taylor & Francis, 1990, 307–48.
Cohen, H.	"Anomia of success and anomia of failure: Study of similarities in opposites." *British Journal of Sociology*, 1972, 23: 329–343.
Collins, H.M.	"Knowledge, norms and rules in the sociology of science." *Social Studies of Science*, 1982, 12: 299–309.
Collins, Randall and Sal Restivo	"Development, diversity and conflict in the sociology of science." *The Sociological Quarterly*, 1983, 24: 185–200.
Coser, Lewis A.	"Merton's uses of the European Sociological Tradition." In L. Coser ed. *The Idea of Social Structure*. New York: Harcourt Brace Jovanovich, 1975, 85–102.
	"Merton und die europäische Tradition der Soziologie." In Wolf Lepenies, ed. *Geschichte der Soziologie*. Frankfurt, A.M.: Suhrkamp, 1981, 4 vols., IV: 237–261.
	"Sociological theory from the Chicago dominance to 1965." *Annual Review of Sociology*, 1976, 2: 145–160.
	Masters of Sociological Thought. New York: Harcourt Brace Jovanovich, 1977, 2nd edn., 562–567.
Cournand, André F. and Harriet Zuckerman	"The code of science: Analysis and some reflections on its future." *Studium Générale*, 1970, 23: 941–962.
Cullen, Francis T.	"Merton and Parsons: General deviance paradigms." In F. T. Cullen, *Rethinking Crime and Deviance Theory*. Totowa, NJ: Rowan & Allanheld, 1984, 74–101 *passim*.

Crozier, Michel   *The Bureaucratic Phenomenon.* Chicago: University of Chicago Press, 1967, Chapter 7.

Dalenius, T., et al.   "Scientists at Work." *Minerva*, 1971, 9: 434–437.

Deflem, Mathieu   "From anomie to anomia and anomic depression: A sociological critique of the use of anomie in psychiatric research." *Social Science and Medicine*, 1989, 29: 627–634.

De Mey, Marc   *The Cognitive Paradigm.* Dordrecht, Holland: D. Reidel, 1982, Chapter 5.

De Zwart, Frank   "Antropologische vergeetachtigheid: Robert K. Merton's transactionalisme 'avant la lettre'." *Sociologische Gids*, 1988, 35: 281–290.

Diekmann, A.   "Anomie und Prozesse der Kriminalitätsentwicklung im sozialen Kontext." *Zeitschrift für Soziologie*, 1979, 8: 330–343.

DiGaetano, Alan   "The rise and development of urban political machines: An alternative to Merton's functional analysis." *Urban Affairs Quarterly*, 1988, 24: 242–267.

Di Lellio, Anna   "Intervista a Robert K. Merton." *Rassegna Italiana di Sociologia*, 1985, XXVI: 3–26.

Donati Pierpaolo   "L'ambivalenza sociologica nel pensiero di R. K. Merton." *Studi di Sociologia*, 1987, 25: 237–253.

Farnworth, Margaret &   "Strain theory revisited: Economic goals, educational
Michael J. Lieber   means, and delinquency." *American Sociological Review*, 24, 1989, 263–274.

Fazey, Cindy   "Merton, retreatism and drug addiction." *The Sociological Review*, August 1973, 31: 417–436.

Feagin, Joe R. and   "Discrimination: Motivation, action, effects and con-
Douglas Eckberg   texts." *Annual Review of Sociology*, 1980, 6: 1–20, esp. 1–2.

Feuer, Lewis F.   "Science and the ethic of Protestant asceticism. A reply to Professor Robert K. Merton." In Robert Alun Jones and Henrika Kuklick, eds., *Research in Sociology of Knowledge, Sciences, and Art.* Greenwich: JAI Press, 1979, 1–23.

Figueira-McDonough, J.   "On the usefulness of Merton's anomie theory: academic failure and deviance among high school students." *Youth & Society*, March 1983, 14: 259–279.

Foley, Donald L.   "The sociology of housing." *Annual Review of Sociology*, 1980, 6: 457–478, esp. 457–458.

Freese, Lee   "Formal theorizing." *Annual Review of Sociology*, 1980, 6: 187–212, esp. 205–207.

Funk, Allie G. and   "Anomie, powerlessness, and exchange: parallel
G. Michael Wise   sources of deviance." *Deviant Behavior*, 1989, 10: 53–60.

Garfield, Eugene   "Citation measures of the influence of Robert K.

	Merton." In Thomas F. Gieryn, ed. *Science and Social Structure: Festschrift for Robert K. Merton.* New York: The New York Academy of Sciences, 1980, 61–74.
	"Robert K. Merton: Among the giants." *Current Contents*, 11 July 1977, 5–7 (Reprinted in E. Garfield, *Essays of an Information Scientist*. Philadelphia: ISI Press, 1980, 176–178.)
Garmendia, Jose A.	"Para una sociologia de la emigracion: A proposito del esquema de formas de adaptación de Robert K. Merton." *Revista de Estudios Sociales*, 1972, 5: 145–155.
Gaston, Jerry	*Originality and Competition in Science.* Chicago: University of Chicago, 1973, Chapter 5.
	The Reward System in British and American Science. New York: Wiley, 1978, *passim.*
Ghandi, R.S.	*Locals and Cosomopolitans of Little India: A Sociological Study of the Indian Student Community at Minnesota, U.S.A.* Bombay: Popular Prakashan, 1974.
Giddens, Anthony	*Studies in Social and Political Theory.* New York: Basic Books, 1977, Chapter 2.
Gieryn, Thomas F.	"Relativist/Constructivist programmes in the sociology of science: redundance and retreat," and "Not last words: one-out dichotomies in the sociology of science." *Social Studies of Science*, 1982, 12: 279–297 and 329–335.
	"Distancing science from religion in seventeenth-century England." *Isis*, December 1988, 79: 582–593.
Gillispie, Charles C.	"Mertonian theses." *Science*, 1974, 184: 656–660.
Goddijn, H.P.M.	"Sociologischie theorie in Amerika." *Sociologische Gids*, 1958, 5: 79–85.
Goddjin, W.	"La diaspora: Essai d'analyse functionell." *Soc. Kompas*, 1958/59, 6: 32–41.
Goldstone, Jack A.	"A deductive explanation of the Matthew effect in science." *Social Studies of Science*, 1979, 9: 385–391.
Gore, M.S.	*Social Movements and the Paradigm of Functional Analysis.* I. P. Desai Memorial Lecture 4. Surat, India: Centre for Social Studies, 1989.
Harris, S.	"Ethos, ideology, and early modern science: Reexamining the Merton thesis in light of Jesuit scientific activity." *Science in Context*, 1989, 3.
Harvey, David L.	"Industrial anomie and hegemony." *Current Perspectives in Social Theory*, 1982, 3: 129–159.
Heilbron, John	"Science in the church." *Science in Context*, 1989, 3.
Hilbert, Richard A.	"Durkheim and Merton on anomie: An unexplored contrast and its derivatives," *Social Problems*, 1989, 36: 242–250.

Hilbert, Richard E. and
Charles W. Wright
"Representations of Merton's theory of anomie." *American Sociologist*, 1979, 14: 150–156.

Hill, Christopher
"Puritanism, capitalism and the scientific revolution." *Past and Present*, 1964, 29: 88–97.
"The intellectual origins of the Royal Society—London or Oxford." *Notes and Records of the Royal Society of London*, 23 December 1968, 144–156.

Himelhoch, Jerome
"Delinquency and opportunity: An end and a beginning of theory." In A. W. Gouldner and M. Miller, eds. *Applied Sociology*, 1965, 189–206.

Hoefer, Carl-Hellmut
Entfremdung: Untersuchungen zu einem Daseinsphänomen im Horizont der Strukturontologie und Anthropologisch-Integrativen Psychotherapie. Würzberg: Julius-Maximilians-Universität, 1983, 585–611.

Hollinger, D.A.
"The defense of democracy and Robert K. Merton's formulation of the scientific ethos." In R. A. Jones and H. Kuklick, *Knowledge & Society: Studies in the Sociology of Culture of Past & Present.* Greenwich: JAI Press, 1983, Vol. 4, pp. 1–15.

Hooykas, R.
"Science and Reformation." *Journal of World History*, 1956, 3: 109–139.
"Answer to Dr. Bainton's comment on 'Science and Reformation.'" *Journal of World History*, 1956, 3: 781–784.
"Science and religion in the seventeenth century." *Free University Quarterly*, 1: 169–183.
Humanisme, Science et Reforme. Leiden: 1958.

Hsu, Lee-da.
(pen name Li Ling-hsia)
"The founder of sociology of science: Merton and Merton's thought, works and his effects." *Information Science* [China], 1981, 2: 57–59.

Hynson, Lawrence
"Anomie: Its history and research application." *Free Inquiry*, 1974, 2: 32–38.

Iadov, V.A.
"Some problems in the theory of and general approach to sociological research." (Part I). *Soviet Sociology*, 1975, 14: 3–32.

Janne, Henri
"Fonction et finalité en sociologie." *Cahiers de international sociologie*, 1954, 16: 50–67.

Jaworski, Gary D.
"Robert K. Merton and Georg Simmel." In *Functionalism, Deviance and the Politics of Postwar Sociology.* New York: New School for Social Research, 1989, unpublished dissertation.

Johnson, Barbara A. and
Jonathan H. Turner
"A formalization and reformalization of anomie theory." *South African Journal of Sociology*, 1984, 15: 151–158.

Johnson, Harry M.
"Some of Robert K. Merton's contributions to sociology: notes toward a tentative assessment." *Journal of the History of the Behavioral Sciences*, January 1984, 20: 63–70.

"Robert K. Merton." *The Social Encyclopedia*, Adam Kuper and Jessica Kuper, eds. London, Boston & Henley: Routledge & Kegan Paul, 1985, 522–523.

Johnson, Larry — "A black perspective on social research: In response to Merton." *Issues in Criminology*. Spring 1974, 55–70.

Jones, Robert Alun — "The new history of sociology: Introduction: Merton and the 'new history of science'." *Annual Review of Sociology*, 1983, 9: 447–469.

"On Merton's 'History' and 'Systematics' of Sociological Theory." In L. Graham, W. Lepenies & P. Weingart, eds. *Functions & Uses of Disciplinary Histories*. Amsterdam: D. Reidel Pub. Co., 1982.

"Presentism, anachronism, and continuity in the history of sociology: a reply to Seidman." *History of Sociology*, 1983, 6: 153–160.

Kagan, Robert A. — *Regulatory Justice*. New York: Russell Sage Foundation, 1978, 92–97.

Kaplan, Norman — "Sociology of science." In R. E. L. Faris, ed. *Handbook of Modern Sociology*. Chicago: Rand McNally, 1964.

Kearney, Hugh F. — "Puritanism, capitalism, and the scientific revolution." *Past and Present*, July 1964, 28: 81–101.

"Puritanism and science: problems of definition." *Past and Present*, July 1965, 31: 104–110.

Origins of the Scientific Revolution. London: Longmans, 1964.

Kemsley, Douglas S. — "Religious influences in the rise of modern science: a review and criticism, particularly of the 'Protestant-Puritan Ethic' theory." *Annals of Science*, 1968, 24: 199–226.

Kent, Stephen A. — "Slogan chanters to mantra chanters: A Mertonian deviance analysis of conversion to religiously ideological organizations in the early 1970s." *Sociological Analysis*, 1988, 49: 104–118.

Knorr-Cetina, Karin D. — "The constructivist programme in the sociology of science: retreats or advances?" *Social Studies of Science*, 1982, 12: 320–324.

Kopp, Manfred and Michael Schmid — "Individuelles Handeln und strukturelle Selektion: Eine Rekonstruktion des Erklärungsprogramms von Robert K. Merton." *Kölner Zeitschrift für Sozialpsychologie*, 1981, 2: 257–272.

Kornhauser, R. Ruth — *Social Sources of Delinquency: An Appraisal of Analytic Models*. Chicago: University of Chicago Press, 1978.

Krohn, Roger — "On Gieryn on the 'relativist/constructivist' programme in the sociology of science." *Social Studies of Science*, 1982, 12: 325–328.

Kuvačić, Ivan	'O Mertonovu obrascu funkcionalne analize u sociologiji." Introduction to Merton, *O Teorijskoj Sociologiji*. Zagreb: Biblioteka Pitanja, 1979, v–x.
Larson, Calvin J.	*Major Themes in Sociological Theory*. New York: David Mckay Co., 1973, 136–140.
Law, John and David French	"Normative and interpretive sociologies of science." *Sociological Review*, 1974, 25: 373–377.
Lazarsfeld, Paul F.	"Working with Merton." In L.A. Coser, ed. *The Idea of Social Structure*. New York: Harcourt Brace Jovanovich, 1975, 35–66.
	"Mit Merton arbeiten." In Wolf Lepenies, ed. *Geschichte der Soziologie*. Frankfurt, A.M.: Suhrkamp, 1981, 4 Vols., I: 237–261.
Lécuyer, Bernard	"Bilan et perspectives de la sociologie de science." *Archives européenes de sociologie/European Journal of Sociology*. September 1978, 19.
	"Le système Mertonien de sociologie de la science: gènese, ramifications, contestation," *Bulletin, Société Française de Sociologie*, 1976, 3–23.
Lee, Gary R.	"Marriage and anomie: A causal argument." *Journal of Marriage and the Family*. 1974, 36: 523–532.
Lepenies, Wolf	"Melancholie als Unordnung bei R. K. Merton." In W. Lepenies, *Melancholie und Gesellschaft*. Frankfurt A.M.: Suhrkamp, 1969, 1981, 12–22.
Link, Bruce and Barry Milcarek	"Selection factors in the dispensation of therapy: The Matthew Effect in the allocation of mental health resources." *Journal of Health and Social Behavior*, 1980, 21: 279–290.
Liska, Allen E.	"Aspirations, expectations and delinquency: stress and additive models." *Sociological Quarterly*, Winter 1971, 12: 99–107.
Löwy, Elana	"Quantification in science and cognition circa 1937." *Science in Context*, 1988, 2: 345–355.
Maniscalco, Maria L.	"L'opera di Robert K. Merton e la sociologia contemporanea: note a margine di un convegno." *Studi di Sociologia*, 1987, 25: 248–252.
Markova, L.A.	"R. Merton's functional analysis in the history of science." In *Science, History and Historiography of the XIX–XX Centuries*. Moscow: Nauka, 1987, 156–176.
Matusewicz, Czelaw	"Accepted values and juvenile delinquency: a review of theories and problems." *Przeglad Psychologiczpny*, 1977, 20: 707–742.
McCullagh, Ciaran	"Merton's view of the norms of science." *Social Studies of Science*, 1974, 4: 249–266.
Medina, Esteban	"Teorías y orientaciones de la sociologia de la ciencia." *Revista Espanola de Investigaciones Sociologicas*, 1982, 20: 7–58.

Meja, Volker and Nico Stehr	"The sociology of knowledge and the ethos of science." in Hermann Strasser, Eileen Leonard and Kenneth Westhues, eds. *Gedenkschrift für Werner Stark*. New York: Fordham University Press, (in press).
Messner, Steven F.	"Merton's 'Social Structure and Anomie': The road not taken." *Deviant Behavior*, 1988, 9: 33–53.
Mihu, Achim	*Sociologia Americana a Grupurilor Mici*. Bucharest: Editura Politica, 1970, 82–86. "Robert K. Merton." *Studia Universitatis Babes-Bolyai Philosophia* [Romania], 1981, XXVI: 18–32.
Milic, Vojin	"On Merton's *Éléments de méthode sociologique.*" *Quarterly Review of Law and Social Sciences, Annals of the Law Faculty of Belgrade*. October-December 1954, 2: 486–489. [In Serbo-Croatian].
Mills, Edgar W. Jr.	"Sociological ambivalence and social order: The constructive uses of normative dissonance." *Sociology and Social Research*, 1983, 67: 279–287.
Mirskaja, E. Z.	"Eticheshie reguliatiny funktsionirovanii nauki." (Ethical regulation of the function of science.) *Voprosy Filosofii* [USSR], 1975, 3: 131–138. "R. Merton and his conception of the sociology of science." In V. Zh. Kelle, E. Z. Mirskaja and A. A. Ignatiev, eds. *Modern Western Sociology of Science: A Critical Analysis*. Moscow: Nauka, 1988, 42–80.
Mitchell, Richard G. Jr.	"Alienation and deviance: Strain theory reconsidered." *Sociological Inquiry*, 1984, 54: 330–345.
Mouzelis, N. P.	"Theories of Bureaucracy." *Encyclopedia Britannica, Micropaedia*, 1974, 15th edition, Vol. III, 494–497.
Mrksic, Danilo	"Mertonove teorije srednjeg obima." *Sociologija*, 1977, 19: 657–677.
Mucha, I.	"Observations on the anomie-concept." *Heilpädagogische Forschung*, 1983, 10: 217–220.
Mulkay, Michael	"Norms and ideology in science." *Social Science Information*, 1976, 1976, 15: 637–655. "The sociology of science in East and West." *Current Sociology*, 1980, 28: 1–184. "Interpretation and the use of rules: The case of the norms in science." In Thomas Gieryn, ed. *Science and Social Structure*. New York: New York Academy of Sciences, 1980, 111–125.
Munger, Frank J. and Douglas Price, eds.	*Readings in Political Parties: Pressure Groups*. New York: Crowell, 1964.
Nagasawa, Richard H.	"Social class differentials in success striving." *Pacific Sociological Review*, April 1971, 14.
Nelson, Benjamin	"The early modern revolution in science and philosophy." In R. S. Cohen and M. Wartofsky, eds.,

Boston Studies in the Philosophy of Science. Dordrecht, Holland: D. Reidel, 1967, Volume 3.

Nelson, Joel and Irving Tallman
"Local-cosmopolitan perceptions of political conformity: a specification of parental influence." *American Journal of Sociology*, September 1969, 75: 193–227.

Opp, Karl-Dieter
Methodologie der Wissenschaften. Hamburg: Rowoholt, 1976, 414–417.

Opp, Karl-Dieter and Frisco D. Heyt
"Zur Integration von Theorie und Forschung in der Soziologie des abweichenden Verhaltens. Eine Integrationsstrategie und ihre Anwendung auf die Anomie Theorie." *Mens en Maatschappj*, 1968, Bd. 43.

Oromaner, Mark
"Professional age and the reception of sociological publications: A test of the Zuckerman-Merton hypothesis." *Social Studies of Science*, 1977, 7: 381–388.

Orrù, Marco
Anomie: History and Meanings. Boston & London: Allen & Unwin, 1987, *passim*.

Patel, Pravin J.
"Robert Merton's formulations in the sociology of science." *Sociological Bulletin*, March 1975, 24: 55–75.

Pelseneer, J.
"L'origine protestante de la science moderne." *Lychnos*, 1947, 246–248.
"Les influences protestantes dans l'histoire des sciences." *Archives Internationale d'Histoire des Sciences*, 1948, 1: 348–353.

Persell, Caroline H.
"An Interview with Robert K. Merton." *Teaching Sociology*, 1984, 11: 355–386.

Phillips, David P. and Richard H. Conviser
"A simple mathematical reformulation of Merton's typology of deviance." *Journal of Mathematical Sociology*, July 1971, 1: 207–211.

Phillips, Derek L.
"Le comunità scientifiche come garanzia sociale dell'oggettività della conoscenza." *Problemi*, 1976, 45: 23–40.

Pinch, T.J.
"Kuhn—the conservative and radical interpretations —Are some Mertonians 'Kuhnians' and some 'Kuhnians' Mertonians?" *4S Bulletin* (Society for Social Studies of Science), Spring 1982, 7: 8–9.

Pinder, Craig C. and Larry Moore, eds.
Middle Range Theory and the Study of Organizations. Boston: Martinus Nijhoff, 1980.

Poloma, Margaret M.
Contemporary Sociological Theory. New York: Collier Macmillan, 1979, 19–30.

Quintyn, J.B.
"Voor een sociologie van wetenschap en technologie." *Tijdschrift voor Sociale Wetenschappen*, 1983, 27: 305–341.

Rabb, Theodore K.
"Puritanism and the rise of experimental science in England." *Journal of World History*, 1962, 7: 46–67.

"Religion and the rise of modern science." *Past and Present*, July 1965, 31: 111–126.

Rafky, David M.
"Police cynicism reconsidered: an application of smallest space analysis." *Criminology: An International Journal*, 1975, 13: 168–192.

Ramos, Alberto
"Latent functions of formalism in Brazil." *Sociology and Social Research*, October 1971, 56.

Reeves, Joy B.
"Merton's adaptation typology: a research tool for applied feminist-oriented sociologists." *Free Inquiry in Creative Sociology*, November 1979, 7: 151–154.

Restivo, Sal
"Some perspectives in contemporary sociology of science." *Science, Technology, and Human Values*, Spring 1981, 6: 22–30.

Rist, Ray C.
"The functionalist paradigm on deviant behavior: towards a new theoretical convergence." *Utah State University Journal of Sociology*, 1972, 3: 78–93.

Ritzer, George
"Robert K. Merton's model of structural functionalism." In *Contemporary Sociological Theory*. New York: Alfred A. Knopf, 1988, 2nd ed., 96–104, 199ff.

Rogers, E.M. and D.K. Bhowmik
"Homophily and heterophily: Relational concepts for communications research." *Public Opinion Quarterly*, 1970, 34: 523–538.

Rosen, George
"Left-wing Puritanism and science." *Bulletin of the Institute of the History of Medicine*, 1944, 15: 375–380.

Rothman, R.A.
"A dissenting view on the scientific ethos." *British Journal of Sociology*, November 1979, 7: 151–154.

Rushing, William A.
"Class, culture and 'Social Structure and Anomie'." *American Journal of Sociology*, March 1971, 76: 857–872.

Rychtarik, Karel
"Mertonov pokus o 'novou syntezu' empirie a teorie." *Sociologicky Casopis*, 1984, 20: 138–155.

Salanick, Gerald R.
"Middle-range theory: Science of a social reality." In Craig C. Pinder and Larry F. Moore, *Middle Range Theory and the Study of Organizations*. Boston/The Hague/London: Martinus Nijhoff, 1980, 408–413.

Samuelson, Paul A.
"Fisher's 'reproductive value' as an economic specimen in Merton's zoo." In Thomas Gieryn, ed. *Science and Social Structure*, 1980, 126–142.

Sandhur, Hayet S.
"Female delinquency: goal obstruction and anomie." *Canadian Review of Sociology and Anthropology*, May 1969, 107–110.

Schacht, Richard
"Doubts about anomie and anomia." In S. Giora Shoham and Anthony Grahame, eds. *Alienation and Anomie Revisited*. Tel-Aviv, Israel: Ramot Publishing Co., 1982, 121–138.

Schaff, Adam
"Anomia e autoalienacja" *Kultura i Spoleczenstwo*, 1977, 21: 35–51.

Schoek, Helmut	*Soziologie: Geschichte ihrer Probleme.* München: Verlag Karl Aber, 1952. *Die Soziologie und die Gesellschaften* Freiburg/München: Verlag Karl Aber, 1964, 2nd edn., 354–356.
Schweiker, W.	"Status consistency in Merton's modes for individual adaptation." *Sociological Quarterly*, 1968, 9: 531–539.
Scott, James C.	"Corruption, machine politics and political change." *American Political Science Review*, December 1969.
Seeman, Melvin	"A prolegomenon on empirical research regarding anomie." In S. Giora Shoham and Anthony Grahame, eds. *Alienation and Anomie Revisited*. Tel-Aviv, Israel: Ramot Publishing Co., 1982, 121–138.
Seidmann, Melvin	"Classics and contemporaries: the history and systematics of sociology revisited." *History of Sociology*, 1981, 6: 121–135.
Shapin, Steven	"Understanding the Merton Thesis." *Isis*, December 1988, 79: 594–605. "The Merton Thesis." W. F. Bynum, E. J. Browne and Roy Porter, eds. *The Dictionary of the History of Science*. London: Macmillan, 1981, 262.
Shapiro, Barbara J.	"Latitudinarianism and science in 17th-Century England." *Past and Present*, 1968, 40: 16–41.
Sharma, R. N.	"Anomie of economic deprivation: Merton re-examined." *Sociological Bulletin*, 1980, 29: 1–32.
Shulman, Lee S.	"The practical and the eclectic: A deliberation on teaching and education research." *Curriculum Inquiry*, 1984, 14: 183–200, esp. 186–188.
Sills, David L.	"Robert K. Merton." In Paula T. Kaufmann, ed. *The Reader's Advisor: The Best in General Reference Literature, the Social Sciences, History, and the Arts*. New York & London: R. R. Bowker Co., 1986, 210–211.
Simon, William and John H. Gagnon	"The anomie of affluence: A post-Mertonian conception." *American Journal of Sociology*, 1976, 82: 356–378.
Skidmore, William	*Theoretical Thinking in Sociology*. Cambridge: Cambridge University Press, 1975, 141–150.
Smith, Robert B.	"Middle-Range Theory." *Handbook of Social Science Methods: An Introduction to Social Research*, Ballinger Publishing Co., 1983, Vol. I., 1–7.
Statera, Gianni	"Origini e sviluppi della sociologia della scienza." *La Critica Sociologica*, 1976, 38, 41–66. "La Sociologia della scienza fra ricerca e ideologia." *Problemi*, 1976, 45: 4–22.
Statera, Gianni et al.	"Sociologia della scienza e politiche della ricerca." *Sociologia e Ricerca Sociale*, 1987, 24: 1–238.
Stearns, Raymond P.	"The scientific spirit in England in early modern times." *Isis*, 1943, 34: 293–300.

"The relations between science and society in the later seventeenth century." In *The Restoration of the Stuarts—Blessing or Disaster?* Washington, DC: The Folger Shakespeare Library, 1960, 67–75.

Steffenhagen, R.A.   "Self-esteem and anomie: an integration of Adler and Merton as a theory of deviance." *Deviant Behavior*, 1984, 5: 23–30.

Stehr, Nico   "Zur Soziologie der Wissenschaftssoziologie." *Kölner Zeitschrift für Soziologie*, 1975, 18: 9–18.

"The ethos of science revisited." *Sociological Inquiry*, 1978, 48: 172–196.

"Robert K. Merton's Wissenschaftssoziologie." In Robert K. Merton, *Entwicklung und Wandel von Forschungsinteressen: Aufsätze zur Wissenschaftssoziologie*, N. Stehr, ed. Frankfurt, A.M.: Suhrkamp, 1985, 7–23.

Stehr, Nico and Volker, Meja   "Robert K. Merton's strukturelle Analyse: Die gesellschaftliche Akkumulation von Vorteilen und Nachteilen." In Karl-Siegbert Rehberg, ed. *Gesellschaftstheorien*. Frankfurt, A.M.: Suhrkamp, 1984.

Stejskal, Karel   "Sociálni podmíněnost vědecké tvorty." *Sociologicky Casopis*, 1988, 24: 32–40.

Stigler, George J.   "Merton on multiples, denied and affirmed." In Thomas F. Gieryn, ed. *Science and Social Structure*. New York: New York Academy of Sciences, 1980, 143–146.

Stinchcombe, Arthur   "Merton's theory of social structure." In L. Coser, ed., *The Idea of Social Structure*, New York: Harcourt Brace Jovanovich, 1975, 11–34.

Struik, Dirk   "Merton in the thirties." *Science in Context*, 1989, 3.

Stzompka, Piotr   "R. K. Mertona konstruktywna destrukcja socjologii wiedzy." *Kultura I Spoleczenstwo*, XXIX, 1985.

"Od Malinowskiego do Mertona. Studium O dziedziczeniu idei." *Miedzy Dwoma Swiatami-Bronislam Malinowski*. Kraków: Jagiellonian University Press, 1985, 59–71.

Szymanski, Albert   "Competing sociological paradigms: A contrast of the sociological systems of Merton, Parsons, and Marx." *Humboldt Journal of Social Relations*, 1975, 2: 57–65.

Thio, A.   "A critical look at Merton's anomie theory." *Pacific Sociological Review*, 1975, 18: 139–158.

Thorner, Isidor   "Ascetic Protestantism and the development of science and technology." *American Journal of Sociology*, 1952, 58: 25–33.

Tilman, R. and J. L. Simich   "On the use and abuse of Thorstein Veblen in Modern American Sociology, II: Daniel Bell and the 'Utopianizing' of Veblen's contribution and its integration by Robert K. Merton and C. W. Mills."

American Journal of Economics and Sociology, 1984, 43: 103–114.

Toomey Richard and Dennis Child — "The development of local and cosmopolitan attitudes among undergraduates and sixth formers." *Sociological Review*, August 1971, 19: 235–242.

Toren, Nina — "The scientific ethos debate: a meta-theoretical view." *Social Science and Medicine*, 1983, 17: 1665–1672.

"The new code of scientists." IEEE *Engineering in Medicine and Biology Magazine*, 1980, EM-7, 78–84.

Unsigned — "Robert K. Merton". In *Contemporary Authors*. Detroit: Gale Research Co., 1974, 423–424.

"Robert K. Merton". In *Current Biography*. Charles Moritz, ed. 1965, Volume 26, 20–33.

"Robert K. Merton." *Encyclopedia Britannica, Micropaedia*, 1974, 15th edition, Volume VI, 813.

Vaccarini, Italo — "Per una rivalutazione della teoria sociologica di Robert K. Merton." *Studi di Sociologia*, 1982, 20: 135–155.

Walker, David — "A path to sociological sanity in the midst of crisis: On the place in American Sociology of Robert K. Merton." *The Times Higher Educational Supplement*, December 1977, 23.

Wallace, Ruth and Alison Wolf — "Robert K. Merton: Middle-range theory." *Contemporary Sociological Theory*, Englewood Cliffs, N.J.: Prentice-Hall, 1980, 53–71.

Wallner, Mathias — "50 Jahre 'Merton These'." *Deutsche Zeitschrift für Philosophie*, January 1988, 12: 268–272.

"Epoche und Erkennen: Die Kreativitätsforschung in den USA als Fallbeispiel". *Deutsche Zeitschrift für Philosophie*, January 1988, 12: 1079–1088.

Webster, Charles — "The origins of the Royal Society: Review essay." *History of Science*, 1967, 6: 106–128.

Weick, Karl E. — "Middle-range theories of social systems." *Behavioral Science*, 1974, 19: 357–367.

"Middle-range theories in organizational thinking". In Craig C. Pinder and Larry F. Moore, *Middle Range Theory and the Study of Organizations*. Boston/The Hague/London: Martinus Nijhoff, 1980, 392–407.

Wells, Alan — "Conflict theory and functionalism." *Teaching Sociology*, July 1979, 6: 429–437.

Wiatr, Jerzy, J. — "Robert K. Merton i socjologia funkcjonalna." In Robert K. Merton, *Teoria Socjologiczna i Struktura Spoleczna*. Warsaw: Pánstowowe Wydawnictwo Naukowe, 1982, xi–xx.

Willie, Charles — "On Merton's insiders and outsiders." *American Journal of Sociology*, March 1973, 78: 1269–1272.

Winslow, Robert W. — "Status management in the adolescent social system:

a formulation of Merton's anomie theory." *British Journal of Sociology*, 1968, 19: 143–159.

Wippler, Reinhard   "Nicht-intendierte soziale Folgen individueller Handlungen." *Soziale Welt*, 1978, 2: 155–179.

Wojtasiewicz, O. A.   "Role and status in Merton." *The Polish Sociological Bulletin*, 1979, 2: 141–143.

Wolfe, Raymond, N.   "Two views of anomie and the nature of normlessness." *Journal of Social Psychology*, 1968, 75: 91–99.

Wright, Charles R.   "Robert K. Merton." In the *International Encyclopedia of Communications*, Erik Barnow, ed. University of Pennsylvania and Oxford University Press, 1988.

Wunderlich, R.   "The scientific ethos: a clarification." *British Journal of Sociology*, 1974, 25: 373–377.

Zeidenstein, Harvey   "The consequences of executive acts: an expanded typology of Merton's functional analysis." *Presidential Studies Quarterly*, Fall 1979, 457–469.

Ziman, John   "Robert K. Merton and science studies." *4S Bulletin*, Society for Social Studies of Science, Winter 1982, 7: 21–22.

"Some very queer fish." In John Ziman, *Puzzles, Problems and Enigmas*. Cambridge: Cambridge University Press, 1981.

Zuckerman, Harriet   "Accumulation of advantage and disadvantage: The theory and its intellectual biography." In Carlo Mongardini and Simonetta Tabboni, eds., *L'Opera di Robert K. Merton e la Sociologia Contemporanea*, 1989.

"The other Merton thesis." *Science in Context*, 1989, 3.

Bibliography

This bibliography, prepared by Jon Clark, contains full references to all the publications cited in the contributions to this book. For a comprehensive bibliography of Merton's writings from 1934 to 1975 see Mary Wilson Miles, 'The Writings of Robert K. Merton—A Bibliography', in Lewis Coser (ed), *The Idea of Social Structure*, New York, Harcourt Brace, pp. 497–522. A 'Supplement' covering Merton's publications from 1975 to 1989, prepared by Mary W. Miles and Rosa Haritos, is contained in the Appendix immediately preceding this bibliography.

Many of Merton's most important articles have been published in one or all of the three editions (1949, 1957, 1968) of his classic work, *Social Theory and Social Structure*, or in the other major collections of his essays, *Sociology of Science* (1973), *Sociological Ambivalence* (1976) and *Social Research and the Practicing Professions* (1982). Reference has been made to the original articles and/or reprints of these books where they have been specifically cited by contributors.

Abraham, G. (1983) 'Misunderstanding the Merton Thesis: A Boundary Dispute between History and Sociology', *Isis*, Vol. 74, pp. 368–87.

Abrams, P. (1982) *Historical Sociology*, Shepton Mallett, Somerset, Open Books.

Albrow, M. (1968) 'The Study of Organizations—Objectivity or Bias?', in J. Gould (ed), *Penguin Social Sciences Survey*, Harmondsworth, Penguin, pp. 259–73.

Albrow, M. (1970) *Bureaucracy*, Praeger, New York.

Alexander, J. (1982) *Theoretical Logic in Sociology*, Vol. 1, Berkeley and Los Angeles, Calif., University of California Press.

Allington, R. (1980) 'Teacher Interruption Behaviors during Primary-Grade Oral Reading', *Journal of Educational Psychology*, Vol. 72, pp. 371–7.

Althusser, L. and Balibar, E. (1970) *Reading Capital*, trans. by B. Brewster, London, New Left Books.

Aquinas, St Thomas (1928) *Summa Contra Gentiles*, Vol. 3, English translation, London.

Aquinas, St Thomas (1945) *Basic Writings of St. Thomas Aquinas*, edited by A. Pegis, New York, Random House.

Arditi, G. (1987) 'Role as Cultural Concept', *Theory and Society*, Vol. 16, pp. 565–91.

Aristotle (1941) *The Basic Works of Aristotle*, ed. by R. McKeon, New York, Random House.

Ashley-Montagu, M. (1939) 'Science and Society in the Seventeenth Century', *University Review*, Vol. 6, pp. 65–6.

Austin, M. and Morrison, C. (1963) *The First R: The Harvard Report on Reading in the Elementary School*, New York, Macmillan.

Babad, E., Inbar, J. and Rosenthal, R. (1982) 'Pygmalion, Galatea, and the Golem: Investigations of Biased and Unbiased Teachers', *Journal of Education Psychology*, Vol. 74, pp. 459–74.

Babchuck, N. and Booth, A. (1969) 'Voluntary Associations', *American Sociological Review*, Vol. 34, pp. 31–45.

Bacharach, S. and Lawler, E. (1980) *Power and Politics in Organizations*, San Francisco, Calif., Jossey-Bass.

Bacon, F. (1960) *The New Organon and Related Writings*, ed. by F. Anderson, Indianapolis, Ind., Bobbs-Merrill.

Bacon, F. (1966) *The Advancement of Learning and New Atlantis*, Oxford, Oxford University Press.

Barbano, F. (1968) 'Social Structures and Social Functions', *Inquiry*, Vol. 2, pp. 40–84.

Barnard, C. (1938) *The Functions of the Executive*, Cambridge, Mass., Harvard University Press.

Barnes, B. (1972) 'Sociological Explanation and Natural Science: A Kuhnian Appraisal', *European Journal of Sociology*, Vol. 13, pp. 373–91.

Barnes, B. (1974) *Scientific Knowledge and Sociological Theory*, London, Routledge and Kegan Paul.

Barnes, B. (1981) 'Über den konventionellen Charakter von Wissen und Erkenntnis', in Stehr and Meja (1981), pp. 163–90.

Barnes, B. (1982) *T.S. Kuhn and Social Science*, London, Macmillan.

Barnes, B. and Dolby, R. (1970) 'The Scientific Ethos: A Deviant Viewpoint', *European Journal of Sociology*, Vol. 11, pp. 3–25.

Barnes, B. and Edge, D. (1982) 'General Introduction' to *idem* (eds), *Science in Context, Readings in the Sociology of Science*, Cambridge, Mass., MIT Press.

Barr, R. and Dreeben, R. (1983) *How Schools Work*, Chicago, Ill., University of Chicago Press.

Barton, A. (1963) *Social Organization under Stress: A Sociological Review of Disaster Studies*, Washington, DC, National Academy of Sciences–National Research Council.

Barton, A. (1969) 'Organizational Measurement', in Etzioni (1969), pp. 259–90.

Bateson, G., Jackson, D., Gealey, J. and Weakland, J. (1956), 'Toward a Theory of Schizophrenia', *Behavioral Science*, Vol. 1, pp. 251–64.

Baxter, R. (1931) *The Autobiography of Richard Baxter* (abridgement of *Reliquiae Baxterianae*, 1627, by J. Lloyd-Thomas), London, J. M. Dent.

Beard, C. (1913) *An Economic Interpretation of the Constitution*, London.

Becker, G. (1984) 'Pietism and Science: A Critique of Robert K. Merton's Hypothesis', *American Journal of Sociology*, Vol. 89, pp. 1065–90.

Bell, D. (1980) *The Winding Passage: Essays and Sociological Journeys*, New York, Basic Books.

Ben-David, J. (1971) *The Scientist's Role in Society*, Englewood Cliffs, NJ, Prentice-Hall.

Bendix, R. (1947) 'Bureaucracy: The Problem and its Setting', *American Sociological Review*, Vol. 12, pp. 493–507.

Bendix, R. (1960) *Max Weber: An Intellectual Portrait*, London, Heinemann.

Benson, J. (1977) 'Innovation and Crisis in Organizational Analysis', *Sociological Quarterly*, Vol. 18, pp. 3–16.

Berlin, I. (1953) *The Hedgehog and the Fox: An Essay on Tolstoy's View of History*, New York, Simon and Schuster.

Bernal, J. (1939) *The Social Function of Science*, New York, Macmillan.

Bernstein, B. (1971) *Class, Codes and Control*, Vol. 1, London, Routledge and Kegan Paul.

Besnard, P. (1978) 'Merton à la recherche de l'anomie', *Revue française de sociologie*, Vol. 19, pp. 3–38.

Besnard, P. (1985) 'The Americanisation of Anomie at Harvard', *Knowledge and Society*, Vol. 6, pp. 41–53.

Besnard, P. (1987) *L'anomie, ses usages et ses fonctions dans la discipline sociologique depuis Durkheim*, Paris, PUF.

Bierstedt, R. (1974) *The Social Order*, 4th ed., New York, McGraw-Hill.

Bierstedt, R. (1981) *American Sociological Theory: A Critical History*, New York, Academic Press.

Bittner, E. (1965) 'The Concept of Organization', *Social Research*, Vol. 32, pp. 239–55.

Bittner, E. (1967) 'The Police on Skid-Row: A Study in Peace Keeping', *American Sociological Review*, Vol. 32, pp. 699–715.

Black, M. (ed) (1961) *The Social Theories of Talcott Parsons*, Englewood Cliffs, NJ, Prentice-Hall.

Blalock, H. (1967a) *Toward a Theory of Minority Group Relations*, New York, Wiley.

Blalock, H. (1967b) 'Status Inconsistency, Social Mobility, Status Integration and Structural Effects', *American Sociological Review*, Vol. 32, pp. 790–801.

Blalock, H. (1982) *Conceptualization and Measurement in the Social Sciences*, Beverly Hills, Calif., Sage.

Blau, P. (1955) *The Dynamics of Bureaucracy*, Chicago, Ill., University of Chicago Press. Revised edition 1963.

Blau, P. (1956) *Bureaucracy in Modern Society*, New York, Random House.

Blau, P. (1964) *Exchange and Power in Social Life*, New York, Wiley.

Blau, P. (1968a) 'The Study of Formal Organizations', in Parsons (1968), pp. 54–65.

Blau, P. (1968b) 'Theories of Organizations', in *Encyclopedia of the Social Sciences*, Vol. 11, pp. 297–305.

Blau, P. (1969) 'Sociological Analysis: Current Trends and Personal Practice', *Sociological Inquiry*, No. 2, pp. 122–5.

Blau, P. (1974) *On the Nature of Organizations*, New York, Wiley.

Blau, P. (ed) (1975a) *Approaches to the Study of Social Structure*, Free Press, New York.

Blau, P. (1975b) 'Structural Constraints of Status Complements', in L. Coser (1975a), pp. 117–38.

Blau, P. (1977) *Inequality and Heterogeneity: A Primitive Theory of Social Structure*, New York, Free Press.

Blau, P. and Duncan, O. (1967) *The American Occupational Structure*, New York, Wiley.

Blau, P. and Merton, R. K. (eds) (1981) *Continuities in Structural Inquiry*, Beverly Hills, Calif., Sage.

Blau, P. and Meyer, M. (1987) *Bureaucracy in Modern Society*, 3rd ed., New York, Random House.

Blau, P. and Schwartz, J. (1984) *Crosscutting Social Circles*, Orlando, Fla., Academic Press.

Blau, P. and Scott, R. (1962) *Formal Organizations*, San Francisco, Calif., Chandler.

Bloch, O. (1971) *La philosophie de Gassendi*, La Haye, Martinus Nijhoff.

Bloor, D. (1974) 'Popper's Mystification of Objective Knowledge', *Science Studies*, Vol. 4, pp. 65–76.

Bloor, D. (1976) *Knowledge and Social Imagery*, London, Routledge and Kegan Paul.

Bloor, D. (1978) 'Polyhedra and the Abominations of Leviticus', *British Journal of Historical Science*, Vol. 11, pp. 245–72.

Bloor, D. (1981) 'Klassifikation und Wissenssoziologie: Durkheim und Mauss neu betrachtet', in Stehr and Meja (1981), pp. 20–51.

Boon, J. (1982) 'Introduction' to English edition of M. Izard and P. Smith, *Between Belief and Transgression—Structuralist Essays in Religion, History and Myth*, Chicago, Ill., University of Chicago Press, pp. v–xiii.

Borko, H., Cone, R., Russo, N. and Shavelson, R. (1979) 'Teachers' Decision Making', in P. Peterson and H. Walberg (eds), *Research on Teaching: Concepts, Findings and Implications*, Berkeley, Calif., McCutchan.

Boudon, R. (1974) *Education, Equality and Social Opportunity*, New York, Wiley.

Boudon, R. (1977) 'Review' of L. Coser (ed), *The Idea of Social Structure*, in *American Journal of Sociology*, Vol. 86, pp. 1356–61.

Boudon, R. (1980) *The Crisis in Sociology—Problems of Sociological Epistemology*, 2nd ed., New York, Columbia University Press.

Boudon, R. (1986) *L'idéologie*, Paris, Fayard (forthcoming in English, Oxford, Basil Blackwell).

Boudon, R. (1988) 'L'acteur social est-il si irrationel (et si conformiste) qu'on le dit?', in *Individu et justice sociale. Autour de John Rawls* (ouvrage collectif), Paris, le Seuil, pp. 219–44.

Bourdieu, P. (1975) 'The Specificity of the Scientific Field and the Social Conditions of the Progress of Reason', *Social Science Information*, Vol. 14, No. 6, pp. 19–47.

Bradley v. Milliken (1971), 338F. Supplement, E.D. Michigan.

Braithwaite, R. (1953) *Scientific Explanation*, Cambridge, Cambridge University Press.

Brophy, J. (1983) 'Research on the Self-Fulfilling Prophecy and Teacher Expectations', *Journal of Educational Psychology*, Vol. 75, pp. 631–61.

Brophy, J. and Good, T. (1970a) 'Teachers' Communication of Differential Expectations for Children's Classroom Performance: Some Behavioral Data', *Journal of Educational Psychology*, Vol. 61, pp. 365–74.

Brophy, J. and Good, T. (1970b) 'The Brophy-Good Dyadic Interaction System', in A. Simon and E. Boyer (eds), *Mirrors for Behavior: An Anthology of Observation Instruments Continued—1970 Supplement, Volume A*, Philadelphia, Pa., Research for Better Schools.

Brophy, J. and Good, T. (1974) *Teacher-Student Relationships: Causes and Consequences*, New York, Holt, Rinehart, and Winston.

Brown v. Board of Education (1954) 347 U.S. 483.

Brown, A. (1978) 'Knowing When, Where, and How to Remember: A Problem of Metacognition', in R. Glaser (ed), *Advances in Instructional Psychology*, Hillsdale, NJ, Erlbaum, pp. 77–165.

Brown, J. and Gilmartin, B. (1969) 'Sociology Today: Lacunae, Emphases and Surfeits', *American Sociologist*, Vol. 4, pp. 285–91.

Brucker, J. (1790) *Institutiones Historiae Philosophicae*, 2nd ed., Leipzig, J.G.I. Breitkopf.

Buddeus, J. (1731) *Compendium Historiae Philosophicae*, Halle.

Bukharin, N. *et al.* (1931) *Science at the Cross Roads*, London, Kniga. Reprinted in 1971 by Frank Cass, London, with an 'Introduction' by Gary Werskey and a 'Foreword' by Joseph Needham.

Burawoy, M. (1979a) *Manufacturing Consent*, Chicago, Ill., University of Chicago Press.

Burawoy, M. (1979b) 'The Anthropology of Industrial Work', *Annual Review of Anthropology*, Vol. 8, pp. 231–66.

Burawoy, M. (1982) 'The Written and the Repressed in Gouldner's Industrial Sociology', *Theory and Society*, Vol. 11, pp. 831–51.

Burke, K. (1935) *Permanence and Change*, New York, New Republic Inc.

Burrell, G. and Morgan, G. (1979) *Sociological Paradigms and Organizational Analysis*, London, Heinemann.

Burtt, E. (1932) *The Metaphysical Foundations of Modern Physical Science*, 2nd ed., London, Routledge and Kegan Paul.

Butterfield, H. (1949) *The Origins of Modern Science 1300–1800*, London, G. Bell and Sons.

Campbell, C. (1982) 'A Dubious Distinction?: An Inquiry into the Value and Use of Merton's Concepts of Manifest and Latent Function', *American Sociological Review*, Vol. 47, pp. 29–44.

Candolle, A. de (1873) *Histoire des sciences et des savants*, Geneva/Bale, H. George, Librairie. Second, considerably enlarged edition, 1885.

Caplow, T. (1964) *Principles of Organization*, New York, Harcourt Brace Jovanovich.

Carter, K., Sabers, D., Cushing, K., Pinnegar, S. and Berliner, D. (1987) 'Processing and Using Information about Students: A Study of Expert, Novice, and Postulant Teachers', *Teaching and Teacher Education*, Vol. 3, pp. 147–57.

Cavalli, A. (1985) 'Introduction' to *idem, Il tempo dei giovani*, Bologna, Il Mulino.

Cavalli, A. (1986) 'L'esperienza del tempo', paper presented to conference on 'Time and the Sacred', Florence, 22–23 May.

Chazel, F. (1967) 'Considérations sur la nature de l'anomie', *Revue française de sociologie*, Vol. 8, pp. 151–68.

Cicourel, A. (1964) *Method and Measurement in Sociology*, New York, Free Press.

Cicourel, A. (1968) *The Social Organization of Juvenile Justice*, New York, Wiley.

Cicourel, A. and Kitsuse, J. (1963) *The Educational Decision Makers*, Indianapolis, Ind., Bobbs-Merrill.

Clark, B. (ed) (1984) *Perspectives on Higher Education*, Berkeley, Calif., University of California Press.

Clark, G. (1935) *The Seventeenth Century*, Oxford, Clarendon Press.

Clark, G. (1937) *Science and Social Welfare in the Age of Newton*, Oxford, Clarendon Press.

Clark, G. (1947) *The Wealth of England 1496–1760*, Oxford, Oxford University Press.

Clark, K. (1955) *Prejudice and Your Child*, Boston, Mass., Beacon Press. Second edition, 1963.

Clark, K. (1963) 'Educational Stimulation of Racially Disadvantaged Children', in Passow (1963), pp. 150ff.

Clark, K. and Clark, M. (1939) 'Development of Consciousness and the Emergence of Racial Identification in Negro Children', *Journal of Social Psychology*, Vol. 10, pp. 591–9.

Clegg, S. (1979) *The Theory of Power and Organization*, London, Routledge and Kegan Paul.

Clegg, S. and Dunkerley, D. (1980) *Organization, Class and Control*, London, Routledge and Kegan Paul.

Clinard, M. (ed) (1964a) *Anomie and Deviant Behavior: A Discussion and Critique*, New York, Free Press.

Clinard, M. (1964b) 'The Theoretical Implications of Anomie and Deviant Behavior', in Clinard (1964a), pp. 1–56.

Cloward, R. (1959) 'Illegitimate Means, Anomie and Deviant Behavior', *American Sociological Review*, Vol. 24, pp. 164–76.

Cloward, R. and Ohlin, L. (1960) *Delinquency and Opportunity: A Theory of Delinquent Gangs*, New York, Free Press.

Cohen, D. and Weiss, J. (1977) 'Social Science and Social Policy: Schools and Race', in R. Rist and R. Anson (eds), *Education, Social Science and the Judicial Process*, New York, Teachers College Press, pp. 72–96.

Cohen, G. A. (1978) *Karl Marx's Theory of History: A Defence*, Oxford, Oxford University Press.

Cohen, G. A. (1982) 'Functional Explanation, Consequence Explanation, and Marxism', *Inquiry*, Vol. 25, pp. 27–56.

Cohen, H. (1970) 'Bureaucratic Flexibility: Some Comments on Robert Merton's "Bureaucratic Structure and Personality"', *British Journal of Sociology*, Vol. 21, pp. 390–9.

Cohen, I. B. (1978) 'James Bryant Conant', *Proceedings of the Massachusetts Historical Society*, Vol. 90, pp. 122–30.

Cohen, I. B. (1988) 'The Publication of *Science, Technology and Society*: Circumstances and Consequences', *Isis*, Vol. 79, pp. 571–82.

Cohen, I. B. (ed) (forthcoming) *Puritanism and the Rise of Modern Science: The Merton Thesis*, New Brunswick, NJ, Rutgers University Press.

Cole, J. and Cole, S. (1973) *Social Stratification and Science*, Chicago, Ill., University of Chicago Press.

Cole, J. and Zuckerman, H. (1975) 'The Emergence of a Scientific Community: The Self-Exemplifying Case of the Sociology of Science', in L. Coser (1975a), pp. 139–74.

Cole, S. (1975) 'The Growth of Scientific Knowledge. Theories of Deviance as a Case Study', in L. Coser (1975a), pp. 175–220.

Cole, S. and Zuckerman, H. (1964) 'Inventory of Empirical and Theoretical Studies of Anomie', in Clinard (1964a), pp. 243–89.

Coleman, J. (1958/59) 'Relational Analysis: The Study of Social Organizations with Survey Methods', *Human Organization*, Vol. 17, pp. 28–36 (reprinted in Etzioni, 1969, pp. 517–27).

Coleman, J., Campbell, E., Hobson, C., McPartland, J., Mood, A., Weinfeld, F. and York, R. (1966) *Equality of Educational Opportunity*, Washington, DC, US Department of Health, Education and Welfare.

Collins, H. and Cox, G. (1976) 'Recovering Relativity: Did Prophecy Fail?', *Social Studies of Science*, Vol. 6, pp. 423–44.

Collins, R. (1975) *Conflict Sociology: Toward an Explanatory Science*, New York, Academic Press.

Collins, R. (1981) *Sociology Since Midcentury*, New York, Academic Press.

Comenius, J. (1642) *A Reformation of Schooles* (English translation of *Prodromus*, 1637, and *Dicucidatio*, 1634), London.

Comenius, J. (1651) *Naturall Philosophie Reformed by Divine Light* (English translation of *Physicae Synopsis*, 1633), London.

Conant, J. (1942) 'The Advancement of Learning during the Puritan Commonwealth', *Proceedings of the Massachusetts Historical Society*, Vol. 66, pp. 3–31.

Conant, J. (ed) (1957) *Harvard Case Histories in Experimental Sciences*, 2 vols, Cambridge, Mass., Harvard University Press.

Conant, J. (1960) 'History in the Education of Scientists', *Harvard Library Bulletin*, Vol. 14, pp. 315–33.

Cooper, H. (1979) 'Pygmalion Grows Up: A Model for Teacher Expectation Communication and Performance Influence', *Review of Educational Research*, Vol. 49, pp. 389–410.

Cooper, H. and Good, T. (1983) *Pygmalion Grows Up: Studies in the Expectation Communication Process*, New York, Løngman.

Corsi, P. (1986) 'Review' of R. Young, *Darwin's Metaphor, Nuncius: Annali di Storia della Scienza*, Vol. 1, No. 2, pp. 144–6.

Coser, L. (1965) 'Introduction' to *idem* (ed), *Georg Simmel*, Englewood Cliffs, NJ, Prentice-Hall, pp. 1–26.

Coser, L. (1971) *Masters of Sociological Thought*, New York, Harcourt Brace Jovanovich.

Coser, L. (1974) *Greedy Institutions: Patterns of Undivided Commitment*, New York, Free Press.

Coser, L. (ed) (1975a) *The Idea of Social Structure*, New York, Harcourt Brace Jovanovich.

Coser, L. (1975b) 'Merton's Use of European Sociological Tradition', in *idem* (1975a), pp. 85–100.

Coser, L. and Coser, R. (1963) 'Time Perspective and Social Structure', in A. Gouldner and H. Gouldner (eds), *Modern Sociology*, New York, Harcourt Brace Jovanovich, pp. 638–50.

Coser, L. and Nisbet, R. (1975) 'Merton and the Contemporary Mind: An Affectionate Dialogue', in L. Coser (1975a), pp. 3–10.

Coser, R. (1961) 'Insulation from Observability and Types of Social Conformity', *American Sociological Review*, Vol. 26, pp. 28–39.

Coser, R. (1974a) 'Authority and Structural Ambivalence in the Middle-Class Family', in R. Coser (1974b), pp. 362–73.

Coser, R. (ed) (1974b) *The Family, Its Structures and Functions*, New York, St Martin's Press.

Coser, R. (1975) 'The Complexity of Roles as a Seedbed of Individual Autonomy', in L. Coser (1975a), pp. 237–64.

Coser, R. (1979) *Training in Ambiguity: Learning through Doing in a Mental Hospital*, New York, Free Press.

Coser, R. (1986) 'Cognitive Structure and the Use of Social Space', *Sociological Forum*, Vol. 1, pp. 1–26.

Coser, R. and Rokoff, G. (1971) 'Women in the Occupational World: Social Disruption and Conflict', *Social Problems*, Vol. 18, pp. 535–54.

Costner, H. and Leik, R. (1963) 'Deductions from Axiomatic Theory', *American Sociological Review*, Vol. 28, pp. 819–35.

Crosby, F. (ed) (1987) *Spouse, Parent, Worker: On Gender and Multiple Roles*, New Haven, Conn., Yale University Press.

Crothers, C. (1987a) *Robert K. Merton*, Key Sociologists Series, London, Ellis Harwood and Tavistock Publications.

Crothers, C. (1987b) 'Influences on and from Robert K. Merton: A Double Case Study', unpublished conference paper, Amalfi.

Crowther, J. (1970) *Fifty Years with Science*, London, Barrie and Jenkins.

Crozier, M. (1964) *The Bureaucratic Phenomenon*, Chicago, Ill., University of Chicago Press.

Crozier, M. (1974) 'Recent Trends and Future Trends for Sociology of Organizations', in M. Archer (ed), *Current Research in Sociology*, Paris, Mouton, pp. 407–14.

Dahme, H.-J. (1981) *Soziologie als exakte Wissenschaft*, 2 vols, Stuttgart, Enke.

Dahrendorf, R. (1968) *Essays in the Theory of Society*, Stanford, Calif., Stanford University Press.

Dalton, M. (1950) 'Conflict between Staff and Line Managerial Officers', *American Sociological Review*, Vol. 15, pp. 342–51.

Dean, D. (1961) 'Alienation: Its Meaning and Measurement', *American Sociological Review*, Vol. 26, pp. 753–8.

Debus, A. (ed.) (1972) *Science, Medicine and Society: Essays to Honor Walter Pagel*, New York, Science History Publications.

Dee, J. (1978) *Propaedeumata Aphoristica, John Dee on Astronomy (1558 and 1568)*, ed. and trans. by W. Shumaker, Berkeley, Calif., University of California Press.

Descartes, R. (1955) *The Philosophical Works of Descartes*, Vols. 1 and 2, trans. by E. Haldane and G. Ross, New York, Dover Reprint.

Dillenberger, J. (1960) *Protestant Thought and Natural Science*, Garden City, NY, Doubleday.

Di Meo, A. (1986) 'Aldo Mieli e la storia della chimica in Italia', *Archives Internationales d'Histoire des Sciences*, Vol. 36, p. 350, quoting *Archeion* (1919), Vol. 1, No. 2, p. 222.

Dolby, R. (1971) 'Sociology of Knowledge in Natural Science', *Science Studies*, Vol. 1, pp. 3–21.

Douglas, J. (ed) (1970) *Understanding Everyday Life*, Chicago, Ill., Aldine.

Douglas, M. (ed) (1982) *Essays in the Sociology of Perception*, London, Routledge and Kegan Paul.

Dreeben, R. (1987) 'Closing the Divide', *American Educator*, Vol. 11, pp. 28–35.

Dreitzel, H.-P. (1968) *Die gesellschaftlichen Leiden und das Leiden an der Gesellschaft. Vorstudien zu einer Pathologie des Rollenverhaltens*, Stuttgart, F. Enke.

Dreyfus, H. (1979) *What Computers Can't Do*, New York, Harper and Row.

Dubin, R. (1951) *Human Relations in Administration*, New York, Prentice-Hall.

Dubin, R. (1959) 'Deviant Behavior and Social Structure: Continuities in Social Theory', *American Sociological Review*, Vol. 24, pp. 147–64.

Duncan, O. and Duncan, B. (1955) 'A Methodological Analysis of Segregation Indexes', *American Sociological Review*, Vol. 20, pp. 210–17.

Durbin, P. (ed) (1980) *A Guide to the Culture of Science, Technology and Medicine*, New York, Free Press.

Durkheim, E. (1893) *De la division du travail social*, Paris, Alcan.

Durkheim, E. (1895) *Les règles de la methode sociologique*, Paris, Alcan.

Durkheim, E. (1897) *Le suicide. Étude de sociologie*, Paris, Alcan.

Durkheim, E. (1912) *Les formes élémentaires de la vie religieuse*, Paris, Alcan.

Durkheim, E. (1928) *Le socialisme*, Paris, Alcan.

Durkheim, E. (1933) *The Division of Labor in Society*, New York, Free Press.

Durkheim, E. (1938) *The Rules of Sociological Method*, New York, Free Press.

Durkheim, E. (1951) *Suicide*, New York, Free Press.

Durkheim, E. (1964) *The Elementary Forms of Religious Life*, London, George Allen and Unwin.

Durkheim, E. and Mauss, M. (1963) *Primitive Classification* (originally 'De quelques formes primitives de classification', *Année Sociologique*, Vol. 6, 1901–02), London, Cohen and West.

Dusek, J. (1975) 'Do Teachers Bias Children's Learning?', *Review of Educational Research*, Vol. 45, pp. 661–84.

Dusek, J. (ed) (1985) *Teacher Expectancies*, Hillsdale, NJ, Lawrence Erlbaum Associates.

Edge, D. (1983) 'Essay Review [on Sociology of Science]', *Isis*, Vol. 74, pp. 250–6.

Elashoff, J. and Snow, R. (1971) *Pygmalion Reconsidered*, Worthington, Ohio, Jones.

Elias, N. (1971) 'Sociology of Knowledge: New Perspectives', *Sociology*, Vol. 5, pp. 149–68, 355–70.

Elias, N. (1982) *The Civilizing Process, Vol. 2: State Formation and Civilization*, English trans. by E. Jephcott, Oxford, Basil Blackwell.

Elias, N. (1986) *Saggio sul tempo*, Bologna, Il Mulino.

Elster, J. (1978) *Logic and Society*, Chichester, Wiley.

Elster, J. (1983) *Explaining Technical Change*, Cambridge, Cambridge University Press.

Elster, J. (1984) *Ulysses and the Sirens*, rev. ed., Cambridge, Cambridge University Press.

Elster, J. (1985) *Making Sense of Marx*, Cambridge, Cambridge University Press.

Emerson, R. (1962) 'Power-Dependence Relations', *American Sociological Review*, Vol. 27, pp. 31–41.

Emerson, R. (1972) 'Exchange Theory, Part II: Exchange Relations and Network Structure', in J. Berger, B. Anderson and M. Zelditch (eds), *Sociological Theories in Progress*, Vol. 2, Boston, Mass., Houghton-Mifflin, pp. 58–87.

Erbring, L. and Young, A. (1979) 'Individuals and Social Structure: Contextual Effects as Endogenous Feedback', *Sociological Methods and Research*, Vol. 7, pp. 396–430.

Etzioni, A. (1961) *A Comparative Analysis of Complex Organizations*, New York, Free Press. Second edition 1975.

Etzioni, A. (1964) *Modern Organizations*, Englewood Cliffs, NJ, Prentice-Hall.

Etzioni, A. (ed) (1969) *A Sociological Reader on Complex Organizations*, 2nd ed., New York, Holt, Rinehart and Winston. First edition, 1961.

Evan, W. (1966) 'Toward a Theory of Inter-Organizational Relations', in J. Thompson (ed), *Approaches to Organizational Design*, Pittsburgh, Pa., University of Pittsburgh Press, pp. 173–92.

Evans, J. and Rosenthal, R. (1969) 'Interpersonal Self-Fulfilling Prophecies: Further Extrapolation from the Laboratory to the Classroom', *Proceedings of the 77th Annual Convention of the American Psychological Association*, Vol. 4, pp. 371–2.

Ewing, C. (1939) 'Review' of Robert K. Merton, *Science, Technology and Society in Seventeenth Century England* (1938), *Southwestern Social Science Quarterly*, Vol. 19, p. 436.

Feingold, M. (1984) *The Mathematicians' Apprenticeship—Science, Universities and Society in England 1560–1640*, Cambridge, Cambridge University Press.

Finley, M. (1983) *Historians, Puritanism and the English Revolution*, Toronto, Toronto University Press.

Firebaugh, G. (1978) 'A Rule for Inferring Individual-Level Relationships from Aggregate Data', *American Sociological Review*, Vol. 43, pp. 557–72.

Forman, P. (1971) *Historical Studies in the Physical Sciences*, 3, pp. 1–115.

Fraisse, P. (1967) *Psychologie du temps*, Paris, PUF.

Francis, R. and Stone, R. (1956) *Service and Procedure in Bureaucracy*, Minneapolis, Minn., University of Minnesota Press.

Frank, R.G., Jr (1975) 'Institutional Structure and Scientific Activity in the Early Royal Society', *Proceedings of the XIVth International Congress of the History of Science*, Tokyo, Vol. 4, pp. 82–101.

Freud, S. (1963) 'Recommendations for Physicians on the Psychoanalytic Method of Treatment', in P. Rieff (ed), *Therapy and Technique*, New York, Collier, pp. 117–26.

Galileo Galilei (1957) *Discoveries and Opinions of Galileo* (including 'The Assayer', 1623), trans. and ed. by S. Drake, New York, Doubleday.

Galileo Galilei (1974) *Two New Sciences* (translation of *Discorsi*, 1638), trans. and ed. by S. Drake, Madison, Wis., University of Wisconsin Press.

Garfield, E. (1980) 'Citation Measures of the Influence of Robert K. Merton', in Gieryn (1980), pp. 61–74.

Garfield, E. (1987) 'The Anomie-Deviant Behavior Connection: The Theories of Durkheim, Merton and Srole', *Current Contents*, Vol. 39, pp. 3–12.

Garfinkel, H. (1967) *Studies in Ethnomethodology*, Englewood Cliffs, NJ, Prentice-Hall.

George, C. and George, K. (1961) *The Protestant Mind of the English Reformation 1570–1640*, Princeton, NJ, Princeton University Press.

Georgiou, P. (1973) 'The Goal Paradigm and Notes towards a Counter-Paradigm', *Administrative Science Quarterly*, Vol. 18, pp. 291–310.

Gerth, H. and Wright Mills, C. (eds) (1946) *From Max Weber: Essays in Sociology*, New York, Oxford University Press; British edition (with identical page numbers) 1947, Kegan Paul, Trench, Trubner; 1948, London, Routledge and Kegan Paul. See also Weber (1946a, b, c).

Gethmann, C. (1981) 'Wissenschaftsforschung—Zur philosophischen Kritik der nach-Kuhnschen Reflexionswissenschaften', in P. Janich (ed), *Wissenschaftstheorie und Wissenschaftsforschung*, Munich, C. H. Beck, pp. 9–38.

Gibbs, J. and Martin, W. (1964) *Status Integration and Suicide*, Eugene, Ore., University of Oregon Press.

Giddens, A. (1971) *Capitalism and Modern Social Theory*, Cambridge, Cambridge University Press.

Giddens, A. (1984) *The Constitution of Society*, Cambridge, Polity Press.

Gieryn, T. (ed) (1980) *Science and Social Structure: A Festschrift for Robert K. Merton*, New York, New York Academy of Sciences.

Gieryn, T. (1982) 'Relativist/Constructivist Programmes in the Sociology of Science: Redundance and Retreat', *Social Studies of Science*, Vol. 12, pp. 279–97.

Gillispie, C. (1960) *The Edge of Objectivity: An Essay in the History of Scientific Ideas*, Princeton, NJ, Princeton University Press.

Gilson, E. (1930) *Études sur la rôle de la pensée médiévale dans la formation du système cartésien*, Paris, Librairie Philosophique J. Vrin.

Glenn, N. (1976) 'Cohort Analysts' Futile Quest: Statistical Attempts to Separate Age, Period and Cohort Effects', *American Sociological Review*, Vol. 41, pp. 900–4.

Goldenweiser, A. (1981) 'History, Philosophy and Culture', *Journal of Philosophy, Psychology and Scientific Methods*, Vol. 15, pp. 561–71, 589–607.

Good, T., Sikes, J. and Brophy, J. (1973) 'Effects of Teacher Sex and Student Sex on Classroom Interaction', *Journal of Educational Psychology*, Vol. 65, pp. 74–87.

Goodchild, B. (1974) 'Class Difference in Environmental Perception', *Urban Studies*, Vol. 11, pp. 157–69.

Goode, W. (1960) 'A Theory of Role Strain', *American Sociological Review*, Vol. 25, pp. 483–96.

Goode, W., Hopkins, E. and McClure, H. (1971) *Social Systems and Family Patterns: A Propositional Inventory*, Indianapolis, Ind., Bobbs-Merrill.

Goodlad, J. (1981) *A Study of Schooling*, New York, McGraw-Hill.

Gould, M. (1976) 'Systems Analysis, Macrosociology, and the Generalized Media of Action', in Loubser *et al.* (1976), pp. 470–506.

Gould, M. (1977) 'Development and Revolution in Science', unpublished manuscript, Max-Planck-Institut, Starnberg, West Germany.

Gould, M. (1985) 'Prolegomena to Any Future Theory of Societal Crisis', in J. Alexander (ed), *Neofunctionalism*, Beverly Hills, Calif., Sage, pp. 51–71.

Gould, M. (1987) *Revolution in the Development of Capitalism*, Berkeley, Calif., University of California Press.

Gould, M. (1989) 'A Theory of Scientific Revolutions', Ms., Haverford College, Pennsylvania.

Gouldner, A. (1947) 'Discussion: Industrial Sociology, Status and Prospects', *American Sociological Review*, Vol. 10, pp. 396–400.

Gouldner, A. (ed) (1950) *Studies in Leadership*, Glencoe, Ill., Free Press.

Gouldner, A. (1954a) *Patterns of Industrial Bureaucracy*, New York, Collier Macmillan.

Gouldner, A. (1954b) *Wildcat Strike*, New York, Antioch Press.

Gouldner, A. (1955) 'Metaphysical Pathos and the Theory of Bureaucracy', *American Political Science Review*, Vol. 49, pp. 496–507.

Gouldner, A. (1957/58) 'Cosmopolitans and Locals: Toward an Analysis of Latent Social Roles', *Administrative Science Quarterly*, Vol. 2, pp. 281–306, 444–80.

Gouldner, A. (1959) 'Organizational Analysis', in Merton, Broom and Cottrell (1959), pp. 400–28.

Gouldner, A. (1962) 'Anti-Minotaur: The Myth of a Value-Free Sociology', *Social Problems*, Vol. 9, pp. 199–213.

Gouldner, A. (1967) 'Reciprocity and Autonomy in Functional Theory', in L. Gross (ed), *Symposium on Sociological Theory: Inquiries and Paradigms*, New York, Harper and Row, pp. 241–70.

Gouldner, A. (1976) *The Dialectic of Ideology and Technology*, London, Macmillan.

Gouldner, A. and Peterson, R. (1962) *Notes on Technology and the Moral Order*, Indianapolis, Ind., Bobbs-Merrill.

Gregory, C. (1922) *Fundamentals of Educational Measurement*, New York, Appleton.

Groethuysen, R. (1927–30) *Die Entstehung der bürgerlichen Welt und Lebensanschauung in Frankreich*, Halle, Saale, N. Niemeyer.

Grusky, O. and Miller, G. (eds) (1970) *The Sociology of Organizations*, New York, Free Press.

Gurin, P. (1987) 'The Political Implications of Women's Statuses', in Crosby (1987), pp. 167–98.

Hage, J. (1980) *Theories of Organization: Form, Process and Transformation*, New York, Wiley.

Hall, A.R. (1952) *Ballistics in the Seventeenth Century*, Cambridge, Cambridge University Press.

Hall, A.R. (1954) *The Scientific Revolution, 1500–1800*, London, Longmans Green.

Hall, A.R. (1963) 'Merton Revisited, or Science and Society in the Seventeenth Century', *History of Science*, Vol. 2, pp. 1–16.

Hall, R. (1963) 'The Concept of Bureaucracy: An Empirical Assessment', *American Journal of Sociology*, Vol. 69, pp. 32–40.

Halmos, P. (ed) (1972), *The Sociology of Science*, Keele, University of Keele.

Hamblin, R., Brooke Jacobsen, R. and Miller, J. (1973) *A Mathematical Theory of Social Change*, New York, Wiley.

Hannan, M. (1971) *Aggregation and Disaggregation in Sociology*, Lexington, Mass., Lexington Books.

Hannaway, O. (1975) *The Chemists and the Word—The Didactic Origins of Chemistry*, Baltimore and London, Johns Hopkins University Press.

Harary, F. (1966) 'Merton Revisited: A New Classification for Deviant Behavior', *American Sociological Review*, Vol. 31, pp. 693–7.

Harvey, W. (1628) *De motu cordis*. Trans. by K. Franklin, London, 1968.

Hawthorn, G. (1976) *Enlightenment and Despair*, Cambridge, Cambridge University Press.

Hayek, F. von (1952) *Scientism and the Study of Society*, Glencoe, Ill., Free Press.

Heilbron, L. (1978) 'Introduction' to Dee (1978), pp. 1–99.

Hempel, C. (1965) *Aspects of Scientific Explanation and Other Essays*, New York, Free Press.

Heritage, J. (1984) *Garfinkel and Ethnomethodology*, New York, Basil Blackwell.

Hessen, B. (1931) 'The Social and Economic Roots of Newton's "Principia"', in Bukharin *et al.* (1931), pp. 147–212.

Heydebrand, W. (1977) 'Organizational Contradictions in Public Bureaucracies: Towards a Marxian Theory of Organizations', *Sociological Quarterly*, Vol. 18, pp. 83–107.

Hilbert, R. A. (1981) 'Toward an Improved Understanding of "Role"', *Theory and Society*, Vol. 10, pp. 207–26.

Hilbert, R. A. (1982) 'Competency Based Teacher Education versus the Real World: Some Natural Limitations to Bureaucratic Reform', *Urban Education*, Vol. 16, pp. 379–98.

Hilbert, R. A. (1986) 'Anomie and the Moral Regulation of Reality: The Durkheimian Tradition in Modern Relief', *Sociological Theory*, Vol. 4, pp. 1–19.

Hilbert, R. A. (1987) 'Bureaucracy as Belief, Rationalization as Repair: Max Weber in a Post-Functionalist Age', *Sociological Theory*, Vol. 5, pp. 70–86.

Hilbert, R. E. and Wright, C. (1979) 'Representations of Merton's Theory of Anomie', *American Sociologist*, Vol. 14, pp. 150–6.

Hill, C. (1965) *Intellectual Origins of the English Revolution*, Oxford, Oxford University Press.

Hirsch, P. (1975) 'Organizational Analysis and Industrial Sociology: An Instance of Cultural Lag', *American Sociologist*, Vol. 10, pp. 3–12.

Hobson v. Hansen (1967), 269F, Supplement 401.

Homans, G. (1950) *The Human Group*, New York, Harcourt Brace.

Homans, G. (1961) *Social Behavior: Its Elementary Forms*, New York, Harcourt, Brace and World.

Homans, G. (1974) Revised edition of Homans (1961).

Hope, K. (1975) 'Models of Status Inconsistency and Social Mobility Effects', *American Sociological Review*, Vol. 40, pp. 322–32.

Hornberger, T. (1937) 'Puritanism and Science: The Relationship Revealed in the Writings of John Cotton', *New England Quarterly*, Vol. 10, pp. 503–15.

Horton, J. (1964) 'The Dehumanization of Anomie and Alienation', *British Journal of Sociology*, Vol. 15, No. 4, pp. 283–300.

Hubert, H. and Mauss, M. (1910) *Mélanges d'histoire des religions*, Paris, Alcan.

Hughes, H. Stuart (1961) *Consciousness and Society—The Reconstruction of European Social Thought 1890–1930*, New York, Random House.

Hunt, M. (1961) 'How Does It Come to Be So?', *New Yorker*, No. 36, pp. 40–63.

Hunter, F. (1953) *Community Power Structure*, Chapel Hill, NC, University of North Carolina Press.

Hunter, M. (1981) *Science and Society in Restoration England*, Cambridge, Cambridge University Press.

Isajiw, W. (1968) *Causation and Functionalism in Sociology*, London, Routledge and Kegan Paul.

Isambert, F. (1985) 'Un programme fort en sociologie de la science', *Revue française de sociologie*, Vol. 26, pp. 485–508.

Jackson, E. (1962) 'Status Consistency and Symptoms of Stress', *American Sociological Review*, Vol. 27, pp. 469–80.

Jahn, J., Schmid, C. and Schrag, C. (1947) 'The Measurement of Ecological Segregation', *American Sociological Review*, Vol. 12, pp. 293–303.

James, W. (1909) *Psychology*, New York, Henry Holt and Co.

Johnston, R. (1976) 'Contextual Knowledge: A Model for the Overthrow of the Internal/External Dichotomy in Science', *Australian and New Zealand Journal of Sociology*, Vol. 12, pp. 193–203.

Jones, R. F. (1936) *Ancients and Moderns: A Study of the Background of the Battle of the Books*, Saint Louis, Washington University Press.

Jones, R. F. (1939) 'Puritanism, Science and Christ Church', *Isis*, Vol. 31, pp. 65–7.

Jones, R. F. (1940) 'Review' of Robert K. Merton, *Science, Technology and Society in Seventeenth Century England* (1938), *Isis*, Vol. 31, pp. 438–41.

Jones, R. F. (1951) *The Seventeenth Century: Studies in the History of English Thought from Bacon to Pope*, Stanford, Calif., Stanford University Press.

Jones, R. F. (1961) *Ancients and Moderns: A Study of the Rise of the Scientific Movement in Seventeenth-Century England*, St. Louis, Washington University Press, revised edition of Jones (1936).

Jones, R. F. (1962) 'The Humanist Defence of Learning in the Mid-Seventeenth Century', in J. Mazzeo (ed), *Reason and the Imagination—Studies in the History of Ideas 1600–1800*, New York and London, Columbia University Press, pp. 71–92.

Jöreskog, K. and Sörbom, D. (1981) *LISREL V: Analysis of Linear Structural Relationships by the Method of Maximum Likelihood*, Uppsala, University of Uppsala.

Jussim, L. (1986) 'Self-Fulfilling Prophecy: A Theoretical and Integrative Review', *Psychological Review*, Vol. 93, pp. 429–45.

Kanter, R. (1972) *Commitment and Community: Communes and Utopias in Sociological Perspective*, Cambridge, Mass., Harvard University Press.

Kassem, M. (1976) 'Introduction: European versus American Organizational Theories', in G. Hofstede and M. Kassem (eds), *European Contributions to Organizational Theory*, Amsterdam, Van Gorcum.

Katz, D. and Kahn, R. (1966) *The Social Psychology of Organizations*, New York, John Wiley.

Kearney, H. (1964) 'Puritanism, Capitalism and the Scientific Revolution', *Past and Present*, Vol. 28, pp. 81–101.

Kearney, H. (1973) 'Merton Revisited (Essay Review)', *Science Studies*, Vol. 3, pp. 72–8.

Kemsley, D. (1968) 'Religious Influences in the Rise of Modern Science: A Review and Criticism, Particularly of the "Protestant-Puritan Ethic" Theory', *Annals of Science*, Vol. 24, pp. 199–226.

Kerman, S. (1979) 'Teacher Expectations and Student Achievement', *Phi, Delta, Kappan*, Vol. 60, pp. 716–18.

King, M. (1971) 'Reason, Tradition and the Progressiveness of Science', *History and Theory*, Vol. 10, pp. 3–32.

Knappen, M. (1965) *Tudor Puritanism* (1st edition 1939), Chicago and London, University of Chicago Press.

Kohn, M. (1963) 'Social Class and Parent-Child Relationships', *American Journal of Sociology*, Vol. 68, pp. 471–80.

Kohn, M. (1969) *Class and Conformity: A Study in Values*, Homewood, Ill., Dorsey Press.

Kopp, C., in collaboration with Kirkpatrick, M. (eds) (1979) *Becoming Female: Perspectives on Development*, New York, Plenum Press.

Koselleck, R. (1979) *Vergangene Zukunft. Zur Semantik geschichtlicher Zeiten*, Frankfurt am Main, Suhrkamp.

Koyré, A. (1957) *From the Closed World to the Infinite Universe*, Baltimore, Md., Johns Hopkins University Press.

Koyré, A. (1965) 'The Significance of the Newtonian Synthesis', in *idem*, *Newtonian Studies*, London, Chapman and Hall, pp. 3–24.

Koyré, A. (1968) *Metaphysics and Measurement*, London, Chapman and Hall.

Krantz, D., Luce, R., Suppes, P. and Tversky, A. (1971) *Foundations of Measurement*, Vol. 1, New York, Academic Press.

Kristeller, P. (1965) 'The Modern System of the Arts', in *idem*, *Renaissance Thought II*, New York, Harper, pp. 163–227.

Krohn, R. (1971) 'Conflict and Function: Some Basic Issues in Bureaucratic Theory', *British Journal of Sociology*, Vol. 22, pp. 115–32.

Kuhn, T. S. (1962) *The Structure of Scientific Revolutions*, Chicago, Ill., University of Chicago Press.

Kuhn, T. S. (1968) 'History of Science', *International Encyclopedia of the Social Sciences*, Vol. 14, pp. 74–8.

Kuhn, T. S. (1970a) 'Reflections on my Critics', in Lakatos and Musgrave (1970), pp. 231–78.

Kuhn, T. S. (1970b) Second extended edition of Kuhn (1962).

Kuhn, T. S. (1974) 'Second Thoughts on Paradigms', in F. Suppe (ed), *The Structure of Scientific Theories*, Urbana, Ill., University of Illinois Press, pp. 459–82.

Kuhn, T. S. (1977) *The Essential Tension—Selected Essays in Scientific Tradition and Change*, Chicago, Ill., University of Chicago Press.

Lagory, N. and Pipkin, J. (1981) *Urban Social Space*, Belmont, Calif., Wadsworth.

Lakatos, I. and Musgrave, A. (eds) (1970) *Criticism and the Growth of Knowledge*, Cambridge, Cambridge University Press.

Lammers, C. (1974) 'The State of Organizational Sociology in the United States: Travel Impressions by a Dutch Cousin', *Administrative Science Quarterly*, Vol. 19, pp. 422–30.

Lander, B. (1954) *Towards an Understanding of Juvenile Delinquency: A Study of 8464 Cases of Juvenile Delinquency in Baltimore*, New York, Columbia University Press.

Langbein, L. and Lichtman, A. (1978) *Ecological Inference*, Beverly Hills, Calif., Sage.

Lansberger, H. (1961) 'Parsons's Theory of Organizations', in Black (1961), pp. 214–49.

Latour, B. (1987) *Science in Action*, Cambridge, Mass., Harvard University Press.

Lazarsfeld, P. (1975) 'Working with Merton', in L. Coser (1975a), pp. 35–66.

Lazarsfeld, P. and Menzel, H. (1969) 'On the Relation between Individual and Collective Properties', in Etzioni (1969), pp. 499–516.

Lazarsfeld, P. and Thielens, W. (1958) *The Academic Mind*, Glencoe, Ill., Free Press.

Lemert, E. (1964) 'Social Structure, Social Control and Deviation', in Clinard (1964a), pp. 57–97.

Lenoble, R. (1971) *Mersenne ou la naissance du mécanisme*, Paris, Librairie Philosophique J. Vrin.

Lenski, G. (1954) 'Status Crystallization: A Nonvertical Dimension of Social Status', *American Sociological Review*, Vol. 19, pp. 405–13.

Lenski, G. (1988) 'Rethinking Macro Sociological Theory', *American Sociological Review*, Vol. 53, pp. 163–71.

Lever, J. (1976) 'Sex Differences in the Games People Play', *Social Problems*, Vol. 23, pp. 478–87.

Lever, J. (1978) 'Sex Differences in the Complexity of Children's Play and Games', *American Sociological Review*, Vol. 43, pp. 471–83.

Levine, D. (1981) 'Sociology's Quest for the Classics: The Case of Simmel', in B. Rhea (ed), *The Future of the Sociological Classics*, London, Allen and Unwin, pp. 60–80.

Levine, D., Carter, E. and Gorman, E. (1976) 'Simmel's Influence on American Sociology', *American Journal of Sociology*, Vol. 81, pp. 813–45, 1112–32.

Liebow, E. (1967) *Tally's Corner*, Boston, Mass., Little Brown and Co.

Lilley, S. (1949) 'Social Aspects of the History of Science', *Archives Internationales d'Histoire des Sciences*, Vol. 28, pp. 378–443.

Linton, R. (1936) *The Study of Man*, New York, Appleton-Century.

Lipset, S. M. (1950) *Agrarian Socialism*, Berkeley, Calif., University of California Press.

Lipset, S. M., Trow, M. and Coleman, J. (1956) *Union Democracy*, New York, Free Press.

Locke, J. (1959) *An Essay Concerning Human Understanding*, Mineola, NY, Dover.

Loomis, C. and Loomis, Z. (1961) *Modern Social Theories: Selected American Writers*, Princeton, NJ, Van Nostrand.

Loubser, J., Baum, R., Effrat, A. and Lidz, V. (eds) (1976) *Explorations in General Theory in Social Science*, Vol. 2, New York, Free Press.

Luhmann, N. (1976) 'Generalized Media and the Problem of Contingency', in Loubser *et al.* (1976), pp. 507–32.

Luhmann, N. (1982) *The Differentiation of Society*, New York, Columbia University Press.

Luhmann, N. (1984) *Soziale Systeme*, Frankfurt am Main, Suhrkamp.

Lynch, K. (ed) (1977) *Growing Up in Cities: Studies of the Spatial Environment of Adolescence in Cracow, Melbourne, Mexico City, Salta, Toluca, and Warszawa*, Cambridge, Mass., MIT Press.

McCloskey, D. (1976) 'On Durkheim, Anomie and the Modern Crisis', *American Journal of Sociology*, Vol. 81, pp. 1481–8.

McClosky, H. and Schaar, J. (1965) 'Psychological Dimensions of Anomy', *American Sociological Review*, Vol. 30, pp. 14–40.

Maccoby, E. and Jacklin, C. (1974) *The Psychology of Sex Differences*, Stanford, Calif., Stanford University Press.

McColley, G. (1939) 'Review' of Robert K. Merton, *Science, Technology and Society in Seventeenth Century England* (1938), *Popular Astronomy*, Vol. 47, pp. 114–15.

McGucken, W. (1984) *Scientists, Society and State: The Social Relations of the Science Movement in Great Britain, 1931–1947*, Columbus, Ohio, Ohio State University Press.

McGuire, J. and Rattansi, P. (1966) 'Newton and the "Pipes of Pan"', in *Notes and Records of the Royal Society of London*, Vol. 21, pp. 108–43.

McGuire, J. and Tamny, M. (eds) (1983) *Certain Philosophical Questions: Newton's Trinity Notebook*, Cambridge, Cambridge University Press.

MacIver, R. (1937) *Society—A Textbook of Sociology*, New York, Farrar and Rinehart.

MacIver, R. (ed) (1949) *Discrimination and National Welfare*, New York and London, Harper Bros.

MacIver, R. (1968) *As A Tale That Is Told*, Chicago, Ill., University of Chicago Press.

MacIver, R. and Page, C. (1949) *Society*, New York, Rinehart.

Macleod, R. (1977) 'Changing Perspectives in the Social History of Science', in I. Spiegel-Rosing and D. de Solla Price (eds), *Science, Technology and Society*, London, Sage, pp. 149–59.

McPherson, J. and Smith-Lovin, L. (1982) 'Women and Weak Ties: Differences by Sex in the Size of Voluntary Organizations', *American Journal of Sociology*, Vol. 87, pp. 883–904.

Mandeville, B. (1714) *The Fable of the Bees*, London, J. Roberts.

Mannheim, K. (1935) *Mensch und Gesellschaft im Zeitalter des Umbaus*, Leiden, A. W. Sijthoff.

Mannheim, K. (1936) *Ideology and Utopia*, London, Routledge and Kegan Paul.

Marburger, C. (1963) 'Considerations for Educational Planning', in Passow (1963), pp. 298–321.

March, J. (ed) (1965) *Handbook of Organizations*, New York, Rand McNally.

March, J. and Simon, H. (1958) *Organizations*, New York, Wiley.

Marcos, L. (1988) 'Dysfunctions in Public Psychiatric Bureaucracies', *American Journal of Psychiatry*, Vol. 145, pp. 331–4.

Martins, H. (1972) 'The Kuhnian Revolution and Its Implications for Sociology', in T. Nossiter, A. Hanson and S. Rokkan (eds), *Imagination and Precision in the Social Sciences*, London, Faber and Faber.

Marx, K. (1978) *The Marx-Engels Reader*, ed. by R. Tucker, New York, W. W. Norton.

Marx, K. and Engels, F. (1947) *The German Ideology*, New York, International Publishers.

Masson, I. (1925) *Three Centuries of Chemistry*, London, Ernest Benn.

Masterman, M. (1970) 'The Nature of a Paradigm', in Lakatos and Musgrave (1970), pp. 59–90.

Matza, D. (1969) *Becoming Deviant*, Englewood Cliffs, NJ, Prentice-Hall.

Mayntz, R. (1964) 'The Study of Organizations', *Current Sociology*, Vol. 13, No. 3, pp. 95–156.

Mead, G. H. (1923) 'Scientific Method and the Moral Sciences', *International Journal of Ethics*, Vol. 33, No. 3, pp. 229–47.

Mead, G. H. (1930) 'The Philosophies of Royce, James and Dewey in their American Setting', *International Journal of Ethics*, Vol. 40, No. 2, pp. 211–31.

Mead, G. H. (1946) *Mind, Self and Society*, Chicago, Ill., University of Chicago Press.

Mentré, M. (1905) 'La simultanéité des découvertes scientifiques', *Congrès International de Philosophie, 4–8 September 1904—Rapports et Comptes Rendus*, IIème session, Geneva, Henry Kundig.

Merton, R. K. (1934a) 'Recent French Sociology', *Social Forces*, Vol. 12, pp. 537–45.

Merton, R. K. (1934b) 'Durkheim's Division of Labor in Society', *American Journal of Sociology*, Vol. 40, pp. 319–28.

Merton, R. K. (1935) 'Science and Military Technique', *Scientific Monthly*, Vol. 41, pp. 542–5.

Merton, R. K. (1936a) 'Puritanism, Pietism and Science', *Sociological Review*, Vol. 28, pp. 1–30.

Merton, R. K. (1936b) 'The Unanticipated Consequences of Purposive Social Action', *American Sociological Review*, Vol. 1, pp. 894–904.

Merton, R. K. (1936c) 'Civilization and Culture', *Sociology and Social Research*, Vol. 21, pp. 103–13.

Merton, R. K. (1937a) 'Some Economic Factors in Seventeenth Century English Science', *Scientia*, Vol. 62, pp. 142–52.

Merton, R. K. (1937b) 'Science, Population and Society', *Scientific Monthly*, Vol. 44, pp. 165–71.

Merton, R. K. (1937c) 'The Sociology of Knowledge', *Isis*, Vol. 27, pp. 493–503.

Merton, R. K. (1938a) *Science, Technology and Society in Seventeenth Century England*, in *Osiris*, Vol. 4, Part 2, Bruges (Belgium), St Catherine Press, pp. 360–632. Reprinted in book form in 1970 (see entry under Merton, 1970a). There have been a number of paperback reprints, the first in 1970 by Harper and Row. For further details see Mary W. Miles and Rosa Haritos, 'The Writings of Robert K. Merton, 1975–1989', printed as an *Appendix* to this volume.

Merton, R. K. (1938b) 'Social Structure and Anomie', *American Sociological Review*, Vol. 3, pp. 672–82. Reprinted in numerous anthologies, including versions in all three editions of *Social Theory and Social Structure* (see Merton, 1949a, for details).

Merton, R. K. (1938c) 'Review' of G. N. Clark, *Science and Social Welfare in the Age of Newton*, *Isis*, Vol. 29, pp. 119–21.

Merton, R. K. (1938d) 'Science and the Social Order', *Philosophy of Science*, Vol. 5, pp. 321–37.

Merton, R. K. (1939a) 'Science and the Economy of 17th Century England', *Science and Society*, Vol. 3, pp. 3–27.

Merton, R. K. (1939b) 'Fact and Factitiousness in Ethnic Opinionnaires', *American Sociological Review*, Vol. 5, pp. 13–28.

Merton, R. K. (1940) 'Bureaucratic Structure and Personality', *Social Forces*, Vol. 18, pp. 560–8. Reprinted in Merton, 1968: 249–60.

Merton, R. K. (1942) 'A Note on Science and Democracy', *Journal of Legal and Political Sociology*, Vol. 1, pp. 115–26.

Merton, R. K. (1945a) 'Sociology of Knowledge', in G. Gurvitch and W. Moore (eds), *Twentieth Century Sociology*, New York, Philosophical Library, pp. 366–405.

Merton, R. K. (1945b) 'Sociological Theory', *American Journal of Sociology*, Vol. 50, pp. 462–73.

Merton, R. K. (1945c) 'Role of the Intellectual in Public Bureaucracy', *Social Forces*, Vol. 23, pp. 405–15. Reprinted in Merton, 1968: 261–78.

Merton, R. K. (1946) *Mass Persuasion*, New York, Harper and Brothers (with the assistance of Marjorie Fiske and Alberta Curtis).

Merton, R. K. (1947) 'The Machine, the Worker and the Engineer', *Science*, Vol. 105, pp. 79–84. Reprinted in Merton, 1968: 616–27.

Merton, R. K. (1948a) 'The Position of Sociological Theory', *American Sociological Review*, Vol. 13, pp. 164–8.

Merton, R. K. (1948b) 'The Self-Fulfilling Prophecy', *Antioch Review* (Summer), pp. 193–210.

Merton, R. K. (1949a) *Social Theory and Social Structure*, New York, Free Press. This edition had six printings, the 1957 edition Merton (1957a) twelve, and the 1968 edition (Merton, 1968) has so far had eleven.

Merton, R. K. (1949b) 'Social Structure and Anomie', in Merton (1949a), pp. 185–214.

Merton, R. K. (1949c) 'Social Structure and Anomie: Revisions and Extensions', in R. Anshen (ed), *The Family: Its Functions and Destiny*, New York, Harper and Brothers, pp. 226–57.

Merton, R. K. (1949d) 'Discrimination and the American Creed', in MacIver (1949), pp. 99–126.

Merton, R. K. (1949e) 'Patterns of Influence: A Study of Interpersonal Influence and Communications Behavior in a Local Community', in P. Lazarsfeld and F. Stanton (eds), *Communications in Research, 1948–49*, New York, Harper and Brothers, pp. 180–219. Reprinted as 'Patterns of Influence: Local and Cosmopolitan Influentials', in Merton, 1968: 441–74.

Merton, R. K. (1949f) 'The Role of Applied Social Science in the Formation of Policy', *Philosophy of Science*, Vol. 16, pp. 161–81. Reprinted in Merton, 1973: 70–98.

Merton, R. K. (1956) 'The Socio-Cultural Environment and Anomie', in H. Witmer and R. Kotinsky (eds), *New Perspectives for Research on Juvenile Delinquency*, Washington, DC, US Government Printing Office, pp. 24–50.

Merton, R. K. (1957a) *Social Theory and Social Structure*, 2nd rev. ed., New York, Free Press. See entry under Merton (1949a) for details of various editions and printings of this volume.

Merton, R. K. (1957b) 'Priorities in Scientific Discovery: A Chapter in the Sociology of Science', *American Sociological Review*, Vol. 22, pp. 635–59.

Merton, R. K. (1957c) 'The Role-Set: Problems in Sociological Theory', *British Journal of Sociology*, Vol. 8, pp. 106–20.

Merton, R. K. (1957d) 'Continuities in the Theory of Social Structure and Anomie', in Merton (1957a), pp. 215–48.

Merton, R. K. (1957e) 'Some Preliminaries to a Sociology of Medical Education', in Merton, Reader and Kendall (eds), pp. 3–79. Reprinted in Merton, 1982a: 135–98.

Merton, R. K. (1958) 'The Functions of the Professional Association', *American Journal of Nursing*, Vol. 58, pp. 50–5. Reprinted in Merton, 1982a: 199–210.

Merton, R. K. (1959a) 'Social Conformity, Deviation and Opportunity-Structures', *American Sociological Review*, Vol. 24, pp. 177–89.

Merton, R. K. (1959b) 'The Scholar and the Craftsman in the Scientific Revolution', in M. Clagett (ed), *Critical Problems in the History of Science*, Madison, Wisc., University of Wisconsin Press, pp. 24–9.

Merton, R. K. (1959c) 'Notes on Problem-Finding in Sociology', in Merton, Broom and Cottrell (1959), pp. ix–xxxiv.

Merton, R. K. (1960) 'The Corporation: Its Coexistence with Men', in M. Ashen and G. Bach (eds) *Management and Corporation 1985*, New York, McGraw-Hill, pp. 57–61.

Merton, R. K. (1961a) 'Now the Case for Sociology: The Canons of the Anti-Sociologist', *New York Times Magazine*, July 16. Reprinted in Merton (1976a), pp. 180–5.

Merton, R. K. (1961b) 'Singletons and Multiples in Scientific Discovery: A Chapter in the Sociology of Science', *Proceedings*, American Philosophical Society, Vol. 105, pp. 470–86. Reprinted in Merton (1973), pp. 343–70.

Merton, R. K. (1963) 'Foreword' to H. J. O'Gorman, *Lawyers and Matrimonial Cases*, Glencoe, Ill., Free Press, pp. vii–xiv.

Merton, R. K. (1964) 'Anomie, Anomia and Social Interaction: Contexts of Deviant Behavior', in Clinard (1964a), pp. 213–42.

Merton, R. K. (1965a) *On the Shoulders of Giants: A Shandean Postscript*, New York, Free Press, Vicennial edition published in 1985 by Harcourt Brace Jovanovich, New York.

Merton, R. K. (1965b) 'The Environment of the Innovating Organization: Some Conjectures and Proposals', in G. Steiner (ed), *The Creative Organization*, Chicago, Ill., University of Chicago Press, pp. 50–65.

Merton, R. K. (1966) 'Dilemmas of Democracy in the Voluntary Association', *American Journal of Nursing*, Vol. 66, pp. 1055–61. Reprinted in Merton, 1976a: 90–105.

Merton, R. K. (1967) *On Theoretical Sociology: Five Essays, Old and New*, New York, Free Press.

Merton, R. K. (1968) *Social Theory and Social Structure*, 3rd enlarged ed., New York, Free Press. See entry under Merton (1949a) for details of various editions and printings of this volume.

Merton, R. K. (1969) 'Behavior Patterns of Scientists', *American Scientist*, Vol. 57, pp. 1–23.

Merton, R. K. (1970a) *Science, Technology and Society in Seventeenth Century England*, New York, Howard Fertig. Reprint of Merton (1938a), together with a new 'Preface' by the author.

Merton, R. K. (1970b) 'The Ambivalence of Organizational Leaders', in J. Oates, *The Contradictions of Leadership* (ed. by B. Billings), New York, Appleton-Century-Crofts, pp. 1–26. Reprinted in Merton, 1976a: 73–89.

Merton, R. K. (1973) *The Sociology of Science: Theoretical and Empirical Investigations*, ed. by N. Storer, Chicago, Ill., University of Chicago Press.

Merton, R. K. (1975) 'Structural Analysis in Sociology', in Blau (1975a), pp. 21–52.

Merton, R. K. (1976a) *Sociological Ambivalence and Other Essays*, New York, Free Press.

Merton, R. K. (1976b) 'Social Problems and Sociological Theory', in Merton and Nisbet (1976), pp. 1–43.

Merton, R. K. (1979a) 'Foreword: The Evolving Grammar of Citation Analysis' in Eugene Garfield, *Citation Indexing: Its Theory and Application in Science, Technology and Humanities*. New York: John Wiley & Sons, pp. vii–xi.

Merton, R. K. (1979b) *The Sociology of Science: An Episodic Memoir*, Carbondale, Ill., Southern Illinois University Press (first published in Merton and Gaston, 1977).

Merton, R. K. (1979c) 'Remembering Paul Lazarsfeld', in *idem*, J. Coleman and P. Rossi (eds), *Qualitative and Quantitative Research: Papers in Honor of Paul F. Lazarsfeld*, New York, Free Press, pp. 19–22.

Merton, R. K. (1979d) 'Introduction' to R. Coser (1979), pp. xi–xiii.

Merton, R. K. (1981a) 'Foreword: Remarks on Theoretical Pluralism', in Blau and Merton (1981), pp. i–vii.

Merton, R. K. (1981b) 'Our Sociological Vernacular', *Columbia* – The Magazine of Columbia University, November, pp. 42–4.

Merton, R. K. (1982a) *Social Research and the Practicing Professions*, edited by A. Rosenblatt and T. Gieryn, Cambridge, Mass., Abt Books.

Merton, R. K. (1982b) 'Socially Expected Durations: A Temporal Component of Social Structure', paper presented to the annual meeting of the American Sociological Association, September.

Merton, R. K. (1984a) 'Socially Expected Durations: A Case Study of Concept Formation in Sociology', in W. Powell and R. Robbins (eds), *Conflict and Consensus: In Honor of Lewis A. Coser*, New York, Free Press, pp. 262–83.

Merton, R. K. (1984b) 'The Fallacy of the Latest Word: The Case of Pietism and Science', *American Journal of Sociology*, Vol. 89, pp. 1091–1121.

Merton, R. K. (1985a) 'George Sarton: Episodic Recollections by an Unruly Apprentice', *Isis*, Vol. 76, pp. 477–86.

Merton, R. K. (1985b) 'The Social Aspects of Duration'. Interview with Robert K. Merton by Anna di Lellio, published in *Rassegna Italiana di Sociologia*, Vo. 26, No. 1, pp. 3–26.

Merton, R. K. (1987) 'Three Fragments from a Sociologist's Notebooks: Establishing the Phenomenon, Specified Ignorance, and Strategic Research Materials', *Annual Review of Sociology*, Vol. 13, pp. 1–28.

Merton, R. K. (1988a) 'Reference Groups, Invisible Colleges, and Deviant Behavior in Science', in H. J. O'Gorman (ed), *Surveying Social Life—Papers in Honor of Herbert H. Hyman*, Middletown, Wesleyan University Press, pp. 174–89.

Merton, R. K. (1988b) 'The Matthew Effect in Science II: Cumulative Advantage and the Symbolism of Intellectual Property', *Isis*, Vol. 79, pp. 606–23.

Merton, R. K. and Barber, B. (1963) 'Sorokin's Formulations in the Sociology of Science', in P. Allen (ed), *P. A. Sorokin in Review*, Durham, NC, Duke University Press, pp. 332–68.

Merton, R. K. and Barber, E. (1963) 'Sociological Ambivalence', in E. Tiryakian (ed), *Sociological Theory, Values and Sociocultural Change*, New York, Free Press, pp. 91–120.

Merton, R. K., Broom, L., and Cottrell, L. (eds) (1959) *Sociology Today: Problems and Prospects*, New York, Basic Books.

Merton, R. K. and Christie, R. (1958) 'Procedures for the Sociological Study of the Value Climate of Medical Schools', in H. Gee and R. Glaser (eds), *The Ecology of the Medical Student*. Evanston, Ill., Association of American Medical Colleges, pp. 125–53.

Merton, R. K. and Devereux, E. (1964) 'Practical Problems and the Uses of Social Science', *Trans-Action*, Vol. 1, pp. 18–21.

Merton, R. K. and Gaston, J. (eds) (1977) *The Sociology of Science in Europe*, Carbondale, Ill., Southern Illinois University Press.

Merton, R. K., Gray, A., Hockey, B., and Selvin, H. (eds) (1952) *Reader in Bureaucracy*, New York, Free Press.

Merton, R. K., Merton, V., and Barber, E. (1983) 'Client Ambivalence in Professional Relationships: The Problem of Seeking Help from Strangers', in B. DePaulo *et al.* (eds), *New Directions in Helping*, Vol. 2, New York, Academic Press, pp. 13–44.

Merton, R. K. and Nisbet, R. (eds) (1976) *Contemporary Social Problems*, 4th ed., New York, Harcourt Brace Jovanovich.

Merton, R. K., Reader, G. and Kendall, P. (eds) (1957) *The Student-Physician*, Cambridge, Mass., Harvard University Press.

Merton, R. K. and Rossi, A. (1950) 'Contributions to the Theory of Reference Group Behaviour', in R. K. Merton and P. Lazarsfeld (eds), *Continuities in Social Research*, New York, Free Press, pp. 40–105.

Merton, R. K. and Thackray, A. (1972) 'On Discipline Building: The Paradoxes of George Sarton', *Isis*, Vol. 63, pp. 473–95.

Mestrovic, S. (1985) 'Anomia and Sin in Durkheim's Thought', *Journal for the Scientific Study of Religion*, Vol. 24, pp. 119–36.

Meyer, W. (1985) 'Summary, Integration and Prospective', in Dusek (1985), pp. 353–70.

Miles, M. (1975) 'The Writings of Robert K. Merton—A Bibliography', in L. Coser (1975a), pp. 497–522.

Mitroff, I. (1974) 'Norms and Counter-Norms in a Select Group of the Apollo Moon Scientists', *American Sociological Review*, Vol. 39, pp. 579–95.

Mongardini, C. (1985) 'L'aspettativa come categoria sociologica', in *idem*, *Epistemologia e Sociologia*, Milano, Angeli, pp. 99–127.

Moore, W. (1963) *Man, Time and Society*, New York and London, Wiley.

Moore, W. (1978) 'Functionalism', in T. Bottomore and R. Nisbet (eds), *A History of Sociological Analysis*, New York, Basic Books, pp. 321–61.

More, H. (1662) *A Collection of Several Philosophical Writings*, Vols. 1 and 2, London.

Morison, S. (1970) *Science in the British Colonies of America*, Urbana, Ill., University of Illinois Press.

Mouzelis, N. (1967) *Organization and Bureaucracy*, London, Routledge and Kegan Paul.

Mulkay, M. (1969) 'Some Aspects of Cultural Growth in the Natural Sciences', *Social Research*, Vol. 36, pp. 22–52.

Mulkay, M. (1975) 'Drei Modelle der Wissenschaftsentwicklung', in N. Stehr and R. König (eds), *Wissenschaftssoziologie*, Opladen, Westdeutscher Verlag, pp. 48–61.

Mullins, N. (1973) *Theory and Theory Groups in Contemporary American Sociology*, New York, Harper and Row.

Namier, L. (1929) *The Structure of Politics at the Accession of George III*, London, Macmillan.

Nasaw, D. (1985) *Children of the City: At Work and at Play*, New York, Anchor Press/Doubleday.

Needham, J. (1934) *A History of Embryology*, Cambridge, Cambridge University Press.

Needham, J. (1938) 'Review' of Robert K. Merton, *Science, Technology and Society in Seventeenth Century England* (1938), *Science and Society*, Vol. 2, pp. 566–71.

Needham, J. and Pagel, W. (eds) (1940) *Background to Modern Science*, Cambridge, Cambridge University Press and New York, Macmillan. Reprinted in 1975 by the Arno Press, New York.

Nelson, B. (1972) 'Review' of Robert K. Merton, *Science, Technology and Society in Seventeenth Century England* (1970a), *American Journal of Sociology*, Vol. 78, pp. 223–31.

Nelson, R. and Winter, S. (1982) *An Evolutionary Theory of Economic Change*, Cambridge, Mass., Harvard University Press.

New, F. (1964) *Anglican and Puritan—The Basis of Their Opposition, 1558–1640*, London, Black.

Nicolson, M. (1946) *Newton Demands the Muse: Newton's Opticks and the Eighteenth Century Poets*, Princeton, NJ, Princeton University Press.

Nicolson, M. (1956) *Science and the Imagination*, Ithaca, NY, Cornell University Press. Reprinted in 1976 by Archon Books, Hamden, Conn.

Nozick, R. (1974) *Anarchy, State and Utopia*, New York, Basic Books.

Oakes, J. (1985) *Keeping Track: How Schools Structure Inequality*, New Haven, Conn., Yale University Press.

Ogburn, W. and Nimkoff, M. (1940) *Sociology*, Cambridge, Mass., Houghton Mifflin.

Olson, M. (1965) *The Logic of Collective Action*, Cambridge, Mass., Harvard University Press.

Ornstein, M. (1938) *The Role of Scientific Societies in the Seventeenth Century*, Chicago, Ill., University of Chicago Press.

Orrù, M. (1983) 'The Ethics of Anomie: Jean Marie Guyau and Emile Durkheim', *British Journal of Sociology*, Vol. 34, pp. 499–518.

Orrù, M. (1985) 'Anomie and Social Theory in Ancient Greece', *Archives européenes de sociologie*, Vol. 26, pp. 3–28.

Orrù, M. (1986) 'Anomy and Reason in the English Renaissance', *Journal of the History of Ideas*, Vol. 47, pp. 177–96.

Orrù, M. (1987) *Anomie: History and Meanings*, Boston, Mass., Allen and Unwin.

Orrù, M. (1989) 'Weber on Anomie', *Sociological Forum*, Vol. 4, pp. 263–70.

Pagel, W. (1935) 'Religious Motives in the Medical Biology of the XVIIth Century', *Bulletin of the History of Medicine*, Vol. 3, pp. 97–128, 213–31, 265–312.

Pagel, W. (1938) 'Review' of Robert K. Merton, *Science, Technology and Society in Seventeenth Century England* (1938), *The Cambridge Review*, 4 November, p. 72.

Pagel, W. (1982) *Paracelsus—An Introduction to Philosophical Medicine in the Renaissance*, Basel, S. Karger.

Parijs, P. van (1981) *Evolutionary Explanation in the Social Sciences*, Totowa, NJ, Rowman and Littlefield.

Parsons, T. (1937) *The Structure of Social Action*, New York, McGraw-Hill. Reprinted 1949, New York, Free Press.

Parsons, T. (1939) 'The Professions and Social Structure', *Social Forces*, Vol. 17, pp. 457–67.

Parsons, T. (1947) 'Introduction' to Weber (1947), pp. 3–86.

Parsons, T. (1948) 'The Position of Sociological Theory', *American Sociological Review*, Vol. 13, pp. 156–64.

Parsons, T. (1951) *The Social System*, New York, Free Press.

Parsons, T. (1956/57) 'Suggestions for a Sociological Approach to the Theory of Organization', *Administrative Science Quarterly*, Vol. 1, pp. 63–85, 225–39. Reprinted in Parsons (1960), pp. 16–58.

Parsons, T. (1960) *Structure and Process in Modern Societies*, New York, Free Press.

Parsons, T. (1966) *Societies: Evolutionary and Comparative Perspectives*, Englewood Cliffs, NJ, Prentice-Hall.

Parsons, T. (ed) (1968) *American Sociology*, New York, Basic Books.

Parsons, T. (1969) *Politics and Social Structure*, New York, Free Press.

Parsons, T. (1970) 'On Building Social Systems Theory', *Daedelus*, Vol. 99, pp. 826–81.

Parsons, T. (1975) 'The Present Status of "Structural-Functional" Theory in Sociology', in L. Coser (1975a), pp. 67–83.

Parsons, T., Bales, R. and Shils, E. (1953) *Working Papers in the Theory of Action*, New York, Free Press.

Parsons, T. and Shils, E. (1951) *Toward a General Theory of Action*, Cambridge, Mass., Harvard University Press.

Parsons, T. and Smelser, N. (1956) *Economy and Society*, New York, Free Press.

Passow, A. (ed) (1963) *Education in Depressed Areas*, New York, Bureau of Publications, Teachers College of Columbia University.

Perrow, C. (1972) *Complex Organizations: A Critical Essay*, Illinois, Scott, Foresman.

Perry, N. (1979) 'Recovery and Retrieval in Organizational Analysis', *Sociology*, Vol. 13, pp. 259–73.

Perry, N. (1981) 'Information Brokerage and Organizational Dependence', *International Journal of Sociology and Social Policy*, Vol. 1, No. 3, pp. 45–57.

Piaget, J. (1971) *Biology and Knowledge*, Edinburgh, Edinburgh University Press; Chicago, Ill., University of Chicago Press.

Pinch, T. (1982) 'Kuhn—The Conservative and Radical Interpretations. Are Some Mertonians "Kuhnians" and Some "Kuhnians" Mertonians?', *Society for the Social Study of Science*, Vol. 7, pp. 10–25.

Pinder, C. and Moore, L. (eds) (1980) *Middle Range Theory and the Study of Organizations*, Boston, Mass., Martinus Nijhoff.

Popper, K. (1959) *The Logic of Scientific Discovery*, New York, Basic Books.

Popper, K. (1967) 'La rationalité et le statut du principe de rationalité', in E. Claasen (ed), *Les fondements philosophiques des systèmes économiques*, Paris, Payot, pp. 142–50.

Porter, R. (1982) 'White Coats in Vogue', *Times Higher Education Supplement*, No. 522, pp. 12–13.

Presthus, R. (1979) *The Organizational Society*, rev. ed., London, Macmillan.

Price, J. (1962) *Handbook of Organizational Measurement*, Lexington, D. C. Heath.

Rabb, T. (1962) 'Puritanism and the Rise of Experimental Science in England', *Journal of World History*, Vol. 7, pp. 46–67.

Rammstaedt, O. (1975) 'Alltagsbewusstsein von Zeit', *Kölner Zeitschrift für Soziologie und Sozial-Psychologie*, Vol. 27, pp. 582–92.

Rattansi, P. (1976) 'Early-Modern Art, "Practical" Mathematics and Matter-Theory', in R. Harre (ed), *The Physical Sciences Since Antiquity*, London, Croom Helm, pp. 63–77.

Rattansi, P. (1988) 'Recovering the Paracelsian Milieu', in W. Shea (ed), *Revolutions in Science—Their Meaning and Relevance*, Canton, Mass., Science History Publications, pp. 1–26.

Ravetz, J. (1971) *Scientific Knowledge and its Social Problems*, Oxford, Oxford University Press.

Reed, M. (1985) *Redirections in Organizational Analysis*, London, Tavistock.

Reingold, N. (1986) 'History of Science Today, 1. Uniformity as Hidden Diversity: History of Science in the United States, 1920–1940', *British Journal of the History of Science*, Vol. 19, p. 243–62.

Rist, R. (1970) 'Student Social Class and Teacher Expectations: The Self-Fulfilling Prophecy in Ghetto Education', *Harvard Educational Review*, Vol. 40, pp. 411–51.

Ritsert, J. (1969) 'Die Antinomien des Anomiekonzepts', *Soziale Welt*, Vol. 20, No. 2, pp. 145–62.

Robinson, C. (1978) 'Sex-typed Behavior in Children's Spontaneous Play', *The Association for the Anthropological Study of Play Newsletter*, Vol. 4, No. 4, pp. 14–17. Champaign, Ill., University of Illinois Children's Research Center.

Robinson, W. (1950) 'Ecological Correlations and the Behavior of Individuals', *American Sociological Review*, Vol. 15, pp. 351–7.

Roethlisberger, F. and Dickson, W. (1939) *Management and the Worker*, Cambridge, Mass., Harvard University Press.

Rohrer, J. and Sherif, M. (eds) (1951) *Social Psychology at the Crossroads*, New York, Harper Bros.

Rose, M. (1975) *Industrial Behaviour: Theoretical Development since Taylor*, Harmondsworth, Penguin. Second revised edition, 1988.

Rose, M. (1979) *Servants of Post-Industrial Power?*, London, Macmillan.

Rosenthal, R. (1966) *Experimenter Effects in Behavioral Research*, New York, Appleton-Century-Crofts.

Rosenthal, R. (1985) 'From Unconscious Experimenter Bias to Teacher Expectancy Effects', in Dusek (1985), pp. 37–65.

Rosenthal, R. and Fode, K. (1963) 'The Effect of Experimenter Bias on the Performance of the Albino Rat', *Behavioral Science*, Vol. 8, pp. 183–9.

Rosenthal, R. and Jacobson, L. (1968a) *Pygmalion in the Classroom: Teacher Expectation and Pupils' Intellectual Development*, New York, Holt, Rinehart, and Winston.

Rosenthal, R. and Jacobson, L. (1968b) 'Self-Fulfilling Prophecies in the Classroom: Teachers' Expectations as Unintended Determinants of Pupils' Intellectual Competence', in M. Deutsch, I. Katz and A. Jensen (eds), *Social Class, Race and Psychological Development*, New York, Holt, Rinehart and Winston, pp. 219–53.

Rosenthal, R. and Jacobson, L. (1968c) 'Teacher Expectations for the Disadvantaged', *Scientific American*, Vol. 218, pp. 19–23.

Rossi, P. (1970) 'Mechanical Arts and Philosophy in the Sixteenth Century', in *idem, Philosophy, Technology and the Arts in the Early Modern Era*, New York, pp. 1–62.

Runciman, W. (1983) *A Treatise on Social Theory*, Vol. 1, Cambridge, Cambridge University Press.

St John, N. (1975) *School Desegregation*, New York, Wiley.

Sarton, G. (1952) *Horus—A Guide to the History of Science*, Waltham, Mass., Chronica Botanica Co.

Savage, S. (1981) *The Theories of Talcott Parsons*, New York, St Martin's Press.

Schneider, L. (1970) *Sociological Approach to Religion*, New York, Wiley (esp. Ch. 6, 'The Case of the Protestant Ethic').

Schneider, L. (1971) 'Dialectic in Sociology', *American Sociological Review*, Vol. 36, pp. 667–78.

Schrödinger, E. (1935) *Science and the Human Temperament*, London, George Allen and Unwin.

Schwartzman, S. (1984) 'The Focus on Scientific Activity', in B. Clark (1984), pp. 199–232.

Scott, M. and Turner, R. (1965) 'Weber and the Anomic Theory of Deviance', *Sociological Quarterly*, Vol. 6, pp. 233–40.

Selznick, P. (1943) 'An Approach to the Theory of Bureaucracy', *American Sociological Review*, Vol. 8, pp. 47–54.

Selznick, P. (1948) 'Foundations of a Theory of Organizations', *American Sociological Review*, Vol. 13, pp. 25–35.

Selznick, P. (1949) *TVA and the Grass Roots*, Berkeley, Calif., University of California Press.

Selznick, P. (1952) *The Organizational Weapon*, New York, McGraw-Hill.

Selznick, P. (1957) *Leadership in Administration*, New York, Harper and Row.

Selznick, P. (1969) 'Rejoinder to Wolin', in Etzioni (1969), pp. 149–54.

Shapiro, B. (1969) *John Wilkins, 1614–1672: An Intellectual Biography*, Berkeley, Calif., University of California Press.

Shavelson, R., Cadwell, J. and Izu, T. (1977) 'Teachers' Sensitivity to the Reliability of Information in Making Pedagogical Decisions', *American Educational Research Journal*, Vol. 14, pp. 83–97.

Sherwood Taylor, F. (1947) 'An Early Satirical Poem on the Royal Society', *Notes and Records of the Royal Society of London*, Vol. 5, pp. 37–46.

Shipton, C. (1934) 'Secondary Education in the Puritan Colonies', *New England Quarterly*, Vol. 7, pp. 646–61.

Shipton, C. (1935) 'A Plea for Puritanism', *American Historical Review*, Vol. 40, 460–7.

Sieber, S. (1974) 'Toward a Theory of Role Accumulation', *American Sociological Review*, Vol. 39, pp. 567–78.

Sills, D. (1957) *The Volunteers*, New York, Free Press.

Sills, D. (1987) 'Paul F. Lazarsfeld, 1901–1976' in *idem*, *Biographical Memoirs*, Washington, DC, The National Academy Press, pp. 251–82.

Simmel, G. (1905) *Die Probleme der Geschichtsphilosophie*, Leipzig, Duncker and Humblot.

Simmel, G. (1908) *Soziologie*, Leipzig, Duncker and Humblot.

Simmel, G. (1950) *The Sociology of Georg Simmel*, trans. by K. Wolff, Glencoe, Ill., Free Press.

Simon, W. and Gagnon, J. (1976) 'The Anomie of Affluence: A Post-Mertonian Conception', *American Journal of Sociology*, Vol. 82, pp. 356–78.

Skinner, Q. (1969) 'Meaning and Understanding in the History of Ideas', *History and Theory*, Vol. 8, pp. 3–53.

Sklair, L. (1972) 'The Political Sociology of Science: A Critique of Current Orthodoxies', in Halmos (1972), pp. 43–59.

Slater, P. (1974) 'Social Limitations on Libidinal Withdrawal', in R. Coser (1974b), pp. 111–33.

Smelser, N. (1962) *Toward a Theory of Collective Behavior*, New York, Free Press.

Snow, R. (1969) 'Unfinished Pygmalion'—'Review' of *Pygmalion in the Classroom, Contemporary Psychology*, Vol. 124, pp. 197–200.

Sorokin, P. (1937/41) *Social and Cultural Dynamics*, 4 vols, New York, American Book Company.

Sorokin, P. (1943) *Sociocultural Causality, Space, Time*, Durham, NC, Duke University Press.

Sorokin, P. (1947) *Society, Culture and Personality*, New York, Harper Brothers.

Sorokin, P. and Merton, R. K. (1935) 'The Course of Arabian Intellectual Development, 700–1300 A.D.', *Isis*, Vol. 22, pp. 516–24.

Sorokin, P. and Merton, R. K. (1937a) 'Social Time: A Methodological and Functional Analysis', *American Journal of Sociology*, Vol. 42, pp. 615–29.

Sorokin, P. and Merton, R. K. (1937b) 'Sociological Aspects of Innovation, Discovery and Scientific Theories', in Sorokin (1937), Vol. 1, pp. 125–80, 439–76.

Srole, L. (1956) 'Social Integration and Certain Corollaries', *American Sociological Review*, Vol. 21, pp. 709–16.

Stahlberg, F. (1987) 'Functional and Dysfunctional Bureaucracies', in J.-E. Lane (ed), *Bureaucracy and Public Choice*, London, Sage, pp. 195–209.

Stearns, R. (1946) 'Colonial Fellows of the Royal Society of London, 1661–1788', *William and Mary Quarterly*, Vol. 3, pp. 208–68. Republished in *Osiris*, Vol. 8, 1948, pp. 73–121; *Notes and Records of the Royal Society*, Vol. 8, 1951, pp. 178–246.

Stearns, R. (1960) 'The Relations between Science and Society in the Later Seventeenth Century', in *The Restoration of the Stuarts, Blessing or Disaster?* A Report of a Folger Library Conference, March 1960, Washington, Folger Shakespeare Library, pp. 67–75.

Stehr, N. (1978) 'The Ethos of Science Revisited', in J. Gaston (ed), *The Sociology of Science: Problems, Approaches and Research*, San Francisco, Calif., Jossey-Bass, pp. 172–96.

Stehr, N. (1985) 'Robert K. Mertons Wissenschaftssoziologie', in R. K. Merton, *Entwicklung und Wandel von Forschungsinteressen. Aufsätze zur Wissenschaftssoziologie*, Frankfurt am Main, Suhrkamp, pp. 7–30, 301–10.

Stern, B. (1939) 'Review' of Robert K. Merton, *Science, Technology and Society in Seventeenth Century England* (1938), *Annals of the American Academy of Political and Social Science*, Vol. 202, p. 262.

Stimson, D. (1931) 'Dr. Wilkins and the Royal Society', *Journal of Modern History*, Vol. 3, pp. 539–63.

Stimson, D. (1932), 'The "Ballad of Gresham Colledge"', *Isis*, Vol. 18, pp. 103–17.

Stimson, D. (1935a) 'Comenius and the Invisible College', *Isis*, Vol. 23, pp. 373–88.

Stimson, D. (1935b) 'Puritanism and the New Philosophy in 17th Century England', *Bulletin of the Institute of the History of Medicine*, Vol. 3, pp. 321–34.

Stimson, D. (1948) *Scientists and Amateurs: A History of the Royal Society*, New York, Henry Schuman.

Stinchcombe, A. (1965) 'Social Structure and Organisation', in March (1965), pp. 142–93.

Stinchcombe, A. (1975) 'Merton's Theory of Social Structure', in L. Coser (1975a), pp. 11–34. Reprinted in revised form as Chapter 7 of this volume.

Storer, N. (1968) 'The Sociology of Science', in Parsons (1968), pp. 199–213.

Storer, N. (1973) 'Introduction' and 'Prefatory Notes' to Merton (1973).

Storing, H. (1962) 'The Science of Administration', in *idem*, *Essays in the Scientific Study of Politics*, London, Routledge and Kegan Paul.

Sutherland, E. (1940) 'White Collar Criminality', *American Sociological Review*, Vol. 5, pp. 1–12.

Sutton-Smith, B. (1979) 'The Play of Girls', in Kopp and Kirkpatrick (1979), pp. 229–57.

Swedberg, R. (1980) 'Communism in American Sociology: A Study of the Relationship between Political Commitment and Social Theory', *American Sociologist*, Vol. 15, pp. 232–46.

Sztompka, P. (1974) *System and Function: Toward a Theory of Society*, New York, Academic Press.

Sztompka, P. (1979) *Sociological Dilemmas: Toward a Dialectic Paradigm*, New York, Academic Press.

Sztompka, P. (1985) 'Introduction' to the Polish edition of J. Turner, *The Structure of Sociological Theory*, Warsaw, Polish Scientific Publishers.

Sztompka, P. (1986) *Robert K. Merton: An Intellectual Profile*, London, Macmillan; New York, St Martin's Press.

Tabboni, S. (1987) 'Il tempo come esperienza e come norma', paper presented in the series 'Costruzione e rappresentazione del tempo', organized by the Institute of Psychology at the Catholic University, 22–23 May 1987.

Tabboni, S. (1988) *La rappresentazione sociale del tempo*, 2nd rev. ed., Milano, Angeli.

Taylor, I., Walton, P. and Young, J. (1973) *The New Criminology—For a Social Theory of Deviance*, London, Routledge and Kegan Paul.

Thomas, K. (1973) *Religion and the Decline of Magic*, Harmondsworth, Penguin Books.

Thorndike, R. (1968) 'Review' of *Pygmalion in the Classroom*, *American Educational Research Journal*, Vol. 5, pp. 708–11.

Trevor-Roper, H. (1960) 'Three Foreigners and the Philosophy of the English Revolution', *Encounter*, Vol. 14, pp. 3–20. Revised version printed in Trevor-Roper (1967), pp. 237–93.

Trevor-Roper, H. (1967) *Religion, the Reformation and Social Change and Other Essays*, London, Macmillan.

Troeltsch, E. (1931) *The Social Teachings of the Christian Churches*, Vols 1 and 2, English translation by O. Wyon, London, Macmillan.

Turner, J. (1980) *The Structure of Sociological Theory*, rev. ed., Homewood, Ill., Dorsey Press.

Turner, Ralph (1947) 'The Navy Disbursing Officer as a Bureaucrat', *American Sociological Review*, Vol. 12, pp. 342–48.

Turner, Ralph (1954) 'Value Conflict in Social Disorganization', *Sociology and Social Research*, Vol. 38, pp. 301–8.

Turner, Roy (ed) (1974) *Ethnomethodology*, New York, Penguin.

Tyacke, N. (1978) 'Science and Religion at Oxford before the Civil War', in D. Pennington and K.

Thomas (eds), *Puritans and Revolutionaries—Essays in Seventeenth Century History Presented to Christopher Hill*, Oxford, Clarendon Press, pp. 73–93.

Walker, D. (1958) *Spiritual and Demonic Magic—From Ficino to Campanella*, London, Warburg Institute.

Wallace, W. (1969) *Sociological Theory*, Chicago, Ill., Aldine, pp. 1–60.

Watkins, J. (1987) 'A New View of Scientific Rationality', *Revue de Synthèse*, Série Générale, Vol. 108, pp. 455ff.

Weber, M. (1930) *The Protestant Ethic and the Spirit of Capitalism*, English translation by Talcott Parsons, London, Unwin University Books.

Weber, M. (1946a) 'Science as Vocation', in Gerth and Mills (1946), pp. 129–58.

Weber, M. (1946b) 'Bureaucracy', in *ibid.*, pp. 196–244.

Weber, M. (1946c) 'The Protestant Sects and the Spirit of Capitalism', in *ibid.*, pp. 302–22.

Weber, M. (1947) *The Theory of Social and Economic Organization*, translated by A. Henderson and T. Parsons, New York, Oxford University Press. Reprinted 1964, New York, Free Press.

Weber, M. (1949) *The Methodology of the Social Sciences*, New York, Free Press.

Weber, M. (1978) *Economy and Society*, ed. by G. Roth and C. Wittich, New York, Bedminster Press.

Weber, Marianne (1975) *Max Weber: A Biography*, New York, Wiley.

Webster, C. (ed) (1974) *The Intellectual Revolution of the Seventeenth Century*, London and Boston, Routledge and Kegan Paul.

Webster, C. (1975) *The Great Instauration—Science, Medicine and Reform 1626–1660*, London, Duckworth.

Weinberg, M. (1975) 'The Relationship between School Desegregation and Academic Achievement: A Review of the Research', *Law and Contemporary Problems*, Vol. 39, pp. 240–70.

Weingart, P. (1972) 'Wissenschaftsforschung und wissenschaftssoziologische Analyse', in *idem* (ed), *Wissenschaftssoziologie I: Wissenschaftliche Entwicklung als sozialer Prozess*, Frankfurt am Main, Athenäum Fischer, pp. 11–42.

Weingart, P. (1974) 'On a Sociological Theory of Scientific Change', in R. Whitley (ed), *Social Processes of Scientific Development*, London, Routledge and Kegan Paul, pp. 45–68.

Weinstein, R. (1976) 'Reading Group Membership in First Grade: Teacher Behaviors and Pupils' Experiences over Time', *Journal of Educational Psychology*, Vol. 68, pp. 103–16.

Weld, C. (1848) *History of the Royal Society*, London, John W. Parker.

West, C. and Anderson, T. (1976) 'The Question of Preponderant Causation in Teacher Expectancy Research', *Review of Educational Research*, Vol. 46, pp. 185–213.

Whitehead, A. N. (1926) *Science and the Modern World*, Cambridge, Cambridge University Press.

Whitley, R. (1972) 'Black Boxism and the Sociology of Science', in Halmos (1972), pp. 61–92.

Whitley, R. (1984) *The Intellectual and Social Organization of the Sciences*, Oxford, Oxford University Press.

Whyte, W. F. (1951) 'Small Groups and Large Organizations', in Rohrer and Sherif (1951), pp. 297–312.

Whyte, W. F. (1961) 'Parsons's Theory Applied to Organizations', in Black (1961), pp. 250–67.

Wieder, L. (1974a) *Language and Social Reality: The Case of Telling the Convict Code*, The Hague, Mouton.

Wieder, L. (1974b) 'Telling the Code', in Roy Turner (1974), pp. 21–6.

Wilkins, J. (1970) *The Mathematical and Philosophical Works of the Right Rev. John Wilkins* (reprint of 1802 edition), London, Frank Cass.

Williams, J. (1948) 'Another Commentary on So-called Segregation Indices', *American Sociological Review*, Vol. 13, pp. 298–303.

Williams, R. (1947) *The Reduction of Intergroup Tensions*, New York, SSRC.

Williamson, G. (1960) 'The Restoration Revolt against Enthusiasm', in *idem*, *Seventeenth Century Contexts*, London, Faber and Faber, pp. 202–39.

Wilson, L. and Kolb, W. (eds) (1949) *Sociological Analysis*, New York, Harcourt Brace Jovanovich.

Wilson, T. (1970) 'Conceptions of Interaction and Forms of Sociological Explanation', *American Sociological Review*, Vol. 35, pp. 697–710.

Wineburg, S. (1988) 'The Self-Fulfillment of the Self-Fulfilling Prophecy: A Critical Appraisal', *Educational Researcher*, Vol. 16, No. 9, pp. 28–37.

Wittgenstein, L. (1953) *Philosophical Investigations*, New York, Macmillan.

Wittgenstein, L. (1956) *Remarks on the Foundations of Mathematics*, Oxford, Basil Blackwell.

Wittgenstein, L. (1958) *The Blue and Brown Books*, Oxford, Basil Blackwell.

Wittrock, B. and Elziga, A. (eds) (1985) *The University Research System*, Stockholm, Almquist and Wiksell.

Wolf, E. (1981) *Trial and Error: The Detroit School Segregation Case*, Detroit, Mich., Wayne State University Press.

Wolin, S. (1961) *Politics and Vision*, London, Garnett and Evans.

Woodhouse, A. (ed) (1974) *Puritanism and Liberty*, London, J. M. Dent.

Woolgar, S. (1986) 'Of the Alleged Distinction between Discourse and Praxis', *Social Studies of Science*, Vol. 16, pp. 309–17.

Woolgar, S. and Latour, B. (1977) *Laboratory Life: The Social Construction of Scientific Facts*, Beverly Hills, Calif., Sage.

Worral, J. (1979) 'Reply to David Bloor', *British Journal of the History of Science*, Vol. 12, pp. 71–81.

Yates, F. (1972) *The Rosicrucian Enlightenment*, London, Routledge and Kegan Paul.

Zerubavel, E. (1981) *Hidden Rhythms: Schedules of Calendars in Social Life*, Chicago, Ill., University of Chicago Press.

Zetterberg, H. (1965) *On Theory and Verification in Sociology*, Totowa, NJ, Bedminster.

Zey-Ferell, M. and Aiken, M. (eds) (1981) *Complex Organizations: Critical Perspectives*, Chicago, Ill., Scott, Foresman and Co.

Zimmerman, D. (1970) 'The Practicalities of Rule Use', in Douglas (1970), pp. 221–38.

Zimmerman, D. (1974) 'Fact as a Practical Accomplishment', in Roy Turner (1974), pp. 128–43.

Zimmerman, D. and Pollner, M. (1970) 'The Everyday World as a Phenomenon', in Douglas (1970), pp. 80–103.

Zuckerman, H. and Merton, R. K. (1971) 'Patterns of Evaluation in Science: Institutionalization, Structure and Functions of the Referee System', *Minerva*, Vol. 9, pp. 66–100.

Zuckerman, H. and Merton, R. K. (1972) 'Age, Aging and Age Structure in Science', in M. Riley, M. Johnson and A. Foner (eds), *A Theory of Age Stratification*, New York, Russell Sage Foundation, pp. 292–356. Reprinted in Merton, 1973: 497–559.

Author Index

Subject Index